LIVES

OF THE

LORD CHANCELLORS OF ENGLAND.

GREAT SEAL OF THE COMMONWEALTH.

LIVES

OF

THE LORD CHANCELLORS

AND

KEEPERS OF THE GREAT SEAL

OF

ENGLAND,

FROM THE EARLIEST TIMES TILL THE REIGN OF QUEEN VICTORIA.

BY

LORD CAMPBELL.

SEVENTH EDITION.

ILLUSTRATED.

VOL. IV.

WILDSIDE PRESS

CONTENTS

OF

THE FOURTH VOLUME.

CHAP.	PAGE.
LXXVIII.—Continuation of the Life of Lord Clarendon till the restoration of Charles II., ...	1
LXXIX.—Continuation of the Life of Lord Clarendon till the meeting of the first Parliament of Charles II., .	11
LXXX.—Continuation of the Life of Lord Clarendon till his acquittal when impeached by the Earl of Bristol, .	28
LXXXI.—Continuation of the Life of Lord Clarendon till his fall, ...	41
LXXXII.—Continuation of the Life of Lord Clarendon till his banishment, ...	54
LXXXIII.—Conclusion of the Life of Lord Clarendon, . .	67
LXXXIV.—Life of Lord Keeper Bridgeman, ...	87
LXXXV.—Life of Lord Chancellor Shaftesbury from his birth till the restoration of Charles II., . . .	102
LXXXVI.—Continuation of the Life of Lord Shaftesbury till his appointment as Lord Chancellor, . . .	117
LXXXVII.—Continuation of the Life of Lord Shaftesbury till his dismissal from the office of Lord Chancellor, .	122
LXXXVIII.—Continuation of the Life of Lord Shaftesbury till the breaking out of the Popish Plot, ...	136
LXXXIX.—Continuation of the Life of Lord Shaftesbury till the dissolution of the Oxford Parliament, . . .	149
XC.—Conclusion of the Life of Lord Shaftesbury, . .	173
XCI.—Life of Lord Chancellor Nottingham from his birth till he was created Lord Chancellor, . . .	190
XCII.—Continuation of the Life of Lord Nottingham till his first quarrel with Lord Shaftesbury, . .	202
XCIII.—Conclusion of the Life of Lord Nottingham, . .	218

CONTENTS.

CHAP.		PAGE.
XCIV.	Life of Lord Keeper Guilford from his birth till he was appointed Solicitor General,	238
XCV.	Continuation of the Life of Lord Guilford till his appointment as Lord Keeper,	251
XCVI.	Continuation of the Life of Lord Guilford till the death of Charles II.,	272
XCVII.	Conclusion of the Life of Lord Guilford,	287
XCVIII.	Life of Lord Chancellor Jeffreys from his birth till he was appointed Recorder of London,	299
XCIX.	Continuation of the Life of Lord Chancellor Jeffreys till his appointment as Lord Chief Justice of the King's Bench,	314
C.	Continuation of the Life of Lord Chancellor Jeffreys till he received the Great Seal,	332
CI.	Continuation of the Life of Lord Chancellor Jeffreys till the Great Seal was taken from him by James II. and thrown into the river Thames,	354
CII.	Conclusion of the Life of Lord Chancellor Jeffreys,	373
CIII.	Lords Commissioners of the Great Seal on the Accession of William and Mary; and Life of Lord Commissioner Maynard from his birth till the Revolution of 1688,	400
CIV.	Conclusion of the Life of Lord Commissioner Maynard,	423
CV.	Life of Lord Commissioner Trevor,	437
CVI.	Life of Lord Somers from his birth till the Revolution,	457
CVII.	Continuation of the Life of Lord Somers till he receives the Great Seal,	482

LIVES

OF THE

LORD CHANCELLORS OF ENGLAND.

CHAPTER LXXVIII.

CONTINUATION OF THE LIFE OF LORD CLARENDON TILL THE RESTORATION OF CHARLES II.

THE new Lord Chancellor, instead of proceeding in state to Westminster Hall, attended by nobles and Judges, and making an inaugural speech before an admiring crowd in the Court of Chancery, or explaining, in the presence of the Sovereign, and the Lords, and the Commons, the reasons for calling a parliament, or presiding in a Council where great national questions were to be determined, had long, for his sole occupation, to provide for the daily necessities of the little domestic establishment, called "the Court of England," at Bruges. The pension from France had entirely ceased, as Charles was now to consider himself at war with that country; and the magnificent promises of a liberal supply from Spain had utterly failed. The consequence was, that the King's finances were in a more dilapidated state than ever, and the debts of his Crown, consisting of his tradesmen's weekly bills, increased most alarmingly. Thus writes his prime minister, who now combined in his own person the duties of Chancellor of the Exchequer and Lord High Chancellor:—"Every bit of meat, every drop of drink, all the fire and all the candles that hath been spent since the King's coming hither, is entirely owed for; and how to get credit for a week more is no easy matter. Mr. Fox[1] was with me yesterday, to move the King that

[1] Afterwards Sir Stephen, and the ancestor of the Holland and Ilchester families.

he would let his own diet fall, and content himself with one dish." So hard was "the Chancellor" pushed, that he was obliged to write the following letter, and to get Charles to copy it, to his sister, the Princess of Orange :— "I know you are without money, and can. not very easily borrow it,—at least upon so little warning; but if you will send me any jewel that I may pawn for £1,500, I do promise you you shall have the jewel again in your hands before Christmas."

The darkest and coldest hour of the night is immediately before break of day. Sexby, meditating assassination, had been detected and shut up in the Tower, but while the royal party were in a state of the deepest despondency at Bruges, a report was spread that Oliver, on whose single life the present *régime* in England was supposed to depend, was dangerously ill of an ague, and in a few days a messenger arrived, announcing that he was no more. Great, at first, was the exultation of Charles and his courtiers, and they all expected in the course of not many days to be in possession of Whitehall. But they were thrown into consternation by the next news— that Richard had been peaceably proclaimed; that his title had been acknowledged by the army as well as all the civil authorities; that addresses, pledging life and fortune in his support, were pouring in from all quarters; and that he had been congratulated on his accession to the Protectorate by all the foreign ambassadors in London. There was now what the lawyers call "a descent cast," whereby, on the death of an ejector, protection is given to the possession of his heir. The restoration of the House of Stuart seemed forever barred by the acknowledged title of a rival dynasty. "We have not," said Hyde, softening the despondence which he felt, that he might not discourage others, "yet found that advantage by Cromwell's death as we rationally hoped; nay, rather, we are the worse for it, and the less esteemed; people imagining by the great calm that hath followed, that the King hath very few friends."[1]

The hopes of the Court at Bruges, however, were soon revived by intelligence of the discontents of the army, and the feuds of its rival chiefs,—which almost from the beginning shook the throne of Richard. When he sum-

[1] Clar. Pap. iii. 428.

moned a parliament, and, departing from his father's reformed system of representation, sent writs to the rotten boroughs, Hyde wrote to the royalists in England, advising that as many of them as possible should quietly get themselves returned to the House of Commons. On the meeting of parliament it was found that they were more numerous than could have been expected, and for the ultimate good of the cause they did not scruple to take the oath of fidelity to the Commonwealth, and abjuration of the Stuarts. Hyde suggested to them an obstructive line of policy—that they should denounce the arbitrary acts of the administration of the late Protector—that they should hold up to particular odium Thurloe and St. John, who were the most influential advisers of the new Protector—that they should oppose all raising of moneys, and whatever might tend to a settlement of the Government—that they should widen the breach between the Cromwellites and the Republicans—and that they should throw their weight into the scale of either party in such manner as might most conduce to the interests of the King.

At this time it was thought that if Richard had been out of the hands of Thurloe and St. John, he would himself have declared for the restoration, "from the difficulties and dangers he met with in his government, and the safe and honorable advantages that he might receive by an accommodation with the exiled family," and Hyde seems to have believed that "he intended wholly for the King."[1]

The small royalist party in the House found it expedient to prevent Richard from being too soon precipitated from power, lest Fleetwood or Lambert, with a considerable share of the military reputation and energy of Oliver, might be elevated on the bucklers of the soldiers. They, therefore, voted for the recognition of his title as Protector, after they had succeeded in expunging the word "undoubted,"—and it was carried by a majority of 191 to 168. They likewise joined in the majority for acknowledging with some qualifications the other House of Parliament, consisting of Oliver's Peers. But they joined most heartily with the republicans in exposing the tyrannical proceedings of Oliver's Major-Generals and High Courts of Justice, which they said far

[1] Clar. Pap. iii. 434, 454.

exceeded in violence any sentences of the Star Chamber or High Commission Court abolished by the late King. They likewise pointed out the enormous increase in the public expenditure, and the arbitrary exactions by which it was supplied,—depicting, in glowing colors, the happy, tranquil, taxless times which the more aged might still remember. All this was supposed to be only out of odium to the Protectorate as against a pure republic, but was meant to bring back the affections of the people to royalty. A favorable impression being made, Hyde wrote to them to move the impeachment of Thurloe and St. John. This they were not strong enough prudently to attempt; but they followed up the blow with great effect on the presentation of Petitions from various persons who had been illegally imprisoned without warrant or cause assigned, or whose relations had been transported without a trial to Barbadoes, and there sold as slaves.

After a session of less than three months, the Protectorate had been so effectually damaged that Richard, as the only step to save himself, resorted to a measure which proved his instant ruin, by dissolving the parliament,—and the army was for a time triumphant. Hyde, watching this movement at Brussels, felt much alarm, which was not quieted by the restoration of the "Rump," where he had no friends. A majority of the survivors of the Long Parliament, though Presbyterians, were for royalty; but the members turned out by "Pride's purge" were still excluded, and those in whom the supreme power was now nominally placed were the section who had voted for the death of Charles I., and were devoted republicans. However, they had no hold of public opinion; and when they affected to assert their independence by cashiering Lambert and Desborough, the nation was rejoiced to see them again expelled, although for a time the government fell into the hands of a self-elected council of state. All these changes aggravated the general confusion, and were favorable to the King. There was now a growing desire for his return, to which Hyde wished to trust rather than to partial insurrections in his favor, saying, "I confess without a general conjunction, and therefore kindling the fire in several parts of the kingdom together, I can not imagine how any single attempt, how bravely soever undertaken by our friends alone, can be attended with success."[1]

A general rising was concerted, with Hyde's concurrence, in the month of July, but fortunately (for it must have lead to much bloodshed) it was prevented by the treachery of Sir R. Willis, who, in an age where, generally speaking, there was unspotted party fidelity, was false, first to the republicans, and then to the royalists.

Charles in the autumn of this year went to the coast of Brittany, intending from thence to make a landing in Wales or Cornwall, and this plan being abandoned, proceeded to join the conference at Fontarabia, in the vain hope of inducing France and Spain to unite in supporting his cause. Hyde meanwhile remained stationary at Brussels, carrying on a secret correspondence with almost all parties and classes of men in England, and seeing more and more clearly the satisfactory prospect of the King being restored by the spontaneous movement of his own subjects. The mode in which the restoration would be accomplished, in the face of the formidable army under Fleetwood and Lambert, composed chiefly of republicans and independents, no one distinctly foresaw; but a general feeling prevailed that it was inevitable, and most men began to speculate how it might best be brought about for their own safety and advantage. Now it was that Whitelock advised Fleetwood to declare for the King,[2] meaning himself to bring over the Commonwealth's Great Seal to Charles,—in which case Monk's real intentions would never have been ascertained, and he would have been almost unknown in history. When Hyde heard the probability of Fleetwood's defection from the republican party, he had no confidence in his firmness, and he thus expressed himself:—"The character which we have always received of the man is not such as makes him equal to any notable design, or to be much relied on to-morrow for what in truth he resolved to do yesterday: however, as his wit is not so great as some of the rest, so his wickedness is much less apparent than any of theirs, and therefore industry and dexterity must be used to dispose and confirm him in his good intentions, and let him take his own time for the manifestation of it."[3]

[1] Thurloe, i. 746. Burton's Diary, iv. 255.   [2] Ante, vol. iii. p. 378 *et seq.*
[3] Clar. Pap. iii. 592.

One of the most amusing proposals made to Hyde was from Lord Hatton, a most zealous royalist,—that Charles should gain over General Lambert by marrying his daughter,—urging "that no foreign aid would be so cheap or would leave the restored monarch at such liberty,— commending withal the beauty and disposition of the lady, the distinguished bravery of the father, and the respectability and antiquity of their lineage." No answer was returned,—that the alliance might not be considered absolutely rejected.

But in common cases, Hyde was not at all scrupulous in trying to gain the support of any party, or any individual, by lavish promises. He distinctly gave the Presbyterians to understand that they were to be favored, and he got the King to write "a great many obliging letters to their leaders to the same effect," so that many of them co-operated in the Restoration hoping that Presbytery was to be adopted as the established religion, and all the rest in the full faith that at all events they would have the same civil rights as the Episcopalians. "The management of all this," says Burnet, "was so entirely the Chancellor's, that there was scarce any other that had so much as a share in it with him."[1] We shall hereafter see whether he kept the word of promise, either to the ear or to the hope, when we relate the passing of "The Corporation Act," "The Act of Uniformity," and "The Conventicle Act."

Hyde early had the penetration to discover Monk's great influence, and the probability of his using it for the King. Soon after Cromwell's death he received a letter from Colepeper, pointing out Monk "as able alone to restore the King, and not absolutely averse to it, neither in his principles nor in his affections," and describing him as likely to be dissatisfied with the advancement of Richard, "being a sullen man, that values himself enough, and much believes that his knowledge and reputation in arms fit him for the title of Highness and the office of Protector better than Mr. Richard Cromwell's skill in horse races and husbandry doth." Hyde therefore wrote a letter, which Charles copied, to be shown to Monk— addressed to Lord Falconbridge, Lord Bellasis, and Sir John Grenville, or either of them:—"I am confident that

[1] Burnet's Own Times, i. 150.

George Monk can have no malice in his heart against me, nor hath he done any thing against me which I can not very easily pardon; and it is in his power to do me so great service that I can not easily reward, but I will do all I can, and I do authorize you, and either of you, with the advice of the rest, to treat with him; and not only to assure him of my kindness, but that I will very tolerably reward him with such an estate in land, and such a title of honor as himself shall desire, if he will declare for me and adhere to my interest; and whatever you shall promise to him on my behalf, or whatever he or you by his advice shall promise to any of his officers in the army under his command (which command he shall still keep), I will make good and perform upon the word of a King."[1]

Charles soon after was induced to write a letter to Monk himself, containing similar assurances; and a brother of Monk, a clergyman in the West of England, was employed, under Hyde's directions, to undertake a journey into Scotland for the purpose of sounding his intentions. But the wary General could not be drawn into any correspondence with the exiled Court. For some reason which has not been explained he showed a marked antipathy to Hyde, and there was no intercourse between them till they met at Dover on the King's landing.

Even when Monk was advancing with his army into England, Hyde, not unreasonably, distrusted him, and suspected that he meant to set up himself for Protector as soon as he should have got the better of Lambert, as "honest George" continued from time to time to declare —"We must live and die for and with a Commonwealth;" —called God to witness "he had no intention to embrace his Majesty's interest, nor ever would he;"—at York caned an officer for saying, "George will at last let in the King;"—and even after his arrival in London made a speech to exclude members about to be restored to their seats in parliament, asserting his preference for "a republican government and a Presbyterian Church." But in the beginning of March Hyde's suspicions were nearly dissipated, and he writes to a friend, "If Monk hath from the beginning intended well, he hath proceeded very wisely in the steps he hath made."[2]

[1] Clar. Pap. ii. 417. [2] Ibid. 694.

After Charles's return from the conference at Fontarabia, Hyde continued with him at Brussels anxiously watching the proceedings in England without being able in any perceptible degree to influence them. His chief task was to restrain indiscreet enterprises, and to induce those around him to wait patiently for the coming events, whose shadows might be so distinctly discerned. He found it particularly difficult to allay the jealousies which broke out among the royalists themselves, all now officiously struggling to make their services conspicuous, and to lay the foundation for future favors. "Those who are trusted a little," said he, "would be trusted more and know more, and are troublesome upon their being disappointed. I know no security but to be obstinate in applying them only to what they are fit for."[1] He was obliged to remonstrate with Lord Mordaunt, whom, under the guise of describing the sentiments of other friends of the King, he thus addressed:—"First, it is said that you take the whole business upon yourself; and therefore they do or pretend to believe that the King hath given the whole power to you, as well in martial as in civil affairs. Secondly, they seem to apprehend that all that is or shall be done is looked upon as your entire work, and the effect of your interest and conduct, and that they are not represented, or shall be considered as copartners in any thing."[2]

The principal anxiety at Brussels now was to ascertain what conditions the Convention parliament, when assembled, would propose. Better than such as had been demanded from the late King while he was in the Isle of Wight were not expected, and these would have been very readily conceded. Almost the last vote of the last parliament—acting freely,—with all its members restored,—and after having resolved to recall the King, was "that Presbyterianism should be the established religion of the kingdom;"—and no one on either side of the water yet appreciated the accelerated strength with which the cavalier spirit, enthusiastic and vengeful, raged throughout the country.

At length Sir Matthew Hale having made his motion for "a Committee to consider the propositions that had been made to, and the concessions that had been offered by, the late King during the war, particularly at the treaty

[1] Clar. Pap. iii. 684.   [2] Ibid.

of Newport, that from thence they might digest such propositions as they would think fit to be sent over to the King," it was strenuously resisted by Monk, who wished to have the glory of an unconditional restoration, and asked, if propositions were fit, "might they not as well prepare them, and offer them to him when he should come over?" Such cheers were elicited by the General's blunt speech, that the motion was dropped. "This," says Burnet, ironically, "was indeed the great service that Monk did!"[1] When the result of the debate was transmitted to Charles and his minister, they saw, with delight, that every thing was now in their discretion, and they deserve credit for the moderate use which, in the first instance, they made of the absolute power over three kingdoms, which, as if by magic, was in a moment conferred upon them.

During this enthusiastic burst of loyalty they were established at Breda, having secretly left Brussels under the apprehension that, in the prospect of Charles's recall to the throne of England, he might have been detained as a hostage by the Spaniards for the restoration of Jamaica and Dunkirk, which had been taken from them by Cromwell. Here gracious letters were written, in the King's name, to Monk and the army, to Montagu and the navy, to the House of Lords, to the House of Commons, and to the Lord Mayor and citizens of London; and here Hyde penned the famous "Declaration from Breda," granting pardon to all such as should claim it within forty days, and return to loyalty and obedience, excepting only such persons as should thereafter be excepted by parliament, providing that *no man should be disquieted or called in question for differences of opinion in matters of religion which do not disturb the peace of the kingdom;* declaring that all questions relating to grants, sales, and purchases of public property should be determined in parliament, and that the army under the command of General Monk should be taken into the King's service, on as good pay and conditions as they then enjoyed.

Nothing now remained, except that Charles should select a port of embarkation, as if, having been long in possession of the Crown, he had been returning to his dominions after a friendly visit to some allied Sovereigns

[1] Burn. Own Times, i. 152.

on the continent;—only that he was more eagerly longed for by his subjects than ever was monarch who had actually reigned.

Hyde accompanied him from Breda to the Hague, amidst the acclamations of the population through which they passed, and was regarded with peculiar interest and favor as the faithful companion of the exiled, and the future minister of the restored Sovereign. On the 23rd of May they embarked on board the English fleet at Scheveling, under the command of Montagu, and on the 25th they landed at Dover.[1] What must have been Hyde's sensations when, under such circumstances, he again set foot on English ground! He had been an exile above fourteen years,—during which he had been exposed to all sorts of perils, privations, and mortifications, and he had often seen reason to abandon himself to despair. Now enjoying both royal favor and popular applause, every thing that an ambitious man could desire had been accomplished by him, or was within his reach;—a splendid provision for his family, so often destitute, was now secured;—he had already achieved a name in history;—and about to guide the destinies of the British empire, he might hope to be long the instrument of conferring blessings on his country and his kind.

Bearing the Great Seal, which had been delivered to him at Bruges, and which was at length transformed into an ensign of real power, he accompanied the King in the grand ovation from Dover,—entering London on the 29th of May, "with a triumph of over 20,000 horse and foot, brandishing their swords, and shouting with inexpressible joy—the ways strewed with flowers—the bells ringing—the streets hung with tapestry—fountains running with wine; the Mayor, Aldermen, and all the Companies in their liveries, chains of gold, and banners; lords and nobles clad in cloth of silver, gold, and velvet; the windows and balconies all set with ladies; trumpets, music, and myriads of people flocking, even so far as from Rochester."[2]

On the arrival of the procession at Whitehall, the two Houses of Parliament were there to receive the King.

---

[1] It is curious enough that Charles selected "the NASEBY" man of war to carry himself and his immediate attendants.

[2] Evelyn, who was an eye witness.—*Mem.* ii. 148.

As Hyde had not yet taken his place as Lord Chancellor on the woolsack, he stood during this ceremony on his Majesty's right hand, and the Earl of Manchester, acting once more as Speaker of the House of Lords, delivered their address of congratulation.

CHAPTER LXXIX.

CONTINUATION OF THE LIFE OF LORD CLARENDON TILL THE MEETING OF THE FIRST PARLIAMENT OF CHARLES II.

ON the 1st of June Hyde entered on the regular discharge of his parliamentary and judicial duties. At the meeting of the House in the morning of that day, though still a Commoner, holding the Great Seal, he took his place on the woolsack as Speaker by prescription.

Soon after the King came in state, and, the Commons being summoned, he made a short speech to both Houses, and then commanded the Lord Chancellor to deliver his mind further to them. The Journals tell us that he did so, but there is no trace of his oration on this interesting occasion any where to be found.[1] The royal assent was then given to a bill for turning the Convention, so irregularly called, into a lawful Parliament, and to some other necessary acts; when "the Lord Chancellor told both Houses with how much readiness his Majesty had passed these important acts, and how willing, they should, at all times hereafter, find him to pass any other that might tend to the advantage and benefit of the people;" in a particular manner desiring, in his Majesty's behalf, that "the Bill of Oblivion, in which they had made so good a progress, might be expedited; that the people might see and know his Majesty's gracious care to ease and free them from their doubts and fears, and that he had not forgotten his gracious declaration made at Breda, but that he would, in all points, make it good."[2]

[1] It must have been, at all events, much to the taste of his audience, for the following day "the House gave the Lord Chancellor thanks for his excellent speech yesterday."—*Lords' Jour.* June 2, 1660. [2] 4 Parl. Hist. 64.

The same day Hyde took his seat in the Court of Chancery, and the oaths of supremacy and allegiance, and the oath of office, were administered to him.[1]

He certainly must have been very unfit for the judicial duties of the office. He never had been a well-grounded lawyer, and he had never practiced much in Courts of Equity. It was now twenty years since he had entirely left the bar. In the interval he had not attempted to keep up any knowledge of his profession; and the important political occupations which constantly harassed him, must have chased from his mind nearly all the judicial notions which had ever entered it, so that by this time he could hardly have recollected the distinction between *legal* and *equitable* estates, or known the difference between a bill of *discovery* and a bill for *relief*. He had cherished the prospect of holding the Great Seal in England, but he had no English law books with him at Bruges, at Brussels, or at Breda; and, while residing in those places, the whole of his time had been engrossed in projecting and watching over measures for the King's restoration.

There were strong efforts made by different parties and individuals to exclude him from the office on political grounds. The Presbyterians, headed by Lords Manchester and Bedford had said that "they could not be secure if they permitted so much as a kitchen-boy to be about the King of his old party," and though they regarded him as "a man to keep out popery," believing him to be "irreconcilable to their form, notwithstanding his fair professions in their favor," they were exceedingly desirous that he should not retain a situation of such power and influence. He was equally obnoxious to the Catholics, notwithstanding the hope he had held out to them that they should be safe by virtue of the dispensing power of the Crown till the penal laws against them

---

[1] "Anno duodecimo Caroli Scdi R*. June 1, 1660.

"The Right Honoble Sr. Edward Hyde, Knt. Lord Chauncr. of England, coming into the Court of Chauncery att Westr. accompanied by the Right Honoble the Lord Culpeper, Mr. of the Rolls, before his Lordsp entering upon anye busynes, took the oathe of the office of Chauncr of England, the booke being held to him by the said Mr. of the Rolls, the first day of June, in the yere aforesaid, being alsoe the first day of his Lop's sitting, and the first day of Terme, the former part not being kept. The Lord Chauncellor took the oathes of supremacye and allegeance, and the oathe of Lord Chauncellor." *Crown Off. Min. B.* fol. 15.

should be duly repealed. Monk was still his secret enemy, and Queen Henrietta, with her friend, Lord Jermyn, retaining her ancient grudge, intrigued against him, particularly with the Presbyterian leaders. It was much pressed upon the King that he should give the Great Seal to Sir Orlando Bridgeman, or Sir Jeffery Palmer, lawyers who had not attached themselves strongly to any party or sect, and from whom all might expect some advantage.[1]

But the judicial qualifications of the persons to be preferred were little thought of. The notion seems still pretty generally to have prevailed, that though to preside properly in a court of common law required a long course of professional study and experience,[2] any man of plain sense and good intentions, might " mitigate the rigor of general rules, and do what was just between the parties in each particular case,"—which was the vulgar notion of equity. Nay, it is asserted that Sir John Grenville, in his first negotiation with Monk, " propounded to the General £100,000 *per annum* for ever, as his Majesty's donation to him and his officers, *with the office of Lord High Chancellor* and Constable of England for himself, and the nomination of any other great officers of the Crown." We may well doubt whether such an offer ever was made—at least with the authority or privity of Hyde; but the circulation of the story shows that men then contemplated the possibility of their having a military Chancellor in Westminster Hall, as there still is in some of our colonies.

The opposition to Hyde's retaining the Great Seal was so formidable, that he seems to have offered to resign it rather than hazard the harmony of the Restoration;[3] but he was warmly supported by Southampton, Ormond, Nicholas, and Colepeper. The King, long accustomed to be guided by him, was " yet wholly in his hands,"—though giving wise and good advice, " he did it too much with the air of a governor or of a lawyer." In truth, for some years " he carried the Crown in his pocket." Clarendon showed his generosity by appointing Bridgeman and Palmer, his rivals for the Great Seal—the one Lord

[1] Clar. Pap. iii. 655, 705, 728, 744.
[2] " Lucubrationes viginti annorum."
[3] Price's Mystery and Method of the Restauration.

Chief Baron of the Court of Exchequer, and the other Attorney General.[1]

As a Judge he conducted himself with such prudence and discretion, and made such wise use of the knowledge and abilities of others, as to escape complaint, and even to be reckoned a good Chancellor. He had always two Masters in Chancery to keep him right in matters of practice, and he never made a decree without the assistance of two of the Judges.[2] He acquired much credit by publishing some salutary regulations for the better administration of the offices of the Masters in Chancery and the Six Clerks, still known and cited under the name of " Lord Clarendon's Orders."[3] These were prepared under his directions by Sir Harbottle Grimston, the Master of the Rolls, assisted by the officers of the Court, and consist chiefly of Lord Keeper Whitelock's orders, and some of the least exceptionable articles in Cromwell's famous Ordinance for reforming the Court of Chancery, which could no longer be directly referred to.[4]

When Clarendon was finally established, and in great favor both with the King and the parliament, his intimate associate, the Duke of Ormond, privately urged him to resign his judicial office and to accept the staff of Lord High Treasurer, stating "that all his best friends wondered that he so much affected the post he was in as to continue in the office of Chancellor, which took up most of his time, especially all the mornings, in *business that many other men could discharge as well as he.*"[5] He replied, " that he would sooner be preferred to the gallows." He probably felt that he would be more exposed to envy, and that his hold of power would be more precarious, in an office purely political. He had resigned the office of Chancellor of the Exchequer, which he had nominally

[1] Burn. Own Times, i. 150.
[2] See note of Speaker Onslow to ed. of Burnet. Oxford, i. 161.
[3] Although it was not till some months after that he was raised to the peerage, it may be convenient that he should now be denominated by the title under which he is familiar to us from the Restoration.
[4] See "Collections of such of the Orders heretofore used in Chancery, with such alterations and additions thereunto as the Earl of Clarendon, Lord Chancellor, and Sir H. Grimston, Master of the Rolls, have thought fit to ordain and publish for reforming of several abuses in the said Court."—12mo. editions, 1661, 1669, 1676, 1688.—*Beames's General Orders*, p. 165.
[5] No reflection being meant upon him as a Judge—and another proof that to preside in the Court of Chancery was not then considered what the Scotch call " a kittle job."—*Life, Continuation*, 14.

held so long under two reigns, and had been succeeded in it by Sir Anthony Ashley Cooper.[1]

We must now attend to his proceedings as prime minister, for it was as a statesman that he was chiefly regarded in his own and succeeding times. He was much embarrassed by the numerous attendance of Privy Councillors, the distinction between the Privy Council and the Cabinet, so familiar to us, not being yet established. To obviate this difficulty, he procured the appointment of a committee, ostensibly for the consideration of foreign affairs, but in reality to discuss all measures, whether of foreign or domestic policy, before they were submitted to a board and formally determined upon.[2] Monk and Morrice

[1] He remained Chancellor of the Exchequer till May 13, 1661, the date of Sir A. A. Cooper's appointment. The Treasury was put into Commission 19th June, 1660, Sir E. Hyde being one of the Commissioners, and named first as Chancellor of England. The other Commissioners were, Marquis of Ormond, Sir George Monk, Earl of Southampton, Lord Roberts, Lord Culpeper, Sir E. Montagu, Sir E. Nicholas, and Sir W. Morrice. Sept. 8, 1660, this Commission ceased, and Lord Southampton was made Lord High Treasurer; and by another patent, dated 12th Sept., was empowered to perform all the duties of Under-Treasurer during the vacancy of that office. May 13, 1661, Sir A. A. Cooper was made Chancellor of Exchequer and Under-Treasurer. It is the Under-Treasurership that is properly the financial office. The Chancellor of the Exchequer, as such, was the Chief Judge, on the equity side of the Court of Exchequer. The two appointments are still kept nominally distinct, and might be conferred on different individuals.

[2] The King was present at all the meetings of this Committee. Lord Culpeper was also a member, but he died very soon. In the State Paper Office are minutes by Sir E. Nicholas, of the meetings of the Committee in the first year after the Restoration. It was arranged at the outset, that it should meet every Monday and Thursday morning at ten, in the Lord Chancellor's Chamber. This Committee was also called the "Cabal" from the first, and long before the so-called "Cabal Ministry." Sir E. Nicholas's minutes are all indorsed C. B. The word "Cabal," derived from the Hebrew, had long before been introduced, both into the French and English languages—originally meaning only *secret* or *mysterious* and gradually savoring of *intrigue* and *conspiracy*. If the fact had not been ascertained that the King attended the meetings of this Committee, it might have been considered the origin of our present Cabinet meetings; but down to the end of Anne's reign, the sovereign in England was always present at state deliberations, and the practice was not altered till the accession of George I., who, being wholly ignorant of our language, absented himself from them, and was content with being told the result in bad Latin, the only medium of communication with his minister. George II., although he knew a little English, naturally fell into the same course, and by the end of his reign this mode of transacting business was considered as permanently engrafted into our constitution; otherwise, George III. would very eagerly and very inconveniently have restored a practice which undoubtedly adds much to the personal influence of the sovereign, although by no means tending to the good government of the country. I must own, however, that our monarchical forms are hardly enough respected, and amidst the talk of "the Duke of Wellington's Govern-

his nominee, were admitted to this secret consultation; but the Chancellor insured his control over them by the presence of Ormond, Southampton, and Nicholas. He had likewise frequent conferences "with such members of the parliament who were most able and willing to serve the King, to concert all the ways and means by which the transactions in the Houses might be carried with the more expedition and attended with the best success."[1] The office of foreign secretary being still unknown, the Chancellor wrote the instructions for all the ambassadors abroad, and regularly corresponded with them, besides superintending the important parliamentary proceedings now necessary to consolidate the Restoration.[2]

The first great measure to be carried was "the Bill of Oblivion and Indemnity," and much praise ought to be bestowed on Clarendon for pushing it through without introducing more numerous exceptions,—notwithstanding the vindictive spirit prevailing in the Commons, and still more in the Lords, where it was denominated "a bill of *oblivion of loyalty and indemnity to treason.*"[3]

The next question was the settlement of the revenue,

ment," "Lord Grey's Government," "Lord Melbourne's Government," and "Sir Robert Peel's Government," it seems to be forgotten that there is a sovereign on the throne.   [1] Life. i. 362.

[2] There were then two principal Secretaries of State, but they were little better than chief clerks, attending the Privy Council and the Committee of Foreign Affairs, and obeying instructions. By and by the world was divided between them, one having to correspond with countries in the north, and the other with countries in the south. This division continued till the middle of the reign of George III., when the Home and Foreign departments were separated, and at last a third secretary was added for the Colonies. But still, in point of law, they have all the same powers and functions. During the time of the northern and southern division, it was said they were like two coachmen on the same box—each intrusted separately with one rein, to the great peril of the passengers.

[3] It was necessary to send several messages to the two Houses in the King's name, praying them to expedite the Bill. The draught of one of these, in Clarendon's handwriting, is preserved in the Bodleian Library: " His Majesty taking notice of the delay in the passinge the Bill of Indemnity, and of the greate obstructions to the peace and security of the kingdome which aryse from that delay, doth very earnestly recommend to the House of Peers that they will use all possible expedicon in passinge the same, and that they will rest satisfyed with the excepcons they have already made of persons, and from henceforwarde that they not thinke of any further excepcons of persons either as to life or estate, or any other incapacity, but endeavor by all means to bury all thoughts of animosity and revenge, that the whole island may returne to those mutuall offices of conversation and friendship which alone can establish a firm and lastinge peace."

and it was proposed by some that the Chancellor should now get for the Crown a perpetual grant, which would for ever render it independent of parliaments; but, believing the scheme to be impracticable or inexpedient, he entirely discountenanced it. "It was believed," says Burnet, "that if two millions had been asked he could have carried it. But he had no mind to put the King out of the necessity of having recourse to his parliament. The King came afterwards to believe that he could have raised both his authority and revenue much higher, but that he had no mind to carry it further or to trust him too much."[1] The grant was limited to £1,200.000, and ways and means were not provided for more than one-half that amount, insomuch that the King was obliged to make the following speech to the two Houses, which, if it was prepared by Clarendon, as we are bound to suppose, shows that pecuniary pressure could make the Historian of the Rebellion lay aside the sesquipedalian words in which he usually delighted. "I must tell you," said the King in his speech to the parliament, on the 29th of August, 1660, "that I am not richer, that is, I have not so much money in my purse as when I came to you. The truth is, I have lived principally ever since upon what I brought with me, which was indeed your money. You sent it to me, and I thank you for it. The weekly expense of the navy eats up all you have given me by the bill of tonnage and poundage. Nor have I been able to give my brother one shilling since I came to England, nor keep any table in my house but where I eat myself; and *that which troubles me most is to see many of you come to me at Whitehall, and to think you must go somewhere else to seek a dinner.*"[2]

The plan was now carried into effect which Clarendon had long contemplated, of sanctioning the abolition of the military tenures, with their incidents of reliefs, wardships and marriages, which brought great profit and patronage to the Crown, but were most burdensome and oppressive to the landed aristocracy, and had been substantially abolished during the Commonwealth by suppressing the Court of Wards and Liveries. The bill, as he introduced it, very equitably charged the £100,000 to be given to the King upon the land, which

---

[1] Burnet, i. 271, 435.   [2] Lords' Jour. Aug. 29, 1660.

was to be relieved; but an amendment was moved throwing it on the Excise, which had been imposed as a temporary tax on articles of consumption. The amendment was stoutly opposed in the House of Commons, and was shown to be so flagrantly unjust, that even some country squires voted against it, so that it was only carried by a majority of 151 to 149. This may be considered the commencement of a new system of legislation by the landed interest for their own immunity: anciently not only was the regular permanent revenue of the Crown chiefly derived from charges upon land, but when extraordinary aids and subsidies were voted, almost the whole fell upon the land,—and, except on the importation of wine and some other foreign commodities, personal property was exempted from almost all fiscal burdens.

Considerable apprehension was still caused by the army of the Commonwealth, which, had it known its own strength, could have commanded the kingdom; but the Chancellor showed great address in the mode adopted for disbanding it. In a speech which he addressed to both Houses in the presence of the King, he said, "it is an army whose order and discipline, whose sobriety and manners, whose courage and success, have made it famous and terrible all over the world; but his Majesty having the felicity of being without danger at home or from abroad, knows that Englishmen will not wish that a standing army should be kept up in the bowels of their own country. Out of regard to public liberty, therefore, the soldiers are to become citizens, and to take delight in that peace which they have so honestly and so wonderfully brought to pass." [1]

The Chancellor's attention was next devoted to the trial of the regicides. Although his name was placed in the commission after that of the Lord Mayor of London, he did not take his place on the Bench during any of the trials, but he was obliged to exercise a general superintendence over the proceedings. It was without difficulty resolved that the indictment should be for "compassing the death of the King"—murdering him not being a substantive treason,—and that the decapitation should be laid only as the overt act to prove the compassing;—but very puzzling questions arose, whether the decapitation

[1] 4 Parl. Hist. 120.

should be alleged to have taken place in the reign of Charles I. or Charles II. ?—and against the peace of which Sovereign the offense should be alleged to have been committed? The Chancellor ordered the Judges to be previously consulted. They agreed that all that was done tending to the King's murder, until the moment before his head was completely severed from his body, was in the time of his own reign, but that the murder was not perfected till the actual severance,—when Charles I. being supposed to have died, a demise of the Crown had taken place, and a new Sovereign must be considered as *de jure* on the throne. They resolved, however, that "the compassing should be laid on the 29th of January, 24 Car. I., and the murder *trecesimo mensis ejusdem Januarii*, without here naming any year of any King; and that the indictment should conclude, *contra pacem nuper domini Regis coron' et dignitat' suas, necnon contra pacem domini nunc Regis coron' et dignitat' suas.*"

I do not think that blame is imputable to Clarendon with respect to any of the unhappy men who suffered, except Sir Harry Vane, who was not concerned in the King's death, and was charged with treason merely for having afterwards acted under the authority of the parliament. No satisfactory answer could be given to the plea that the parliament was then *de facto* the supreme power of the state, and that it could as little be treason to act under its authority as under the authority of an usurper on the throne,—which is expressly declared by the statute of Henry VII. not to be treason; and it was miserable sophistry to which the Court was obliged to resort, that, as there was no one else acknowledged as King in England, Charles II., while in exile, must be considered King *de facto* as well as *de jure*. The high cavaliers might be excused for wishing, by any means, to bring down vengeance on VANE, because he was the chief cause of the death of STRAFFORD; but Hyde should have remembered that he himself voted for Strafford's impeachment, and for his attainder.

He must likewise be severely blamed for suffering the exhumation of the bodies of Cromwell and some of his associates, who had died before the Restoration,—hanging them on a gibbet, cutting off their heads, and offering other revolting insults to their remains.— These atrocities were committed not by order of the executive government, not by an act of the legislature, but by the joint resolution of the two Houses of parliament, who were now exceeding their jurisdiction as clearly as they had ever done in the time of the Commonwealth. Hyde must have put the resolution from the woolsack, and, as Speaker of the House of Lords, have issued the directions to the Sheriff of Middlesex and the other officers of the law to carry it into effect. If he did not actually support the motion, he offered it no opposition or discountenance.[1]

During the sitting of the Convention Parliament, which continued about eight months, Hyde, on some points, had rather a difficult game to play, for he was not sure of a majority of the House of Commons. After much trouble he succeeded in carrying an equitable settlement respecting lay property which had been alienated during the troubles. There was a strong party who thought this a favorable opportunity for redistributing ecclesiastical property, and making a better provision for the working clergy; but Hyde successfully resisted any such interference, "showing himself," says Burnet, "more the Bishop's friend than the Church's,"[2] and delaying those reforms which have been introduced by Lord John Russel and Sir Robert Peel in the nineteenth century.

With regard to church government, being no doubt very sincere and conscientious in the object he had in view, he was exceedingly disingenuous and crafty as to the means he employed to accomplish it. He seems to have considered it his duty to crush the Presbyterians, and to re-establish the Church of England on the most exclusive principles. But as the Restoration was to be brought about through the Presbyterians, he held out to them flattering hopes by the Declaration from Breda; and, as they were found still to be very powerful on the King's return, ten of their most distinguished ministers, including Baxter and Calamy, were made royal chaplains, preaching in turn before the Court. Manchester and other Presbyterian Peers were introduced into offices in the household, and a modified Episcopacy, according to

[1] 4 Parl. Hist. 158. Even the corpse of the illustrious Blake was disinterred, and removed from its place of sepulture in Henry VII.'s chapel.
[2] Burnet, i. 321.

the model of Archbishop Usher, was announced,—to which they were ready to agree. A deputation of the Presbyterian clergy having delivered an address to the King, declaring their readiness to make a union with the Episcopalians, Charles, in the presence of the Chancellor, expressed his willingness to promote it; adding, that such union must be effected, "not by bringing one party over to the other, but by abating somewhat on both sides; that he was inclined to see it brought to pass, and that he would draw them together himself;"—which made a member of the deputation "burst into tears of joy, and to declare the gladness this promise of his Majesty had put into his heart."[1]

Conferences now took place between the divines on both sides, and a manifesto was actually published in the King's name as Head of the Church,—but the avowed production of the Lord Chancellor,—announcing the basis of the settlement. This paper, after commending the Church of England as "the best fence against Popery," and extolling the moderation of many of the Presbyterians, and asserting that on all essential points the two parties cordially agreed, specified the modifications of Episcopacy to which the King intended to assent. 1. To take away all notion of the Bishops being restored to the House of Lords, "that they do very often preach themselves *in some church of their diocese*, except they be hindered by sickness or other bodily infirmities, or some other justifiable occasion, which shall not be thought justifiable if it be frequent." 2. That such number of suffragan Bishops should be appointed as might be sufficient for the service of the church. 3. That Bishops should not censure or ordain without the advice of their Presbyters, and that the Bishop should act not singly, but as the president of an ecclesiastical board. 4. That the Liturgy should be revised by an equal number of divines of both persuasions. 5. Subscription to the thirty-nine articles was not to be required for ordination, institution, or induction, or for degrees at the Universities.

There seems no doubt that all these proceedings were with a view of amusing the Presbyterians till the Convention Parliament might be dissolved and another assembled, more devoted to the purposes of the Court. The Presby-

[1] Kennet, 183, 187. Calamy's Life of Baxter, 144.

terian leaders suspecting such an artifice, procured a select committee of the Hou e of Commons to be appointed to frame a bill which should immediately convert the royal declaration into a law. This committee met, and for their chairman elected the famous Sir Matthew Hale, who without delay framed the bill and introduced it. Immediately after, he received an intimation from the Chancellor that he was appointed Lord Chief Baron of the Court of Exchequer. A more laudable appointment never took place in Westminster Hall; but we may well suspect that it was prompted by a desire to remove from the House of Commons the framer and supporter of this bill, as well as by a knowledge of his great learning, ability, and piety. The dependents of the Court now received instructions to vote against the bill; Morrice, the Secretary of State, made a long speech, abusing it as inconsistent with the true doctrine of apostolical succession, and it was thrown out on the second reading by a majority of 26 in a House of 340 members.[1]

The Convention Parliament was soon after dissolved. The language of the Chancellor's parting speech to the two Houses on this occasion was most conciliating, although he had certainly made up his mind to stand at all hazards by the ultra-Episcopalians. "The King is a suitor to you," said he, "that you will join with him in restoring the whole nation to its primitive temper and integrity; to its old good manners, its old good humor, and its old good nature,—good nature, a virtue so peculiar to you that it can be translated into no other language, and hardly practiced by any other people."[2]

I have now to relate a sad perplexity into which Hyde was thrown, and from which he did not extricate himself with much dignity. His daughter, Annie, having been placed, as we have related, in the family of the Princess of Orange, accompanied her mistress to Paris on a visit to the Queen Henrietta. James, Duke of York, then living with his mother, had early displayed that taste for plain women which distinguished him through life,[3] and he fell in love at first sight with Anne Hyde, who, though possessed of wit and agreeable manners, was without personal

---

[1] 4 Parl. Hist. 141, 152.   [2] Ibid. 126.
[3] Charles said that James's mistresses seemed to have been given to him for a penance by his priests.

charms.¹ She had the address to draw from him first a verbal promise, and then a written contract to marry her before she admitted him to her bed. When she rejoined her father's family at the Restoration, she was in a state of pregnancy. Notwithstanding his overacted surprise and horror when the news was afterwards publicly announced to him by the King's orders, there seems little doubt that she had communicated what had passed to both her parents, and that as he knew that this amounted, in point of law, to a valid marriage, they regarded her as the wife of the Duke of York. Long before any open declaration of the union, "the Earl of Southampton and Sir Anthony Ashley Cooper having dined together at the Chancellor's—as they were returning home, Sir Anthony said to Lord Southampton, *Yonder Mrs. Annie Hyde is certainly married to one of the brothers.* The Earl, who was a friend to the Chancellor, treated this as a chimera, and asked him how so wild a fancy could get into his head. *Assure yourself*, replied he, *it is so. A concealed respect (however suppressed) showed itself so plainly in the looks, voice, and manner wherewith her mother carved to her, or offered her of every dish, that it is impossible but it must be so.*" ²

Before the birth of her child, the lady (probably prompted by her father, that there might be clear evidence to prove her *status*) prevailed upon the Duke to have the marriage celebrated according to the rites of the Church of England; and this ceremony took place privately at Worcester House, the Lord Chancellor's residence,—Dr. Crowther, chaplain to James, officiating,—in the presence of Lord Ossory, who gave away the bride, and of her maid-servant for another witness.

The Duke now disclosed what had happened to the King, and requested that he might be permitted to own her publicly as his Duchess. Charles sent for Ormond and Southampton, and desired them to consult the Chan-

---

[1] "La Duchesse de York est fort laide; la bouche extraordinairement fendue, et les yeux fort écailleux, mais très courtoise."—*Journal de Monceris*. p. 22. Count Anthony Hamilton is more courtly, saying she had "l'air grand, la taille assez belle, et beaucoup d'esprit."—*Mém. Gram.* i. 149. But honest Pepys, on whom beauty was never thrown away, tells us, after having had the honor to kiss her hand, that "she was a plain woman like her mother."—i. 188.

[2] Kennet's Register, 381. "My Lord S., who thought it a groundless conceit then, was not long after convinced, by the Duke of York's owning of her, 'that Ashley was no bad guesser.'"

cellor. They began by telling him, "that the Duke of York had owned a great affection for his daughter, and that the King much doubted she was with child by the Duke, and that his Majesty required their advice what was to be done." According to his own statement, "he broke out into a very immoderate passion against the wickedness of his daughter,"—said, in coarse terms, he had rather she should be the Duke's mistress than his wife,—shed floods of tears,—said he would consent to an act of Parliament "for cutting off her head,"—and hoped that her presumption in aspiring to a royal alliance might be punished, in the first instance, by an immediate commitment to the tower.[1]

Southampton, taken in by this ebullition, exclaimed, in the King's presence, "that the Chancellor was mad, and had proposed such extravagant things that he was no more to be consulted with."[2]

Hyde now affected, in the exercise of his paternal rights, to shut his daughter up in his house in order to prevent all further interviews between her and the Duke of York,—at which, however, he privately connived; for, alluding to his wife, he says that the attempt was rendered unsuccessful by "those who knew they were married." In the meantime, we learn from James himself, that, "with great caution and circumspection, he did his part to soften the King, in that matter, which, in every respect, seemed so much for his advantage."[3] Charles, with his usual careless good-nature, was disposed to acquiesce; but the *mésalliance* made his mother and his eldest sister furious. Henrietta hastened over to prevent so foul a disgrace to the royal houses of England and France, and declared that, "whenever *that woman* should be brought into Whitehall by one door, she herself would leave the palace by another, and never enter it again." And the Princess of Orange, who had recently arrived from Holland, declared that "she would never yield precedence to a girl who had stood as a servant behind her chair." The Duke of Gloucester, the youngest brother, is

[1] Life, i. 378. I see no reason to doubt the accuracy of this statement as others have done; nor do I consider it at all inconsistent with Clarendon's subsequent attempt " to soften the King."—See Lister's *Life of Clar.* ii. 69.
[2] Life, i. 378.
[3] Life of James II., i. 287, which is considerably at variance with Clarendon's own representation, that he would not hear of the marriage.

likewise said to have declared that "she smelt so strong of her father's green bag, that he could not get the better of himself whenever he had the misfortune to be in her presence."[1]

The courtiers were much puzzled as to the course they should pursue, and James himself was thought to waver,—when Sir Charles Berkeley, a profligate favorite of the Duke of York, boldly came to their aid, by affirming, with oaths, that Anne had been his mistress under a promise of marriage, and by bringing forward the Earl of Arran, Jermyn, Talbot, and Killigrew, as witnesses of her loose and wanton behavior,—"tous gens d'honneur," says the courtly author of the MEMOIRES DE GRAMMONT, "mais qui préféroient infiniment celui du Duc de York à celui de Mademoiselle Hyde." Berkeley went so far as to say that he claimed her as his own wife. Pending these false accusations Anne was taken in labor; and, while she lay in the throes of childbirth, her spiritual guide, Dr. Morley, Bishop-elect of Worcester, standing by the bedside, adjured her, in the name of the living God, to speak the truth before the noble ladies who attended by order from the King. To his questions she replied that the Duke was the father of her child,—that they had been married to each other by a priest before witnesses,—and that, having met him a virgin, she had ever been faithful to his bed. She then brought a male child into the world.

James, deeply touched by her situation, and pleased with the birth of a son, who might one day mount the throne, on her recovery showed a strong disposition to acknowledge her if her character were cleared,—when Berkeley made an open confession that the charges against her were wholly groundless, and that he had been induced to bring them forward, and to suborn the witnesses to prove them, purely out of his regard for the honor of the royal family. James, having returned warm thanks for such extraordinary proofs of devoted zeal, hurried off to the King, and had a long interview with him.[2] The

[1] Burnet, i. 291, n.
[2] The following letter from Charles to Hyde, which must have been written a few days before, is extant in the British Museum.—*Landsdown MSS.* 1236. "Tuesday morning.
"My brother hath spoken with the Queen yesterday concerning the owning of his sonn; and in much passion she tould him that from the time he did

particulars were never made known, but the result was favorable, for Berkeley and Lord Ossory were desired to meet the Duke in an hour at Worcester House. Thither they went, not at all foreseeing the dénouement. This we have from the Mémoirs of De Grammont. "Ils trouvèrent à l'heure marquée son Altesse dans la chambre de Mademoiselle Hyde. Ses yeux paroissoient mouillés de quelques larmes, qu'elle s'efforçoit de retenir. Le Chancellier appuyé contre la muraille, leur parut bouffi de quelque chose. Ils ne doutèrent point que ce ne fut de rage et de désespoir. Le Duc d'York leur dit de cet air content et serein dont on annonce les bonnes nouvelles: 'Comme vous etes les deux hommes de la Cour que j'estime le plus, je veux que vous ayez les premiers l'honneur de saluer la Duchesse d'York. La voilà.'"

Not the least wonderful part of the story is the Duchess's conduct to her calumniator. Clarendon says, "the Duke had brought Sir Charles Berkeley to the Duchess, at whose feet he had cast himself with all the acknowledgment and penitence he could express; and she, according to the command of the Duke, accepted his submission, and promised to forget the offense;" but, according to Hamilton, she went further, and praised the conduct of Berkeley and his associates, telling them "that nothing marks more plainly the self-devotion of an honorable man than *de prendre un peu sur sa probité*,[1] to serve the interest of a master or a friend." All this we may believe of the daughter, when the stern old father gives us this evidently subdued account of his own complaisance:—" He came likewise to the Chancellor with those professions he could easily make; and *the other was obliged to receive him civilly.*"[2]

The restoration of harmony in the royal family was facilitated by the sudden death of the Princess of Orange and the Duke of Gloucester, and by a message from Cardinal Mazarine to the Queen mother, "that if she wished to be well received when she returned to the Court of France, she must be exceedingly civil to the Lord Chancellor, whom he was anxious to oblige." On the any such thing, she would never see his face more. I would be glad to see you before you go to the parliament, that I may advise with you what is to be done; for my brother tells me he will do whatever I please."

[Superscribed]—" For the Chancellor."

[1] Anglicè, "to tell a calumnious falsehood."   [2] Life, ii. 385, 393, 397.

day before she left England, the Duke brought his wife to be presented to her for the first time, and the "Queen," says Pepys, "is said to receive her now with much respect and love."[1] The new Duchess supported her rank at Court with as much ease and dignity as if she had never moved in an inferior station.

Her elevation by no means tended to the permanent stability of the Chancellor; but for a short time he was on terms of cordiality with his son-in-law, and, if possible, in higher favor with the King.

He was now raised to the peerage by the title of Baron Hyde of Hindon, and shortly after he was created Viscount Cornbury and Earl of Clarendon. On the application of the Duke of York he was likewise offered the Garter; but though several of his predecessors had borne this distinction, he wisely declined it, thinking that it would bring him more envy than advantage. He accepted a more substantial proof of royal gratitude in a present of £20,000. Charles at the same time made him an offer of 10,000 acres of Crown land; but this he declined, saying, that "it was the principal part or obligation of his office to dissuade the King from making any grants of such a nature (except when the necessity or convenience was very notorious), and even to stop those which should be made of that kind, and not to suffer them to pass the Seal till he had again waited upon the King, and informed him of the evil consequence of these grants, which discharge of his duty could not but raise him many enemies, who should not have that advantage to say that he obstructed the King's bounty towards other men, when he made it very profuse towards himself."[2]

[1] Pepys, i. 166. [2] Life ii. 408.

CHAPTER LXXX.

CONTINUATION OF THE LIFE OF LORD CLARENDON TILL HIS ACQUITTAL WHEN IMPEACHED BY THE EARL OF BRISTOL.

SOON after the ceremony of the coronation, at which the Chancellor appeared with his lately conferred dignity of an Earl, he had to meet the new parliament. Before its dissolution, at the end of eighteen years, it gave abundant opposition to the inclinations of the Court, but the great difficulty at first was to repress its exuberant loyalty. Although the Presbyterians had been so powerful in the Convention Parliament, only fifty-six of that persuasion were returned to the present House of Commons, and almost all the other members were taken from the hottest of the Cavaliers. The House of Lords was tempered by a considerable number of liberal and moderate Peers; but the House of Commons was, at its outset, the most intolerant, bigoted, slavishly inclined legislative assembly which ever met in England, and greatly exceeded the other House in the desire to fix the Church on the narrowest foundation, and to persecute all who should not rigidly conform to its doctrines and discipline.[1]

On the first day of the session, the King, having spoken at greater length than usual, still referred the two Houses for a further explanation of his views to the Lord Chancellor. Clarendon, knowing that the ecclesiastical measures which he approved of were now completely in his power, prepared the parliament for receiving them, and took a very unfair advantage of the late mad and wicked insurrection of Venner and the "Millenarians," which was in reality as much condemned and deplored by the Presbyterians, as by the members of the Church of England. However, to check the Cavalier impetuosity of the new

---

[1] "The representatives," says Rapin, "for the most part were elected agreeably to the wishes and without doubt by the influence of the Court. This parliament may be said to be composed by Chancellor Hyde, prime minister." The insane insurrection of Venner and the Millenarians had thrown much discredit on all dissenters.

parliament, he strongly inculcated upon them the propriety of adhering to the Act of Indemnity.

The Commons, whether prompted by him I know not, showed their spirit by beginning the session with a most unconstitutional resolution, which was to be acted upon without the consent of the Lords or the King,—"that all their members should forthwith take the sacrament according to the rites of the Church of England, on pain of expulsion from the House."[1] To exasperate the public mind, he certainly encouraged the Lords to join the Commons in an order that "the solemn League and Covenant" (which the reigning King had signed) should be burnt by the hands of the common hangman,—along with the ordinances for the trial of the late King, for establishing a commonwealth, and for the security of the person of the Lord Protector.[2] No wonder that he afterwards found extreme difficulty in prevailing upon them to confirm the Act of Indemnity, notwithstanding his earnest representations that the promise of it had brought about the Restoration, and that the faith of the King and of the nation was pledged to it.[3]

The declaration for union and comprehension which Clarendon had drawn, and the King had published during the Convention Parliament, and Sir Mathew Hale's bill founded upon it, of course were thought of no more. The first church bill which Clarendon introduced met with very little opposition,—being to restore the Bishops to their seats in the House of Lords. The act for their exclusion had passed in times of great violence, and there was a general feeling that for the dignity of the assembly of which they had ever formed a constituent part, and for the honor and protection of the church, they should again exercise their parliamentary functions along with the hereditary nobility.

Next came Clarenden's famous "Corporation Act," which, contrary to the Declaration of Breda,—contrary to the repeated promises of the King and the Chancellor after their return,—contrary to the plain principles

---

[1] 4 Parl. Hist. 208.
[2] Ib. 209. Such proceedings show that from the late troubles men of all parties had forgotten the limits of the constitutional powers of the two Houses. This House of Commons made orders directly on the Attorney and Solicitor General to prosecute for high treason, without even the form of an address to the Crown.   [3] 4 Parl. Hist. 209–213.

of justice and expediency,—contrary to the respect
and reverence due to the most solemn institution of our
holy religion which was to be desecrated,—provided that
no one should be elected to any corporate office, who had
not, within a year before his election, taken the sacrament
of the Lord's supper according to the rights of the Church
of England,—laying down a rule which was soon to be
applied to all civil offices and public employments. It
was violently opposed, but passed by large majorities, and
it continued the opprobrium of the Statute Book till, by
the unwearied exertions in the cause of civil and religious
liberty of an illustrious patriot, it was repealed in our own
times.

Clarendon followed up this blow by the Act of Uniformity,—which, on St. Bartholomew's day following, ejected 2,000 ministers from their livings,—which, if rigidly enforced (as it was intended to be), would have established a system of persecution unparalleled in any Protestant country,—and which, notwithstanding the succeeding Act of Toleration, annual indemnity acts, and other relaxations, has deprived the Church of England of the support of those who now form the Wesleyan and other powerful and pious persuasions, and has considerably impaired her influence and usefulness.

It is remarkable that, although Clarendon himself presided in the House of Lords, these and all the other violent measures of the session were much less cordially received in that assembly than in the House of Commons, where it was hardly possible to restrain members from proceeding to extremities against all who had ever submitted to the authority of the Commonwealth, or questioned the infallibility of Archbishop Laud. For example, the Act of Uniformity was abundantly stringent as Clarendon himself framed it ; but he tells us, that no sooner did it come down to the Commons, " than every man, according to his passion, thought of adding somewhat to it that might make it more grievous to somebody whom he did not love." The Lords had set apart one-fifth of the profits of the livings from which the nonconforming clergy were to be ejected, for their support,—as had been done by Elizabeth when she enforced her Liturgy, and even by the Puritanical Parliament when imposing the Presbyterian discipline ;—but to this the Commons would by no means now consent;—and they insisted, that the required subscription should be extended to schoolmasters and tutors, to be enforced against them by fine and imprisonment, as they had no livings to lose. These alterations were not very disagreeable to the Chancellor, for, after a conference between the two Houses, he advised the Lords to agree to them.

At the conclusion of the session was celebrated the King's inauspicious union with Catherine of Braganza. Clarendon afterwards incurred great, and, I think, undeserved, odium for having concurred in this match. It certainly would have been much more desirable for the sake of the national religion that Charles should have selected a Protestant princess from Germany or the North of Europe. But to this he had an insuperable objection, and the match with Catherine seemed as little objectionable as an alliance with any other Roman Catholic family. Although the Spanish ambassador, who wished by all means to break it off, publicly declared that the Princess never could have children, this was properly treated as a mere gratuitous and malignant assertion, and there is not the slightest color for the imputation afterwards cast upon Clarendon of having designedly married the King to a barren wife, that his own grandchildren might succeed to the Crown.[1]

He is not so easily defended for the part he took soon after in trying to persuade the Queen to consent to Lady Castlemaine, the King's avowed mistress, being one of the ladies of the bed-chamber. Catherine, having fainted away when this person was presented to her, and having resisted the shameless application of the King to receive her as an attendant, the Chancellor at first remonstrated with him by letter upon the monstrous impropriety of his conduct,—when he received the following reply: "I wish I may be unhappy in this world and in the world to come, if I faile in the least degree of what I have resolved, which is making of my Lady Castlemaine of my wife's bed-chamber. I am resolved to go through with this matter, let what will come on it; which again I solemnly sware before Almighty God; therefore, if you wish to have the

[1] From Charles's very minute and circumstantial letters to the Chancellor after meeting the Queen, it appears that he was at first highly pleased with her, and there seems to be no doubt that she afterwards miscarried.

continuance of my friendship, meddle no more with this business, except it be to bear down all false and scandalous reports, and to facilitate what I am sure my honour is so much concerned in; and whosoever I find to be my Lady Castlemaine's enemy in this matter, I do promise, upon my word, to be his enemy as long as I live. You may show this letter to my Lord Lieutenant, and if you have both a mind to oblige me, carry yourselves like friends to me in this matter."

Considering that Clarendon wished to be a contrast to Buckingham and Charles's other companions, who thought there was no harm in such violations of morality and decency,—considering that he would not allow his own wife to visit any of the royal mistresses,—that, unlike most of the other ministers of state, he refused to call upon these ladies himself, or to hold councils at their lodgings,—and he affected uniform primness and fastidiousness of demeanor in the midst of a dissolute Court,—it does seem most strange that such a mission should have been proposed to him, and still more strange that he should have accepted it. Certain it is, however, that he had several interviews with Catherine, in which he in vain tried to argue her into compliance. "The fire," he himself tells us, "flamed higher than ever. The King reproached the Queen with stubbornness and want of duty, and she him with tyranny and want of affection; he used threats and menaces (which he never intended to put in execution), and she talked loudly how ill she was treated, and that she would return again to Portugal. He replied, *she would do well first to know whether her mother would receive her*, and he would give her a fit opportunity to know that, by sending to their home all her Portuguese servants; for to them and their counsel he imputed all her perverseness."[1] The grave and reverend head of English judicature, the apostle of orthodoxy, the patron saint of the Church of England, after an interval, again undertook the negotiation, and earnestly advised the Queen that she should submit cheerfully to that which she could not prevent. She replied, "that her conscience would not suffer her to consent to what she could not but suppose would be an occasion and opportunity of sin." Foiled by the native good sense and right feeling

[1] Life, ii. 184.

of this uneducated woman, who had hardly ever been out of a convent till she sailed for England, he threw up the commission, and prayed the King "that he might be no more consulted with nor employed in an affair in which he had been so unsuccessful."[1] Charles at last, by a series of personal insults, himself contrived to break her spirit, and to induce her to take Lady Castlemaine into special favor, so that "she was merry with her in public, and in private used nobody more friendly."

Clarendon's own solicitations are not more disgraceful to him than his taunts upon the poor Queen for her tardy compliance. "But," says he, "this sudden downfall and total abandoning her own greatness, this low demeanor to a person she had justly abhorred and worthily contemned, made all men concluded that it was a hard matter to know her, and consequently to serve her. And the King himself was so far from being reconciled by it, that the esteem which he could not hitherto but retain in his heart for her grew much less. He concluded that all her former aversion expressed in those lively passions, which seemed not capable of dissimulation, was all fiction, and purely acted to the life by a nature crafty, perverse, and inconsistent. He congratulated his own ill-natured perseverance by which he had discovered how he was to behave himself hereafter, and what remedies he was to apply to all future indispositions; nor had he ever after the same value of her wit, judgment, and understanding which he had formerly; and was well enough pleased to observe, that the reverence others had for all three was somewhat diminished."[2] It is impossible not to suspect from such language, that the minister participated in the exultation of the King, and that they mixed their discussions upon the dry subject of the necessity for passing the "Corporation Act" and the "Act of Uniformity" for the purpose of promoting pure religion, with a few sallies upon the vanquished prudery of the Queen, and the superior skill with which her husband had brought her to reason, when "the Keeper of his Conscience" had failed.

Nevertheless, the superior virtue of the Chancellor shone out very conspicuously in another affair which he has related to us, very much to his own advantage. *Bastide,*

---

[1] Life, ii. 180. [2] Ibid. 195.

the French ambassador, having several points which he wished much to carry for his court, particularly the restitution of Nova Scotia—in a conference with him at Worcester House, alluded very mysteriously to the privations which had been endured by him before the Restoration, to the jealous rivals who probably surrounded one so powerful, and to the expediency of his creating friends by acts of bounty,—and at last came out with the declaration "that he had brought with him a present, which in itself was small, but was only the earnest of as much every year, which should be constantly paid, and more if he had occasion to use it." His Excellency then produced bills of exchange for £10,000, which would be paid that afternoon to any persons who might be sent to receive the money. "The Chancellor had heard him with much indignation, and answered him warmly, that if this correspondence must expose him to such a reproach, he should not willingly enter into it, and wished him to tell M. Fouquet that he would only receive wages from his own Master. The gentleman so little looked for a refusal, that he would not understand it, but persisted to know who should receive the money, which should be paid in such a manner that the person who paid it should never know to whom it was paid, and that it shall always remain a secret, still pressing it with importunity till the other went with manifest anger out of the room."

Soon after the King and the Duke, who were privy to all Bastide's proceeding's, called at Worcester House, and seeing the Chancellor much discomposed, asked whether any thing unfortunate had happened to him? He stated to them, " with much choler," the attempt that had been made upon his virtue, whereupon they both burst out in loud laughter at him, saying, "*the French did all their business that way,*" and the King told him "*he was a fool.*" He then, as he assures us, read the King a lecture on his levity and want of principle, "beseeching him not to appear to his servants so unconcerned in matters of this nature, and desiring him to consider what the consequences of his receiving that money, with what secresy, soever, must be ; that the French King must either believe that he had received it without his own Sovereign's privity, and so look upon him as a knave fit to be depended upon in any treachery against his Master, or that it was with his Majesty's approbation, which must needs lessen his esteem of him that he should permit his servants of the nearest trust to grow rich at the charge of another Prince, who might, the next day, become his enemy." Charles smiled, and merely replied, "Few men are so scrupulous;" but before going away charged him to cherish the correspondence with the French minister, which might be useful, and could produce no inconvenience.[1] The bribe was shortly after again offered, and refused, but Clarendon consented to accept for his library a present from the French King of all the books printed at the Louvre.

Our Chancellor's private purity, as illustrated by this transaction, is very much to be commended; but we must deeply condemn his conduct as a constitutional minister in shortly after soliciting a bribe for his Master, and teaching him to be a pensioner of the French King. Bastide having once more made an offer to him of pecuniary aid, "for the furthering the King of England's or his own interest at the next parliament," he wrote for answer: —" We can not have more reason to be confident of any thing than of the good temper and great affection of the parliament, which is now shortly to meet, and we have many matters of greater importance to settle with them than the procuring of money till the other things are done, and yet you will easily believe that the King, before that time, may be in some straits which he will not willingly own. If this should fall out to be the case, do you believe, if the King desires it, that the King of France will lend him £50,000 for ten or twelve months, in which time it shall be punctually repaid?" This petition was, of course, joyfully granted.

Although the money was to be received from a foreign state without the knowledge of parliament, and was to be partly employed in bribing members of the House of Commons, and the receipt of it was necessarily to make England subservient to France, it is remarkable that Clarendon does not seem to have had the least consciousness of any impropriety in negotiating the bribe under the name of loan, and seems to have thought his own conduct as innocent as in obtaining contributions to pay Charles's tradesmen at Cologne or Bruges. But he must

[1] Life of Clarendon, ii. 521—524. Burnet, i. 285.

be considered answerable for having originated and sanctioned that shameful dependence of Charles upon Louis XIV., which is the greatest reproach of this reign. He afterwards used some big words in the dispute about our naval rights, which made the French King complain of the hauteur of the Chancellor; but the encourager of bribes soon found himself obliged to submit.

Clarendon was next engaged in a transaction which raised a terrible cry against him, and in which, I think, his conduct was by no means blameless—the sale of Dunkirk. There is no ground whatever for believing that, in the course of it, he was guilty of private corruption by the secret receipt of money for his own use. The retention of the place by England was, perhaps, hardly desirable, from the expense it occasioned, and the temptation it offered to engage in continental wars, although it greatly flattered the pride of the nation, who delighted in this acquisition as a substitute for Calais, and it was regarded, like Berwick and Gibraltar in other times, as a proof of the prowess of England in possessing a strong fortress on the territory of a rival state. But the manner in which it was alienated in the time of profound peace, without the knowledge of parliament, for a sum of money to supply the expense of the profligate pleasures of the Sovereign, seems to me deserving of severe censure,—which falls almost exclusively on the Chancellor.

So lately as the 19th of May, 1662, he himself had said in a speech in the House of Lords, "Whosoever unskillfully murmurs at the expense of Dunkirk and the other new acquisitions, which ought to be looked upon as jewels of an immense magnitude in the royal diadem, do not enough remember what we have lost by Dunkirk, and should always do, if it were in an enemy's hands." Yet in the month of October following, he signed a treaty by which Dunkirk was sold to France for five millions of livres, to be paid into the private purse of the King of England. He stoutly denies that he was the author of the measure, and Louis XIV. boasts that his ambassador, d'Estrades, dexterously put it into the head of Charles, although Charles himself said that it was first proposed to him by the Chancellor. The former supposition is more probable, but hardly in any appreciable degree mitigates the misconduct of the minister, for he admits that he adopted it, and earnestly carried it forward. He even privately instructed the King how it was to be propounded to the Council, as we learn from a written communication between them, which is still extant: *King.* "Am not I to break this business of Dunkirke?"—*Chan.* "Yes: and first declare that you have somewhat of importance to propose, and therefore that you will have a close counsell, and that the clarke withdraw: then state it as you resolved."—*King.* "I think the first opening of the matter must be upon Monsieur d'Estrades's desire of having the place."—*Chan.* "No: but upon several representacions my Lord Treasurer hath made to you: Of your expences how farr they exceed your receipts: That you have spent some time in the consideracions how to improve the one and to lessen the other: That you finde the expence of Dunkirke to be £130,000 a yeere: You finde if it were fitt to parte with it, you could not only take off that expence, but do believe you might get a good sum of money. Aske the advice of the Board in an affayre of this moment."

Clarendon strove hard to make a good pecuniary bargain, and probably could not have got a higher price from any other customer, although Louis boasted of having overreached him by pretending that he had no ready money, and then discounting his own acceptances.[1] The proceeds were thrown into the lap of the Countess of Castlemaine, and the Chancellor's splendid new mansion now rising in Piccadilly, received from the multitude the name of "DUNKIRK HOUSE."

Hitherto the King had been entirely under the guidance of Clarendon; but at length they had a difference, and though it was only by slow degrees that the pupil could get rid of his master, all cordiality between them was gone. Charles, while in exile had been secretly reconciled to the Catholic Church, and though, in general, very little subject to religious impressions, yet at times he was desirous of making atonement for his immoralities by doing what might be agreeable to his spiritual guides. The Act of Uniformity, if strictly enforced, would operate most oppressively against the Roman Catholics. He was willing to give them some relief, but could here expect no assistance from the Chancellor. Nicholas was removed

[1] Œuvres de Louis XIV. i. 175. D'Estrades, i. 286, 343.

from the office of Secretary of State, and was replaced by Sir Henry Bennet, afterwards Earl of Arlington, who "had the art of managing the temper of the King beyond all other men of that time,"[1] and, to please him, had himself become a Papist. The question of indulgence was now brought forward before the Council, when Bennet maintained that the King, as Head of the Church possessed the right of suspending all penal laws in matters of religion,—a doctrine which Clarendon now controverted. In spite of his opinion, and as he asserts, without his being consulted on the propriety of such a step, a royal Declaration, drawn by Bennet, came out, in which his Majesty was made to say, "as for what concerns the penalties upon those who, living peaceably, do not conform themselves to the discipline and government of the Church of England, through scruple and tenderness of misguided conscience, but modestly and without scandal perform their devotions in their own way, he should make it his special care, so far as in him lay, without invading the freedom of parliament, to incline their wisdom next approaching session to concur with him in making such act for that purpose as may enable him to exercise, with a more universal satisfaction, that power of dispensing which he conceived to be inherent in the Crown."

When Parliament met Clarendon was confined by illness, and the King opened the session with a speech expressing his zeal for Protestantism, but caused a bill to be introduced in the House of Lords, by the Lord Privy Seal, to enable him to dispense with all laws requiring subscription or obedience to the doctrine and discipline of the established Church. In the first day's debate on this bill, in the absence of Clarendon, it was stoutly opposed by Lord Southampton and the Bishops, but boldly supported by Lord Ashley, Lord Robartes, and other Peers, who wished to pay court to the Sovereign. The debate was adjourned, and the result considered doubtful. Under these circumstances the Chancellor, next morning, left his sick bed, came down to the House, and made such an uncompromising and powerful speech against the bill, that the second reading was postponed, and it was never again resumed.

But his favor with the King was turned into loathing,

[1] Burnet.

and this change being visible, there was a general disposition among the courtiers to annoy him,—which induced him to write to his friend Ormond, "I have had so unpleasant a life as that, for my own ease and content, I rather wished myself at Breda, and have hardly been able to restrain myself from making that suit."[1]

Pepys gives us a most lively description of the state of the Court at this time. "It seems the present favorites now are my Lord Bristol, Duke of Buckingham, Sir H. Bennet, my Lord Ashley, and Sir Charles Berkeley: who, amongst them, have cast my Lord Chancellor on his back past ever getting up again, there being now little for him to do; and he waits at Court, attending to speak to the King, as others do. The King do mind nothing but pleasure. If any of the counselors give him good advice, and move him to anything that is to his good and honor, the other part, which are his counselors of pleasure, take him when he is with my Lady Castlemaine, and in a humor of delight, and then persuade him that he ought not to listen to the advice of those old dotards or counselors that were heretofore his enemies, when, God knows! it is they that, now-a-days, do most study his honor."[2]

Clarendon was saved from the impending peril, and enabled to continue some years longer in office, by the rash attempt of an enemy to precipitate his fall. On the 10th of July, to the astonishment of all, except a very few who were in the secret, the Earl of Bristol rose in his place in the House of Lords, and produced a paper in his own hand-writing, and signed with his name, containing "Articles of impeachment for high treason and other misdemeanors against the Lord High Chancellor." He told the Lords "that he could not but observe that, after so glorious a return with which God had blessed the King and the nation, so that all the world had expected that the prosperity of the kingdom would have far exceeded the misery and adversity that it had for many years endured, and after the parliament had contributed more to it than ever parliament had done; notwithstanding all which it was evident to all men, and lamented by those who wished well to his Majesty, that his affairs grew every day worse and

---

[1] April 11, 1663.   [2] Pepys, ii. 38.

worse; the King himself lost much of his honor and the affection he had in the hearts of the people; that, for his part, he looked upon it with as much sadness as any man, and had made inquiry, as well as he could, from whence this great misfortune, which every body was sensible of, could proceed; and that he was satisfied, in his own conscience, that it proceeded principally from the power and credit of the Chancellor; and therefore he was resolved, for the good of his country, to accuse the Lord Chancellor of high treason." He concluded by desiring that the articles might be read. They charged that the Chancellor had arrogated to himself the direction of all his Majesty's affairs, both at home and abroad; that he had applied to the Pope for a Cardinal's cap for Lord Aubigny; that some of his friends had said, "Were it not for my Lord Chancellor standing in the gap, Popery would be introduced;" that he had concluded the King's marriage without due agreement how it should be solemnized: that he and his adherents had uttered gross scandals against the King's course of life; that he had advised and effected the sale of Dunkirk; that he had told the King the House of Lords was weak and inconsiderable; and that he had enriched himself and his creatures by the sale of offices.

The Chancellor, leaving the woolsack, made a pointed and animated defense, contending that all the charges which were not quite frivolous were false; that none of them amounted to treason; and that an impeachment for treason could not thus be commenced by one Peer against another,—upon which points he desired that the Judges might be consulted.

The Judges being summoned pronounced their unanimous opinion, by the mouth of Lord Chief Justice Bridgeman, that the prosecution was not duly commenced, and that if the charges were all admitted to be true, there was nothing of treason in them. The King, seeing the result, very irregularly sent a message to the Lords, telling them that in the articles he finds many matters of fact charged, which, upon his own certain knowledge are untrue. The Lords resolved *nemine dissentiente*, that they concurred with the Judges, and they dismissed the prosecution, with a strong censure of the Earl of Bristol for the manner in which he had brought it forward. Warrants were issued for his apprehension, and he was obliged to remain in concealment for some years.¹

Clarendon's enemies were completely disheartened and confounded by this failure, and he seemed again firmly seated in power; but although the chief direction of affairs was restored to him, Charles watched impatiently for a favorable opportunity entirely to emancipate himself from his minister.²

CHAPTER LXXXI.

CONTINUATION OF THE LIFE OF LORD CLARENDON TILL HIS FALL.

CLARENDON was prevented by illness from being present at the opening of the session of parliament, which began in March, 1664, but he prompted Charles's address to the two Houses, delivered on that occasion. The doctrine was not yet recognized that the Royal speech is the speech of the minister, or he would have been liable to very sincere censure for the language now uttered. The House of Commons having sat three years, objections were started that under the Triennial Act, to which Charles I. had regularly given his assent, it had, in point of law, ceased to exist. "I confess to you, my lords and gentlemen," said the King, "I have often myself read over that bill, and though there is no color for the fancy of the determination of this parliament, yet I will not deny to you that I have always expected that you would, and even wondered that you have not, considered the wonderful clauses in that bill, which passed in a time very uncareful for the dignity of the Crown, or the security of the people. I need not tell you how much I love parliaments. Never King was so much beholden to parliaments as I have been; nor do I think the Crown can ever be happy without frequent parliaments. But assure yourselves, if I should think otherwise, *I would never suffer a parliament to come together by the means prescribed by that bill.*"

"So audacious a declaration, equivalent to an avowed

¹ 4 Parl. Hist. 276.   ² Life, ii. 256.   Burnet, i. 358.

design in certain circumstances of preventing the execution of the laws by force of arms, was never before heard from the lips of an English King, and would in any other times have awakened a storm of indignation from the Commons."[1] But a repealing act rapidly passed both Houses, providing merely that parliaments should not be intermitted more than three years, but furnishing no remedy for the enforcement of the rule,—a provision which was found nugatory in the course of this very reign. Clarendon's ecclesiastical policy has excited so much attention, that he has escaped the blame he deserves for having been instrumental in removing this constitutional barrier, whereby he hurried on the destruction of the family whose power he wished to extend.

He now gained immense applause from the ultra-high-church party, by passing the "Conventicle Act," the object of which was wholly to prevent the public celebration of religious worship, except according to the ceremonies of the Church of England,—by enacting that every meeting of more than five persons, in addition to the members of the family, for religious purposes, not in accordance with the established Liturgy, should be held to be a seditious and unlawful conventicle, and that any person above sixteen years of age, on conviction before a single justice, might be punished by a fine of £5, or imprisonment during three months for the first offense, £10, or six months for the second offense, and £100, or transportation for the third offense.

This was followed up a few months after with the " Five Mile Act," which completed the " Clarendonian Code," enacting that all nonconforming clergymen should make oath that it was not lawful, upon any pretense whatsoever, to take arms against the King or against those commissioned by him, and *that they would not at any time endeavor any alteration of government in Church or State,—* and that whoever would not swear this oath should be rendered incapable of teaching in schools, and should be forbidden under pain of fine and imprisonment to abide within five miles of any city, corporate, or borough town

[1] Hall. Const. Hist. ii. 448. It has been suggested that the speech meant no more than that the King would take care, by the frequent calling of parliaments, that the compulsory clauses of the Triennial Act should never come into operation ; but I think the plain meaning is, that he would set them at defiance.—See Lister's *Life of Clarendon*, ii. 289.

sending members to parliament, or any place where he had exercised his ministry. This outrageous bill, though brought in by the ministry, was opposed by Southampton, the Lord Treasurer, who declared he could take no such oath himself; for how firm soever he had always been to the Church, yet as things were managed he did not know but he himself might see cause to endeavor an alteration;[1] but Clarendon rebukes his friend for too great indulgence to the Presbyterians, and praises the parliament which passed this act " for entirely sympathizing with his Majesty, and having passed more acts for his honor and security than any other had ever done in so short a session."[2] No one can doubt his sincerity or his disinterestedness, for he was not only making himself obnoxious both to the dissenters and the Roman Catholics, but he was likewise fully aware that the line of policy he pursued on these questions was highly distasteful to the King, who was for liberty of conscience and of worship, for the sake of the religion he had embraced. We can only deeply regret the Chancellor's growing bigotry, and his utter forgetfulness of the solemn engagements into which he had entered.

The Dutch war was now undertaken, from commercial jealousy on the part of the English nation, and from the King's hope of diverting to private purposes a part of the supplies voted by parliament for carrying it on. To the honor of Clarendon, he, with his friend Southampton, steadily opposed it as unjust and impolitic. According to the maxims which then prevailed, he considered himself authorized, however, to remain in office and publicly to defend the policy of the Government which he privately condemned. Being still unable to be present at the opening of a new session, in November, he prepared "a Narrative of the late Passages between his Majesty and the Dutch, and his Majesty's Preparations thereupon," which the King, after his own speech, handed in, and which was read in his presence. This was in the nature of a manifesto to justify hostilities, and concluded with an earnest exhortation to the two Houses to enable the King, by liberal supplies, to prosecute the war with vigor, and so to obtain an honorable peace. Conferences were held at Worcester House with the leading members of the House of Commons as to the most expedient mode

---

[1] Burnet, i. 390.   [2] Life, iii. 1.

of conducting the business of the government in that assembly, where motions of supply were still made by independent members, and the ostensible office of government leader was unknown. Charles himself used occasionally to attend these meetings. Clarendon has left us a curious account of one of them held in his own bed-chamber, when he was confined by the gout, the question being, "whether the government should agree to a proposal, strongly supported in the House of Commons, that the money voted should be appropriated to particular services, instead of forming a general fund to be applied at the pleasure of the Crown?" Sir George Downing ventured to express an opinion in favor of this course,—which threw the old Chancellor into a towering passion, and,—joined to "the extremity of the pain which at that time he endured in his bed,"—drew from him this reprimand, "that it was impossible for the King to be well served whilst fellows of his condition were admitted to speak as much as they had a mind to, and that in the best times such presumption had been punished with imprisonment by the Lords of the Council." But the King was not pleased to see a leading member of the House of Commons so put down, and took his side—probably from the fear that, without the appropriation, the supply would not be granted, and hoping when he had once got the money to divert it to his own purposes.

The next motion in the House of Commons alarmed the Chancellor much more, being for the appointment of Commissioners to superintend the expenditure of the poll tax and other taxes. This was carried by a majority of 119 to 83, though, according to Pepys, "it was mightily ill taken by all the Court party, as a mortal blow that struck deep into the King's prerogative, and, though when the division was expected the King had given order to my Lord Chamberlain to send to the playhouses and brothels to bid all the parliament-men that were there to go to the parliament presently."[1]

It seems very strange to us that Clarendon should advise the King to resist the inquiry into the public expenditure—which he considered as bad as anything attempted by the Long Parliament, saying, "that this was such a new encroachment as had no bottom; and that the scars

[1] Pepys, iii. 102, 103.

were yet too fresh and green of those wounds, which had been inflicted upon the kingdom from such usurpation: and therefore he desired his Majesty to be firm in the resolution he had taken and not to depart from it."[1]

Charles pretended to follow his advice, by appointing Lord Ashley treasurer of prize-money, with a provision "that he should account for all moneys received by him to the King himself, and to no other person whatsoever." Clarendon remonstrated, arguing that such a patent was unprecedented; that it would cause the King to be defrauded; and that it was an offensive encroachment on the office of Lord Treasurer. He might have added, that it was an expedient to facilitate the peculation meditated by his Majesty. Charles here was "firm in the resolution he had taken, and would not depart from it, for the King sent the Chancellor a positive order to seal the commission, which he could no longer refuse."[2]

In the next controversy in which Clarendon was engaged he gained much credit with the judicious, although he was denounced by the landed interest as "a friend of free trade." The importation of cattle from Ireland had lately considerably increased, and the landlords of England, headed by the Duke of Buckingham, instead of pretending to stand up as the advocates of the tenant-farmers, or of the laborers, or of the public, plainly spoke out, "that, from a fall in the price of cattle, their rents were lowered to the amount of £200,000 a year, which they could not afford." A bill was therefore brought in absolutely to prohibit such importation in future; this was followed by another bill, equally to prohibit the importation of any cured meat or provisions from Ireland, and to guard against the pretense that these were merely fiscal regulations, which the King might render nugatory by his dispensing power, the prohibited trade was declared to be "a nuisance." Both bills passed the Commons by great majorities, and when they came to the Lords, the Duke of Buckingham observed that "they could not be opposed

---

[1] Life, iii. 132.
[2] Life of Clarendon, ii. 340. We have here another instance of the notion then prevailing that any act was excused by the personal order of the Sovereign. The correlative maxims of royal impeccability and ministerial responsibility were yet imperfectly understood. Resignation instead of compliance was never thought of.—See Life of Lord Keeper Herbert, *ante*, vol iii. p. 399.

by any who had not Irish estates or Irish understandings."[1] The Chancellor, however, had the courage to deliver a most admirable speech against them, pointing out the injustice of these measures to our fellow-subjects in Ireland, and the impolicy of them with a view to English manufactures, the demand for which from Ireland must cease,—and even to English agriculture, which could not fail to prosper with the increased prosperity produced by a free interchange of commodities between the two islands. He was told, however, that the heavily-taxed English could not enter into a competition in the breeding of cattle with the lightly-taxed Irish, and that without the proposed "protection" tenants would be bankrupt, laborers must come upon the parish, and the kingdom must be ruined. He was shamefully beaten in all the divisions on the bill, and all that he could effect was, in the Committee, to carry an amendment, by 63 to 47, to strike out the word "nuisance," and to insert "detriment and mischief" in its stead. The Chancellor's amendment set the Commons in a flame, and many sarcasms were uttered upon the presumption of a lawyer, who had hardly inherited an acre from his father, either in Ireland or England, pretending to speak upon such a subject. Several conferences took place between the two Houses, the King for some time, at the request of the Duke of Ormond, supporting the Chancellor; but the Squires declared that they had not yet completed the supplies, and that they would stop them at all hazards if they were to be thus dictated to by wild theorists, who had no practical knowledge of the breeding of cattle, or of the true interests of the country. Charles became alarmed lest no more money should be granted to carry on the war and to satisfy the rapacity of his mistresses; the friends of the Court in the House of Lords were instructed to agree to the contested word, and the bill received the royal assent with the clause declaring that the importation of Irish cattle and provisions was "to the common nuisance of all his Majesty's subjects residing in England."[2] This happened in the "*annus mirabilis,*" and was of more permanent injury to the country than the Plague or the Fire of London.

[1] Ossory, the son of the Lord Lieutenant, in consequence sent him a challenge, but they were both taken into the custody of the Black Rod.
[2] Lords' Jour. Dec. 20, 29, 1666. Jan. 3, 12, 14, 1667.

I have no doubt that the part which Clarendon took on the Irish question contributed to his fall quite as much as the unfortunate termination of the Dutch war, to which it has been generally ascribed.

For the conduct of that war he was not answerable more than for its commencement. He strove to influence the votes of both Houses in its favor, and likewise to obtain supplies from the Commons for carrying it on, but these were handed over to Charles's profligate companions, and shamefully misapplied. The consequence was, that while the negotiations for a peace were going forward,—by the energy of De Witt, the Dutch fleet, under the command of De Ruyter, took Sheerness, burnt the dockyard at Chatham, sunk several English ships of war in the Thames, sailed up the river as high as Gravesend, were expected next tide at London Bridge, and after blockading the port of London, and insulting the English coast on the German Ocean, and on the Channel for some weeks, withdrew at their leisure to their own harbors. The peace of Breda soon removed the apprehensions of invasion; but the disgrace which the nation had suffered sunk deep into the public mind, and the present times were necessarily contrasted with those when Blake humbled the power of Spain, and the English flag rode triumphant on every sea.

Other circumstances concurred to depress the spirits of the nation to an unparalleled degree. Most families were in mourning for the loss of relations in the plague; the metropolis was still lying in ruins from the great fire by which it had been destroyed in the autumn of the preceding year; foreign trade was almost extinguished; and numerous classes of laborers at home were entirely without employment or support.

Clarendon was ostensibly the prime minister, and the multitude, without giving themselves the trouble of any discrimination, passionately pronounced him the author of all their sufferings. Soon after the Restoration, he had been thus addressed by Dryden:

> "Such is the mighty swiftness of your mind,
> That, like the earth, it leaves our sense behind;
> While you so smoothly turn and roll our sphere,
> That rapid motion does but rest appear;
> Yet unimpaired with labors or with time,
> Your age but seems to a new youth to climb."

But when the alarming news arrived that the Dutch fleet was at Gravesend, a mob broke in the windows of his new palace, and painted a gibbet on his gate, with this rude rhyme:

> "Three sights to be seen,
> Dunkirk, Tangiers, and a barren Queen."

This magnificent structure had risen amidst the national disasters, and he had very recently taken possession of it. Reckless charges being circulated against him of bribery from the Dutch and Portuguese, as well as the French, its usual name of "Dunkirk House" was sometimes made to give place to that of "Holland House" and "Tangier Hall."[1] Even sacrilege was imputed to him because he had purchased certain materials which had been destined for the repair of St. Paul's Cathedral. Persons of superior condition sanctioned, without believing these calumnies; and the following epigram from Andrew Marvell, though more remarkable for malignity than wit, suited the general taste, and was in everybody's mouth:—

> "Here lie the sacred bones
> Of Paul, beguil'd of his stones;
> Here lie golden briberies,
> The price of ruin'd families;
> The cavalier's debenture wall,
> Fix'd on an eccentric basis:
> Here's Dunkirk town and Tangier Hall,
> The Queen's marriage and all;
> The Dutchman's *templum pacis*."[2]

Clarendon had lately lost his firm friend and supporter, Lord Southampton; and unfortunately, there was no sect or party in the country to stand by him when assailed by such a tide of unpopularity. The Dissenters regarded him with abhorrence, as the perfidious schemer of all the measures by which they had been oppressed. He was equally disliked by the Catholics, as the person who defeated all the King's intentions to favor them. Even the ungrateful Bishops, he tells us, were dissatisfied with him, for not doing more to put down schism, "which produced a greater coldness from some of them towards him, and a greater resentment from him, who thought

---

[1] Pepys, iii. 251. Tangiers, part of the dowry of Queen Catherine, he had boasted of as an important acquisition to the Crown, but it had been found only a source of useless expense. The other two taunts are obvious enough.
[2] Marvell's Works, iii. 342.

he had deserved better from their functions and their persons, than was in a long time, if ever, perfectly reconciled."[1] The orthodox clergy generally regarded him with ill will, as the author of a proclamation in which they had been charged with drunkenness.[2] The unrewarded cavaliers, because he had stopped some improvident grants, ascribed to him all their disappointments. He had given mortal offense to the present House of Commons by an opinion, in which the best constitutional authorities concur with him, that the parliament, having been prorogued on the 8th of February to the 10th of October, the King could not summon it to meet at an earlier day, even on the apprehension of a Dutch invasion, and that the only legal course was to dissolve the existing parliament, and instantly to call another.

The King had never forgiven his opposition to the bill "for indulgence to tender consciences," and now rather rejoiced both at the well and the ill founded accusations brought against him. Buckingham, Killigrew, and the other wits of the Court, who were in the habit of ridiculing the Chancellor for the amusement of Charles and Lady Castlemaine, ventured more and more boldly upon the broad buffoonery of exhibiting him marching in procession with pompous gait to the Court of Chancery,—a pair of bellows and a fire-shovel being carried before him, like the Great Seal and the mace. These mimicries, which the King encouraged by his laughter, while he affected to reprove them, by degrees entirely obliterated his respect for his old monitor, and gave him courage to assert his own freedom.[3]

But what most deeply affected the royal mind was, the Chancellor's conduct respecting "la belle Stuart." Charles

[1] Life of Clar. ii. 150.   [2] 4 Parl. Hist. 382.
[3] The part of the Chancellor was supported by Buckingham, who is said most felicitously to have imitated "the stately stalk of that solemn personage." Colonel Titus was the mace-bearer, and carried the fire-shovel on his shoulder with such gravity and self-importance, that the courtiers called out, "Like master like man." The name of the actor who played "purse-bearer" is not recorded. The fame of this masque came round to the Chancellor. "For wit's sake they sometimes reflected upon somewhat he had said, or acted some of his postures and manner of speaking, the skill in mimicry being the best faculty in wit many of them had. But by these liberties, which at first only raised laughter, they by degrees got the hardiness to censure both the persons, counsels, and actions of those who were nearest his

was believed to have been more tenderly attached to this lady than to any of her sex, for whom he had ever professed admiration; but she, though admitting his approaches in a manner not very consistent with discretion, had resolutely defended the citadel of her virtue. His passion being inflamed by this resistance, he contemplated offering her his hand in marriage, after obtaining a divorce on some pretext from his present wife. So serious was he that he consulted Archbishop Sheldon on the subject, who, without giving him an answer, communicated what had passed between them to the Chancellor. There were evidently strong objections to the scheme, on the ground of justice and expediency; and these were greatly strengthened in the mind of Clarendon by the consideration that it would probably cut off the chance of his grandchildren succeeding to the throne, which had for some time been considered certain. It is believed that he went straightway to Miss Stuart, and, by strong representations of what was for her honor and advantage, induced her immediately to consent to a clandestine marriage with the Duke of Richmond, who had long been her suitor. Charles discovering the secret, and, from an accidental meeting with Lord Cornbury, the Chancellor's son, at Miss Stuart's lodgings, suspecting the author of his disappointment,—expressed his indignation in the most unmeasured terms.' This being reported to Chancellor, he in a very undignified manner (which considerably detracts from the merit of his boasted demeanor to the royal mistresses) denied peremptorily, in the King's presence, that he had any concern in Miss Stuart's marriage to the Duke of Rich-

Majesty's trust with the highest malice and presumption, and too often suspended or totally disappointed some resolutions which had been taken upon very mature deliberation."—*Life*, ii. 324. The ladies of the Court joined, by saying to the King as the Chancellor appeared, "Here comes your schoolmaster!"

¹ The following is Ludlow's malicious account of this affair written in Switzerland: "The Chancellor sent for the Duke of Richmond, and pretending to be sorry that a person of his worth should receive no marks of his favor, advised him to marry Mrs. Stuart as the most certain way he could take to advance himself. The young man unwarily took in the bait, and credulously relying on what the old *Volpone* had said, made immediate application to the young lady, who was ignorant of the King's intentions, and in a few days married her. The King being thus disappointed, and soon after informed by what means this match had been brought about, banished the Duke with his new Duchess from the Court, and kept his resentment against the Chancellor to a more convenient opportunity."—*Mem.* 417.

mond; and finding that the King still imputed to him the failure of his hopes, condescended to repeat the denial in writing. Charles still remained incredulous, and viewed the Chancellor with more and more dislike.

While the political horizon was blackening on all sides around the aged statesman, he suffered a severe domestic affliction, which he thus records: "His wife, the mother of all his children, and *his companion in all his banishment*,[1] and who had made all his former calamities less grievous by her company and courage, having made a journey to Tunbridge for her health, returned from thence without the benefit she expected, yet without being thought by the physician to be in any danger, and within less than three days died; which was so sudden, unexpected, and irreparable a loss, that he had not courage to support; which nobody wondered at who knew the mutual satisfaction and comfort they had in each other."[2]

While he secluded himself from public business and from society, his ruin was consummated by the reconciliation of the King to Buckingham, who had been for some time in disgrace and skulking from a warrant of commitment to the Tower. This was brought about by the mediation of Lady Castlemaine, who succeeded by often calling Charles "fool," and telling him "that if he was not a fool he would not suffer his business to be carried on by fools that did not understand them, and cause his best subjects and those best able to serve him to be imprisoned."

As soon as Buckingham was restored to the Court, he was impatient for the formation of the new administration, which afterwards acquired such infamy under the name of the CABAL; and Lady Castlemaine and he would give the indolent King no rest till he sent a message to the Chancellor through the Duke of York, intimating that he had been secretly informed that the parliament would certainly impeach him at their next meeting, not only for his having opposed them in all those things upon which they had set their hearts, but because he had proposed and advised their dissolution, and recommending

---

[1] There is no reason to suppose that he was not a very good husband; but he is here *rhetorical* in his grief, for his wife was hardly ever with him during his exile, although she pressed him to send for her.   [2] Life, iii. 282.

that he should appease their wrath by an immediate surrender of the Great Seal.[1]

Clarendon expressed his regret that the King should have no better opinion of his innocence and integrity than to conclude that he could not repel such an attack, and requested an audience before returning any answer to his commands.

This request could not be refused, and the King appointed him to come to him after breakfast on the 26th of August. The approaching interview was known to all the courtiers, and excited the liveliest interest among them, as each was sanguine enough to hope some personal advantage from the expected change.

Clarendon being admitted to the royal presence, said he had no suit to make to his Majesty, nor the least thought of diverting him from the resolution his Majesty had taken, but he wished to receive his Majesty's determination from his Majesty himself, and that he therefore came to know what fault he had committed. The King disclaimed having anything to object to him, but professed that he had adopted this resolution for his good and preservation, saying that taking the Seal from him at this time would so well please the parliament, that he might thereby be preserved, and his Majesty himself might, in all other things, have what he desired,—adding that the business was already so publicly spoken of that he knew not how to change his purpose.—*Clarendon.* " Your Majesty has the undoubted right to dispose of my office as seemeth you best, and forthwith to deprive me of the Seal; but I, your Majesty's humble liege subject, have a right to defend mine honor, and I will by no means suffer it to be believed that I voluntarily give up the Seal, as confessing wrong, nor, if I am deprived of it, will I acknowledge this deprivation to be done in my favor, or in order to do me good; and so far am I from fearing the justice of the parliament, that I renounce your Majesty's protection or interposition towards my preservation."—*King.* " You have not enough reflected on the power of the parliament, or their hostility to you, however groundless that may be; and my own condition, after recent miscarriages, is such that I can not dispute with them, and am myself at their mercy."—*Claren-*

[1] Life, iii. 282.

don. "Whatever resolution your Majesty may take in my particular, let me beseech you not to suffer your spirits to fall, nor yourself to be dejected with the apprehension of the formidable power of the parliament, which is more, or less, or nothing, as you please to make it. It is yet in your power to govern them; but if they find it in theirs to govern you, nobody knows what the end will be." He then made a short relation of the manner in which Richard II. had been bullied by his parliament, and how his misfortunes might have been prevented.

All this Charles took in tolerably good part; but when Clarendon began to warn him more directly against the bad advice of those by whom he was surrounded, and pointedly to allude to the Countess of Castlemaine, anger and impatience were visibly depicted on the royal visage. The noble historian's narrative admits that, in the course of the conversation, "he mentioned *the lady* with some reflections and cautions, which he might more advisedly have declined." After two hours' discourse the King rose and retired without announcing any resolution on the subject. The Duke of York, who was the only third party present, expressed a fear that "he was offended with the last part of it."[1]

Such curiosity was excited among the courtiers and mistresses by this conference, that they were eager to guess at the result of it by watching the countenances of the King and the Chancellor when it was over; but they could only discover that "both looked very thoughtful."[2] Great alarm prevailed among them when some days passed over without a resignation or dismissal. Sir William Coventry and Arlington saw that they could not place reliance on the unsteady and careless temper of the King, particularly as it was understood that the Duke of York had been attempting to soften his father-in-law's harsh expressions at the late interview, and to restore him to

[1] Life of Clar. iii. 286.
[2] Pepys gives a particularly lively description of the demeanor of Lady Castlemaine as the Chancellor was leaving Whitehall: "When he went from the King on Monday morning she was in bed (though about twelve o'clock) and ran out in her smock into her aviary looking into Whitehall Garden; and thither her woman brought her her nightgown, and stood blessing herself at the old man's going away; and several of the gallants of Whitehall (of which there were many staying to see the Chancellor's return) did talk to her in her birdcage; among others, Blancford, telling her she was a bird of passage."—*Pepys*, iii. 334.

favor. They, therefore, strongly represented to Charles that he had proceeded too far to retire, and that he would be looked upon as a child if he should now hesitate; they taunted him with his subserviency to the Chancellor, and the awe in which he stood of him; they represented the Chancellor as a cunning old lawyer, who only sought his own ends, and who, to add to his own consequence, had kept the Crown dependent on the parliament by refusing the offer of a great permanent revenue. Not yet sure of having inspired the King with necessary courage and energy, they again set Lady Castlemaine upon him, "who nearly hectored him out of his wits." She, strange to say, asked him if this was his return for her complaisance in trying to further his suit with "la belle Stuart?"[1] At this name Charles instantly asked forgiveness of her upon his knees for his delay, and sent Morrice, the Secretary of State, with a warrant under the sign-manual, to require and receive the Great Seal from the present holder of it. Clarendon was employing it in sealing the formal proclamation of the Peace of Breda, and as soon as this ceremony was finished, he delivered it up with an expression of submission to the royal will, and of satisfaction that his last official act was to restore harmony between two nations who ought to be united. Morrice returned with the Seal to Whitehall, and put it into the King's hands while he still remained in Lady Castlemaine's apartments, surrounded by Clarendon's enemies,—when May, one of the basest of them, embracing his Majesty's knees, exclaimed, "Sir, you are now a King!"[2]

CHAPTER LXXXII.

CONTINUATION OF THE LIFE OF LORD CLARENDON TILL HIS BANISHMENT.

CLARENDON bore his reverse of fortune with firmness. He put some faith in the representation that after the loss of his office no further steps would be taken against him; but he was prepared resolutely to

---

[1] At his request she had frequently invited Miss Stuart to her parties, and left them alone together. [2] Life, iii. 294. Pepys, iii. 321, 335, 338, 407.

defend himself should he be assailed on the meeting of parliament.[1] As yet he had no suspicion that the King would sanction any attempt to destroy him or to offer him further molestation. Charles at first imputed the act of dismissing him entirely to his bad temper. "The truth is," said his Majesty in a letter to Ormond, "his behavior and humor was grown so insupportable to myself and all the world else, that I could no longer endure it, and it was impossible for me to bear with it and those things with the parliament that must be done, or the government will be lost."[2] Being asked by some holding offices under the government, "whether their visiting him, to whom they had been formerly much beholden, would offend his Majesty," he answered, *No, he had not forbid any man to visit him.*

The Ex-Chancellor himself gives rather a satisfactory account of the behavior of the world to him immediately after his dismissal. "Many persons of honor and quality came every day to visit him, with many expressions of affection and esteem, and most of the King's servants, except only those few who had declared themselves his enemies."[3] Evelyn, at this time, makes a less favorable entry in his Journal:—"I dined with my late Lord Chancellor, where also dined Mr. Ashburnham and Mr. W. Legge, of the bed-chamber; his Lordship pretty well in heart, though many of his friends and sycophants abandoned him. But there were great apprehensions at Court that if he were spared, the storm having blown over, his influence might revive, and that, being restored to power, he might take ample vengeance on his enemies." The King's confidence was now enjoyed by the members who afterwards formed the CABAL, and who entertaining the most criminal designs, were resolved to ruin him of whom it had been said in the hearing of some of them,—"He is a true Protestant and an honest English-

---

[1] "The Chancellor believed that the storm had been now over; for he had not the least apprehension of the displeasure of the parliament, or of any thing they could say or do against him; yet he resolved to stay at his house till it should meet (without going thither, which he was informed would be ill taken), that he might not be thought to be afraid of being questioned, and then to retire into the country and live there very privately."—*Life*, iii. 835.

[2] Ellis's Original Letters, iv. 30.   [3] Life of Clar. iii. 295.

man, and while he enjoys power we are secure of our laws, liberties, and religion."[1]

The King on this occasion, for the first time, gave clear proof of that thorough want of heart and principle which appeared more and more distinctly, and which, notwithstanding his outward good qualities, ultimately rendered his reign inglorious and his memory contemptible. He zealously joined in the persecution of Clarendon, who, from boyhood, had been his adviser, companion, and friend, and against whom he could urge nothing except "defect of temper." Notwithstanding the first professions of good-will, an intimation was soon given "that the King would take it ill from all his servants who visited the late Chancellor, and it appeared more every day that they were best looked on who forbore going to him."[2]

But he was not to escape with the mere punishment of being frowned on by the Sovereign and deserted by all who aspired to promotion at Court. A parliamentary impeachment was resolved on,—not to bring him to the scaffold, but to drive him forever from his native country;—and although it was well known that nothing could be proved against him amounting to high treason, or any serious crime, entire reliance was placed on the prejudices of the parliament and of the nation.

The fall of Clarendon was certainly hailed with almost universal satisfaction, and further joy was expressed when the plan was announced of bringing him to justice for his supposed delinquencies.

On the 10th of October parliament re-assembled, and the King alluded to the dismissal of Clarendon in these words, which constituted the whole of his speech:—"When we last met here, about eleven weeks ago, I thought fit to prorogue the parliament to this day, resolving that there should be a session now, and to give myself time to do some things I have since done, which I hope will not be unwelcome to you, but a foundation for a greater confidence between us for the future."

It had been hitherto the custom merely by a general vote to thank his Majesty for his gracious speech, without an address, according to modern fashion, re-echoing all the sentiments of the speech, and specifically concurring

---

[1] By Lord Southampton, in council, shortly before his death.
[2] Life, iii. 295.

in them. But on this occasion, as a preliminary to further proceedings against the Ex-Chancellor, there was a joint address of both Houses, thanking his Majesty for the recent measures of his government, and thus concluding:—
"We are grateful for your Majesty's care in quickening the execution of the Act against the importation of foreign [Irish] cattle, and more especially that your Majesty hath been pleased to displace the late Lord Chancellor, and remove him from the exercise of public trust and employment in the affairs of state."[1]

The King made the following answer, dictated by Buckingham:—"I thank you for your thanks. I am glad the things I have done have given you so good satisfaction, and for the Earl of Clarendon, I assure you I will never employ him again in any public affairs whatsoever."

The motion for impeachment was made in the House of Commons by Sir Edward Seymour, a man able, ambitious, and "supposed to decline no means that tended to his advancement." No orator ever addressed a more favorable audience, and he fully availed himself of his advantage by bringing forward charges in vague and declamatory language to suit the passions of every section of the House; but the indignation excited by the sale of Dunkirk, by the alleged plan of keeping up a standing army, and by the disgrace at the conclusion of the Dutch war, was nothing compared to the fury which burst forth when he came to "the importation of Irish cattle," and the crowning accusation—"that the Earl of Clarendon, in dissuading the assembling of parliament on an earlier day than that to which it had been prorogued, although an invasion of the realm was threatened by a foreign foe, had audaciously and treasonably spoken these scandalous and abominable words of and concerning the representatives of the people in the Commons' House of Parliament. — *Four hundred country gentlemen are only fit to give money, and do not understand how an invasion is to be resisted.*"[2]

---

[1] "The Lords at first objected to this address, but the King said "it should go worse for the Chancellor" if his friends in the Lords opposed it; and he sent a message to the Archbishop of Canterbury that he should, in his Majesty's name, command all the Bishops' bench to concur in it, and if they should refuse it he would make them repent it."—*Life of Clar.* iii. This may be considered the commencement of the *constitutional* career of the CABAL.   [2] North's Lives, ii. 51.

Sheridan's famous speech in the House of Commons against Warren Hastings was not more successful; and the only question was, how the prosecution should be conducted? At last "a committee was appointed to look into ancient precedents of the method of the proceedings of this House in cases of impeachment for *capital offenses*," which was followed by a committee " to reduce into heads the accusations against the Earl of Clarendon."

This committee, consisting of his bitterest enemies, in their report proposed seventeen articles of impeachment most preposterously vague and absurd. I can only give the first as a specimen. " 1. That the Earl of Clarendon hath designed a standing army to be raised and to govern the kingdom, thereby advised the King to dissolve this present parliament, to lay aside all thoughts of parliament for the future, to govern by a military power, and to maintain the same by free quarters and contribution." By the others he was charged with having said that *the King was a papist in his heart, or popishly affected, or words to that effect*,—with receiving money for passing illegal patents—with causing divers persons to be illegally imprisoned, and sent to remote islands and garrisons,[1]—with procuring his Majesty to pay debts for which he was not liable,—with receiving money from the Vintners' Company for enhancing the price of wines,—with gaining a great estate more rapidly than was possible by lawful means,—with introducing arbitrary government into the plantations,—with advising and effecting the sale of Dunkirk, together with the artillery and stores, and for no greater value than the artillery and stores were worth,—with arbitrary proceedings at the council table,—with illegally causing writs of *quo warranto* to issue,—and with betraying his Majesty in negotiations relating to the late war.

[1] This was the best founded charge. As yet little regard was paid to personal liberty; there were arbitrary commitments by the Council and the Secretary of State, and writs of *habeas corpus* were disregarded. The long imprisonment of Colonel Hutchinson, which caused his death, may be taken as an example. Large sums were given occasionally to be discharged from illegal imprisonment, and there is reason to apprehend that a portion of these sometimes found their way to the Lord Chancellor. —See *Pepys*, iii. 220, 221, 285. Lister's *Life of Ld. Cl.* ii. 500. Men's minds were not yet accustomed to regular and constitutional government, and in this transition state very arbitrary proceedings occasionally took place without much notice.

But some of the country gentlemen who had such a horror of Clarendon for his defense of the importation of Irish cattle and provisions, seeing that this was not made a substantive charge, doubted whether any of those brought forward amounted to high treason, and an opinion was expressed that the prosecution should only be for "high crimes and misdemeanors,"—so as not to affect his life.

The motion that he should be impeached for high treason on the first charge was nevertheless persisted in, and, wonderful to relate, after a two day's debate it was negatived by 172 to 103. The others, taken *seriatim*, had the same fate, till that one was reached which charged him with betraying his Majesty in negotiations,—when Lord Vaughan, eldest son of the Earl of Carberry, moved the addition of these words, "and discovered and betrayed his secret counsels to the enemy,"—asserting that he was credibly informed that this could be made out by a person of honor, whose name he for the present had good reasons for concealing. The words were inserted, and the motion that the Earl of Clarendon on this charge be impeached for high treason was carried by 161 to 89.

Still they were ashamed to exhibit these articles specifically at the bar of the House of Lords, and Seymour, going up there, preferred the impeachment in the following general words: "The Commons assembled in parliament having received information of divers traitorous practices and designs of a great Peer of this House, Edward, Earl of Clarendon, have commanded me to impeach the said Earl of treason and other high crimes and misdemeanors, and I do here, in their names and in the names of all the Commons of England, impeach Edward, Earl of Clarendon of treason and other high crimes and misdemeanors. I am further commanded by the House of Commons to desire your Lordships that the Earl of Clarendon may be sequestered to safe custody. They further commanded me to acquaint your Lordships that they will, within a convenient time, exhibit to your Lordships the articles of charge against him."[1]

This is one of the many occasions in our constitutional history when the Lords, with all their faults, have shown much more regard to the principles of justice and liberty, than the inflamed and prejudiced elected representatives

[1] 4 Parl. Hist. 586.

of the people. After four days' debate it was resolved, "that the House would not comply with the desire of the House of Commons concerning the commitment of the Earl of Clarendon and sequestering him from Parliament, *because the House of Commons have only accused him of treason in general, and have not assigned or specified any particular treason.*"

This resolution being communicated to the Commons, a conference took place between the two Houses in the Painted Chamber, when the Commons insisted on their right to demand the commitment of a Peer on a general impeachment for treason, citing the recent cases of the Earl of Strafford, Archbishop Laud, and Lord Keeper Finch, and greatly praising the gravity and wisdom of the early proceedings of the Long Parliament. The Lords answered, that these precedents had occurred in times of great heat and violence; that if they ought always to commit upon impeachment by the Commons, they were rather executors of process than Judges; that, *excellent as was the composition of the present House of Commons*, there might be a House of Commons inclined to faction, who, by the abuse of the power now claimed, might make dangerous inroads upon the justice and ancient government of the kingdom, terrify and invade the highest jurisdiction, and indeed bring the House of Lords to as small a number as they please to leave unaccused; that as all inferior courts and magistrates were bound to examine upon oath the particular crimes wherewith a man is charged before depriving him of his freedom, the parliament should be careful herein to give a good example; and that the Petition of Right having declared that no man ought to be imprisoned or detained without being first charged with something to which he might make answer according to law, it would be a plain infraction of that rule to commit upon generals, which do not allow answer or defense.

Each House adhered to its resolution,—even after another conference, which was "free," and in which the question was debated warmly between the managers.

The Commons then resolved, "that the Lords not having complied with the desires of the Commons for the commitment of the Earl of Clarendon, and sequestering him from parliament upon the impeachment of this House, is an obstruction to the public justice of the kingdom, and a precedent of evil and dangerous consequences."[1]

This was the most direct and seemingly the most dangerous collision which had ever taken place between the two Houses. "It is much to be feared," wrote an intelligent observer, "all future intercourse between them will stop. The consequence none can foresee. A worse position of affairs this government does not admit, his Majesty wanting a considerable sum for the payment of the navy and other debts; the people full of complaint for their late miscarriages; our neighbors arming, and we exposed to all kinds of hazards from abroad and at home."

What was to be done? A new creation of Peers to carry a ministerial measure, was a *coup d'état* which had not then been thought of, and if a dissolution had taken place, the public mind was in such an inflamed state that, notwithstanding the unanswerable reasoning of the Lords, the commitment on a general accusation would have been demanded by a new and more violent House of Commons.

It was suggested by the courtiers that Clarendon might extricate all parties from this dilemma by withdrawing beyond the seas; but he scorned the proposal. Some of his own friends, thinking that it would be the wisest course for himself, represented to him the danger in which he was, and spread reports to reach him that the Duke of Albemarle, his old enemy, was now plotting against him; that he was to be arrested in his house by a guard of soldiers, and carried to the Tower; that directions had been given to the Lieutenant of the Tower to treat him with severity; and that the intention was to keep him always in prison without bringing him to trial. Still he remained firm, urging that his flight would be interpreted as a confession of guilt,—would be a triumph to his enemies,—and would bring lasting disgrace upon himself.

Being told that his withdrawing would be grateful to the King, he took a step the real motives for which it is very difficult to fathom. Perhaps he expected that Charles would disclaim any such wish, or might be melted by a personal appeal to him; though still it is impossible to account for his topics and his tone. He wrote a letter to the King, in which, imputing his Majesty's displeasure to his having brought about the marriage between the Duke

---

[1] 4 Parl. Hist. 388—390.

of Richmond and "la belle Stuart," he again denied all previous knowledge of it. He expressed his earnest desire, at all times, to act according to his Majesty's wishes, and to regain his favor, and thus concluded:—"I do most humbly beseech your Majesty, by the memory of your father, who recommended me to you with some testimony, and by your own reflection upon some one service I may have performed in my life that hath been acceptable to you, that you will, by your royal power and interposition, put a stop to this severe prosecution against me; and that my concernment may give no longer interruption to the great affairs of the kingdom; but that I may spend the small remainder of my life, which can not hold long, in some part beyond the seas, never to return."

This letter was put into the King's own hands by Bridgman, the new Lord Keeper. As soon as Charles had perused it, he burned it in the flame of a candle, merely saying, with an air of *nonchalance*, "There is something here which I do not understand; but I wonder Lord Clarendon doth not withdraw himself." If anything could palliate the King's abandonment or persecution of his old friend, it would be this letter, in which the writer directly imputes such a base motive (though it might be the true one) for the royal displeasure, and pretty plainly intimates that he himself should have been pleased to aid his Majesty's designs on Miss Stuart, whatever they might have been.

The laconic and insulting response, reported to Clarendon by the Lord Keeper, rather induced him to remain in England at all hazards. The next move was a visit to him from the Bishop of Hereford, who intimated, that if he would quit the kingdom, to prevent the mischief which must arise from the difference between the two Houses,—the Bishop would undertake, "upon his salvation," that he should not be interrupted in his journey, nor be afterwards prosecuted, or suffer during his absence in honor or in fortune. Clarendon demanded written evidence of the King's wishes, and a pass signed by the King, lest his enemies should arrest him as a fugitive from justice. The Bishop sent him word that the pass could not be granted, from the apprehension of giving displeasure to the parliament, but that he might as securely go as if he had it. Ruvigni, the French embassador, to induce him to fly, assured him of kind treatment in France. But while he could reckon on a friendly majority in the House of Lords he considered himself safe, and was resolved to remain at his post.

He became alarmed by being told that, for the purpose of convicting him capitally parliament was to be prorogued, and that an indictment for treason would then be found against him by a grand jury, upon which he would be tried before the Lord High Steward and a small number of Peers, selected by the Government from among his enemies. This turned out to be no idle rumor. A positive resolution had been taken to force him fly, or to proceed to extremities against him. The King, at some risk of infection, went to the Duke of York, who had been confined by the small pox, and told him to advise his father-in-law to be gone,—blaming him for not giving credit to what had been said to him by the Bishop of Hereford. The Duke immediately sent a message to Clarendon, by the Bishop of Winchester, "that it was absolutely necessary for him to be gone, and that he had the King's word for all that had been undertaken by the Bishop of Hereford."

The Duke having continued always to behave to him with kindness and sincerity, he thought there was no longer room for hesitation, and he resolved to set off for France that very night. His friend, Sir John Wolstenholme, agreed to have a boat ready to receive him at Erith. As soon as it was dark the Ex-Chancellor got into his coach, at Clarendon House, with two servants, and, guarded by his two sons and two or three friends on horseback, he passed rapidly, by Temple Bar, through the city, crossed London Bridge, and proceeded along the right bank of the river to his place of embarkation. At eleven o'clock in the night of Saturday, the 29th of November, 1667, he hurried on board the boat which was waiting for him at Erith, and bid a last adieu to his native country. Evelyn gives us a very interesting account of a visit he had paid him in the morning of the same day, before his communication from the Duke of York: "I found him in his garden at his new-built palace, sitting in his gout wheele chayre, and seeing the gates setting up towards the north and the fields. He looked and spoke very disconsolately. After some while deploring his condition to me, I took my leave. Next morning I heard he was gone. I am persuaded," adds Evelyn, that had he gone sooner, though but to Cornbury, and there lain quiet, it would have satisfied the parliament. That which exasperated them was his presuming to stay and contest the accusation so long as it was possible ; and they were on the point of sending him to the Tower."[1]

I must express my surprise, that he did not persist in his resolution still to remain and face the accusation. He owed no sacrifice to the King for the purpose of extricating the government from the embarrassment in which they were placed by this scandalous prosecution ; he had a reasonable safeguard from violence in the firmness of the House of Lords; and he might have braved the threat of sending him to the Tower, and bringing him to trial before a packed tribunal.

Although he does not expressly mention that he was influenced by the wishes of his children, I cannot help believing that the Duchess of York joined with her husband in advising him to withdraw ; and that his sons, who had gallantly defended him in the House of Commons, in their pious fears exaggerated to him the danger arising from the blind fury of that assembly.

He probably hoped, ere long, safely to return ; and, at all events he confidently relied upon the royal pledge, so solemnly given, that no further steps would be taken against him while he was in exile.

His flight was greatly condemned at the time ; and " made a greater impression upon many worthy persons, to his disadvantage, than any particular that was contained in the charge that had been offered to the House."[2]

He left behind him a letter, addressed to the Lords, which was delivered by Lord Cornbury to the Earl of Denbigh ; and by him presented to the House. This contained a vindication of his conduct. To the charge of having suddenly accumulated great wealth, which weighed most with the public, he said he never received from his office more than its just emoluments, as sanctioned by Lords Ellesmere and Coventry, who had escaped all reproach; that he had received from the King presents, in all amounting to £26,000, and some small grants of land, having refused to accept much greater ; that his whole

[1] Evelyn. ii. 299.   [2] Life, iii. 300.

estate, after payment of his debts, would not amount to £2,000 a year; and that, instead of having a large hoard of ready money by him,—since the time the Seals were taken from him he had lived upon the produce of his plate. With respect to the management of public affairs, he answered, that after the parliament at Oxford, his credit had greatly declined; that since the introduction of Arlington into the Council, he had been little attended to; that it was notorious he had opposed the Dutch war; and that he had not, during the whole of the last year, been above twice alone with the King, who had preferred other advisers. He solemnly denied that he had ever "upon all the treaties or otherwise, received the value of 1s. from all the Kings and Princes in the World, except the books of the Louvre prints, sent him by the Chancellor of France." He accounts for his present position from having made enemies in the faithful discharge of his public duties, and thus concludes: "I most humbly beseech your Lordships, that I may not forfeit your Lordships' favor and protection by withdrawing myself from so powerful a prosecution, in hopes I may be able, by such withdrawing, hereafter to appear and make my defense; when his Majesty's justice, to which I shall always submit, may not be obstructed nor controlled by the power and malice of those who have sworn my destruction."[1]

Arlington, who was here so distinctly pointed out as the author of the late pernicious measures, spoke vehemently against this letter, denouncing it as "a libel," and asserting that "there was not one word of truth in it." Buckingham, at whom it distinctly glanced, moved that it should be communicated to the Commons as "a scandalous and seditious paper," and himself being appointed to be the messenger, at a conference between the two Houses, he performed the task in his usual strain of insult and ridicule: "The Lords have commanded me to deliver to you this scandalous and seditious paper sent from the Earl of Clarendon: they bid me to present it to you, and desire you, in convenient time, to send it to them again; for *it is a style which they are in love with, and therefore desire to keep it*,"—mimicking the tones and gestures of the Ex-Chancellor.

[1] Life, iii. 346.

The Commons resolved that it should be burnt by the hands of the common hangman, and sent up this resolution to the Lords, who so far forgot their dignity as to concur in it. This pitiful mode of showing spite against writings which perhaps could not be refuted, continued in fashion for a century afterwards.

By way of preparation for the solemnity on this occasion, the address was printed and cried through the streets, with this opprobrious title: "News from Dunkirk House, or Clarendon's Farewell to England; in his seditious Address to the Right Honorable the House of Peers, on the 3rd of December, 1667." The burning took place in Palace Yard in the presence of the Sheriffs of London and Middlesex, amidst tremendous shouts of applause from the populace.

The Commons added a resolution on their own sole authority as to the obligation of the Lords to commit on a general impeachment for treason,—with this qualification, that "the Lords may limit a convenient time for bringing the particular charge before them." But this struggle put an end to general impeachments,—and ever since, upon an impeachment voted by the Commons before a demand of commitment, the different charges, articulately framed, have been delivered in writing at the bar of the House of Lords.

According to the agreement which was to be observed "on the salvation of the Bishop of Hereford,"—Clarendon having withdrawn beyond the seas, was not to suffer further in his honor or his estate. But unfortunately for the devoted Prelate, the enemies of the Ex-Chancellor, with the full concurrence of the King, immediately introduced a bill in the House of Lords, which, under pretense that he had voluntarily fled from justice, enacted, "that unless he returned and surrendered himself before the 1st of February next, he was to be banished for life, disabled from ever again holding any office, subjected, if he afterwards returned to England, to the penalties of high treason, and rendered incapable of pardon without the consent of the two Houses of Parliament." An amendment to extend the day for his appearance to the 10th of February was negatived, and the bill was carried by a considerable majority, all the influence of the government being exerted to support it. A strong protest against it was signed by several Peers, on the grounds that it was unjust to punish a man for withdrawing, against whom no legal charge had been brought, and for whose appearance there had been no regular process or order: that the day mentioned in the bill was so near at hand, that he had no fair opportunity of surrendering and taking his trial; and that the bill encroached on the royal prerogative by depriving the King of the power to pardon.

When it came down to the Commons, the objection chiefly made to it was that it was too mild,—and it was carried only by a majority of 65 to 42,—the minority consisting mostly of men who thought that the impeachment for high treason ought not to be stopped, and if there was to be legislation, it should be by a present and absolute attainder.

Charles supported the bill in all its stages,—the only symptom of shame which he displayed in the breach of all his duties and engagements being, that he gave the royal assent to it by commission, and not in person.

The name of the Ex-Chancellor was immediately erased from the list of the Privy Council, and from every public commission in which it appeared.[1]

CHAPTER LXXXIII.

CONCLUSION OF THE LIFE OF LORD CLARENDON.

THE victim of these arbitrary proceedings was now in France, experiencing by turns kind and harsh treatment, as Louis XIV. was guided by his own inclination to ostentatious generosity, or by the apprehension of giving offense to the King of England. Although the Ex-Chancellor had set sail from Erith with a favorable wind, he was soon driven back by a tempest, and it was only after beating about in the mouth of the river Thames and in the English Channel three days and nights that he reached Calais. From thence he applied to the French Government for permission to reside at Rouen. Louis wrote him a letter with his own hand, acceding to his request, and informing him that orders were issued to the

[1] Life, iii. 970.

Governors of Calais, Boulogne, and Montreuil, to treat him as a person whom their King esteemed, and to afford him a sufficient escort; that a coach should meet him at Abbeville to conduct him to Rouen, and that there every thing should be done to render his residence safe and agreeable. He accordingly proceeded on his journey, and was received with great distinction as he passed through Artois and Picardy. At Montreuil, the Duc d'Elbœuf, the governor, lent him his own carriage and horses as far as Abbeville. There he found the equipage promised by Louis, which was to convey him to Rouen. He preferred the route by the sea-shore, that he might revisit some of the scenes of his former exile, and he spent a few days very pleasantly at Dieppe. His spirits now rallied, and he almost became reconciled to his fate, thinking of the repose he was about to enjoy under the protection and patronage of the *Grand Monarque*. But proceeding on his journey,—when about half-way between Dieppe and Rouen, a gentleman, attended by two servants, rode up to his carriage window and delivered a letter to him from Louis, merely desiring him to give credit to whatever the bearer of it should communicate, and to obey his orders. This was M. Le Fonde, who held a considerable office at Court, and who then, with much formality, declared, in the name of the King his Master, that "inasmuch as any favor shown in France to the banished Conte de Clarendon would give offense to his ally, the King of England, and might cause a breach between the two Crowns, his most Christian Majesty must desire the said Conte de Clarendon to quit his dominions immediately; but that Mons. le Conte might want no accommodation for his journey to the frontier, he, the bearer of this message, was commanded to do himself the honor of accompanying him thither." So Clarendon found himself a prisoner in the custody of M. Le Fonde. He asked and obtained permission to proceed to Rouen. Whether by accident or design, the coach which conveyed him was three times overturned before reaching that place, and he was very seriously bruised. He arrived at Rouen late at night, exceedingly ill. Next day he was quite unable to move, and a courier was sent off to Paris to mention his condition to the French Government, and to ask for fresh instructions. The former harsh command was reiterated, that he should immediately quit the French territory. "The fatigues of the journey, and the bruises he had received from the falls and overturnings of the coach, made him not able to rise out of his bed, and the physicians, who had taken much blood from him, exceedingly dissuaded it."[1] M. le Fonde still urging his departure, he dictated a letter to the French minister, intimating his submission to the orders laid upon him; that he had selected Avignon, under the rule of his Holiness the Pope, for his place of residence; and that he would proceed to it with all possible expedition,—but requesting that he might remain a short time longer at Rouen, waiting his recovery, and that, on account of the state of his health, he might be permitted to stop occasionally on his journey to recruit his strength, and particularly a few days at Orleans. The reply was, that he must immediately set off for his destination, and that in traveling to Avignon he would only be permitted to stop every tenth day.

A few hours after, he received letters from his sons informing him of the steps which had been taken against him in his absence, and containing a copy of the Act by which he was to be banished for life, and branded as a traitor, unless he surrendered himself by the 1st of February. There was just time for him, by expeditious traveling to be in London by that day. Instead of proceeding to Avignon, he resolved to face his enemies, and not to submit to the cruel sentence which, in violation of the royal pledge, had been conditionally pronounced upon him. Ill as he was, he immediately set off for Calais,—which he was allowed to do on his representation that he should from thence quit France, in obedience to the royal mandate. But when he arrived there, after a fatiguing journey in the depth of winter, he was so much worse that his life was considered in danger, and bleeding was deemed necessary to allay his fever. The weather was tempestuous, and he could not embark. While he thus lay on a bed of sickness, a peremptory order arrived from the French Government, that under no circumstances should Lord Clarendon be allowed to remain a day longer at Calais. "The King, your Master," said he to the messenger, "is a very great and powerful Prince, but he is not so omnipotent as to make a dying man undertake a

[1] Life, iii. 355.

journey. I am at your King's mercy, and must endure whatever it is his pleasure to inflict. He may send me a prisoner to England, or cause me to be carried dead or alive into the Spanish territories, but I will not commit suicide by voluntarily attempting what it is impossible for me to perform." He requested the Lieutenant-Governor of Calais, and the President of the Court of Justice, with whom he had formerly been acquainted, to visit him, and they seeing his deplorable condition, and fortified by a certificate from the physicians who attended him, that he could not be removed without danger to his life, made a representation which obtained a permission for him to remain at Calais till he should recover from his illness.

This concession was probably facilitated by rumors of the "Triple Alliance" which had just been concluded by Sir William Temple and De Witt, for curbing the ambition of the French King, now beginning to alarm Europe. When the certain news of this treaty was received, the French minister sent a dispatch to Clarendon, assuring him "that he had the same respect for him which he had always professed to have in his greatest fortune; that it was never the purpose of his Christian Majesty to endanger his health by making a journey that he could not well bear; and, therefore, that it was left entirely to himself to remove from Calais when he thought fit, and to go to what place he would."

The day for his surrender was gone by; he was now a banished man for life, and he could not set foot on English ground without being liable to be immediately executed as a convicted traitor. He resumed his intention of settling at Avignon; but for many weeks he was confined to his bed at Calais, and it was not till the spring had made some progress that he was able to begin his journey. Having bought a large easy coach from his friend the President, who had continued to show him great attention, he then set forward for Rouen, where, in the hurry of his departure, some of his effects had been left. Louis, smarting under the restraint of the Triple Alliance, to which Charles, although his virtuous fit was nearly over, still reluctantly adhered, Clarendon on his arrival there found fresh assurances of the good-will of the French Government, and permission to reside (with the exception of Paris) in any part of France.

He still looked to Avignon as the place of his residence, but resolved in his way thither to try to recruit his strength by taking the waters of Bourbon. The first night after he left Rouen, he stopped at Evreux,—where he encountered a peril which strongly shows his unpopularity at this time with almost all classes of Englishmen, and their disposition to attribute all their grievances to his misconduct. A company of English seamen who had been employed in the French artillery lay in the town, and being told of the arrival of Lord Clarendon, the famous Chancellor, whom they had heard spoken of in their own country as the author of the bad measures which had enabled the Dutch to get to Chatham, and the person who had applied the money voted for the support of the navy to the embellishment of Dunkirk House, flocked round his inn, declaring "that there were many months' arrears due to them from England, and that they would make him pay the whole before he should leave the place." On account of his lameness, he was lodged in a room on the ground floor. The door being strongly barricaded, they attempted to enter by the window; but they were some time kept at bay by Le Fonde, who still attended him as a commissioner on the part of the French Government, and by the devoted efforts of his own servants. From a discharge of fire-arms Le Fonde and one of the servants were wounded and fell,—when the ringleader entered at the window, threw open the door, and admitted the rest of the rioters. The Ex-Chancellor was found sitting on his bed, and was knocked down and stunned by a blow on the head from the flat side of a broad-sword. Fortunately they differed among themselves what they should do with him,—some crying that they would instantly kill him, and others that they would carry him prisoner to England. In the mean time they rifled his pockets, broke open his trunks, and plundered his goods. The ringleader protested against stabbing him in his bed-room as conduct unworthy of English seamen, and proposed that a gibbet should be erected in the court-yard, in the fashion of a yard-arm, from which he should be suspended. To this they all assented by acclamation, and they were dragging him through a corridor to the intended place of execution when their commanding officer arrived accompanied by some of the magistrates and the city guard—and their victim was rescued from impending death. He obtained an asylum in the house of the Duc de Bouillon. After a foolish dispute between two sets of French functionaries respecting jurisdiction, the outrage having been committed in the suburbs of the town, the rioters were seized, and the ringleader and two others of the most culpable were afterwards broken on the wheel.

It turned out that on this occasion, though much frightened, he had not received any serious hurt, and he was soon able to prosecute his journey to Bourbon. There he remained some weeks, deriving material benefit to his health from the waters, from the soothing attentions of the company, and from the tranquillity he was at last enabled to enjoy. He made another agreeable rest at Lyons, and about midsummer he arrived at Avignon. Here he was well received by the dignitaries and magistrates, and he had reason to be satisfied with the cheapness of living and the beauty of the surrounding country. But he began to think it might have a strange appearance that he who had always been such a zealous Protestant, should voluntarily choose to live and die under the temporal dominion of Pope. He was attracted by the climate and society of Montpellier. After an experimental visit he established himself there, and during the two years that it was his residence, he enjoyed as much happiness as was consistent with separation from his country, his family, and his friends. He was treated with great respect and civility by the Governor, the inhabitants of the place, and all strangers of distinction who visited it, and he was solaced by talking the English language and of English affairs with the Earl and Countess of Mordaunt, who were much attached to him, and from the lady's delicate state of health were at this time resident at Montpellier.

He had to struggle against bodily pain and weakness by which an ordinary man's mental activity would have been subdued. "His indisposition and infirmity, which either kept him under the actual and sharp visitation of the gout, or when the rigor of that was abated, in much weakness of his limbs when the pain was gone, were so great that he could not be without the attendance of four servants about his own person; having in those seasons when he enjoyed most health and underwent least pain, his knees, legs, and feet so weak that he could not walk, especially up or down stairs, without the help of two men."[1]

But his love of literature was again his true support. He now proceeded to complete his "History of the Rebellion," which had been so long suspended by his political and judicial occupations; he wrote his "Justification" against the charges contained in his recent impeachment; and he began his "Autobiography," which was to contain a narrative of his private life, with some account of public affairs after the Restoration. He likewise composed a number of Essays in imitation of Lord Bacon's, and went on with his devotional work on the Psalms, which he had begun at Jersey. In the midst of all these occupations he took pains to improve himself in the French language, of which he had never been quite master, not having been familiar with it when he was young,—and he began the study of Italian, "towards which he made competent progress."[2]

He carried on an affectionate intercourse by letter with his family, and he was now perhaps enjoying life more than among the excitements, disappointments, and mortifications of ambition,—when he heard that his daughter, the Duchess of York, had openly embraced the Romish religion, he was dreadfully shocked, but hoped to bring her back to the true Protestant faith. With this view he wrote a long and elaborate letter, in which he found himself obliged to depart from the high-church ground he had so boldly taken up against the Presbyterians, and on which he had successfully resisted the scheme of comprehension. "The common argument," he tells her, "that there is no salvation out of the church is both irrational and untrue. There are many churches in which salvation may be obtained as well as in any one of them, and were many even in the apostolic time; otherwise, the apostles would not have directed their epistles to so many several churches, in which there were different opinions received and very different doctrines taught. There is, indeed, but one faith in which we can be saved—the steadfast belief of the birth, passion, and resurrection of our Saviour. *And every church that receives and embraces*

[1] Life, iii. 968.   [2] Ibid. 373—376.

that faith is in a state of salvation." If he had still dwelt on the apostolical succession, the necessity for receiving the sacraments from a priest, episcopally ordained, and the duty of implicitly believing with child-like docility all that the church teaches, her Royal Highness might have sent a triumphant answer to her father, and shown him that, on his own principles, if he did not abjure the Protestant heresy, his soul was in great peril, and he must renounce the covenanted mercies of the Gospel.

Clarendon at the same time dispatched a similar missive to the Duke, her husband. Choosing to assume that his Royal Highness still remained a steady Protestant, (although there was now little doubt with the public of his having been reconciled to Rome, and of the Duchess having gone over to please him), the Ex-Chancellor condoled with him on the grief he must suffer from her defection, and (as he thought), with a refinement of policy, pointed out the danger to the Catholics from such an open conversion, as they would be sure to be treated with increased rigor. But in spite of these pious efforts James soon after professed himself to be a Roman Catholic in the face of the world, and the Duchess steadily adhered to that faith till her death.

This event took place in March, 1671, and the intelligence of it plunged her father into the deepest affliction. He was tenderly attached to her, and he had complacently anticipated the time (although he could not hope to live to see it) when she would sit upon the throne, and teach her children who were to reign after her to honor and to defend his memory. His grief was soon after aggravated by hearing of the death of her only surviving son, and he trembled lest her daughters, Mary and Anne, should, like their brothers and sisters, be doomed to an early grave.

He was so overset that he could no longer follow his usual occupations, and change of scene being recommended to him, he retired from Montpellier to Moulins.

Here he was consoled by the society of Lawrence, his second son, who, with some difficulty, obtained permission from the English government to visit him. His spirits gradually rallied, and he resumed his studies. Having finished his "History of the Rebellion," he wrote to Charles II., and after trying to soften him with an account of his desolate condition in exile, he says, " I have performed a work under this mortification, which I began with the approbation and encouragement of your blessed father, and when I had the honor to be near your Majesty, and which, if I do not overmuch flatter myself, may be for the honor of both your Majesties."[1] He concluded by entreating, in pathetic terms, "that an old man, who had served the Crown above thirty years in some trust and with some acceptation, might be permitted to end his days, which could not be many, in his own country and in the society of his children." He entertained sanguine hopes that this appeal would be successful, and he at the same time sent directions for the management of his house and lands in England in the tone of one who expected soon to revisit them. But Charles, by the advice of *C*lifford, *A*rlington, *B*uckingham, *A*shley, and *L*auderdale, having broken the Triple Alliance, shut up the Exchequer, tried to favor popery, and fallen into complete dependence upon the French King, could not bear the idea of again seeing the face of his ancient monitor, under whose guidance his measures and his character had been comparatively respectable. One might have supposed that he would have felt curiosity to peruse the great historical work to which he himself had formerly contributed some materials; but now, absorbed in present pleasure, he was wholly indifferent to the opinion entertained of his father or himself by the present age or by posterity.

The disappointment to Clarendon was severe, but he bore it with fortitude. His steady props were literature and religion. On the 8th of June, 1672, he commenced the Continuation of his Life, which he entitled "Reflections upon the most material Passages which happened after th: King's Restoration to the Time of the Chancellor's Banishment, out of which his Children, for whose information only they are collected, may add some important Passages to his Life as the true cause of his misfortunes." During a visit to Pezenas he steadily went on with it, and he finished it on his return. At Moulins he also wrote "A View and Survey of Hobbes's Leviathan;" "Animadversions on a Controversy between Dr. Stillingfleet and Mr. Crossy respecting the Catholic Church;" and "An Historical Discourse upon the Jurisdiction assumed by the Popes." He even contemplated a new history of Eng-

[1] Clar. Pap. iii. Sup. xi.

land, "that it may be more profitably and exactly communicated than it hath yet been."[1]

But in the midst of these labors he perceived that his bodily strength gradually declined, and that each fresh access of his constitutional disorder, the gout, became more formidable. As his career was visibly drawing to a close, his desire to revisit his native land constantly increased; and that he might at least have the satisfaction of being nearer it,—in the summer of 1674 he removed from Moulins to Rouen, destined to be his last place of abode. Here he made another effort upon the obdurate heart of Charles, by a petition that he might be allowed to die among his children. "Seven years," he observed, "was a time prescribed and limited by God himself for the expiation of some of his greatest judgments, and it is full that time since I have, with all possible humility, sustained the insupportable weight of the King's displeasure. Since it will be in nobody's power long to prevent me from dying, methinks the desiring a place to die in should not be thought a great presumption."[2] But Charles would not even vouchsafe to return him an answer.

After this disappointment he abandoned all hope in this world, and prepared for a better. On the 1st of December he, with difficulty, wrote his will in these words:—

"I, Edward, Earl of Clarendon, do order this to be my last will and testament. Imprimis, I commit my soul to God, and make the executors of this said last will my two sons, Henry, Viscount Cornbury and Lawrence Hyde, Esq., and commend to them the care of my servants, who have behaved themselves very carefully and honestly to me. And likewise recommend their sister, Francis Hyde, and their brother, James Hyde, Esq., to their kindness, to whom I am able to leave nothing but their kindness. Item, I give and bequeath to my said two sons all my papers and writings of what kind soever, and leave them entirely to their disposal, as they shall be advised, either by suppressing or publishing, by the advice and approbation of my Lord Archbishop of Canterbury and the Bishop of Winchester, whom I entreat to be the overseers of this my will. And that they would be both suitors to his Majesty on my children's behalf, who have all possible need of his Majesty's charity, being children

[1] Life. iii. 481.   [2] Clar. Pap. iii. Sup. xliv.

of a father who never committed fault against his Majesty.   CLARENDON."

His eldest son had come over to Rouen to attend him on the news of his danger, and was with him to the last. We have no further particulars of his death-bed. He expired on the 9th of December, 1674, in the 65th year of his age.

By an arret of the French Government during a temporary difference with England, the "*droit d'aubaine*" was remitted in favor of the heirs of the Earl of Clarendon if he should die in France,—and this was still respected. His body was sent over to his native country, and on the 4th of January, 1675, was privately interred on the north side of Henry VII.'s chapel, in Westminster Abbey—an honor conceded, I presume, on account of his alliance to the royal family. But although his two granddaughters successively reigned in England, no monument was ever erected to his memory, and there is no inscription even to point out the spot where his dust reposes.

He himself has left us more lasting memorials of his existence than marble or brass could furnish; and he certainly is a memorable personage in our annals, both by his actions and his writings. Without the original genius and comprehensive grasp of intellect which distinguished his predecessor, Bacon, he had an acute and vigorous understanding, which, united with unwearied industry, made him a man of most respectable acquirements, and admirably adapted him for the scenes through which he was to pass. In ordinary times he would have been known during his life merely to his own family, his personal friends, and his profession, and would have been forgotten as soon as the tomb had closed over him; but amidst civil strife and revolutions, he was qualified to take a leading part, and to influence the opinions and the conduct of mankind. For delicacy of observation and felicity of delineation of the characters of contemporaries, he is almost without a rival.

In his conduct we have much more to commend than to censure. His early career was without a blemish; and it is only in considering how few would have done the same, that we can properly appreciate his merit in seeking to gain distinction by the liberal practice of his profession, instead of retiring to obscure indolence upon the competence left him by his father,—and in readily renouncing that profession when it had become to him a source of large emolument, that he might be free to discharge his duties as a member of the legislature at the great crisis of his country's fate. His efforts at the opening of the Long Parliament for the punishment of the Judges, and the correction of abuses, showed him to be a sincere friend of constitutional freedom ; and if he proceeded too far in supporting the attainder of Strafford, he might well be excused, from the general enthusiasm then prevailing, and the countenance of the virtuous men with whom he acted. He went over to the King at a time when the disinterestedness of his motives was above all suspicion ; and the sound advice which he then gave, if it had been followed, would either have warded off a rupture, or would probably have insured success to the royal cause. We shall nowhere find better illustrated than in the state papers he then wrote, the sound principles of representative government and limited monarchy. In his first exile we are called upon to forgive the jealousy and hatred he displayed towards his rival, Lord Keeper Herbert—which we can do, while we admire his fidelity, his industry, and his fortitude.

We see him on a more trying scene, when in possession of supreme power; and I think it is impossible to defend, or much to palliate, the gross breach of his solemn engagements to the Presbyterians—his extreme illiberality in matters of church discipline—his long-continued negotiation with the Queen to induce her to take the King's mistress into her establishment as one of her ladies of honor—his earnest disavowals of having counteracted the King's designs on Miss Stuart—his affected indignation at the announcement of his daughter's marriage with the Duke of York, and his pretended wish that she were his mistress—his encouraging the King to receive money privately from France—his sale, for the purpose of contributing to the King's profligate pleasures, of an important fortress. which had been added by the Commonwealth to the dominions of England—his repeal of the Triennial Act, without any effectual provision to limit the duration, or to prevent the intermission of parliaments—or his violent opposition to the appropriation of the supplies and the revision by parliament of the public expenditure. But, on the other hand, we must bear in mind his steady adherence to the promise of indemnity, notwithstanding the odium he thereby incurred with the dominant party—his opposition to the plan of rendering the crown independent of parliament by the grant of a large permanent revenue—his confirmation of the abolition of military tenures and re-enactment of other good laws of the Commonwealth—his opposition to the Dutch war—his steady support of the reformed religion, at the risk of losing the favor of the King—and his efforts to stem the tide of open immorality, which, flowing from the Court, was threatening to corrupt the manners of the whole nation. If disposed to blame him very severely for remaining in office when his advice was not followed and he disapproved of the measures of the government, we should remember that then a unanimous cabinet was not considered by any means necessary—persons once appointed to the offices of Treasurer, or Chancellor, or Secretary of State, no more thought of voluntarily resigning than a common law judge—and, till the King dismissed them, they went on doing the duties of their departments and giving their opinions at the council table when required to do so, leaving the Sovereign to decide when his ministers were divided. In forming a judgment of Clarendon's administration we must likewise always bear in mind what a character he had to manage in Charles II.,—and we should look to that King's subsequent conduct under other counselors.

His judicial duties he seems to have discharged to the satisfaction of the public. Burnet says, "He was a good Chancellor, only a little too rough; but very impartial in the administration of justice;" and Pepys, having heard some cases decided by him, makes this entry in his journal, "I perceive my Lord is a most able and ready man." These testimonies are not very high as to legal capacity, but show strongly the favorable impression made on the public by his manner and deportment. In the Court of Chancery he was kept right by his assessors. The judicial business of the House of Lords was then exceedingly small. From the long discontinuance of parliaments in the reign of Charles I. and the disturbances which had prevailed for the twenty years which followed the meeting of the Long Parliament, the House of Lords had ceased to be regarded as the highest court of justice in the kingdom, as it had formerly been; and in Clarendon's time, luckily for him, it had hardly recovered its appellate jurisdiction. He was the only Law Lord in the House, and his opinion on legal questions would not have carried with it much weight.

He admirably performed one of the most important duties of a Chancellor by raising the best men he could find to the bench. The aggregate of evil inflicted on the community by a bad judicial appointment is so enormous, that it would be less mischievous to the public if a Chancellor were to accept a bribe for pronouncing an unjust decree, than if, yielding to personal favor or party bias, he should make an incompetent Judge. Hale was supposed to owe his promotion to a desire to take from the House of Commons the active supporter of the Comprehension Bill; but Bridgeman, Twisden, Foster, and Windham, with respect to whom there could be no suspicion of improper motive, were placed by his side.

Clarendon likewise has the merit of having listened favorably to the suggestion of Hale and other enlightened jurists, who were for following up the law reforms begun under the Commonwealth; and under his auspices, on the 5th of October, 1666, the House of Commons appointed "a Committee to confer with such of the Lords, the Judges, and other persons of the long robe who have already taken pains and made progress in perusing the statute law; and to consider of repealing such former statute laws as they shall find necessary to be repealed, and, if expedient, of reducing all laws of one nature under such a method as may conduce to the more ready understanding and better execution of such laws,"[1]—an exploit still remaining for the glory of some future Lord Chancellor.

He was charged in his impeachment with the sale of offices, and with receiving money for passing illegal patents, but nothing like judicial corruption was established against him.

He certainly put the Great Seal to proclamations which we should consider beyond the power of the prerogative—as that all who had served in the army of the

[1] Com. Jour. Oct. 5, 1666.

Commonwealth should retire above twenty miles from London ; and that after the fire of London, the new edifices should be after a specified design, and of specified materials. Nay, he wished to issue a commission to shut up all coffee-houses, by reason of dangerous talk in them. But the boundary between things that may be done by royal authority, and things requiring a legislative act, was then very undefined in England, as it still is in the continental states in which a constitutional monarchy has been attempted. Thus, before any statute had passed to regulate the press, Clarendon, without exciting any remark, issued an order for seizing all copies of Buchanan's "History of Scotland" and his Dialogue "De jure regni apud Scotos," as pernicious to monarchy and injurious to his Majesty's blessed progenitors.

But we must seriously blame Clarendon, as head of the law, for sanctioning the prosecution and execution of Twyn for high treason, because he had published a book alleged to be seditious;—the doctrine being laid down, and acted upon, "that the publishing of this book is all one and the same as if he had raised an army to dethrone the King."[1]

The reports of his parliamentary speeches which have come down to us do not by any means answer the expectation we are led to form of him as an orator, for he is one of the earliest instances of a man rising to high office through success in parliament. He was undoubtedly a powerful debater in both Houses, and he seems to have gained great public reputation by these efforts, without the assistance of Hansard or the newspapers. Evelyn mentions "his eloquent tongue," and Pepys says, in his characteristic quaint style, 'I am mad in love with my Lord Chancellor, for he do comprehend and speak out well, and with the greatest easiness and authority that ever I saw man in my life." The authority with which he addressed the Lords may be gathered from Evelyn's admiration of " his manner and freedom of doing it, as if he played with it, and was informing only all the rest of the company."[2] Yet his addresses to the two Houses by

[1] 6 St. Tr. 531.
[2] Pepys, iii. 62. From the same source we learn that like other great and good men, he was sometimes *caught napping.* " Nov. 20th, 1666. By coach to Barkeshire House, and there did get a very great meeting; the Duke of York being there, and much business done, though not in proportion to the

order of the King, and the other specimens of his oratory which are preserved, though showing good judgment and discretion, are without anything at all striking in thought or expression, and are greatly inferior to his writings. On these his reputation safely reposes.

It is easy to point out faults in his "History of the Rebellion,"—its redundancies, its omissions, its inaccuracies, its misrepresentations, its careless style, and its immethodical arrangement. But of all history contemporary history is the most valuable; of contemporary histories that is to be preferred which is written by one who took a part in the events related; and of all such contemporary histories, in our own or any other language, this great work is the most to be admired, for graphic narration of facts, for just exposition of motives, and for true and striking delineation of character.[1] We find in it a freshness, a spirit, a raciness, which induce us, in spite of all its imperfections, to lay it down with regret, and to resume it with new pleasure. With regard to its *sincerity*, which has been so much contested, perhaps the author may be acquitted of willfully asserting what is false; but he seems to have considered himself fully justified in suppressing what is true, when he thought he could do so for the advantage of his party. He made no secret with his friends, that he was writing an apology for the King, which "should give no information to posterity, where it could not give that it would, and should leave his memory happy, though his reign had been so unfortunate."[2] The reader of the History is surprised at finding in it no allusion to the King's negotiation with Glamorgan and the Catholics of Ireland; but this omission is explained by the historian's private letter to Secretary Nicholas: "I care not how little I say of that business of Ireland, since those strange powers and instructions given to your favorite, Glamorgan, which appear to me so inexcusable to justice, piety, and prudence."[3]

Perhaps, unconsciously, he makes his History the vehicle for his personal partialities and antipathies; and

greatness of the business, *and my Lord Chancellor sleeping and snoring the greater part of the time.*"

[1] Of course I do not allude to such narratives as Cæsar's Commentaries, or the Memoirs of De Retz.
[2] Letter to Colepeper, Clar. Pap. ii. 327.
[3] Clar. Pap. ii. 337.

what it thus gains in liveliness it certainly loses in authority.¹

There are likewise to be found in the work statements of dates, speeches, and occurrences, entirely at variance with the journals of the two Houses and other authentic records, and which, being against his party as often as in favor of it, we can only account for by his want of opportunity to consult original papers. His memory failing him, he seems occasionally, to have filled up the interval with what he deemed probable and characteristic, as if he had been writing an historical romance.²

With all these abatements, the "History of the Rebellion" was a great accession to English literature; and it will continue to be read when Hume may be superseded by another compiler, equally lively and engaging, and more painstaking and impartial.³

Clarendon's "Life"⁴ and "Continuation"⁵ are inferior productions. His genius and his style do not bend to the familiarity of personal narrative; he seldom interests us in his individual adventures or feelings; he hardly ever introduces us to his domestic circle; and his great object is to defend himself, as a public man, from the imputations which had been made against him, or to which he thought he was liable. Writing so long after the occurrences he narrates, and with his impaired memory only to rely upon, he is generally vague and unsatisfactory, and sometimes falls into unaccountable blunders. He furnishes us with few interesting anecdotes of himself or his

---

¹ See Hallam's Const. Hist. ii. 302. Edinburgh Review, No. ciii. cxxxix. Quarterly Review, No. cxxiv.

² I have had occasion to point out the spite which he ever betrays in mentioning the name of Sir Edward Herbert, his rival for the Great Seal. His injustice to John Ashburnham, who held an office in the King's household, and accompanied him on his flight from Oxford and Hampton Court, is strongly exposed by the Earl of Ashburnham. See a Narrative by John Ashburnham, and edited by the Earl of Ashburnham, his lineal descendant. 2 vols. 8vo. 1830.

³ Whitelock's Memorials, being a diary, are far more accurate than Clarendon's History, and are a most valuable repertory; but seldom assume the form of continuous narration. The only contemporary writer to be compared to him is Ludlow, whose Memoirs, for brilliancy of description, vigor of sentiment and elegance of style, certainly are delightful. I may mention as a benefit to learning conferred by the "History of the Rebellion," that its profits founded the CLARENDON PRESS, at Oxford, from which so many valuable works have issued.

⁴ Commenced at Montpellier, July, 1668.

⁵ Commenced at Moulins, June, 1672.

contemporaries; and when he does give us a glimpse of private life,—from the unsuitableness of his manner and style, he is not so entertaining as when with *verve* he describes proceedings of the legislature or campaigns in the field.

With the other writings which amused his exile, I am not sufficiently acquainted to pronounce any opinion upon them; but, from a glance at them, I am convinced that his answer to Hobbes could not do much to correct the errors of that philosopher, and that the rest have deservedly fallen into oblivion.

Although his letters have been highly commended, I own they seem to me extremely stiff and heavy; and it seems hardly possible to believe that he lived in the same age and country with Dryden, who had shown so strikingly the power of the English language in this as in almost every other species of prose and metrical composition.

While he was himself uninitiated in science, he had the merit, as Chancellor, of promoting the establishment of the Royal Society; and that learned body, then so illustrious, thanked him for his conduct, which they were pleased to say had "wiped away the aspersion that had been scandalously cast on the profession of the law, that it is an enemy to learning and the civil arts."[1]

On the Restoration he was elected Chancellor of the University of Oxford, where his ecclesiastical policy was highly prized, in spite of his political moderation, and where his memory is held in the deepest veneration; but he had reason to believe that when he had lost the favor of the court, he would have been deposed from his office; and to avoid this disgrace, as soon as he reached Calais, in 1667, he resigned it.

From his early entrance into good society, and from his long travels abroad, we should have expected his manners to be remarkably disengaged and agreeable; but although Burnet says "he had too much levity in his wit, and did not always observe the decorum of his post," all other authorities represent him as formal, haughty, and supercilious. It is clear that he attached infinite importance to the possession of the Great Seal, and so sweetly did

---

[1] Sprat's History of the Royal Society, p. 143.

the word " Chancellor " sound in his ear, that by this title he constantly designates himself, and represents others addressing him, long before he had received the appointment, and after he had lost it. It is quite clear that he stood upon his dignity much more than Charles ; and he must have been an admirable subject of ridicule for the mimic statesmen who surrounded this merry monarch. Yet he was capable of forming warm friendships with such men as Falkland, Southampton, and Ormond.

After the Restoration, he lived in great splendor. For a short time he occupied Dorset House in Salisbury Court, once the residence of the bishops of Salisbury. But he soon received a letter from the Marquis of Worcester, soliciting favors, and saying, " Be pleased to accept of Worcester House to live in, farr more comodious for yr. Lo. than where you now are, without requiring from yr. Lo. one penny rent (yet that only knowne between yr. Lo. and me)." This was evidently intended as a bribe ; but Clarendon says he insisted on paying for it a yearly rent of £500.[1] Here he resided during almost the whole of his administration ; and when he was laid up by the gout, here the King used to come to attend councils held in his bed-room. In 1666, during the great fire of London, which was expected to destroy the west end of the town as well as the city, all his furniture and goods were sent off to a villa he had at Twickenham. After a short residence in Berkshire House, near St. James, he moved, when his fall was approaching, to his new palace, which he had been constructing some years, on a piece of ground granted to him by the Crown, on the road to Kensington, where Albemarle-street now stands. Evelyn says it was " the first palace, the best contrived, the most useful, graceful, and magnificent house in England—nothing abroad pleased him better — nothing at home approached it."[2] The estimate of the architect stated the expense at £20,000; but it actually came to near three times that amount. The furnishing was suitable to the architecture. His library was one of the finest ever collected in England, and he had a picture gallery filled with the *chefs-d'œuvre* of the best masters. Evelyn states " that many of these were gifts ; and that when his design

[1] Life, iii. 486. Worcester House stood in the Strand, on the ground now occupied by Beaufort Buildings.   [2] Ev. ii. 280.

was once made known, everybody who either had them of their own, or could purchase them at any price, strove to make their court by these presents." The erection of this palace he considered the capital error of his life, as "it more contributed to that gust of envy, which had so violently shaken him than any misdemeanor that he was thought to have been guilty of, and it infinitely discomposed his whole affairs and broke his estate."[1] He had likewise a magnificent country house at Cornbury, in Oxfordshire, where he exercised hospitality on a grand scale during the long vacations. It is related that on one occasion all the gentry of the surrounding country flocking into his hall to pay their court to him, Lenthal, the Speaker of the Long Parliament, went among the number, and being "much fleered at by the company," he said, in the hearing of them all, "My Lord, pray observe these very gentlemen, who are now so eager to bow to your Lordship, have done the very same to me, and may before long turn their backs upon you"—"a just reprimand to the gentlemen," says my authority, "and a prudent caution to the Chancellor."[2]

From such splendor was he indeed at once reduced to live in a miserable lodging in a provincial town in a foreign country. But the resignation and fortitude he then displayed have inclined us to forgive his faults and to revere his memory, and he is more to be admired and envied while composing his immortal work at Montpellier and Moulins, than when, flattered by treacherous courtiers, he reclined amidst the splendors of Clarendon House and Cornbury.

Besides his daughter, the Duchess of York, through whom he was the grandsire of sovereigns, he left three sons, who gained some distinction in the reigns of James II. and William III. The most eminent was Lawrence, the second, created Earl of Rochester, celebrated in "Absalom and Achitophel."

> "HUSHAI, the friend of David in distress,
> In public storms of manly stedfastness:
> By foreign treaties he inform'd his youth,
> And join'd experience to his native truth."

But the Chancellor's male line failed about the middle of the last century. He is now represented through a

---

[1] Life, iii. 971.   [2] Life of Edward, Earl of Clarendon (L. C.), 320.

female, by the present Earl of Clarendon, destined to add new luster to the title which he bears.[1]

CHAPTER LXXXIV.

LIFE OF LORD KEEPER BRIDGEMAN.

CLARENDON had been dismissed from office, not by the intrigues of a competitor for the Great Seal, or from a desire of the Court to confer it upon some aspiring lawyer who by talent or subserviency had raised himself to political eminence. The disposal of it in fact caused great perplexity. After many doubts and conflicting plans among the King's male and female advisers, it was put into the hands of a grave common-law Judge, Sir ORLANDO BRIDGEMAN, Lord Chief Justice of the Common Pleas,—at first merely as a temporary arrangement, till another Lord Keeper could be fixed upon; but he held it, with that title, for five years; and his life, therefore, must now engage our attention.

He was the son of Dr. John Bridgeman, Bishop of Chester, descended from a respectable family in Devonshire. His mother was a daughter of Dr. Keylar, canon of Exeter, and Archdeacon of Barnstaple. Having been well grounded in classical learning under his father's tuition, he was entered of Queen's College, Cambridge, in July, 1619, and there took his degree of B. A. in January, 1623. In the following year he was entered of the Inner Temple. He certainly must have studied at his Inn of Court with great assiduity, for he was a profound master of the common law. To his profession he chiefly devoted himself through life, affording little of his time to literature or politics. He was particularly famous for diligent attendance in court at all interesting arguments; and while a student he took very full and accurate notes of cases, which he afterwards cited from the bench.[2] He was called to the bar in 1632. Although he was to inherit a good estate from his father, he addicted himself to business; and though not much distinguished for elo-

[1] Grandeur of the Law, p. 70.   [2] Bridg. Rep. 27.

quence, his great learning and industry procured him considerable employment.

At the meeting of the Long Parliament he was returned for the borough of Wigan. He took the King's side zealously from the beginning, but he did not venture to encounter Pym, St. John, or Hyde, in debate, and contented himself with giving silent votes against the abolition of the Star Chamber, and the other reforms then introduced. Once he had the courage to say a few words against Strafford's attainder.

When hostilities commenced he did not throw aside the gown for the sword; but he repaired to his native place, that, by his advice and influence as a civilian, he might there support the royal cause. "The city of Chester," says Lord Clarendon, "was firm to the King by the virtue of the inhabitants, and the interest of the Bishop and Cathedral men; but especially by the reputation and dexterity of Mr. O. Bridgeman, son to the Bishop, and a lawyer of very good estimation; who not only informed them of their duty, and encouraged them in it, but upon his credit and estate, both which were very good, supplied them with whatsoever was necessary for their defense." The citizens thus roused and encouraged were eager to defend their walls, and Sir Nicholas Byron, a gallant and experienced soldier, being sent to command them as governor, they carried the war into the enemies' quarters at Nantwich.

But the activity of the honorable member for Wigan in those parts being reported at Westminster, on the 29th of August, 1642, he was unanimously expelled the House for deserting its service, and assisting in the defense of Chester against the Parliament.[1]

When the King summoned the members of the two Houses who were faithful to him, to assemble at Oxford, in January, 1645, Bridgeman, still considering himself the lawful representative for Wigan, took his seat in Christ Church Hall, and joined in the resolutions of the supposed House of Commons, and subscribed the Letter to the Earl of Essex. As a reward for his services, by patent, under the Great Seal at Oxford, passed by Lord Keeper Littleton, he was appointed "Attorney General to the Court of Wards and Liveries," an office, when actually

[1] 2 Parl. Hist. 611.

exercised, of great importance and emolument, but now a mere feather in his cap. Even this the Parliament would not allow him to wear in their sight. When the treaty of Uxbridge was to take place, Bridgeman was named one of the King's Commissioners, and was designated by his new title; but the Westminster potentates having voted that all grants under the Great Seal were void after it had been carried to Charles, at York, in 1642, would not recognize his promotion, and insisted that he should appear in the commission and passport as plain " Orlando Bridgeman." [1]

When the treaty began, the grand question as to the militia, or the power of the sword,—upon which the rupture took place, and which ever prevented a settlement,—was assigned to Bridgeman and three other great lawyers, Lane, Gardiner, and Palmer. They here clearly had right on their side, and when they made the demand of the power of the sword by the parliament appear to be without law or justice, their opponents never offered to allege any other argument than "the determination of the parliament," from which they could not recede. The parliamentary Commissioners seem to have admitted privately that the law was against them, but to have urged that the command of the army was absolutely necessary for their security, and that the refusal of it could proceed from nothing but a resolution to take the highest vengeance upon them for their resistance.[2]

The subsequent struggle in the field having terminated in the triumph of the parliament, and Oxford having capitulated to Fairfax, Bridgeman first withdrew to his house in the country, and then came privately to London. But he would not recognize the usurped authority of the parliament so far as to put on his gown and plead, even before a Rolle or a Hale. During the Commonwealth he practiced as a conveyancer and chamber counsel. Lord Holt, in referring to this period of his life, says, " My Lord Chief Justice Bridgeman was a very studious gentleman; and, though he kept to his chamber, yet he had an account brought him of all that passed in the Courts." He looked forward to better times, but thought it more

[1] The same objection was made to the designation of Colepeper as Master of the Rolls, Hyde as Chancellor of the Exchequer, Lane as Chief Baron, and Gardiner as Solicitor General.   [2] Hist. Reb. b. viii.

politic to trust to the growing discontent of the nation
than to engage in any of the premature royalist plots,
which ended in ruining the authors of them, and strength-
ening the existing government.

When Monk marched to the South, Bridgeman crept
out from his hole, and exerted himself actively, though
cautiously, to further the Restoration. Another representative having been returned for Wigan after his expulsion, he does not seem to have attempted to resume his
place in the House of Commons on the last re-establishment of the Long Parliament (or the "Rump"), and the
readmission of the secluded members. One would have
expected to find him returned with other distinguished
cavalier lawyers to the Convention Parliament, but his
name does not appear in the list of its members. Nevertheless, he must have been in communication with the Court,
and high in the confidence of Hyde; for two days after
the King's return to Whitehall a writ was issued under
the Great Seal for calling him to the degree of a Sergeant
at law, and in two days more he was created Lord Chief
Baron of the Court of Exchequer.[1] He was soon after
appointed to sit as Speaker of the House of Lords, in the
absence of the Lord Chancellor.

In October, the same year, he presided at the trial of
the regicides. We find handed down to us some of the
flowers of his eloquence, in charging the grand jury on
this occasion. Having explained to them that the treason consisted "in *imagining* and *compassing* the King's
death," and stated that the prisoners had gone further,
and "*executed* him on a scaffold in front of his own
palace," he said, "Certainly this is so much beyond the
imagination and compassing, as it is not only laying
the cockatrice's egg, but brooding upon it till it hath
brought forth a serpent." After stating that the crown
of England is an imperial crown, he asks, "What is an
imperial crown? It is that which, as to the coercive part,
is subject to no man under God. The King of Poland
has a crown; but what is it? At his coronation he is
conditioned with the people, that if he shall not govern
them according to such and such rules, they shall be
freed from their homage and allegiance; but the crown
of England is, and always was, an imperial crown,—not

[1] June 2, 1660. Dug. Or. Jur. 1660.

subject to any human tribunal or judicature whatever. As to the person of the King, he is not to be touched. *Touch not mine annointed.* Is is true (blessed be God!) we have as great liberties as any people have in Christendom, but let us owe them where they are due; we have them by the concession of our Princes. Our Princes have granted them and the King now grants them." Having stirred up their indignation by a rhetorical description of the King's death, he thus concludes,—" No story that ever was,—I do not think that any romance—any fabulous tragedy,—can produce the like. You are now to inquire of blood—of royal blood—of sacred blood—blood like that of the saints under the altar, crying, *Quousque, Domine.* This blood cries for vengeance; and it will not be appeased without a bloody sacrifice. He that conceals the guilt of blood takes it upon himself—willfully, knowingly takes it upon himself; and we know that when the Jews said, *Let his blood be on us and our seed,* it continued and continues to bring a curse unto them and their posterity to this day." [1]

I can not say there is any bad law here, but the political doctrines promulgated must have drawn a disagreeable gaze on the Duke of Albemarle, the Earl of Manchester, Lord Hollis, and others, who, having been active Commonwealth's men, had the bad taste to be present as Judges on their *collaborateurs*. It has been said that when the indictments were found by the Grand Jury, and the prisoners were tried *seriatim* before Bridgeman, "he distinguished himself by his acrimony, intemperance and inhumanity;"[2] but though I do not agree in the panegyric upon him, that "he was a man of great learning and *greater temperance*,"[3] I do not discover much to censure in his conduct on these trials. He was bound to require the parties to plead guilty or not guilty, before they addressed the Court. The observation which General Harrison was beginning, "Divers of those who sat upon the Bench were formerly as active——" though true, could not be decently permitted. The defense, that the King's trial was under an Ordinance of the House of Commons, required to be overruled; and the suggestion that "the whole proceeding had been approved by God,"

[1] Manning's Report of the Sergeant's Case, 5 St. Tr. 998.
[2] Serviens ad Legem, 181. [3] Siderfin, 3.

might well justify strong remarks upon its criminality. We should think it rather strange if a Judge were to tell the Jury that a capital charge was so clearly proved that they ought to find a verdict of *guilty* without leaving the box; but even fair Judges were not so squeamish in those days, and the case was made out in law, and in fact, beyond all possibility of doubt. He checked the applause which burst out at the verdict, stating that it was more fitting for a stage play than a Court of Justice.[1]

As soon as the trials were over he was made a Baronet, and promoted to be Chief Justice of the Court of Common Pleas. "While he presided in this Court," says Granger, "his reputation was at the height; then his moderation and equity were such that he seemed to carry a chancery in his breast. His own reports of his decisions certainly show that he was a very learned, acute, and pains-taking Judge."[2]

Presiding in a court which merely decided questions of property between party and party, he had few opportunities of showing his political bias, but such as occurred he very eagerly improved. His most celebrated judgment is that in the case of Benyon *v.* Evelyn,[3] which has endeared his memory to the enemies of parliamentary privilege. In an action for a debt, which was clearly barred by "the Statute of Limitations," the defense was likewise grounded on a resolution of the House of Commons with respect to the commencement of an action against a member during the sitting of parliament. The Chief Justice, who, as we have seen, thought that all our liberties were *octroyed* or granted by the Crown, and wished that they should still be considered as depending on the good pleasure of the reigning sovereign,—of course highly disapproved of the notion that there was any privilege constitutionally inherent in the Houses of Parliament. He had himself been expelled the House of Commons by an abuse of an assumed privilege; he had ob-

---

[1] 5 St. Tr. 947.
[2] Vol. iii. 361. In the arguments of Chief Justice Bridgeman methinks I find that *evisceratio causæ*, as the Roman orator calls it, an exact anatomy of the case, and a dexterous piercing into the very bowels of it; and it was no small commendation of an eminent professor of our law, and one that afterwards was advanced to the highest office a person of that profession can be capable, " That he always argued like a lawyer and a gentleman."—*Preface to Carter's Reports.* [3] Bridg. Rep. 324.

served the great advantage which parliament had derived from the doctrine of privilege in its struggles with the Crown during the last reign; and, though parliament was at present abundantly subservient, he had the sagacity to foresee that similar struggles might again arise. His object, therefore, was to aim a blow at privilege, by very unnecessarily and wantonly denying that any weight was to be attached to resolutions of the two Houses respecting their privileges, and asserting that parliamentary privilege was to be defined, limited, and determined by the King's Judges. The judgment in favor of the defendant being clearly right on other grounds, it could not be brought before any other tribunal; and no member of parliament being affected by the result, it could not be noticed by either House. In truth, not the slightest particle of public attention seems to have been bestowed upon it at the time; but being recently discovered, it has placed Lord Chief Justice Bridgeman on a pinnacle, and we are now called upon to honor him as the champion of our laws and liberties.[1]

That he was not a Judge of very enlarged views we may conjecture from his celebrated construction of the clause of MAGNA CHARTA, providing for the due administration of justice. The Court of Common Pleas, in the reign of Charles II., was held in Westminster Hall, near the great northern gate, and the Judges, counsel, attorneys, suitors and by-standers, being much annoyed by the cold and the noise, there was a general wish that the Court should be removed to an adjoining recess, from which the voice of the Sergeants, when eloquent, might still have been heard in the Hall; but the Chief Justice would by no means agree to this innovation, "as the Great Charter enacts that the Court of Common Pleas, instead of following the King in his progresses, shall be held *in aliquo certo loco;*" so that, after the proposed removal, all the proceedings of the Court would be "*coram non judice* and void."[2]

During the illnesses of the Lord Chancellor, the Chief Justice Bridgeman frequently sat Speaker in the House

[1] See Lord Campbell's Speeches, p. 316.
[2] North's Life of Guilford, i. 185. This decision rather supports Erasmus's account of English lawyers: "Doctissimum genus indoctissimorum hominum."

of Lords, but he seems to have been very little connected with any political party or leader, and not to have aimed at any higher promotion. He was not at all mixed up in the intrigues which ended in the removal of Clarendon; and Lady Castlemaine, Buckingham, Ashley, and Arlington only thought of him as a person who might be safely trusted to hold the Great Seal till they could fix upon some one likely more actively to promote the measures or jobs which they had in contemplation.[1] It was arranged that he should still retain his office of Chief Justice of the Common Pleas, and, in fact, he did retain it near a year after he was appointed Lord Keeper.[2]

The ceremony of delivering the Great Seal to him took place at Whitehall, on Saturday, the 31st of August, 1667; and "on the Wednesday following, in full council, he took the oaths of supremacy and allegiance, and of the office of Lord Keeper, and of a Privy Councillor."[3] He had the long vacation to prepare himself for the duties of his new office, but not expecting to hold it, or being insuperably unfit for it, he never made any progress in his Equity studies, and all accounts represent him to have turned out a most execrably bad Equity Judge. We find constant complaints of him, even amidst compliments to Clarendon, his predecessor, and Shaftesbury, who succeeded him—who, notwithstanding their utter ignorance of equitable and legal principles, contrived, by *representing* the part more skillfully, to delude many into an opinion of their sufficiency.

On the first day of Michaelmas term he went in grand procession, attended by the Judges and King's Counsel, in coaches, from Sergeant's Inn to Westminster Hall; and "soe soone as he came to his place in the midst of the Court of Chancery, standing, tooke the oathe of the office of Lord Keeper of the Great Seale of England, the booke being held by the oldest Master of the Chancery, in the

[1] In a very artful letter written on the very evening of Bridgeman's appointment, by Arlington to break the news to the Duke of Ormond, Clarendon's fast friend—after stating that the King had sent for the seals by Secretary Morrice, he says, "and this night his Majesty hath given them to my Lorde Bridgeman, *with whome hee sayes hee will advise concerning his Lop.'s successour.* I can not but still be of ye opinion that not only the publique affaires will bee bettered by this change, but that my Lord Chancell^r will find greater ease by it than he seemes yet to believe hee shall."

[2] He was succeeded by Lord C. J. Vaughan, on the 23rd of May, 1668.

[3] Cr. Off. Min. 1667.

absence of the Master of the Rolls, being sick, who, had he been present, ought to have held it."[1]

The high expectation entertained by some from seeing an experienced lawyer appointed to this great judicial office, was immediately disappointed. He departed from the discreet practice of Lord Clarendon, always to have Judges and Masters of Chancery on the Bench with him to assist him; and, though very desirous to do what was right, he gave universal dissatisfaction to the parties, to the profession, and to the public. Burnet says, that, "as Chief Justice of the Common Pleas he was in great esteem, which he did not long maintain after his advancement. His study and practice lay so entirely in the common law, that he never seemed to apprehend what Equity was; nor had he a head made for the business of such a Court."[2] But of all the writers who fleered at him, Roger North gives us the liveliest picture of the Lord Keeper himself and those about him. "He had been a celebrated lawyer, and sat with high esteem in the place of Lord Chief Justice of the *Common Pleas*. The removing him from thence to the Chancery did not at all contribute any increase to his fame, but rather the contrary, for he was timorous to an impotence, and that not mended by his great age. He labored very much to please everybody, and that is a temper of ill consequence in a Judge. It was observed of him, that if a case admitted of divers doubts, which the lawyers call points, he would never give all on one side, but either party should have somewhat to go away with. And in his time the Court of Chancery run out of order into delays and endless motions in causes, so that it was like a field overgrown with briars. And what was worst of all, his family was very ill qualified for that place—his lady being a most violent intriguess in business, and his sons kept no good decorum whilst they practiced under him; and he had not a vigor of mind and strength to coerce the cause of so much disorder in his family."[3]

[1] Cr. Off. Min. 1667.   [2] Burnet, i. 253.
[3] Life of Lord Keeper, i. 168. In another place he says, "The Lord Bridgeman, who was a very good common law judge, made a very bad Chancellor. For his timidous manner of creating and judging abundance of points, some on one side and some on another, and if possible contriving that each should have a competent share, made work for registers, solicitors, and counsel, who dressed up causes to fit his humor," ii. 74.—See also *Granger*, iii. 361. *Life of James II.* vol. i. 429.

The printed Reports of his decisions in Chancery are so scanty, that the perusal of them does not enable us to form any opinion of him as an Equity Judge. The points to be found there are of small importance, and seem generally to have been properly ruled.[1] But so little progress had Equity then made as a science, that the Lord Keeper having on one occasion called in the three chiefs to assist him, and Chief Justice Keyling having quoted the decision of a former Chancellor, supposed to be in point, Chief Justice Vaughan, a very accomplished lawyer, thus broke out: "I wonder to hear of citing precedents in matters of equity; for if there be equity in a case, that equity is an universal truth; and there can be no precedent in it. So that in any precedent that can be produced, if it be the same with this case, the reason is the same in itself; and if the precedent be not the same case with this, it is not to be cited, being not to that purpose."[2]

We must now view him in his political capacity. Never being created a Peer, his only duty in the House of Lords was to put the question, and to address the two Houses in explanation of the royal will on the assembling of parliament. His first essay in this line was at the opening of the session which began on the 10th of October, 1667. His address was short and becoming; and he did not refer to the dismissal of his predecessor, unless, perhaps, in these general terms: "His Majesty hath reason to believe that some disaffected persons have spread abroad discourses and rumors reflecting on the government. It is an easy thing to take exceptions: *Cum neque culpam humana infirmitas, neque calumniam regnandi difficultas evitat.*" But he had to read the joint address of both Houses to the King: "thanking his Majesty for having been pleased to displace the late Lord Chancellor, and remove him from the exercise of public trust and employment in the affairs of state."[3] He appears to have behaved with generosity to his former patron and friend, when all the world was abandoning him; and, at the risk of soon losing the Great Seal, to have done what lay in his power to stop the impeachment, and to prevent the necessity for flight. He was the messenger who carried to the King the last letter which Clarendon wrote to him in

[1] Cases in Chancery, Part I. Mod. I. [2] A. D. 1670. [3] 4 Parl. Hist. 366.

England, denying his privity with the marriage between the Duke of Richmond and " La belle Stuart ;" and if he at last counseled him to withdraw, according to the strong hint which Charles then so insultingly gave,— Clarendon's own family, and most attached friends, now joined in the same advice.[1] Whatever influence the new Lord Keeper had, was used to make the bill of pains and penalties, which the King and the Court party insisted on, operate with as little prejudice as possible to Clarendon and his property; and he behaved with kindness to the sons and dependents of the banished Earl.

There was no one else on whom the courtiers could agree to confer the office of Lord Keeper. Meanwhile, Bridgeman affixed the Great Seal to grants to Lady Castlemaine and others which Clarendon had stopped, and proved for a long time entirely submissive to them in all things. He was, therefore, allowed to hold it till the measures of the CABAL were so atrocious, and the orders imposed upon him were so revolting, that even *he* scrupled, and protested, and resisted—when it was snatched from him by the most daring and profligate of mankind. Bridgeman interfered with the general policy of the government less than any of his predecessors had ever done. If he can claim no merit for proposing or furthering the Triple Alliance, he was not implicated in the secret treaty with France for violating it, nor in the conspiracy deliberately formed to overturn the religion and the liberties of the country.

There are preserved to us speeches which he made a the opening of parliament in October, 1669, February, 1670, and October, 1671; but they merely refer, in general terms, to the state of public affairs, and press for a supply to pay the King's debts.

He was in office when the Triple Alliance was negotiated, and he must have put the Great Seal to that treaty,[2] but the only two public measures with which his name has been connected are " the Declaration of Indulgence," and " the Shutting-up of the Exchequer "—and these led to his fall.

Clifford, who had planned the re-establishment of Popery, and the King's open profession of that religion, —in February, 1672, proposed in Council that a royal

[1] Ante, p. 62.   [2] See Sir W. Temple's Letters.

Declaration should be published "for indulgence to tender consciences, suspending by the supreme power in ecclesiastical matters inherent in the Crown, and recognized by several acts of parliament, all manner of penal laws in matters ecclesiastical, against whatsoever sort of non-conformists or recusants." As the Great Seal must be affixed to such a Declaration to give it any color of validity, the Lord Keeper had been summoned to attend this Council. A most bigoted Protestant, he had been always eager for putting in force the penal laws against the Catholics, and his religion now warped his opinion upon constitutional law; for though he had often stood up for the King's dispensing power,—when he saw that such a use was to be made of it, he expressed great doubts whether it existed, and positively refused, without further consideration, to allow the Declaration to pass the Great Seal.[1] As it must have caused great alarm directly to dismiss him from his office on the ground (as it would be said) that he had shown himself the champion of the Church of England and of the Protestant faith, Clifford proposed a proviso which he hoped might be soon got rid of, or not enforced, "that the benefit of public worship should not be extended to the Catholics, who, to avoid molestation, must confine their religious assemblies to private houses."[2]

The Lord Keeper agreed to this compromise, but at the same time expressed his determination never to consent to the legalizing of the idolatry and will-worship of the Church of Rome in this Protestant land. The Declaration came out, and he retained his office for some months, though thenceforth an object of suspicion and dislike to the existing administration.[3]

The proximate cause of this removal was his refusal,

---

[1] He here imitated the example of a greater man, Lord Clarendon, who, though a stickler for the dispensing power, flatly denied it when it was to be exercised in favor of liberty of conscience.—Ante, p. 37.

[2] 4 Parl. Hist. 515.

[3] Burnet and others have said that the Lord Keeper refused to affix the Great Seal to the Declaration, and was for that reason dismissed from h s office; whereas the Declaration issued in March, and he held the Great Seal till November. A curious account of this transaction is to be found in "A Letter from a Person of Quality to his Friend in the Country," which was written by Locke under the directions of Shaftesbury, and in which it is said that it was "the vanity of the Lord Keeper" which caused the Catholics to be named in the Declaration.—See 4 Parl. Hist. App. No. v. p. xxxviii.

when sitting as a Judge in the Court of Chancery, to grant injunctions which were applied for in consequence of the most fraudulent and foolish act that any government ever resorted to. The object was to enable the King to carry on a war against Holland, in violation of the Triple Alliance, and in conjunction with Louis XIV., to crush the liberties of the United Provinces, preparatory to the introduction of absolutism and Romanism into England. Large sums had been advanced by the bankers of London, for the repayment of which orders on the Exchequer had been issued, and the King having solemnly promised "that he would not, on any occasion whatever, suffer any interruption of payment of these orders of the Exchequer,"[1]—the honest men and profound political economists now at the head of affairs, resolved that the Exchequer should be suddenly shut, and that no payment should be made to any public creditor for a twelvemonth. The approach of the Dutch fleet to Gravesend, or the Great Plague, hardly produced a greater sensation in the city. An unexampled shock was given to commercial credit; trade was paralyzed; many mercantile houses became bankrupt; numbers of annuitants, widows, and orphans were reduced to a state of the lowest distress,—and though, by this contrivance, a sum of £1,300,000 was, in the first instance, placed at the disposal of the ministers, the regular revenue failed, and the finances were in a state of greater disorder than ever.

The bankers to whom the large payments were due, were the first victims. The money which they had advanced to the government at eight or ten *per cent.*, they had borrowed at six or seven from their customers, who, not receiving principal or interest, brought actions against them, and threatened them with statutes of bankruptcy. When they stated the hardship of their case to Shaftesbury, who had the chief management of affairs at the Treasury board, he, vaguely recollecting something he had heard or read when a student in the Inns of Court about *Injunctions*, said, " Why do you not apply to the Lord Keeper for *an injunction* against all such proceedings, to which you must be clearly entitled, as your inability to pay your customers proceeds entirely from an act of the King, resorted to for the safety of the State?"

[1] 14 St. Tr. 1.

They communicated this advice to their solicitors and counsel, who never had dreamed of such an expedient. But bills were immediately filled, and injunctions were moved for. The Lord Keeper was prepared for these motions by an intimation from Shaftesbury and his other colleagues, that it was indispensably necessary that all actions and proceedings against the bankers in consequence of the shutting of the Exchequer should be stopped. Nay, a message was brought to the perplexed Bridgeman from the King himself, that "he deemed himself bound in honor to shelter the bankers whose money he had had locked up in the Exchequer from the pursuit of their creditors."

But when the application was made in open Court, no principle or precedent could be cited to support it, although a feeble attempt was made on the ground that the fulfillment of the contract had been prevented by *vis major* or *casus fortuitus*,[1]—while the opposite counsel argued conclusively that the debt being admitted, and there being no legal defense, the inability of the debtor to pay could constitute no equity in his favor; that the rights of the creditor could not be prejudiced by the fraud or force of a third party; and that the shutting up of the Exchequer, whatever might be its character, was entirely *res inter alios acta*.

The case was so clear to the bar and the bystanders, as well as to the Lord Keeper himself, that he durst not grant the injunction; but in hopes to find out some by-point upon which he might intimate an opinion for the bankers, and so soften their disappointment, he said he should take the papers home with him, and pronounce judgment another day.

Shaftesbury, who was the real *actor*, was not a man so to be dealt with. He resolved that he would grasp the Great Seal, and grant the injunctions himself. He posted off to the King, swore that Bridgeman was an old dotard, quite unequal to his situation; declared that he (Shaftesbury) was himself much fitter for it; pointed out how the recent example proved the little use of black letter learning in teaching what is just and equitable; and vowed that if he were made Chancellor the appointment would greatly redound to the King's ease and the public

[1] See Reports in Chancery, i. 24.

welfare. Charles, at first, thought that Shaftesbury was in jest, and received the proposal with a laugh; but Buckingham, Arlington, and Clifford were brought to support it,—probably from the hope that a colleague, whom they began to find very troublesome, might ruin his credit by such a freak, and at any rate would find plenty to occupy him without interfering with their departments. The King acquiesced, and Secretary Coventry, without any thing having been done to prepare the Lord Keeper for such a blow, was sent for the Great Seal, and demanded it from him,—while he was thinking of the least unpalatable terms in which he might refuse the injunction, and was hesitating whether he could with any decency refuse to punish the bankers with the costs of the application. Charles kept the Great Seal in his own custody one night, and next morning it was delivered to Shaftesbury with the title of Lord Chancellor.

Burnet, in relating this event, says that Lord Keeper Bridgeman "had lost all credit at Court, with the reputation he had formerly acquired, and that they had some time been seeking an occasion to get rid of him."[1]

In addition to the refusal of the injunctions Roger North assigns another direct cause of his removal, of which I no where else find any trace,—his refusal to seal "a commission for martial law," observing "he was pressed, but proved restive on both points. For the sake of his family, that gathered like a snow-ball while he had the Seal, he would not have formalized with any tolerable compliances: but these impositions were too rank for him to comport with."[2]

After his fall he lived in entire seclusion at his villa at at Teddington, and died there, 25th June, 1674.

Lord Chancellor Nottingham, referring to one of his decisions, said,—"It is due to the memory of so great a man, whenever we speak of him, to mention him with reverence and with veneration for his learning and integrity;" and Lord Ellenborough pronounces him "a most eminent Judge, distinguished by the profundity of his learning and the extent of his industry." But greatness will only be attributed to him by lawyers: he knew nothing beyond his own art; in only one department of that was he distinguished,—and such distinction, with op-

[1] Own Times, i. 198, 535.   [2] Examen, 38.

portunity, may be attained by any man of ordinary intellect and extraordinary industry. He is very much to be honored for his steady and consistent adherence to his royalist principles, but he has received unmerited praise for having denied the dispensing power, and for having favored toleration,—seeing that rather than give up his office he put the Great Seal to the Declaration suspending the penal laws when he had got the Catholics excluded from it,—and that he fully partook of the horror felt by Clarendon, his patron, against all who were not high Protestant Episcopalians.

He is said to have favored men of learning. Bishop Cumberland, author of the *De Legibus Naturæ*, was his chaplain, and received from him the living of All-hallows, Stamford.

He was twice married—first to Judith, daughter and heiress of John Kynaston, Esq., of Morton, in the county of Salop; and secondly, to Dorothy, daughter of Dr. Saunders, Provost of Oriel College, Oxford, by both of whom he left issue. Sir Henry Bridgeman, the fifth Baronet (whose mother was the daughter and heiress of Thomas, the last Earl of Bradford, of the family of Newport), was created Baron Bradford by George III. in the year 1794; and in 1815 his son was raised to the Earldom of Bradford, now enjoyed by the lineal representative in the male line of the Lord Keeper.[1]

CHAPTER LXXXV.

LIFE OF LORD CHANCELLOR SHAFTESBURY FROM HIS BIRTH TILL THE RESTORATION OF CHARLES II.

WE pass at once from a mere lawyer—" leguleius quidam cautus et acutus, præco actionum, cantor formularum, auceps syllabarum "—to a Chancellor who did not affect to have even a smattering of law, but who possessed brilliant accomplishments as well as talents, and who, as a statesman, is one of most extraordinary characters in English history.

[1] Grandeur of the Law, 97.

> "For close designs and crooked counsels fit,
> Sagacious, bold, and turbulent of wit;
> Restless, unfix'd in principles and place;
> In power unpleas'd, impatient of disgrace;
> A daring pilot in extremity,
> Pleas'd with the danger when the waves ran high,
> He sought the storms; but for a calm unfit,
> Would steer too near the sands to boast his wit.
> In friendship false, implacable in hate,
> Resolv'd to ruin or to rule the state.
> Then seiz'd with fear, yet still affecting fame,
> Usurp'd a patriot's all-atoning name."

From the birth and boyish position of ANTHONY ASHLEY COOPER, so enterprising, so energetic, so aspiring, so reckless, it might have been expected that he would have quietly devoted himself to dogs and horses, and that if his breast was ever fired by ambition, it would only have been to be High Sheriff of the county, or Chairman of Quarter Sessions. While a schoolboy, he was a Baronet in possession of large landed estates, yielding him a revenue of £8,000 a year.

The subject of this memoir was the son of Sir John Cooper, of Rockborne, in Hampshire, who was created a baronet by James I., and Anne Ashley, only daughter and heiress of Sir Anthony Ashley, of Wimborne St. Giles, in the county of Dorset, who had been Clerk of the Council in the reign of Elizabeth, and had acted as secretary to the council of war in the expedition against Cadiz in 1596.[1] He was born at Wimborne St. Giles, July 22, 1621. His grandfather died in 1627, and his father in 1631, when the title, with the fortunes of both families, descended upon him.

His early education was intrusted to Mr. Guerdean, a Fellow of Queen's College, Cambridge, selected by Sir Anthony for strictness of principle and severity of temper,—the old gentleman often saying, "that youth could not have too deep a dye of religion, for business and conversation in the world would wear it to a just moderation."[2] It can not be objected that the pupil from this early discipline showed himself over strait-laced and stiff.

It is related that the youth while only thirteen years of age, showed the energy of his character by defeating a scheme of his trustees to deprive him of a large part of his

---

[1] Arch. xxii. 172. [2] Life by Martyn, 35.

property. Being a ward of the Crown, he went alone to Noy, the Attorney-General, and acquainted him with the proceedings,—observing that he had no one to depend upon but him, who had been the friend of his grandfather. Noy, pleased with his spirit, zealously undertook his cause in the Court of Wards, and succeeded for him without taking any fees.[1]

In 1636 he was entered of Exeter College, Oxford, where he early distinguished himself by refusing to submit to some traditionary tricks attempted to be put upon him as a freshman, and by stirring up a rebellion against the seniors. I find nothing more recorded of his academical life, except that his wit, affability, and courage gained him the good-will of the University. He improved himself more by conversation than by study, and though not grossly deficient in acquirements becoming a gentleman, he might well have been designated "*acerrimi ingenii—paucarum literarum.*"

Having remained about two years at Oxford,—to finish his education he was transferred to Lincoln's Inn, where he remained for a short time,—associating with other young men of fortune like himself,—frequenting the theaters and fencing schools,—but without any thought of being called to the bar or studying the law.

While only eighteen he married a young lady of great beauty and accomplishments, a daughter of Lord Keeper Coventry. After his marriage he lived with his father-in-law; and now in a legal atmosphere, he must have imbibed the few loose notions of jurisprudence which he ever possessed. But instead of listening to the coifed sages of the law who frequented Durham House, he delighted himself, when accompanying the family into Worcestershire, to act the part of a fortune-teller,—which he did with brilliant reputation, by the assistance of a servant who got into all the love stories of the houses which he visited. But such a mixture of contradictions was he, that, according to Bishop Burnet, he himself "had the dotage of astrology in him to a high degree," and he declared, "that a Dutch doctor, had from the stars foretold him the whole series of his life."

In one of these visits to the country, he was invited to a public dinner given by the Bailiffs of Tewkesbury. Sir

[1] Life, 38.

Harry Spiller, "a vain man, that despised all whom he thought his inferiors," thought fit to put many affronts on the Bailiffs and their entertainment, in the presence of the first gentlemen of the county, before whom they were desirous of appearing to the best advantage. Young Sir Anthony rose in defense of the corporation, and retorted on the assailant his rough raillery with such wit and success as to gain the victory, and completely to silence him.

This occurrence had an important influence on Shaftesbury's future destiny. The invasion of the Scots and the general discontents rendering a parliament indispensable, after an experiment of above eleven years' duration, to rule by prerogative,—a writ came down to elect members for Tewkesbury, and the burgesses unanimously chose their champion as one of their representatives,—in his absence,—without his knowledge,—and when he was only nineteen years of age.[1]

Before parliament met, his father-in-law, the Lord Keeper, died, and he was thenceforth his own master, or rather the slave of his own passions and caprice.

He took his place in the House of Commons during the short parliament which met in April, 1640; but I can not find an account of any of his speeches, although it seems impossible that he should have remained silent during the three weeks which elapsed before the dissolution. It is said that he diligently attended the House of Commons, and every day practiced the useful lesson of writing out a report of their proceedings. We can not doubt that he warmly supported the Court in the grand struggle which was led on opposite sides by Hyde and Hampden, whether the supply demanded should be granted before the consideration of grievances? Till he met with the affront about the garrison of Weymouth, hereafter to be related, he was an ardent friend of high prerogative.

For this very reason, probably, he had given dissatisfaction to his constituents at Tewkesbury; and it was now very difficult for a man of such principles, in the universal rage for reform, to find a seat. He stood for Downton, and was beaten. He petitioned against the return, but

---

[1] The son of the Duke of Albemarle sat in parliament, after the Restoration, at the age of fifteen.

the decision of the House of Commons was against him.¹ Thus he never was a member of the Long Parliament till immediately before the Restoration, when,—twenty years from its first assembling,—it met for the last time under the name of the " Rump."

However, although, to his deep mortification, prevented from defending Strafford and ship-money, out of parliament he exerted himself to the utmost in support of the royal cause. When hostilities were about to commence he attended the king to the north, and he was present at the ceremony of erecting the royal standard at Nottingham. In 1643, after various conferences with the leading royalists at Oxford, he was ordered to his house at Wimborne St. Giles, in the hope that he might get some of the towns in the western counties which were held for the parliament to declare for the King. He now declaimed with much eloquence at public meetings on the tyranny of the parliament, and the good intentions of Charles I.; and he displayed such boldness and address in the intrigues he carried on, that he prevailed on the inhabitants of Weymouth to expel the parliamentary garrison, and to receive him as governor of the town in the King's name. Poole, Dorchester, and other places in that county were about to follow their example. But Prince Maurice, who held a superior command in the west, superseded him as governor of Weymouth, refused to recognize the terms on which he had induced it to come over to the Crown, and treated the young baronet with marked disdain. Sir Anthony took a journey to Oxford to lay his case before the King, and meeting with no redress, "he was thereby so much disobliged that he quitted the King's party, and gave himself up body and soul to the services of the parliament, with an implacable animosity against the royal cause." ²

¹ Com. Jour. 10 Feb. 1641.
² Clarendon This account of Shaftesbury's first change of party differs considerably from that given in the Memoir of his Life by Locke. I should have had no difficulty in preferring Locke to all other authority, had he been narrating from his own knowledge and observation ; but during these events he was a boy at school, and he did not form an acquaintance with Shaftesbury till the year 1666. Then, struck by his conversation, and fascinated by his kindness, he was blind to his vices, and gave implicit credit to all he heard from a man of such distinction. The memoir, and the " Letter from a Person of Quality," were both written at Shaftesbury's request, and on his representations. The converted patriot, in vindication of his consistency,

Upon this, as upon every subsequent change, however violent,—claiming the credit of being a perfectly consistent politician, and contending that the friends whom he abandoned had left those principles to which he steadily adhered,—he pretended that the aspect of public affairs had suddenly changed,—and he now affirmed that all who had a true regard for the monarchy ought to fight under the Earl of Essex. But it must be related to his honor, that he was now governed by a rule which he always afterwards rigidly observed, and which went far to redeem him from the odium of his frequent tergiversations,—that he never betrayed the secrets of a party he had left, or made harsh personal observations on the conduct of his old friends;—not only trying to keep up a familiar private intercourse with them, but abstaining from vindictive reflections upon them in his speeches or his writings.

Having traveled secretly from Oxford to London, he there formally sent in his adhesion to the parliament. He was received, as may be supposed, with great cordiality; but a committee of the House of Commons being appointed to confer with him and to examine him, he absolutely refused to make any discovery either as to persons or the management of affairs of what he had observed while he had been on the King's side, saying, that the maxim ought to be acted upon in public as well as private life,—"that there is a general and tacit trust in conversation whereby a man is obliged not to report anything to the speaker's prejudice, though no intimation may be given of a desire not to have it spoken of again."[1]

The parliament was contented to receive him on his own terms; and by an ordinance of the two Houses, on the 14th of August, 1644, he was appointed one of the committee of the western counties for governing the army. A military district was assigned to him, and he was placed in the command of a brigade consisting of Colonel Popham's and Colonel Cooke's regiments. At the head of these, he marched to Wareham, a royal garrison, which he

was desirous that it should be supposed that he had been at the head of a middle party between the King and the parliament; whereas there is no doubt that, in the language of Clarendon, "he gave himself up body and soul," first to the one, and then to the other. The accurate Whitelock says, "he professed his great affection for the parliament, and his enmity to the King's party, from whom he had revolted; and was now in great favor and trust with the parliament." [1] Life, 142. Locke's Memoir, Works, ix. 270.

resolved to take by assault. Having carried one of the outworks, he drove the enemy into the town; and they, intimidated by this onset, surrendered, upon the terms that 300 of them should serve the parliament against the rebels in Ireland.

He next laid siege to Corfe Castle, which soon surrendered at discretion; and as a precaution against any attempt of the royalists to retake it, he threw a considerable body of foot and horse into the adjoining stronghold of Lulworth. Drawing together a large force from the garrisons of Weymouth, Poole, and Wareham, he marched to Abbotsbury, then a considerable place on the sea-coast, and took it by storm, after a gallant defense by Colonel Strangeways.[1] Having refreshed his men in Dorchester, he successively attacked the remaining garrisons in that part of England, and reduced them to obedience to the parliament.

He then marched to the relief of Taunton, where the gallant Blake (afterwards so illustrious as an admiral) was the governor, and his ammunition and provisions being exhausted, was on the point of capitulating. Shaftesbury first routed an auxiliary force coming to the assistance of the besiegers, and then their main body, and compelled them to raise the siege. He wrote a flaming account of this exploit to the parliament,—taking greater credit to himself than Cromwell in his dispatch announcing his victory at Dunbar.

But he was suddenly satiated with military glory, and after this brilliant campaign never again appeared in the field. Whether he retired from some affront, or from mere caprice, is not certainly known.[2]

There is a considerable obscurity as to the manner in which he employed himself during the several years which followed, while with envious eyes he saw Cromwell mounting to supreme power. To his unspeakable mortification he never was a member of the Long Parliament, all his attempts to get himself returned upon a vacancy being defeated from a suspicion of his unsteady and dangerous character. Had he succeeded in obtaining a

---

[1] Vicars, Part IV. 67.
[2] Some have supposed that the "self-denying ordinance" drove him from the army; but this could not possibly be the case, as he was not then in parliament.

seat, it is not at all improbable that he might have prevented the ascendency of the Independents and their Chief; for the Presbyterians, till "Pride's purge," were a majority in the House, and they only wanted a bold and resolute leader to have successfully opposed such crafty schemes as the "self-denying ordinance" by which they were crushed.

Some accounts state that in the year 1645, Sir Anthony Ashley Cooper was High Sheriff of Norfolk; but his name does not appear in the list of High Sheriffs for that county, and during this year the office was served by Sir Jacob Astley. The following year he certainly was appointed High Sheriff of Wiltshire, under an ordinance which gave him leave to reside in Dorsetshire. He is said at this time to have distinguished himself as an active magistrate—exciting the admiration of the country people by his eloquence at sessions,—quarter and petty.

When he occasionally came to London, he associated himself chiefly with the Presbyterian leaders; and he strongly dissuaded Hollis from the indiscreet move which terminated in Cromwell escaping to the army and practically assuming supreme power. It is said that the Lord General, some time after, meeting him, said to him jeeringly, "I am holden to you for your kindness to me; for you, I hear, were for letting me go without punishment; but your friend, God be thanked! was not wise enough to take your advice."[1]

In the beginning of 1652, he became a member of the famous commission for the reform of the law; but he soon found this very dull work; and being shut out from all military and civil distinction, he became highly discontented, and muttered so loud against the reigning authorities, that he was actually taken up as a delinquent; but nothing could be proved against him except some intemperate speeches, and it was resolved by the House "that Sir Anthony Ashley Cooper be pardoned of all delinquency."[2]

After the expulsion of the Long Parliament he intrigued with Cromwell, who was anxious to secure him, and held out to him the prospect of being appointed Lord Keeper of the Great Seal,—an office for which he was quite as fit as Lisle or Fiennes, who actually held it.

[1] Life, 159.   [2] Com. Jour. March 17, 1652.

Shaftesbury at this moment saw no other course than to temporize with Oliver. He, therefore, in his own country, pretended to have received "the new light," after the fashion of the Independents; and when Barebones' Parliament was to be called, he contrived to get his name included in the list of "godly men" returned by the county of Wilts to the Council of State, from whom a selection was to be made of fit representatives of the people in the legislature, Cromwell actually appointed him one of this motley assembly.

Sir Anthony found himself in strange company; but, on the meeting of the House, he joined zealously in "seeking the Lord," along with the great body of fanatics of which it was composed. His views on the Great Seal were considerably dashed by the bill " for the immediate and total abolition of the Court of Chancery;" which, after it had been read a second time, he contrived to obstruct in the committee, by suggesting difficulties as to the determination of existing suits, and as to the enforcement of certain important rights, for which the courts of common law afforded no remedy.

Hence it has been said that he opposed Cromwell in this parliament—which is supposed to be further proved by his having powerfully supported the motion made on the 12th of December, "that the sitting of the parliament any longer would not be for the good of the Commonwealth." But I think it is probable that the good understanding between these two extraordinary men still subsisted; and it is quite certain that the motion referred to was highly agreeable to Cromwell, who wished to get rid of the parliament immediately, and had "the Instrument of Government" all prepared and ready, by which, as soon as a dissolution took place, he was to be declared LORD PROTECTOR.

But there was a decided estrangement between them soon after, probably arising from the promise about the Great Seal not being fulfilled—Cromwell's intuitive insight into character telling him that Shaftesbury was not to be trusted.

When the Protector's second parliament was called, on the excellent model so much praised by Lord Clarendon, and the basis of Lord Grey's Reform Bill, Shaftesbury was one of the ten members returned for the county of

Wilts; and, after a keen contest, he was at the head of the poll.¹

When the parliament met, he strongly co-operated with the party who were for beginning to inquire into the validity of "the Instrument of Government;" and the motion being made, "that the House do approve that the government be in one single person and a parliament," he supported the amendment, "that the Instrument of Government be examined, article by article, in a committee of the whole House." After a debate of three days, the amendment was carried by a majority of 141 to 136.²

This made the Protector resolve by a strong hand to exclude all such refractory spirits as Sir Anthony Ashley Cooper; and after sending for the Commons to Whitehall, and giving them a lecture, they found on their return a military guard at their door, who would allow no one to enter without signing the following declaration :—

"I do hereby freely promise and engage to be true and faithful to the Lord Protector and the Commonwealth of England, Scotland, and Ireland; and shall not, according to the tenor of the indenture whereby I am returned to serve in this present parliament, propose or give my consent to alter the government as it is settled in one person and a parliament."³

Shaftesbury absolutely refused to sign the declaration. Thus excluded, he intrigued actively against Cromwell, with the members who had signed it; and such an opposition was organized, that a dissolution took place within the five months, during which, by "the Instrument of Government," the parliament ought at all events to have been continued.

The Protector, finding his opponent so troublesome, soon after made a bold attempt to gain him over by appointing him a member of "the Council of State," with promises of further advancement. This gracious demeanor roused in the bosom of Sir Anthony the ambitious project of forming an alliance with the Protectoral house, and, having been some time a widower, he actually demanded in marriage "the musical glib-tongued Lady Mary,' afterwards united to Lord Fauconberg. Probably on account

---
¹ He was likewise returned to this parliament by Tewkesbury and by Poole—but elected to serve for his native county.
² 3 Parl. Hist. 1445.   ³ Parl. Hist. 1454.   ⁴ Ludlow.

of his dissolute morals,[1] he met with a flat refusal. Thereupon he finally broke with Oliver, and became a partisan of the banished royal family.[2] When he had only twice or thrice sat in the Council of State, he sent in his resignation, alleging that "the government by one person was against his conscience." Cromwell complained that "of all the difficult characters he had met with, the most difficult to manage was MARCUS TULLIUS CICERO—*the little man with three names.*"[3]

When the Protector's third and last parliament was called, in 1656, Sir Anthony Ashley Cooper was again at the head of the poll for the county of Wilts; but all that he was permitted to do, as a member, was on the first day of the session to hear a sermon in the Abbey Church, and to be present in the Painted Chamber when Oliver, in royal state, delivered his speech explaining the cause of the summons. No member was allowed to enter the House of Commons without a certificate of approbation from the Council of State, which was peremptorily withheld from *him*, on the pretense of some former acts of delinquency. Thus he took no part in the discussions about offering the Crown to Cromwell; but he was secretly leagued with the republicans, and without doing any act to render himself liable to be tried before "a high court of justice," he keenly intrigued against the government.

Bishop Burnet, in contradiction to all other authorities, says that Shaftesbury advised Cromwell "to take the Kingship,"—although with a secret design to destroy him. But to render this story incredible, it is enough to observe that Shaftesbury remained excluded from the House of Commons, and that he was not one of the new Peers; whereas his aid would have been eagerly courted in either House. This is as little to be believed as another story Burnet tells us, that "Cromwell offered to make Shaftes-

---

[1] At this very time the match which actually took place between Cromwell's youngest daughter, Lady Fanny, and Lord Rich, had nearly been broken off by a report to his disadvantage. See an extremely interesting letter on the subject from Lady Mary to her brother Henry.—Carlyle's Cromwell, iii. 181.

[2] This anecdote has been very lately discovered from a suppressed passage of *Ludlow's Memoirs*, in the handwriting of Locke, copied by him for his Life of the Earl of Shaftesbury, preserved among the MSS. of Lord Lovelace. See Carlyle's Cromwell, 183.

[3] Double Christian or surnames were then almost unknown in England.

bury King." The truth is, that when, in subsequent times, Shaftesbury became acquainted with the good Bishop, he took undue advantage of his credulity, and mystified him exceedingly.[1] Shaftesbury certainly continued in opposition to the government, professing republican principles, till Oliver's death.

On Richard's accession he was again returned to the House of Commons for Wiltshire, although the old system of representation was revived, each county sending only two members; but Sir William St. John had now the greatest number of votes. Sir Anthony did not scruple to take the oaths to the new Lord Protector, and solemnly to abjure the family of Stuart; but he had the penetration speedily to discover that Richard's government could not stand, and that to put an end to the general discontent, the old dynasty would ere long be restored. He therefore left the republicans, and intrigued with the royalists. He used, in after times, to take to himself almost the whole merit of the Restoration, representing Monk as merely his tool; and in the preamble to his patent of Peerage, he introduced a statement that "this happy event was chiefly brought about by the efforts of our right trusty and well beloved Sir Anthony Ashley Cooper." But he really was of considerable use, by embarrassing the government of Richard,—by rendering a dissolution of parliament necessary,—by successively bringing into discredit the Rump and the Council of Officers,—and by thickening the general confusion, which made all men turn their eyes to the exiled King. There is preserved to us a full report of his speech in Richard's House of Commons, in the only important debate which took place while it sat,—the question being,—"Whether the other House, consisting of Oliver's Peers, should be recognized?" Having for some time inveighed bitterly against them and their maker, he thus proceeded:

"I acknowledge, Mr. Speaker, the mixture of the other House to be like the composition of apothecaries, who mix something grateful to the taste to qualify their bitter drugs, which else, perhaps, would be immediately spit out.[2] So, Sir, his Highness of deplorable memory, to

---

[1] Burnet, i. 133.
[2] —— "Velutei pueris absinthia tetra medentes
Quum dare conantur, prius oras, pocula circum,
Contingunt mellis dulci flavoque liquore."

countenance as well the want of quality as honesty in the rest, has nominated some against whom there lies no other reproach but only that nomination,—but not out of any respect to their quality, or regard to their virtues, but out of regard to the *no quality*, the *no virtues* of the rest ; which truly, Mr. Speaker, if he had not done, we could easily have given a more express name to this other House than he hath been pleased to do ; for we know a house designed for beggars and malefactors is *a House of Correction*, and so termed by our law. But, Mr. Speaker, setting those few persons aside who, I hope, think the nomination a disgrace, and their ever coming to sit there a much greater, can we without indignation think of the rest? He who is first in their roll,[1] a condemned coward: one that out of fear and baseness did once what he could to betray our liberties, and now does the same for gain. The second,[2] a person of as little sense as honesty, preferred for no other reason but his no-worth—his no-conscience, —except cheating his father of all he had, was thought a virtue by him, who, by sad experience, we find hath done as much for his mother—his country. The third,[3] a Cavalier, a Presbyterian, an Independent—for the Republic—for a Protector—for everything—for nothing— but only that one thing—money. It were endless, Sir, to run through them all—to tell you of the Lordships of £17 a year land of inheritance, of the farmer Lordships, draymen Lordships, cobbler Lordships, without one foot of land but what the blood of Englishmen has purchased. These, Sir, are to be our rulers, these the Judges of our lives and fortunes. To these we are to stand bare, whilst their pageant Lordships deign to give us a conference on their breeches. The House of Lords are the King's great hereditary Council; they are the highest court of judicature : they assist in making new laws and abrogating old; from amongst them we take our great officers of state ; they are commonly our generals at land and our admirals

> "Cosi all' egro fanciul porgiamo aspersi
> Di soave licor gli orli del vaso ;
> Succhi amari ingannato intanto ei beve,
> E dall' inganno suo vita riceve."

[1] Fiennes, who had been found guilty of cowardice in **surrendering the** Great Seal, but afterwards restored and made Keeper.
[2] Lisle, an officer and Keeper of the Great Seal.
[3] Lawrence, one of the King's Judges.

at sea. In conclusion, they are both of the essence and constitution of our old government; and have besides the greatest and noblest share in the administration. Now, certainly, Sir, to judge, according to the dictates of reason, one would imagine some small faculties and endowments to be necessary for discharging such a calling; and such are not usually acquired in shops and warehouses, nor found by following the plow; and what other academies most of their Lordships have been bred in but their shops—what other arts they have been versed in but those which more required good arms and good shoulders than good heads, I think we are yet to be informed."

The recognition was carried by a majority of 177 to 113; but this attack hastened the dissolution, which terminated the Protectorate, and put an end to the danger, once so formidable, of a Cromwell dynasty.

Shaftesbury's present policy was to assist in weakening each party that successively gained an ascendency, till, by some expression of the national will, the King should be recalled. He intrigued against the officers at Wallingford House till the "Rump" was restored. He was then named a member of the "Council of State;" but, instead of taking his seat in it, he did all that he could to introduce disunion and discord among the members. Monk, calculating upon his influence, wrote to him, soliciting that none of the officers of the army in Scotland might be removed. He returned a favorable answer, and a friendly correspondence was established between them. He secretly encouraged a royalist rising in Dorsetshire, and incurred so much suspicion, that he was taken into custody, and brought before the Council of State; but they were obliged to release him for want of evidence; and the parliament, on the motion of a friend of his, resolved, "that Sir Anthony Ashley Cooper is clear from the accusation laid against him, and that there is not any just ground of jealousy or imputation upon him."

But the majority of this assembly being for the desperate experiment of a pure republic without any head,

---

[1] See Old Parliamentary History, xxi. 297. Biog. Brit.: "Cooper." Life, 199. I have given only a short specimen of Sir Anthony's tirade, which is much more lively than well founded: for, with very few exceptions, Cromwell's Peers were men of family, wealth and reputation. See Carlyle's Cromwell, iii. 389, 390.

he encouraged them to cashier Lambert and Desborough,
—which led to another expulsion of the " Rump." He
had next to agitate against " the Committee of Safety,"
consisting of officers who wished to restore " the Protectorate" under one of themselves; and he was mainly
instrumental in upsetting them, by heading the mob
which met in Lincoln's Inn Fields,—by leading them to
the Rolls House, in Chancery Lane,—and by insisting
that Lenthal should proceed to Westminster, and again
take the chair as Speaker.[1]

The first act of the restored " Rump " was to appoint
Sir Anthony one of the Commissioners for the command
of the forces ; and he was enabled, by sudden orders for
changing their officers and moving their quarters, to paralyze the power of Lambert. He next contrived to get
himself seated in the House of Commons as representative for Downton, on the plea that he had been duly
elected, and ought to have been returned for that place
in the year 1640,[2] and he thenceforth mainly guided their
proceedings with a view to the Restoration. Monk was
advancing from the North, and, notwithstanding his dissimulation, little doubt was entertained as to his ultimate
intentions. Shaftesbury wrote to him to hasten his march,
and assured him that he need apprehend no resistance.
Soon after Monk's arrival, he instigated him to make the
declaration at Guildhall for " a free parliament," which was
as much as for the King's recall. Bonfires being lighted,
at which rumps were roasted, as Shaftesbury was returning from the city with Colonel Popham, the mob surrounded the carriage, and, knowing them to be members
of the House of Commons, loudly shouted, " down with
the Rump!" Shaftesbury looked out, and, smiling, exclaimed, " What, gentlemen, not one good steak in the
whole rump?" The mob were tickled with the jest, and
some of them asserting that he was "a brave boy," they
accompanied him with acclamations to his lodgings.

Shaftesbury warmly supported the act for putting an
end to the Long Parliament, and he was appointed one
of the new Council of State who were to carry on the government till the Convention Parliament could assemble.

[1] 3 Parl. Hist. 1571.
[2] He had twice unsuccessfully renewed his petition, in September, 1645,
and in May, 1659. See Com Jour. 7th January, 1660.

To this parliament he was again returned as member for the county of Wilts; and he had completely recovered his popularity in the West, for he was now at the head of the poll. When the House met, nothing remained but to arrange the ceremonial of the King's return. Sir John Grenville having delivered his Majesty's letter, Shaftesbury was appointed one of a select committee to draw up the answer; and he was chosen one of the Commissioners of the Commons to repair to Breda with the humble invitation and supplication of the parliament, *"*that his Majesty would be pleased to return, and take the government of the kingdom into his own hands."

In this journey he met with a dangerous accident. Being overturned in his carriage on a Dutch road, he received a wound between the ribs, which ulcerated many years after, and was opened when he was Chancellor. By way of compensation, this misfortune was the cause of his subsequent introduction to the famous John Locke. For the present he seemed to recover, and accompanying the other Commissioners, he was able to throw himself at the King's feet. At this first interview they little anticipated either the extraordinary intimacy, or the extraordinary enmity, which was afterwards to prevail between them. The King received Sir Anthony very courteously, and told him "he was very sensible with what zeal and application he had labored for his restoration."[1]

CHAPTER LXXXVI.

CONTINUATION OF THE LIFE OF LORD SHAFTESBURY TILL HIS APPOINTMENT AS LORD CHANCELLOR.

SOON after the King's return, Sir Anthony Ashley Cooper, in recompense of his services, was successively made a Privy Councillor, Chancellor of the Exchequer, Lord Lieutenant of the county of Dorset, Governor of the Isle of Wight, and Baron Ashley of Wimborne St. Giles.

His conduct for the next seven years seems wholly

[1] Life, 203.

inexplicable; for he remained quite regular, and seemingly contented. He had a little excitement by sitting as a judge on the trial of the regicides, and joining in the sentence on some of his old associates. Not being a member of the Long Parliament, he had not joined in this particular treason, but he had often actually "levied war" against Charles I., and he had on several occasions acted under the parliament as zealously as Sir Harry Vane, for the purpose of keeping out Charles II., so that his life had been forfeited to the law by his co-operation with the prisoners. Still he thought it right and decent that he should countenance the proceedings against them.

These trials being over, he seemed to sink down into a Treasury drudge. The office of Chancellor of the Exchequer, which he held, though a Peer, was not then of much importance, and chiefly imposed the duty of attending to accounts. He was not a member of the Committee of the Council to whom, under Clarendon, the conduct of foreign affairs and the management of the business in parliament were intrusted. Strange to say, it was some years before he began seriously to try to undermine Clarendon. The only solution is, that his uncle, Southampton, the Lord Treasurer, who had become very infirm, left to him almost the sole direction of the Exchequer, with all its patronage, and, being strongly attached to Clarendon, probably labored to induce him to abstain from any turbulent measures. Shaftesbury, along with Southampton, gave some opposition to the "Corporation Act" and the "Act of Uniformity;" and when Dunkirk had been sold, he expressed some disapprobation of that transaction. He strongly supported the "Bill for Indulgence," which was brought in to please the King, and was rejected by the hostility of Clarendon. But during these years he did not take by any means a prominent part in parliament, and he devoted himself much to the duties of his office. He considered himself bound regularly to attend the King at Whitehall, to pay court to Lady Castlemaine, and to cultivate with unwearied assiduity his reputation for licentiousness—which he did so successfully as even to rival that of his Master, .

But he became tired of routine business and the life of a mere *roué;* and seeing with satisfaction the King's growing dislike to Clarendon, he took every opportunity

of widening the breach between them. By the death of
Lord Southampton, in May, 1667, all restraint was removed,
and he entered into a strict alliance with Arlington and
Clifford for Clarendon's overthrow. The Treasury was
put into commission against Clarendon's strong opinion,
and Shaftesbury contrived to get himself named the first
efficient Commissioner, still retaining his office of Chancellor of the Exchequer. His influence from henceforth
grew daily; he managed to make all the odium of the
Dutch war fall upon the Chancellor, who had from the beginning disapproved of it; he aggravated the discontent
of Cavaliers, Dissenters, and Roman Catholics, pointing out the Chancellor as the author of all their grievances; and he incited Lady Castlemaine to seek revenge
upon the man who, to be sure, had earnestly tried to
prevail upon the Queen to receive her as a lady of the
bedchamber, but who had given her mortal offense by
forbidding his wife to visit her. After a hard struggle
they spirited up the King to take the Great Seal from
Clarendon, and as a temporary arrangement, to give it
to Sir Orlando Bridgeman. Shaftesbury probably had
thought of it for himself ever since it was promised to
him by Cromwell; but neither the Court nor the public
were yet at all prepared to see such a successor of Sir
Thomas More and Lord Ellesmere, and his pretensions
could not at pressnt be put forward. If either Sir Jeffrey
Palmer or Sir Heneage Finch, who with reputation filled
the offices of Attorney and Solicitor General, had been
appointed, there might have been some difficulty in removing them; but Bridgeman, from his age, could not
hold the Seal many years; and from his want of political
importance might be set aside at pleasure.

The expectant Chancellor zealously co-operated with
those whose object it was,—not to bring Clarendon to the
scaffold, but to compel him to fly the country,—so that
neither by the interest of the Duke of York, nor a relenting of the King he might ever recover power. When
the impeachment for high treason came up from the Commons, with a requisition that the accused should be immediately imprisoned, Shaftesbury strenuously resisted
the application, on the ground that the Commons had
specified no particular act of treason; but he supported
the bill by which Clarendon was banished for life; and

was rendered liable to instant execution if he ever again set foot on English ground.¹

The first act of the new administration (constituting an exception to the whole foreign policy of this reign) was wise and virtuous —"the Triple Alliance," by which the free state of Holland was saved from the rapacity of a tyrant openly aspiring to the dominion of Europe. Sir William Temple has all the merit of this deviation into rectitude; and the surprise is, that those about the King permitted him, even for a time, to desert his cherished connection with France, which brought them plenteously avowed pensions and secret bribes. But the wax which sealed the treaty of Aix-la-Chapelle was hardly cold before they began to plot against it. Shaftesbury's apologists have contended that he was always an enemy to the French Alliance; but this is contrary to all contemporary testimony, as well as to all probability. I believe he did not take money from Louis, like his colleagues, for he was always above pecuniary corruption; but there can not be a doubt that, with a view to gratify the King, and to consolidate his own power, he acceded to the conspiracy for crushing the liberties of Holland, and for establishing, with French assistance, Popery and arbitrary government in England.

> "To compass this the triple bond he broke,
> The pillars of the public safety shook,
> And fitted England for a foreign yoke."

It has been suggested that, being now as keen a Protestant as when he denounced the Popish plot, it was on the enlightened principles of toleration that he supported "the Declaration of Indulgence," to which he induced the Lord Keeper Bridgeman to put the Great Seal. Unluckily, at this time he knew that Charles had been reconciled to Rome, and that the Declaration was a measure preparatory to the King's avowal of his conversion. He was too penetrating a genius not to discover that religious toleration was highly expedient; but for the sake of his ambition, he would have been ready to prosecute Catholics or Protestants with indiscriminate zeal.

Although Clifford certainly was the first to propose the shutting up of the Exchequer to the Council, there is a great reason to think that Shaftesbury, who had the

¹ 4 Parl. Hist. 373.

sole management of the finances as Chancellor of the Exchequer and Lord Commissioner of the Treasury, originated the nefarious scheme; and, at all events he supported and defended it.

By this conduct he rose into unbounded favor with the King, who, though he afterwards pronounced him "the weakest and wickedest man of the age," now professed the highest admiration not only of his agreeable manners, but of the boldness, energy, and originality of his genius as a statesman. In anticipation of greater advancement, as a reward for his services in closing the Exchequer, he was created Earl of Shaftesbury. It is said that he was offered the Treasurer's staff, but that, on account of the national insolvency, for which he knew no real cure, he declined it.

The CABAL was now in the zenith of its power. There were considerable jealousies among the members of the administration; but the energy of Shaftesbury prevailed, and he was the mainspring of all its operations. His reputation was not at all impaired by the general distress which followed the shutting up of the Exchequer—when he came forward with his remedy of stopping, by injunctions, all the suits against the bankers—whereby commercial credit was to be restored.

I have stated, in the Life of Lord Keeper Bridgeman, the refusal of that Judge to grant these injunctions, and his consequent dismissal.[1]

The ceremony of delivering the Great Seal to Shaftesbury, with the title of Lord Chancellor, took place next morning at Whitehall, I presume, in the apartments of Lady Castlemaine.[2] "And the said Earle having received the said Great Seale as Lord Chancellor, he presently attended his Majesty at his chappell in Whitehall in that capacity, bearing the said Seale before his Majesty."[3]

The event was thus announced to the public in the London Gazette:—

"Whitehall, Nov. 17, 1672.

"His Majesty, reflecting upon the age and infirmities of Sir Orlando Bridgeman, Lord Keeper of the Great Seal of

[1] Ante, p. 100.
[2] While she retained her ascendency, the ministers met the King in her apartments every Sunday morning, and attended him from thence to the chapel—even when they were to receive the communion.
[3] Crown Off. Min. 1672.

England, hath thought fit to admit of his resignation thereof, with all demonstration on his Majesty's part of his kindess and esteem of the said Lord Keeper's merit towards him; and his Majesty, willing to gratify the uninterrupted good services of the Earl of Shaftesbury, Chancellor of the Exchequer, and one of the Lords Commissioners of the Treasury, was pleased this day to give unto him the keeping of the said Great Seal, with the title of Lord Chancellor of England."

CHAPTER LXXXVII.

CONTINUATION OF THE LIFE OF LORD SHAFTESBURY TILL HIS DISMISSAL FROM THE OFFICE OF LORD CHANCELLOR.

I CAN not find how the new appointment was at first received by the profession of the law or by the public; but it seems entirely to have turned the head of the Lord Chancellor himself, and, notwithstanding his excellent good sense, and his discernment of the impression to be made by his conduct, he now played fantastic tricks which could be expected only from a fool and a coxcomb. "After he was possessed of the Great Seal, he was in appearance the gloriousest man alive; and no man's discourse in his place ever flew so high as he did, not only against the House of Commons where, perhaps, he expected a party to sustain him, but against the tribe of the Court of Chancery officers and counsel, and their methods of ordering the business of the Court. As for the Commons, he did not understand by what reason men should sit and vote themselves privileges. And for the Chancery, he would teach the bar that a man of sense was above all their forms. So with all the gayety *de cœur* imaginable and a world of pleasant wit in his conversation (as he had indeed a very great share, and showed it upon all occasions), he composed himself to perform the duties of his office." [1]

Such confidence had he in his judicial powers derived from " the light of nature," that, unlike Lord Keeper

[1] Examen, 46.

Williams and some of his sneaking predecessors, who, being "minus sufficientes in lege," had painful misgivings as to their ability to acquit themselves decently, and therefore put off as long as possible the time of taking their seat in the Court of Chancery, he was impatient to show that he was superior as a Judge to all who had ever before sat in the marble chair. "The next day, being the xviii[th] day of November, his Lo[p] went to the Chancery Co[rt] in Westm[r] Hall, and there standing in his place, tooke the oathes as Lord Chancellor, the booke being held to him by the Master of the Rolls, the Dukes of Lauderdale and Ormond, the Earle of St. Alban's, the Earle of Arlington, and several other persons of honor accompanyinge his Lo[p] to and in the Co[rt] untill his Lo[p] was sworne, all the said persons of honor, with the Judges and Chancery officers, attending his Lo[p] from his house in the Strand, to the Chancery Co[rt], in Westm[r] Hall."[1]

There is no further account of this installation. Having been got up so suddenly, it could not have been very splendid. But to compensate for the disappointment, Shaftesbury determined to amuse the metropolis with a sight that had not been seen for half a century. Coaches were introduced into England in the latter end of the reign of Elizabeth, and had for many years become so common that the ancient custom of the Chancellors and the Judges riding on horseback to Westminster Hall to open the term had been entirely laid aside, and the Chancellor had headed the procession in a grand gilt state carriage, almost as large as a house,—being followed by the Judges, the King's Sergeants, the King's Counsel, &c. in modern equipages. They still continued to "ride the circuit" on sober pads, but the *ménage* for learning to sit on the great horse, which used to be frequented by the gentlemen of the Inns of Court, was very much neglected, and the practice of riding managed horses in the streets of London had fallen into entire disuse. Shaftesbury, who had been bred a country squire, and had been colonel of a regiment of cavalry, piqued himself much upon his horsemanship, and to gratify his morbid appetite to be talked of, and out of malice to some of the old Judges, who he heard had been sneering at his decisions, he issued an order that on the first day of Hilary term, 1673, there

[1] Crown Off. Min. 1672.

should be a judicial cavalcade according to ancient form, from Exeter House, in the Strand, the place of his residence, to Westminster Hall. On that day he gave a sumptuous breakfast not only to noblemen, judges, and other dignitaries, but to all the barristers, all the students of the Inns of Court, and the sixty clerks, with all the other officers of the Court of Chancery. He then mounted his richly caparisoned charger,—preceded by those who bore the insignia of his authority,—his master of the horse, page, groom, and six footmen walking along by his stirrup.

This procession marched by the Strand through the quadrangle at Whitehall to King Street, then the only entrance to Palace Yard,—and so to Westminster Hall. It is described by several contemporary writers,[1] but Roger North's account of it is the most graphic.

"His Lordship had an early fancy, or rather, freak, the first day of the term (when all the officers of the law, King's Counsel, and Judges, used to wait upon the Great Seal to Westminster Hall), to make this procession on horseback, as in old time the way was, when coaches were not so rife. And accordingly the Judges, &c., were spoken to get horses, as they and all the rest did, by borrowing and hiring, and so equipped themselves with black footcloaths in the best manner they could: and divers of the nobility, as usual, in compliment and honor to a new Lord Chancellor, attended also in their equipments. Upon notice in town of this cavalcade, all the show company took their places at windows and balconies, with the foot guard in the streets to partake of the fine sight, and, being once well settled for the march, it moved, as the design was, statelily along. But when they came to straights and interruptions, for want of gravity in the beasts and too much in the riders, there happened some curveting, which made no little disorder. Judge Twisden, in his great affright and the consternation of his grave brethren, was laid along in the dirt;[2] but all at length arrived safe, without loss of life or limb in the service. This ac-

[1] See Rawleigh Redivivus, 75.
[2] According to tradition this disgrazia happened from meeting a line of brewer's drays at Charing Cross. When Twisden recovered himself, he declared *in furore*, "that no Lord Chancellor should ever make him mount on horseback again.

cident was enough to divert the like frolic for the future, and the very next term after, they fell to their coaches as before. Usages that are most fitting at one time appear ridiculous at another. As here the sitting of grave men used only to coaches, upon the *ménage* on horseback, only for the vanity of show, to make men wonder and children sport, with hazard to most, mischief to some, and terror to all, was very impertinent, and must end, as it did, in ridicule."

We now come to consider how Shaftesbury comported himself in the Court of Chancery. The general opinion of subsequent times has been, that, with all his faults as a statesman, he proved a consummate Judge.[1] I believe that this opinion is wholly erroneous and that it is entirely to be ascribed to the celebrated lines in praise of his judicial character in "ABSOLOM AND ACHITOPHEL."

> "Yet fame deserv'd no enemy can grudge,
> The statesman we abhor, but praise the judge;
> In Israel's courts ne'er sat an Abethdin
> With more discerning eyes or hands more clean.
> Unbrib'd, unsought, the wretched to redress,
> Swift of dispatch, and easy of access.
> Oh! had he been content to serve the Crown,
> With virtues only proper to the gown!"

Had Dryden been sincere and honest in praising Shaftesbury, his testimony ought not to have much weight, for the great poet probably never was in the Court of Chancery in his life, and though the first of English critics in polite literature, he could not have formed a very correct opinion as to the propriety of an order or decree in Equity. But the panegyric was purchased, and was a mere poetical picture drawn from the imagination of the *beau idéal* of a good Chancellor. It did not appear in the first edition of the poem, which, in describing the character of Achitophel, contained unmixed invective, and represented him as unredeemed from his vices by any semblance of virtue. Shaftesbury, nevertheless, while the town was ringing with the abuse of him, and he was universally pointed to as "the false Achitophel,"—being a governor of the Charter House, sent to Dryden a nomi-

---

[1] "It is remarkable that this man, whose principles and conduct were in all other respects so exceptionable, proved an excellent Chancellor."—*Hume*. And all the historians of the eighteenth century, reading Dryden or copying each other, write to the same effect.

nation to that establishment for his son,—which was highly valuable to him, and was joyfully accepted. A second edition was called for. The bard could not soften the political character of his hero without utterly destroying the poem, and breaking with the Court, who had paid him well for it; but in the fulfillment of an implied obligation, he set his wits to work to consider what a Chancellor should be in administering justice, and so produced the lines which have induced posterity to believe that such a Chancellor was Shaftesbury. King Charles is said to have been very indignant when he saw the second edition, and to have declared that the portrait of Achitophel was so disfigured that he no longer recognized the original.[1]

Shaftesbury never took bribes. Luckily he had only one political case before him; and he would not listen to private solicitation in favor of litigants. But except being free from gross corruption, he was the worst Judge that had ever sat in the Court. This was inevitable, for he might as well have tried to sustain a principal part in an opera, without having learned the first rudiments of music.

There was no refusal to practice before him on account of his ignorance of law, as in the case of Lord Chancellor Hatton and Lord Keeper Williams. The bar took a more effectual mode of exposing and subduing him. Had he

[1] Malone, in his "Life of Dryden," has attempted to refute this story, but in my humble opinion he has utterly failed. He has shown satisfactorily that it could only be applied to the poet's third son, the two elder being educated at Westminster School, and he has given a copy of the admission of this youth in the following words:—

"Feb. 6th, 1682-3. Erasmus Henry Dryden admitted for his Majesty (in the room of Orlando Bagnall) aged 14 years 2nd of May next."

He reasons that as the admissions did not take place in the end of Nov. 1681, between the two editions of the poem, there could be no connection between the poetry and the presentation. But on inquiry I find that at the Charter House the admission sometimes does not take place till years after the nomination. The expression here "for his Majesty," may be inaccurate, and if accurate may be explained by an exchange of one nomination for another (not an unusual practice) to suit the ages of the boys,—and it is nothing when we consider that the anecdote rests on the authority of a most respectable lawyer, STRINGER, the intimate friend and protégé of Shaftesbury, who was Secretary of Presentations to him while he was Chancellor, and probably would be the person by whom the act would be done;—that it is confirmed by Martyn, who wrote the life of the first Lord Shaftesbury under the superintendence of his grandson;—and that it is repeated in the eulogistic Life of Lord Shaftesbury in the "Biographia Britannica," written by Dr. Kippis, who is said to have received £500 from the family for the pains he bestowed upon it. It has been said that Dryden could not have composed

been ruled by his assessors,[1] he might have avoided any palpable absurdities; but despising all learning that he did not know, he thought he was fitter to decide than any of them, and he scorned their advice. To show his contempt for all who had gone before him, as well as his contemporaries, he would not be habited like his predecessors, "for he sat upon the bench in an ash-colored gown silver-laced, and full-ribboned pantaloons displayed, without any black at all in his garb unless it were his hat."[2] Roger North's account of the result of all his boasts may be relied upon. "He slighted the bar, declared their reign at an end. He would make all his own orders his own way, and in his discourse trampled on all the forms of the Court. And to be as good as his word, at his first motion-day, although the counsel (as always out of respect to a new judge) were easy and inclined of themselves to yield to what was fit to be ordered, and not to perplex him with contention upon forms; yet he would not accept of their civility, but cut and slashed after his own fancy; and nothing would down with him that any of them suggested, though all were agreed upon the matter. They soon found his humor, and let him have his caprice; and after, upon notice, moved him to discharge his orders; and thereupon, having the advantage upon the opening to be heard at large, they showed him his face, and that what he did was against common justice and sense. And this speculum of his own ignorance and presumption coming to be said before him every motion-day, did so intricate and embarrass his understanding, that, in a short time, like any haggered hawk that is not let sleep, he was entirely reclaimed. And from a trade of perpetually making and unmaking his own orders, he fell to be the tamest Judge, and, as to all forms and modes of proceeding, the most resigned to the disposition of the bar, that ever sat on the bench."[3] "He swaggered and vapored what asses he would make

" the MEDAL," after receiving such a favor from Shaftesbury,—but this is explained by the royal solicitation and the 100 broad pieces.—*See post.*
[1] By a reference to the minutes in the Registrar's Office, it appears that on the 18th Nov. 1672, the Master of the Rolls and Mr. Baron Windham sat with him, and that he had the Master of the Rolls, or a common law Judge, and Masters in Chancery by him, every day he sat, till the end of the term.
[2] Examen, 60. He is said to have been "more like a rakish young nobleman at the University than a Lord High Chancellor."   [3] Examen, 57.

of all the counsel at the bar, but like the month of March, as they say, '*In like a lion, and out like a lamb.*'"[1]

There are a few of his decisions to be found in the books,[2] but none of these are of the slightest importance, except "the Bankers' case," for which he assumed the Great Seal. The application for the injunctions was immediately renewed before him. Having told the King, "that it was only a morose scrupulosity and humor in his old Keeper that made him averse to passing them," he could not flatly refuse them, although, "it was said to be no new device to shove men out of their places by contriving incompartable hardships to be put upon them, and after bespeaking the succession by officious undertaking to do all that was required, to break the condition of the advancement."[3] He was a good deal perplexed; for on the renewed argument it was made to appear more clearly than ever that the illegal act of shutting up the Exchequer could not be a ground for preventing actions against the bankers to recover acknowledged debts long since payable. After a little blustering at the unreasonableness of the creditors, he resorted to the expedient of granting injunctions unless cause should be shown at a distant day, and,

---

[1] Life of Guilford, ii. 74. The only contradictory authority, if such it may be called, is "Rawleigh Redivivus," which being an unmixed and unqualified eulogy of the whole life of Shaftesbury, contains lines extolling not only the purity of his morals, but his judicial excellence :—

———— "His choice sagacity
Straight solv'd the knot that subtle lawyers tyed,
And through all fogs discern'd the oppressed side ;
Banish'd delays, and so this noble peer
Became a star of honor in our sphere."—Part i. 88.

It has been supposed that he was the author of a new code for regulating the practice of the Court of Chancery; and there is extant a paper entitled "A collection of the Orders heretofore used in Chancery, with such alterations and additions thereunto as the Right Honorable ANTHONY, EARLE of SHAFTESBURY, Lord High Chancellor of England, by and with the advice and assistance of the Honorable SIR HARBOTTLE GRIMSTONE, Baronet, Master of the Rolls, hath thought fit at present to ordaine and publish: For reforming of severall abuses in the said Court, preventing of multiplicity of suites and unnecessary charge to the suitors, and for their more expeditious and certaine course for reliefe." This collection is exceedingly well digested, and might have been very useful; but it can confer no credit on Shaftesbury, for he left his office without ever having signed it, and the probability is, that he never even read it. It had been drawn up for his consideration, but he had thrown it aside. The regulations it contains against the idleness and malpractices of counsel are particularly curious.—*See Saunders's Orders*, i. 344, n., ii. 1056, 1075. Martyn, by Cooke, ii. 81.

[2] See Reports in Chancery 24 & 25 Car. II.   [3] Examen, 39.

by some contrivance, the day of hearing was postponed from time to time till he went out of office.

In swearing in Mr. Sergeant Thurland a Baron of the Exchequer, the Chancellor gave him a lecture on his duties after ancient custom, saying, amongst other things,—" Let not the King's prerogative and the law be two things with you, for the King's prerogative is law and the principal part of it ; and therefore, in maintaining that, you maintain the law. So manage the King's justice and revenue as the King may have most profit and the subject least vexation. Give me leave also to remind you of your oath that *the King's needs ye shall speed before all other*, that is, the business of the revenue of the Crown you are to dispatch before all other, and not turn your Court into a Court of Common Pleas, and let that justle out what you were constituted for. Let me conclude with what concerns all my Lords the Judges, as well as you,—let me recommend to you the port and way of living suitable to the dignity of your place and what the King allows you."

He wished the Treasury to have remained in Commission, and was rather annoyed by Clifford receiving the white staff, and being placed above him in the ministry. When the new Lord Treasurer was sworn in before him, he made a speech in which, after applying to the King the character of the Emperor Titus—" *Deliciæ humani generis*," he said, " no subtle insinuations of any near him, nor the aspiring interest of a favorite, shall ever prevail against those that serve him well, nor can his servants fear to be sacrificed to a more swelling popular greatness."

Parliament had not met for nearly two years, being prorogued from time to time that the CABAL might more quietly carry on their operations,—but the state of the Exchequer at length rendered a session indispensable. To strengthen his party in the House of Commons, Shaftesbury resorted to the bold measure of issuing writs by his own authority for the election of new members to fill up all the vacancies which had occurred. These writs were delivered to his creatures who were to be candidates, and who, being able to fix the time of election, generally succeeded. He likewise maintained that, the writs issuing under the Great Seal, it was for the Chancellor to decide the validity of the elections, in spite of the resolutions of the House of Commons usurping a jurisdiction on this subject.

On the 4th of February, 1673, the session began, and the King having addressed the two Houses, was followed by Shaftesbury in a speech which for impudence and effrontery far exceeds any to be found in our parliamentary records. He begins in a protecting, condescending, patronizing style, by praising his royal Master:—" My Lords, and you, the knights, citizens, and burgesses of the House of Commons, the King hath spoken so fully, so excellently well, and so like himself, that you are not to expect much from me." He justifies the two years' adjournment on the ground that the King wished to give the members ease and vacancy for their own private concerns. He boldly defends the breach of the Triple Alliance, and the league with the French King against the Dutch:—" Both Kings knowing their interest resolved to join against them who were the common enemies to all monarchies, and I may say especially to ours, their only competitor for trade and power at sea, and who only can stand in their way to an universal empire as great as Rome. But you judged aright. *Delenda est Carthago*, and therefore the King may well say to you, ' *it is your war.*' " The shutting up of the Exchequer he treats without any apparent consciousness of the measure being liable to the slightest blame, saying, that " the King had made use of his own revenue, which had enabled him to effectually carry on the war, and to check exorbitant interest obtained by the bankers." " But," he mildly adds, " though he hath put a stop to the trade and gain of the bankers, yet he would be unwilling to ruin them, and oppress so many families as are concerned in those debts." This he lays as a ground for a large supply which he requires to be speedily granted before any inquiry into the manner in which the public difficulties had arisen. He then comes to " the Declaration of Indulgence," and if he was not a party to the original treaty with Louis, originated by Clifford for the establishment of the Roman Catholic religion in England, being now well acquainted with its contents, he ascribes the suspension of the penal laws to the King's regard for toleration. " He loves not blood nor rigorous severities, but where mild or gentle ways may be used by a wise prince, he is certain to choose them. The Church of England and all good Protestants have reason to rejoice in such a Head and such a Defender. His Majesty doth declare his care and concerns for the Church, and will maintain her in all her rights and privileges equal, if not beyond, any of his predecessors." Having urgently pressed for a supply, we have this modest peroration, with a sneer at " *The Triple Alliance.*" " Let me conclude, nay, let us all conclude, with blessing God and the King. Let us bless God that he hath given us such a King. Let us bless the King for taking away all our fears, and leaving no room for jealousies. Let us bless God and the King that our religion is safe; that the Church of England is the care of our Prince; that Parliaments are safe; that our properties and liberties are safe. What more hath a good Englishman to ask but that this King may long reign, and that this 'TRIPLE ALLIANCE' of King, parliament, and people may never be dissolved."[1]

Shaftesbury, much ashamed of this speech when he had become a patriot, pretended that it had been "settled in the Council," and that it expressed the King's sentiments only, not his own. But it is so racy and characteristic that no man in England could have composed it except Shaftesbury himself; and he could not palliate his guilt by the unconstitutional doctrine that, instead of the speech of the King being liable to censure as the speech of the Minister, the speech of the Minister is sacred from censure as the speech of the King. The truth is, that, at this moment, he thought of nothing but how he might outstrip all others in complying with the royal inclination; and he succeeded so well, that Charles declared, " My Chancellor knows more law than all my Judges, and more divinity than all my Bishops."

Even in Shaftesbury, hardly ever was there such a sudden change of conduct as he now exhibited. Parliament had not sat a week, when, perceiving the disposition which it manifested, he entirely altered his plan of operations, and began to intrigue with the country party against his colleagues of the CABAL. The Commons immediately attacked his writs, issued in vacation, of his own authority, and declared the elections under them void. He wished to resist, but the King, backed by Clifford and the Duke of York, would not enter into the controversy,

[1] 4 Parl. Hist. 503.

and he was obliged to succumb.¹ He had his revenge by secretly fomenting the proceedings of the House of Commons against "the Declaration of Indulgence." Upon the resolution passing, "that penal statutes, in matters ecclesiastical, can not be suspended but by act of parliament,"—while Clifford, Buckingham, and Lauderdale advised defiance, Shaftesbury said, "his individual opinion continued unshaken in favor of the prerogative, but he would not venture to place it in the balance against the authority of so august a body as the House of Commons.". While he was speaking, the Duke of York, enraged at him, whispered to the King, who was standing at the fire, " What a rogue you have for a Lord Chancellor !" The King answered, "Cods-fish, what a fool have you of a Lord Treasurer!"² Clifford was outwitted, and Charles finding himself thus deserted by the Keeper of his conscience, sent for the Declaration, canceled it at the Council Board, and forwarded a promise to the Lords and Commons that " what had been done with respect to the suspension of the penal laws should never be drawn into consequence." Bonfires illuminated the streets of the metropolis.

Shaftesbury's present plan was to take advantage of the popular feeling that he might rid himself of the Romanizing ministers, and get all power into his own hands as the head of the Protestant party. He therefore warmly encouraged the Test Act, and contrived the introduction into it of the famous declaration against " Transubstantiation," which no Catholic could possibly make.³ The King's scruples were overcome by the observation, that, in the present temper of the House of Commons, he could on no other terms hope for a supply, and that his brother James would not be so insensate as to sacrifice the possession of office to the profession of his religion.

To please the Dissenters, Shaftesbury pretended to support the bill for their relief, on the promise of which they had agreed to the Test Act ; but the latter act, which he thought was to secure his supremacy in the Cabinet, having passed, he grew indifferent about the other, and suffered it to be lost by a parliamentary manœuvre of the high Churchmen.

As soon as parliament had adjourned, the Duke of

¹ 4 Parl. Hist. 507.   ² Echard.   ³ Stat. 25 Car. 2, c. 2.

York, now openly professing himself a Roman Catholic, resigned all his employments, and Clifford, surrendering the Treasurer's staff, it was given to Sir Thomas Osborne, afterwards Earl of Danby. Shaftesbury was far from enjoying the undivided power he had expected, and the King was already taught to look upon him with distrust and dislike. Notwithstanding this apparent coldness, "it was not fit to lay him aside till it should appear what service he could do them in another session of parliament,"[1] and knowing his extraordinary energy, they were obliged to deliberate whether he would be more formidable to them in office or in opposition.

During the recess, which lasted above six months, never were the councils of any country in a more distracted state. A sanguine hope was entertained that Shaftesbury would be ruined by the question of Martial Law. Thus wrote Sir W. Coventry to a friend:—"I believe that Lord Chancellor will now have a great plunge upon Martial Law. His old supports at Court, I apprehend, have left, or will leave him upon this point; and on the other side, if he pass it, adieu to the popularity he hath seemed to pretend to of late: and when it is passed, it will make some difficulties even in the army, for if ever Parliament sit again, whoever shall have sat at condemning any man for life or limb, will, I believe, be questioned, this point and matter of money being the only guard the people have against an army they so much dread." But the great measure in agitation was the Duke of York's marriage with the Princess of Modena—against which Shaftesbury, holding the Great Seal, intrigued with the malcontents, joining in the popular cry, "that it was dangerous to the established religion." The two Houses being adjourned to the 20th of October, the Lord Chancellor had received orders to see that they should adjourn to a subsequent day without then transacting any business; but he thought fit to delay the adjournment till the Commons had, with great zeal and unanimity, agreed upon an address to the Crown against the Modenese match. The King was much exasperated, but had not yet the courage to dismiss him; and at the regular opening of the session, on the 29th of October, after the King's speech, he, as

---

[1] Burnet.

Chancellor, again addressed the Lords and Commons; but as even *he* could hardly, on such an occasion, openly attack the government, and as he would say nothing in its praise, he was brief and tame, reminding his hearers of his former liveliness only by one sally: "There is not so lawful or commendable a jealousy in the world as an Englishman's of the growing greatness of any prince at sea. If you permit the sea, our British wife, to be ravished, an eternal mark of infamy will stick upon us." Anticipating that he should soon be in opposition, and in want of the support of the City, he put in a good word for the goldsmiths or bankers, saying, "You all know how many widows, orphans, and particular persons the public calamity hath overtaken, and how hard it is that so disproportionate a burden should fall upon them even to their utter ruin."¹

Nothing was done in the Lords; but the Chancellor's associates were very active in the Commons, and during a supper at the Duchess of Portsmouth's, when the King was a good deal excited by wine, it was resolved that, to put an end to their machinations, parliament should instantly be dissolved. On cooler reflection, next morning, Charles mitigated his resolution to a prorogation, and, sending for Shaftesbury, asked him if he had brought his parliamentary robes? This led to an explanation, in which Shaftesbury, according to his own account, warned the King against the measures into which "the Popish faction" were hurrying him. Retiring from the closet, he sent a servant for his robes, and on his way to Westminster met a friend to whom he related this conversation.²

The King was in the House of Lords almost as soon as the Chancellor, and the Black Rod was sent to summon the Commons. An effort was made to keep him out till certain factious resolutions might be carried; but before the motion could be seconded, "that the Duke of Lauderdale was a grievance," he had thrice knocked, and the door was thrown open to him. When the Commons came to the bar of the House of Lords, the King ordered the Lord Chancellor to prorogue the two Houses in his name till the 7th of January. Shaftesbury obeyed, and was virtually out of office.

It was now thought that he could not be more danger-

---
¹ 4 Parl. Hist. 586. ² Stringer.

ous in any position than in his present, and the Duke of York extracted a royal promise that he should be immediately dismissed. The morning of Sunday, the 9th of November, before chapel, at Whitehall, was fixed for the transfer of the Great Seal to Sir Heneage Finch, the Attorney General, who had been summoned then and there to receive it. We have a very amusing account of Shaftesbury's last appearance as Chancellor. As soon as he arrived at Court, he retired with the King into the closet, while the prevailing party waited in triumph to see him return without the purse. The first salutation being over, he said, "*Sir, I know you intend to give the Seals to the Attorney General, but I am sure your Majesty never designed to dismiss me with contempt.*" The King, always good humored, replied, "*Cods-fish, my Lord, I will not do it with any circumstance as may look like an affront.*" "*Then, Sir,*" said the Earl, "*I desire your Majesty will permit me to carry the Seals before you to chapel, and send for them afterwards to my own house.*" To this his Majesty readily assenting, Shaftesbury entertained him with news and diverting stories till the very minute he was to go to the chapel, purposely to amuse the courtiers and his successor, who, he knew, were upon the rack for fear he should change his mind. The King, and the Chancellor still holding the purse, came out of the closet talking together and smiling, and marched together to chapel, without an opportunity being given for the King to say a word to any of the by-standers. They were all in great consternation; and some ran immediately to tell the Duke of York all their measures were broken, and others declared themselves to be inconsolable. The Attorney General nearly fainted away.[1]

At the conclusion of the service Shaftesbury carried the Great Seal home with him to Exeter House, and in the afternoon it was fetched from him by Mr. Secretary Coventry, who said, "I desired to be excused from this office; but, being your relation and friend, they put it as an affront upon me." Shaftesbury gave up the Seal with an air of great cheerfulness, exclaiming—" It is only laying down my gown, and putting on my sword!"[2] This emblem of hostility he actually ordered to be brought to him by his servant, and he immediately buckled it on.

[1] Echard.   [2] Crown Off. Min. 1673.

The same evening Sir HENEAGE FINCH'S fears were all dissipated by his receiving the Great Seal from the King, with the title of Lord Keeper.

CHAPTER LXXXVIII.

CONTINUATION OF THE LIFE OF LORD SHAFTESBURY TILL THE BREAKING OUT OF THE POPISH PLOT.

WHILE the ceremony of delivering the Great Seal to Sir Heneage Finch, as Lord Keeper, was going on in the palace at Whitehall, Exeter House was crowded with the leading men of the country party, and Shaftesbury was by acclamation installed as their chief. He found the name of "patriot" all-atoning, —and the disgraced minister who had been the adviser of the most arbitrary measures, proclaiming himself the adversary of the Court, was hailed as the champion of the liberties of the people.

Next morning, accompanied by some of the young nobility, he went to the Royal Exchange, where all the great merchants and bankers then daily congregated,— entered into familiar conversation with them,—and feelingly deplored to them the depression of trade, and the miseries of the nation, arising from profligate measures, which he had in vain done his utmost to resist, till at last he had been dismissed for his integrity and boldness. They gathered round him with enthusiasm as a persecuted philanthropist, and vowed to live and die in his cause. But it was religion that gave him the prodigious power which from this time he wielded. He was regarded as the saviour of the nation from Popery, and, though among his private friends it was doubtful whether or not he believed in revelation, theologians were found to proclaim him from the pulpit as the saviour of the true faith, and to foretell that his fame, like that of the woman mentioned in the Gospel, should live throughout all future generations.[1]

During the short session of parliament, in the spring of 1674, he carried addresses for a public fast "to implore the protection of the Almighty for the preservation of

[1] Parker, 206, 271. Macph. Pap. i. 69. Life of James, i. 488

church and state against the undermining practices of Popish recusants;"—" for the removal from office of all counselors Popishly affected, or otherwise obnoxious or dangerous;" and specifically " for the dismissal of the Dukes of Lauderdale and Buckingham." He next attempted the impeachment of Arlington, but here he was baffled; and he likewise failed in the attempts which he made to exclude the Duke of York from sitting in the House of Lords, as his Royal Higness submitted to abjure the temporal power of the Pope, and a bill for a more stringent test to be taken by all the ministers of both Houses was lost.[1] The parliamentary reports of this period are so defective, that there are but scanty remains of his speeches in the House of Lords during the subsequent part of his career.

In the following session his party in the Lords was strengthened by the Duke of Buckingham, who, having quarreled with Charles, now joined in raising the cry of " No Popery." But Danby imitated the arts of his opponents, and greatly appeased the Protestants by marrying the Princess Mary, in spite of her father's remonstrances, to the Prince of Orange, and issuing a proclamation against Popish recusants. Though these measures were denounced as *artifices* of the " Popish party," the impeachment which had been moved against the minister was dropped.

The Court, to pursue its success, introduced a bill into the Lords, which was either to expel Shaftesbury from the House of Lords, or to degrade him. This was entitled " An Act to prevent the Dangers which may arise from Persons disaffected to the Government," and required, from all persons in office, and all members of parliament, a declaration in favor of passive obedience, with an oath " never to endeavor the alteration of the government in church or state." It had very nearly become the law of the land, and utterly extinguished our free constitution. Its defeat we owe entirely to Shaftesbury's unexampled energy and boundless resources. Unfortunately, we can by no means laud the purity of his motives, but we are exceedingly beholden to his exertions; and this much I think I may fairly say for him, that although he would not scruple for his private ends to abet the most arbi-

[1] 4 Parl. Hist. 611–666.

trary principles and the most profligate measures, yet he seems to have acted more heartily and joyously in a good cause when his ambition called upon him to support it.

On this occasion, heading a small party in the Lords, and with a decided majority against him in the Commons,—by his skillful management he defeated the Court and saved the country. Not until after five days' debate would he suffer the bill to be read a second time, and, in a protest circulated throughout the nation, he asserted that "it struck at that freedom of debating and voting which is necessary for those who have the power to alter and make laws, and that the bill obliged every man to abjure all endeavors to improve the government of the church, without regard to anything that Christian compassion or the necessity of affairs might at any time require." The Lords resolved, "that the reasons given in the said protest did reflect upon the honor of the House, and were of dangerous consequence;" but this only produced a more violent protest from Shaftesbury against the resolution.

He kept the bill twelve days in the committee,—the House sitting from an early hour in the morning till eight in the evening, and sometimes till midnight. The Government proposed, as an amendment, that the oath should be, "not to endeavor to alter *the Protestant religion*, or the government either of church or state." He asked, "where are the boundaries, or how much is meant by the Protestant religion?"

The Lord Keeper Finch, his successor, exclaimed, "*Tell it not in Gath, nor publish it in the streets of Ascalon*, that a Peer of so great parts and eminence as my noble and learned friend, a member of the Church of England, and the champion of the Reformation, should confess that he does not know what is meant by the Protestant religion." Several Bishops followed, explaining that the Protestant religion is comprehended in the thirty-nine articles, the liturgy, the catechism, the homilies, and the canons of the Church of England. From the few preserved fragments of Shaftesbury's reply, it seems to have been most splendid—pointing out the defects in these standards of orthodoxy, with the opposite interpretations put upon them by different parties in the Church,—and asking whether it should be a crime to propose to restore the liturgy to what it was in the days of Queen Elizabeth? Overhearing a Bishop, who had become very indolent since his elevation, say to another Bishop, "I wonder when he will have done preaching," he said in an under tone to be heard distinctly all over the House, "When I am made a Bishop, my Lord,"—and then proceeded triumphantly with his speech.[1] The King attended the debates very regularly, sometimes sitting in his chair of state, but more frequently standing by the fire. He eagerly supported the bill, which he was told was a panacea for all the evils of faction, and would make the rest of his reign quiet and happy. Yet he could not but smile at this jest upon the Bishop. Buckingham was stimulated by envy to make a ruder assault upon the right reverend bench, but he was not equally felicitous.[2]

The Bill at last passed and was sent down to the Commons, where preparations were ordered to be made for its good reception by a very copious distribution of bribes.

It was read a second time by a large majority, and it was now thought quite safe,—when Shaftesbury arrested its progress, and defeated it, by stirring up a quarrel between the two Houses on a question of privilege. This he dexterously inflamed to such a pitch of violence, that it threatened a public convulsion; and it could only be appeased by putting a sudden end to the session.

At this time it happened that appeals were brought to the House of Lords from the Court of Chancery in three suits, in which members of the House of Commons were the respondents, and they received notice to appear at the bar of the House of Lords to hear the appeals argued and adjudged.

Writs of error from the Courts of Common law had been brought in the House of Lords without dispute from a very remote era; but appeals in Equity suits were of very recent origin, and their legality had been denied. On Shaftesbury's suggestion, the matter was taken up in the Commons, and all those over whom he had influence

---

[1] Inconvenience seems to have been felt then, as now, from the room in which the Lords assemble being too small, so that remarks in private conversation are heard across the table. From this and other causes, a meeting of the Lords has more the appearance of a club for idle lounging than of a deliberative assembly to pass laws. A.D. 1845. The spacious and splendid hall in which the Lords now assemble has deprived them of all excuse for their errors on the score of *locality*. A. D. 1848.   [2] 4 Parl. Hist. 714.

joined in a vote which was nearly unanimous and seemed wholly unconnected with politics, "that the notice served upon the members of that House to appear at the bar of the House of Lords was a breach of privilege." Shaftesbury himself, in the Upper House, strongly insisted on their right to hear appeals from the Courts of Equity, and that it could make no difference whether the parties were or were not members of the House of Commons; otherwise a denial of justice must follow. The Commons in a fury, which court and country party shared, committed Shirley and Stoughton, two of the appellants, to the Tower,—resolved "that to prosecute in the House of Lords any cause against a member of their House was a breach of privilege;"—declared "that no appeal lay from the Courts of Equity to any other tribunal;"—and ordered that the four barristers who, by order of the Lords, had pleaded before the House in one of the appeals, should be taken into custody. Shaftesbury, delighted to see the quarrel go on so gloriously, made a long and inflammatory speech in defense of the rights of the peerage,—and describing the imprisonment of the four barristers as an unsupportable insult, moved that they should be immediately set at liberty by order of the House. The resolution was carried with tumultous applause, and the captive barristers were forcibly rescued by the Usher of the Black Rod, the officer of the Lords,—from the Sergeant at Arms, the officer of the Commons,—who was so frightened by his loss that he suddenly absconded, to escape the punishment of his pusillanimity. But the enemies of the Test Bill declared in the Commons, that "if this outrage were submitted to, not only the privileges of the Commons, but the liberties of England were for ever subverted," and an order was made that the four barristers should be recaptured. Next morning, Speaker Seymour passing up Westminster Hall, saw one of them, Pemberton, (afterwards Chief Justice), and with the assistance of some of the officers of the House took him prisoner, and lodged him in "Little Ease."[1] The other three[2] were arrested in the Court of King's Bench by the new Sergeant at Arms, eager to show his superior courage, — and all the four, being

[1] For this exploit the Speaker received the special thanks of the House. 4 Parl. Hist. 733.
[2] Sir John Churchill, Mr. Sergeant Pecke and Mr. Porter.

brought to the bar of the House were committed to the Tower.

At the suggestion of the ministers, the King attempted to appease the feud, and addressing the two Houses at Whitehall, told them "they were the dupes of men enemies to him and to the Church of England, who were indifferent about privilege, and only sought a dissolution, whereby a measure of great importance to the peace of of the kingdom might be defeated." He then very unadvisedly talked in a slighting manner of questions of privilege, and intimated an intention of deciding this controversy in a summary manner by his own authority.[1]

Shaftesbury took advantage of this indiscretion, and the *esprit de corps* absorbing for the moment the love for the test, he hurried on the Lords to make an order on the Lieutenant of the Tower to set the four barristers at liberty, and, on a refusal, to resort to the novel process of issuing writs of *habeas corpus*, commanding the Lieutenant to produce his prisoners before the King in his High Court of Parliament. The Lord Keeper, who well saw the drift of this proceeding, was himself ordered to sign and seal the writs, and send them to be executed with sufficient force. The Commons, on the other hand, resolved "that the Sergeant at Arms attending this house be protected against all persons that shall any ways molest or hinder him from executing his office;" and they passed resolutions "that no commoners of England, committed by the order or warrant of the House of Commons for breach of privilege, ought, without order of the House, to be by any writ of *habeas corpus*, or any other authority whatever, made to appear, or answer, or receive any determination in the House of Peers." 2. "That the order of the House of Peers for issuing writs of *habeas corpus* concerning the four barristers committed by the House, is insufficient and illegal." 3. "That the Lord Keeper be informed of these resolutions, so that the said writs of *habeas corpus* may be superseded as contrary to law and the privileges of this House."

Thus was this dispute brought to the verge of civil war —and, to preserve the public tranquillity, the Government was driven to abandon the Test Bill. The morning after these resolutions had been passed, the King came to

[1] 4 Parl Hist. 721.

the House of Lords, and the Commons being summoned, he declared that "those unhappy differences between his two Houses were grown to such a height that he found no possible means of putting an end to them but by a prorogation."[1]

I conceive that for tactics there is no parliamentary campaign more brilliant than this of Shaftesbury. Bishop Burnet says, that "in one of the debates on the Test Bill he spoke a whole hour against the non-resistance clause; and that, though his words were watched so that it was resolved to send him to the Tower if he had uttered any thing that could be laid hold of, he spoke both with so much boldness and so much caution that, while he provoked the Court extremely, no advantage could be taken against him."[2] But all this was nothing compared to his dexterity in playing off the two Houses against each other on the question of privilege. Such fervor did he excite in the Commons, that no courtier had the courage to oppose the resolutions against the encroachments of the Lords, and they passed *nemine dissentiente*. In the Lords, although at the head of a very small political party, he so manœuvred, that the resolutions against the illegal proceedings of the Commons were carried by a large majority, composed chiefly of supporters of the "Test Bill," which they were framed to defeat, and he carried along with him the whole House, except a few Bishops and placemen. He now published a pamphlet under the title of "A Letter from a Person of Quality to a Friend in the Country," in which he was assisted by Locke, purporting to detail the debate on the subject of the non-resisting test.

Both Houses meeting after a recess of four months, the Court hoped that now a supply might be granted, which would make way for the reintroduction of the "Test Bill;" but a most injudicious motion was made and carried, "that the pamphlet entitled *A Letter from a Person of Quality to a Friend in the Country* was a lying, scandalous, and seditious libel, and that it be burned by the hands of the common hangman." Shaftesbury durst not avow the publication, and could hardly resist the motion; but he had his revenge by moving "that a day be appointed

---

[1] 4 Parl. Hist. 740. Lords' Jour. 1675. Com. Jour. 1675. Marvell, i. 517. Burnet, ii. 75.   [2] Burnet, i. 384.

for hearing at the bar the appeal of *Shirley* v. *Fagg*."
A most animated debate ensued, in which the courtiers
tried to get rid of the difficulty by a proposal to adjourn
all judicial business for six weeks. We have a full report
of his reply, which shows us the great dexterity with
which he addressed himself to the feelings and prejudices
of his audience. He thus began: " My Lords, our all is
at stake, and therefore you must give me leave to speak
freely before we part with it." He then goes over the
different topics adduced by his opponents—dwelling with
peculiar severity on the arguments of the Bishop of Salisbury and the Lord Keeper. He reminds them, in a
taunting manner, of the arrest of the four barristers for
pleading by their order at their bar: " How far the pretended privilege of the House of Commons, their servants, and those they own, doth extend, Westminster
Hall may with grief tell your Lordships. And, my Lords,
we are sure it doth not stop here, for they have already,
nem. con., voted against your Lordships' power of appeals
from any Court of Equity; so that you may plainly see
where this caution and reason of state means to stop—
not one jot short of laying your whole judicature aside.
The poorest Lord, if birthright of the peerage be maintained, has a fair prospect before him for himself or his
posterity; but the greatest title, with mere present power
and riches, is but a mean creature, and maintains nobles
in absolute monarchies no otherwise than by servile and
low flatteries. My Lords, it is not only your interest, but
the interest of the nation, that you maintain your rights;
for let the House of Commons and gentry of England
think what they please, there is no Prince that ever governed without a nobility or an army; if you will not have
one you must have the other, or the monarchy can not
long support or keep itself from tumbling into a demo-
cratical republic. My Lords, would you be in favor with
the King? Do not put yourselves out of a future capacity to be considerable in his service. I will serve my
Prince as a Peer, but will not destroy the Peerage to serve
him." He next attacks the Bishops in a manner which
shows that the venerable heads of the Church were not
held in such reverence then as in our time. Defending
the purity of the judicial decisions of the House of Lords,
in spite of attempts by the Court to corrupt them, he

says, "It was come to that pass, that men even hired or borrowed of their friends, handsome sisters or daughters, to deliver their petitions; but yet for all this, I must say that your judgments have been sacred, unless in one or two causes, *and those we owe most to that Bench from whence we now apprehend the most danger*." He felt that he carried the House so completely along with him, that he did not hesitate to ridicule the "Laudean doctrine of *the Divine right of Kings*," and he thus practically concluded: "You see your duty to yourselves and the people, and that it is not really the interest of the House of Commons, *but may be the inclination of the Court*, that you lose the power of appeals. But I beg our House not to be *felo de se*, but that your Lordships would take in this affair the only course to preserve yourselves, and appoint a day, this day three weeks, for the hearing of this appeal." The motion was carried by a large majority, and notice was served on Sir John Fagg, M.P., to appear at the bar of the House on the day appointed. An order was made at the same time that the appellant and his counsel should have the protection of the House.[1]

The Commons were instantly in a flame, and renewed all the violent resolutions of the former session. Shaftesbury followed up the blow by inducing Lord Mohun to move an address to dissolve the parliament, which had now sat fourteen years, and could no longer be considered as justly representing the people. The Duke of York and the Catholic Peers were so disgusted with Danby's ultra-Protestant policy, that they joined Shaftesbury on this occasion; the Minister was outvoted by the Peers present, and by calling proxies obtained only a majority of two.

A violent protest, drawn by Shaftesbury, against the rejection of the address, was entered next morning in the Journals. Fifteen Peers had signed it, and others were preparing to sign it, when the King made his appearance on the throne, and at one blow prorogued parliament for the unexampled period of one year and three months.[2]

Shaftesbury was assailed by many pamphlets, imputing to him the loss of the Test Bill, the quarrel about privilege, and the distracted state of the country. One of them described him as "a fairy fiend that haunted and

[1] 4 Parl. Hist. 791.   [2] Ibid. 803.

deluded both Houses." He brought an action of defamation against Lord Digby, for saying to him at county meeting, "You are against the King, and for seditions and factious aid for a Commonwealth, and, by God, we we will have your head next parliament," and he recovered a verdict with £1,000 damages.[1]

After this protracted and stormy recess, the same parliament again met (its 15th session) in February, 1677. The ground now seized by Shaftesbury was, that in point of law the parliament must be taken to have been dissolved, and that there was no longer any lawful parliament in existence. As soon as the King had withdrawn he put up Buckingham to make this objection, and to deliver an argument he himself had prepared, "that a continuous prorogation for more than a year was tantamount to a dissolution, by virtue of the statutes 4 Ed. III. c. 14, and 36 Ed. III. c. 10, which require *that a parliament be holden every year once, and more often if need be:* now, on the last prorogation, the present parliament could not meet within a year,—and as the King could not be supposed to have meant to have put it out of his power to obey the law, the just intendment was that he dissolved the old parliament, so that he might within the year call a new one as the law requires,—an intendment greatly strengthened by the consideration that nearly seventeen years had elapsed since this parliament had been elected, and that it would be indecent to impute a design to the King to make it last during his whole reign."

As soon as Buckingham sat down, a motion was made that he be called to the bar for the insult which he had offered to the House, and the Lord Keeper resorted to the miserable quibble, that the words, "if need be" override the whole clause, leaving it to the King to consider whether there was any occasion to call a parliament even once a year,—and went so far as to hint at the doctrine that no act of parliament interfering with the essential prerogative of the Crown in calling or dissolving parlia-

---

[1] Juries were then sometimes much more liberal, giving £100,000 in actions of defamation and scan. mag. On this occasion the foreman said, "they would have given larger damages, but that they considered Lord Digby's father (Earl of Bristol) was still alive, Lord Digby had a very small estate in hand, and they did not wish to perpetuate a feud between the two families."

ments is binding. Shaftesbury was in hopes of aid from the Catholic Peers; but they remaining silent, he was called up, and he gallantly insisted that the individuals by whom he was surrounded were no House of Parliament, and that no one was bound to respect their proceedings, —treating with scorn the Lord Keeper's construction of the statute, and his unconstitutional limitation of the supremacy of parliament,—"for which the Lord Keeper ought to be called to the bar, instead of the Duke of Buckingham." He was supported by Lords Salisbury and Wharton.

After a debate of five hours, it was resolved that Buckingham, Shaftesbury, Salisbury, and Wharton should retract their opinion, acknowledge that their conduct was "ill-advised," and beg pardon of the King and the House. Shaftesbury, as the chief delinquent, was first commanded to submit, and, on his refusal, was committed to the Tower "during the pleasure of the King and the House." There he lay above a year—and he could not recover his liberty without considerable humiliation.

This was a bold but an imprudent move of the Ex-Chancellor, for he might have foreseen that "a virtual dissolution" would be highly distasteful to members of the House of Commons, and not well relished by the Lords, so that the support of it would place him at the mercy of his enemies. Buckingham, Salisbury, and Wharton, who were committed along with him, after an imprisonment of a few months, made their submission and were discharged; but he still disdained such a course, and suing out a writ of *habeas corpus* before the Court of King's Bench, he insisted that the commitment was illegal, and that he was entitled, as a matter of right, to be unconditionally set fee, or at all events to be bailed.

It must have been a scene of considerable interest when an Earl, an ex-Lord Chancellor, and the head of a great political party was brought up in custody, and, after arguments from his counsel, pleaded his own cause. He put very strongly the objection that the warrant of commitment was bad, being merely " for high contempts against this House," without specifying what the contempts were, so that he might have been committed for something wholly frivolous, as the cut of his beard, or something he had done in the strict discharge of his duty,—as obeying the process of the law,—which either House of parliament might construe into a contempt. He powerfully urged that, as a warrant in this form by the King or any other magistrate would be void, there could be no reason why we should bind our necks to the yoke of assemblies established to protect—not to extinguish—our liberties. To the taunt of the Attorney General, that being a Peer he should stand up for the privileges of the Peerage, he said, "It is true I am a Peer, and no man hath a greater reverence or esteem for the Lords than myself; but I hope my being a Peer shall not lose my being an Englishman, or make me to have less the title to MAGNA CHARTA and the other laws of English liberty. I desire your Lordships well to consider what rule you make in my case, for it will be a precedent that in future ages may concern every man in England."

Rainsford, C. J.—" This Court hath no jurisdiction of the cause, and therefore the form of the return is not considerable. We ought not to extend our jurisdiction beyond its due limits."[1]

Shaftesbury was remanded, and found himself in "a false position." He was, at first, visited by all the factious; but an order was made that no one should be admitted to him without the King's express permission. He languished in the Tower without any prospect of getting himself liberated, and he had the mortification to learn that, meanwhile, in his absence, things were marvelously quiet in the House of Lords, and that Danby was carrying every thing before him. He in vain wrote spirited and pathetic letters to the King and the Duke of York, appealing to their justice and generosity.

At last, in February, 1678, he condescended to petition that he might be brought to the bar to apologize for the offense he had given. His application to the Court of King's Bench was now represented as the great aggravation of his crime, and Danby tried to shut him out from a hearing, on account of some contemptuous words respect-

[1] 6 St. Tr. 1296. The precedent hitherto has been respected. In the case of the Sheriffs of Middlesex, which occurred when I was Attorney General and a Member of the House of Commons, I settled the warrant of commitment, and took care that it should be in this general form. Some observations were made by the Court of King's Bench as to the impropriety of preventing them from seeing the true cause of commitment but they held it sufficient.

ing the House of Lords he was charged with then using—but the witness called could not prove them.

On his knees was the "Patriot" compelled to repeat, after the Lord Chancellor, the following mortifying palinode: "I, Anthony, Earl of Shaftesbury, do acknowledge that my endeavoring to maintain that the parliament is dissolved was an ill-advised action, for which I humbly beg the pardon of the King's Majesty, and of this most Honorable House; and I do also acknowledge that my bringing of a *habeas corpus* in the King's Bench was a high violation of your Lordships' privileges, and a great aggravation of my former offense, for which I likewise most humbly beg the pardon of this most Honorable House."

The Lords, with white staves, were ordered to inform the King that the House was satisfied, and Shaftesbury was allowed to resume his seat.

During the short glimpse of power and favor which he enjoyed two years after, he contrived by a vote of the House of Lords to have all these proceedings condemned as unparliamentary and unconstitutional, "and that the entry of them on the Journals should be vacated, so that they might never be drawn into precedent for the future."[1]

Upon his discharge, he found his influence very much diminished. Danby, whose policy in the race for popularity was to take the wind out of the sails of his competitor, had gained great popularity with the Protestants. The marriage of the Princess Mary, the eldest daughter of the Duke of York and next in succession to the Crown, with the Prince of Orange, now at the head of the Protestant interest in Europe, had been followed up by the treaty of Nimeguen, which drew the Protestant states into closer amity, and placed on a respectable footing the foreign relations of the country. Shaftesbury resumed his opposition with vigor, but down to the prorogation in the end of June, could find no opportunity of seriously embarrassing the measures of the government, and he agitated against the Duke of York and the Papists with little hope of ever again being the idol of a great party.[2]

This was only a lull; the hurricane soon burst forth;

[1] Lords' Jour. Nov. 13, 1680. [2] 4 Parl. Hist. 977-1004.

Shaftesbury directed it,—and he was more formidable than at any former period of his career.

CHAPTER LXXXIX.

CONTINUATION OF THE LIFE OF LORD SHAFTESBURY TILL THE DISSOLUTION OF THE OXFORD PARLIAMENT.

THE charge stoutly adduced against Shaftesbury of having been the inventor of the Popish plot, and of having suborned Titus Oates to bring it forward, is unsupported by any reasonable evidence, and is, I think, wholly unfounded; but no one can deny that he early caught at this delusion as an engine of annoyance to his adversaries, and that he unscrupulously used it for his ambitious purposes, regardless of the ruin which it brought on individuals, and of the public calamities which it caused. As the monstrous improbability of the tale negatives the notion that he framed it, so it prevents us from supposing that he believed in it. Yet he pretended to give implicit credit to all its wildest fictions; he was mainly instrumental in propagating the general panic on the opportune murder of Sir Edmonsbury Godfrey; he joined in the cry that this worthy Protestant magistrate had been assassinated by the Papists for having taken Oates's evidence; he suggested to the Londoners to prepare for the defense of the City, as if a foreign enemy were at its gates; and he was supposed to have suggested to Sir Thomas Player, the Chamberlain, the noted saying, "that were it not for these precautions, all the Protestant citizens might rise next morning with their throats cut."

On the meeting of parliament, Danby, that he might anticipate Shaftesbury, brought forward the subject of the Popish plot in the Lords, contrary to the advice of the King, who said, "You will find you have given the parliament a handle to ruin yourself as well as to disturb all my affairs, and you will surely live to repent it." Shaftesbury soon took the matter entirely out of Danby's hands, and carried resolutions for a committee to inquire into the horrible conspiracy,—for the removal of Popish recusants from London,—for appointing the train-bands of London and Westminster to be in readiness,—for sending Lords Powis, Stafford, Arundel, Peters, and Bellasis to the Tower, as Papists and traitors, and for declaring " that there hath been and still is a damnable and hellish plot continued and carried on by Popish recusants for assassinating the King, subverting the government, and rooting out and destroying the Protestant religion."[1] He was chairman of the Committee of the House of Lords for prosecuting the inquiry ; and, superseding the government who wished to conduct it, took the whole management of it into his own hands. He was always at his post—receiving informations, granting warrants for searches and arrests, examining and committing prisoners, and issuing instructions to officers, informers, and jailers. He converted, with consummate art, every succeeding occurrence into a confirmation of the plot, and by inflaming the passions of the people was able to direct them at his pleasure. From being lately nearly isolated as a party leader, and somewhat contemned for his inglorious release from imprisonment, the popular delirium now placed him at the head of a decided majority in both Houses, and the ministers were allowed to remain in office only till it suited his purpose to remove them.

The exorbitant power which he now enjoyed he grossly abused. His first measure was the bill for a Test by which Roman Catholics should be excluded from sitting in either House of Parliament. He began it in the House of Commons, where it passed by acclamation. In the upper House there was a strong feeling with many in favor of the Roman Catholic Peers,—men of undoubted honor and loyalty,—and the representatives of the most illustrious families. The bill likewise caused alarm as an attack on the hereditary rights of the peerage; for if one class might be disqualified from acting in their legislative capacity for adhering to the religion of their ancestors, the same injustice might be done to others on some new pretext, and the whole body would depend upon the arbitrary will of the minister, or the capricious tyranny of the multitude, prompted by an unprincipled demagogue.

Shaftesbury overcame these obstacles by the fresh discoveries of Titus Oates; and a clause being introduced

---

[1] 4 Parl. Hist. 1022.

into the Bill for excepting the Duke of York from its operation, it received the royal assent.[1] The injustice of this statute, which was passed in a moment of delusion and violence, could not be remedied for a period of 150 years; and still we continue to feel its mischievous consequences. If our Roman Catholic brethren had been allowed to sit in parliament as they had continued to do since the Reformation, the enmity between the followers of the two religions would probably soon have died away, and, all enjoying the same civil rights in England and in Ireland, all might have been equally attached to the law and constitution, and we might have escaped the discords and jealousies which have long weakened the empire, and have sometimes threatened its dismemberment. This statute, so eagerly clung to by the pious and the orthodox as the safeguard of our religion, was undoubtedly the handiwork of the profligate and sceptical Shaftesbury. He ere long made some compensation, by a law for securing personal liberty; but in estimating his merits, the disqualification of Roman Catholics to sit in parliament must be considered a tremendous set off against "the Habeas Corpus Act."

The factious leader further moved the House of Lords for an address to the King to remove the Duke of York from his presence and councils. This was defeated by James getting up in his place and declaring that he had already ceased to be a member of the Privy Council;—whereupon the candid and virtuous Lord Russell was induced to withdraw a similar motion, which, from the purest motives he had made in the Commons.[2]

To show the versatility of his powers, in the midst of these violent struggles, he calmly delivered, as Ex-Chancellor, a character he felt it for his influence to maintain, a long and learned argument on the question argued at the bar in the Viscount Purbeck's case, "whether a peerage can be surrendered to the King?" He contended that *Honors* are not within the *statute de Donis*, and that the heir to the peerage could only lose his right by *forfeiture*, although the law of Scotland upon this subject was different. The House was guided by his opinion.[3]

The trials now began—the most disgraceful in our

[1] 30 Car. 2, st. 2. 4 Parl. Hist. 1024.   [2] Ibid. 1025.
[3] Shower's Parl. Cases, p. 1,

judicial history—against those accused of being implicated in the Popish plot. Shaftesbury had only to look quietly on while Judge Scroggs and demented juries were eager to credit perjury, that they might convict innocent men whom they had prejudged.

Some victims being offered up to feed the popular fury, it was thought full time that Danby, the Lord Treasurer, should be precipitated from power. Montague, the ambassador at Paris, arrived as a useful ally, and disclosing the secret negotiations with the court of France, a motion was carried in the House of Commons for Danby's impeachment for high treason. The King, during some time stood by his minister, and, to procure him a respite, dissolved the parliament, that he might get rid of a House of Commons which, having sat nearly eighteen years, had entirely altered its character, and from being the most obsequious to the Court, had become one of the most formidable that had ever been assembled,—notwithstanding the notorious bribery practiced to corrupt its members.[1]

The state of the exchequer rendered a parliament indispensable, and a new one was called, to meet in forty days. Shaftesbury was indefatigable in superintending the elections, and, as might easily have been anticipated, from the present ferment in the public mind, they turned out decidedly in his favor. Danby thought to avert the storm which was pending over him, by contriving that, before the opening of the session, the Duke of York should withdraw to Brussels; but the Court was beaten in the choice of a Speaker, and the King resorted to the ungracious exercise of the prerogative, of disallowing the Speaker elected by a majority of the House.

The impeachment was immediately revived. To stop it, a pardon was granted to the minister, to which the King affixed the Great Seal with his own hand; but Shaftesbury maitained the doctrine, that a pardon can not be pleaded in bar to a parliamentary impeachment, so as to prevent inquiry and sentence, although, after sentence, the Crown may remit the punishment. The Lords yielded to this doctrine, and issued a warrant to arrest the Earl of Danby. Upon this he absconded; and a bill was passed to attaint him, unless he should surrender. He did sur-

---

[1] 4 Parl. Hist. 1074.

render, and Shaftesbury had the gratification of seeing his adversary sent off to the Tower on a capital charge.

To leave the Court no breathing-time he made a motion in the Lords, for a committee of the whole House "on the state of the nation," which he prefaced with a most inflammatory speech, in his peculiar style, on the danger to the Protestant faith :—

"'*We have a little sister, and she hath no breasts; what shall we do for our sister in the day when she shall be spoken for? If she be a wall, we will build on her a palace of silver; if she be a door, we will inclose her with boards of cedar.*' We have several little sisters without breasts— the French Protestant churches; the two kingdoms of Ireland and Scotland. The foreign Protestants are a wall, the only wall and defense of England; upon it you may build palaces of silver, glorious palaces. The protection of the Protestants abroad is the greatest power and security the Crown of England can attain to, and which alone can help us to give check to the growing greatness of France. Scotland and Ireland are two doors, either to let in good or mischief upon us; they are much weakened by the artifice of our cunning enemies, and we ought to inclose them with boards of cedar. Popery and slavery, like two sisters, go hand in hand; and sometimes one goes first, sometimes the other; but wheresoever the one enters, the other is always following close at hand. In England, Popery was to have brought in slavery; in Scotland, slavery went before, and Popery was to follow." [1]

Charles, without a minister, had sent for Sir William Temple, who produced a new-invented plan of government—very plausible—but wholly inconsistent with our parliamentary constitution, which requires that the King shall have advisers possessing the confidence of the two Houses, and that when they lose that confidence they shall be changed. Temple recommended a permanent council, to the number of thirty, taken from different parties and ranks, fifteen being with, and fifteen without office—great property being an indispensable qualification —and that the King having no prime minister, should consult them on all affairs of state, and be governed by their opinion. Charles, in his present difficulties, agreed

[1] 4 Parl. Hist. 1116. It is said that 30,000 copies of this speech were printed and circulated in a few days after it was delivered.

to try the experiment, and himself proposed that Shaftesbury should be a member of the new council. Against this Temple strongly remonstrated. The King said, he might be dangerous as a friend; but he was now irresistible as a foe. Shaftesbury, being sounded, consented to join the new government, on the condition that he was President of the all-directing Council. This was consented to, and he was sworn in accordingly.

The King in person informed the two Houses that he had established a new Privy Council, not to exceed thirty; that he had made choice of such persons as were worthy and able to advise him, and was resolved in all his weighty and important affairs, next to the advice of his great Council in parliament, to be guided by this Privy Council.[1]

Being installed as Lord President of the new-fangled Board, Shaftesbury was presented to the public as the most prominent member of the government. But he felt that he had only the appearance of power; that he could not rely upon the Court; that he was marked out for vengeance by the Duke of York; and that the proclamation of this Prince as inheritor of the throne, if that event should ever happen, would be his death-warrant. He seems now deliberately to have taken up the plan which had probably often previously presented itself to his imagination, of setting up the Duke of Monmouth as heir apparent, on the ground that there had been a contract of marriage between the King and Lucy Walters. Notwithstanding Charles's solemn denial of any such contract, a hope was entertained that he would acquiesce in the scheme, from his affection for his son and his regard for his own ease.

Shaftesbury felt that success was to be obtained only from the continuance of his personal popularity. This had not been at all impaired by his unexpected elevation, which was considered the triumph of the people, and which he construed into a proof that the King in his heart would be pleased with his brother's exclusion, and the legitimation of Monmouth. To retain his influence with the multitude, on which alone he could depend, he

[1] Of this most aristocratic body twenty were members of the House of Lords, and of the remaining ten, several were the eldest sons of peers, or men in office under the Crown. The annual income of the thirty was estimated at £300,000, and that of the House of Commons at £400,000.

still worked the plot as ingeniously as ever, and encouraged the new discoveries and the new prosecutions which marked its frightful progress; although Charles not only treated with scorn the attempt to implicate the Queen, but in private manfully declared his conviction that the whole was a fabrication. The ex-Chancellor likewise still assiduously cultivated his connection with the City. He lived in Thanet House, in Aldersgate Street; he declared his resolution to offer himself as a candidate for the office of Lord Mayor, and was pleased in the mean time to be addressed by his sobriquet of "Alderman Shaftesbury,"—Buckingham being his brother citizen, and intriguing with him in the Court of Aldermen, in the Common Council, and in every Wardmote.[1]

But to establish his reputation on a permanent basis, he happily completed a reform, which almost makes his name respectable, notwithstanding all his follies and all his crimes. The personal liberty of the subject, the first end of good government, was yet very insecure in England. The common law declared that no man could be lawfully imprisoned, except upon a warrant specifying the crime of which he was accused, and that every man accused should be speedily brought to trial,—but had not provided any adequate remedy; and these salutary principles were constantly violated, by commitments in the name of the King in Council, by sending prisoners to distant jails, by omitting to put their names in the calendar on a jail delivery, by refusing writs for producing before the judges persons illegally imprisoned, and by jailers disobeying such writs when they were sued out. Shaftesbury had several times attempted in vain to remedy such abuses; and he now with admirable skill, framed a statute, by which personal liberty has been more effectually guarded in England than it has ever been in any other country in the world. This he caused to be introduced in the House of Commons, where it was generally supported. But a strong opposition to it was concerted in the House of Lords. Although avowedly the measure of the Lord President, all the weight of the Court was exerted against it, and several amendments were introduced in the Committee with a view of defeating it, under the belief that the Commons would not agree to them. The

[1] Mem. James II. 651.

third reading is said to have been carried by an accident. According to Bishop Burnet, "Lords Grey and Norris were named to be tellers. Lord Norris being a man subject to vapors, was not at all times attentive to what he was doing. So a very fat Lord coming in, Lord Grey counted him for ten, as a jest, at first; but seeing Lord Norris had not observed it, he went on with his misreckoning of ten, so it was reported to the House, and declared that they who were for the bill were the majority, though it indeed went on the other side."[1]

The majority being declared from the woolsack in favor of the bill, Shaftesbury perceived a great commotion among the courtiers at a result so little expected on either side. With much presence of mind he instantly started on his legs, and after speaking near an hour, during which many members entered and left the House, concluded with a motion on some indifferent subject. It was now impossible that the House could be retold, and no further question could be made upon the bill in the Lords. There was a strong hope that the Commons would disagree to the amendments,—upon which they had to determine at a "conference," while the King was coming to put an end to the session. But they at last waived all their objections; and Shaftesbury, who managed the conference for the Lords,—before the King entered, reported that, "the bill had been delivered back, closed up and perfected." Charles being seated on the throne, the title of it was read, along with several others, and the words "*Le Roy le voet*" being pronounced, it for ever became law.[2]

[1] In the Oxford edition of Burnet's History, there is the following note by Speaker Onslow: "See minute book of the House of Lords with regard to this bill, and compare there the number of Lords that day in the House, with the number reported to be in the division, which agrees with the story. —O." There must certainly have been some mistake, accidental or willful, for the numbers were declared to be 57 to 55; and by the minute book of the Lords it appears that there were only 107 peers in the House. We must suppose that before the Lord Chancellor was aware of the mistake, he had put the additional motion, "that this bill do pass," and that it had been agreed to as a matter of course after the division.

[2] 31 Car. 2, c. 2. It is a common saying, without any foundation, that Jenkes's case produced the Habeas Corpus Act. His illegal imprisonment occurred in 1666 (6 St. Tr. 1190), and had been forgotten in the subsequent excitement of the Popish plot. Shaftesbury's attention had been particularly drawn to the subject from the charges brought against Lord Clarendon, and from his own imprisonments. He had introduced bills which partially met

The prorogation was hurried by the progress in the House of Commons of the Bill for excluding the Duke of York from the succession to the Crown, which, by a large majority, had been there read a second time. This bill, which Shaftesbury openly countenanced, paved the way for Monmouth's pretensions, by enacting that on the death or resignation of his present Majesty, the Duke of York should not inherit the crown; and that if he landed in England he should be attainted. The apparent object was merely to let in the Princess Mary and the Princess Anne; but Shaftesbury expected, that if the King's brother, who had long been considered next heir, could be set aside, there would be little difficulty in bringing forward the youth in whose name he intended to govern. Over the existing House of Commons he had a complete control, and he had been able to carry the most important questions against all the influence of the Court in the House of Lords.

But Charles dreaded his ascendency, and, forgetting his promise to do nothing without the advice of his new Council, resorted to the prorogation without consulting any one, except the Lord Keeper, Essex and Halifax. Shaftesbury considered himself secure while this House of Commons remained,—which he thought in no danger, as it had sat little more than twelve months, while the last preceding House of Commons had existed near eighteen years.

The prorogation had been to the 14th of August; and he indiscreetly boasted of the measures he should then bring forward, and was sure to carry, to crush his opponents. What then must have been his astonishment when, sitting one day as President of the Council, the King, suddenly turning to the Chancellor, ordered him to prepare a proclamation for the dissolution of the present and the calling of another parliament,—whereupon the Council immedi-

the evils complained of in 1668, 1670, 1674, and 1675. The final measure, carried in 1679, was long called "Lord Shaftesbury's Act."—*Life of Shaftesbury*, ii. 221.

James II., in the true spirit of tyranny, to his dying day thought this one of the worst acts ever passed. "It was a great misfortune to the people," says he, "as well as to the Crown, the passing of the Habeas Corpus Act, since it obliges the Crown to keep a greater force on foot to preserve the government, and encourages disaffected, turbulent, and unquiet spirits to carry on their wicked designs; it was contrived by the Earl of Shaftesbury to that effect."—Life, vol. ii. 621.

ately broke up, without any opportunity having been given for deliberation or remonstrance! This was the result of a secret consultation which the King had held with Sunderland and Temple, who thought a more dangerous House of Commons could not be elected, and that delay gave some hope of reaction. When Shaftesbury had left the council-chamber, he passionately swore "that he would have the head of the man who had given such advice."

He had presently to watch the elections for the House of Commons, which turned out as favorably as he could desire; and he looked forward with impatience to the first day of a new session; but he was again confounded, while sitting in council, by the King ordering the Chancellor to prepare a Commission for the prorogation of parliament for a twelvemonth. The members not in the secret gazed on each other with signs of wonder, and the President rose to speak; but Charles commanded silence, saying, "he had foreseen and weighed every objection, and that having taken his resolution he would be obeyed." He was emboldened to take this decisive part by a secret treaty with France, by which, in consideration of preventing the meeting of the English parliament, he received a bribe of a million of livres.

Shaftesbury was immediately removed from his office of President, and his name was struck out of the list of Privy Councillors. Lord Russell, and the other popular leaders, seeing that the Council was not consulted in matters of the highest moment, resigned their seats in it, acknowledged Shaftesbury as their chief, and organized a regular opposition to the government. The names of "Court and Country parties" gave way to the other appellations, at first used in derision, and afterwards proudly adopted by those to whom they were applied,— and the grand struggle began between the TORIES and the WHIGS. The former consisted chiefly of the old Cavaliers and High Churchmen, who stood up for passive obedience and the divine right of kings; the latter, of more moderate Churchmen, with many dissenters, who insisted that government was established for the welfare of the governed.[1]

[1] The two parties, always being distinguished by their respective devotion to prerogative and to liberty, exchanged sentiments on several points, and on none more strikingly than their feeling towards Roman Catholics,—at start-

The Whigs had among them some men of pure patriotism, as well as great talents; but their cause was for a long time tainted by the reckless Shaftesbury, who pretended to adopt their principles, while he cared for nothing but the gratification of his own ambition. His chief object now was to keep up an excitement in the public mind till parliament should meet.

On the 5th of November he had a grand gunpowder-plot procession, headed by Guy Fawkes, to keep up a horror of the Papists; but this was nothing to a new pageant he got up for the 17th of November, the anniversary of the accession of that Protestant princess, Queen Elizabeth. First appeared a bellman with a slow and solemn pace, exclaiming at intervals, in a sepulchral tone, "Remember Godfrey!" next came a representation of the body of the murdered magistrate borne by one habited like a Jesuit; then followed nuns, monks, priests, Catholic bishops in copes and mitres, Protestant bishops in lawn sleeves, six cardinals with their red hats, and last of all, the Pope, in a litter, attended by "Arch-Chancellor, the Devil." The procession having marched through the city at night amidst the glare of several thousand flambeaux, the whole population turning out to witness it, and to call down vengeance on the heads of those who paid homage to the SCARLET LADY, halted at Temple Bar,—when, at a concerted signal, the Pope and his attendants were precipitated into the flames with a shout, "the echo of which," according to the account published by Shrewsbury's orders, "reached by continued reverberations to Scotland, and France, and Rome itself, damping them all with dreadful astonishment." This exhibition was so much applauded, that the contriver of it had it repeated the two following years with additional embellishments and enormous effect.

Elated with the certain prospect of carrying his plan for changing the succession, he soon recalled Monmouth from Brussels, where the son of Lucy Walters had been living in a sort of royal exile. On the young man's arrival, the bells were rung, bonfires were kindled, and the city was illuminated. Charles, on his refusal to quit the

ing, the Tories favoring them, and the Whigs persecuting them; while many years before the Roman Catholic Relief Bill passed, they were supported by the Whigs and discountenanced by the Tories.

kingdom, deprived him of all his employments; but he still went about receiving the homage of the mob. Shaftesbury factiously defended his obstinacy, on the pretense that "as a dutiful son, he was bound either to preserve the King's life from the daggers of the Papists, or to revenge his death, if he should fall by their treason."

Pamphlets were written under Shaftesbury's superintendence, pointing out the horrors of a Popish successor, recommending Monmouth in preference, for his religion, his conduct, and his courage, and suggesting that the objection to his title should not be regarded, as "the worst title makes the best king," and "what the prince wants in right, he must supply by concession."

He obtained petitions to the King for the speedy meeting of parliament from almost every county and town in England; but some of these were presented in such a tumultuary way as to cause great alarm, and to induce an apprehension that there was to be a renewal of civil war.

The Duke of York having returned from Scotland, and having met with rather a cordial reception in the City, Shaftesbury, to keep up the worship of his idol, propagated rumors that the King only denied his marriage with Lucy Walters from pride, that the witnesses to the ceremony were still alive, and that the contract itself, inclosed in a black box, had been intrusted by the late Bishop of Durham to the custody of his son-in-law, Sir Gilbert Gerard, who had it ready to produce before parliament.

Finally, he resorted to the daring expedient of prosecuting the King's brother, and the heir presumptive to the throne, as a Popish recusant. In Trinity Term, 1680, he proceeded to Westminster Hall, in company with the Earl of Huntingdon, Lord Grey of Werke, Lord Gerard of Brandon, Lord Russell, Lord Cavendish, and several other persons of high rank; he appeared before the Grand Jury for the County of Middlesex in the Court of King's Bench,—and in due form submitted to them "a **present**ment against his Royal Highness, James, Duke of **Y**ork, as a Popish recusant,"—whereby it was alleged the defendant had forfeited two-thirds of his property, and was liable to divers other heavy penalties and disabilities. Six reasons or grounds were offered, in a separate document, as proof of the charge. To excite still greater alarm at

Whitehall, he publicly asserted before the Grand Jury that the Duchess of Portsmouth should likewise be indicted as a national nuisance.

The attempt for the present was defeated by the Judges very irregularly discharging the Grand Jury, while they were deliberating; but it produced a great effect all over the nation. There could be no doubt that, according to the statutes then in force, the Duke was liable to the prosecution, which might be at any time renewed; and Shaftesbury having committed himself in mortal strife with the next heir to the Crown, had shown that he had nerve to take any advantage which the law might offer him, without regard to the consequences. The Duke was immediately ordered to return to Edinburgh; while Monmouth made a progress through the provinces,—visiting the most celebrated fairs, races, and assemblies of amusement. On these occasions he was much admired for his fine person and courteous manners, and, without putting forth any distinct claims, he was addressed as " His Highness," and was generally received as the King's legitimate son.

Nearly a year and a half had elapsed since parliament was summoned, and its meeting could no longer be delayed. In the House of Commons Shaftesbury's supremacy was unshaken; but in the Lords he was looked upon with suspicion and alarm, on account of the violence of his recent proceedings. He planned the campaign with his usual skill. After several votes in support of the right of petitioning, and condemning the efforts of the government to crush it, he brought forward DANGERFIELD and his " NARRATIVE," to frighten the isle from its propriety; and then he obtained resolutions of the House of Commons, which no one ventured to oppose: " That it is the opinion of this House that parliament ought to proceed effectually to suppress Popery, and to prevent a Popish succession:" " That the Duke of York being a Papist, the hopes of his coming to the Crown have given the greatest countenance and encouragement to the present designs and conspiracies against the King and the Protestant religion:" " That in defense of the King's person and government, and Protestant religion, this House doth declare they will stand by his Majesty with their lives and fortunes; and that if his Majesty should come to any violent death, which God forbid, they will revenge it to the utmost on the Papists."[1]

On this foundation he ordered the Exclusion Bill to be again introduced.

The bill passed rapidly through the House of Commons; and, on the 15th of November, was brought up by Lord Russell to the House of Lords, amidst loud cheers from members below the bar. Here was to be the mortal struggle. The King warmly espoused the cause of his brother, openly canvassed for votes in his favor, and himself attended the debates upon it,—showing his inclination by significant looks and loud whispers while Peers were addressing the House.

Shaftesbury, nothing daunted, unflinchingly supported his bill; and, after showing the absurdity of indefeasible hereditary right,—the well-settled authority of parliament to alter the succession to the Crown,—the repugnancy of the Romish religion to our constitution,—the violent temper and bigotry of the Duke,—the certain overthrow of our liberties as well as our religion, if he should ever mount the throne,—and the superiority of the remedy of setting him aside, to that of limiting his powers, as had been proposed,—he turned towards the Bishops, of whom he was most distrustful, and, in a pathetic tone, implored them to have a regard to the civil rights of their fellow-subjects, and to the best interests of the Church of which they were the fathers,—reminding them that they then had it in their power to exclude a Popish Prince by law, and thereby preserve their religion and liberties; but that, if they should lose the present opportunity, they must afterwards either run into rebellion to save themselves, or sit down with the melancholy portion of bondage, ignominy, and repentance.

He was answered by Lord Halifax, who displayed an extent of capacity and a force of eloquence which had never been surpassed in that assembly. This aspiring orator was animated by the greatness of the occasion, by the presence of the King, and by a rivalship with his uncle Shaftesbury, whom, during that day's debate, he for the first time eclipsed. He seems with much felicity to have ridiculed the hypocritical ambition of Monmouth,

[1] 4 Parl Hist. 1162.

who had spoken in support of the bill;[1] and, without saying anything personally offensive, to have admirably developed the arts, intrigues, and objects of the leader of the Exclusionists. After a debate which lasted till near midnight, the bill was thrown out by a majority of sixty-three to thirty, proxies not being called.[2]

Shaftesbury was no doubt actuated by the most factious and unworthy motives; but I must nevertheless give my humble opinion that the bill was a constitutional proceeding. James's conduct as king, and the Revolution of 1688, amply excused its defenders.

This defeat did not quell the courage of the great agitator, conscious of the power he still possessed in the House of Commons and in the country. A few days after, there was a committee on a supply bill, which he strongly opposed. He printed and published his Reply, which, if its accuracy may be relied upon, shows that he indulged in the most cutting personalities against the King, who was one of his hearers. A few specimens may be amusing:—

"My Lords, this noble Lord near me hath found fault with that precedent which he supposes I offered to your Lordships concerning the chargeable ladies at Court. I remember no such thing, I said. But if I must speak of them, I shall say as the prophet did to King Saul—'*What meaneth this bleating of the cattle?*' and I hope the King will make the same answer,—'*That he reserves them for sacrifice, and means to deliver them up to please his people;*' for there must be, in plain English, my Lords, a change. We must neither have a Popish favorite, nor Popish mistress, nor Popish counselor at Court. What I spoke was about another lady, that belongs not to the Court, but, like Sempronia in Catiline's conspiracy, does more mischief than Cethegus."—"My Lords, it is a very hard thing to say we can not trust the King, and that we have already been deceived so often, that we see plainly the apprehension of discontent is no argument at Court; and though our Prince be himself an excellent person, that the people have the greatest inclinations to love, yet I must say he is such an one as no story affords us a parallel of."
—"The transactions between him and his brother are ad-

---

[1] Charles, at this expression, exclaimed in a stage whisper, "The kiss of Judas!"   [2] All the bishops present, fourteen in number, voted against it.

mirable and incomprehensible. The match with a Portugal lady, not likely to have children, was contrived by the Duke's father-in-law, and no sooner effected, but the Duke and his party make proclamation to the world that we are like to have no children, and that he must be the certain heir. He takes his seat in parliament as Prince of Wales,—has his guards about him,—the Prince's lodgings at Whitehall,—his guards on the same floor, without any interposition between him and the King. This Prince changes his religion to make himself a party, and such a party that his brother must be sure to die or be made away with to make room for him."—" The prorogations, the dissolutions, the cutting short of parliaments—not suffering them to have time to look into anything, have showed what reason we have for confidence in the Court. We are now come to a parliament again—by what fate or riddle, I can not guess."—" The Duke is sent away; the House of Commons have brought up a bill to disable him of the Crown; and I think they are, so far, extremely in the right; but your Lordships are wiser than I, and have rejected it. Yet you have thought fit, and the King himself hath made the proposition, to adopt such expedients as shall render him but a nominal prince."—" However, we know who hears us; and I am glad of this, that your Lordships have dealt so honorably and so clearly in the King's presence, that he can not say he wants a right state of things. He hath it before him, and may take counsel as he thinks fit." [1]

His next move was to lay on the table of the House of Lords, " A Bill to dissolve the King's marriage with Catherine of Portugal," which he thought might breed a quarrel between the two royal brothers, and greatly embarrass the ministers. In introducing the bill, he professed the most profound respect for the monarchy, and deep reverence for the Protestant religion—describing this measure as the only means for saving both, by enabling his Majesty to marry a Protestant princess, by whom he might have legitimate issue, and thus to exclude a Popish successor without violating the usual rule of succession to the Crown, which a majority of their Lord-

---

[1] I can not help suspecting that in the Report which he published of this speech, he introduced several things which he could not have spoken without being sent to the Tower.—See *Life*, by Martyn, ii. 252.

ships deemed so sacred. Charles, however, with a fairness and firmness which should make us look with lenience at some of his errors, declared that he would never consent to the disgrace of an innocent woman, and openly canvassed the Peers against the bill—so that Shaftesbury, seeing that he was likely to have a smaller minority upon it than upon the Exclusion Bill, postponed the consideration of it, on different pretenses, from time to time, and never brought it to a second reading.[1]

But he was abundantly active in the House of Commons, where a large majority was at his beck. He caused several bills to be introduced there, the original drafts of which are still extant in his handwriting—one, to revive the Triennial Act, which had been so improperly repealed by Lord Clarendon; a second, to enact that the Judges should hold their offices *quamdiu se bene gesserint;* a third, to make the levying of money without consent of parliament, high treason; and a fourth, to constitute an association for the safety of his Majesty's person, for defense of the Protestant religion, and preventing the Duke of York or any Papist from succeeding to the Crown. None of these met with any serious opposition in the Lower House.

Next, he carried an impeachment against Lord Chief Justice Scroggs, for illegally discharging the Grand Jury of the County of Middlesex while they were deliberating on the indictment he had preferred against the Duke of York as a Popish recusant; and he instituted proceedings against the Lord Chief Justice North, and Jeffreys the Recorder of London, for interfering with the right of petitioning.[2]

The severe chastisement he had received from his nephew, Lord Halifax, rankled deeply in his mind, and he caused a motion to be made in the Commons for an address to the King to remove this nobleman from his presence and councils for ever. The attempt to defeat it only showed the weakness of the Court, for an adjournment of the debate, moved by Halifax's friends, was negatived by a majority of 219 to 95; and the address was then carried without a division. When the Committee appointed to draw up the address made their report,

[1] James's Memoirs, 618. Macpherson, i. 109.
[2] 4 Parl. Hist. 1224, 1291, 1274.

the ministerialists unexpectedly rallied, and were in hopes by a manœuvre to reject it ; but the debate was kept up till Shaftesbury's adherents arrived in great numbers, and it was then agreed to by a majority of 213 to 101. They did not venture to ask the Lords to concur; but the King, by the advice of the Earl of Halifax, having returned for answer, "that he doth not find the grounds in the address to be sufficient for removing the Earl of Halifax," Shaftesbury got the Commons to pass fresh resolutions, "That there is no security for the Protestant religion, the King's life, or government of this nation, without passing a bill for disabling James, Duke of York, to inherit the imperial crown of this realm ;"—"That until such a bill do pass, this House can not give any supply to his Majesty ;"—and "That George, Earl of Halifax, having advised his Majesty against such a bill, has given pernicious counsel to his Majesty, as a promoter of Popery, and is an enemy to the King and kingdom." A sudden termination to the session being now apprehended, these were soon backed by resolutions, "That whoever advised his Majesty to prorogue parliament is a betrayer of the King, the Protestant religion, and of the kingdom of England, a promoter of the French interest, and a pensioner to France ;"—"That whoever shall lend any money on the revenue arising from customs or excise, or accept or pay any tally in anticipation of the public revenue, shall be considered a hinderer of the sitting of parliament, and responsible to parliament for the same ;"—"That the city of London was burnt by the Papists, in 1666, for the introduction of Popery and arbitrary power;" and,—"That his Majesty should be addressed to restore the Duke of Monmouth to the offices of which he had been deprived by the influence of the Duke of York."

The last resolution had scarcely been put when the Black Rod knocked at the door, and commanded the Commons forthwith to attend his Majesty in the House of Lords, where a prorogation was announced, which was, in a few days, followed up by a dissolution, and a summons for a new parliament to assemble at Oxford.[1]

Shaftesbury immediately penned a petition to the King, which was signed by sixteen Peers, attributing the choice of Oxford to the counsels of wicked men, favorers of

[1] 4. Parl. Hist, 1175–1295.

Popery, promoters of French interests, and enemies to the happiness of England, as in such a place the two Houses would be deprived of freedom of debate, and exposed to the swords of the Papists who had crept into the ranks of the King's guards. Many addresses of thanks were presented to the Peers who signed it. Halifax, equally active, published a pamphlet, entitled "A Seasonable Address to both Houses of Parliament concerning the Succession, the Fears of Popery, and Arbitrary Government,"—insinuating very plainly that the two great pillars of the Protestant religion, Shaftesbury and Buckingham, had no religion at all, and broadly asserting that the former had only a few months before offered his services to the Duke of York if he might be restored to the office of Lord Chancellor.

The City of London began with returning its four former popular members by an immense majority, and instructing them to adhere to their illustrious fellow-citizen, who had proved himself the bulwark of the Protestant faith. The example was generally followed throughout the kingdom, the electors insisting on paying all the expenses of the popular candidates,—and when the elections were over, Shaftesbury found himself as strong in numbers as he had been in the last parliament,—but many members of the country party privately expressed great alarm at his violence, and to the eyes of the discerning the reaction against him had palpably begun. Unconscious of his danger, he prepared a circular form of instructions to be sent by the different constituencies to the newly-elected members, particularly pressing them to pass a bill to exclude the Duke of York and all Popish successors from the Crown—to insist on an adjustment of the King's prerogative of calling, proroguing, and dissolving parliaments,—to restore the liberty enjoyed by their forefathers of being free from guards and mercenary soldiers—and to refuse all supplies till the nation was secure from Popery and arbitrary power.[1]

The King was emboldened by a secret treaty with France, by which he was to receive a subsidy of 2,000,000 of livres for the current year, and 500,000 crowns for the two following years—in consideration of which he was to withdraw himself from Spain, and to abet the scheme of

[1] This paper, in Shaftesbury's handwriting, is still extant

Louis for the conquest of the Netherlands. He then proceeded to Oxford, escorted by his horse guards. Shaftesbury, the representatives of London, and the popular leaders followed, armed, and attended by a numerous band of armed men wearing round their hats a ribbon, with the inscription " No Popery! No Slavery!" Oxford had the appearance of the place of meeting of a Polish diet. During the rapid week which the parliament was allowed to sit, Shaftesbury played his part with all his wonted energy,—though not with his wonted discretion.

He opened the business in the House of Lords by denouncing a most irregular proceeding on the last day of the last parliament. Both Houses had passed "a Bill for repealing the 35th of Elizabeth against Protestant Dissenters who do not attend public worship on Sundays in their parish church." This was disagreeable to the King, who wished to keep them dependent on his dispensing power, and to prevent them from being in a better situation than the Roman Catholics, and yet did not like to incur the odium of openly rejecting it by his veto. He therefore directed the clerk privately to remove it from the table of the House of Lords, and the prorogation took place without any notice being taken of it. Shaftesbury now affecting to lay the blame upon the officers, pointed out the gross impropriety of the manner in which the bill had been unconstitutionally got rid of; and the ministers could not refuse him the committee he moved for to inquire into the affair, although they were aware that if the committee ever sat, the truth must come out. They succeeded in getting the meeting of the committee deferred to a distant day,—before which the parliament was dissolved. In the mean time he introduced another bill, in the same terms, to repeal the 35th of Elizabeth, to which they did not venture to offer any opposition.

But the two grand measures on which the fate of this parliament turned, were " the Exclusion Bill" and "the impeachment of Fitzharris." The King in his speech had declared his willingness to assent to any expedient by which, in the event of a Catholic Prince succeeding to the throne, the administration of government might be retained in the hands of Protestants, but said he would never depart from his resolution of keeping the succession unbroken. Halifax immediately laid before the House the details of this plan,—by which the Duke of York was to be banished 500 miles from the British dominions during his life; on the demise of the crown he was to assume the title of King, but all the powers of government were to be transferred to a Regent, to be exercised in the name of the absent Sovereign; the regency to belong, in the first instance, to the Princess of Orange, after her to the Lady Anne, and if James should have a legitimate son educated a Protestant, to continue during the minority of such son and no longer. If Shaftesbury had acted wisely, he would have closed with this proposal, which was only made in the belief that it would be rejected; but, betrayed into an overweening confidence of victory, he undertook to compel the King to assent to the measure on which he staked all,—total exclusion. He gave the very insufficient reason, that as, according to the doctrine of the lawyers, the descent of the Crown takes away all disabilities from the next heir on whom it descends, James becoming King would claim an indefeasible right to the Sovereign authority, unimpaired by statute;—not observing that the same futile argument might be applied with equal force against his own favorite Exclusion Bill. This, after a two days' debate, was again ordered to be introduced in the House of Commons, and was read a first time by a great majority; but the public began more strongly to take part with the King, and to apprehend a civil war from an attempt to put Monmouth on the throne,—which now appeared to be the object of the total exclusion of the Duke of York,—rather than a regard for religion or liberty.

Shaftesbury fell into a still graver error by his unconstitutional attempt to try a commoner on a capital offense before the House of Peers. There had been a great struggle between the two parties, which of them should have as a tool a miscreant of the name of Fitzharris, who was ready to accuse himself and others of any atrocities to suit the purposes of those who should pay him best. He was to have been brought by Shaftesbury to Oxford to make some terrific discoveries in support of the Popish plot, and it was thought a masterly stroke on the part of the King to shut him up in the Tower, and to order the Attorney General to proceed against him for high treason in the

Court of King's Bench. But Shaftesbury ingeniously devised a scheme by which he might completely recover his control over his creature. A motion was made and carried in the Commons for impeaching Fitzharris before the Lords for high treason,—with a view to supersede the King's prosecution, and enable the exclusionists to turn him to what use they pleased. In the wantonness of triumph the victorious party ordered that Sir Leoline Jenkins, the Secretary of State, who had signed the warrants for his committal to the Tower, should carry up the impeachment, and this grave functionary was obliged, however reluctantly, to obey,—that he might escape imprisonment and expulsion. The objection was immediately started in the Lords, that the accused, being a commoner, he could not be tried for his life by them who were not his peers.

Shaftesbury, forgetting Charles I.'s prosecution for high treason before the Lords of the five members of the House of Commons,—which had been so much condemned and which had cost him so dear,—rashly and obstinately contended that the Commons had in all ages justly exercised the right of impeachment against all subjects for all offenses;—that impeachment being at the suit of the people what an indictment is at the suit of the King, and the House of Lords being the only Court in which the people can sue, to reject the impeachment would be a denial of justice; and that although Magna Charta says a man is to be tried by his peers, it adds, "or by the law of the land," referring no doubt to parliamentary impeachment, which knows no distinction, as far as jurisdiction is concerned, between misdemeanor, felony, and treason.

On the other side, the Lord Chancellor argued irresistibly, that whatever instances there might be to the contrary, in times of confusion and violence, a commoner was as little liable to be tried for his life by the House of Peers as a Peer by a petty jury, and he produced from the rolls of parliament (what had great weight) an "accord" made before Edward III. in full parliament, stating "that the judgment for high treason given by the Lords against the murderers of Edward II. should never be drawn into a precedent whereby they might be called upon to judge any other than Peers." The House resolved that Fitzharris should be proceeded with according to the course of the common law and not by way of impeachment.

Shaftesbury could only get nineteen other Peers to join him in opposing this resolution in the Lords but the Commons in a flame immediately voted for him almost unanimously, " that it amounted to a denial of justice, a violation of the constitution of parliament, and an obstruction to the further discovery of the Popish plot; and that if any inferior Court should proceed to the trial of Fitzharris, it would be guilty of a high breach of the privileges of the House of Commons."[1]

It so happened that these resolutions were passed on Saturday, the 26th of March, the same day that there was a vote in favor of the Exclusion Bill. Charles thereupon formed his determination forthwith to dissolve the parliament, but he kept it a profound secret till the very mo-

---

[1] Mr. Hallam, a most respectable authority on all constitutional questions, has condemned this resolution of the Lords, contending that a commoner may be lawfully impeached before the Lords for a capital offense (*Const. Hist.* ii. 603); but I adhere to the opinion of those great lawyers, Hale (*Jurisdiction of House of Lords*, c. xiv.) and Blackstone (*Com.* iv. c. 19), who lay down the contrary doctrine in the most explicit terms. 1. The provision of Magna Charta " nec super eum ibimus nisi per legale judicium parium suorum," which is a statutory declaration of the common law, I think embraces every mode of prosecution. 2. De Beresford's case (4 Ed. 3), in which the Lords with one voice said that he was not their peer, and that they were not bound to judge him as a peer of the land, is conclusive to show the state of the law at that time, even if the proviso were not an act of parliament, which, being " in full parliament," it seems to be. 3. Parliamentary impeachments were of more recent origin, and could not justly deprive English commoners of their birthright. 4. The instances of impeachments of commoners for high treason are very irregular, and more resemble acts of attainder than judicial proceedings. 5. The waiver of the objection in such instances amounts to little. The five members prosecuted for high treason by the Attorney General before the Lords, allowed to be improperly prosecuted, did not plead to the jurisdiction more than Scroggs when impeached by the Commons. 6. The liability of a commoner to be impeached for a *misdemeanor* does not break in upon the rule,—which has always been confined to capital cases. Thus for a misdemeanor, a Peer may be tried before a jury, as a commoner may before the Peers. 7. The resolution of the House of Lords to proceed against Sir Adam Blair and others, in 1690, after the opinion of the Judges that the record of 4 Ed. 3 was a statute, is entitled to no weight, as there never was any intention to do more than to frighten the defendants for publishing a libel; and the understanding in the profession ever since has been that a commoner can not be tried for his life by the House of Lords. For a century and a half there has been no such proceeding, and although Lord Nottingham's position is said to be "dangerous and unfounded," such a proceeding we may venture to say will never again be attempted.—See *St. Tr.* viii. 223, xii. 1207. *Hat. Prec.* iv. 50. *Pamphlet* by Sir W. Jones, 1681.

ment of its execution. The Commons having complained of the inconvenience of the Convocation house where they met, the public theater was fitted up for them, and during this day the King repeatedly came to the spot, and himself gave directions as to the most convenient manner of carrying on the works. During the Sunday he made "the wonderful accommodation he was providing for his faithful Commons," the frequent subject of his discourse, —and everything indicated a protracted session. On the Monday morning the King came to the House of Lords, as he was wont, in a sedan chair, the crown being secretly carried between his feet. Another chair followed with the curtains drawn, supposed to contain the Lord in waiting. The lid being raised it was found stuffed with the King's robes. But here a formidable difficulty arose, for they were found to be by mistake the robes of the order of the Garter. So the chair was sent back again for the parliamentary robes and a member of the House of Lords, who wished to escape from the room to tell what he had seen, was locked up till the chair returned. The King having instantly thrown the proper robes over him, and taken his seat on the throne in the House of Lords, the Black Rod was sent for the Commons, and found them listening in a very careless manner to some tedious remarks of Sir William Jones, an old lawyer, on the Lord Chancellor's "Accord, temp. Ed. III." Going up to the bar of the House of Lords, there they saw the King with the Crown on his head, and heard him say, "My Lords and Gentlemen,—all the world may see we are not like to have a good end when the divisions at the beginning are such. Therefore, my Lord Chancellor, do as I have commanded you." *Lord Chancellor.*—"My Lords and Gentlemen, his Majesty has commanded me to say that it is his Majesty's royal will and pleasure that this parliament be dissolved, and this parliament is accordingly dissolved."[1]

Charles instantly stepped into his carriage and set off at full speed for Windsor. Shaftesbury, when he had recovered his breath, talked of sitting for the dispatch of business in spite of the dissolution, called on his friends not to separate, and sent several messengers to the Commons, entreating them to wait, as the Lords were still

[1] 4 Parl. Hist. 1339. Examen, 104.

sitting. But the members of the popular party in both Houses gradually withdrew; Shaftesbury, almost deserted, went out into the streets, where he saw a general dispersion; in a few hours he found Oxford in its wonted state of torpidity, and, by way of relief to his troubled thoughts, he himself hurried off for London."[1]

CHAPTER XC.

CONCLUSION OF THE LIFE OF LORD SHAFTESBURY.

FOR some time after his arrival in London, Shaftesbury flattered himself that the dissolution of the parliament at Oxford, like former violent dissolutions, would aggravate the public discontent; but the victory of his opponents was complete, and Charles was enabled from henceforth for the rest of his reign to rule by prerogative,—to carry into execution all his plans— and, though the victim he most panted for escaped him, to execute a bloody revenge upon others who had incurred his resentment.

There remained a most formidable popular party, and it was fortunate for the King that neither pecuniary difficulties nor the state of public affairs imposed upon him such a necessity for calling a parliament as, forty years before had been felt by his father on the Scottish invasion; but there can be no doubt that there was now a considerable reaction in his favor, which arose partly from the general fickleness of the public mind, partly from Shaftesbury's dangerous character and designs being more clearly developed, partly from the proffered concessions to guard against a Popish succession; but, above all, from the discredit into which the Popish plot had fallen, and the desire of mankind to blame others for their own credulity and folly.

Shaftesbury entrenched himself in the city of London, but saw that he would soon be assailed there. The government began the celebration of their triumph with the

[1] He had been lodged in Baliol College, to which he presented a magnificent piece of plate as a mark of his gratitude. *Rawleigh Redivivus*, Part II. 101.

conviction and execution of Fitzharris, in spite of the resolution of the House of Commons, that, after their impeachment of him, his trial by the course of the common law would be a high breach of their privileges.[1] Still more alarming was the fate of COLLEGE, "the Protestant Joiner," who, after a bill of indictment against him had been thrown out by a Middlesex grand jury, was carried down into Oxfordshire, under pretense that he had been guilty of an overt act of treason in that county, by going armed to the parliament,—and was there found guilty and put to death,—although nothing was satisfactorily proved against him, except that he was a turbulent demagogue, who had gained great distinction by bawling out "No Popery."[2]

Soon the eyes of England and of all Europe were turned to the fate of the man who had so long held a divided sway with his Sovereign, and by whose destruction it was hoped that all further opposition to the plans of the Court would for ever cease. Early in the morning of the 2nd of July, 1681, under a warrant from the Secretary of State, the Earl of Shaftesbury was apprehended at Thanet House, in Aldersgate Street, on a charge of high treason, his papers were seized, and he was carried, under a military escort, to be examined before the Council at Whitehall. Arriving there, he found the Council assembled, and the King had the bad taste to be present, having come from Windsor that morning for the pleasure of seeing his old friend and arch enemy in custody on a capital charge.

Certain depositions were read against him, made by Irish witnesses, who were to have been examined against the Duke of York and the Queen, and who, accusing Shaftesbury of having suborned them, swore that he had entered into a conspiracy with them, in case he should be worsted in the parliament, at Oxford, to carry his measures by an open insurrection, and that he had used many violent and threatening expressions against the King. The prisoner treated this charge with the utmost scorn, desiring to be confronted with the witnesses; and observing that, if he really could treat of such matters with such persons, he was fitter for Bedlam than the Tower. Among his papers was found the draft of an association

[1] 3 St. Tr. 243.   [2] Ibid. 549.

rather of a dangerous nature; but it was not in his handwriting, and there was nothing to show that he had ever perused it. Upon such evidence he could not be fairly convicted; but, in the hope of the case being strengthened, or of a partial tribunal, he was committed to take his trial. In James's Memoirs[1] it is said, that his boldness forsook him when the warrant for his commitment was signed, and that the very rabble hooted him on his way to the Tower. Martyn asserts, with much more probability, that he remained undaunted; that, as he was conducted to prison, he was saluted by vast multitudes with wishes and prayers for his prosperity; and that one among the rest having cried out, "God bless your Lordship! and deliver you from your enemies," he replied, with a smile, "I thank you, sir, but I have nothing to fear: they have much, therefore pray God to deliver them from me." A few days after, one of the Popish Lords, whom he had been instrumental in sending to the Tower, affecting great surprise to find him among them, he coolly answered, "that he had been lately indisposed with an ague, and was come to take some *Jesuits' powder*."[2]

It seems certain, however, that while in the Tower, he offered to expatriate himself, and to spend the remainder of his days in Carolina, a colony which he had assisted to settle, and where he had property,[3] but the King declared "*he should be tried by his Peers.*"

The difficulty of the government was to get a bill of indictment found against him by a grand jury. Parliament not sitting, and there being a determination that a parliament should never sit again, this was the only mode of commencing the prosecution. But the first step being gained, all the rest of the process would have been most easy, for the indictment being removed before the Court of the Lord High Steward, consisting of Peers selected by the King—his subsequent trial would have been mere matter of form—as much as after sentence the warrant to behead him.

All regard to truth and justice being set aside, the clever course would have been for the witnesses to have

---

[1] Vol. i. 713.
[2] Life, by Martyn, ii. 288. Life and Death of Earl of Shaftesbury, published immediately after his death.—*Harl. Misc.*
[3] The aristocratic constitution for this colony was drawn up at his request by Mr. Locke.—*Locke's Works*, x. 175.

sworn to an overt act of treason in some county where there was a manageable grand jury; but they had not been properly drilled upon this point, and they represented all the treasonable consults to have taken place in Thanet House, in the City of London. By a London grand jury alone, therefore, could the bill of indictment be found; and London was still in the power of the old liberal corporation. The grand jury was to be summoned by the Sheriffs, and the Sheriffs were Whigs. There were Old Bailey Sessions held on the 7th of July, at which regularly the indictment ought to have been preferred; but the Attorney General waited in the hope of better Sheriffs. Shute and Pilkington, the next couple, were " Whigs and something more."

The trial being delayed, Shaftesbury repeatedly applied, by counsel, at the Old Bailey and Hicks's Hall, that, according to his own HABEAS CORPUS ACT, he might be bailed; but on the suggestion that the Tower was not under the jurisdiction of the Court, and other frivolous excuses, the application, to which he was clearly entitled, was refused. He prepared an indictment against the Justice who had taken the depositions on which he was committed, and against several of the witnesses for a conspiracy to convict him by perjury; but Pemberton, and the other Judges who wished to please the King, would not suffer the indictment to be submitted to a grand jury.

In the mean time, every exertion was made to poison the public mind, and to prejudice against the accused those who were to decide upon his fate. Innumerable pamphlets issued from the press, denouncing him as " the great agitator, without whose baleful presence all resistance to sound principles in church and state would be at an end." The pulpits rang with the dangers to true religion from the non-conformist, and he was reviled by name as "the Apostle of Schism." The Catholics very excusably joined loudly in the cry against him, and called him " the Man of Sin." Political vituperators branded him as " Mephistophiles," " the Fiend," and " Alderman *Shift*sbury." For the purpose of lowering his reputation, a story was revived of his having boasted that he might have been King of Poland when John Sobieski was elected; and a whimsical Narrative was published, giving an account of his election, under the name of " Count

Tapsky," which, in one sense, applied to an operation performed on his side, in consequence of the abscess formed there from his wound, and in another to his towering genius, leading him to penetrate the firmament and to touch the stars. But the grand engine which the Court hoped would turn the full flood of public indignation against him was the poetry of Dryden. On the 17th of November, 1681, exactly one week before the bill of indictment was to be prepared against him at the Old Bailey, came out "ABSALOM AND ACHITOPHEL,"[1] the most lively, the most entertaining, the most poetical, the most captivating personal satire ever written. It had the greatest sale of any publication issuing from the press in England down to the end of the reign of Queen Anne, except the sermon for which Dr. Sacheverell was impeached.[2] In a few months it had gone through seven large editions, and in a few hours the character of Achitophel was in the mouth of every one. Shadwell and Settle published answers, but of very inferior merit. High hopes were expressed that the witnesses would gain credit with the grand jury against a man so degraded; but such reasoners knew little of faction; for the more Shaftesbury was assailed, the more resolutely did his admirers adhere to him, and they now regarded him with respect, affection, and tenderness, as a martyr in their cause.

The 24th of November was the critical day, and when it dawned there seemed a strong probability to many that the STATE TRIALS would be ornamented with "an account of the conviction of Anthony, Earl of Shaftesbury, for high treason, and of his gallant behavior on the scaffold." The two Chief Justices, Pemberton and North, presided at the Old Bailey, both devoted tools of the government. The former charged the Grand Jury, and, instead of tell-

[1] Although Dryden has the merit of the ingenious parallel between Jewish and English history, he was not the first to fix the name on Shaftesbury. On the 9th of July, 1681, exactly a week after his arrest,—came out a doggerel poem against him, entitled, "The Badger in the Fox-trap," containing these lines:—

"Besides, my titles are as numerous,
As all my actions various, still, and humorous;
Some call me Tory, some ACHITOPHEL,
Some Jack-a-Dandy, some old Machiavel;
Some call me devil, some his foster-brother,
And turn-coat, rebel, all the nation over."

[2] On the authority of Dr. Johnson's father, who was a bookseller.—See *Life of Dryden*, in the "Lives of the Poets."

ing them "that though the proceeding was *ex parte*, and not conclusive, a case must be made out against the prisoner, which, if not answered, would be sufficient to convict him of high treason," said, "That which is referred to you is, to consider whether, upon the evidence given to you, there be any reason or ground for the King to call this person to an account. You are not to judge the person; for the honor of the King and the decency of the matter it is not thought fit by the law that persons should be accused and indicted where there is no color or ground for it; where there is no kind of suspicion of a crime, nor reason to believe that the thing can be proved, it is not for the King's honor to call men to an account; therefore, you are to inquire whether what you hear be any cause or reason for the King to put the party to answer it." The cunning Judge knew well that "BILLA VERA" would have been Shaftesbury's death warrant.

The Attorney General made the extraordinary application that the witnesses for the Crown might be examined in open Court—so that the Grand Jury might be overawed by the authority of the Judges.

The foreman suggested, that it had been the constant rule from all time for Grand Juries to examine the witnesses privately in their own chamber; and, to show the secrecy of this preliminary inquiry, he quoted the words of the Grand Juror's oath,—"the King's counsel, your fellows', and your own you shall keep secret,"—which could not apply to a proceeding before all the world. But C. J. North ruled that the King might dispense with this secrecy, and that the application could not be refused.

The indictment was upon the 25th of Edward III. "for compassing and imagining the death of the King,"—and the overt acts were designing to raise an insurrection at Oxford,—asserting "that the King was a man of no faith, and deserved to be deposed like Richard II.," and declaring "that he, the Earl of Shaftesbury, would make England into a Commonwealth like Holland." Notwithstanding all the pains that had been taken for four months, the case was not stronger than at the time of commitment; and the witnesses, telling a most improbable story, contradicted each other and themselves, although the Judges interposed from time with friendly questions, and tried to keep them in countenance.

The evidence being closed Pemberton said—" You are to inquire whether it be fitting for the King to call my Lord Shaftesbury to question upon this account of treasonable words." *North*, C. J.—" Gentlemen, I hope you will consider your oaths, and give all things their due weight."

The Grand Jury were then allowed to retire, carrying the indictment along with them. They soon returned, and quietly handed it to the Court. Never before or since, on the decision of a Grand Jury, did so much depend, or was there such breathless anxiety. When the officer, looking on the back of the indictment, read aloud the word "IGNORAMUS," a shout arose which lasted above an hour; and, before it concluded, there were bonfires and illuminations in every street in the metropolis.

The messenger who carried the news of the *Ignoramus* to the Tower found Shaftesbury playing a game at piquet with his Countess,—which he calmly continued,—the cards having probably been provided by design for the occasion, like Richard's prayer-book at Crosby House when he expected the offer of the Crown. King Charles being told the cause of the rejoicings, he said, without any art, " It is a hard case that I am the last man to have law and justice in the whole nation." [1]

The event was celebrated by a MEDAL, bearing the bust of Shaftesbury, and the inscription, "ANTONIO COMITI DE SHAFTESBURY;" on the reverse, the sun bursting through a cloud over the city and Tower of London, with the date, 24th of November, 1681, and the motto, " LÆTAMUR."

This gave rise to Dryden's famous poem of "THE MEDAL," said to have been suggested by the King himself, who, walking with him one day soon after in the Mall, said, " If I were a poet (and I think I am poor enough to be one), I would write a poem on Lord Shaftesbury's escape from justice in the following manner," and then gave him the plan of it. Dryden took the hint, carried the poem, as soon as it was written, to the King, and had a present of a hundred broad pieces for it. It was published in March, 1682. The satire is, if possible, more cutting than anything in "' Absalom and Achitophel." This is the description of Shaftesbury's ministerial career:

[1] 8 St. Tr. 759.

> "Behold him now exalted into trust
> His counsels oft convenient, never just;
> E'en in the most sincere advice he gave,
> He had a grudging still to be a knave:
> At least as little honest as he could,
> And, like white witches, mischievously good.
> To his first bias longingly he leans,
> And rather would be great by wicked means."

Such a withering prophecy as the following was enough to bring on the decrepitude it portrays:

> "If true succession from our isle should fail,
> And crowds profane with impious arts prevail,
> Not thou, not those thy factious arms engage,
> Shall reap that harvest of rebellious rage,
> With which thou flatterest thy decrepit age."

But the poem brought the actual "*Medal*" into greater vogue, and the whole Whig party wore it depending by a ribbon from their button-hole, to show their numbers and their spirit.

Charles was so delighted with the manner in which Dryden avenged him upon Shaftesbury, that he pressed for a second part of "Absalom and Achitophel." This task the great poet turned over to Nahum Tate, contributing the 200 admirable lines beginning—

> "Next these a troop of busy spirits press,
> Of little fortunes, and of conscience less;
> Shall that false Hebronite escape our curse,
> Judas that keeps the rebels' pension purse,
> Judas that pays the treason writer's fee,
> Judas who well deserves his namesake's tree?"

This poem did not appear till November, 1682, and had small success, but was little wanted; for by this time the King had got a Lord Mayor and Sheriffs of his own in the city, while Shaftesbury, rapidly declining in reputation and in influence, had ceased to be formidable to his enemies, and from the extravagant notions which had taken possession of his diseased mind, was looked upon by his friends with compassion, distrust, and alarm.

Immediately after the indictment had been *ignored*, the noble prisoner moved for his discharge; but he was illegally detained in custody in the Tower till the end of the following Hilary term. He then resumed his residence in Thanet House, taking special care not to go beyond the limits of the city of London and county of Middlesex.

He instituted a prosecution against the principal witnesses who had conspired maliciously to prosecute him for high treason. The indictment being found at the Old Bailey, it was removed by *certiorari* into the Court of King's Bench, and the Judges granted a rule to show cause why it should not be tried in another county. He showed cause in person, and offered to try it in Middlesex. The Court insisted on a more distant county. He declared that he abandoned the prosecution, as in every other county, since the dissolution of the Oxford Parliament, passive-obedience sheriffs and magistrates had been appointed, to the exclusion of all fair men, and no justice could be obtained.

In the course of a few months he had the mortification to find, that London and Middlesex were as much enslaved and as unsafe as any part of the kingdom.[1] By recurring to an obsolete custom of appointing one Sheriff in the City by the Lord Mayor drinking his health, and by the expedient of holding an illegal poll, Sir Dudley North and Rich, the passive-obedience candidates, got possession of the office of Sheriffs of London and Middlesex, instead of Papillon and Dubois, liberals, who were duly elected; and though, at the election of Lord Mayor, Gould, the liberal candidate, had a large majority of lawful votes,— by a partial scrutiny, Pritchard, his passive-resistance competitor, was placed in the civic chair.

Now were vigorously prosecuted the proceedings in the Court of King's Bench for disfranchising the city of London, and other municipal corporations,—and the plan of destroying all free institutions in England, and establishing arbitrary rule, was openly avowed and very generally encouraged.

Shaftesbury in despair for the State, and knowing that he was himself still marked out for vengeance, began to contemplate a most criminal enterprise. There had as yet been no misrule but what might be corrected by constitutional means and by the returning good sense of the public; and at any rate, the strength of the government was so great that resistance could only involve those who

[1] The unlearned reader should be informed, that the office of Sheriff of Middlesex, by a very ancient grant, belongs to the city of London, and is exercised by the two individuals who are elected Sheriffs of London, and who thus have the power of returning juries for the county as well as for the city.

attempted it in ruin, and defer the hope of redress. Yet Shaftesbury was for an immediate insurrection,—professing that he would respect the monarchy and the person of the King, but that he would forcibly set aside the Duke of York as successor to the crown and get rid of evil counselors. He flattered himself that he had the City at his command, and that his "brisk boys" suddenly rising and putting him in possession of this citadel, the rest of the kingdom would by a general effort throw off the galling yoke now imposed upon it. He solicited Lord Russell, Sydney, and the other Whig leaders to join him. They had various conferences with him, in which they agreed in reprobating the arbitrary policy of the government, and even deliberated with him on the necessity and the possibility of saving the constitution by force; but they positively refused to join in an instant rising, and by way of tranquilizing him, strongly pressed for delay, till his plans should be better matured, and the times should be more propitious. Even the rash Monmouth cautioned him to be more prudent. It is said that Shaftesbury's mind was now greatly enfeebled by bodily suffering, and that his temper, formerly cheerful, equal, and bland, had become morose, irritable, and gloomy. At times, his former gayety of heart broke forth. He declared to his friends, "That he would lead the army himself;" and jesting on his infirmities he said, "They must be convinced he could not run away, and they should see he knew better how to die fighting for their liberties than on a scaffold,—the only alternative that remained for him." They were in hourly apprehension of his engaging in some mad enterprise which would involve the whole party in destruction.

Having information, in the beginning of November, that there was an intention to arrest him, he settled his estate so that it should, in any event be secure to his family; and, leaving Thanet House, he lay concealed among his intimates in different parts of the city, always shifting his quarters and putting on different disguises. At last, being told by his friend, Lord Mordaunt, of a suspicious conference in the apartments of the Duchess of Portsmouth, of which he was supposed to be the subject, he said, "My Lord, you are a young man of honor, and would not deceive me: if this has happened, I must be gone to-night." Accordingly he immediately left the house in which he was concealed, and in a few hours it was searched by the King's messengers.

The following night, having tenderly taken leave of his Countess and his friends, he quitted London, and, dressed in the habit of a Presbyterian minister, he traveled to Harwich, that he might embark from thence for the Continent. There he was detained eight or ten days by contrary winds. During this time he remained at an obscure inn with a handsome young friend of the name of Wheelock, who was likewise disguised under a black peruke, and passed as his nephew. It so happened, that one day the maid of the house came suddenly into the room of this youth, and, to her surprise and admiration, saw him with a fine light head of hair. She instantly told her mistress, who acquainted the Presbyterian minister and his nephew of the maid's discovery. "As to herself," she said, "she did not know, nor desire to know, who they were, and that they might depend upon her silence, but she could not be sure of her maid's, and therefore advised them to leave the house and town directly." Shaftesbury, thanking her for her information, declared that "he should have no apprehension from one who had such a sense of honor. As for the maid," said he, turning with a pleasant air to Wheelock, "you must go and make love to her, and this will secure her secrecy."

One of his servants, whom he dressed up in a similar disguise to his own, was stopped and taken into custody,—which facilitated the master's escape. Changing his habiliments, he got off in an open boat, and after a tempestuous and perilous voyage, arrived at Amsterdam.

He was afraid of being reclaimed by the English government, and sent over as a criminal, of which there had been several instances during these revolutionary times. But acting with his usual assurance, and confiding in the forgiveness of political injuries when circumstances are changed, he immediately petitioned to be admitted into the magistracy,—and his prayer was complied with by the Capital of the United Provinces in the following form:—"Carthago, non adhuc deleta, Comitem de Shaftesbury in gremio suo recipere vult."[1]

[1] Bibliothèque Choisie, vi. 367. "C'est un honneur," says Le Clerc,

He took a large house, in which he was beginning to live very elegantly, out of compliment to his adopted country. The principal men of the city waited upon him, saying, he had at present no enemies but such as were theirs, and the municipality of Amsterdam ornamented their public hall with a portrait of their new fellow-citizen.

In the midst of the fetes he was giving and receiving as a Dutchman, he was seized with a violent fit of his old distemper, the gout. It seemed to yield to the prescibed remedies, and he thought he should soon recover, when it suddenly flew to his stomach and proved fatal. He expired in the arms of his faithful companion, Wheelock, on the 21st of January, 1683, in the 62nd year of his age.

Their High Mightinesses, the Lords of the States, showed all respect for his memory by putting themselves into mourning, and ordering that his corpse and effects should be exempt from all toll, fees, and customs, in every place they should be carried through in order to their passage to England. A vessel hung with black, and adorned with streamers and scutcheons, conveyed the body to Poole in Dorsetshire; and on its arrival there the principal gentlemen of the county, forgetting past animosities, and for the time recollecting only what was praiseworthy in their distinguished countryman, attended his funeral to Wimborne St. Giles, where he was honorably interred.

In the year 1732, the fourth Earl erected in the church there a splendid monument to him, with an inscription, which, after his genealogy and his offices, thus records his services to the King, the country, liberty, and Protestantism :—

> " Et principi et populo fidus, per varias rerum vicissitudines
> Saluti publicæ invigilavit ; Regnum Anarchiâ penitus obrutum
> Restituit, stabilivit. Cùm vero despotici imperii fautores,

---

"pour la ville d'Amsterdam d'avoir reçu et d'avoir protégé un si illustre réfugié, sans avoir égard aux sinistres impressions qu'on avoit voulu donner de lui, a cause d'un discours qu'il avoit prononcé comme Chancellier dans le parlement 1672. Les descendans de ce Seigneur en conservent une mémoire pleine de reconnoissance, comme M. le Comte, son petit fils, me l's témoigne plus d'une fois." From the view I have felt myself obliged to take of some parts of Lord Shaftesbury's character and conduct, I have not felt myself at liberty to ask for access to the family archives, but there seems no reason to suppose that they would afford any contradiction to these statements.

> Servum pecus, et Roma, scelerum artifex, patriæ intentarent ruinam,
> Civilis et Ecclesiasticæ libertatis Assertor extitit
> Indefessus, Conservator strenuus. Humanitate, in patriam amore,
> Ingenii acumine, probitate, facundia, fortitudine, fide,
> Cæterisque eximiis animi dotibus, nullum habuit superiorem.
> Vitæ, publicis commodis impensæ, memoriam et laudes,
> Stante libertate, nunquam abolebit Tempus edax, nec edacior Invidia."

But the impartial historian can not concur in this eulogy. We readily allow that Shaftesbury not only had splendid talents and an energy of mind almost unparalleled, but that he had very valuable qualities calculated to secure attachment and respect both in private and in public life. He was a high-bred gentleman, and strictly observed all the conventional rules of honor. In an age of great pecuniary corruption he never took bribes from individuals at home or from foreign governments. Although frequently changing his party, he had the address to gain the confidence of his new associates without incurring the personal ill-will of those whom he left. The satire of Hudibras is unjust upon his betraying the different administrations to to which he had belonged :

> " Was for them and against them all,
> But barbarous when they came to fall ;
> For my trepanning th' old to ruin,
> He made his interest with the new one."

Yet the attempts of his apologists to show that he was through life the consistent friend of liberty and toleration, with the exception of being carried rather too far by his zeal for the reformed faith, rest upon a total perversion of facts and a confusion of the distinctions between right and wrong. He began by supporting the worst abuses of the reign of Charles I. which had prevailed under his father-in-law, Lord Keeper Coventry ; and when he went over to the parliament he was distinguished by his democratic fervor and his antipathy to the royal family. He then eagerly joined those who were for restoring Charles II. without condition or any security for the constitution ; and as long as he shared in exercising the power of the prerogative, he eagerly assisted in extending it, and would have been pleased to see the King of England as absolute as the King of France. His love for the natural rights of mankind and for the Protestant religion he testified by his exclamation, " Delenda est Carthago," and his accession to Clifford's treaty, by which Popery was to be established in England. Although he did not himself take bribes, he knew that the King and his colleagues were the pensioners of Louis, and he countenanced a policy by which England would have been degraded into a province of that kingdom which she has conquered, and of which she ought ever at least to be the rival and the equal.

I must likewise enumerate among his faults his grasping the office of Chancellor, for which, if he was a man of sense, he must have known that he was wholly incompetent. To gratify his ambition, or vanity, or caprice, he turned a court of justice into a lottery office,—sporting with the property and the dearest interests of his fellow-subjects.

When he went over to the popular side, he was of great service in opposing unconstitutional measures, such as "the Test for establishing passive obedience." His "Exclusion Bill" was a glorious effort, and he did accomplish the grand safeguard for personal liberty,—for which we must be for ever grateful to him. But for his own crooked purposes, he inflamed religious animosity to a pitch of fury wholly unexampled in England, he patronized the monstrous fictions and murders of the Popish plot, and he passed the Catholic Disqualification Bill, the bitter fruits of which our children will taste. When by the extreme violence of his machinations he had alarmed the friends of constitutional government, and given an ascendency to the arbitrary principles adopted by the Court, he planned an insurrection, which, if attempted according to his eager wishes, could only have terminated in the utter ruin of the liberal party, and the permanent establishment of despotism. The final result of his excesses and vagaries was, that he lost influence with all parties, and that his death in exile caused little grief to his friends or exultation to his enemies.

His great passion was for intense political excitement; and he was never so happy as in the crisis of some bold enterprise in which he hazarded his own safety and that of the state.

From the specimens of his oratory which have come down to us, he appears to have been the first man in this country whom we can designate a great parliamentary debater. Compare his dexterous appeals to party feeling, his cutting personalities, and his epigrammatic turns, to the eternal divisions and subdivisions of Pym, or the mixed pedantry and cant of the other leaders on either side in the Long Parliament. Halifax, formed on his model, if more refined, was less impressive, and till the elder Pitt arose, he probably was not excelled for eloquence in the English senate.

As to his literary merits, he was infinitely inferior to Bolingbroke; and I must agree with Horace Walpole, "that he was rather a copious writer for faction, than an author, and that he wrote nothing which he could wish to be remembered." As the occasion required, he threw off a pamphlet containing some burning words, but reckless as to facts, sentiments, and even style.

We have deeply to regret the loss of his autobiography, which he intrusted to Mr. Locke, and which was burnt in the panic occasioned by the execution of Algernon Sydney for having in his possession a speculative treatise upon government. The philosopher has by no means made atonement for his timidity by his "Memoirs relating to the Life of Anthony, first Earl of Shaftesbury,"—an extremely jejune and perfunctory performance. Indeed, it is difficult to conceive how any one of common intelligence, who had been long in habits of familiar intercourse with such an eminent and interesting personage, should have professed to give any account of him without communicating more to instruct or amuse the reader.[1]

Shaftesbury seems to have been a most delightful companion, and the following anecdote is handed down to us to show his tact in society. While yet a young man, he was invited to dine with Sir John Denham, an aged widower (as was supposed), at Chelsea, who, when the guests had assembled, said to them that he had made choice of the company on account of their known abilities and particular friendship to him, for their advice in a matter of the greatest moment to him. He had been, he said, a widower for many years, and began to want somebody that might ease him of the trouble of housekeeping, and take some care of him under the growing infirmities of old age; and to that purpose had pitched upon a

[1] Doubts have been entertained whether this sketch be by Locke; but I can not doubt the fact, although there is a copy of it among Locke's papers in the possession of Lord Lovelace not in Locke's handwriting.

woman well known to him by the experience of many years, in fine, his housekeeper. A gentlemen present, to dissuade him from this step, out of regard to his grown-up children, was beginning a very unflattering description of the object of his choice—when Shaftesbury begged permission to interrupt the debate by a question to their host—"whether he was not already married to her?" Sir John, after a little demur, answered, "Yes, truly, I was married to her yesterday." "Well, then," exclaimed Sir Anthony Ashley Cooper, "there is no more need of our advice; pray let us have the honor to see my lady and wish her joy, and so to dinner." He afterwards said privately, in returning home, to the gentleman whose speech he had cut short, "The man and the manner gave me a suspicion that having done a foolish thing, he was desirous to cover himself with the authority of our advice. I thought it good to be sure before you went any further and you see what came of it."[1] Another instance of his sagacity was his discovery of Miss Hyde's marriage to the Duke of York, long before it was made public, from the deference with which she was treated by her mother.[2]

He lived in great splendor, and entertained the King sumptuously at Wimborne St. Giles. Like his principles, he changed his style of cookery. In 1669, when there was a coolness with the French court, he received a visit from Cosmo de' Medici, Duke of Tuscany. Regulating his table entirely in the English manner, he declared that "he was neither an admirer of the French taste nor friend to French interests, while some with the servile maxims of that country had imbibed its luxury. Others might treat him like a Frenchman; his desire was to entertain him like an Englishman." The Prince politely answered, "It was the greatest compliment he could make him;" and, on his return to Italy, sent him every year presents of wine as a testimony of his regard.[3]

Complying fully with the Court fashion, he seems to have aimed at distinction in licentiousness as much as in any other pursuit. Even when he was Lord Chancellor, he sought to rival the King by the variety and notoriety of his amours. This is quaintly intimated to us by Roger North: "Whether out of inclination, custom, or policy, I will not determine, it is certain he was not behindhand

[1] Locke, ix. 273.   [2] Ante, p. 23.   [3] Martyn, 383.

with the Court in the modish pleasures of the time. There was a deformed old gentleman called Sir P. Neal, who, they say, sat for the picture of Sydrophel, in Hudibras, and about town was called *the Lord Shaftesbury's groom*, because he watered his mares in Hyde Park with Rhenish wine and sugar, and not seldom a bait of cheesecakes." [1]

Otway most indecently brought his vices on the stage, in the character of ANTONIO, in VENICE PRESERVED[2]— which, that it might not be mistaken, was thus boastfully announced in the prologue:—

> " Next is a senator that keeps ———
> In Venice none a higher office bore ;
> To lewdness every night the lecher ran,
> Show me all London such another man."

But though eager for reputation as a man of gallantry he modestly yielded the palm to his master. Charles having said to him one day, " Shaftesbury, you are the most profligate man in my dominions," he coolly replied, " Of a subject, sir, I believe I am."

Yet he was not altogether negligent of domestic duties. He was thrice married, and behaved to his wives with courtesy. The first, as we have related, was the daughter of Lord Keeper Coventry. By her he had no issue. Nor had he any by his third wife, who survived him,—a daughter of William, Lord Spencer, of Wormlington. But by his second wife, the daughter of the Earl of Exeter, he had a son, Anthony, who was not at all remarkable for genius, but who was the father of the third Earl, the pupil of Locke, and the author of " The Characteristics." In the education of this grandson, amidst all his distractions, he took the most unceasing and tender interest.

Shaftesbury in his person was short and slender, but well made, and when young, strong and active, but from the life he led, he early showed symptoms of premature old age.

---

[1] Examen, 60. Sir P. Neal, thus contemptuously mentioned, is said to have been a physician ; a friend of Locke's and a fellow of the Royal Society.

[2] It seems utterly impossible to believe that the scenes between Antonio and Aquilina could ever have been publicly performed. To make the matter, if possible, worse, the tragedy of " Venice Preserved " was brought out in February, 1681, when Shaftesbury was to be tried for his life,—with a view to render him odious. Dr. Johnson says in his Life of Otway, that this play was not acted ti'l 1685, but he is mistaken. See Malone's Life of Dryden p. 168.

"A fiery soul, which working out its way,
Fretted the pigmy body to decay.
And o'er-inform'd the tenement of clay."

I wish, for many reasons, that I could have spoken of him more favorably. It is delightful to think that his honors and estates are now enjoyed by descendants who, inheriting a large portion of his talents, are adorned by every public and private virtue.

CHAPTER XCI.

LIFE OF LORD CHANCELLOR NOTTINGHAM FROM HIS BIRTH TILL HE WAS CREATED LORD CHANCELLOR.

WE now pass from a Chancellor destitute of all juridicial requirements—to the "Father of Equity." Lord Shaftesbury was succeeded by Lord Nottingham who fully deserves all the praise that has been bestowed upon him as "a consummate lawyer," although I am afraid we shall not be able to regard him always as "a zealous defender of the constitution."[1]

Heneage Finch, afterwards Earl of Nottingham, and Lord Chancellor of England, was born at Eastwell, in Kent, on the 23rd of December, 1621. He was of the ancient family of the Finches, whose descent from Henry Fitzherbert, Chancellor to Henry I., we have already noticed.[2] He was the son of Sir Heneage Finch, who was the younger son of Sir Moyle Finch, and consequently he was first-cousin to the Lord Keeper of that name. This Sir Heneage, the father, was Recorder of London, and Speaker of the House of Commons in the second parliament of Charles I., which met in 1626, and he delivered to the King the address for the removal of the Duke of Buckingham. He had been the friend of Lord Bacon, and gallantly stood by that great man when charged with bribery and corruption. He never rose to greater distinction, but he made a large fortune by his profession, and lived splendidly in Kensington Palace, which was sold by his grandson to King William III.

Young Heneage, unlike his kinsman, who gained

[1] 3 Bl. Com. 56.   [2] See Life of Lord Keeper Finch, Ante, Vol. II.

the Great Seal by such evil arts, was ever remarkable for his steadiness of conduct and diligent application to study. He was educated at Westminster School, and was thence transferred to Christ Church, Oxford, where he was entered a gentleman commoner in Lent Term, 1635. Here he remained between two and three years, reading very diligently; but on account of the sudden death of his father, he withdrew from the University without taking a degree. Left so young his own master, with a considerable patrimony, there was great danger of his plunging into dissipation; but he resolved to rise to distinction by the profession of the law as several of his family had already done. He therefore entered himself of the Inner Temple, not merely like other cavaliers of fortune, to give a fashionable finish to his education, but with the fixed resolve of mastering the science of the law. The present practice of students at the Inns of Court becoming pupils of special pleaders, conveyancers, and equity draughtsmen, was then unknown, and a knowledge of the law was acquired by hearing lectures called "readings," by the habit of "*case putting*" at "moots," and by taking notes of arguments in the courts of justice. In the whole of this discipline, young Finch was remarkable for his regularity and zeal. He laid to heart a maxim of his uncle, Sir Henry Finch, that "a law student ought to read all the morning and to talk all the afternoon."[1] He therefore regularly attended the disputations after supper in the Cloister Walks[2] in the Temple, which seem to have supplied the place of our modern debating clubs,—and, being a noted "*put case*," he acquired great fluency of speech and readiness in reply.

He was likewise a diligent note-taker when cases of importance were argued at Westminster, and these he digested for his own use, there being no "Term Reports" in those days. This useful exercise he continued for some years after he was in practice. In a MS. treatise of

[1] Roger North makes the Earl of Nottingham himself the original author of this saying.—*Life of Lord Guildford*, i. 25.
[2] These "Walks" were burnt down in the great fire of London, in 1666. The benchers of the Middle Temple wished to build chambers on the site—but this plan was stopped by our Finch, then a bencher of the Inner Temple, from a grateful recollection of the benefit of case-putting. Sir Christopher Wren afterwards reconstructed the Cloisters with chambers over them, as they now remain, at the bottom of Inner Temple Lane.

his, composed when he was Chancellor, he thus refers to a case decided in Michaelmas Term, 1656:—"*Vide meas notas in diebus illis.*"

He was called to the Bar on the 30th of January, 1645,—although then of little more than six years standing on the books of the Inner Temple,—the required period of seven years being abridged in his case from favor, or from extraordinary proficiency.[1] About the same time he married the daughter of Mr. William Harvey, merchant of London,—a lady of beauty and merit, with whom he long lived in a state of great connubial happiness.

During the next fifteen years, except in domestic life, we know nothing of him. His name is not mentioned in any public records or private memorials of the time, and we are left to the probable conjecture that being a keen royalist in his heart, he would not accept of any employment under the Commonwealth, and that not being of a nature very chivalrous or adventurous,—instead of entering into plots against the established government, he calmly and steadily pursued his profession, in the hope that a change of opinion might bring round better times. The prosecution and flight of his cousin, Lord Keeper Finch, from whose patronage he no doubt expected promotion, must have been a heavy blow to him, but he did not consider himself bound either to rush forward in his defense or to share his exile.

At last, Oliver died, Richard abdicated, Monk marched from the North, and royalist principles might be safely proclaimed. Finch emerged into public life, and was returned for the city of Canterbury to the Convention Parliament. To mark his loyal enthusiasm, he got up "a declaration and vindication of the loyal-hearted nobility, gentry, and others of the county of Kent and city of Canterbury, that they had no hand in the murder of the King."—wherein it is set forth, "that the generality, and

[1] This period has been gradually shortened. When Lord Coke was a student, it was eight years, but from his stupendous acquirements he was called at the end of six. There were then regular and severe examinations during the studentship, and a man might either have been accelerated or plucked. The period at the Middle Temple and Gray's Inn is now reduced to three years, and at Lincoln's Inn and the Inner Temple to five years—abridging it to three in favor of those who have taken the degree of A. M. at Oxford, Cambridge, or Dublin. At all, the examinations have become merely formal and farcical—the student being stopped in "putting his case" as soon as he has pronounced the words " John Danvers seised in fee—,"

as for the number, much the greater, so also for the quality, much the better part of this famous and populous county and city hath, from the alpha to the omega, from the first to the last of these distracted, distempered, and unhappy times, been truly cordial, constant, and steady in the matter of their fidelity and loyalty to their Prince and Sovereign, without the least thought or desire to deviate, apostatize, or turn out of the good old way of due allegiance."

On the King's return, Finch was rewarded with the office of Solicitor General,—to the disappointment of several cavalier lawyers, who had run more risks, and made greater sacrifices in the royal cause; but considering his deep learning, his solid abilities, his professional eminence, and his fair character, no one could justly blame the appointment. To grace it, he was first knighted, and immediately after made a baronet. Sir Jeffrey Palmer, the Attorney General, a very able lawyer, having been in the service of Charles I., was now old and infirm; and not being a member of the House of Commons, the great weight of the government business was thrown upon the Solicitor, who got through it very creditably. While the Convention Parliament lasted, he seconded Clarendon's policy, by obstructing all the plans that were brought forward for comprehending the Presbyterians in the establishment, and still giving them hopes of favor.[1] When the bill of indemnity was passing, he successfully supported the amendment of the Lords, not only to except the King's Judges, but Vane, Haslerig, Lambert, and Axtell—urging that they could only be pardoned on the saying of David, "Slay them not, lest my people forget it;"[2] but he was unable to resist the proviso "that Vane and Lambert should not be executed without the further authority of the two Houses."[3]

A troublesome motion being made for an address that the King would marry a Protestant, Mr. Solicitor parried it by urging that "they had no reason to think the King would marry a Papist, as he had not done so when living in the courts of Catholic princes." He said, "they should, at all events, first have a convenient Protestant match to propose;" and he denied that the marriage of the King's

---

[1] 4 Parl. Hist. 119.   [2] Ibid. 100, 102, 108.   [3] Ibid. 79, 95, 154.

father to a Papist had been a chief cause of the late troubles.¹

Finch strenuously supported a very foolish motion for the impeachment of Mr. Drake, author of a book published to show, what was undoubtedly correct in point of law, "that the Long Parliament had never been legally put an end to," as the Act for that purpose was a mere ordinance of the Commons, without the concurrence of the King or the Lords,—and that the present parliament was not legally assembled," the writs being issued in the name of "the Keepers of the Liberties of England."²

As a lawyer, I blush for my order while I mention Finch's last appearance in the Convention Parliament. John Milton, already the author of COMUS and other poems, the most exquisite in the language,—after being long detained in the custody of the Sergeant-at-Arms, was released by order of the House—most men, however "cavalierly" inclined, being disposed to forget his political offenses. The Sergeant had exacted from his prisoner fees to the amount of £150,—a sum which, with great difficulty, he had borrowed from his friends. The famous Andrew Marvell brought the matter before the House, and moved that the money should be refunded. He was supported in this motion by Colonel King and Colonel Shapcot, two officers of undoubted loyalty as well as gallantry; but Mr. Solicitor-General Finch strongly opposed it, saying that "this Mr. Milton had been Latin Secretary to Cromwell, and, instead of paying £150, well deserved hanging."³ However, the matter was referred to a committee of privileges, who, I hope, decided for the poet.

The trials of the regicides coming on, they were chiefly conducted by Mr. Solicitor Finch on the part of the Crown; and through the whole of the proceedings he seems to have acted with moderation and firmness. He can not fairly be made answerable for the objectionable Judges named in the Commission, or for the harshness with which some of the prosecutions against those who had not concurred in the King's death were instituted.

Next year he was chosen "Autumn Reader of the Inner Temple," and he performed his duties with an ability and splendor never surpassed. He took for the subject of his

¹ 4 Parl. Hist. 120.   ² 5 St. Tr. 1363.   ³ 5 St. Tr. 162.

lectures " the Payment and Recovery of the Debts of the Crown," which he treated with great depth of learning and felicity of illustration.—The feasting lasted six days. On the first of these he entertained the nobility and Privy Councillors; on the second, the Lord Mayor, Aldermen, and principal citizens of London; on the third, the whole College of Physicians, who came with caps and gowns; on the fourth, the Long Robe—Judges, Advocates, Doctors of the civil law, and all the society of Doctors' Commons; on the fifth, the Archbishops, Bishops, and other dignitaries of the Church; and on the last, the King, the Duke of York, and all the great officers of the Court. There had not been such a royal visit since Henry VIII. and Queen Catherine honored a Sergeant's feast kept in Ely House, as commemorated by Stowe,—although Henry VII. and preceding sovereigns had often thus shown their respect for the Law and its Professors. On this occasion, we are told that his Majesty came from Whitehall in his state barge, and landing at the Temple stairs, was there received by the Reader, and the Chief Justice of the Common Pleas. Passing thence through a double file of the Reader's servants clothed in scarlet cloaks and white doublets, he took his way through a breach made expressly for the occasion in the wall, which at that time inclosed the Temple Garden,—and moved on through a lane formed of Benchers, Utter-barristers, and Students belonging to the Society,—till mounting the Terrace, he arrived at the Inner Temple Hall. A band of many wind instruments and twenty violins saluted the royal ear with lively and soothing airs. After the sumptuous dinner, there was much dancing and merriment, which continued to a late hour. His Majesty entered with a hearty good humor into the frolics of the place; and the Duke of York and Prince Rupert were admitted members of the society.[1]

In the parliament called in 1661, which sat near eighteen years, Finch represented the University of Oxford, which was proud of him, but not quite satisfied with his services, as he did not procure a remission of the tax upon hearths, which weighed heavily on the Colleges. While the parliament was held at Oxford in 1665, on account of the

[1] A similar honor was soon after conferred on Lincoln's Inn, where the royal signatures are still to be seen.

plague raging in London, the member for the University greatly distinguished himself in supporting "the Five-mile Act," much valued by his constituents, as it forbade any nonconformist minister to dwell in, or come within five miles of, any market town; and they resolved gratefully to confer upon him the honorary degree of Doctor of Civil Law; "which creation being concluded," says Anthony Wood, "in the presence of several parliament men, the Vice Chancellor stood up and spoke to the public orator to do his office: Whereupon he made a most admirable harangue, and amongst other things, to this effect, *that the University wished they had more Colleges to entertain the parliamentary men, and more chambers*, BUT BY NO MEANS MORE CHIMNEYS,—at which Sir Heneage changed his countenance, and drew a little back."

During this short session at Oxford he incurred the high displeasure of the landed interest, by opposing the bill to prohibit the importation of Irish cattle and provisions. "He was never known," says Carter, "to exert himself so much; but had an angel spoken, it would have signified nothing."[1] He could not even prevail on the House to pause or to give a copy of the Bill to Sir William Petty, and the other deputies sent over from Ireland to oppose it,—who were told "that it might be once read over to them, and then they must immediately say what they had to offer in objection."[2]

I do not find any further notice of his parliamentary efforts while he was Solicitor General, except on the impeachment of Lord Clarendon. It has been falsely said that he then turned against his patron;[3] but it is quite clear that he manfully stood by him,—admitting "that an impeachment there must be if there be cause, and that such accusations are not to be passed over in silence,"—but arguing with irresistible force that none of the articles amounted to high treason under 25 Ed. III., and scouting the notion that there may be a prosecution for treason in parliament more than in the inferior courts for any offense not declared to be treason by the statute: "How then doth the bringing it into parliament alter the case?

---

[1] Life of Ormond, ii. 322.
[2] Com. Journ. I am proud to think that the opposition to this iniquitous measure was led in either House by a lawyer.—*Life of Clarendon*, ante, p. 46.
[3] L. C. i. 165.

If the parliament set aside laws in this case, we should be happy to see a law declaring what is the power of parliament."[1]

But, in the mean time, his reputation for fine speaking at the bar rose so high that he was now often called the "English Cicero" and the "English Roscius." Evelyn styles him "the smooth-tongued Solicitor;" and in his Diary, under date October 26th, 1664, he writes, "At the Council I heard Mr. Solicitor Finch plead most eloquently for the merchants trading to the Canaries, praying for a new charter." We have a similar testimony from the simple and trustworthy Pepys respecting the hearing of an appeal at the bar of the House of Lords. "The cause was managed for my Lord Privy Seal by Finch, the Solicitor General, but I do really think that he is a man of as great eloquence as ever I heard or ever hope to hear in all my life."[2]

On the trial of Lord Morley for the murder of Mr. Hastings, before the Lord High Steward and the Peers, he made a most elaborate speech, laying down with great precision the distinction between murder and manslaughter. Some of his observations on the effect of the prisoner being a Peer are curious: "I do acknowledge to your Lordships (for why should I conceal any thing that makes for my Lord Morley's advantage?) I do confess that an affront or indignity offered to a Peer is much more heinous than that which is offered to a private gentleman. But I must needs say withal, that the law hath provided another manner of reparation for a Peer than that which it gives a gentleman. The same words that being spoken of a gentleman will bear no kind of action, when they are spoken to a Peer become *scandalum magnatum*. The Peer recovers great damage; the King inflicts fine or imprisonment; so that upon the matter the offender is bound in chains, and brought and laid at my Lord's feet. Now, for him whose honor is thus guarded by the law, to avenge himself by his sword is a most unpardonable excuse. I do not pretend, I do not offer to say, that the killing of a man is more capital in the case of a Peer than it would be in the case of a private gentleman: but I do presume to affirm, that no provocation in the world can make that to be but manslaughter in the

[1] 4 Parl. Hist. 375.   [2] May 3, 1664.

case of a Peer that would be murder in the case of a gentleman." The noble prisoner was acquitted of murder by all except two Peers (Ashley and Wharton), and being found guilty of manslaughter, pleaded his privilege, and was discharged.[1]

Sir Jeffrey Palmer, after a lingering illness, dying in 1670, Sir Heneage Finch, as a matter of course, succeeded him in the office of Attorney General, the duties of which he had long performed. He now took a more prominent part in the House of Commons, and stoutly defended the measures of the Government, which had become of a very unconstitutional and dangerous character.

He strongly opposed the "Coventry Act,"[2] and proposed that the punishment of "cutting to disfigure" should only be forfeiture of goods and imprisonment for life,[3]—actuated, I fear, less by a dislike of capital punishment than by a desire to please the Court, who highly approved of the dastardly atrocity which gave rise to this piece of legislation.[4]

He successfully opposed a measure for enforcing the attendance of members of parliament, by enacting that defaulters should be doubly assessed to the subsidy, saying, "You have a power to fine them, and you may appoint a day to pay it, on penalty of expulsion from the House." It was rejected only by a majority of 115 to 98.[5]

In 1671, a keen controversy arose between the two Houses as to the right of the Lords to alter money bills, particularly in lowering rates voted by the Commons, the Lords having unanimously resolved, "that the power exercised by them in making amendments and abatements on a bill for imposing duties on foreign commodities, both as to the matter, measure, and time concerning the rates and impositions on merchandise, is a fundamental, inherent, and undoubted right of the House of Peers, from which they can not depart." There were various conferences on the subject, which were managed, on the part of the Commons, by Mr. Attorney General Finch,

---

[1] 6 St. Tr. 786. So the Duchess of Kingston, being found guilty of bigamy in 1776, was discharged with a caution from the Lord High Steward "not to do the like again."

[2] 22 & 23 Car. 2, c. 1.   [3] 4 Parl. Hist. 466, 467.

[4] Slitting the nose of Sir John Coventry by hired bravoes for a pleasantry uttered by him in the House of Commons upon the amorous propensities of the King.   [5] 4 Parl. Hist. 472.

who in vain tried to persuade the Lords, by citing precedents, and by appealing to their regard for the wishes and interests of the King, to abandon their amendments, and to pass the bill as it was sent up to them. Neither party would yield, and the bill was lost by a prorogation.[1] But the Commons ultimately prevailed; and, allowing it to be highly proper that they should guard to themselves the exclusive right of granting supplies, they have carried their jealousy of amendments by the Lords in money bills to a pitch unnecessary, coxcombical, and often highly detrimental to the public service.

The promotion of such an interloper as Shaftesbury to the office of Lord Chancellor, upon the removal of Lord Keeper Bridgeman, must have been a heavy disappointment to Finch, who, having been now above twelve years a law officer of the Crown, and having served with applause, must have expected to succeed him "as the night the day." He found it convenient, however, to smother his indignation, and zealously to support his new master, even in the attempt to issue writs for the election of members of the House of Commons of his own authority, without the privity of the Speaker. When this subject came to be debated, Mr. Attorney, forgetting his late fight for the privileges of the Commons, boldly argued that it belonged to the Chancellor to issue the writs in vacation time, saying, "It is a necessity to the public that things may not be carried in a thin House; a Peer may knock at the door, and call for his writ to the Chancellor." It was nevertheless resolved, "that all elections upon the writs issued by the Chancellor since the last session are void, and that Mr. Speaker do issue out warrants to the Clerk of the Crown, to make out new writs for those places." And this important and necessary privilege of the House of Commons has never since been disputed.

Finch boldly defended the famous "Declaration of Indulgence"—on the King's universal and absolute dispensing power. "There is no question," said he, "of the King's power of dispensation where the forfeiture is his own. Where half the penalty is to the informer, the King may inform for the whole and dispense for the whole. The question is, whether the King cannot dispense with the laws in order to the preservation of the

---
[1] 4 Parl. Hist. 480, 487.

kingdom; and we are all miserable if he cannot."[1] This is the vaunted champion of the laws and constitution of his country![2] He first contends for the power of dispensing with all penal laws, on the reasoning that they are only enacted to provide pocket money for the King, who may therefore renounce what was intended for his private benefit;[3] and having established this point, he invests the King with the prerogative of dispensing with all laws which he or his ministers may think inconsistent with the public safety, or, in other words, disagreeable to themselves!

His last appearance in the House of Commons was on the 31st of October, 1673, when Shaftesbury, openly intriguing with the heads of the country party, was about to be turned out. The question was, whether the redress of grievances or the grant of supply should have the precedence?—and the aspirant to the Great Seal argued, "that *not first to give money* is at this time a grievance not to be redressed in many ages."[4]

It was presently intimated to him that he was to be Lord Keeper, and the morning of Sunday, the 9th of November, was appointed for his investiture. We have already related the terrible fright he was then thrown into by Shaftesbury's waggery, and how, in the evening of the same day, he was made happy by the Great Seal being actually put into his hand, and his carrying it home with him as the true Lord Keeper.[5] This is the official record of the event:—

"S^r. Heneage Finch, K^t. & Bar^t., the King's Ma^{ty*} Atturny Generall, received the Great Seale of England as Lord Keep^r, from his Ma^{ty}, at Whitehall, on Sunday, in the evening, being the 9th of Nov^r., 1673, in the 25th year of his said Ma^{ty*} raigne. The King sent for it the same day from the Earl of Shaftesbury, Lord Chancellor, by Mr. Secretary Coventry."[6]

His first act was to seal a pardon to his predecessor, which had been stipulated for when Shaftesbury took the office, foreseeing that he might probably do many things for which a pardon might be required, and wishing to have the pleasure of sinning with an indulgence in his

---

[1] *q* Parl. Hist. 522. [3] 3 Bl. Com. 56.
[2] "Cuique licet renunciare juri pro se introducto." [4] 4 Parl. Hist. 592.
[5] *ante*, p. 136. [6] Crown Off. Min. Book, fol. 73.

pocket. He then sealed a commission authorizing the Master of the Rolls and others to hear causes in his absence.

On the 11th of November, the new Lord Keeper had a grand procession from his house, in Queen Street, Lincoln's Inn Fields, to Westminster Hall, attended by the Lord Treasurer, the Lord Privy Seal, the Duke of Buckingham, the Duke of Ormond, the Marquis of Worcester, many others of the nobility, the Judges, the King's Counsel, and all the gentlemen of the Society of the Inner Temple. Entering the Court of Chancery, he took the oaths of office, the Master of the Rolls holding the book.

According to ancient usage he ought then to have delivered an inaugural address, of which high expectations were formed from his rhetorical reputation; but he immediately called upon the Solicitor General to move, and proceeded to business.' He probably was deterred from attempting a task which, in ordinary circumstances, he could have performed so easily and so gracefully, by the embarrassment of touching upon his predecessor, whom, according to the precedents, he ought to have praised for his learning and exemplary conduct, and proposed to himself as an example to stimulate his love of law and of virtue.

In a note to his MS. cases, he himself favors us with the following autobiographical account of these occurrences:

"Sunday, 9th November, 1673.

"At six at night I received the Great Seal from his Majesty at Whitehall, and was made C. S.—10th. I recipi'd my Lord Shaftesbury's pattent, which came to me from the Privy Seal. It was reported his Lordship kept the bill signed by him above a year and a half, for it was signed before he was Chancellor, as is said, and never meant to send it to the Seals till there was great necessity, and so hath covered all his misdemeanors as Chancellor. But this was a malicious report to his prejudice and mine, as if he had been false, and I too easy in this matter; for in truth the pardon did extend to the 6th of November, which could not possibly be by virtue of any old warrant; but the Chancellor, foreseeing his fall, ob-

---

[1] Sir Francis North was then Solicitor General, and was made Attorney General the following day.

tained a warrant for a new pardon, signed by Mr. Secretary Coventry, and Mr. Solicitor North passed it on Saturday, the 8th of November, and his Lordship intended to have sealed it as Chancellor, for the Privy Seal was directed to him by that name; but it was razed in the King's presence, and directed to me by name, with a *nuper Cancellarius* interlined where it mentioned him. Also, I sealed a commission to the Judges and Master of the Rolls to hear causes, for by the change of the C. or C. S. the commission fayles.—11th. I took my seat and was sworne in Chancery; but I made no speech, as some of my predecessors have done, upon the occasion."

On the 10th of January, 1674, he was created Baron FINCH, of Daventry, in the county of Northampton; on the 19th of December, 1675, Lord Chancellor of England;[1] and on the 12th of May, 1681, Earl of NOTTINGHAM, which has become his historical name, and by which I shall henceforth designate him.

CHAPTER XCII.

CONTINUATION OF THE LIFE OF LORD NOTTINGHAM TILL HIS FIRST QUARREL WITH LORD SHAFTESBURY.

HE held the Great Seal and presided in the Court of Chancery nine years, during the whole of which time he devoted himself with indefatigable labor and with brilliant success to the discharge of his judicial duties. I have sincere delight in relating, for the in-

---

[1] Of this further elevation we have the following account in his MS. Reports:—"Sunday morning. The King going to chapell declared me Lord Chancellor, whereupon I kist his hand, and presently had the compliments of all the Court, and not long after from all the ambassadors and foreign ministers."

"The Right Honble. Heneage L^d. Finch, Baron of Daventre, took the oath of Lord Chancellor of England in the High Court of Chancery, on Monday the 24th of January in the 27th year of his Ma^{tys}. reign, being the first day of Hilary Terme; the book being held to him by S^r. Harbottle Grimston, M^r. of the Rolls, and the oath read by Mr. Bucher, Clerk of the Crown.

"His Majesty having been pleased on the 19th day of December before to take the seal into his own hands, and to deliver it to him again by the stile of Lord Chancellor.

"M^d. he took only the oath of Chancr."—*Crown Off. Min.* 54.

struction and improvement of those who may aspire to rival his fame, the course he pursued. He did not consider his office as chiefly political, nor, anxious only to retain it, did he entirely occupy himself with court intrigues, or the management of a party in parliament ; nor did he become indolent and remiss on reaching the great object of his ambition ; nor did he dissipate his attention among a variety of pursuits,—from the vulgar ambition of being admired for universality of genius,—which leads generally to universal shallowness of acquirement. Placed at the head of the magistracy of a great country, he deemed it his first duty adequately to administer justice from his own tribunal; and for this purpose he did not think it enough merely to sit in public a certain number of hours, and to bestow decent pains upon each particular case which came before him. Justly regarding jurisprudence as a science which rests on general principles, and is illustrated and defined by the writings and rules of former jurists, he bore in mind that without a familiarity with these it was impossible that his own decisions should be consistent, systematic, and sound. He had peculiar difficulties to struggle with,—that Equity, which he was to administer, had sprung up originally in England, more from a desire to get at what was thought the justice of a particular case between litigating parties, than to lay down methodical rules,—that many of his predecessors had been men not educated in the profession of the law, and incapable of apprehending legal distinctions,—that their judgments had been generally allowed to fall into oblivion as more likely to mislead than to guide,—and that no attempt had been made to classify or to systematize those which had been preserved. He had the sagacity to discover that Equity might be molded into a noble code, supplying the deficiencies of the old feudal doctrines, and adapted to the altering necessities of a people whose commerce and wealth were so rapidly increasing.

Lord Nottingham had laid the indispensable foundation for being a great equity lawyer, by a profound knowledge of the common-law. His notes on Coke upon Littleton, published by Hargrave and Butler, in their edition of that great work, show how deeply he had studied it,—and several of his arguments handed down to us prove that our other institutional writers were equally familiar to him. He resorted early to a practice, without which great proficiency cannot be attained,—of writing on legal subjects. Besides his digested reports of cases which he had heard argued and determined, he wrote Treatises or Essays "on the King's Prerogative," and "on the Power of Parliament." Later in his career, "EQUITY" fixed his attention, and while in full practice at the bar—either for his own use in Court, or anticipating that he should one day hold the Great Seal, he composed a book, "*De Officio Cancellarii.*"

But all this preparation, joined with most extensive practical experience at the bar, he now considered quite insufficient to enable him to preside creditably in the Court of Chancery. As soon as he received the Great Seal, he began, and he worked indefatigably every moment he could spare from other duties till he had completed two new treatises,—one on the practices and the other on the principles and doctrines of the Court. The first he entitled "A System or Collection of such Rules and Orders in Chancery as have at any time heretofore been printed or published; together with some explanations and alterations thereof, and additions thereunto, as also some observations,—what rules have been lately discontinued and yet may be fit to be revived, and what are fit to be laid aside. By F. C. S."[1] The other and more important work he entitled " Prolegomena of Equity." This, written in the piebald style then usual among lawyers, a mixture of bad Latin, bad French, and bad English,—contains, under methodical divisions, all that was then known of Equity, as contradistinguished from common law. The reader may be amused with some of the titles: Cap. 6. " Equity versus purchasor ne sera." 7. " Equity relieves en plusors cases l'ou les printed livres deny it." 12. " Of trusts in general, quid sint." 30. " De Anomolies." 31. " L'ou les juges del common ley

---

[1] In one of his note books he thus refers it : " I took this occasion to show that the Court of Chancery hath always had an Admiralty jurisdiction, not only *per viam appellationis*, but *per viam evocationis* too, and may send for any cause out of the Admiralty to determine it here, of which there are many precedents in Noy's MS. 88, and in my little book in the preface · De Officio Cancellarii,' sec. 18, and in my ' Parliament Book,' sec. 8, title 'Admiralty.' "

[2] These letters C. S. show that the work was completed before Dec. 1675, when he was made Chancellor.

ont agreed to alter it, sans act de parlement, et l'ou nemy," [or "*of Judge-made law.*"][1]

Thus was he much better acquainted with the practice and with the principles and doctrines of the Court than any of the advocates pleading before him, and having previously considered them systematically, he could readily see how they were to be applied, or extended, or restrained.[2]

But what perhaps still more raised his judicial fame was the admirable habit which he adopted, and which has been revived and recommended by illustrious judges still living,—of writing the judgment to be delivered in every case of importance,—whereby the judge is forced to apprehend accurately both facts and law,—becomes fully acquainted with all difficulties and objections before he has publicly committed himself by any opinion,—and lays down and qualifies his positions with more nicety than it is possible for him to do in an extempore speech. In Lord Nottingham's MSS. still extant, are to be found almost all the important judgments he delivered while he held the Great Seal.[3]

It may well be believed that he found the causes in a state of great confusion from the rashness and the timidity

---

[1] The value of this treatise may be appreciated by the observations of that accomplished lawyer, Mr. Hargrave, on a copy of it made by himself: "In this copy of Lord Chancellor Nottingham's 'Prolegomena,' I have adhered closely to Mr. Heneage Legge's copy, except that I have avoided the numerous abbreviations in the latter, and that I have translated all the French words, and so made what was almost throughout a mixture of French and English, entirely English. The whole of this copy, except a few lines in page 2, is in my own handwriting. But from the interesting and valuable nature of the contents, I did not feel the labor of copying and translating as any fatigue."—See Preface to Hale's *Jurisdiction of Lords*, p. 153. This MS. treatise is likewise mentioned very respectfully by Sir W. Grant, in the Bishop of Winchester *v.* Paine, 11 Vesey, 200.

[2] Chief Justice Pemberton used to boast "that while he was a Judge, he had for his own share made more law than King, Lords, and Commons, since the time he was born."

[3] There are in all 1170. In the folio volume containing them are to be found a few scattered memoranda, which show what a valuable Diary he might have kept. Under date Feb. 21, 1675, there is an account of Sir Matthew Hale coming into Chancery, to enroll the resignation of his office of Chief Justice,—and another details how on Sunday, the 12th of Feb., 1678, the King, on returning from Chapel, sent for the Chancellor to wait upon him alone in his closet at Whitehall, and there desired him to attest a document written with his own hand, the purport of which was "that he had never been married to the Duke of Monmouth's mother, or to any one except Queen Katherine."

which had marked the beginning and the close of the short judicial career of his eccentric predecessor. The new Keeper made no parade of differing from him;—insomuch that it has been said that hardly any of Lord Shaftesbury's decrees were reversed, (a compliment I find paid almost to every Chancellor,) but on rehearings, he quietly corrected irregularities and mistakes; and soon the business of the Court was in a better state even than in the time of Lord Keeper Coventry, whose successors had almost demolished the system of equity which he was beginning to create.

He exerted himself to the utmost to prevent delay, with which, partly from a deficient judicial staff, but more from the nature of the suits, Equity has always been unjustly taunted by the multitude. A case once being mentioned to him in which he was told the bill had been filed previous to the commencement of the civil war, and had been heard and reheard before all the Lord Chancellors, Lord Keepers, and Lords Commissioners of the Great Seal who had sat in Chancery ever since, he instantly appointed a time for its being finally disposed of, and declared that he would rather sit on five or six days, himself making inquiries and taking accounts, than it should again be referred to a Master and continue the opprobrium of the Court.[1]

Lord Nottingham never incurred the suspicion of bribery, or of being influenced by the solicitations of King or Courtiers. Luckily for him, no political case came before him in the Court of Chancery, and his fame is untarnished by the charge of having given way to party bias. We are therefore allowed to look up to him as a Judge with unmixed admiration. He was one of the most distinguished and meritorious of the great men who have adorned the magistracy in England, and who, if they have not hitherto acquired such general celebrity, may well bear a comparison with the Oxenstierns, Molés, and D'Aguesseaus of the continental nations.

[1] The late Mr. Jekyll told me that soon after he was called to the bar, a strange solicitor coming up to him in Westminster Hall, begged him to step into the Court of Chancery to make a motion of course, and gave him a fee. The young barrister pleased, but looking a little surprised, the solicitor said to him, "I thought you had a sort of right, sir, to this motion, for the bill was drawn up by Sir Joseph Jekyll, your great-granduncle, in the reign of Queen Anne."

I wish I could be excused from following his track as a statesman, where, although his conduct may be palliated, it can not possibly be defended. Taking no lead in the cabinet, he is not chargeable with originating bad measures, like Shaftesbury; but he gave himself up implicitly to those ministers who successively ruled in the King's name, concurring in their policy, and openly and indiscriminately justifying it, whatever it might be. He seems to have considered himself merely as the retained advocate of the Court, bound in duty to do the best for his clients, according to the instructions he received from them, without any misgivings that he compromised his own character by trying to show that criminal acts were innocent, or by using arguments which he must have known to be fallacious.

It has been urged in his defense, that his only choice was to go over to the country party, whose measures, at this time were still more reprehensible; but it will be seen that, to weaken that party, he was willing to advance beyond them in their worst excesses; and if, after vigorous efforts, he could not influence the counsels of the government to which he belonged, he had always before him an honorable retreat in a private station.

We have very scanty accounts of his parliamentary efforts after he held the Great Seal,—except of his speeches on the opening of parliament, which are not at all interesting, being vague and dull, and instead of containing, as formerly, lively personal sallies, evidently bearing marks of having been, like modern royal speeches, elaborated in the cabinet.

The first of these he delivered on the 7th of January, 1674,—according to the absurd fashion of the Lord Keeper addressing the two Houses, when the King had concluded, and after kneeling down and receiving directions from his Majesty,—reciting an oration before his Majesty in his Majesty's praise. Having enumerated the recent measures of the government, which he imputes to the wisdom and virtue of the King, he says, on this occasion, "These are not single and transient acts, but such acts as flow from habits; these are not leaves and blossoms, but true, solid, and lasting fruits. Long! long! may that royal tree live and flourish upon which these fruits do grow!" He is not less complimentary, nor more sincere, in speaking of the parliament, which had become very troublesome and factious. "Posterity will have cause to doubt which was the greater felicity of the two, that Providence which restored the Crown, or that which sent us such a parliament to preserve it when it was restored. What may not the King now hope from you? What may not you assure yourselves from him? Can anything be difficult to hearts so united, to interests so twisted and interwoven together as the King's and yours are? Doubtless the King will surpass himself at this time, in endeavoring to procure the good of the kingdom. Do you but excel yourselves, too, in the continued evidences of your affections, and then the glory of reviving the state will be entirely due to this session. Then they who wait for the languishing and the declination of the present government will be amazed to see so happy a crisis, so blest a revolution; and ages to come will find cause to celebrate your memories as the truest physicians, the wisest counselors, the noblest patriots, and the best session of the best parliament that ever King or kingdom met with."[1]

The response was an address for a fast for the heinous sins of the nation, and the introduction of measures for the impeachment of the Duke of Buckingham, the Duke of Lauderdale, and the Earl of Arlington.

In the session of 1675, the policy of the Court was to outbid the Opposition in zeal for Protestantism; and the Lord Keeper said, "His Majesty has considered religion first, in general, as it is Protestant, and stands opposed to Popery; and upon this account it is that he has awakened all the laws against the Papists: there is not one statute extant in all the volume of our laws but his Majesty has now put it in a way of taking its full course against them. His Majesty, with equal and impartial justice, hath revived all the laws against dissenters and nonconformists, but not with equal severity; for the laws against the Papists are edged, and the execution of them quickened by new rewards proposed to the informers; those against dissenters are left to that strength which they have already."[2] The only subject which shares his solicitude for the true religion is "the excess of new buildings near London and Westminster; a growing mischief which

[1] 4 Parl. Hist. 612. [2] Ibid. 673.

nothing but a new law can put a stop to; a mischief which, for a long time, hath depopulated the country, and now begins to depopulate the city, too, by leaving a great part of it uninhabited.¹

The cry of "*No Popery*," which the ministers now bawled out more loudly than their antagonists, brought them into such favor that they thought to crush Shaftesbury for ever by "the Passive Obedience Test Bill," requiring an oath never to attempt any change in the law respecting either church or state. This was strenuously supported by Lord Nottingham, and being carried in the Lords after seventeen days' debate, was considered as having for ever extinguished free discussion in parliament and in the country,—when it was defeated by the controversy got up between the two Houses, respecting the right of the Lords to entertain appeals from Courts of Equity.² The Chancellor had the sagacity to see the trap laid for the government; but he had not the address to avoid it. He was bound to second the resolutions which Shaftesbury moved, asserting the jurisdiction of the Lords for the alleged benefit of the community, "who must otherwise depend on the caprice of the Sovereign to grant or to refuse a commission of appeal,"—and he could not control the fervor of the friends of the government in the other House, who, mad on this question of privilege, disregarded all party predilections and stood up for their own notions of the rights of their order.

During these debates, the Ex-Chancellor and the reigning Lord Chancellor being pitted against each other, the latter suffered severely. I have already related his discomfiture, when, thinking Shaftesbury had committed himself by declaring, "I know not what is meant by the Protestant religion," he rashly exclaimed, "*Tell it not in Gath.*"³ On a subsequent day, having been hard pressed by some taunts upon his late measures,—instead of vindicating himself, he sought to recriminate by thanking God that he did not advise the breaking up of the Triple Alliance; that he did not advise the shutting up of the Exchequer; and that he did not advise the Dutch war. The King being present, Shaftesbury, with much dexterity, conveyed an impression that he himself was not responsible for proposing these measures—without naming the

¹ 4 Parl. Hist. 674.   ² Ante, p. 137.   ³ Ante, p. 138.

author of them. Lord Arlington, who disliked the Chancellor, asked the King which of the two had acted most respectfully towards him; since he knew how open Lord Shaftesbury could have laid those affairs, and yet, under such provocations, he only cleared himself, and still kept the secret. The King thereupon rebuked the Chancellor for meddling with the secrets of the Council in so public a place, and told him "he knew nothing of those matters." [1]

But in the vicissitudes of political warfare, Nottingham had, by-and-by, the satisfaction to witness Shaftesbury's blunders, in contending that, after an adjournment for fifteen months, the parliament was *ipso facto* dissolved. He was obliged, it is true, to resort in debate to the miserable quibble that the words "yearly, and oftener if need be," in the statute of Edward III., for the frequent holding of parliaments, gave the King a discretion to decide whether there *be need* to summon a parliament yearly; but he addressed a willing audience, eager to swallow any sophistry which flattered their prejudices; and, finding it his "painful duty" to move the commitment of the four leaders of the opposition to the Tower, he saw them marched off in custody, and himself and his friends left in undisputed possession of the field of battle.

The happiest period of his life probably was the fifteen months during which Shaftesbury lay a prisoner in the Tower,—particularly after the Court of King's Bench refused to discharge him, and it was quite certain that, being at the mercy of a ministerial majority in the Lords, the agitator must make humiliating concessions, or continue in a state of suspended animation. But his most swelling moment, no doubt, was that when Shaftesbury, seeming to have fallen, like Lucifer, never to rise again,—on bended knee,—amidst the scoffs of foes, and the blushes of his friends,—repeated after him the abject apology, "I, Anthony,"[2] &c.,—acknowledging his heinous transgression,—expressing his deep contrition,—and promising amendment of life.

The Popish plot soon saved Shaftesbury from shame and insignificance,—and that breaking out, he was, in a moment, more formidable than he had ever been.

In viewing Lord Nottingham's conduct at this crisis,

[1] Martyn's Life of Shaftesbury, i. 423.   [2] Ante, p. 149.

we must charitably suppose that, like Lord Russell, and other very sensible persons, he was the dupe of Titus Oates; for otherwise, we must set him down as one of the most infamous of mankind,—premeditatedly dealing in calumny and murder to serve his own selfish ends. At the opening of the session of 1679, he said,—

"At home we had need to look about us; for his Majesty's royal person hath been in danger by a conspiracy against his sacred life, maliciously contrived and industriously carried on by those Seminary Priests and Jesuits, and their adherents, who think themselves under some obligation of conscience to effect it; and having vowed the subversion of the true religion amongst us, find no way so likely to compass it as to wound us in the head, and to kill the Defender of the Faith. It hath ever been the practice of those votaries first to murder the fame of princes, and then their persons; first to slander them to their people as if they favored Papists, and then to assassinate them for being too zealous Protestants. Enough hath appeared to bring some capital offenders to public justice; some of the traitors have been executed; several priests have been arrested and imprisoned; all are hiding themselves and lurking in secret corners, like the sons of darkness. But their expectations are vain, as their designs are wicked; for his Majesty hath already begun to let them see with what severity he means to proceed against them. He hath passed a law to disable all the nobility and gentry of that faction ever to sit in Parliament; and not content with that, he did offer to the last parliament, and does again renew the same offer to this parliament, to pass any further laws against Popery."[1]

There is, therefore, no foundation for the attempts which have been made to fix the odium of the Popish plot, and of all the atrocities perpetrated in consequence of it, exclusively on the liberal party; for the Tories, represented by Danby and Nottingham, either under delusion,—or, what would be infinitely worse,—knowingly,— from sinister motives,—joined with eagerness in inflaming the multitude, and hallooing them on to blood.

While the disgraceful ceremony was proceeding of the sacrifice of Lord Stafford, Nottingham gave the most decided proof of his own fanaticism or rascality. Presiding

[1] 4 Parl. Hist. 1087, 1111.

as Lord High Steward,—I am afraid he showed, by his address to the prisoner, at the very opening of the trial, that this virtuous man was prejudged. "As it is," said he, "impossible for my Lords to condemn the innocent, so it is equally impossible that they should clear the guilty. If, therefore, you have been agitated by a restless zeal to promote that which you call the Catholic cause; if this zeal has engaged you in such deep and black design as you are charged with, and this charge shall be fully proved, then you must expect to reap what you have sown; for every work must and ought to receive the wages that are due to it."[1]

When a verdict of *guilty* had been given by a majority of fifty-five, consisting of the Lord High Steward, the Lord President of the Council, the Lord Privy Seal, and many high-church Peers, against thirty-one, comprising Lord Holles, and several other Presbyterian Peers, and a motion in arrest of judgment had been overruled,—his Grace proceeded to pass sentence (according to the expression of Evelyn, who was present) "with greate solemnity and dreadful gravity."

Lord High Steward. "My Lord Stafford, my part which remains is a very sad one; for I never yet gave sentence of death upon any man, and am extremely sorry that I must begin with your Lordship. Who would have thought that a person of your quality, of so noble an extraction, of so considerable estate and fortune, so eminent a sufferer in the late ill times, so interested in the preservation of the government, so much obliged to the moderation of it, and so personally obliged to the King and his royal father for their particular favors to you, should ever have entered into so infernal a conspiracy as to contrive the murder of the King, the ruin of the state, the subversion of the religion, and, as much as in you lay, the destruction of all the souls and bodies of three Christian nations? And yet the impeachment of the House of Commons amounts to no less a charge, and of this charge their Lordships have found you guilty. That there hath been a general and desperate conspiracy of the Papists, and that the death of the King hath been all along one chief part of the conspirators' design, is now apparent beyond all possibility of doubting. What was the meaning of all

[1] 7 St. Tr. 1297.

those treatises, which were published about two years since, against the oath of allegiance, in a time when no man dreamt of such a controversy? What was the meaning of Father Conyers's sermon upon the same subject, but only because there was a demonstration of zeal, as they call it, intended against the person of the King, which the scruples arising from that oath did somewhat hinder? To what purpose were all the correspondencies with foreign nations? the collections of money among the Fathers abroad and at home? What was the meaning of their governing themselves here by such advices as came frequently from Paris and St. Omer's? And how shall we expound that letter which came from Ireland, to assure the Fathers here, that all things were in readiness there too, as soon as the blow should be given? *Does any man now begin to doubt how London came to be burnt? Or by what ways and means poor Justice Godfrey fell? And is it not apparent, by these instances, that such is the frantic zeal of some bigoted Papists, that they resolve no means to advance the Catholic cause shall be left unattempted, though it be by fire and sword?* My Lord, as the plot in general is most manifest, so your Lordship's part in it hath been too plain. What you did in Paris, and continued to do at Tixall, in Staffordshire, shows a settled purpose of mind against the King; and what you said at London touching honest Will shows that you were acquainted with that conspiracy against the King's life, which was carrying on here, too: and in all this there was a great degree of malice; for your Lordship at one time called the King '*heretic*,' and '*traitor to God*,' and at another time you reviled him for misplacing his bounty, and rewarding none but traitors and rebels. And thus you see, that which the wise man forewarned you of, is come upon you: '*Curse not the King, no not in thy heart; for the birds of the air shall reveal, and that which hath wings will declare the matter.*' Three things I shall presume to recommend to your Lordship's consideration. In the first place, your Lordship sees how it hath pleased God to leave you so far to yourself, that you are fallen into the snare, and into the pit which you were digging for others. Consider, therefore, that God Almighty never yet left any man who did not first leave him. In the next place, think a little better of it than hitherto you have done, what kind of religion that is in which the blind guides have been able to lead you into so much ruin and destruction as is now like to befall you. In the last place, I pray your Lordship to consider, that true repentance is never too late. A devout, penitential sorrow, joined with an humble and hearty confession, is of mighty power and efficacy both with God and man. There have been some of late who have refused to give God the glory of his justice, by acknowledging the crimes for which they were condemned; nay, who have been taught to believe that it is a mortal sin to confess that crime in public for which they have been absolved in private, and so have not dared to give God that glory which otherwise they would have done. God forbid your Lordship should rest upon forms! God forbid your Lordship should be found among the number of those poor forsaken souls whom the first thing that undeceives is death itself! Perhaps your Lordship may not much esteem the prayers of those whom you have long been taught to miscall heretics; but whether you do or no, I am to assure your Lordship, that all my Lords here, even they that have condemned you, will never cease to pray for you, that the end of your life may be Christian and pious, how tragical soever the means are that must bring you thither. And now, my Lord, this is the last time that I can call you 'My Lord,' for the next words I am to speak will attaint you. The judgment of the law is, and this Court doth award that, 'You go to the place from whence you came; from thence you must be drawn upon a hurdle to the place of execution; when you come there, you must be hanged up by the neck, but not till you are dead, for you must be cut down alive,'" &c. &c.

Lord Stafford begged that he might no longer be kept a close prisoner as he had long been, and that his wife and children might be admitted to see him till his death.

L. H. S. "My Lord Stafford, I believe I may with my Lords' leave tell you one thing further, that my Lords, as they proceed with rigor of justice, so they proceed with all the mercy and compassion that may be; and therefore my Lords will be humble suitors to the King, that he will remit all punishment but the taking off your head."

His Grace, complacently swelling with the consciousness of his humane intentions, then broke his white staff, and dissolved the Commission.¹

He received the thanks of the House of Lords for his speech in passing sentence, and was desired to print it.² Nevertheless, his conduct upon this occasion, it must be acknowledged, reflects deep disgrace upon his memory, and greatly detracts from the respect with which we should regard him as a civil Judge. Assuming that he was carried away by the general frenzy—not imputing to him the diabolical purpose of trying to gain a wretched popularity to the government by shedding innocent blood —he is still to be severely censured. Placed in his elevated position—

> "Despicere unde queas alios passimque videre
> Errare, atque viam palanteis quærere vitæ "—

it was his duty to have guided the peerage of England to the rescue of an innocent man, instead of acting as their high priest to offer him up a victim to the idols of bigotry and prejudice.

If he was sincere, it may mitigate our censure of his credulity to recollect that it was shared by the virtuous Lord Russell, who upon this occasion went so far as even to question the power of the King to mitigate the sentence in the manner suggested by the Lord Chancellor,—on the ground that the prosecution was not by the King, but by the House of Commons. The repugnance to cruelty which can never be extinguished in the English nation, operated so powerfully upon this occasion, that the Chancellor prevailed, without difficulty, in having the whole of the sentence remitted except the beheading, and the House of Commons magnanimously resolved, " that this House is content that the sheriffs of London and Middlesex do execute William, late Viscount Stafford, by severing his head from his body only."³

The Chancellor found himself involved in a most serious

---

¹ 7 St. Tr. 1217–1558.
² Lords' Jour. Dec. 7, 1668. Burnet says, " Lord Nottingham, when he gave judgment, delivered it with one of the best speeches had he ever made. But he committed one great indecency in it: for he said, ' Who can doubt any longer that London was burnt by the Papists?' though there was not one word in the whole trial relating to that matter."
³ Com. Jour. Dec. 23, 1680. It is some consolation to think, that this infamous attainder has been reversed, and that his honors and estates are now enjoyed by his descendants.

controversy with the Commons, from the attempt made to stop their prosecution of the Earl of Danby. The impossibility was at last discovered of longer retaining this minister, who, notwithstanding all his arts to court popularity, had become generally odious.[1] Charles was now willing to abandon him; but he dreaded the trial of the impeachment, which would have brought out his secret treaties with France, the bribes he had received from that country, and various other secrets of his misrule. The expedient resorted to was to grant a pardon to Danby, which should be pleaded in bar of the impeachment. But a parliamentary impeachment never had been so stopped; and although Nottingham would probably have got over his doubts as to the regularity of the proceeding, if it had been perfectly safe to himself,—he knew that he must give deep offense to the House of Commons by putting the Great Seal to such an instrument, and that the power of the country party was there at that time almost irresistible. He therefore refused to pass the pardon. Still the impeachment must be stopped. He would not voluntarily resign. There was no desire of getting rid of a Chancellor usually so complying. Under such circumstances this most unworthy trick was practiced,—devised by whom I know not,—but, I am ashamed to say, sanctioned by Nottingham. The pardon, being drawn up in proper form, was delivered to the King; Nottingham was summoned to Whitehall, and desired to bring the Great Seal with him. On his arrival, he was desired to seal the pardon. He begged leave respectfully to inform his Majesty that he had such scruples as to the regularity of granting a pardon pending a parliamentary impeachment, that he must be excused doing so without further consideration. The King then took the seal from him, and either affixed it to the pardon with his own hand, or caused this to be done by an officer of the Court acting under his orders. He then handed the pardon to the Earl of Danby, and taking up the Seal, returned it to the Earl of Nottingham, saying, "Take it back, my Lord; I know not where to bestow it better."

[1] Nottingham was the last to give up the Lord Treasurer: "The Lord C. is more my Lord Danby's friend than any body: he got him to keep his stall ten days, which cost the King £200 000."—*H. Sydney's Diary*, vol. i. p. 3.

The pardon being pleaded in bar of the further prosecution of the impeachment, the Commons were thrown into a fury, and appointed a select committee to inquire into the manner in which it had been granted. The committee finding no entry of the pardon in any of the public offices, requested information on the subject from the Lord Chancellor, who stated to them how "his Majesty commanded the seal to be taken out of the bag, which his Lordship was obliged to submit unto, it not being in his power to hinder it, and then writing his name on the top of the parchment, had the pardon sealed; and that at the very time of affixing the Seal to the parchment he did not look upon himself to have the custody of the Seal."[1] The Commons sent a message to the Lords demanding justice on the Earl of Danby, and an address to the King, complaining of the irregularity and illegality of the pardon.

Although Danby, after a temporary concealment, surrendered himself, and was committed to the Tower, where he lay under this charge five years,—on account of the temporary introduction of Shaftesbury into the ministry, and the rapid events which followed till the dissolution of the Oxford parliament, the impeachment was not prosecuted, and the grand question which the plea in bar raised was never judicially determined. Nor was it even expressly set at rest by the Bill of Rights, notwithstanding a vote of the House of Commons at the time of the Revolution, that a pardon is not pleadable in bar of an impeachment. But at last, by the Act of Settlement, 12 & 13 W. 3, c. 2, it was *enacted* "That no pardon under the Great Seal of England be pleadable to an impeachment by the Commons in parliament." This restriction is necessary for discovering and exposing ministerial delinquency; but after conviction the power of pardon is vested in the Crown, to be exercised by responsible advisers,—where the prosecution has been by impeachment as well as in the name of the King,[2] although, according to the law, where a capital prosecution was instituted by appeal at the suit of the party injured the prosecutor might pardon, but the King could not.[3]

[1] 4 Parl. Hist. 1114.   11 St. Tr. 766.
[2] After the conviction on impeachment of the six rebel lords in 1715, three of them were pardoned.   [3] 4 Bl. Com. 400.

It must have been an amusing sight, immediately after this controversy about Danby's pardon, during which Shaftesbury had vowed that "he would have Nottingham's head," to have seen the two sitting next each other in council, and seemingly on terms of cordiality. But they hated each other as much as ever, and secretly prepared for a rupture. Nottingham, not venturing openly to oppose Shaftesbury's Habeas Corpus Bill, in vain intrigued to have it thrown out by the expedient of a difference between the two Houses, which had been so successfully worked against himself.

Hopes were entertained that Shaftesbury might now be prevailed upon to give up his Exclusion Bill; but he, feeling that his only chance of permanent power was to compel the King to take him for his sole minister, and to recognize Monmouth for his successor, thwarted the measures of Nottingham and the inner cabinet, and showed himself as hostile as ever to the Duke of York. It was no surprise to Nottingham, although it was to Shaftesbury, when the King, without any previous deliberation with the Council, suddenly turned round to him, and ordered him first to prepare a commission for proroguing parliament, and then a proclamation to dissolve it.[1]

Shaftesbury being immediately turned out office, Nottingham and he for the rest of their days were at open and mortal enmity with each other.

CHAPTER XCIII.

CONCLUSION OF THE LIFE OF LORD NOTTINGHAM.

DURING the short parliament which met in October, 1680, Nottingham, under the Earl of Halifax, assisted the ministerial majority in the House of Lords to counteract the schemes of Shaftesbury, who made a stout fight in his own House, and dictated all the resolutions of the other. The Exclusion Bill being renewed in the Commons was followed up by addresses to remove Halifax and Seymour, who opposed it, and by

[1] Ante, p. 134.

impeachments of Scroggs, Jeffreys, and North, for their obstruction of the prosecution of the Duke of York as a Popish recusant, and their interference with the right of petitioning. In spite of Nottingham's very superior legal acquirements, Shaftesbury seems generally to have had the advantage over him in debate, even on constitutional questions,—the "Patriot" making up for his deficiency in knowledge by boldness of assertion and bitterness of sarcasm. The poor Lord Chancellor, leading such an uneasy life, must have very heartily concurred in the resolution to put a sudden end to this parliament; and, thankful for the respite, must joyfully have pronounced the words by which it was dissolved, although another was summoned to meet at Oxford, as a last experiment, before laying parliaments entirely aside.

On the last day of the session he assisted the King in a most unworthy manœuvre,—to steal from the table a disagreeable Bill, which both Houses had passed, "for the Protection of Dissenters from being prosecuted for not going to their parish church,"—so that it was defeated without the odium of a public exercise of the royal veto.[1] This affair might have led to very serious consequences to the Chancellor if he had been questioned for it by a patriotic House of Commons, backed by an approving public; but the House of Commons was outrageously factious,—the public were disgusted with their representatives,—and he escaped.

When the Oxford Parliament met, fortune favored him in every thing. The Commons took up, with much eagerness, the stealing of the Dissenters' Relief Bill; but they rejected with contumely all the King's proffered concessions to guard the reformed religion from the Popish successor by banishing him from the kingdom for life, and providing that the next Protestant heir should govern as Regent in his name;—and, to defeat the government prosecution of their informer, Fitzharris, they resolved that they would themselves impeach him for high treason before the House of Lords. This last was Shaftesbury's fatal blunder. A great many Protestant zealots still stuck by him for the "exclusion," while the more discerning members of his party now saw through his design of gaining power to himself by trying to establish the legiti-

[1] Ante, p. 165.

macy of the Duke of Monmouth,—but nearly all were shocked by observing a capital prosecution sported with as an instrument of faction, and an attempt to try a commoner for his life before those who were not his peers.

Nottingham dexterously seized the advantage presented him, and advised the Lords to reject the impeachment, on the ground that Fitzharris, as a commoner, was entitled to be tried for this offense by a jury of commoners. We have a very imperfect report of his speech on this occasion; but he seems very successfully to have thrown odium on the House of Commons for betraying the rights of their constituents, under pretense of supporting their own privileges; and he brought forward, with prodigious effect, the precedent of the judgment on the murderers of Edward II., where it was declared in full parliament that commoners should not thereafter be tried on a capital charge by the House of Lords.[1]

While the Commons voted the rejection of the impeachment "a denial of justice," the nation on this question took part with the Lords; and the sudden dissolution of the parliament gave a decided victory to the Court.[2]

Here ended Nottingham's senatorial career, the King ruling by high prerogative alone during the rest of his reign.

He had on two other occasions, which I have not mentioned, presided in the Lords as High Steward on the trial of Peers. The first was that of the Earl of Pembroke and Montgomery, for the murder of a Mr. Cony in an affray in a tavern. In a note to his MS. Reports, Nottingham has left an account of the ceremonial on this occasion, to which he seems to have attached great importance. "Being come to the Lords' House, and retired to putt on my robes, after prayers said, wee adjourned the House into Westminster Hall, and went, in the order prescribed, through the Painted Chamber, Court of Requests, and Court of Wards, into the Hall. In which procession the Duke of York and Prince Rupert,[3] to do honor to the King's Lieutenant (for so they called me), gave me the precedence, and suffered me to come last all the while, till the tryall was over and the white staff

[1] See ante, p. 170. Hale's Jurisdiction of the House of Lords, c. xiv.
[2] 4 Parl. Hist. 1298-1339.
[3] Duke of Cambridge,—but he still went by his *nom de guerre.*

broken. When we came into Westminster Hall, the Court was prepared like the House of Peers in all points; with scaffolds on each side for the spectators, and a place for all the foreign ministers. So the Lords spirituall and temporall did quickly know their own places. I took my place upon the woolsack, near the cloth of state, but not directly under it, having first made my obeysance to the chaire, and then to the King and Queen, who satt by al *incognito.*"

The Lord High Steward is reported to have delivered a preliminary address to the noble prisoner, by way of encouraging him, which seems to have been in a strange taste: "Let not the disgrace of standing as a felon at the bar too much deject you; no man's credit can fall so low but that if he bear his shame as he should do, and profit by it as he ought to do, it is in his own power to redeem his reputation. Therefore, let no man despair that desires and endeavors to recover himself again; much less let the terrors of justice affright you; for though your Lordship have great cause to fear, yet whatever may be lawfully hoped for, your Lordship may expect from the Peers."

Lord Pembroke, being found guilty of manslaughter, was discharged with an admonition, that upon a second conviction for the like offense he would be liable to be hanged.[1]

The other case occurred soon after, and excited considerable interest, being that of a minor peer, a schoolboy, prosecuted for the murder of a companion, with whom he had quarreled in the palace, at Whitehall. The Lord High Steward's address to encourage the accused, was again anything but encouraging: "My Lord Cornwallis, the violation of the King's peace, in the chief sanctuary of it, his own royal palace, and in so high a manner, as by the death of one of his subjects, is a matter that must be accounted for. It is your Lordship's great unhappiness, at this time, to stand prisoner at the bar under the weight of no less a charge than an indictment of murder. And it is not to be wondered at if so great a misfortune as this be attended with some sort of confusion of face; when a man sees himself become a spectacle of misery in so great a presence, and before so noble and so illustrious an as-

[1] 6 St. Tr. 1309.

sembly. But be not yet dismayed, my Lord, for all this: let not the terrors of justice so amaze and surprise you as to betray those succors that your reason would afford you, or to disarm you of those helps which good discretion may administer, and which are now so necessary. It is indeed a dreadful thing to fall into the hands of justice, where the law is the rule, and a severe and inflexible measure both of life and death."

It turned out, however, that the poor young Lord was hardly at all to blame; and notwithstanding strong speeches against him by Sir William Jones, the Attorney General, and old Sergeant Maynard, and that he was not allowed counsel to assist him, he was acquitted both of murder and manslaughter, to the great joy of the by-standers.[1]

Nottingham survived the dissolution of the Oxford parliament nearly two years, and, continuing Chancellor, is chiefly responsible for the unconstitutional system of government by which justice was perverted, and every institution was attacked which had a tendency to check the abitrary will of the Sovereign. He sanctioned the execution of Fitzharris for publishing a libel, and of College, "the Protestant joiner," for making violent speeches at public meetings;—he approved of the plan of wreaking the vengeance of the Court on the popular leaders, by prosecuting them for high treason;—he signed the warrant for the arrest of Shaftesbury, and his commitment to the Tower, on the unfounded charge of having conspired to control the King at Oxford by military violence;—he kept his political opponent many months illegally imprisoned, refusing either to discharge him or to bring him to trial;—and he concurred in the irregular attempts to prevail on a grand jury to find an indictment for high treason against him,—intending, if the indictment had been found, to sit upon his trial as Lord High Steward, and, with the assistance of Peers to be selected for the occasion, to have consigned him to the scaffold. What is still more culpable, he poisoned the fountains of justice. He removed from the Commission of the Peace, throughout England, all magistrates whose political principles were adverse to his own, substituting for them the men that could be found most noted for their love of passive obedi-

[1] 7 St. Tr. 143.

ence, and their hatred of religious toleration. By the same rule did he universally appoint Sheriffs, by whom juries were to be returned,—except the Sheriffs for London and Middlesex, who, by ancient charters held sacred through a long succession of ages, were elected by popular choice. In violation of these charters, he procured the nomination of men who were the mere tools of the Government to be Sheriffs for London and Middlesex;—he instituted arbitrary proceedings in the Court of King's Bench to have those charters canceled; and he unblushingly removed and appointed Judges in this Court, that, contrary to the established law of the land, his purpose might be accomplished.

But he has not to answer for the blood of Russell and of Sydney, as he was removed from this mortal scene before the worst atrocities of the reign of Charles II. were completed. He had long suffered from the gout; and his attacks from that disorder had become so frequent and severe, that he was for months together prevented from attending the House of Lords, the Court of Chancery, or the Council. Chief Justice North used to sit for him frequently as Speaker of the House of Lords, and sometimes in the Court of Chancery, although his love of his work there induced him to struggle to perform it in person, when from bodily suffering he might well have been excused for throwing it on others. "I have known him," observes Roger North, "sit to hear petitions in great pain, and say that his servants had led him out, though he was fitter for his chamber."[1] His frame becoming more and more enfeebled,—soon after the flight of Shaftesbury to Holland, and about a month before the death of his predecessor in office and perpetual rival, Nottingham's career was for ever closed. He expired on the 18th of December, 1682, at his house in Great Queen Street, Lincoln's Inn Fields, in the 61st year of his age.

His remains were interred in the parish church of Ravenstone in Buckinghamshire, where he had an estate which

[1] Life of Lord Guildford, i. 49. His absences from Parliament were occasionally suspected to be from the apprehension of encountering Shaftesbury as we learn from a stanza in "a loyal song:"—

"Ask me no more why little Finch
From parliament began to winch;
Since such as dare to hawk at kings,
With ease can clip a Finch's wings."

had belonged to Cardinal Wolsey, and reverting to the Crown, had been granted to Sir Moyle Finch, the Chancellor's grandfather. A splendid monument was erected to his memory by his eldest son, which thus describes him:—

> "A Person
> Of extraordinary natural endowments, and for manly and unaffected eloquence,
> Universal learning, uncorrupted justice, and indefatigable diligence,
> Most exemplary piety, large and diffusive charity, not unequal to any
> That have gone before him, and an eminent example to posterity.
> In whom all the virtues that make a great and good man
> Were very conspicuous, without the blemish of any vice." [1]

It is impossible, with the slightest regard to justice, to concur in the unqualified praise bestowed upon him as a statesman. Although he had no gratuitous love of despotic government, yet his respect for the constitution was always ready to give way to his own interest, and there were no measures, however arbitrary, brought forward by the Court while he was in office, that he did not zealously assist in executing and defending. His wanton accusation against the Catholics in pronouncing sentence upon Lord Stafford, "that they had burnt the city of London and murdered Sir Edmondsbury Godfrey," I am afraid we must set down to a desire to acquire popularity to the administration,—and he must have regretted it in his heart, though he was rewarded for it with an earldom.

In every other point of view we are at liberty to regard him with unmixed admiration. Considering how very few individuals have distinguished themselves in the profession of the law in England, who have not been urged by necessity to the labor and the sacrifices which it demands, we must honor the energy and steadfastness of purpose which enabled him, the early possessor of large hereditary wealth, to devote himself to the dry study of jurisprudence, and when he had mastered it, to renounce the alluring pursuits which were open to him, that he might attend to the business of his clients in Westminster Hall.

When he had received the Great Seal, he had not yet reached the summit of his ambition,—which was to acquire the reputation (hardly aimed at by his prede-

---

[1] His origin, offices, and alliances are detailed at great length. The monument likewise contains a Latin inscription still more florid. I am indebted for a copy of this to the kindness of the Rev. Mr. Godfrey, the present Vicar of Ravenstone.

cessors) of being a consummate Equity Judge, and of reducing "Equity" as contradistinguished from the common law of England into a scientific system. I have already tried to describe the noble efforts which he made for that purpose.¹

Unfortunately, the brilliancy of his success is impaired to us by the imperfect record of it. His name as a Judge has not utterly perished from the entire want of Reporters; but the printed accounts of his decisions are wretchedly bad. Much inconvenience does arise from the multiplicity and copiousness of Reports in modern times; but we ought to recollect the great advantage we derive from full and accurate statements of all that passes in our courts of justice,—whereby Judges speaking to the nation, are constantly on their good behavior, and while what is trivial soon sinks from notice, that which is important is imperishably preserved. The art of Equity-reporting, though still capable of improvement, has advanced exceedingly, and the worst Equity Reports now are better than the best of the reign of Charles II.

For what Lord Nottingham did and said in the Court of Chancery, we have chiefly to trust to a folio published in 1725, entitled "Reports Tempore Finch,"—being a selection of cases decided by him from 1673 to 1680, in which the Reporter himself was counsel;—but they are miserably executed, containing a defective narrative of the facts,—hardly any statement of the points made by the counsel or the authorities relied on,—and, without the reasons of the Judge, giving only an abstract of the Decree, with the introductory words,—"The Court ordered," or "The Court directed," or "The Court allowed." We have next an anonymous octavo volume, dated 1694, and entitled "Reports of Cases taken and adjudged in the Court of Chancery, from the 20th of Charles II. to the 1st of William and Mary," containing a number of cases by Lord Nottingham, not given in a style more

¹ He issued several orders for regulating the practice of the Court which were generally of a very beneficial nature, but one of them, I am afraid, was prompted by the prevailing desire to vilify and to persecute Quakers. It recites that Quakers, when required to answer bills and interrogatories on oath, got others to personate them, and provides that when Quakers are to put in answers to bills, or to be examined on interrogatories, two previous days' notice shall be given, so that the plaintiff or his solicitor may attend to see them duly sworn.—*Sand. Ord.* I. 348.

satisfactory. Then there is a black-letter folio, published in 1697, under the name of " Cases argued and decreed in the High Court of Chancery from the 12th of Charles II to the 31st, compiled from the Papers of Sir Anthony Keck,"—if possible still worse than than the preceding

There are a few decisions of Lord Nottingham, of little value, to be found in " Reports in Chancery," in " Modern Reports," in " Dickens," in " Vernon," in " Nelson," and in " Freeman;" but till the recent labors of Mr. Swanston, the public had no better means of forming an opinion of his judicial powers. That gentleman, who so ably reported the later decisions of Lord Eldon, has published in the Appendix to his second and third volumes, from the folio MS. volume of Lord Nottingham's judgments in his own handwriting, a number of very important and interesting cases, which strikingly exhibit the characteristics of his judicial style and manner.

It will not be found (as might have been expected from some of the panegyrics upon him that Lord Nottingham was much distinguished from his predecessors by the nature or extent of the particular equitable doctrines which he established. His great merit lay in the scientific method which he pursued. Instead of disposing of a case with a few random observations, like a Chairman at Quarter Sessions, we find his written judgments methodical, and logical even to formalism, reminding one of the resolution of cases of conscience by the schoolmen. His great object continued to be to redeem Equity from the disgrace of being supposed to depend upon the individual opinion or caprice of the Lord Chancellor. With this view he put a strict limit to implied trusts, by which everything might be brought within the jurisdiction of the Court. "A general rule," said he, "to which there is no exception, is this: the law never implies, the Court never presumes, a trust, but in case of absolute necessity. The reason of this rule is sacred; for, if the Chancery do once take liberty to construe a trust by implication of law, or to presume a trust unnecessarily, a way is opened to the Lord Chancellor to construe or presume any man in England out of his estate; and so at last every case in Court will become *casus pro amico*."[1]

Another admirable rule guided him,—never in the

[1] Cook v. Fountain, 3 Swanst. 592.

absence of fraud, to interfere with contracts, or with obligations solemnly contracted. "If a man," said he, "will improvidently bind himself up by a voluntary deed, and not reserve a liberty to himself by a power of revocation, this Court will not loose the fetters he hath put upon himself, but he must lie down under his own folly."[1]

Bishop Burnet concludes his life of Hale with a character of that great judge, "furnished to him by one of the greatest men of the profession of the law," who was no other than Lord Nottingham, and who, after mentioning that Sir Matthew was frequently called into the Court of Chancery to advise the Lord Chancellor or Lord Keeper, says:—" He looked upon Equity as a part of the common law, and one of the grounds of it; and, therefore, as near as he could, he did always reduce it to certain rules and principles, that men might study it as a science, and not think the administration of it had anything arbitrary in it." There Lord Nottingham may be considered as having drawn his own portrait, and to have revealed the secret of his own pre-eminence.[2]

Roger North blames him for too much facility in hearing counsel; but, I believe, he only showed the desire, which is most shown by Judges who least want it, to have the best assistance of the bar in coming to a right conclusion. It is related that Mr. Somers, afterwards the great Lord Chancellor, when a very young man, rising after five or six seniors, said, "that he was of the same side, but that so much had been already said, he had no room to add any thing, and therefore he would not take up his Lordship's time by repeating what had been so well urged by the gentlemen who went before him." "Sir," said Lord Nottingham, "pray go on. I sit in this place to hear everybody. You never repeat, nor will you take up my time, and therefore I shall listen to you with pleasure."

His most important decision, while he held the Great Seal, probably was, that the obligation on constituencies to pay wages to their representatives in the House of Commons, still continues. After the dissolution of parliament, in 1681, Thomas King, Esq., late member for Harwich, presented a petition, stating "that he had

[1] Villars *v.* Beaumont, 1 Vern. 101.
[2] See Preface to Hale's P. C. by Evelyn, vii. n. *h.*

served as burgesse in parliament for the said borrough severall yeares, and did give his constant attendance therein; but that the said borrough had not paid him his wages, though often requested so to do." Notice being given to the corporation of Harwich, and the facts being verified, the Lord Chancellor ordered the writ to issue *De expensis burgensium levandis*.[1]

It is now ascertained that Lord Nottingham was the author of the most important and most beneficial piece of juridical legislation of which we can boast,—the famous "Statute of Frauds,"[2] the glory of which was long divided between Lord Hale and Sir Leoline Jenkins. In his judgment in the case of *Ash* v. *Abdy*, lately published from his MS. by Mr. Swanston,—commenting on the Statute of Frauds, he says, "I have some reason to know the meaning of this law; for it had its first rise from me, who brought in the bill into the Lord's House, though it afterwards received some additions and improvements from the Judges and the civilians."[3]

He never aspired to authorship beyond the printing of a few of his speeches as pamphlets soon after they were spoken,—in imitation of Shaftesbury,—looking more to the temporary impression he might make on public opinion than to permanent reputation. The manuscript reports of his judgments he wrote merely that he might be better enabled to perform his judicial duties. He inserts in his collection a few notes in the form of a journal, but without any thought of appearing to posterity as an autobiographer. His different treatises on the juridical and

---

[1] Reg. Lib. A. 1679, p, 215. I believe this is the last order made for payment of wages. Some say that Andrew Marvell was regularly paid his wages as long as he served for Hull, but I believe he only received from his constituents yearly a complimentary cask of herrings. I know no reason in point of law, why any member may not now insist on payment of his wages, or, if he never means to stand again for the same or any other place, why, in point of prudence, he may not insist on his rights. In most cases the proceeding would be what in the law of Scotland is called "an action of repetition," to recover back money *wrongously* received. For this point of the People's Charter—payment of wages—no new law is required.

[2] 29 Charles 2, c. 3.

[3] 3 Swanston, 664. Lord Hale and Leoline Jenkins may have been two of the Judges and civilians who assisted in improving it.—See Gilb. *Rep. in Eq.* 171. North's *Life of Guilford*, i. 209. 1 Burr. 418. 5 East, 17. If Lord Nottingham drew it, he was the less qualified to construe it, the author of an act considering more what he privately intended, than the meaning he has expressed.

constitutional subjects he composed entirely for his own use, without any view to publication, either during his life or after his death. That "On the King's power of granting Pardons in Cases of Impeachment," written while proceedings were depending against Lord Danby, was published by Mr. Hargrave, in the year 1791, from a MS. in Lord Lansdowne's library, as it was supposed to throw light on some of the questions agitated during the impeachment of Mr. Hastings. He appears to have written well for one accustomed to pore over the musty folios which then formed the lawyer's library, and which were more immethodical in their arrangement, and more barbarous in their diction, as they were more recent; but he is at an immeasurable distance from the ease and elegance which now characterized the prose of Sir William Temple and of Dryden.[1]

He was a great patron of learning. Bishop Burnet, in the preface to the History of the Reformation, pays the following compliment to his liberality and kindness:—
" The Right Honorable the Lord Finch, now Lord High Chancellor of England, whose great parts and greater virtues are so conspicuous, that it were a high presumption in me to say anything in his commendation, being in nothing more eminent than in his zeal for and care of this Church, thought it must be of some importance to have its history well digested; and therefore, *as he bore a large share of my expense*, so he took it more particularly under his care; and, under all the burdens of that high employment which he now bears, yet *found time for reading it in manuscript*, of which he must have robbed himself, since he never denies it to those who have a right to it on any public account, and *hath added such remarks and corrections as are no small part of any finishing it may be judged to have*."[2]

A still more striking tribute to his protection of men distinguished by their literary acquirements we have in a letter from the famous Bishop Warburton to the granddaughter of Lord Nottingham, who was married to the first Lord Mansfield, the celebrated Chief Justice of the King's Bench:—

---

[1] I have recently been much struck by an admirable paper written by Lord Nottingham, justifying the privileges of the Commons in granting supplies—and denying the power of the Lords to alter a money bill.   3 Hatsell, p. 371. —*Note to 4th Ed.*
[2] Pref. to 2nd Part, p iv.

"Madam,—You ought not to think strange of an address of this kind from a churchman to the granddaughter of that great magistrate, who, while he held the Seals for the King and constitution, besides the most exemplary attention to the proper business of his office, was elegantly ambitious to give the last polish to his country by a patronage of learning and science.

"He took early into his notice, and continued long in his protection every great name in letters and religion, from Cudworth, who died in the reign of Charles II. to Prideaux, who lived under George I. It was the care and culture of an age, and, in spite of a dissolute and abandoned Court, he made the reign of Charles II. to be what it is now likely to be always esteemed,—our golden age of literature. The glory of bearing this relation to *so faithful a guardian of the human faculties in their nonage*, Providence, in reward of your virtues, hath doubled in a still nearer relation to one who, in his high station, may, with the same justice, be esteemed the great support of civil liberty, and is now engaged in the like generous task for the very being of a free community, which the other so successfully accomplished for that chief ornament of it, literature and science.

"But the honors you derive from others you preserve untarnished by the splendor of those you have acquired for yourself in the course of a sober and enlightened piety, which makes you an example to the rest of your sex, as the patriotic virtues of your illustrious consort will make him to the wisest of his."[1]

Lord Nottingham was particularly praised by his contemporaries for the conscientious impartiality with which he disposed of the church preferment in his gift as Chancellor. His anxiety on this subject is feelingly expressed in a letter to his chaplain, Dr. Sharp, afterwards Archbishop of York, whom he considered more competent than himself to exercise the duty of judicious selection: "The greatest difficulty I apprehend in my office, is the patronage of ecclesiastical preferments. God is my witness that I would not knowingly prefer an unworthy person; but as my course of life and studies has lain another way, I can not think myself so good a judge of the merits

---

[1] Nichol's Literary Anecdotes, ix. p. 626. Additions to the fifth vol.: "Warburton."

of such suitors as you are. I therefore charge it upon your conscience as you will answer it to Almighty God, that upon every such occasion you make the best inquiry and give me the best advice you can, that I may never bestow any favor upon an undeserving man; which if you neglect to do, the guilt will be entirely yours, and I shall save my own soul."

He was most strictly decent and moral in private life,— setting an example peculiarly useful and praiseworthy, when we consider that, to show a hatred of puritanism, and to gain favor at Court, it was thought necessary to assume vices if men had them not, and that his predecessor having bandied compliments with the Sovereign on their rival claims to profligacy, his successor was strongly and seriously advised, if he would retain his office, openly to keep a mistress.

Lord Nottingham had the misfortune to lose his wife after she had brought him fourteen children, and he continued for the rest of his days as a widower affectionately to cherish her memory.

It is related of him, that he comforted himself by taking the Great Seal to bed with him, and that thus on the 7th of February,[1] 1677, he saved it from the fate which then befell the mace, and afterwards the Great Seal itself, in the time of Lord Chancellor Thurlow, who had not treated it so tenderly. "About one in the morning," says Wood, "the Lord Chancellor Finch his mace was stole out of his house in Queen Street. The Seal laid under his pillow, so the thief missed it. The famous thief that did it was Thomas Sadler, soon after taken and hanged for it at Tyburn."[2]

He was much applauded for the dignity with which he kept up the state of his high office. Besides his townhouse, in which he gave sumptuous banquets to all classes of men, he had a villa at Kensington, to which he could retire with a few chosen friends, and enjoy fresh air and repose amidst the gardens and meadows which surrounded it.[3] He was so wealthy, that after he had held the Great Seal a few years he gave up to the King the allowance of £4,000 a year assigned to him for the expense of his

---

[1] A. Wood's Life, ii. 264.   [2] Ath. Ox.
[3] On the site of this stands the royal palace of William III.—an enlargement of Lord Nottingham's house.

tables, and he never solicited any grant of land, or bargained for any pension upon his retirement.

He seems to have been fanciful about his health, and to have been a believer not only in the occult powers of medicine, but in astrology. In the diary of the famous Elias Ashmole, under date 23rd October, 1682, we find this entry: "My Lord Chancellor Finch sent for me to cure him of his rheumatism. I dined there, but would not undertake the cure." On calculating the Lord Chancellor's nativity, I presume it was ascertained that the aspect of the stars was unfavorable. If he joined Dryden in such vagaries, need we be much astonished when we find grave characters believing in *clairvoyance* at the present day?

Instead of attempting any general character of him myself, I shall conclude with some conflicting observations made upon him by others, which may better assist the reader to appreciate his merits and defects. "He was a formalist," says Roger North, "and took pleasure in hearing and deciding, and gave way to all kinds of motions the counsel would offer; supposing, that if he split the hairs, and with his gold scales determined reasonably on one side of the motion, justice was nicely done. Not imagining what torment the people endured, who were torn from the law and there (in Equity) tossed in a blanket."[1]

"He was a man of probity," says Bishop Burnet of his patron, reposing at Ravenstone, "and well versed in the laws; but very ill-bred, vain, and haughty. He was long much admired for his eloquence; but it was labored and affected, and he saw it as much despised before he died. He had no sort of knowledge in foreign affairs, and yet he loved to talk of them perpetually; by which he exposed himself to those who understood them. He thought he was bound to justify the Court in all the debates in the House of Lords, which he did with the vehemence of a pleader rather than with the solemnity of a senator. He was an incorrupt Judge, and in his Court he could resist the strongest applications, even from the King himself, though he did it nowhere else. He was

---

[1] Life of Guilford, ii. 74. I should have thought that smothering between two feather beds,—or starving to death in a dungeon, would have been a better illustration of the fate of a Chancery victim.

too eloquent: on the bench, in the House of Lords, and even in common conversation, that eloquence became in him ridiculous."[1]

Duke Wharton out of spite to Shaftesbury, bestows upon Nottingham unmixed commendation—" He had no pimps, poets, and buffoons to administer to pleasure or flattery. His train was made up of gentlemen of figure, men of estates, barristers at law, and such as had a reputation in the profession, and were suitable and becoming so high a station. His decrees were pronounced with the greatest solemnity and gravity; no man's ever were in higher esteem, had more weight, or carry greater authority at this very day than his do. He was a great refiner, but never made use of nice distinctions to prejudice truth, or color over what deserves the worst of names. He frequently declared he sat there to do justice, and as long as his Majesty was pleased to continue him on that seat, he would do it by the help of God impartially to all,—to the officer as well as the suitor. If the officer exceeded his just fees, or played tricks with the client, he would fine or punish him severely; at the same time, the trouble and attendance of the officer (he thought) justly entitled him to his fees. His reprimands were mixed with sweetness and severity, and so pointed as to correct, not confound the counsel. He was, indeed, difficult of access; but when once you had admittance, you found nothing from him but what was fair, just, and honorable; so that he had the happiness to send most people away with pleasure and satisfaction. His morals were as chaste as his writings, and they who have pretended to criticise the one, could never find the least fault with the other. His conversation was always with the greatest deference to decency and good manners. He was ever on his guard to parry the thrusts of witty courtiers and men of pleasantry. To figure this great and inestimable man aright, and to paint him in his true colors, and with some warmth of imagination, but still with the greatest submission to strict justice, I would seat him on his throne with a ray of glory about his head, his ermines without spot or blemish, his balance in his right hand, mercy on his left, splendor and brightness at his feet, and his tongue dispensing truth, goodness, virtue, and justice to mankind."[2]

[1] Own Times, vol. ii. 28—137.   [2] True Briton, No. 69.

From the author of the interesting Life of Bishop Bull we have the following warm testimony to the merits of Lord Nottingham:—" His Lordship was justly esteemed the great oracle of the law in his time, and so perfect a master in the art of speaking, that he passed for the English Cicero. Yet his great understanding, his eloquent tongue, and his titles of honor, did not give his name so lasting a luster as that piety and virtue wherewith he adorned his high station, which is but too often starved in so rich a soil, and thriveth best in a private life." [1]

He is again favorably contrasted with Shaftesbury in the second part of " Absalom and Achitophel:"—

> " Sincere was AMRI, and not only knew,
> But Israel's sanctions into practice drew;
> Our laws that did a boundless ocean seem,
> Were coasted all and fathomed all by him
> No Rabbin speaks like him their mystic sense,
> So just, and with such charms of eloquence;
> To whom the double blessing does belong,
> With Moses' inspiration, Aaron's tongue."

All juridical writers, both in this country and in America, worship him as the first of lawyers. Blackstone in his enthusiasm having described him as "the zealous defender of the laws and constitution," goes on truly to say he was " endued with a pervading genius that enabled him to discover and to pursue the true spirit of justice, notwithstanding the embarrassments raised by the narrow and technical notions which then prevailed in the Courts of Law, and the imperfect ideas of redress which had possessed the Courts of Equity. The reason and necessities of mankind arising from the great change in property by the extension of trade, and the abolition of military tenures, co-operated in establishing his plan, and enabled him, in the course of nine years, to build a system of jurisprudence and jurisdiction upon wide and rational foundations." [2]

The great Chancellor Kent, after repeating this eulogy on Lord Nottingham, adds, " We have but few reports of his decisions that are worthy of his fame. They are diffused through several works of inferior authority. It is from his time, however, that Equity became a regular and

---

[1] Nelson's Life of Bishop Bull, 277, 278.   [2] 3 Bl. Com. 56.

cultivated science, and the judicial decisions in Chancery are to be carefully studied."[1]

Finally, Professor Story, who has treated this subject more systematically than any English jurist, in giving a history of Equity, observes, " With Lord Nottingham a new era commenced. He was a person of eminent abilities and the most incorruptible integrity. He possessed a fine genius and great liberality of views, and a thorough comprehension of the true principles of Equity, so that he was enabled to expand the remedial justice of the Court far beyond the aims of his predecessors. He built up a system which served as a model for succeeding judges to the Court ; and hence he has been emphatically called *the Father of Equity.*"[2]

His descendants were most distinguished members of the peerage of England. Daniel, his eldest son, not only succeeded to his titles, but, on the failure of the older branch of the Finch family, to the earldom of Winchilsea, and they are all now enjoyed by his lineal representative, the present Earl of Winchilsea and Nottingham.

The Chancellor's second son, Heneage, was bred to the law, and almost rivaled his father in the brilliancy and success of his professional career. An innate gift of eloquence was held at that time to be an hereditary talent in the blood of Finch. North, in his discourse on the study of the law, where he is expatiating on the necessity of a lawyer's endeavoring to acquire volubility of talk, after quoting the well-known saying of Sergeant Maynard, that the law is "ARS BABLATIVA," adds, " that all the learning in the world will not set a man up in bar practice without the faculty of a ready utterance, and that is acquired by habit only, unless there be a natural felicity of speech, *such as the family of the Finches is eminent by*." This displayed itself conspicuously in young Heneage, who was called "silver-tongued Finch," and with general approbation was appointed Solicitor General while his father held the Great Seal. From this post he was removed soon after the accession of James II. for his opposition to the arbitrary measures of the Court. He then joined the Whig party, was one of the principal counsel for the seven Bishops, and assisted in bringing in King William. Early in the reign of Queen Anne, he was

[1] Kent's Com. 491. [2] Story's Equity, i. 46.

called to the Upper House as Baron Guernsey, and on the accession of George I. he was created Earl of Aylesford, the title now borne by his great-great-grandson. He completed the list of the eminent men who have made the name of Finch so conspicuous in our legal annals.

Although Charles II. survived Lord Chancellor Nottingham above two years—as he never called another parliament, this may be the most convenient opportunity for taking a short review of the changes introduced into the law while he was upon the throne. Blackstone goes so far as to say, that "notwithstanding much practical oppression in this reign, wicked, sanguinary, and turbulent as it was, the constitution of England had arrived to its full vigor, and the true balance between liberty and prerogative was happily established by law."[1] Certainly great benefits were conferred upon the public by converting military tenures into common soccage—by entirely sweeping away purveyance and pre-emption—by abolishing the writ "*De hæretico comburendo*,"[2] which might otherwise now have been called into action against Unitarians and other dissenters—by "the Statute of Distributions,"[3] which makes a most equitable disposition of personal property in case of intestacy; by "the Statute of Frauds," admirably regulating the forms of entering into contracts and making wills;[4] and above all, "the Habeas Corpus Act," the safeguard under which personal liberty has continued to be protected in England to a degree elsewhere unknown. Among the juridical improvements of the reign must likewise be enumerated the practical settlement of certain important constitutional doctrines, such as that the Peers have no original civil jurisdiction, but that they have an appellate jurisdiction from Courts of Equity as well as from Courts of Law;[5] that the King's pardon can not be pleaded in bar of a parliamentary impeachment; and that no commoner can be tried for his life except before his own peers—an English jury. But I believe, regret is now generally felt that some of the clauses of the "Act of Uniformity" are so rigorous and exclusive, and that "the Coventicle Act" and "the Five

---

[1] 4 Bl. Com. 439.   [2] 29 Car. 2. c. 9.   [3] 22 & 23 Car. 2, c. 10.
[4] 29 Car. 2, c. 3. Lord Nottingham used to say, "that every line of it was worth a subsidy."—R. North's *Life of Guilford*, i. 209.
[5] Hale's Jurisdiction of the House of Lords, by Hargrave, cx., clxv., clxxix.

Mile Act" ever passed. I must likewise be permitted to deplore the passing of "the Test and Corporation Acts," and "the Act for excluding Roman Catholics from sitting in Parliament," which have at last been repealed in our own time. Nor do I understand Blackstone's alleged theoretical perfection of the constitution, at a time when the Judges might lawfully be removed on any occasion at the will of the Crown,—when there was no security for the meeting of parliament,—and when his own constitutional oracle, Lord Chancellor Nottingham, laid down, *ex cathedrâ*, that the King of England has a right to dispense with all laws.

At the commencement of the reign, the laudable eagerness for rational legal reform which had distinguished the Commonwealth still prevailed, and a Committee was appointed by the House of Commons, "to confer with such of the Lords, the Judges, and other persons of the long robe, who have already taken pains and made progress in perusing the statute laws, and to consider of repealing such former statute laws as they shall find necessary to be repealed, and of expedients of reducing all statute laws of one nature under such a method and head as may conduce to the more ready understanding and better execution of such laws."[1] The Solicitor General Finch, Sergeant Maynard, Prynne, and many other eminent lawyers, were members of the Committee; but the codification of the statute law is still reserved for the glory of the present or some future government. Under Charles II. political faction and religious controversey soon absorbed all attention and interest, and nothing effectual was done to correct the abuses prevailing either in the Courts of Law or Equity, so that the satire of the poet met with a response from the public voice, when he sang:—

> "He that with injury is griev'd
> And goes to law to be reliev'd,
> Is sillier than a sottish chouse,
> Who, when a thief has robb'd his house,
> Applies himself to *cunning men*,
> To help him to his goods again;
> When all he can expect to gain
> Is but to squander more in vain.—
> Does not in Chancery ev'ry man swear
> What makes best for him in his answer?
> And while their purses can dispute,
> There is no end of th' *immortal suit.*"[2]

---

[1] Com. Journ. viii. 631.   [2] Hudibras, part iii. cant. 2.

CHAPTER XCIV.

LIFE OF LORD KEEPER GUILFORD FROM HIS BIRTH TILL HE WAS APPOINTED SOLICITOR GENERAL.

WE now come to one of the most contemptible men who ever held the Great Seal of England. He had not courage to commit great crimes; but—selfish, cunning, sneaking, and unprincipled,—his only restraint was a regard to his own personal safety, and throughout his whole life he sought and obtained advancement by the meanest arts. Nottingham was succeeded by FRANCIS NORTH, known by the title of "Lord Keeper GUILFORD."

Our hero, although he himself ascribed his success to his poverty, was of noble birth. The founder of his family was Edward North, a Sergeant at law, Chancellor of the Augmentations, and created a Baron by writ in the reign of Henry VIII.[1] Dudley, the third Baron, "having consumed the greatest part of his estate in the gallantries of King James's Court, or rather his son, Prince Henry's," retired and spent the rest of his days at his seat in Cambridgeshire. When the civil war broke out, he sided with the parliament, and, on rare occasions, coming to London, he is said to have sat on the trial of Laud, and to have voted for his death. Having reached extreme old age, he died in the year 1666.[2]

Dudley, his heir, who at the age of sixty-three, stood on the steps of the throne in the House of Lords "as the eldest son of a Peer," was a great traveler in his youth, and served with distinction in the Low Countries, under Sir Francis Vere. Yet he never would put on his hat nor sit down in the presence of his father, unless by the old Peer's express commands. Being returned to the Long Parliament for the county of Cambridge, he strenuously opposed the Court, and signed the Solemn League and Covenant; but, adhering to the Presbyterian party, he was turned out by *Pride's purge*,[3] and lived in retirement till the Restoration. He married Anne, one of the daughters and coheirs of Sir Charles Montagu, brother of the

[1] April 5. 1554 [2] Grandeur of Law. Collins. [3] 2 Parl. Hist. 600.

Earl of Manchester, by whom he had a very numerous family.

The subject of this memoir was their second son, and was born on the 22nd of October, 1637.[1] Though he turned out such a zealous royalist and high churchman, it is curious to think that his early training began among republicans and fanatics. As soon as he left the nursery, he was sent to a preparatory school at Isleworth, the master of which was a rigid Presbyterian. His wife was a furious Independent, and she ruled the household. "She used to instruct her babes in the gift of praying by the Spirit, and all the scholars were made to kneel by a bedside and pray; but this petit spark was too small for that posture, and was set upon the bed to kneel with his face to a pillow. She then led off their devotions, as one specially inspired; but all that North could distinctly recollect of them was, that *he prayed for his distressed brethren in Ireland.*"[2]

His family becoming disgusted with the extravagance of the ruling powers, and beginning to look to royalty as the only cure for the evils the nation was suffering, he was removed from Isleworth, and put to a grammar school at Bury St. Edmunds, under a cavalier master. Here principles of loyalty were secretly instilled into him; and as a proof of his proficiency in the Latin tongue, he made out a list of all the verbs neuter, which was printed in an appendix to Lilly's Grammar.

In 1653 he was admitted a fellow commoner at St. John's College, Cambridge. He is said to have remained there two or three years, applying diligently to the studies of the place; but he seems to have devoted much of his time to the bass-viol, and he left the university without a degree.

He was then transferred to the Middle Temple. When he was entered, the treasurer was Chaloner Chute, the eminent counsel, famous for having been the Speaker of Cromwell's parliaments, and more famous among lawyers for his habits, when he wished to pass a few months in pleasure after his own humor, of saying to his clerk,—

---

[1] Roger North, his biographer, does not mention the time of his birth, and it has been generally laid in the year 1640; but I have clearly ascertained this date by an inscription on his tombstone in the parish church of Wroxton, near Banbury, in Oxfordshire. [2] North's Life of Guilford. i. 11

"Tell the people I will not practice this term,"—being able, when he pleased, to resume his business, which was nothing shrunk by the discontinuance. The Treasurer, who was nearly connected by marriage with the North family, having the power of fixing the admission fee, which was seldom less than five pounds, asked Sir Dudley, the father, what he was willing to give; and he answering, "Three pounds ten," and the money being laid down, the Treasurer swept it all into the hat of young Frank, marking the admission *nil*, and saying,—" Let this be a beginning of your getting money here."[1]

His father bought him a very small set of chambers, in which he shut himself up, and dedicated himself to the study of the law. He early learned and often repeated this saying of the citizens to their apprentices,—" Keep your shop, and your shop will keep you." He did not frequent riding-schools, or dancing-schools, or play-houses, or gaming-houses,—so dangerous to youth at the Inns of Court. Though he could " make one at gammon, gleek, piquet, or even the merry-main, he had ever a notable regard to his purse to keep that from oversetting, like a vessel at sea that hath too much sail and too little ballast."[2]

While a student, he paid frequent and long visits to his grandfather, who seems to have become a most singularly tyrannical and capricious old man. Frank exerted himself to the utmost to comply with all his humors, being allowed by him £20 a year; but lost his favor and his pension by conveying to him, at the request of Sir Dudley, the father, some caution about the appointment of a steward. He had at last a qualified pardon in a letter concluding with these words—" *In consilium ne accesseris antequam voceris*—do not offer your advice before it is asked." He was always industrious, and during these visits, though he could not altogether avoid bowling, fishing, hunting, visiting, and billiards, he spent the greater part of his time in reading and common-placing the law books brought down to him by the carrier.

While in town, he always dined in the hall,—twelve at noon being the hour of dinner,—and supped there again at six;—after which " case-putting" began in the cloister

---

[1] It appears by the books of the Middle Temple, that he was admitted Nov. 27, 1655. [2] Life, i. 17.

walks,—and he acquired the character of a great "put-case." He kept a common-place book, which seems to have been almost as massive as "Brooke's Abridgment of the Law." He made himself well acquainted with the Year Books, although not altogether so passionately attached to them as Sergeant Maynard, who, when he was taking an airing in his coach, always carried a volume of them along with him, which, he said, amused him more than a comedy. He attended all famous legal arguments, particularly those of Sir Heneage Finch, and taking notes in the morning in law French, he employed himself most usefully at night in making out in English a report of the cases he had heard.

By way of relaxation he would go to music meetings, or to hear Hugh Peters preach. Nothing places him in such an amiable point of view as the delight he is said to have taken, on rare occasions, in "a petit supper and a bottle," —when there really seems to have been a short oblivion of anxiety about his rise in the world; but, to show his constitutional caution, his brother Roger assures us that, " whenever he was a little overtaken, it was a warning to him to take better care afterwards."

We are told that while he was a student he "under-pulled" or managed suits for his grandfather, father, and other friends—an occupation which rather puzzles us—for it was not merely superintending a solicitor who conducted them, but he himself made out to his clients a bill of fees and disbursements, in which his grandfather violently suspected that he was guilty of great frauds. Yet a solicitor was employed, who likewise made out a bill, on which he offered North a percentage, saying that " it was their way, and they were allowed at the offices somewhat for encouragement to them that brought business."[1] There are many things to show that the administration of justice between party and party, as well as between the crown and the subject, is much purer now than in former times.

Long before he was called to the bar, "he undertook the practice of court-keeping;" that is, he was appointed the steward of a great many manors by his grandfather and other friends, and he did all the work in person, writing all his court rolls, and making out his copies with

[1] Life, i. 36.

his own hand. I am afraid he now began his violation of the rights and liberties of his fellow-subjects by practicing some petty extortions upon the bumpkins who came before him. "His grandfather," says Roger, with inimitable simplicity, " had a venerable old steward, careful by nature and faithful to his Lord, employing all his thoughts and time to manage for supply of his house and upholding his rents,—*in short, one of a race of human kind heretofore frequent, but now utterly extinct,*—affectionate as well as faithful, and diligent rather for love than self-interest. This old gentleman, with his boot-hose and beard, used to accompany his young master to his court-keeping, and OBSERVING HIM REASON THE COUNTRY PEOPLE OUT OF THEIR PENCE FOR ESSOINES, &c., he commended him, saying, ' If you will be contented, Master Frank, to be a great while getting a little, you will be a little while getting a great deal ;' wherein he was no false prophet."[1]

Having been the requisite time on the books of the society of the Middle Temple, and performed all his moots (upon which he bestowed great labor), Francis was called to the bar, *ex debito justitiæ*. He might have been called earlier, *ex gratia ;* but he wisely remembered Lord Coke's warning against *præpropera praxis*, as well as *præpostera lectio*, and he acted upon the maxim which still holds true, that "he who is not a good lawyer before he comes to the bar, will never be a good one after it."

The allowance of sixty pounds a-year which he had hitherto received from his father was now reduced to fifty, in respect of the pence he collected by court-keeping and the expected profits of his practice. He highly disapproved of this reduction, and wrote many letters to his father to remonstrate against it. At last he received an answer which he hoped was favorable, but which contained only these words:—" Frank, I suppose by this time, having vented all your discontent, you are satisfied with what I have done." The reduced allowance, however, was continued to him as long as his father lived, who said " he would not discourage industry by rewarding it when successful with loss."

The young barrister was now hard put to it. He took "a practicing chamber" on a first floor in Elm Court, "a

[1] Life, i. 33.

dismal hole—dark next the Court, and on the other side a high building of the Inner Temple standing within five or six yards of the windows." He was able to fill his shelves with all useful books of the law from the produce of certain legacies and gifts collected for him by his mother, and he seems still to have had a small pecuniary help from his grandfather.[1] For some time he had great difficulty in keeping free from debt; but he often declared that " if he had been sure of a hundred pounds a-year to live upon, he had never been a lawyer."

He is much praised by his brother, because it is said " he did not (as seems to have been common), for the sake of pushing himself, begin by bustling about town and obtruding himself upon attorneys or bargaining for business, but was contented if chance or a friend brought him a motion as he was standing at the bar taking notes." These, however, came so rarely that he fell into a very dejected and hypochondriacal state. Thinking himself dying, he carried a list of his ailments to a celebrated physician, Dr. Beckenham of Bury, who laughed at him and sent him away, prescribing fresh air and amusement.

He was in danger of utterly sinking in the slough of despond, when he was suddenly taken by the hand by the great lawyer, Sir Jeffrey Palmer, who was made Attorney General on the restoration of Charles II., and who, if he had lived must have been Lord Chancellor. His son, Edward, a very promising young man, lately called to the bar, died about this time in the arms of Francis North, who had been at college with him, and had shown him great attention during his illness.

All the business destined for young Palmer now somehow found its way to his surviving friend. Patronage, recommendation, and canvassing to push a young lawyer into business, were not in those days deemed irregular. We are told, without any suspicion of impropriety, that North was now supported " through the whole relation and dependence of Sir Jeffrey " and that " his wheel of good fortune turned upon the favor of Mr. Attorney Palmer." This powerful protector rapidly brought him forward by employing him in government prosecutions,[2]

---

[1] At that time not more than fifty volumes were required. Now, unfortunately a law library is "multorum camelorum onus."

[2] 6 St. Tr. 520, 540, 830.

and even when he himself was confined by illness, by giving him his briefs in smaller matters to hold for him in Court. North, we may be sure, was most devotedly assiduous in making a suitable return for this kindness, and in flattering his patron. Instead of the sentiments he had imbibed from his family in his early days, he now loudly expressed those of an ultra-prerogative lawyer, exalting the power of the King both over the church and the parliament.

Being considered a rising man, his private friends and near relations came to consult him. He was once asked if he took fees from them. "Yes," said he; "they, no doubt, come to do me a kindness; and what kindness have I if I refuse their money?"

Soon after he was called to the bar he went the Norfolk circuit, where his family interest lay; but here again he chiefly relied upon his grand resource of flattering his superiors, and accommodating himself to their humors. "He was exceeding careful to keep fair with the cocks of the circuit, and particularly with Sergeant Earl, who had almost a monopoly. The Sergeant was a very covetous man, and when none would starve with him in journeys, this young gentleman kept him company."[1] They once rode together from Cambridge to Norwich without drawing bit, to escape the expense of baiting at an inn, and North would have been famished if the Sergeant's man, knowing his master's habits, had not privately furnished him with a cake. He asked the Sergeant, out of compliment to his riches, how he kept his accounts, "for you have," said he, "lands, securities, and great comings in of all kinds." "Accounts, boy'" exclaimed the Sergeant, "I get as much as I can, and I spend as little as I can; and there is all the account I keep." In these journeys the Sergeant talked so agreeably of law, and tricks, and purchases, and management, that North's hunger was beguiled, and he thought only of the useful knowledge he was acquiring, and the advantage to be derived from the countenance of a man so looked up to.

In court he stood in great awe of the leaders, "for they having the conduct of the cause, take it ill if a young man blurts out anything, though possibly to the purpose, because it seems to top them."[2] Therefore he would not

[1] Life, i. 69. [2] Ibid. i. 70.

make himself too conspicuous, "and when he had a point he always communicated it to his leader, who would sometimes desire him to move it himself, and would be sure thereafter to try to have his assistance."[1]

His business was increased on the circuit by his becoming a Commissioner of the Bedford Level, by his rise to be Chief Justice of Ely, and by his acting as Counsel for the Crown in a grand Eyre to visit all the forests south of Trent. But still nothing pleased him so much as to get on by personal favor.

Lord Chief Justice Hyde generally rode the Norfolk circuit and so completely had North taken the measure of his foot, that my Lord called him "Cousin" in open Court, " which was a declaration that he would take it for a respect to himself to bring him causes." The biographer to whom we are so much indebted lays it down that there is no harm in a Judge letting it be known " that a particular counsel will be easily heard before him, and that his errors and lapses, when they happen, will not offend his Lordship or hurt the cause, *beyond which* the profession of favor is censurable both to judge and counsel." The morality of the bar in those days will be better understood by the following observations of simple Roger: " In circuit practice there is need of an exquisite knowledge of the Judge's humor, as well as his learning and ability to try causes ; and he, North, was a wonderful artist at watching a Judge's tendency, to make it serve his turn, and yet never failed to pay the greatest regard and deference to his opinion: for so they get credit, because *the Judge for the most part thinks that person the best lawyer that respects most his opinion.* I have heard his Lordship say, that sometimes he hath been forced to give up a cause to the Judge's opinion when he (the Judge) was plainly in the wrong, and when more contradiction had but made him more positive ; and, besides, that in so doing he himself had weakened his own credit with the Judge, and thereby been less able to set him right when he was inclined to it. A good opinion so gained often helps at another time to good purpose, and sometimes to ill purpose ; as I heard it credibly reported of Sergeant Maynard, that being the leading counsel in a small-fee'd cause, would give it up to the Judge's mistake, and not

[1] Life, i. 70.

contend to set him right, that he might gain credit to mislead him in some other cause in which he was well fee'd."[1] These gentlemen of the long robe ought to have changed places in Court with the highwaymen they were retained to prosecute.[2]

There was no nonsense, however arrant, a silly Judge might speak, in deciding for North, which he would not back. Thus a certain Mr. Justice Archer, who seems to have been the laughing-stock of the profession, having, to the amusement of the juniors, " noted a difference between a renunciation of an executorship upon record and *in pais*," North said, " Ay, my Lord ; just so, my Lord"—upon which his Lordship became as fierce as a lion, and would not hear the argument on the other side.[3] But even such a learned and sensible Judge as Chief Justice Hale, North could win by an affectation of modesty, diffidence, and profound veneration. Early in his career, when he found it difficult to get to his place in a very crowded court, Sir Matthew said from the Bench, " Good people, make way for this little gentleman ; he will soon make way for himself."

His consultations were enormously long, and he gained vast applause at them by his care and dexterity in probing the cause, starting objections, inventing points, foretelling what would be said by the opposite counsel and by the Judge, and showing how the verdict might be lost or was to be secured. But, to make security doubly sure, after mastering the record and perusing the deeds to be given in evidence, he himself examined the witnesses, and thus had an opportunity of presenting the facts properly to their minds.

Need we wonder that, from an humble beginner, rejoicing in a cause that came to him, he soon became " Cock of the Circuit," all who had trials rejoicing to have him on their side ?

[1] Life, i. 71.
[2] I have heard a circuit leader avow that he sometimes feebly made bad points, to give the Judge the credit of overruling them, lest it should be thought his Lordship was under undue influence by always deciding in favor of the good points which the counsel strenuously pressed ; but this is the extent of my *nisi prius* confidences.
[3] Archer's incapacity at last excited so much scandal that they tried to remove him from his office, but could not, as, by some accident, he had been appointed *quamdiu se bene gesserit ;* but he was prohibited from sitting on the bench.—Sir. T. Raym. Rep. 217.

I shall give only one specimen of his conduct as a leader. He was counsel for the defendant in an action tried before his friend, JUDGE ARCHER, for not setting out tithes—in which the treble value was to be recovered. Finding that he had not a leg to stand upon, he manœuvred to get his client off with the single value—so he told his Lordship that this was a cause to try a right of a very intricate nature, which would require the reading of a long series of records and ancient writings, and that it ought not to be treated as a penal action ; wherefore, they should agree upon the single value of the tithes, for which the verdict should be taken conditionally, and then proceed fairly to try the merits. The Judge insisted on this course being adopted ; and the other side, not to irritate him, acquiesced in North's proposal. " Then did he open a long history of matters upon record, of bulls, monasteries, orders, greater and lesser house, surrenders, patents, and a great deal more, *very proper if it had been true*, while the counsel on the other side stared at him ; and, having done, they bid him go to his evidence. He leaned back, as speaking to the Attorney, and then, '*My Lord*,' said he, '*we are very unhappy in this cause. The Attorney tells me they forgot to examine their copies with the originals at the Tower ;*' and (so folding up his brief), '*My Lord*,' said he, '*they must have the verdict, and we must come better prepared another time.*' So, notwithstanding all the mooting the other side could make, the Judge held them to it, and they were choused of the treble value." [1]

I shall conclude his circuit life with a redeeming anecdote. " Being invited with the rest of the counsel to dine at Colchester, with the recorder, Sir John Shaw, who was well known to be one of the greatest kill-cows at drinking in the nation, he, with the rest of his brethren, by methods too well known, got very drunk. They were obliged to go on, and in that condition mounted, but some dropped and others proceeded. His Lordship (North) had a clerk, one Lucas, a very drunken fellow, but at that time not far gone. He thought it his duty to have a tender care of

[1] Life, i. 87. Very different was the practice of Sir Matthew Hale. "He abhorred those too common faults of misrepresenting evidence, quoting precedents or books falsely, or asserting anything confidently by which ignorant juries and weak Judges are too often wrought upon."—Burnet's *Life of Sir M. Hale*, 72.

his master, who, having had one fall (contrary to the sound advice of his experienced clerk), would needs get up again, calling him all to nought for his pains. His Lordship was got upon a very sprightly nag, that trotted on very hard, and Lucas came near to persuade him not to go so fast, but that put the horse upon the run, and away he went with his master full speed, so as no one could follow him. The horse, when he found himself clear of pursuers, stopped his course by degrees, and went with his rider (fast asleep upon his back) into a pond to drink, and there sat his Lordship on the sally." We are then told how a barrister's clerk came up, and rescued his Lordship as he was about to fall into the water,— how he was carried to a public house and put to bed, while "the rest of the company went on for fear of losing their market;"—and how his Lordship was astonished when he awoke next morning, having forgotten everything that had happened since his horse ran away with him. It would seem that "his Lordship" could occasionally dismiss from his mind his briefs, his fees, and his tricks, and enjoy good fellowship, ever preserving his characteristic caution; —for Roger says, "he had strength of head to bear a great deal; and when he found that infirmity coming upon him, he used to sit smiling, and say little or nothing." Once, when he was Attorney General, having dined with the Earl of Sandwich, he went in the afternoon to the Privy Council, to plead upon a petition before the King. Next day the Earl asked a Lord who had been present how Mr. Attorney behaved himself. "*Very well*," said the Lord. "*I thought so*," answered the Earl, "*for I sent him instructed with at least three bottles in his belly.*" [1]

But we must now come to more serious matters, in which, instead of the entertaining Roger, we must take for our guides State Trials, Parliamentary Debates, Law Reports and contemporary Histories.

While North had such success on the circuit, he was equally flourishing in Westminster Hall. By answering cases and preparing legal arguments for Sir Jeffrey Palmer, and by flouting at parliamentary privilege, he was still higher than ever in favor with that potential functionary. It happened that in the year 1668, after the fall of the

[1] Life, i. 90.

Earl of Clarendon, a writ of error was brought in the House of Lords upon the judgment of the Court of King's Bench in the great case of "*The King* v. *Sir John Elliot, Denzil Hollis, and Others*," decided in the fifth year of the reign of Charles I.,—Denzil Hollis, now Lord Hollis, being the only defendant surviving. This, it will be recollected, was a prosecution by the King against five members of the House of Commons for what had been done in the House on the last day of the preceding session, when Sir John Finch was held in the chair, while certain resolutions, alleged to be seditious, were voted, and one of the defendants said "that the Council and Judges had all conspired to trample under foot the liberties of the subject." They pleaded to the jurisdiction of the Court of King's Bench, " that the supposed offenses were committed in parliament, and ought not to be punished or inquired of in this Court or elsewhere than in parliament." But their plea was overruled, and they were all sentenced to heavy fine and imprisonment.[1]

Although there had been resolutions of the House of Commons on the meeting of the Long Parliament condemning this judgment, it still stood on record, and Lord Hollis thought it was a duty he owed his country, before he died, to have it reversed.

Sir Jeffrey Palmer, as Attorney General, pleaded *in nullo est erratum;* but having returned his writ of summons to the House of Lords, and being in the habit of sitting there on the woolsack as one of the assessors to the Peers, he could not himself argue the case as counsel at the bar. The King's Sergeants declined to do so out of respect for the House of Commons. Francis North thinking this a most favorable opportunity to make himself known at Court as an antiparliamentarian lawyer, volunteered to support the judgment, and his services were accepted. He says himself " he was satisfied he argued on the right side, and that on the record the law was for the King." Accordingly, on the appointed day, he boldly contended that, as the Information averred that the offenses were *against the peace*, as privilege of parliament does not extend to offenses in breach of the peace, as they had not been punished in the parliament in which they were committed, and as no subsequent parliament could take notice

[1] 3 St. Tr. 294. Lord Campbell's Speeches, p. 202.

of them, they were properly cognizable in a Court of common law. The judgment was reversed,[1]—but North's fortune was made. The Duke of York was pleased to inquire " who that young gentleman was who had argued so well? " Being told that " he was the younger son of the Lord North, and, what was rare among young lawyers at that time, of loyal principles," his Royal Highness undertook to encourage him by getting the King to appoint him one of his Majesty's counsel. North was much gratified by receiving a message to this effect, but was alarmed lest the Lord Keeper Bridgeman, who, by his place, was to superintend preferments in the law, might conceive a grudge against him for this interference with his patronage. The Lord Keeper acquitted him of all blame, wished him joy, and with peculiar civility desired him to take his place within the bar.

The job, however, seems very much to have shocked the grave Benchers of the Middle Temple, or Frank had offended them by the insolent airs which he assumed, for they refused to call him to the Bench, " alleging, that if young men by favor so preferred came up straight to the Bench, and by their precedence topped the rest of the ancient Benchers, it might in time destroy the government of the society." He went round to the Judges complaining of this as a slight to the King. " The very next day, in Westminster Hall, when any of the Benchers appeared at the Courts, they received reprimands from the Judges for their insolence, as if a person whom his Majesty had thought fit to make one of his counsel extraordinary was not worthy to come into their company, and so dismissed them unheard, with declaration, that until they had done their duty in calling Mr. North to their Bench, they must not expect to be heard as counsel in his Majesty's Courts. This was English; and that evening they conformed and were reinstated."[2]

Things went on very smoothly with him now till the death of Sir Jeffrey Palmer, when Sir Heneage Finch being promoted to be Attorney General, the Solicitor's place was vacant.[3] North being the only King's Counsel, and having been long employed in Crown business, had a fair

---

[1] 3 St. Tr. 333.
[2] Life, i. 65, 66. He was the only King's counsel then at the bar, and there were very few till after the Revolution. [3] Dug. Or. Jur. 117.

claim to succeed, and he was warmly supported by the Lord Keeper, as well as the new Attorney General, who was desirous of having him as a colleague. But the Duke of Buckingham, at this time considered Prime Minister, preferred Sir William Jones, who was North's chief competitor in the King's Bench, and over whose head he had been put when he received his silk gown.

To terminate the difference they were both set aside, and the office of Solicitor General was given to Sir Edward Turner, Speaker of the House of Commons, who held it for a twelvemonth; at the end of which he was made Chief Baron of the Exchequer, in the room of Sir Matthew Hale, promoted to be Chief Justice of the Common Pleas.

Buckingham's influence had now greatly declined, and North was made Solicitor General without difficulty, Jones being solaced with a silk gown, and the promise of further promotion on the next vacancy.[1]

CHAPTER XCV.

CONTINUATION OF THE LIFE OF LORD GUILFORD TILL HIS APPOINTMENT AS LORD KEEPER.

THE CABAL was now in its full ascendency; and as the leaders did not take any inferior members of the government into their councils, and contrived to prevent the meeting of parliament for nearly two years, the new Solicitor had only to attend to his profession. Of course he gave up the circuit, and he set the example, generally followed for 150 years, of making the Court of Chancery his principal place of practice, on being promoted to be a law officer of the Crown,—henceforth going to other Courts only in cases in which the Crown was concerned, or which were of very great magnitude. To keep up his law,—when he could be spared from the Court of Chancery, he stepped across the Hall and seated himself in the Court of King's Bench, "with his note book in his hand, reporting as the students about the Court did, and, during the whole time of his practice, every Christmas he read over 'Littleton's

[1] Dug. Or. Jur. 117.

Tenures.'" He had hitherto practiced conveyancing to a considerable extent; but he now turned over this business to Siderfin the Reporter, whom he appointed to serve him in the capacity of "*Devil*," as he himself had served Sir Jeffrey Palmer. He was on very decent terms with Sir Heneage Finch, who had much assisted his promotion; but he showed his characteristic cunning by an expedient he adopted to get the largest share of the patent business. According to immemorial usage, all patents of dignity belong exclusively to the Attorney General; but the warrants for all other patents may be carried either to the Attorney or Solicitor. North, with much dexterity, took into his employment a clerk of Sir Jeffrey Palmer, who was reputed to have a magazine of the best precedents, and who had great interest among the attorneys, whereby many patents came to his chambers which otherwise would have gone to the Attorney General's.

But if he was eager to get money, he spent it freely. He was now appointed "Autumn Reader" of the Middle Temple, and though the festivity was not honored with the presence of royalty, like Finch's in the Inner Temple, it was conducted sumptuously, and cost him above £1,000. He took for his subject "the Statute of Fines," which he treated very learnedly, and the arguers against him, the best lawyers of the Society, did their part very stoutly. On the "Grand Day" all the King's chief ministers attended and the profusion of the best provisions and wine led to such debauchery, disorder, tumult, and waste, that this was the last public Reading in the Inns of Court, the lectures being discontinued and the banqueting commuted for a fine.

I must not pass over his loves, although they were not very romantic or chivalrous. He was desirous of being married—among other reasons,—because he was tired of dining in the Hall and eating "a costelet and salad at Chastelin's in the evening with a friend,—and he wished to enjoy the pleasures of domestic life. One would have thought that the younger son of a Peer—of great reputation at the bar,—Solicitor General at thirty-one, and rising to the highest offices in the law,—might have had no difficulty in matching to his mind,—but he met with various rebuffs and disappointments. Above all, he required a wealthy bride,—not then easily to be obtained without the display of a long rent roll. He first addressed the daughter of an old usurer in Gray's Inn, who speedily put an end to the suit by asking him "what estate his father intended to settle upon him for present maintenance, jointure, and provision for children?" He could not satisfy this requisition by an "Abstract" of his "profitable rood of ground in Westminster Hall." He then paid court to a coquettish young widow; but after showing him some favor, she jilted him for a jolly knight of good estate. The next proposition was made to him by a City alderman, the father of many daughters, who, it was given out, were to have each a portion of £6,000. North dined with the alderman, and liked one of them very much, but, coming to treat, the fortune shrunk to £5,000. He immediately took his leave. The alderman ran after him, and offered him to boot £500 on the birth of the first child, but he would not bate a farthing of the £6,000.

At last his mother found him a match to his mind in the Lady Francis Pope, one of the three daughters and coheirs of the Earl of Down, who lived at Wroxton, in Oxfordshire, with fortunes of £14,000 a-piece. We are surprised to find that, with all his circuit and Westminster Hall earnings, he was obliged to borrow £600 from a friend before he could compass £6,000 to be settled upon her. He then ventured down with grand equipage and attendance, and, in less than a fortnight, obtained the young lady's consent, and the writings being sealed, the lovers were happily married. The feasting and jollities in the country lasted three weeks, and Mr. Solicitor, heartily tired of them, was very impatient to get back to his briefs. However, he seems always to have treated his wife, while she lived, with all due tenderness. He took a house in Chancery Lane, near Sergeant's Inn, and acquired huge glory by constructing a drain for the use of the neighborhood,—a refinement never before heard of in that quarter. This was the happiest period of his life.

In the beginning of 1673, the meeting of parliament could be deferred no longer, and it was considered necessary that the Solicitor-General should have a seat in the House of Commons. Lord Chancellor Shaftesbury was now to try his scheme of issuing writs for the election of members without the warrant of the Speaker. It happened that there was a vacancy for Lynn, in Norfolk, by the death of Sir Robert Stuart, and North having great family and personal interest in the town and neighborhood, became a candidate to succeed him. After giving a handsome treat to the electors, he was returned without opposition,—but not without grumbling on their part, that there was no competition to make the money fly. Some of them testily exclaimed, that " Hobson's choice was no choice." But, alas for Mr. Solicitor! before he was allowed to take his seat, all the elections under these writs were declared void by the House of Commons,[1] and he had still the sea to drink. To the great joy of Lynn, a second candidate was at last obtained in Sir Simon Taylor, a wealthy wine-merchant in the town.[2] Butts of sherry were opened in the market-place, gin was as plentiful as water, every spigot in the town ran beer without intermission, and the greatest exertions were used to induce the electors to vote for their townsman. However, the government was not to be disgraced by the rejection of their law officer, and he was so considerably at the head of the poll, that Sir Simon Taylor signed the indenture of his return. There were good hopes that, on account of the corrupt practices to which his friends had resorted, he would have been thrown out upon a petition; but, according to the notion of election law which then prevailed, the step of acquiescence which his opponent had taken precluded the attempt, and he was allowed quietly to keep his seat.

He remained member for Lynn till he was made Chief Justice of the Common Pleas, in January, 1675; but I can hardly find any trace of his ever having spoken in the House of Commons. During two short sessions, in 1673, he was Solicitor-General, and things were in such confusion from Lord Shaftesbury being in opposition while he remained Chancellor, that the members of the government were quite at a loss what part to take in the Lower

[1] 4 Parl. Hist. 507. Ante, p. 132.
[2] I can testify from having witnessed it, that the scene of the greatest exultation and joy in this world, is the procession of the "third man" entering a borough during a canvass for the election of members of parliament. Those who do not mean to support him, and know that he has no chance of success, equally rejoice—in the consciousness of their own increased importance;—and from his worship the Mayor down to the beggar in the street all expect to derive some gratification from the coming contest.

House, and the subordinates seemed to have remained silent.

Shaftesbury was at last turned out, and the Great Seal was given to Sir Heneage Finch, who, being asked by the King to name his successor, said, "Who should succeed the Captain but the Lieutenant?" and North became Attorney General.[1] He had for his colleague as Solicitor his old rival, Sir William Jones, who seems to have been a considerable man,—who afterwards had the virtue voluntarily to give up office that he might join the popular party,—and who, if not cut off by an early death, would probably have acted the part of Lord Somers at the Revolution, and left a great name in history. The account we have of the demeanor of North and Jones to each other is creditable to them, if not to the general courtesy of the bar in their time: "although in the course of their practice they were often chosen on purpose to resist each other, especially in hot factious causes, yet they never clashed in words, or made any show of private animosity, *as commonly in such cases is done with great noise and indecency.* But they conversed, visited, and entertained familiarly, though less frequent after the times grew hot, and preferment of the one made a greater distance between them.[2]

Parliament met in a few weeks after North's promotion. In those good old times when, according to Blackstone, the English constitution was "theoretically perfect," the appointment to an office of profit under the Crown did not vacate a seat in the House of Commons,[3]—but a notice was given to question North's right to sit longer as representative of Lynn, on the ground that, as Attorney General, he had a writ of summons to the House of Lords, and was bound to give his attendance there. He diligently prepared to meet this objection, and had got up all the precedents and authorities, but as these were decidedly in his favor, the notice was suffered to drop. It is rather lucky for his parliamentary fame, that the motion against him was not brought forward; for he

[1] Or Jur. 118. [2] Examen, 514.
[3] In a note upon this sentence of my work by some laborious editor in a future age, it will be said, "the author here talks very feelingly; for I find that when he himself was promoted from being Solicitor to be Attorney General, in the year 1834, he lost his seat for Dudley, and was kept out of parliament nearly a whole session till re-elected for the city of Edinburgh."

must have defended himself; he probably would have done it ably; the House had always listened favorably to the answer to a personal attack,—and after a successful maiden speech he might have become a distinguished debater. He still remained mute. We are told that "little or nothing of the King's business in the House of Commons leaned upon him, because Mr. Secretary Coventry was there, who managed for the Court."[1] The skill, readiness, and influence of this leader of the House of Commons seem to have superseded the efforts of all the other members of the government, who were reminded by him of the useful maxim, "*Least said is soonest mended.*" He is celebrated as "an ancient member who had the nice step of the House, and withal was wonderfully witty;" and we are assured (which could not be truly said respecting all his successors who may have merited the same panegyric for talent and dexterity), that "he had never said anything in the House which afterwards proved a lie, and had that credit, that whatever he affirmed the House believed. North once or twice spoke a few words, "in resolving the fallacies of the country party," but did not venture beyond an opinion upon a point of law which incidentally arose.

"He could not attend the House constantly, but took the liberty of pursuing his practice in Westminster Hall."[2] There he was easily the first; and the quantity of business which he got through in Chancery ("his home") and the other Courts where he went *special* seems to have been enormous. His mode of preparation was (like Lord Erskine's) to have a consultation in the evening before reading his brief, when "he was informed of the history of the cause and where the pinch was." Next morning at four he was called by a trusty boy, who never failed, winter or summer, to come into his chamber at that hour,[3] and by the sitting of the Court he had gone through his brief, and was ready to do ample justice to his clients.

Fees now flowed in upon him so fast that he hardly knew how to dispose of them. He seems to have taken

---

[1] Henry Coventry, youngest son of Lord Chancellor Coventry.
[2] Life, i. 177. The hours then kept must have been very inconvenient for lawyers in parliament, as all the Courts and both Houses met at eight in the morning, and sat till noon.
[3] This early rising rendered it necessary for him to take "a short turn in the other world after dinner."

them from his clients with his own hand. At one time, he had had a fancy for his health, to wear a sort of skullcap. He now routed out three of these, which he placed on the table before him, and into these he distributed the cash as it was paid to him. "One had the gold, another the crowns and half-crowns, and another the smaller money." When these vessels were full, they were committed to his brother Roger, who told out the pieces, and put them into bags, which he carried to Child's, the goldsmith, at Temple Bar.[1]

But still Mr. Attorney was dissatisfied with his position. He could not but be mortified by his insignificance in the House of Commons. The country party there was rapidly gaining strength, and although it was not then usual for the Crown to turn out its law officers on a change of ministers, he began to be very much frightened by threats of impeachment uttered against all who were instrumental in executing the measures of the government. Shaftesbury was in furious opposition. While only at the head of a small minority in the House of Lords, the House of Commons was more and more under his influence. North was exceedingly timid, always conjuring up imaginary dangers, and exaggerating such as he had to encounter. He now exceedingly longed to lay his head on "the cushions of the Common Pleas," instead of running the risk of its being laid on the block on Tower Hill.

Vaughan, the Chief Justice of that Court, died, and his wishes were accomplished,—notwithstanding some intrigues to elevate Sir William Jones or Sir William Montagu.[2] When it came to the pinch, North was rather shocked to think of the sacrifice of profit which he was making, "for the Attorney's place was (with his practice) near £7,000 *per annum*,[3] and the cushion of the Common Pleas not above £4,000. But accepting, he accounted himself enfranchised from the Court brigues and attendances at the price of the difference."[4]

North held the office of Chief Justice of the Common Pleas near eight years, which may be divided into two

---

[1] Life, i. 171. Roger assures us he did not purloin any part of the treasure, —for which he takes infinite credit to himself.
[2] Or. Jurid. 118.
[3] The official fees seem to have fallen off greatly since Bacon's time, which probably arose from the abolition of the military tenures and the Court of Wards. [4] Life, i. 183.

periods:—1st, From his appointment till the formation of the council of thirty, on the recommendation of Sir William Temple, in the year 1679;—2ndly, From thence till he received the Great Seal in the end of the year 1682. During the former he mixed little in politics, and devoting himself to his juridical duties, he discharged them creditably.

At this time, and for long after, the emoluments of the Judges in Westminster Hall depended chiefly upon fees, and there was a great competition between the different Courts for business. The King's Bench, originally instituted for criminal proceedings, had, by a dexterous use of their writ of "*latitat*," tricked[1] the Common Pleas of almost all civil actions; and when the new Chief Justice took his seat, he found his Court a desert. There was hardly sufficient business to countenance his coming every day in term to Westminster Hall, while the Sergeants and officers were repining and starving.[2] But he was soon up with the King's Bench, by a new and more dexterous use of the "*capias*," the ancient writ of that Court—applying it to all personal actions. "After this process came into common use, it is scarce to be conceived how the Court revived and flourished, being, instead of vacation in term, rather term in vacation, so large was the increase of trials by *nisi prius* out of the Court, as also of motions and pleas in the Court."[3] Hence Anstey sings in the Pleader's Guide—

> "If haply John-a-Stile provoke
> The legal fight 'gainst John-a-Noke,
> The 'LATITAT' the foe besieges,
> And baffles him in BANCO REGIS;
> Skill'd with *ac etiams* to perplex,
> And foil with *bill of Middlesex*.
> While 'CAPIAS' is rejoic'd to seize,
> And plunder him in Common Pleas."[4]

The Sergeants were for some time most grateful to the Chief Justice, and hailed him as their deliverer from the usurpation of the King's Bench; but before long he got

---

[1] It was called "Trickum in lege."
[2] The Court of C. P. in point of business seems then to have been as badly off as I remember the Exchequer,—when it was said that the Barons "met punctually at half-past eleven, and rose half an hour before twelve:" and that if, having a stray motion, you wished to take a shot at them, "they were like a covey of partridges in November, you could never find them *sitting*."   [3] Life, i. 193.   [4] Pl. G. Lect. v.

into very bad odor with them for allowing his brother Roger, not of the order of the Coif, to make certain motions, which they said belonged exclusively to them. To show their resentment, they one day refused to bring forward any business. The Chief Justice, in great indignation, adjourned the Court, saying, that the following day they would hear common barristers, or attorneys, or the suitors themselves plead in spite of the monopoly of the Sergeants, that there might not be a failure of justice. "This was like thunder to the Sergeants, and they fell to quarreling one with another about being the cause of this great evil they had brought upon themselves. In the afternoon they attended the Chief and the other Judges of the Court, and in great humility owned their fault and begged pardon, and they would be careful not to give the like offense for the future. The Chief told them that the affront was in public and in the face of the Court, and they must make their recognition there next morning in such manner as the greatness of their offense demanded, and then they should hear what the Court would say to them. Accordingly they did, and the Chief first, and then the rest in order, gave them a formal chiding with acrimony enough—all which, with dejected countenances, they were bound to hear. When this discipline was over, the Chief pointed to one to move, which he did more like one crying than speaking; and so ended the comedy, as it was acted in Westminster Hall, called '*The Dumb Day.*'"[1]

At this time a Judge, when appointed, selected a circuit, to which he steadily adhered, till another, which he preferred, became vacant. Chief Justice North for several years "rode the Western;" and in his charges to juries, as well as in his conversation with the country gentlemen, he strongly inculcated the most slavish Church-and-King doctrines, insomuch that the Cavaliers called him "*Deliciæ Occidentis*," or, "the Darling of the West."

Though careful to avoid all fanatics, he was once completely taken in by a Mr. Duke, who had a very handsome house in Devonshire. This gentleman asked the Chief Justice and his brother Judge to pass a night with him, and they, believing him to be perfectly orthodox, accepted the invitation. But instead of getting a priest to

[1] Life, i. 195–198. Serjeant's case, by Manning.

read prayers before their Lordships, "he himself got behind the table in his hall, and read a chapter, and then gave them a long-winded prayer after the Presbyterian way. The Judges took it very ill, but did not think fit to affront him in his own house. Next day, when they came early in the morning to Exeter, all the news was, that the Judges had been at a conventicle, and the Grand Jury intended to present them and all their retinue for it; and much merriment was made upon the subject."[1] As they were above the allowed number, and not of the family of the master of the house, they were all certainly liable to be prosecuted under "the Conventicle Act," which the High Church party then prized so dearly.

The Chief Justice afterwards went the Northern Circuit. attended by his brother Roger, who gives a most entertaining account of his travels, and who seems to have thought the natives of Northumberland and Cumberland as distant, as little known, and as barbarous, as we should now think the Esquimaux or the aborigines of New Zealand.

Till the Popish plot broke out, Chief Justice North had no political trials before him; and the only cases which gave him much anxiety were charges of witchcraft. He does not appear, like Chief Justice Hale, to have been a believer in the black art; but, with his characteristic timidity, he was ashamed to combat the popular prejudice, lest the countrymen should cry, "This Judge hath no religion,—he doth not believe witches." Therefore he avoided trying witches himself as much as possible, and turned them over to his brother Judge, Mr. Justice Raymond, whom he allowed to hang them. He was once forced to try a wizard; but the fraud of a young girl, whom the prisoner was supposed to have enchanted and made to spit pins, was so clearly exposed to the witnesses, that the Chief Justice had the boldness to direct an acquittal.[2]

The Popish plot he treated as he did witchcraft. He disbelieved it from the beginning, but was afraid openly to express a doubt of its reality. He thought it might be exposed by the press, and he got a man to publish an anonymous pamphlet against it, to which he contributed· but sitting along with Chief Justice Scroggs, who pre-

[1] Life i. 226. [2] Ibid. 255.

sided at the trial of those charged with being implicated in it, he never attempted to restrain this "butcher's son and butcher" from slaughtering the victims.[1]

So on the trial of Lord Stafford, though he privately affected severely to condemn the proceeding, he would not venture to save Lord Nottingham, the High Steward, from the disgrace of assisting in that murder; and he dryly gave his own opinion, that two witnesses were not necessary to each overt act of treason.[2]

We have still more flagrant proof of his baseness on the trial of Reading, prosecuted by order of the House of Commons for trying to suppress evidence of the plot. North himself now presided, and having procured a conviction,—in sentencing the defendant to fine, imprisonment, and the pillory, he said,—"I will tell you your offense is so great and hath such a relation to that which the whole nation is concerned in, because it was an attempt to baffle the evidence of that conspiracy, which, if it had not been, by the mercy of God, detected, God knows what might have befallen us all by this time."[3]

We now come to present North on the political stage, where he continued to act a very conspicuous and disreputable part down to the time of his death. In the year 1679, when the King adopted his new plan of government by a Council of thirty, of which Shaftesbury was made President, and into which Lord Russell and several of the popular leaders were introduced, it was thought fit to balance them by some determined ultra-royalists; and the Lord Chief Justice of the Common Pleas, who had acquired himself the reputation of being the most eminent of that class, was selected,—although he had not hitherto been a Privy Councillor. At first he seldom openly gave any opinion in Council, but he secretly engaged in the intrigues which ended in the abrupt prorogation and dissolution of the parliament, in the dismissal of Shaftesbury, and the resignation of Lord Russell and the Whigs. The

---

[1] "At the Old Bailey," says his apologist, "where the Oatesian storms were most impetuous, the Lord Chief Justice of the King's Bench steered the vessel, and the other Judges had little or no share in the conduct, whereby his Lordship (North) in the main was rather an observer than an actor in these proceedings, to which hung the issues of life and death. And nothing can qualify the silence but the inconceivable fury and rage of the community, gentle and simple, at that time, and the consequences of an open opposition to the chief, whose part it was to act as he did, demanding no assistance from any of them."—Life, i. 302.   [2] 7 St. Tr. 1527.   [3] Ibid. 310.

scheme of government was then altered, and a Cabinet, consisting of a small number of Privy Councillors, was formed, North being one of them. To his opinion, on legal and constitutional questions, the government was now disposed to show more respect than to that of Lord Chancellor Nottingham.

There being much talk against the Court in the London coffee-houses, it was wished to suppress them by proclamation; and our Chief Justice being consulted on the subject, gave this response,—that " though retailing coffee may, under certain circumstances, be an innocent trade, yet as it is used at present in the nature of a common assembly to discourse of matters of state, news, and great persons, it becomes unlawful; and as the coffee-houses are nurseries of idleness and pragmaticalness, and hinder the consumption of our native provisions, they may be treated as common nuisances." Accordingly, a proclamation was issued for shutting up all coffee-houses, and forbidding the sale of coffee in the metropolis; but this caused such a general murmur, not only among politicians and idlers, but among the industrious classes connected with foreign and colonial trade, that it was speedily recalled.[1]

The meeting of the new parliament summoned in the end of 1675 having been repeatedly postponed, there arose the opposite factions of " Petitioners " and "Abhorrers,"—the former *petitioning* the King that parliament might be speedily assembled for the redress of grievances, and the latter, in their addresses to the King, expressing their *abhorrence* of such seditious sentiments. The " Petitioners," however, were much more numerous and active, and a Council was called to consider how their proceedings might be stopped or punished. Our Chief Justice recommended a proclamation, which the King approved of, and ordered the Attorney General, Sir Creswell Levinz, to draw. Mr. Attorney, alarmed by considering how he might be questioned for such an act on the meeting of parliament, said, " I do not well understand what my Lord Chief Justice means, and I humbly pray of your Majesty that his Lordship may himself draw up the proclamation."—*King.* " My Lord, I think then you must draw this proclamation."—*Chief Justice.* " Sire,

[1] Examen, 140. Life, i. 298.

it is the office of your Majesty's Attorney General to prepare all royal proclamations, and it is not proper for any one else to do it. I beg that your Majesty's affairs may go in their due course; but if in this matter Mr. Attorney doubts anything, and will give himself the trouble to call upon me, I will give him the best assistance I can."

Sir Creswell having written on a sheet of paper a formal commencement and conclusion of a royal proclamation, carried it to the Chief Justice, who filled up the blank with a *recital* that, "for spurious ends and purposes relating to the public, persons were going about to collect and procure the subscriptions of multitudes of his Majesty's subjects to petitions to his Majesty,—which proceedings were contrary to the known laws of this realm, and ought not to go unpunished,"—and a *mandate* to all his Majesty's loving subjects of what rank or degree soever, "that they presume not to agitate or promote any such subscriptions, nor in anywise join in any petition in that manner to be preferred to his Majesty, upon pain of the utmost rigor of the law, and that all magistrates and other officers should take effectual care that all such offenders against the laws be prosecuted and punished according to their demerits."[1]

Parliament at last met, and strong measures were taken against the "Abhorrers," who had obstructed the right of petitioning. An inquiry was instituted respecting the Proclamation. Sir Creswell Levinz was placed at the bar, and asked by whose advice or assistance he had prepared it. He several times refused to answer, but being hard pressed, and afraid of commitment to the Tower, he named the Lord Chief Justice North,—against whom there had been a strong suspicion, but no proof. A hot debate arose, which ended in the Resolution, "That the evidence this day given to this House against Sir Francis North, Chief Justice of the Common Pleas, is sufficient ground for this House to proceed upon an impeachment against him for high crimes and misdemeaners."[2]

He was a good deal alarmed by the vote of impeachment, but it raised him still higher in favor at Court. Next day, presiding in the House of Lords as Speaker,

[1] Examen, 547.   [2] Com. Journ. Nov. 25, 1679. 4 Parl Hist. 1229.

in the absence of the Lord Chancellor, and seeming very much dejected, King Charles (according to his manner) "came and clapped himself down close by him on the woolsack, and, '*My Lord,*' said he, '*be of good comfort; I will never forsake my friends, as my father did.*'" His Majesty, without waiting for a reply, then walked off to another part of the House.

A committee was appointed to draw up the articles of impeachment against the Chief Justice; but before they made any report, this parliament too was dissolved.

Soon after the summoning of Charles's last parliament, North was obliged to set off upon the spring circuit; and notwithstanding his best efforts to finish the business rapidly, he could not arrive at Oxford till the two Houses had assembled, and had entered into the controversy respecting the trial of Fitzharris. He lodged in Trinity College, as his lady was one of the coheirs of the founder, and there he kept a table for the well-affected members of either House,—being "allowed to battle in the butteries."

As Lord Nottingham was able to be present and preside in the House of Lords, North had no opportunity for any public appearance; but we need not doubt that he was very active in private intrigues, and that he warmly supported the opportune doctrine, however much he might inwardly condemn it, that a Commoner may not be tried for his life by the House of Lords. He was of the small junto to whom was intrusted the secret of immediate dissolution, The moment the deed was done, he set off for London. pretending to be afraid of what he called "the positive armament against the King, which manifestly showed itself at Oxford."

As soon as the Cabinet met at Whitehall, North advised the issuing of a declaration to justify the dissolution of the three last parliaments which had met respectively at Westminster and at Oxford,—and himself drew an elaborate one, which was adopted. This state paper certainly puts the popular party in the wrong, upon the "exclusion question" and other matters, with considerable dexterity, and it was supposed to have contributed materially to the reaction going on in favor of the government.

So far his conduct was legitimate, and in the fair exercise of his functions as a Privy Councillor; but I am sorry to say that he now sullied his ermine by a flagrant disregard of his duties as a Judge. The Grand Jury for the city of London having very properly thrown out the bill of indictment against Stephen College, "the Protestant joiner," it was resolved to try him at Oxford; and for this purpose a Special Commission was issued,—at the head of which was placed Lord Chief Justice North. Burnet says mildly, "North's behavior in that whole matter was such that, probably, if he had lived to see an impeaching parliament, he might have felt the ill effects of it."[1] After perusing the trial, I must say, that his misconduct upon it was most atrocious. The prisoner, being a violent enemy to Popery, had attended the City members to Oxford as one of their guard, with "No Popery" flags and cockades,—using strong language against the Papists and their supporters, but without any thought of using force. Yet the Chief Justice was determined that he should be found guilty of compassing and imagining the King's death, and levying war against him in his realm. College's papers, which he was to use in his defense, were forcibly taken from him, on the ground that they had been written by some other persons, who gave him hints what he was to say. They were in reality prepared by his legal advisers, Mr. Aaron Smith and Mr. West.[2] The prisoner was checked and browbeaten as often as he put a question or made an observation. His defense was much more able than could have been expected from a person in his station of life;—but, of course, he was convicted. The Chief Justice, in passing sentence, observed, "Look you, Mr. College; because you say you are innocent, it is necessary for me to say something in vindication of the verdict, which I think the Court were all well satisfied with. I thought it was a case, that, as you made your own defense, small proof would serve the turn to make any one believe you guilty. For, as you defend yourself by pretending to be a Protestant, I did wonder, I must confess, when you called so many witnesses to your religion and reputation, that none of them gave an account that they saw you receive the Sacrament

[1] O. T. i. 504.
[2] Examen, 589. Roger North was himself one of the counsel for the Crown.

within these many years, or any of them particularly had seen you at church in many years, or what kind of Protestant you were. But crying aloud against the Papists,—it was proved here who you called Papists. You had the boldness to say the King was a Papist, the Bishops were Papists, and the Church of England were Papists. If these be the Papists you cry out against, what kind of Protestant you are I know not,—I am sure you can be no good one. How it came into your head, that were but a private man, to go to guard the Parliament, I much wonder. Suppose all men of your condition should have gone to have guarded the Parliament, what an assembly had there been! And though you say you are no man of quality, nor likely to do anything upon the King's guards or the King's person, yet if all of your quality had gone upon the same design, what ill consequences might have followed! We see what has been done by Massaniello, a mean man in another country,—what by Wat Tyler and Jack Straw in this kingdom." College asked him to fix the day of his death, but he answered that that depended on the King; adding, in a tone of great humanity, "that he should have due notice of it to prepare, by repenting of his crimes."[1] College's innocence was so manifest, that even Hume, eager to palliate all the atrocities of this reign, says, "that his whole conduct and demeanor prove him to have been governed by an honest but indiscreet zeal for his country and his religion." On the 31st of August, 1681, the sentence, with all its savage barbarities, was carried into execution. "Sir Francis North," observes Roger Coke, "was a man cut out, to all intents and purposes, for such a work."[2]

He was next called upon to assist at the immolation of a nobler victim, who escaped from the horns of the altar. Shaftesbury had been for some time very careful never to open his mouth on politics out of the city of London and county of Middlesex, and during the Oxford parliament had touched on no public topic except in the House of Lords. It was resolved, at all hazards, to bring him to trial; but this could only be done by an indictment to be found at the Old Bailey. There did North attend when the indictment was to be preferred, and resolutely assist Lord Chief Justice Pemberton in perverting

[1] 8 St. Tr. 550–723.   [2] Detection, ii. 358.

the law, by examining the witnesses in open Court, and by trying to intimidate and mislead the Grand Jury; but he was punished by being present at the shout which lasted an hour when "*Ignoramus*" was returned.[1]

He next zealously lent himself to the scheme of the Court for upsetting the municipal privileges of the city of London, and of obtaining sheriffs for London and Middlesex, who would return juries at the will of the government. The Lord Mayor having been gained over, and the stratagem devised of creating a sheriff by the Lord Mayor drinking to him, instead of by the election of his fellow-citizens,—the difficulty was to find any freeman of fair character who would incur all the odium and risk of being so introduced to the shrievalty. It so happened that at that time there returned to England a brother of the Chief Justice, Mr. Dudley, afterwards Sir Dudley, North, who was free of the city from having been apprenticed there to a merchant, and who had amassed considerable wealth by a long residence in Turkey. It being suggested at Court that this was the very man for their Sheriff,[2] "the King very much approved of the person, but was very dubious whether the Chief Justice, with his much caution and wisdom, would advise his brother to stand in a litigious post. But yet he resolved to try; and one day he spoke to Sir Francis with a world of tenderness, and desired to know *if it would be too much to ask his brother Dudley to hold Sheriff on my Lord Mayor's drinking?*" The wily Chief Justice immediately saw the advantage this proposal might bring to the whole family, and returned a favorable answer. "For matter of title," says Roger, "he thought there was more squeak than wool, for whatever people thought was at the bottom, if a citizen be called upon an office by the government of the city and obeys, where is the crime? But then such a terrible fear was artificially raised up in the city as if this service was the greatest hazard in the world." Sir Francis gently broke the matter to his brother, saying, "that there was an opportunity which preferred itself whereby he

---

[1] Ante, p. 179.
[2] It was said, by way of jest, on the other side, that he was only selected by the Court to answer their purposes, as in Turkey he had often been before the Kadi, and he had become well acquainted with the use of the bow-string.

might make a fortune if he wanted it, and much enlarge
what he had, besides great reputation to be gained, which
would make him all the days of his life very considerable,
laying open the case of the Lord Mayor's right very clear
and plain, against which in common sense there was no
reply." Dudley, however, made many objections, and
talked of the terrible expense to which he should be exposed. The Chief Justice urged that if he served, the obligation was so transcendent, that there could be no employment by commission from the Crown which would
not fall to his share, "and as for the charge," said he,—
"here, brother, take £1,000 to help make good your account, and if you never have an opportunity by pensions
or employments to reimburse you and me, I will lose my
share; else I shall be content to receive this £1,000 out
of one-half of your pensions when they come in, and
otherwise not at all."[1] The merchant yielded; and under this pure bargain, proposed by the Judge before whom
the validity of the appointment might come to be decided,—when his health was given by the Lord Mayor as
Sheriff of London and Middlesex, he agreed to accept
the office.

But the old sheriffs insisted on holding a Common Hall
for the election of their successors, according to ancient
usage, on Midsummer day,—when Lord Chief Justice
North had the extreme meanness, at the King's request,
to go into the city and take post in a house near Guildhall, belonging to Sir George Jeffreys, "who had no small
share in the conduct of this affair, to the end that if any
incident required immediate advice, or if the spirits of the
Lord Mayor should droop, which in outward appearance
were but faint, there might be a ready recourse." It is
true, the opposite faction had the Lord Grey de Werke
and other leaders from the west end of the town, to advise and countenance them; but this could be no excuse
for a Judge so degrading himself. The poll going for the
popular candidates, the Lord Mayor, by Chief Justice
North's advice, under pretense of a riot, attempted to adjourn the election; but the Sheriffs required that the
polling should continue, and declared Papillon and Dubois
duly elected.[2]

This causing great consternation at Whitehall, a coun-

[1] Life, ii. 16-20. [2] Ibid. ii. 20.

cil was called, to which the Lord Mayor and Aldermen were summoned. Lord Chief Justice North, by the King's command, addressed them, saying, "That the proceedings of the Sheriffs at the Common Hall after the adjournment were not only utterly null and void, but the persons were guilty of an audacious riot and contempt of lawful authority, for which, by due course of law, they would be severely punished; but, in the meantime, it was the Lord Mayor's duty, and his Majesty's pleasure, that they should go back to the city and summon the Common Hall, and make election of Sheriffs for the year ensuing." The Lord Mayor having been told that the courtiers would bamboozle him and leave him in the lurch,—when North had concluded, said, "My Lord, will your Lordship be pleased to give me this under your hand?" The King and all the councillors were much tickled to see the wily Chief Justice thus nailed, "expecting some turn of wit to fetch himself off, and thinking to have sport in seeing how woodenly he would excuse himself." But to their utter astonishment, for once in his life Francis North was bold and straightforward, and cheating them all, he answered, without any hesitation, "Yes, and you shall have it presently." Then seizing a pen, he wrote, "I am of opinion, that it is in the Lord Mayor's power to call, adjourn, and dissolve the Common Hall at his pleasure, and that all acts done there, as of the Common Hall, during such adjournment, are mere nullities, and have no legal effect." This he signed, and handed to the Lord Mayor, who then promised obedience.[1]

Accordingly, another Common Hall was called, at which it was pretended that Sir Dudley North and Rich were elected, and they were actually installed in the office of Sheriff. By the contrivance of Lord Chief Justice North, the office of Lord Mayor for the ensuing year was likewise filled by a thorough passive-obedience tool of the Court. Gould, the liberal candidate, had a majority of legal votes on the poll, but under a pretended scrutiny, Pritchard was declared duly elected, and Sir John More, the renegade Mayor, willingly transferred to him the insignia of Chief Magistrate, so that the King had now the city authorities completely at his devotion. Shaftesbury fled to Holland; and it was for the Court to determine

[1] Life, ii. 23.

when the blow should be struck against the popular leaders who remained.

Such were the services of Lord Chief Justice North, which all plainly saw would ere long be rewarded by higher promotion. The health of Lord Nottingham, the Chancellor, was rapidly declining, and the Court had already designated his successor. Lord Craven, famous for wishing to appear intimate with rising men,—in the circle at Whitehall now seized Lord Chief Justice North by the arm and whispered in his ear;—and the foreign ambassadors so distinctly saw the shadow of the coming event, that they treated him with as great respect as if he had been prime minister, "and when any of them looked towards him and thought he perceived it, they very formally bowed."

We are told, that in many things North acted as "Co-Chancellor" with Nottingham; and for the first time the office of Chancellor seems to have been like that of Sheriff of Middlesex, one in its nature, but filled by two officers of equal authority. It is said, that "the *aspirant* dealt with all imaginable kindness and candor to the *declinant*, and that never were predecessor and successor such cordial friends to each other, and in every respect mutually assistant, as those two were."[1]

Such hopes on an expected vacancy of the Great Seal are sometimes disappointed, but here there were very solid reasons for entertaining them. While the Lord Chancellor was languishing, the Chief Justice being at Windsor, the King plainly intimated to him, that when the fatal event, which must be shortly looked for, had taken place, the Great Seal would be put into his hands. He modestly represented himself to his Majesty as unfit for the place, and affected by all his art and skill to decline it. In truth, he really wished to convey to the King's mind the impression that he did not desire it, although he had been working so foully for it,—as he knew it would be pressed upon him, there being no competitor so knowing and so pliant, and he had an important stipulation to make for a pension before he would accept it. When he came back to London, and confidentially mentioned what had passed between him and the King, he pretended to be annoyed, and said, "that if the Seal were offered to

[1] Life, ii. 64, 75.

him he was determined to refuse it;" but it is quite clear that he was highly gratified to see himself so near the great object of his ambition, and that his only anxiety now was, that he might drive a good bargain when he should consent to give up "the cushion of the Common Pleas."

Lord Nottingham having died about four o'clock in the afternoon of Monday, the 18th of December, 1682,[1] the Great Seal was carried next morning, from his house in Great Queen Street, to the King at Windsor. The following day his Majesty brought it with him to Whitehall, and in the evening sent for the Lord Chief Justice of the Common Pleas to offer it to him. When North arrived, he found Lord Rochester, the Treasurer, and several other ministers, closeted with Charles. As yet, there was no distinction between the funds to be applied to the King's private expenses and to the public service. Therefore, the Exchequer being now very empty—and the resolution being taken never more to summon a parliament for supplies—it was considered an object that the Keeper of the Great Seal should be contented with the fees of his office, without any allowance or pension from the Crown. Charles himself was careless about such matters, but the Treasurer had inculcated upon him the importance of this piece of economy. As soon as North entered, his Majesty offered him the Seal, and the ministers began to congratulate the new Lord Keeper; but, with many acknowledgments for his Majesty's gracious intentions, he begged leave to suggest the necessity, for his Majesty's honor, that a pension should be assigned to him, as it had been to his predecessor, for otherwise the dignity of this high office could not be supported. Rochester interposed, pointing out the necessity, in times like these, for all his Majesty's servants to be ready to make some sacrifices; that the emoluments of the Great Seal were considerable; and that it would be more becoming to trust to his Majesty's bounty than to seek to drive a hard bargain with him. But Sir George Jeffreys being yet only a bustling city officer, who could not with any decency have been put at the head of the law; the Attorney and Solicitor General not being considered men of mark or likelihood; Sir Harbottle Grimston, the Master of the Rolls, being at

[1] 1 Vernon, 115.

death's door, and no other common-law Judge besides himself being producible—the little gentleman was firm, and positively declared that he would not touch the Great Seal without a pension. After much haggling, a compromise took place, by which he was to have £2,000 a year instead of the £4,000 a year assigned to his predecessor. The King then lifted up the purse containing the Seal, and putting it into his hand, said, "Here, my Lord, take it; you will find it heavy." "Thus," says Roger North, "his Majesty acted the *prophet* as well as the *King;* for, shortly before his Lordship's death, he declared that, *since he had the Seal he had not enjoyed one easy and contented minute.*"[1]

CHAPTER XCVI.

CONTINUATION OF THE LIFE OF LORD GUILFORD TILL THE DEATH OF CHARLES II.

WHEN the new Lord Keeper came home, at night, from Whitehall to his house in Chancery Lane, bringing the Great Seal with him, and attended by the officers of the Court of Chancery—instead of appearing much gratified, as was expected by his brother and his friends, who were waiting to welcome him, he was in a great rage—disappointed that he had not been able to make a better bargain, and, perhaps, a little mortified that he had only the title of "Lord Keeper," instead of the more sounding one of "Lord Chancellor." Recriminating on those with whom he had been so keenly acting the chapman, he exclaimed, "To be haggled with about a pension,[2] as at the purchase of a horse or an ox! After I had declared that I would not accept without a pension, to think I was so frivolous as to insist and desist all in a moment! As if I were to be wheedled and charmed by their insignificant tropes! To think me worthy of so great a trust, and withal so little and mean as to endure

[1] Life, ii. 68, 69. Crown Off. Min. fol. 108.
[2] By this word "pension," I conceive we are to understand *salary* while the Lord Keeper was in office, and not, as might be supposed, an allowance on his retirement.

such usage! It is disobliging, inconsistent, and insufferable. What have I done that may give them cause to think me of so poor a spirit as to be thus trifled with?"[1] It might have been answered, that, though the King and the courtiers made use of him for their own ends, they had seen his actions, understood his character, and had no great respect for him. Till Jeffreys was a little further advanced, they could not run the risk of breaking with him—but then he was subjected to all sorts of mortifications and insults.

The day after his appointment "he kept a private seal for writs at his house in Chancery Lane,"[2] and on the first day of the following Hilary term he took his place in the Court of Chancery. By this time he was in possession of his predecessor's house in Great Queen Street, Lincoln's Inn Fields; and he had a grand procession from thence to Westminster Hall, attended by the Duke of Ormond, the Earls of Craven and Rochester, the great officers of State, and the Judges. He took the oaths, the Master of the Rolls holding the book. He does not appear to have delivered any inaugural address. The attendant Lords stayed and heard a motion or two, and then departed, leaving the Lord Keeper in Court.[3]

They might have been well amused if they had remained. For the crooked purposes of the Government, with a view to the disfranchising of the City of London by the *quo warranto* depending against it, Pemberton was this day to be removed from being Chief Justice of the King's Bench to be Chief Justice of the Common Pleas, and Edmund Saunders was to be at once raised from wearing a stuff gown at the bar to be Chief Justice of the King's Bench. This keen but unscrupulous lawyer was previously to be made a Sergeant, that he might be qualified to be a Judge, and, coming into the Court of Chancery, he presented the Lord Keeper with a ring for himself, and another for the King, inscribed with the courtly motto, "Principi sic placuit." The Lord Keeper then accompanied him into the Court where he was to preside, called him to the bench, and made him a speech on the duties of his office. The ceremonies of the day were concluded by his Lordship afterwards going to his old Court, the Common Pleas, and there swearing in Pember-

---
[1] Life, i. 415   [2] 1 Vernon, 115.   [3] Cr. Off. Min. fol. 105.

ton as his successor, whom he congratulated upon "the ease with dignity" which he was now to enjoy.

Parasites and preferment-hunters crowded the levee of the new Lord Keeper. He was immediately waited upon by the courtly Evelyn, who discovered in him a thousand good qualities.[1]

In the midst of these blandishments, he applied himself with laudable diligence to the discharge of his judicial duties. He declared that he was shocked by many abuses in the Court of Chancery, and he found fault with the manner in which his two predecessors, Bridgeman and Nottingham, had allowed the practice of the Court to lead to delay and expense. It was properly understood at the bar and on the bench, that nothing done in Lord Shaftesbury's time should ever be referred to as a precedent on account of his rashness and ignorance. But it was even the fashion to talk of Bridgeman as "a splitter of hairs," and Nottingham as "a formalist,"[2] and to lament how justice was obstructed by the slow process, the motions, the exceptions, the injunctions, and the rehearings which they had encouraged.

North's conduct as a law reformer was extremely characteristic. He talked much of issuing a new set of "Rules and Orders" to remedy all abuses, but he was afraid "that it would give so great alarm to the bar and officers, with the solicitors, as would make them confederate and demur, and by making a tumult and disturbance, endeavor to hinder the doing anything of that kind which they would apprehend to be very prejudicial to their interests."[3] Then, when he wished to simplify the practice and to speed causes to a hearing and final decree, he considered that he was not only to regard the suitors, but that " there was a justice due as well to the Crown, which had advantage growing by the disposition of places, profits, by processes of all sorts, as also the Judges and their servants, and counsel at the bar, and solicitors, who were all in possession of their advantages, and by public en-

---

[1] "Sir F. North being made Lord Keeper on the death of the Earl of Nottingham, the Lord Chancellor, I went to congratulate him. He is a most knowing, learned, and ingenious person ; and, besides having an excellent person, of an ingenuous and sweet disposition, very skillful in music, painting, the new philosophy, and political studies."—*Mem.* i. 513.

[2] This is like the slighting manner in which Lord Mansfield was spoken of in the time of Lord Kenyon. [3] *Life*, ii. 76.

couragement to spend their youth to make them fit for them, and had no other means generally to provide for themselves and their families, and had a right to their reasonable profits, if not strictly by law, yet through long connivance."[1]

He pretended to have an intention to abolish the usage of selling the places of the Masters in Chancery, which were in the disposal of the Lord Chancellor or Lord Keeper, as "the Court had not so much power to coerce exorbitances or to control their profits, when they bought their places, as if they were conferred gratis, for, upon the least rumor of a reform, they cry out—*Purchase!—Valuable consideration!*" But he very prudently doubted how far he could effectually cure the evil if he were to dispose of the offices without taking money for them. He also reflected how indifferently such a generous act would be accepted by the public. He thought, judging by his own standard of right, that "it would have been termed either vanity or folly, and perhaps both; and all the skillful had reported no better of him, and so, instead of having the action approved, he had been rendered contemptible for it, as one that did not understand his own advantages; if selling such places was inconvenient, constant usage that established it must answer."[2] So, after due deliberation, his Lordship thought it the most becoming course "*stare super antiquas vias*"—to follow the steps of his predecessors, and to dispose of those places for a price, as they had done before him.

But he retrenched "Heraldry," or motions for giving precedence to causes, "which had become so common that Sir John Churchill, a famous Chancery practitioner, used to take as much as £28 in walking from Lincoln's Inn to the Middle Temple Hall, where the sittings were held out of term, with breviates respecting the booking and retarding of hearings." He abolished the rule that an injunction for want of answer must continue after the coming in of the answer, if exceptions were taken to it for insufficiency. He likewise checked vexatious exceptions to Master's Reports; and he is said to have been very particular in granting rehearings. He very laudably dictated the material parts of his decrees; and he encouraged the registrars to come to him privately in ca-

[1] Life, ii. 83. [2] Ibid. ii. 13.

any difficulty, to avoid the frequent disputes in Court about minutes after the decree has been pronounced.

Such being the amount of his reforms, I think we must say that his alleged merit consists chiefly in the profession of good intentions; that he allowed the practice of the Court to remain pretty much as he found it; and that if he saw and approved what was right, he followed what was wrong—aggravating his errors by disregarding the strong dictates of his conscience.

Nevertheless, he applied himself very assiduously to the business of his Court—which, from his experience at the bar, and from his having often sat for his predecessor, was quite familiar to him—and he seems to have disposed of it satisfactorily. He was not led into temptation by having to decide in equity any political case; and no serious charge was preferred against him of bribery or undue influence.[1] Till the meeting of parliament in the reign of James, and the failure of his health, he prevented the accumulation of arrears; and, upon the whole, as an Equity Judge, he is to be praised rather than censured.

I wish as much could be said of his political conduct while he held the Great Seal. He may have *wished* " to bring the King to rule wholly by law, and to do nothing which, by any reasonable construction, might argue the contrary;" but for this purpose he would make feeble efforts, and no sacrifice; and all the measures cf the Court, however profligate, when resolved upon, he strenuously assisted in carrying into execution.

The ministers who now bore sway, and who were on several points opposed to each other, were Halifax, Sunderland, and Rochester. The Duke of York, restored to the office of Lord High Admiral and to the Privy Council, in direct violation of the " Test Act," had so much influence, that it was said that " to spite those who wished to prevent him from reigning at the King's death, he was permitted to reign during the King's life." The Duchess of Portsmouth was likewise at the head of a party at Court, although Mrs. Gwin, her Protestant rival, did not

---

[1] In the short notice of him, in a Collection of Lives published in 1712, there is allusion to " an odd story of a Chancery suit between the Duke of N—— and Sir P—— H——, and of some gold plate in a box." i. 177, but no particulars are given, and it is entitled to no weight.

interfere with politics. With none of these would the Lord Keeper combine. His policy was to study the peculiar humors of the King—to do whatever would be most agreeable personally to him—to pass for "the King's friend"—and to be " solus cum solo."[1]

Charles, although aware of his cunning and his selfishness, was well pleased with the slavish doctrines he laid down, and with the devoted zeal he expressed for the royal prerogative; and till Jeffrey's superior vigor, dexterity, and power of pleasing gained the ascendency, usually treated him with decent consideration. Every Sunday morning when the King was in town, the Lord Keeper went with the other great officers to Whitehall, to wait on the King to chapel. "That was usually a grand assembly of the Court; and the great men had opportunity to speak in discourse to the King as he gave them occasion, of which his Majesty was no niggard; and very excellent things said there, on the one side and on the other, were an high regale to such has had the advantage to stand within hearing."[2] A Cabinet Council was held almost every Sunday evening. When the Court was at Windsor, this made Sunday a traveling day. The Lord Keeper had a lodging provided for him there in the Dean's house. For the ease of attendance, the King would come from Windsor to hold a public Council at Hampton Court. There, and at Whitehall, the Lord Keeper had a lodging in the palace. If at any time he wished to see the King privately, he went directly to the royal bedchamber and took possession of it. "In that part of the Court were always attendants who straight found where the King was, and told him my Lord Keeper was there; and the King, knowing he had something to say to him, never failed to come to him, and that without any delay."[3]

He never would give any opinion on foreign affairs, nor attend a committee of Council summoned specially to consider them, professing himself, for want of a fit education and study, incompetent to judge at all of these matters, and declaring, like a true courtier, that "King Charles II. understood foreign affairs better than all his councils and councillors put together."[4] But he regularly attended all other Cabinet meetings, and when there was

[1] Life, ii. 163, 165, 169. [2] Ibid. ii. 168. [3] Ibid. ii. 178. [4] Ibid. ii. 181.

any business of a judicial nature to be done at the council table, he always presided there, "the Lord President not having the art of examining into and developing cases of intricacy."[1]

The first of these in which he had to display his powers was the disfranchisement of the City of London. Saunders, counsel in the *quo warranto*, having been appointed Chief Justice, to decide in favor of the sufficiency of the pleadings which he himself had drawn, the opinion of the Court of King's Bench had been pronounced for the Crown, "that all the City charters were forfeited," because a toll had been demanded alleged to be illegal, and a petition had been presented alleged to be seditious—notwithstanding the argument that these could not be considered the acts of the *Ens Legis*, called the Corporation, which was to be punished for them, and that if the offenses of extortion and libel had been committed, they should be visited only upon the *individuals* who were guilty of them. Formal judgment was not yet entered on the record—to give an opportunity to the Mayor, Aldermen, and Citizens to make their submission, and to accept terms which might henceforth annihilate their privileges and make them the slaves of the government. They accordingly did prepare a petition to the King, imploring his princely compassion and grace—which they presented to him at a Council held at Windsor on the 18th of June, 1683. The petition being read, they were ordered to withdraw, and when they were again called in, the Lord Keeper thus addressed them, disclosing somewhat indiscreetly the real motives for the *quo warranto:* "My Lord Mayor, I am by the King's command to tell you that he hath considered the humble petition of the City of London, where so many of the present magistrates and other eminent citizens are of undoubted loyalty and affection to his service; that for their sakes his Majesty will show the City all the favor they can reasonably desire. It was very long before his Majesty took resolutions to question their charter; it was not the seditious discourses of the coffee houses, the treasonable pamphlets and libels daily published and dispersed thence into all parts of the kingdom, the outrageous tumults in the streets, nor the affronts to his Courts of Justice could provoke him to it. His Majesty had pa-

[1] Life, ii. 169.

tience until disorders were grown to that height, that nothing less seemed to be designed than a ruin to the government both of Church and State." After pointing out the mischief of having factious magistrates, he adds, "It was high time to put a stop to this growing evil. This made it necessary for his Majesty to inquire into the abuses of franchises, that it might be in his power to make a regulation sufficient to restore the City to its former good government." He then stated the regulations to which they were required to assent, among which were —"That no Lord Mayor, Sheriff, or other officer should be appointed without the King's consent; that the King might cashier them at his pleasure; that if the King disapproved of the Sheriffs elected, he might appoint others by his own authority; and that the King should appoint all magistrates in the City by his Commission, instead of their being elected as hitherto." In conclusion he said: "The City ought to look upon this as a great condescension on his Majesty's part, it being in the nature of a reservation of a small part of what is already in his power by the judgment. My Lord Mayor, it is his Majesty's pleasure that you return to the City and consult the Common Council, that he may speedily know your resolutions thereupon, and accordingly give his directions. That you may see the King is in earnest, and the matter is not capable of delay, I am commanded to let you know he hath given order to his Attorney General to enter up judgment on Saturday next, unless you prevent it by your compliance in all these particulars."[1]

The citizens refused to comply with these terms, and judgment was entered up. Thus, on the most frivolous pretext, and by a scandalous perversion of the forms of law, was the City of London robbed of the free institutions which it had enjoyed, and under which it had flourished for many ages. The proceeding was less appalling to the public than the trial and execution of eminent patriots, but was a more dangerous blow to civil liberty. London remained disfranchised, and governed by the agents of the Crown, during the rest of this reign, and till the expected invasion of the Prince of Orange near the conclusion of the next,—when, too late, an offer was made to restore its charters with all its ancient privileges

[1] 8 St. Tr. 1039-1350.

Immediately after the Revolution, they were irrevocably confirmed by act of parliament.[1]

The Lord Keeper's conduct in this affair gave such high satisfaction at Court, that, as a reward for it, he was raised to the peerage by the title of Baron Guilford. His brother says that he did not seek the elevation from vanity, but that he might be protected against the attacks which might hereafter be made upon him in the House of Commons. He obtained it on the recommendation of the Duke of York, who overlooked his dislike of Popery in respect of his steady hatred to public liberty.[2]

To show his gratitude, the new Peer directed similar proceedings to be commenced against many other corporations,—which ended in the forfeiture or surrender of the charters of most of the towns in England in which the liberal party had enjoyed an ascendency.

Gilbert Burnet, about this time appointed Preacher at the Rolls, thought he had secured a protector in the Lord Keeper; but as soon as this Whig divine had incurred the displeasure of the Court, his Lordship wrote to the Master of the Rolls that the King considered the Chapel of the Rolls as one of his own chapels, and that Dr. Burnet must be dismissed as one disaffected to the government. In consequence he was obliged to go beyond seas, and to remain in exile till he returned with King William.[3]

Soon after followed the disgraceful trials for high treason, which arose out of the discovery of the Rye-House Plot. The Lord Keeper did not preside at these; but having directed them,—superintending the general administration of justice, and especially bound to see that the convictions had been obtained on legal evidence, —he is deeply responsible for the blood that was shed. He must have known that if, in point of law, the witnesses made out a case to be submitted to the jury against Lord Russell, that virtuous nobleman was really prosecuted for his support of the Exclusion Bill; and he must have seen that against Algernon Sydney no case had been made out to be submitted to the jury, as there was only one witness that swore to anything which could be construed into an overt act of treason, and the attempt to supply the defect by a MS. containing a speculative essay on government, which was found in his study, and

---

[1] 2 W. & M. sess. i. c. 8.   [2] Life, ii. 234.   [3] Own Times, ii. 269.

had been written many years before—was futile and flagitious.[1] Yet did he sign the death-warrants of both these men,—whose names have been honored, while his has been execrated in all succeeding times.

It is edifying and consolatory to think that he was outdone by his own arts, and that the rest of his career was attended by almost constant mortification, humiliation, and wretchedness. Saunders enjoyed the office of Chief Justice of the King's Bench only for a few months, being carried off by an apoplexy, soon after the decision of the great London *quo warranto* cause.[2] An intrigue was immediately set on foot to procure the appointment for Jeffreys, who had more than ever recommended himself to the Court by his zeal on the trial of Lord Russell, in which he had eclipsed the Attorney and Solicitor General —and he was anxiously wanted to preside at the trial of Sydney, against whom the case was known to be so slender, but who was particularly obnoxious on account of his late quarrel with the Duke of York, and his sworn enmity to despotism. The pretensions of Jeffreys were supported by Sunderland, probably out of ill will to the Lord Keeper, who had intuitively shown a great jealousy of the new favorite. But the proposal produced great opposition and bickerings among different sections of courtiers. The Lord Keeper of course resisted it *totis viribus*, representing to the King that the office, according to ancient and salutary usage, ought to be offered to the Attorney and Solicitor General, who had been irregularly passed over on the appointment of the late Chief Justice, to gain an object of such magnitude as the forfeiture of the City Charters; that Saunders was a man of immense learning, which countenanced *his* sudden elevation; but that *Jeffreys*, though gifted with a fluency of speech, was known to be unequal to so high an office ; and that the whole profession of the law, and the public would condemn an act so arbitrary and capricious. Charles was, or pretended to be, impressed by these arguments, which he repeated to Sunderland, and the office was kept vacant for three months after the death of Saunders.[3] But on

[1] 8 St. Tr. 578, 818.
[2] Although this decision was his, he was too ill to be present when it was pronounced by the seinor puisne Judge.
[3] See Sunderland's Letter, Clar. Corr. i. 82.

the 29th of September, the Lord Keeper had the mortification to put the great Seal to the writ constituting Jeffreys "Chief Justice of England," and on the first day of the following Michaelmas term to make a speech, publicly congratulating him on his rise to the supreme seat of criminal justice—so well merited by his learning, his abilities, and his services.

What was worse, the new Lord Chief Justice was not only sworn as a Privy Councillor, but, in a few weeks, was admitted into the Cabinet, where he, from the first, set himself to oppose the opinions, and to discredit the reputation, of him who he knew had opposed his appointment, and whom (his ambition being still unsatiated) he was resolved, in due time, to supplant.

Jeffreys began with interfering very offensively in the appointment of puisne Judges,—which of right belonged to the Lord Keeper. At first he was contented with the reputation of power in this department. The Lord Keeper having announced privately to Sergeant Bedingfield that he was to be made a Judge, Jeffreys worked upon him by the threat of stopping his promotion, to make him publish to the world that he owed it exclusively to the Chief Justice of the King's Bench.[1]

He next resolved to make a Judge, by his own authority, of a man almost as worthless as himself. This was Sir Robert Wright, who had never had any law, who had spent his patrimony in debauchery, and who, being in great distress, had lately sworn a false affidavit to enable him to commit a fraud on his own mortgagee. There being a vacancy on the bench, the Lord Keeper waited on his Majesty to "take his pleasure" on the appointment of a fit person, whom he named.—*King.* "My Lord, what think you of Sergeant Wright? Why may not he be the man?"—*Guilford.* "Because, Sir, I know him too well, and he is the most unfit person in England to be made a Judge."—*King.* "Then it must not be." Upon this they parted; but the next time that the Lord Keeper was in the royal presence, the King again said, "Why may not Wright be a Judge? He is strongly recommended to me; but I would have a due respect paid to you, and I would not make him without your concurrence. Is it impossible, my Lord?"—*Guilford.* "Sir,

[1] Life, ii. 93.

the making of a Judge is your Majesty's choice, and not my pleasure. I am bound to put the Seal as I am commanded, whatever the person may be. It is for your Majesty to determine, and me, your servant, to obey.[1] But I must do my duty by informing your Majesty of the truth respecting this man, whom I personally know to be a dunce and no lawyer; who is not worth a groat, having spent his estate by debauched living; who is without honesty, having been guilty of willful perjury to gain the borrowing of a sum of money. And now, Sir, I have done my duty to your Majesty; and am ready to obey your Majesty's commands in case it be your pleasure that this man shall be a Judge."—*King.* "My Lord, I thank you." (*Exit* King).—Next day there came a warrant for the appointment of "our right trusty and right well beloved Sir Robert Wright to be one of the Justices of our Court before us."

Jeffreys was not satisfied with his triumph without proclaiming it to all Westminster Hall. "Being there that same morning, while the Court of Chancery was sitting, he beckoned to Wright to come to him, and giving him a slap on the shoulder, and whispering in his ear, he flung him off, holding out his arms towards the Lord Keeper. This was a public declaration *that, in spite of that man above there, Wright should be a Judge.* His Lordship saw all this, as it was intended he should, and it caused him some melancholy." But he found it convenient to pocket the insult; he put the Great Seal to Wright's patent, and assisted at the ceremony of his installation. There is no trace of the Lord Keeper's speech on this occasion, so that we do not know in what terms he complimented the new Judge on his profound skill in the law, his spotless integrity, and his universal fitness to adorn the judgment-seat.[2]

When heated with liquor, Jeffreys could not now conceal his contempt for the Lord Keeper, even in the King's presence. It is related that, upon the hearing of a matter before the Council, arising out of a controversy for juris-

---

[1] Till the Revolution, and even for some time after, the King's personal command was considered a justification to every functionary.

[2] This wretch became so great a favorite in the next reign, that Herbert was turned out of the office of Chief Justice of the King's Bench to make way for him, and he presided at the trial of the seven Bishops, thereby greatly accelerating and furthering the Revolution.—12 *St. Tr.* 189.

diction between two sets of magistrates, Guilford proposed some sort of compromise between them, when the Lord Chief Justice, " flaming drunk," came from the lower to the upper end of the board, and " talking and staring like a madman," bitterly inveighed against " Trimmers," and told the King " he had *Trimmers* in his Court, and he never would be easy till all the *Trimmers* were sent about their business." " The Lord Keeper, knowing that these darts were aimed at him,¹ moved the King that the whole business should be referred to the Lord Chief Justice, and that he should make a report to his Majesty in Council of what should be fit to be done." This was ordered, and Guilford seems to have entertained a hope that Jeffreys, from the state of intoxication he was in, would entirely forget the reference, and so might fall into disgrace.²

But the most serious difference between them in Charles's time was on the return of Jeffreys from the northern circuit, in the autumn of 1684—when, backed by the Duke of York, he had a deliberate purpose of immediately grasping the Great Seal. At a Cabinet Council, held on a Sunday evening, he stood up, and addressing the King, while he held in his hands the rolls of the recusants in the north of England—" Sir," said he, " I have a business to lay before your Majesty which I took notice of in the north, and which well deserves your Majesty's royal commiseration. It is the case of numberless members of your good subjects that are imprisoned for recusancy; I have the list of them here to justify what I say. They are so many that the great jails can not hold them without their lying one upon another." After tropes and figures about " rotting and stinking in prison," he concluded with a motion to his Majesty " that he would, by his pardon, discharge all the convictions for recusancy, and thereby restore air and liberty to these poor men." This was a deep-laid scheme, for besides pleasing the royal brothers, one of whom was a disguised, and the other an avowed, Papist, he expected that Guilford must either be turned out for refusing to put the Great Seal to

¹ It is curious that Roger gravely states, that " he was dropped from the Tory list and turned Trimmer."—*Life*, i. 404.
² Life, ii. 179. It should be recollected that, at this time, the Council met in the afternoon, between two and three—dinner having taken place soon after twelve, and a little elevation from wine was not more discreditable at that hour, than in our own time between eleven and twelve o'clock at night.

the pardon, or that he would make himself most obnoxious to the public, and afterwards to parliament by compliance. A general silence prevailed, and the expectation was, that Halifax, or Rochester, who were strong Protestants, would have stoutly objected. The Lord Keeper, alarmed lest the motion should be carried, and seeing the dilemma to which he might be reduced, plucked up courage, and said, " Sir, I humbly entreat your Majesty that my Lord Chief Justice may declare whether all the persons named in these rolls are actually in prison or not ?" *Chief Justice:* "No fair man could suspect my meaning to be that all these are actual prisoners ; for all the jails in England would not hold them. But if they are not in prison, their case is little better; for they lie under sentence of commitment, and are obnoxious to be taken up by every peevish sheriff or magistrate, and are made to redeem their liberty with gross fees, which is a cruel oppression to them and their families." *Lord Keeper:* " Sir, I beg your Majesty will consider what little reason there is to grant such a general pardon at this time. For they are not all Roman Catholics that lie under sentence of recusancy, but sectaries of all kinds and denominations; perhaps as many, or more, who are all professed enemies to your Majesty and your government in church and state. They are a turbulent people, and always stirring up sedition. What will they not do when your Majesty gives them a discharge at once? Is it not better that your enemies should live under some disadvantages, and be obnoxious to your Majesty's pleasure, so that, if they are turbulent or troublesome, you may inflict the penalties of the law upon them? If there be any Roman Catholics whom you wish to favor, grant to them a particular and express pardon, but do not by a universal measure set your enemies as well as your friends at ease. The ill uses that would be made of such a step to the prejudice of your Majesty's interests and affairs are obvious and endless."[1] The King was much struck with these observations, urged with a boldness so unusual in the Lord Keeper. The other Lords wondered, and the motion was dropped.

The Lord Keeper, not without reason, boasted of this as the most brilliant passage of his life. When he came

[1] Life, ii. 150, 153, 334.

home at night he broke out in exclamations: "What can be their meaning? Are they all stark mad?" And before he went to bed, as a memorial of his exploit, he wrote in his almanac, opposite to the day of the month, "Motion *cui solus obstiti.*"

By such an extraordinary exhibition of courage to which he was driven by the instinct of self-preservation, he escaped the peril which Jeffreys had planned for him, and he retained the Great Seal till the King's death.

In the morning of Monday, the 2nd of February, 1685, he was sent for to Whitehall, by a messenger announcing that his Majesty had had an apoplectic seizure. According to the ancient custom and supposed law when the sovereign is dangerously distempered,— the Privy Council was immediately assembled; and the Lord Keeper examined the King's physicians.[1] "Their discourse ran upon indefinites—what they observed, their method intended, and success hoped. He said to them, *that these matters were little satisfactory to the Council, unless they would declare, in the main, what they judged of the King's case; whether his Majesty was like to recover or not?* But they would never be brought to that; *all lay in hopes.*"[2]

With short intervals, the Council continued to sit day and night. After a time, the physicians came into the council chamber, smiling, and saying they had good news, for the King had a fever.—*Lord Keeper.* "Gentlemen, what do you mean? Can anything be worse?"—*First Physician.* "Now we know what to do."—*Lord Keeper.* "What is that?"—*Second Physician.* "To give him the cortex." The exhibition of Jesuits' bark was sanctioned by the Council, but proved fatal,—and being continued

---

[1] Lord Coke lays down, that upon such an occasion there ought to be a warrant by advice of the Privy Council, as in 32 H. 8, to certain physicians and surgeons named, authorizing them to administer to the royal patient "potiones, syrupos, confectiones, laxitivas, medicinas, clysteria, supposituria, capitis purgea, capitis rasuram, fomentationes, embrocationes, emplastra," &c.; still that no medicine should be given to the King but by the advice of his Council; that no physic should be administered except that which is set down in writing, and that it is not to be prepared by any apothecary, but by the surgeons named in the warrant—4 *Inst.* 251. These were the precautions of times when no eminent person died suddenly without suspicion of poison. Even Charles II. was at first said to have been cut off to make way for a Popish successor, although, when the truth came out, it appeared that he had himself been reconciled to the Roman Catholic church.

[2] Life, ii. 184.

while the poor King grew weaker and weaker, at the end of four days he expired. The Lord Keeper and the Council were kept in ignorance of the fact, that Chiffinch (accustomed to be employed on royal errands of a different sort) had been sent for a Roman Catholic priest to receive his confession and administer the sacraments to him, when he had declined the spiritual assistance of a Bishop of the Church of England.

CHAPTER XCVII.

CONCLUSION OF THE LIFE OF LORD GUILFORD.

THE Council was still sitting when the news was brought that Charles was no more. After a short interval, James, who, leaving the death-bed of his brother, had decently engaged in a devotional exercise in his own closet, entered the apartment in which the Councillors were assembled, and all kneeling down they saluted him as their Sovereign. When he had seated himself in the chair of state, and delivered his declaration, which, with very gracious expressions, smacked of the arbitrary principles so soon acted upon, Lord Guilford surrendered the Great Seal into his hands, and again received it from him with the former title of Lord Keeper.[1] James would, no doubt, have been much better pleased to have transferred it to Jeffreys; but it was his policy, at the commencement of his reign, to make no change in the administration, and he desired all present to retain the several charges which they held under his deceased brother,—assuring them that he earnestly wished to imitate the good and gracious sovereign whose loss they deplored.

Jeffreys, though continued a member of the Cabinet, was probably a good deal disappointed, and he resolved to leave nothing undone to mortify the man who stood between him and his object, and to strike him down as soon as possible.

The first question upon which James consulted the Coun-

[1] On the 10th of February, before proceeding to business, he took the oaths, standing in his place in the Court of Chancery, the Master of the Rolls holding the book.—*Cr. Off. Min.* fol. 117.

cil, was respecting the levying of the duties of Customs and Excise, which had been granted by parliament only during the life of the late King. The Lord Keeper intimating a clear conviction that parliament would continue the grant as from the demise of the Crown, recommended a Proclamation requiring that the duties should be collected and paid into the Exchequer, and that the officers should keep the product separate from other revenues till the next session of parliament, in order to be disposed of as his Majesty and the two Houses should think fit. But the Lord Chief Justice represented this advice as low and trimming, and he moved that "his Majesty should cause his royal proclamation to issue, commanding all officers to collect, and the subjects to pay, these duties for his Majesty's use, as part of the royal revenue." The Lord Keeper ventured humbly to ask his Majesty to consider whether such a proclamation would be for his service, as it might give a handle to his Majesty's enemies to say that his Majesty, at the very entrance upon his government, levied money of the subject without the authority of parliament. The Chief Justice's advice was far more palatable. The proclamation which he recommended was therefore ordered to be drawn up, and was immediately issued. The Lord Keeper had the baseness to affix the Great Seal to this proclamation, thinking as he did of its expediency and legality. But rather than resign or be turned out of his office, he was ready to concur in any outrage on the constitution, or to submit to any personal indignity.

A parliament was found indispensable; and, counting on the very loyal disposition manifested by the nation, writs for calling one were issued, returnable the 19th of May.

As that day approached, the Lord Keeper began to write the speech which he expected to deliver in the presence of the King to the two Houses on their assembling. He was much pleased with this performance, on which he had taken uncommon pains, and when finished, he read it to his brother and his officers, who highly applauded it.[1] But what was his consternation when he

---

[1] See the speech at full length. Life, ii. 192. There is nothing in it very good or bad.

was told that he was not to be allowed to open his mouth upon the occasion!¹

Parliament meeting, the course was adopted which has been followed ever since. Instead of having on the first day of the session, before the choice of a Speaker by the Commons, one speech from the King, and another from the Lord Chancellor or Lord Keeper, to explain the causes of the summons—the Commons being sent for by the Black Rod, the Lord Keeper merely desired them to retire to their own Chamber and choose a Speaker, and to present him at an hour which was named, for his Majesty's approbation. The Speaker being chosen and approved of, and having demanded and obtained a recognition of the privileges of the Commons—on the following day the King himself made a speech from the throne and immediately withdrew.²

But this speech was not in modern fashion settled at the Cabinet; nor was it read the evening before at the Cockpit, or to the chief supporters of the government in both Houses at the dinner-table of the two leaders respectively; nor was it to be treated as the speech of the minister. "At least the Lord Keeper had no hand in it; for he was not so much as consulted about either the matter or expressions the King intended to use, as one might well judge by the unguarded tenor of it."³

Yet he still was mean enough to cling to office, and to do what he could for a government impatient to get rid of him. He had been very active in the elections; and by his influence had procured the return of a good many zealous Church-and-King members. "And to make the attendance easy to these gentlemen, whose concerns were in the country, he took divers of them to rack and manger in his family, where they were entertained while the parliament sat."⁴ But nothing which he could do would mitigate the hostility of those who had vowed his destruction.

At the meeting of parliament, Jeffreys was made a Peer,⁵ that he might have the better opportunity to thwart and insult the Lord Keeper—although there had been no previous instance of raising a common-law judge to the peerage.

¹ Life, ii. 120.   ² Ibid. 191.   ³ Ibid. 197.
⁴ 4 Parl. Hist. 1349.   ⁵ May 15, 1685.

There were several appeals from decrees of the Lord Keeper speedily brought to a hearing. "Jeffreys affected to let fly at them, to have it thought that he was fitter to be Chancellor." He attended, neglecting all other business; and during the argument, and in giving his opinion, took every opportunity of disparaging the Lord Keeper's law, preparatory to moving reversals. He was particularly outrageous in the case of Howard *v.* the Duke of Norfolk—being emboldened to talk confidently on matters with which he was not much acquainted, by having to rest on the reputation of Lord Nottingham. That great equity lawyer, contrary to the opinion of the two Chief Justices and the Chief Baron, whom he had called in to assist him, had held that an equitable estate tail might be created in a term of years; but his successor had reversed his decree, and the decree of reversal was now under appeal. "Lord Chief Justice Jeffreys, by means of some encouragement he had met with, took upon him the part of slighting and insulting his Lordship on all occasions that proffered. And here he had a rare opportunity; for, in his rude way of talking, and others of a party after him, he battered the poor decree; not without the most indecent affronts to his Lordship that in such an assembly ever were heard." The courtesy now prevailing between law Lords of opposite political parties was not then known between colleagues sitting in the same cabinet; and the poor Lord Keeper was assailed by the coarsest vituperation, and the most cutting ridicule. The second Earl of Nottingham, son of the Chancellor, "who hated him because he had endeavored to detract from his father's memory," likewise took this oportunity to attack him, and got together many instances of his ill-administration of justice, and greatly exposed him. He was not roused into retaliation or resistance; and he contented himself with a dry legal argument. The decree was reversed; and when he announced that the *contents had it*, he must have felt as if he had been sounding his own death-knell. The lay Lords who voted could have known nothing of the merits of such a nice question; and must have been guided by favor or enmity to the Lord

---

[1] Burnet, ii. 357. It was believed that this reversal "gave the crisis to the uneasiness and distraction of mind he was laboring under."

Keeper or the Lord Chief Justice.[1] What rendered the defeat and contemptuous usage more galling was the presence of the King; for James, like his brother, attended in the House of Lords when anything interesting was coming on; and walked about the House, or stood by the fire, or sat in his chair of state, or on the woolsack, as suited his fancy.[2]

"Having opened this scene," says Roger, "we are not to expect other than opposition, contempt, and brutal usage, of that Chief towards his Lordship while he lived."

There were few debates in the House of Lords during this short session; but, even in going through the common forms of the House, Jeffreys found opportunities publicly to testify his contempt for the Lord Keeper; and in the Cabinet, in discussing the dispensation to be granted to Catholic officers to serve in the army, and other subjects, he constantly laid traps for him, with a view of either making him obnoxious to the King, or odious to the public,—who considered him the author of every declaration or dispensation which passed the Great Seal.

Sunderland and other members of the cabinet openly joined in this persecution, and "he was little less than derided by them. Being soon to be laid aside, he was not relied upon in anything, but was truly a seal-keeper rather than a minister of state, and kept on for dispatch of the formularies, rather than for advice or trust."[3] Why did he not resign? It is difficult to understand the reasoning of his brother, who thus accounts for his continuing to bear such insults:—"His Lordship was so ill used at Court by the Earl of Sunderland, Jeffreys, and their sub-sycophants, that I am persuaded if he had had less pride of heart, he had been tempted to have delivered up the Seal in full health. But he cared not to gratify, by

---

[1] It is insinuated that some, to please the King, were influenced by the consideration that the appellant was a Roman Catholic, while the respondent was a Protestant.—See 1 *Vernon*, 162. *Life*, ii. 93.

[2] By a reference to the Journals of the House of Lords, it appears that the King attended almost every day during the whole of this session. The argument of Howard *v*. Duke of Norfolk occupied two days. It was decided, June 19, 1685, by a very full House, there being present, besides the King, eighteen bishops, and sixty-seven temporal peers, although there was no other business to be done. There was no division on the motion to reverse, so that the Lord Keeper must have been almost entirely without support.

[3] *Life*, ii. 132.

that, such disingenuous enemies. He cared not to humor these barkers, or to quit his place before he might do it with safety to his dignity. He intended to stay till the King would bear him no longer, and then make it his Majesty's own act to remove him."[1]

He felt keenly a sense of the insignificance and disfavor into which he had fallen; and the anticipation of "the worse remaining behind," when he was to be finally kicked out, preyed upon his spirits. No longer was he ear-wigged by the Lord Cravens, who worship a favorite; no more did the foreign ambassadors bow low when they thought that he observed them: his levee was now deserted; he seemed to himself to discover a sneer on every countenance at Whitehall; and he suspected that the bar, the officers of the Court, and the by-standers in Chancery, looked at him as if they were sure of his coming disgrace. To shade himself from observation, while he sat on the bench he held a large nosegay before his face.[2]

Dreadfully dejected, he lost his appetite and his strength. He could not even get through the business of the Court; and *remancts* multiplying upon him kept him awake at night, or haunted him in his sleep. He drooped so much, that for some time he seemed quite heart-broken. At last, he had an attack of fever, which confined him to his bed.

The coronation was approaching, and it was important that he should sit in the "Court of Claims." Having recovered a little by the use of Jesuit's bark, he presided there, though still extremely weak—and he walked at the coronation "as a ghost with the visage of death upon him, such a sunk and spiritless countenance he had."[3]

While he was in this wretched state, news arrived that the Duke of Monmouth had landed in the West of England and raised the standard of rebellion. The parliament, having come to a number of loyal votes, having attainted the Duke, and granted a supply, was adjourned, that the members might assist in preserving tranquillity in their several districts.

The Lord Keeper talked of resigning, and wrote a letter to the Earl of Rochester, to ask leave to go into the country for the recovery of his health, saying, "I have put myself into the hands of a doctor, who assures me of

---

[1] Life, ii. 222, 239.   [2] Ibid. 133.   [3] Ibid. ii. 205.

a speedy cure by entering into a course of physic." Leave was given, and he proceeded to Wroxton, in Oxfordshire, the seat which belonged to him in right of his wife.[1]

Here he languished while the battle of Sedgemoor was fought—Monmouth, after in vain trying to melt the heart of his obdurate uncle, was executed on Tower Hill under his parliamentary attainder—and the inhuman Jeffreys, armed with civil and military authority, set out on his celebrated "campaign." Roger North would make us believe that the dying Guilford was horrified by the effusion of blood which was now *incarnadining* the western counties by command of the Lord General Chief Justice, and that he actually interposed to stay it: "Upon the news returned of his violent proceedings, his Lordship saw the King would be a great sufferer thereby, and went directly to the King, and moved him to put a stop to the fury, which was in no respect for his service, but in many respects for the contrary. For though the executions were by law just, yet never were the deluded people all capitally punished; and it would be accounted a carnage, and not law or justice; and thereupon orders went to mitigate the proceeding. I am sure of his Lordship's intercession to the King on this occasion, being told it at the very time by himself." It is painful to doubt the supposed exertion of mercy and firmness by the Lord Keeper; but an attention to dates, of which this biographer is always so inconceivably negligent, shows the story to be impossible. Jeffreys did not open his campaign by the slaughter of the Lady Lisle, at Winchester, till the 27th of August, and he carried it on with increased cruelty till the very end of September.[2] On the 5th of September died Lord Keeper Guilford, at Wroxton, after having been for some weeks in a state of such debility and exhaustion, that, able only to attend to his spiritual concerns, he thought no more of domestic treason or foreign levy than if he had already slept in the grave.[3]

---

[1] Roger praises him much for the humility which he now exhibited: "It had been usual heretofore for all writs to bear teste where the Lord Keeper resided, though the King was not there; which was looked upon as a mark of honor to their families upon record. But his Lordship, thinking it mere vanity, ordered none to bear teste *apud Wroxton*, but *apud Westmonastrium* only."—*Life of Lord Keeper*, vol. ii. 144. [2] 11 St. Tr. 297, *et seq.*

[3] Roger (I will not say from any bad motive) does not mention the day of his brother's death; but this is placed beyond all doubt by the entry on the

For a short time after his arrival there, he rallied, by the use of mineral waters, but he soon had a relapse, and he could with difficulty sign his will. He was peevish and fretful during his sickness, but calmly met his end. "He advised his friends not to mourn for him, yet commended an old maid-servant for her good will that said, *As long as there is life there is hope.* At length, having strove a little to rise, he said, *It will not do,*—and then, with patience and resignation, lay down for good and all, and expired."[1]

He was buried in Wroxton Church, in a vault belonging to his wife's family, the Earls of Down. There is no other monument to him than a large marble slab in the middle of the floor of the chancel, bearing the following inscription:—

"Here lyeth the body of the Right Hon[ble] Francis Lord Guilford, Lord Keeper of the Great Seale of England.
He was borne the 22d of October, 1637, and departed this life the 5th of September, in the year of our Lord 1685."

"He was a crafty and designing man," says Bishop Burnet. "He had no mind to part with the Great Seal, and yet he saw he could not hold it without an entire compliance with the pleasure of the Court. Nothing but his successor made him be remembered with regret. He had not the virtues of his predecessor; but he had parts far beyond him. They were turned to craft; so that whereas the former (Lord Nottingham) seemed to mean well even when he did ill, this man was believed to mean ill even when he did well."[2] I accede to this character, with the exception of the estimate of North's "parts," which I think are greatly overrated. He was sharp and shrewd, but of no imagination, of no depth, of no grasp of intellect,—any more than generosity of sentiment. Cunning,

record respecting the appointment of his successor.—*Cr. Off. Min. Book,* 121. This is like a story he tells, equally incredible and impossible, of a caution given by the Lord Keeper in an interview with the King, after Monmouth's execution, to beware of the Prince of Orange.—*Life,* ii. 227. Monmouth was executed on the 15th of July, and the Lord Keeper and the King never could have met afterwards.—See *Ralph,* i. 893; 11 *St. Tr.* 303.—*Note to 1st Edition.*

Mr. Macaulay (Hist., vol. i. p. 638) supposes the alleged remonstrance to have taken place before Guilford retired from London; but this seems impossible, for the battle of Sedgemoor was fought while he was residing at Wroxton.—*Note to 4th Edition.*

[1] *Life,* ii. 215.   [2] O. T. ii. 155, 387.

industry, and opportunity may make such a man at any time. A Nottingham does not arise above once in a century.

Guilford had as much law as he could contain, but he was incapable of taking an enlarged and commanding view of any subject. The best specimen of his juridical powers is his judgment, when Chief Justice of the Common Pleas, in the great case of Soames *v.* Barnardiston, in which it was decided that an action at common law does not lie against a Sheriff for the false return of a member of parliament, as the validity of the return ought to be determined by the House of Commons.[1] In equity, he did nothing to rear up the system of which the foundations had been so admirably laid by his predecessor. His industry was commendable; and I think he may be fairly acquitted of corruption, notwithstanding his indiscreet acceptance of a present of £1,000 from the Six Clerks, when they had a dispute with the Sixty, on which he was to adjudicate.

He labors under the imputation of once having expressed a constitutional sentiment, "that his Majesty's *defensive* weapons were his *guards*, and his *offensive* weapons the *laws*, and that *rebels* were to be *overcome* by opposing force to force, but to be *punished* only by law,"—which from its rarity caused a great sensation. But where he was not under the apprehension of personal responsibility, there was nothing which he would not say or do to exalt the prerogative, and to please his patrons. I shall add only one instance. Sir Thomas Armstrong was outlawed for high treason while beyond the seas unless he surrendered within a year. Being sent over a prisoner from Holland within a year, he insisted that he was entitled to a writ of error to reverse the outlawry, and to be admitted to make his defense; but the Lord Keeper refused him his writ of error, first, on the pretense that there was no fiat for it by the Attorney General, and then, that he had no right to reverse his outlawry, as he was present by compulsion. Thus, the unhappy victim was sent to instant execution without trial.[2]

So zealous a conservative was Guilford, that "he

---

[1] 6 St. Tr. 1092, 1098. His judgment was confirmed on a writ of error by the House of Lords after the Revolution.—See *Lord Campbell's Speeches*, 277. [2] 10 St. Tr. 106.

thought the taking away of the tenures," (*i. e.* the abolition of wardship and the other oppressive feudal burdens introduced at the Conquest) a desperate wound to the liberties of the people."

The Court wags made great sport of him, the Earl of Sunderland taking the lead, and giving out the signal, while Jeffreys was always ready to join in the laugh. I may offer as an example "the story of the Rhinoceros." My Lord Keeper went one day into the City, accompanied by his brother, Sir Dudley, to see a Rhinoceros of enormous size lately imported, and about to be exhibited as a show.[1] Next morning, at Whitehall, a rumor was industriously spread, that the Lord Keeper had been riding on the Rhinoceros, " and soon after dinner, some Lords and others came to his Lordship to know the truth from himself: for the setters of the lie affirmed it positively, as of their own knowledge. That did not give his Lordship much disturbance, for he expected no better from his adversaries. But that his friends, intelligent persons, who must know him to be far from guilty of any childish levity, should believe it, was what *roiled* him extremely, and much more when they had the face to come to him to know if it were true. So it passed; and the Earl of Sunderland, with Jeffreys and others of that crew, never blushed at the lie of their own making, but valued themselves upon it as a very good jest."[2]

To try how far his compliance with the humors of the Court would go, they next persuaded his own brother-in-law (that he might not suspect the hoax) to wait upon him, and in strict confidence, and with great seriousness, to advise him to keep a mistress, " otherwise he would lose all his interest with the King; for it was well understood that he was ill looked upon for want of doing so, because he seemed continually to reprehend them by not falling in with the general custom; and the messenger added, that if his Lordship pleased he would help him to

---

[1] Evelyn tells us that this was the first rhinoceros ever introduced into England, and that it sold for £2,000. Shakespeare may have seen "the Hyrcan Tiger," but he could only have heard, or read, or seen a picture of "the armed rhinoceros."

[2] Life, ii. 167. The marginal note to this anecdote by Roger is amusing: —"The foolish lie of the rhinoceros. His Lordship much roiled thereat." The word "roiled" was transported to the American plantations, where it may still be met with.—See the *Clockmaker*.

one." He declined the offer,—with much politeness, however, lest he should give offense. But with his familiar friends " he made wonderfully merry with this state policy, especially the procuring part, and said, *that if he were to entertain a madam, it should be one of his own choosing, and not one of their stale trumpery*."[1]

Although he never aimed at oratory, it is said that he meditated a " History of his own Times." He might have transmitted to us many curious anecdotes, but the performance must have been without literary merit; for some of his notes which he had written as materials are in the most wretched style, and show that he was unacquainted with the first principles of English composition, and even with the common rules of grammar. He did publish two or three short tracts " on Music " and other subjects,—which were soon forgotten. He was well versed in music, conversed with Sir Peter Lely about painting, speculated with natural philosophers on the use of the bladder of fishes, and learned several of the continental languages; but he seems never to have looked into a classical writer after he left college, and to have had the same taste for the *belles lettres* as his brother Roger, who, placing them all in the same category, talks with equal contempt of "departed quacks, *poets*, and almanack makers."[2] Although his two immediate predecessors were libeled and lauded by popular verses in the mouths of every one, I can find no allusion in any fine writer either of the Court or Country party to North; and it may be doubtful whether he knew anything of the works of Butler, of Dryden, of Waller, or of Cowley, beyond the snatches of them he may have heard repeated in the merry circle at Whitehall.

He lived very hospitably,—receiving those who retailed the gossip of the day in his house in Great Queen Street, Lincoln's Inn Fields,—then the fashionable quarter of the town for the great nobility as well as for eminent lawyers. He had a large range of stables near his house, under the superintendence of his " Master of the Horse," an old Cavalier officer who could smoke tobacco and taste claret, though not very skillful or careful in his office. There were various tables in the house daily,—from that of the Major Domo, or the " prefect of eating," down to that of

---

[1] Life, ii. 239.   [2] Preface, vi.

the inferior servants who "ate like harpies at the catch, and, to say truth, most scandalously." The nobility and chief gentry coming to London frequently dined with him. The dinner was at a very early hour, and did not last long. "After a solemn service of tea in a withdrawing-room, the company usually left him."[1] He had a Court room fitted up on the ground floor, which he then entered,—and there he continued hearing causes and exceptions, sometimes to what was considered a late hour. About eight o'clock came supper, which he took with a few private friends, and relished as the most agreeable and refreshing meal of the day.[2]

In the vacations, when he could be spared from London, he retired to his seat at Wroxton. For some years he likewise rented a villa at Hammersmith, but this he gave up soon after his wife's death.

He had the misfortune to lose her after they had been married only a few years. She seems to have been a very amiable person. She found out when her husband had any trouble upon his spirits, and she would say, "*Come, Sir Francis,* (as she always styled him,) *you shall not think; we must talk and be merry, and you shall not look on the fire as you do. I know something troubles you; and I will not have it so.*"[3] He would never marry again, which in his last illness he repented, for "he fancied that in the night human heat was friendly."

He was extremely amiable in all the relations of domestic life. Nothing can be more touching than the account we have of the warm and steady affection subsisting between him and his brother, who survived to be his biographer.

The Lord Keeper was a little but handsome man, and is said to have had "an ingenuous aspect," his motto being, "Il volto sciolto, i pensieri stretti."

He left behind him Francis, his son and heir, the second Baron Guilford, father of Francis, the third Baron Guilford, on whom descended the Barony of North, by failure of the elder branch of the family, and who, in 1752, was created Earl of Guilford, and was the father of Lord North, the prime minister, so celebrated for his polished oratory, his refined wit, and amiable manners. His daughter, Lady Charlotte Lindsey, still survives, the

[1] Life, ii. 167.   [2] Ibid. 195–210.   [3] Ibid. 316.

grace and ornament of her sex, in the reign of Queen Victoria.[1]

The title of Guilford is now enjoyed by Francis, the sixth Earl.[2]

When we estimate what the Lord Keeper achieved, we should bear in mind that he died at *forty-eight*, an age considerably more advanced than that reached by his immediate successor; yet under that at which other Lord Chancellors and Lord Keepers began to look for promotion. Although I have brought him into existence three years sooner than former biographers—he was in truth Solicitor General at *thirty-four*, Attorney General at *thirty-seven*, Chief Justice of the Common Pleas at *thirty-eight*, and Lord Keeper and a Peer at *forty-five*. It is probably well for his memory that his career was not prolonged. He might have made a respectable Judge when the constitution was settled; but he was wholly unfit for the times in which he lived.

I ought not to conclude this memoir without acknowledging my obligations to " Roger North's Life of the Lord Keeper;" which, like " Boswell's Life of Johnson," interests us highly, without giving us a very exalted notion of the author. Notwithstanding its extravagant praise of the hero of the tale, its inaccuracies, and its want of method, it is a most valuable piece of biography, and with Roger's Lives of his brothers, " Dudley and John," and his " Examen," it ought to be studied by every one who wishes to understand the history and the manners of the reign of Charles II.

CHAPTER XCVIII.

LIFE OF LORD CHANCELLOR JEFFREYS[3] FROM HIS BIRTH TILL HE WAS APPOINTED RECORDER OF LONDON.

IT is hardly known to the multitude that this infamous person ever held the Great Seal of England; as, from the almost exclusive recollection of his presiding on criminal trials, he has been execrated under the designa-

[1] Written in 1844. [2] Grandeur of the Law, p. 64.
[3] The name is spelt no fewer than eight different ways:—" Jeffries," " Jefferies," " Jefferys," " Jeffereys," " Jefferyes," " Jeffrys," " Jeffryes," and " Jeffreys,"

tion of "JUDGE JEFFREYS,"—which is as familiar in our mouths as household words. Yet was he Chancellor a considerably longer time than Chief Justice,—and in the former capacity, as well as the latter, he did many things to astonish and horrify mankind.

He has been so much abused, that I began my critical examination of his history in the hope and belief that I should find that his misdeeds had been exaggerated, and that I might be able to rescue his memory from some portion of the obloquy under which it labors; but I am sorry to say, that, in my matured opinion, although he appears to have been a man of high talents, of singularly agreeable manners, and entirely free from hypocrisy, his cruelty and his political profligacy have not been sufficiently exposed or reprobated; and that he was not redeemed from his vices by one single solid virtue.

George Jeffreys was a younger son of John Jeffreys, Esq., of Acton, near Wrexham, in Denbighshire, a gentleman of a respectable Welsh family, and of small fortune. His mother was a daughter of Sir Thomas Ireland, Knight, of the County Palatine of Lancaster. Never was child so unlike parents; for they were both quiet, sedate, thrifty, unambitious persons, who aspired not higher than to be well reputed in the parish in which they lived, and decently to rear their numerous offspring. Some imputed to the father a niggardly and covetous disposition; but he appears only to have exercised a becoming economy, and to have lived at home with his consort in peace and happiness, till he was made more anxious than pleased by the irregular advancement of his boy George. It is said he had an early presentiment that this son would come to a violent end; and was particularly desirous that he should be brought up to some steady trade, in which he might be secured from temptation and peril. The old gentlemen lived till he heard, after the landing of the Prince of Orange, of the Lord Chancellor being taken up at Wapping, disguised as a sailor, being assaulted by the mob, being carried before the Lord Mayor, and dying miserably in the Tower of London.[1]

and he himself spelt it differently at different times of his life; but the last spelling is that which is found in his patent of peerage, and which he always used afterwards.

[1] Pennant saw a likeness of this old gentleman at Acton House, taken in 1690, in the 82nd year of his age.—See Pennant's *Tour in Wales*, i. 296.

He of whom such tales were to be told, was born in his father's lowly dwelling at Acton, in the year 1648.[1] He showed, from early infancy, the lively parts, the active temperament, the outward good humor, and the overbearing disposition which distinguished him through life. He acquired an ascendency among his companions in his native village by coaxing some and intimidating others, and making those most opposed to each other believe that he favored both. At marbles and leap-frog he was known to take undue advantages; and, nevertheless, he contrived notwithstanding secret murmurs, to be acknowledged as "Master of the Revels."

While still very young he was put to the free school at the town of Shrewsbury, which was then considered a sort of metropolis for North Wales. Here he continued for two or three years: but we have no account how he demeaned himself. At the end of this time, his father, though resolved to bind him apprentice to a shopkeeper in Wales, sent him for a short time to St. Paul's School, in the City of London. The sight of the metropolis had a most extraordinary effect upon the mind of this ardent youth, and exceedingly disgusted him with the notion of returning into Denbighshire, to pass his life in a small provincial town as a mercer. On the first Sunday in every term he saw the Judges and the Sergeants come in grand procession to St. Paul's Cathedral, and afterwards go to dine with the Lord Mayor—appearing little inferior to this great Sovereign of the City in power and splendor. He heard that some of them had been poor boys like himself, who had pushed themselves on without fortune

---

[1] This is generally given as the year of his birth, but I have in vain tried to have it authenticated. There is no entry of his baptism, nor of the baptism of his brothers, in the register of Wrexham, the parish in which he was born, nor in the adjoining parish of Gresford, in which part of the family property lies. I have had accurate searches made in these registers by the kindness of my learned friend, Mr. Sergeant Atcherly, who has estates in the neighborhood. It is not improbable that, in spite of the Chancellor's great horror of dissenters, he may have been baptized by "a dissenting teacher."— 1*st Edition*.

This conjecture is strongly confirmed by a passage which I have since found in a Life by Matthew Henry, the Commentator on the Bible, of his father, Philip Henry, a famous Presbyterian minister, to the effect that Judge Jeffreys, notwithstanding his harsh character, always, while he was Chief Justice of Chester, refused to put the *Fine Mote Act* in force against *Philip Henry*, because this pious divine had been his mother's friend and pastor.— *4th Edition*.

or friends; and though he was not so presumptuous as to hope, like another Whittington, to rise to be Lord Mayor, he was resolved that he would be Lord Chief Justice or Lord Chancellor.

Now it was that he acquired whatever scholarship he ever possessed. The Master of St. Paul's School, at this time, was Samuel Cromleholme, or Crumlum, who, for his skill in languages, obtained the name of Πολυγλωττος, and under him Jeffreys applied with considerable diligence to Greek and Latin, though occasionally flogged for idleness and insolence. He at last ventured to disclose his scheme of becoming a great lawyer, to his father, who violently opposed it, as wild and romantic and impossible,—and who inwardly dreaded that, from involving him in want and distress, it might lead to some fatal catastrophe. He wrote back to his son, pointing out the inability of the family to give him a University education, or to maintain him at the Inns of Court till he should have a chance of getting into practice—his utter want of connections in London—and the hopelessness of his entering into a contest in an overstocked profession with so many who had the advantage of superior education, wealth, and patronage. Although the aspirant professed himself unconvinced by these arguments, and still tried to show the certainty of his success at the bar, he must have stood a crop-eared apprentice behind a counter in Denbigh, Ruthyn, or Flint, if it had not been for his maternal grandmother, who was pleased to see the blood of the Irelands break out, and who, having a small jointure, offered to contribute a part of it for his support. The University was still beyond their means; but it was thought this might be better dispensed with if he should be for some time at one of our great schools of royal foundation, where he might form acquaintances afterwards to be useful to him. The father reluctantly consented, in the hope that his son would soon return to his sober senses, and that the project would be abandoned with the general concurrence of the family. Meanwhile, young George was transferred to Westminster School, then under the rule of the celebrated Busby.

There is reason to fear that the zeal for improvement which he had exhibited at St. Paul's soon left him, and that he here began to acquire those habits of intemperance which afterwards proved so fatal to him. His father hearing of these had all his fears revived, and when the boy was at Acton during the holidays, again tried in vain to induce him to become a tradesman. But finding all dissuasions unavailing, the old gentleman withdrew his opposition, giving him a gentle pat on the back, accompanied by these words,—" Ah, George, George, I fear thou wilt die with thy shoes and stockings on!"

Yet the wayward youth while at Westminster had fits of application, and carried away from thence a sufficient stock of learning to prevent him from appearing in after-life grossly deficient when any question of grammar arose. He was fond of reminding the world of the great master under whom he had studied. On the trial before him as Chief Justice, in the year 1684, of Rosewell, the dissenting minister, for high treason in a sermon delivered from the pulpit, an objection was taken to the sufficiency of the indictment, in which it was alleged that the defendant had said, "We have had two wicked Kings together, who have permitted Popery to enter in under their noses, whom we can resemble to no other person but to most wicked Jeroboam; and if *they* would stand to their principles, he did not fear but *they* would overcome their enemies, as in former times with rams' horns, broken platters, and a stone in a sling." The counsel insisting that it was not sufficiently averred who were thus to overturn the government by physical force, the Chief Justice, who, on account of a suggestion from the government, wished in this case to procure an acquittal, favored the objection, and said, " I think it must be taken to be an entire speech, and you lay it in the indictment to be so, and then the relative must go to the last antecedent, or else Dr. Busby (that so long ruled in Westminster School) taught me quite wrong, and who had tried most of the grammars extant, and used to lay down as a positive rule of grammar, *that the relative must refer to the last antecedent.*"[1]

[1] 10 St. Tr. 299. The bitter spite always shown against Jeffreys by Roger North is explained by this trial. As junior counsel for the Crown he had drawn the indictment, and was eager to defend it against the intimation of the opinion of the Bench. *Mr. North—*" Will your Lordship please to spare me a word?" *L. C. J.—*" Aye, sir, let every man be heard, in God's name." Roger makes some observations, which I must acknowledge are rather foolish, and then the C. J. thus puts him down :—" Mr. North, the argument

His confidence in his own powers was so great, that, without conforming to ordinary rules, he expected to overcome every obstacle. Being now in the neighborhood of Westminster Hall, his ambition to be a great lawyer was inflamed by seeing the grand processions on the first day of term, and by occasionally peeping into the Courts, when an important trial was going forward. He must have been much struck by the grandeur of the Earl of Clarendon, who then presided in the Court of Chancery. In his waking moments he could scarcely have hoped to succeed him, but such visions passed before his imagination, and when he was actually Lord Chancellor, he used to relate that, while a boy at Westminster School, he had a dream, in which a Gipsy read his fortune, foretelling, "that he should be the chief scholar there, and should afterwards enrich himself by study and industry, and that he should come to be the second man in the kingdom, but, in conclusion, should fall into disgrace and misery."

He was now sixteen, an age after which it was not usual to remain at school in those days. A family council was called at Acton, and as George still sanguinely adhered to the law, it was settled that, the University being quite beyond their reach, he should immediately be entered at an Inn of Court; that, to support him there, his grandmother should allow him forty pounds a year, and that his father should add ten pounds a year for decent clothing.[1] The aid which has since been found available to poor students, from literary labor, and of which, when a student at Lincoln's Inn, I availed myself, was then unknown; so that this was the whole revenue he could calculate upon till it should be augmented by the distant and uncertain accession of clients and fees.

However, he believed in his dream, and, on the 19th of May, 1663, to his great joy, he was admitted a member of the Inner Temple.[2] He got a small and gloomy chamber, in which, with much energy, he began his legal studies.

turns both ways upon that. It is so loose a hung-together indictment, as truly I have scarce seen." The Court took time to consider, and the prisoner was pardoned.

[1] Though so small, it was not much less than that of Lord Keeper Guilford, the son of a peer, ante, p. 242.

[2] "Jefferies (Gs.) Georgius Jefferies de Acton in Comitatu Denbigh generosus admissus est in hanc Societatem, &c." May 1663. *Admission Book, Inner Temple*, folio 918.

He not only had a natural boldness of eloquence, but an excellent head for law. With steadiness of application he would have greatly excelled Lord Keeper Guilford, and in the mastery of this science would have rivaled Lord Hale and Lord Nottingham. But he could not long resist the temptations of bad company. Having laid in a very slender stock for a Counsel or a Judge, he forsook Littleton and Plowden,[1] "moots and readings," for the tavern, where was his chief delight. He seems to have escaped the ruinous and irreclaimable vice of gaming, but to have fallen into all others to which reckless Templars were prone. Nevertheless, he had ever a keen eye to his own interest; and in these scenes of dissipation he assiduously cultivated the acquaintance of young attorneys and their clerks, who might afterwards be useful to him. He could not, like Mr. Surrebutter in the Pleader's Guide, give them rich treats at his chambers,[2] but, when they met over a bowl of punch at the Devil tavern, or some worse place, he charmed them with songs and jokes, and took care to bring out before them, opportunely, any scrap of law which he had picked up, to impress them with the notion that, when he put on his gown and applied to business, he should be able to win all the causes in which he might be retained. He was exceedingly popular, and he had many invitations to dinner; which, to make his way in the world, he thought it better to accept, than to waste his time over the midnight oil, in acquiring knowledge which it might never be known that he possessed.

[1]
"He scorned Littleton and Plowden too;
With mouldy authors he'd have nought to do."
Jefferys' Elegy on Old Parr.

[2] This great Nisi Prius leader, in narrating his rise, thus describes his guests.—
"*To wit*, Old Buzzard, Hawk, and Crow,
Item, Tom Thornback, Shark, and Co.,
Attorneys all as keen and staunch
As e'er devour'd a client's haunch.
Nor did I not the clerks invite,
To taste said venison hash'd at night;
For well I knew that hopeful fry
My rising merits would descry;
The same litigious course pursue,
And when to fish of prey they grew,
By love of food and contest led,
Would haunt the spot where once they fed."
Pl. Guide, part i. lect.

After the first fervor of loyalty which burst out at the Restoration had passed away, a malcontent party was formed, which gradually gained strength. In this most of the aspiring young lawyers, not actually employed by the government, were ranged,—finding it politic to begin in "the sedition line,"[1] that their value might be better appreciated by the Court, and a better price might be bid for them.[2] From such reasoning, or perhaps, from accidental circumstances, Jeffreys associated himself with the popular leaders, and in the hour of revelry, would drink on his knees any toasts to "the good old cause," and to "the immortal memory of old Noll." The Calves Head Club had not yet been established, or he probably would not have scrupled to belong to it, and to have drunk with devotion the two standing toasts of the brethren,— "to the man in the mask," and "the man that would do it without a mask."

He was often put to great shifts from the embarrassed state of his finances, the £10 for "decent clothing" for a year being expended in a single suit of cut velvet, and his grandmother's £40 being insufficient to pay his tavern bills. But he displayed much address in obtaining prolonged and increased credit from his tradesmen. He borrowed adroitly; and it is said that such an impression was made by his opening talents, that several wealthy men on the popular side voluntarily made him presents of money in the hope of the important services they were speedily to receive from his support.

It is very much to be regretted that we have not from a Roger North more minute information with respect to the manner in which his character was formed, and his abilities were cultivated. He seems to have been a most precocious young man. While still in his twentieth year, he was not only familiarly acquainted with the town, and

---

[1] This expression is said to have been invented by that famous Stenographer, celebrated in the "Pleader's Guide":—

"Sit behind some fat attorney,
And make a friend of Mr. Gurney."

—the father of that very worthy man, the late Mr. Baron Gurney. The old gentleman being asked about the year 1792, when State Trials were so rife, how his son John was getting on at the bar, replied, "Remarkably well ; he has taken to the sedition line, and I hope he will make his fortune in it."

[2] Sir Francis North valued himself much on having been an exception to this rule, and always loyal.

completely a man of the world, exciting confident expectations of great future eminence, but he was already received among veteran statesmen as a member of an important party in the state, consulted as to their movements, and regarded as their future leader.

We are now actually to see him on the stage of public life. It has been constantly asserted, that he made his entrance most irregularly into the profession of the law. A story was propagated soon after his death, and has been repeated ever since, that he was never called to the bar, and that for lack of counselors,—who are all supposed to have been killed or frightened away by the plague,—at the Kingston assizes, in 1666, being then a lad of eighteen, he boldly put on a bombazine gown, walked into Court as a barrister, was intrusted with briefs by the attorneys, won verdicts, and continued to practice with applause ever after. But it bears such improbabilities on the face of it, that hardly any evidence could support it. The plague of 1666 did not rage anywhere out of London so as to interfere with the common affairs of life. It must have been fatal indeed before it would induce the members of the circuit established in business, or candidates for it, to give up their profits and their position to adventurous rivals.[1] In such a state of things neither judge, nor jury, nor witnesses, nor attorneys, nor parties, would have attended. If there had been any presumptuous stripling so absurd as to make the supposed attempt, he could not have inspired confidence into any one. We must further bear in mind that the regulations, by which no person was allowed to practice as a barrister without being called to the bar by one of the four Inns of Court, were then quite as strict and as rigidly enforced as they now are. If, by any unaccountable accident, the sham barrister had been permitted to plead a cause in the country, he would have been silenced on his return to London, and if contumacious, he would have been

---

[1] At the Gloucester summer assizes, 1832, the Asiatic cholera was raging in that city; tar barrels were burnt all day in the streets,—no one entered the county hall except on some sort of compulsion, and every one who entered held in his hand some charm against the infection. Yet of a bar above fifty in number only one man fled the field. There were many deaths daily in Leather Bottle Lane, close by my lodgings, but I thought that I, the leader of the circuit, was bound to remain at my post, and to give a chance to my juniors.

disgracefully expelled from the Society whose discipline he had defied. The story rests on vague rumor, not corroborated by any name, circumstance, or authority. But at once to demolish it, I find upon a reference to the books of the Inner Temple, which I have been kindly permitted to examine, that the same George Jeffreys admitted on the 19th of March, 1663—after keeping all his terms, and doing all his exercises, was regularly called to the bar on the 22nd day of November, 1668—having been on the books of the Society five years and six months—and the requisite period of probation having been previously, by a general regulation, reduced from seven to the present period of five years. I can not offer direct proof that he did not practice as a barrister in Westminster Hall in the intermediate time; but when I show the exact date of his actual call, surely the inevitable inference is, that till then he continued *in statu pupillari* as a student of law.

Although he does not appear ever to have been chosen "Reader" or "Treasurer" of the Society, yet in the year 1678, on being elected Recorder of London, he was made a Bencher,[1] and he continued to be so till he took the coif, when he necessarily left it for Sergeants' Inn.

During his early career, he was involved in difficulties, which could only have been overcome by uncommon energy. Pressed by creditors, and at a loss to provide for the day that was passing over him, he had burdened himself with the expenses of a family. But this arose out of a speculation, which, in the first instance, was very prudent. Being a handsome young fellow, and capable of making himself acceptable to modest women—notwithstanding the bad company which he kept, he resolved to repair his fortunes by marrying an heiress; and he fixed upon the daughter of a country gentleman of large possessions, who, on account of his agreeable qualities, had invited him to his house. The daughter, still very young, was cautiously guarded, and almost always confined to her chamber; but Jeffreys contrived to make a confidant and friend of a poor relation of hers, who was the daughter of a country parson, and lived with her as a

---

[1] "Jan. 26, 1678. At this parliament it is ordered, that Sir George Jefferyes, Knt. be and is called to be one of the Masters of the Bench of this Society."—Entry in Books of I. T.

companion. Through this agency he had established a correspondence with the heiress, and an interest in her affections, so that on his last visit she had agreed, if her father's consent could not be obtained, to elope with him. What was his disappointment, soon after his return to his dismal chamber in the Inner Temple, which he had hoped soon to exchange for a sumptuous manor-house, to receive a letter from the *companion*, informing him " that his correspondence with the *heiress* had been discovered by the old father, who was in such a rage, that, locking up her cousin, he had instantly turned herself out of doors, and that having taken shelter in the house of an acquaintance in Holborn, she was there in a state of great destitution and distraction—afraid to return to her father, or to inform him of what had happened!" The conduct of Jeffreys on this occasion may be truly considered the brightest passage in his history. He went to her, found her in tears, and considering that he had been the means of ruining her prospects in life (to say nothing of her being much handsomer than her rich cousin), he offered her his hand. She consented. Her father, notwithstanding the character and circumstances of his proposed son-in-law,—out of regard to his daughter's reputation, sanctioned their union, and to the surprise of all parties gave her a fortune of £300. Accordingly, " on the 23rd of May, 1667, at Allhallows Church, Barking, George Jeffreys of the Inner Temple, Esq., was married to Sarah, the daughter of the Reverend Thomas Neesham, A.M." [1]

She made an excellent wife, and I do not find any complaint of his having used her ill—till near the time of her death, a few years after, when he had cast his affections upon the lady who became the second Mrs. Jeffreys. Meanwhile he left her at her father's, occasionally visiting her; and he continued to carry on his former pursuits, and to strengthen his connections in London, with a view to his success at the bar, on which he resolutely calculated with unabated confidence.

He was not disappointed. Never had a young lawyer risen so rapidly into practice. But he cut out a new line for himself. Instead of attending in Westminster Hall to take notes in law French of the long-winded arguments of Sergeants and eminent counsel, where he would have had

[1] Parish Reg. of Allhallows, Barking.

little chance of employment in actions real, and trials at bar, as he was utterly unacquainted with "Fitzherbert's Natura Brevium," or "the Doctrina placitandi,"—he did not go near any of the superior Courts for some years, but confined himself to the Old Bailey, the London Sessions, and Hicks's Hall. There he was soon "the cock of the walk."

But at his outset there was no art, however low, to which he would not resort with a view to "get on." "He used to sit in coffee-houses, and order his clerk to come and tell him *that company attended him at his chamber.* At which he would huff and say,—*Let them stay a little; I will come presently;*—and thus made a show of business."[2]

Some of his pot companions were now of great use to him in bringing him briefs, and recommending him to business. All this pushing would have been of little avail if he had not fully equaled expectation by the forensic abilities which he displayed. He had a very sweet and powerful voice, having something in its tone which immediately fixed the attention, so that his audience always were compelled to listen to him, irrespective of what he said.[3] "He was of bold aspect, and cared not for the countenance of any man." He was extremely voluble, but always perspicuous and forcible, making use of idiomatic, and familiar, and colloquial, and sometimes of coarse language. He never spared any assertion that was likely to serve his client. He could get up a point of law so as to argue it with great ability, and with the Justices, as well as with Juries, his influence was unbounded. He was particularly famous for his talent in cross-examination, indulging in ribaldry and banter to a degree which

[1] Considering his recorded habits as a student, it is possible he might have made the same use of this treatise to acquire the reputation of learning among the attorneys as the celebrated Mr. Surrebutter, who, on their approach, having conveyed into the coal-hole what interested him more, thus describes his own demeanor:—

"At once with serious look profound,
Mine eyes communing with the ground.
I seem'd like one estrang'd to sleep,
'And fix'd in cogitation deep;'
Sat motionless, and in my hand I
Held my DOCTRINA PLACITANDI!"

[2] North's Life of Guilford, ii. 96.

[3] A few such voices I have known in my time,—particularly that of the late Sir William Garrow,—whose early professional career was pretty much like that of Jeffreys, although he was free from his vices.

would not now be permitted. The audience being ever ready to take part with the persecuted witness, the laugh was sometimes turned against him. It is related that, about this time, beginning to cross-examine a witness in *a leathern doublet*, who had made out a complete case against his client, he bawled fourth, "You fellow in the leathern doublet, pray what have you for swearing?" The man looked steadily at him, and, "Truly, sir," said he, "if you have no more for lying than I have for swearing, you might wear a leathern doublet as well as I." This blunt reply got to the west end of the town, and was remembered among the courtiers against Jeffreys when he grew to be a great man.

While a trial was going on he was devotedly earnest in it; but when it was over, he would recklessly get drunk, as if he never were to have another to conduct.[1] Coming so much in contact with the aldermen, he ingratiated himself with them very much, and he was particularly patronized by a namesake (though no relation) of his own, —Jeffreys, alderman of Bread Street Ward, who was very wealthy, a great smoker (an accomplishment in which the lawyer could rival him, as well as in drinking), and who had immense influence with the livery.[2]

Pushed by him, or rising rapidly by his own buoyancy, George, our hero, before he had been two years and a half at the bar, and while only twenty-three years of age, was elected Common Sergeant of the city of London,— an office which has raised a Denman as well as a Jeffreys to be Chief Justice of England. This first step of his elevation he obtained on the 17th of March, 1671, on a vacancy occasioned by the resignation of Sir Richard Browne.

But his ambition was only inflamed by this promotion, which disqualified him for a considerable part of his bar practice, and he resolved entirely to change the field of his operations,—making a dash at Westminster Hall. He

---

[1] Mackintosh says, "His professional practice was low, and chiefly obtained from the companions of his vulgar excesses, whom he captivated by that gross buffoonery which accompanied him to the most exalted stations."—Works, vol. ii. 14.

[2] There were two aldermen of this name in the reign of Charles II.—John, elected alderman of Bread Street in 1661, of whom we are speaking, and Robert, elected Alderman of Cordwainer's Ward in 1676, and Lord Mayor in 1686.

knew well that he could not be employed to draw declarations and pleas, or to argue demurrers or special verdicts; but he hoped his talent for examining witnesses and for speaking might avail him. At any rate, this was the only road to high distinction in his profession, and he spurned the idea of spending his life in trying petty larcenies, and dining with the City companies.

Hard drinking was again his grand resource. He could now afford to invite the great City attorneys to his house as well as carouse with them at taverns, and they were pleased with the attentions of a rising barrister, as well as charmed with the pleasantry of the most jovial of companions. He likewise began to cultivate fashionable society, and to consider how he might contrive to get an introduction at Court. "He put himself into all companies,--for which he was qualified, by using himself to drink hard."—Now was the time when men got forward in life by showing their hatred of puritanism, their devotion to Church and King, and an affectation of vice, even if actually free from it.

Yet such was the versatility of Jeffreys, that for the nonce he could appear sanctimonious and even puritanical. Thus he deceived the religious, the moral, the immaculate Sir Mathew Hale, then Chief Justice of the King's Bench. Roger North, in drawing the character of this extraordinary man, says, "Although he was very grave in his own person, he loved the most bizarre and irregular wits in the practice of the law before him most extravagantly. So Sir George Jeffreys gained as great an ascendant in practice over him as ever counsel had over a judge."

As a King's Bench practitioner, Jeffreys was first employed at Nisi Prius in actions for assaults and defamation; but before long the City attorneys gave him briefs in commercial causes tried at Guildhall, and though in *banc* he could not well stand up against regularly-bred lawyers, like Sir Francis North, Sir William Jones, Sir Creswell Levinz, and Heneage Finch, the son of the Lord Chancellor Nottingham,—he was generally equal to them before a jury, and he rapidly trod upon their heels.

He anxiously asked himself how was he to climb to high office. He had started with the disaffected party, and they had been of essential use to him; but though they were growing in strength, no chance existed of their being able to make Attorney Generals, Chief Justices, or Chancellors. At the same time, he did not like yet to break with those who might still serve him,—particularly in obtaining the Recordership, which he coveted as a stepping stone to something better. He resolved so to manage as to be a favorite of both parties till he could devote himself entirely and exclusively and openly to the one which should be dominant ;—and he again succeeded.

From his well known influence in the City he found no difficulty in making the acquaintance of Will Chiffinch, " the trusty page of the back stairs," who, besides other employments of a still more confidential nature, was intrusted by Charles II. to get at the secrets of all men of any consequence in every department of life. " This Mr. Chiffinch," says Roger North, " was a true secretary as well as page, for he had a lodging at the back stairs, which might have been properly termed 'the Spy Office,' where the King spoke with particular persons about intrigues of all kinds ; and all little informers, projectors, &c., were carried to Chiffinch's lodging. He was a most impetuous drinker, and in that capacity an admirable spy ; for he let none part with him sober, if it were possible to get them drunk, and his great artifice was pushing idolatrous healths of his good master, and being always in haste ; *for the King is coming*, which was his word. Nor, to make sure work, would he scruple to put his master's salutiferous drops (which were called the King's, of the nature of Goddard's) into the glasses ; and being an Hercules well breathed at the sport himself, he commonly had the better ; and so fished out many secrets, and discovered men's characters, which the King could never have obtained the knowledge of by any other means. It is likely that Jeffreys being a pretender to main feasts with the citizens, might forward himself, and be entertained by Will Chiffinch, and that which at first was mere spying turn to acquaintance, if not friendship, such as is apt to grow up between immense drinkers, and from thence might spring recommendations of him to the King, as the most useful man that could be found to serve his Majesty in London."[1]

Thus while Mr. Common Sergeant was caballing in the

[1] Roger North's Life of Guilford, ii. 98.

City with Lord Shaftesbury, who had established himself in Aldersgate Street, and talked of becoming Lord Mayor, he had secretly got a footing at Court, and by assurances of future services disposed the government to assist him in all his jobs. His opposition friends were a little startled by hearing that he had been made Solicitor to the Duke of York; but he assured them that this was merely a professional employment, unconnected with politics, which, according to professional etiquette, he could not decline; and when he was knighted as a mark of royal favor, with which he was silly enough to be much tickled, he said that he was obliged reluctantly to submit to the degradation as a consequence of his employment.

By some mischance, which is not explained, he missed the office of Recorder on the vacancy occasioned by the resignation of Sir John Howel, who so outraged public decency on the trial of Penn and Mead;[1] but Sir William Dolbein, the successful candidate, being made a Judge on the 22nd of October, 1678, Jeffreys was then elected his successor. Upon this occasion there were three other candidates—Mr. Richardson, a Judge of the Sheriff's Court; Mr. Turner, a bencher of Gray's Inn; and Mr. Robert Belwood, a barrister of the Middle Temple—but he was so warmly supported by both parties in politics, that they all withdrew before the day of nomination, and he is said in the City Records to have been "freely and unanimously elected."

CHAPTER XCIX.

CONTINUATION OF THE LIFE OF LORD CHANCELLOR JEFFREYS TILL HIS APPOINTMENT AS LORD CHIEF JUSTICE OF THE KING'S BENCH.

THE new Recorder had hardly been sworn in, when, feeling that the liberals could do nothing more for him, he utterly cast them off, becoming, for the rest of his life, the open, avowed, unblushing slave of the Court, and the bitter, persecuting, and unappeasable

---

[1] 6 St. Tr. 951.

enemy of the principles he had before supported, and of the men he had professed to love.

He entirely forsook Thanet House, in Aldersgate Street, and all the meetings of the Whigs in the City; and instead of secret interviews with Will Chiffinch in "the Spy Office," he went openly to Court, and, with his usual address, he contrived, by constant assiduities and flatteries, to gain the good graces both of Nell Gwin and of the Duchess of Portsmouth, who, since the fall of Lady Castlemaine, held divided empire at Whitehall, balancing the Roman Catholic and Protestant parties. To each of these ladies, it would appear from the libels of the day, his rise was attributed.[1]

However, not long after he had openly ratted, an accident happened that had like to have spoiled all his projects; and that was, the breaking out of the Popish plot. Although there is no reasonable ground for saying that it was contrived by Shaftesbury, he made such skillful and unscrupulous use of it, that suddenly, from appearing the leader of a small, declining, and despairing party, he had the City and the nation at his beck, and with a majority in both Houses of Parliament, there seemed every probability that he would soon force himself upon the King, and have at his disposal all the patronage of the government. Jeffreys was for some time much disconcerted, and thought that once in his life he had made a false move. He was utterly at a loss how to conduct himself; and his craft never was put to so severe a trial. It is even said that he had the meanness to try to reconcile himself to his old friends. But I do not believe that he seriously made or contemplated such an attempt, as it would have been foolish; for he had, in the insolence of his triumph,

[1] " 'Well,' quoth Sir G., ' the Whigs may think me rude,
Or brand me guilty of ingratitude ;
At my preferment they, poor fools, may grudge :
And think me fit for hangman more than Judge ;
But though they fret and bite their nails, and brawl,
I'll slight them, and go kiss dear *Nelly Wall.*' "*
Midsummer Moon.

" Monmouth's tamer, *Jeff's advance,*
Foe to England, spy to France,
False and foolish, proud and bold,
Ugly as you see, and old."
Duchess of Portsmouth Picture.

---

* Said to have been Nelly's *maiden name.*

left himself no retreat, and he had not only deserted but vituperated and insulted the leaders of the opposition.

I have little doubt, therefore, that he soon recovered his courage, and with his usual intuition saw the right course to be pursued, for, like the man whose notice he once humbly courted, but to whom he was now opposed, he showed himself—

> "A daring pilot in extremity,
> Pleas'd with the danger when the waves ran high."

Being called into council, he recommended that the government should profess to credit the plot, and should outvie the other side in zeal for the Protestant religion,— but should contrive to make Shaftesbury answerable for the reality of the conspiracy, so that, if hereafter it should blow up, or the people should get tired of it, all that was done to punish the supposed authors of it might be laid to his account.

I can not understand why he was not now brought into parliament, where his services were much wanted, and where one would have expected from his bold, ready, and sarcastic style of speaking, his success was certain. On the Exclusion Bill it might have been thought that his patron, the Duke of York, would have mainly relied upon him; and when Danby was to be impeached, that minister might well have availed himself of such a powerful advocate. Mr. Recorder had no longer a chance to be returned for the city of London, but most of the Cornish boroughs were then in the power of the government, and if there had been a difficulty in finding a seat for him near the conclusion of the parliament which had sat seventeen years, he might easily have been introduced in the two Westminster parliaments, and the Oxford parliament which followed. Yet Jeffreys remained the only lawyer of the 17th century who took a prominent part in politics, and was never a member of the House of Commons.

Perhaps there were jealousies among the ministerialists in the House, which prevented his being permitted to join them, it being foreseen that he would immediately struggle for the lead; perhaps it was thought that the Court would be less benefited by his talents than damaged by his bad character, which was now notorious; and there might be a dread of his habit of intoxication, in which he occasionally indulged to great excess, and which might have led him in debate to divulge Cabinet secrets, and have brought the administration into difficulties.

However this may be, we find that he immediately began diligently to work the Popish plot according to his own scheme. Coleman, Whitbread, Ireland, and all whom Oates and Bedloe accused being committed to prison,—it was resolved to prosecute them for high treason in having compassed the death of the King, as well as the overthrow of the Protestant religion,—and their trials were conducted by the government as state trials, partly at the bar of the Court of King's Bench, and partly at the Old Bailey. In the former, Jeffreys acted as a counsel, in the latter as a Judge.[1] It is asserted, and not improbably, that he had a real horror of Popery, which, though he could control it in the presence of the Duke of York, and when his interest required, at other times burst out with sincerity as well as fierceness.

Scroggs presided at the Old Bailey,[2] but Jeffreys whetted his fury by telling him that the King was a thorough believer in the plot,[3] and by echoing his expressions; as, when

---

[1] 7 St. Tr. 6, 167, 312, 487, 609, 769, 842, 908, 959, 1050, 1081, 1208. 8 St. Tr. 128, 287, 301, 524, 573, 640, 653.   [2] St. Tr. vol. ii.

[3] As the name of this wretch is so often coupled with that of Jeffreys, it may be proper to give a short account of him. The story of his being the son of a butcher, though generally circulated and believed in his own time, was a fiction. He was the son of a private gentleman in Oxfordshire, and took a degree at the University; he was intended for the church, but in the civil war took arms for the King. He was then called to the bar, and although he was exceedingly dissolute in his morals, and so much embarrassed that when a Sergeant he was arrested for debt in Westminster Hall,—he was made, on account of his subserviency, first a Puisne Judge of the Common Pleas, and then Chief Justice of the Common Pleas. When he convicted the Popish conspirators with such zeal, he believed that the government was sincere in prosecuting them, and he was confirmed in this notion by seeing Shaftesbury taken into office; but when he was told that "the President of the Council had no more influence with the King than his footman," he threw cold water on the plot,—for which he was impeached. He was obliged to give up his office, but was allowed to die in peace. A few stanzas of a ballad then published upon him, will show how he was regarded by his contemporaries:—

> "A Butcher's son's Judge capital,
> Poor Protestants to enthral,
>   And England to enslave, sirs;
> Lose both our laws and lives we must,
> When to do justice we intrust
>   So known an errant knave, sirs.
>
> "His father once exempted was
> Out of all juries; why, because

the Chief Justice said to the jury, "You have done like honest men," Jeffreys exclaimed, in a stage whisper, "They have done like honest men." As mouthpiece of the Lord Mayor, the head of the Commission,—after conviction he had the pleasing duty of passing sentence of death by the protracted tortures which the law of treason prescribed. He said to Ireland, Grove, and Pickering, the Jesuits, "Thus I speak to you, gentlemen, not vauntingly; 'tis against my nature to insult upon persons in your sad condition: God forgive you for what you have done; and I do heartily beg it, though you don't desire I should: for, poor men! you may believe that your interest in the world to come is secured to you by your masses, but do well consider that vast eternity you must, ere long, enter into, and that great tribunal you must appear before, where masses will not signify so many groats to you; no, not one farthing. And I must say it, for the sake of those silly people whom you have imposed upon with such fallacies, that the masses can no more save you from future damnation than they do from a present condemnation. The sen- of the law is," &c.; and then came from his delighted lips the hurdle, the hanging, the cutting down alive, and other particulars too shocking to be repeated.[1]

He had a still greater treat in passing the like sentence on Richard Langhorn, an eminent Catholic barrister, with whom he had been familiarly acquainted. He first addressed generally the whole batch of the prisoners convicted—whom he thus continues to upbraid for trying to root out "the best of religions;" "I call it the best of religions, even for your sakes; for had it not been for the sake of our religion, that teaches us not to make such requitals as yours seems to teach you, you had not had

> He was a man of blood, sirs;
> And why the butcherly son (forsooth!)
> Should be Judge and Jury both,
> Can not be understood, sirs.
> "The good old man with knife and knocks
> Made harmless sheep and stubborn ox
> Stoop to him in his fury;
> But the brib'd son, like greasy oaf,
> Kneels down and worships golden calf,
> And massacres the jury."
>
> *Justice in Masquerade.*

[1] 7 St. Tr. 138

this fair, formal trial, but murder would have been returned to you for the murder you intended to commit both upon the King and most of his people. What a strange sort of religion is that whose doctrine seems to allow them to be the greatest saints in another world who have been the most impudent sinners in this! Murder and the blackest of crimes were the best means among you to get a man to be canonized a saint hereafter." Then he comes to his brother lawyer. "There is one gentleman that stands at the bar whom I am very sorry to see, with all my heart, in this condition, because of some acquaintance I have had with him heretofore. To see that a man who hath understanding in the law and who hath arrived at so great an eminency in that profession as this gentleman hath done, should not remember that it is not only against the rules of Christianity, but even against the rules of his profession to attempt any injury against the person of the King! He knows it is against all the rules of law to endeavor to introduce a foreign power into this land. So that you have sinned both against your conscience, and your own certain knowledge." Last of all, he offers his friend the assistance of a Protestant divine to prepare him for a speedy departure, and, referring him to the statute whereby the ministration of a Catholic priest is made illegal, he, himself, though "a layman," gives him some "pious advice." —He had carried the sympathies of his audience along with him, for, when he had concluded with the "quartering," he was greeted with a loud shout of applause.[1]

Thus, by the powerful assistance of the Recorder, did the government obtain popularity for prosecuting the plot till the people at last actually did get tired of it, and Shaftesbury was prevented from deriving any fruit from it, beyond the precarious tenure, for a few months, of his office of President of the Council.

The Recorder was equally zealous, on all other occasions to do what he thought would be agreeable at Court. With the view of repressing public discussion, he laid down for law, as he said, on the authority of all the

---

[1] 7 St. Tr. 487. After this the story is credible which Sir Walter Scott used to tell of a Scotch Judge, who, having sentenced to death an old friend tried before him for murder, by whom he had often been beaten at chess, concluded by saying, " and now, I think I have checkmated you!"

Judges, "that no person whatsoever could expose to the public knowledge anything that concerned the affairs of the public without license from the King, or from such persons as he may think fit to intrust with that power."[1]

The Grand Jury having several times returned "*ignoramus*" to an indictment against one Smith for a libel, in respect of a very innocent publication, though they were sent out of Court to reconsider the finding, he at last exclaimed, "God bless me from such jurymen! I will see the face of every one of them, and let others see them also." He accordingly cleared the bar, and calling the jurymen one by one, put the question to them, and made each of them repeat the word "ignoramus." He then went on another tack, and addressing the defendant, said, in a coaxing tone, "Come, Mr. Smith, there are two persons besides you whom this jury have brought in *ignoramus;* but they have been ingenious enough to confess, and I can not think to fine them little enough: they shall be fined two pence for their ingenuity in confessing. Well, come, Mr. Smith, we know who hath formerly owned both printing and publishing this book." —*Smith.* "Sir, my ingenuity hath sufficiently experienced the reward of your severity; and, besides, I know no law commands me to accuse myself; neither shall I; and the jury have done like true Englishmen and worthy citizens, and blessed be God for such a jury." Jeffreys was furious, but could only vent his rage by committing the defendant till he gave security for his good behavior.

Such services were not to go unrewarded. It was the wish of the government to put the renegade Jeffreys into the office of Chief Justice of Chester, so often the price of political apostacy; but Sir Job Charlton, a very old gentleman, who now held it, could not be prevailed upon voluntarily to resign, for he had a considerable estate in the neighborhood, and was loth to be stripped of his dignity. Jeffreys, supported by the Duke of York, pressed the King hard, urging that "a Welshman ought not to judge his countrymen," and a message was sent to Sir Job that he was to be removed. He laid this heavily to heart, and desired only that he might speak to the King, and receive his pleasure from his own mouth; but was told that it was a thing resolved upon. Once, how-

[1] 7 St. Tr. 929, 1114, 1127.

ever, he went to Whitehall, and placed himself "like hermit poor," where the King, returning from feeding his ducks in St. James's Park, must pass; but his Majesty was now so much ashamed of the affair, that, when he spied Sir Job, he turned short round and went another way. The old gentleman was imperfectly consoled with the place of Puisne Judge of the Common Pleas, which, in the reign of James II., he was subsequently allowed to exchange for his beloved Chester. Meanwhile he was succeeded by Jeffreys, "more Welshman than himself," who was at the same time made counsel for the Crown, at Ludlow, where a Court was still held for Wales.

Immediately afterwards the new Chief Justice was called to the degree of the Coif, and made King's Sergeant, whereby he had precedence in Westminster Hall of the Attorney and Solicitor General. The motto on his rings, with great brevity and point, inculcated the prevailing doctrines of divine right and passive obedience— "A Deo Rex, a Rege Lex." As a further mark of royal favor, there was conferred upon him the hereditary dignity of a Baronet. He still retained the Recordership of London, and had extensive practice at the bar,

We have notices of a few important causes in which he was engaged as counsel. A new translation of the Psalms had been published under the title of "the King's Psalter," and the Stationers' Company applied to the King in Council to protect their property from invasion. Charles was present when the case came on to be heard, and thus was he addressed by the learned Recorder:— "They have teemed, sir, with a spurious brat, which being clandestinely midwived into the world, the better to cover the imposture they lay it at your Majesty's door." We may know, from the introductory lines of "Absalom and Achitophel," that his Majesty was well pleased with any allusion, however public, to his gallantries. On the present occasion he whispered, " This is a bold fellow," and did not try to disguise his satisfaction. Jeffreys got a decree for his clients.

He was equally successful in an important suit he conducted in the King's Bench for the Duke of York, to whom the revenue of the post-office had been granted, and who had prosecuted a person by the name of Dockra for establishing "the penny post" in London for his own benefit. The Court decided that this was an infraction of the Duke's right. His Royal Highness therefore continued to have "the penny post" for the rest of this reign; and, from his own accession it was under the immediate management of the Crown, the profits going into the public revenue.[1]

The great prosperity which Jeffreys now enjoyed had not the effect which it ought to have produced upon a good disposition, by making him more courteous and kind to others. When not under the sordid dread of injuring himself by offending superiors, he was universally insolent and overbearing. Being made Chief Justice of Chester, he thought that all Puisne Judges were beneath him, and he would not behave to them with decent respect, even when practicing before them. At the Kingston Assizes, Baron Weston having tried to check his irregularities, he complained that he was not treated like a counselor, being curbed in the management of his brief.—*Weston, B.* "Sir George, since the King has thrust his favors upon you, and made you Chief Justice of Chester, you think to run down everybody; if you find yourself aggrieved make your complaint; here's nobody cares for you."—*Jeffreys.* "I have not been used to make complaints, but rather to stop those that are made."—*Weston, B.* "I desire, sir, that you will sit down." He sat down, and is said to have wept with anger. His intemperate habits had so far shaken his nerves, that he shed tears very freely on any strong emotion.[2]

[1] Life of Guilford, ii. 99.
[2] The manner in which Jeffreys was regarded by the public at this time is very strikingly illustrated by an anonymous letter received by him, which had fallen into the hands of Sir Peter King, Recorder of London, afterwards Lord Chancellor, and is now preserved among the papers of the Earl of Lovelace. This effusion of malignity, like the famous letter of Mary to Elizabeth, which cost the Scotch queen her life, professes in a candid and friendly spirit to communicate the ill-natured things said of the party addressed:—

"May it please your Lordship,—You were once counsel for me at a trial where you spoke so brave and loud that we carried the cause, and I have loved you for it ever since;* and having an opportunity now to show it, I send you the following account, for it is useful for men who design to be great, to know what the people say of them. The other day I was at the election of the Sheriffs,† where one of my neighbors commended the former part of your speech exceedingly, and said your fellow servant Coleman's de-

* Satire on his bullying style of doing business at the bar.
† 24th June, 1680, when Jeffreys as Recorder conducted the proceedings.

We may be prepared for his playing some fantastic tricks before his countrymen at Chester, where he was subject to no control; but the description of his conduct

claration was not better penned; yet he could not believe that the D. of York's solicitor could be very hearty in the Protestant religion. But he thought you a very proper man for the office you hold in the city, to be our mouth and lungs, when Sir Richard Clayton is our head, because now those parts are good in their kind. 'But I wonder,' continued he, ' that they two agree no better, for I am sure my Lady Jefferies the longest day she has to live can not forget the kindness Miss Bludworth met with at his house one night.'*
' Aye, but,' says another, 'all Lord Mayors have an antipathy against him ever since he betrayed his client, the Lord Mayor of York, at the council table.'
' What you call a betraying,' said I, ' was but prevailing with his client to submit to the council board, who are in the wrong, and might appear to have the better on't. But for that and some other like services, he was lately made Chief Justice of Chester, and soon will be Attorney General.' ' What is the manner of making an Attorney General?' said my neighbor. I told him I thought it was by entering a form of words (as the City of London does at my Lord Mayor's day, in the Courts of Westminster Hall): *Dominus Rex ponit loco suo Georgium Jeffries,* &c. ' If that be all,' said a stander-by, ' Sir George has got that already, for that was the form of his marriage license.' † Whereat some of the company fell a laughing, but I can not imagine why. However I desired them to be civil and mannerly, and not to laugh at you whom they ought to respect, as being the mouth of the City. My neighbors presently snapt me up, and said that you were the 'foul mouth of the City,' and pointing to you on the hustings cried, ' That's our mountebank lawyer, and that you could no more make an argument at law than you could speak softly; and though you bragged that as long as Nelly Wall was the mistress, and the D . of P. was her mistress and our master's mistress, you could have what you would at Court; ‡ yet he said you were already come to the highest, and we should see you dwindle to nothing, like your wife's jointure. I replied that he might be mistaken; we should live to see you Lord Chancellor, and then the lady would be sure to have a good jointure, and to have her train held up. ' I know,' said he, ' an addition to his wife's jointure would be very welcome, but for his coals they were taken up in her maiden days.' I was extremely vexed at that, but I thought it best not to stir in such a business, and 'tis no great matter what he says, for he is a rascal and a rebel,—a very fanatic, and in my next letter you shall know his name. In the mean time, I will be a spy for you at the Rainbow and the Amsterdam Coffeehouses, where the fanatics speak oftentimes very saucily of you. One of them told me a lie there t'other day, ' that my lady was bt to bed before her time, and that you reckoned without her host, and that you were the Bull and Moses of the City,' and said, ' when you come to be put in the pillory, as Harris was, you will never be able to get your head out again.' But when we get them into the Crown Office, you and I will make them pay for all. ‖ After all this intelligence, pray take my advice, be patient; for the fretting and blowing is as improper to extinguish the fire that is now smoking all over the City, as the ——§ was to blow out the great bonfire that Holy Catholic

---

* Alluding to some scandalous anecdote respecting his second wife, whose maiden name was *Bludworth.*
† Vide post, an account of the lady's frailties.   ‡ Vide ante, p. 315.
‖ A threatened prosecution for defamation in the Court of King's Bench.
§ Illegible.

there by Lord Delamere (afterwards Earl of Warrington), in denouncing it in the House of Commons, must surely be overcharged:—

"The county for which I serve is Cheshire, which is a county palatine; and we have two Judges peculiarly assigned us by his Majesty. Our puisne Judge I have nothing to say against; he is a very honest man, for aught I know; but I can not be silent as to our chief Judge; and I will name him, because what I have to say will appear more probable. His name is Sir GEORGE JEFFREYS, who, I must say, behaved himself more like a Jack-pudding than with that gravity which becomes a Judge. He was witty upon the prisoners at the bar. He was very full of his jokes upon people that came to give evidence, not suffering them to declare what they had to say in their own way and method, but would interrupt them because they behaved themselves with more gravity than he. But I do not insist upon this, nor upon the late hours he kept up and down our city: it's said he was every night drinking till two o'clock, or beyond that time, and that he went to his chamber drunk; but this I have only by common fame, for I was not in his company; I bless God I am not a man of his principles and behavior—but in the mornings he appeared with the symptoms of a man that overnight had taken a large cup. That which I have to say is the complaint of every man, especially of them that had any law-suits. Our Chief Justice has a Church made in Pudding Lane.* And if you would but observe, the poor mad folks about the streets the naughty boys don't use to follow them and call them names, unless like you they make a noise, and throw dirt. And be not so free of speech: that which you take to be your talent—speech-making, you love it but it loves not you. It will have no better success than Scroggs's still prefaced apology in Wakeman's case,† which did no more clear his innocence than Pilate's speech did: that Scroggs fell short in this, that he did not wash his hands. And all he said was largely and abundantly answered by Pemberton's saying nothing—who knew better than to believe him, and was better bred than to tell him he lied.

"I am,

"Your Worship's humble Servant,

"A LIVERYMAN OF THE CITY OF LONDON.

"Cheapside, July 17th 1680.
* To Sir George Jeffries, the Recorder."

---

* The Fire of London, which began in *Pudding Lane* and ended in *Pie Corner.*

† Alluding to some proceedings lately instituted by Shaftesbury against his tool Scroggs.

very arbitrary power in appointing the assize when he pleases, and this man has strained it to the highest point; for whereas we were accustomed to have two assizes, the first about April or May, the latter about September—it was this year the middle (as I remember) of August before we had any assize; and then he dispatched business so well that he left half the causes untried, and, to help the matter, has resolved we shall have no more assizes this year."[1]

Being tired of reveling in Chester, he put a sudden end to his first assize there, that he might pay a visit to his native place—to which I am afraid he was less prompted by a pious wish to embrace his father, who had been so resolutely bent on making him a shopkeeper, and who, from the stories propagated about his conduct as a Judge, still expressed some misgivings about him—than to dazzle his old companions with the splendor of his new state. Accordingly, he came with such a train that the cider-barrels at Acton ran very fast, and the larder was soon exhausted; whereupon, the old gentleman, in a great fret, charged his son with a design to ruin him, by bringing a whole country at his heels, and warned him against again attempting the same prodigality.

But a violent political storm now arose, which threatened entirely to overwhelm our hero, and from which he did not escape unhurt. In the struggle which arose from the long delay to assemble Parliament,[2] he had leagued himself strongly with the "Abhorrers" against the "Petitioners," and proceedings were instituted in the House of Commons, on this ground, against him, along with Chief Justice Scroggs and Chief Justice North.[3]

A petition from the City of London, very numerously signed, having been presented, complaining that the Recorder had obstructed the citizens in their attempts to have Parliament assembled for the redress of grievances, a select committee was appointed—who, having heard evidence on the subject, and examined him in person, presented a report—on which the following resolutions were passed:—

"That Sir George Jeffreys, Recorder of the City of

---

[1] Wool. 66. Chandler's Debates, ii. 163.   [2] Ante, p. 262 *et seq.*
[3] Burnet, in referring to these proceedings, says, "They fell also on Sir George Jeffries a *furious declaimer at the bar.*"—Vol. ii. 121.

London, by traducing and obstructing petitioning for the sitting of this Parliament, hath destroyed the right of the subject.

"That an humble address be presented to his Majesty, to remove Sir George Jeffreys out of all public offices.

" That the members of this House serving for the City of London do communicate these resolutions to the Court of Aldermen for the said City."

The King was stanch, and returned for answer to the address the civil refusal " that he would consider of it;" [1] but Jeffreys, who, where he apprehended personal danger, was "none of the intrepids," quailed under the charge, and, afraid of further steps being taken against him, came to an understanding that he should give up the Recordership, which his enemies wished to be conferred upon their partisan, Sir George Treby. The King was much chagrined at the loss of such a valuable Recorder, and said sarcastically that " he was not parliament proof." But he was obliged to acquiesce, and Jeffreys, having been reprimanded on his knees at the bar, was discharged. The address of Speaker Williams was very bitter, and caused deep resentment in the mind of Jeffreys.[2] On the 2nd of December he actually did resign his office, and Treby was chosen to succeed him.[3]

In a few days after, there was exhibited one of Lord Shaftesbury's famous Protestant processions, on the anniversary of the accession of Queen Elizabeth.[4] In this rode a figure on horseback to represent the Ex-Recorder, with his face to the tail, and a label on his back—" I am an Abhorrer." At Temple Bar he was thrown into a bonfire, coupled with the Devil—the preceding pair, who suffered the same fate, being Sir Roger L'Estrange and the Pope of Rome.[5]

However, all these indignities endeared him to the Court; and his pusillanimity was forgiven from the recollection of past and the hope of future services. A peti

---

[1] " Le Roy s'avisera," the royal veto to a bill passed by the two Houses.
[2] North's Life of Guilford, ii. 108.   4 Parl. Hist. 1216. Wool. 75.
[3] " On the second of Decr. Sir George Jeffreys, Bart., Sergeant-at-Law, Recorder of the city here present, did freely surrender up into this court his place of Recorder, and all his right and interest therein, of which surrender the Court did accept and allow. George Treby, of the Middle Temple, London, Esq., was elected the same day."—*City Books.*
[4] Ante, p. 159.   [5] Wool. 80.

tion from the city being presented to the King at Hampton Court, he attended as a liveryman, though no longer the mouth-piece of the corporation,—when he was treated with marked civility by Charles, and detained to dinner,—while the Lord Mayor and Aldermen, and the new Recorder, were sent off with a reprimand.

To oblige the Court, and to assist them in their criminal jobs, he accepted the appointment of Chairman of the Middlesex Sessions at Hicks's Hall; although it was somewhat beneath his dignity, and it deprived him of a portion of his practice.[1] Here the Grand Jury were sworn in; and as they were returned by sheriffs whom the City of London elected, and who were still of the liberal party, the problem was to have them remodeled, so that they might find bills of indictment against all whom the government wished to prosecute. With this view, Jeffreys declared that none should serve except true Church of England men; and he ordered the under-sheriff to return a new panel purged of all sectarians. He had a particular spite against the Presbyterians, who had mainly contributed to his being turned out of the Recordership. The under-sheriff disobeying his summons, he ordered the sheriffs to attend next day in person; but in their stead came the new Recorder, who urged that, by the privileges of the City of London, they were exempted from attending at Hicks's Hall. He overruled this claim with contempt, and fined the sheriffs £100. It was found, however, that while the City retained the power of electing the sheriffs, all these attempts to pervert justice would be fruitless.[2]

Jeffreys remained in a state of painful anxiety during Charles's last Westminster parliament, and during the few days of the Oxford parliament. The popular party had such a majority in the House of Commons, and seemed so powerful, that it is said the renegade again expressed deep regret that he had left them: but late at night, on Monday, the 28th day of March, 1681, news arrived in London, that early that morning the King had dissolved the parliament, and had declared his firm determination never to call another. If Jeffreys was still sober, and got drunk that night, we ought to excuse him.

[1] Wool. 85.   [2] Ibid. 86.

Now his talents were to be brought into full play. In the conflict, the ranks of the enemy being thrown into disorder, the brigade of the lawyers, who had been kept back as a reserve, was marched up to hang on their broken rear insulting, and to sweep them from the field.

First came on the trial of Fitzharris for high treason. Jeffreys, as counsel for the Crown, argued the demurrer to the plea of the pendency of the impeachment: and then, having assisted the Duchess of Portsmouth to evade the questions which were put to her, for the purpose of showing that the prisoner had acted under the King's orders, he addressed the Jury with great zeal after the Solicitor General, and was mainly instrumental in obtaining the conviction.[1]

Next came the trial of Archbishop Plunkett, the Roman Catholic Primate of Ireland; in which Jeffreys was so intemperate, that the Attorney General was obliged to check him, that the prisoner might have some show of fair play.[2] But it was on the trial of College, "the Protestant joiner," that he gave the earliest specimen of his characteristic ribaldry, and his talent for jesting in cases of life and death, which shone out so conspicuously when he was Lord Chief Justice of the King's Bench. He began with strongly justifying the act of taking from the prisoner the papers he was to use in his defense, saying, that to allow him to see them would be "assigning counsel to him with a vengeance." A witness having stated that pistols were found in the prisoner's holsters when he was attending the City members at Oxford, Jeffreys exclaimed with a grin, "I think a *chisel* might have been more proper for a *joiner.*"

There was called as a witness by the prisoner one Lun, who being a waiter at the Devil Tavern, and a fanatic, had some years before been caught on his knees praying against the Cavaliers, saying "Scatter them, good Lord! Scatter them!"—from whence he had ever borne the nickname of "SCATTER'EM." Jeffreys thus begins his cross-examination:—"We know you, Mr. Lun; we only ask questions about you that the jury too may know you as well as we."—*Lun.* "I don't care to give evidence of any thing but the truth. *I was never on my knees before the parliament for any thing.*"—*Jeffreys.* "Nor I neither

[1] 8 St. Tr. 223.   [2] Ibid. 447.

for much, yet you were once on your knees when you cried, '*Scatter them, good Lord.*' Was it not so, Mr. Scatter'em?"

He had next an encounter with the famous Titus Oates, who was called by College, and who, when cross-examined by him, appealed to Sir George Jeffreys's own knowledge of a fact about which he was inquiring.—*Jeffreys.* " Sir George Jeffreys does not intend to be an evidence I assure you."—*Dr. Oates.* " I do not desire Sir George Jeffreys to be an evidence for me; I had credit in parliaments, and Sir George had disgrace in one of them."—*Jeffreys* " Your servant, doctor; you are a witty man and a philosopher.'" He had his full revenge when the Doctor himself was afterwards tried before him.

We may judge of the Counselor's general style of treating witnesses by his remark on the trial of Lord Grey De Werke for carrying off the Lady Henrietta Berkley; when his objection was overruled to the competency of the young lady as a witness for the defendant, although she was not only of high rank and uncommon beauty, but undoubted veracity,—he observed, "Truly, my Lord, we would prevent perjury if we could."[2]

We now come to transactions which strikingly prove the innate baseness of his nature in the midst of his pretended openness and jolly good humor. He owed everything in life to the Corporation of the City of London. The freemen, in the exercise of their ancient privileges, had raised him from the ground by electing him Common Sergeant and Recorder, and to the influence he was supposed to have in the Court of Common Council and in the Court of Aldermen must be ascribed his introduction to Whitehall, and all his political advancement. But when, upon the failure of the prosecution against Lord Shaftesbury, the free municipal constitution of the City became so odious to the government, he heartily entered into the conspiracy to destroy it. It is said that he actually suggested the scheme of having a sheriff nominated by the Lord Mayor, and he certainly took a very active part in carrying it into execution. On Midsummer-day, having planted Lord Chief Justice North in his house in Aldermanbury that he might be backed by his authority, he himself appeared on the hustings in Guildhall, and

[1] 8 St. Tr. 405.   [2] 9 Ibid. 127.

when the poll was going against the Court candidates, illegally advised the Lord Mayor to dissolve the Hall, and afterwards to declare them duly elected. He did everything in his power to push on and to assist the great *Quo Warranto*, by which the City was to be entirely disfranchised.

When success had crowned these efforts, and Pilkington and Shute, the former sheriffs, with Alderman Cornish and others were to be tried before a packed jury for a riot at the election, finding that he had the game in his hand, his insolence knew no bounds. The defendants having challenged the array, on the ground that the sheriffs who returned the panel were not lawfully appointed—as soon as the challenge was read he exclaimed, "Here's a tale of a tub indeed!" The counsel for the defendants insisted that the challenge was good in law, and at great length argued for its validity.

Jeffreys. "Robin Hood Upon Greendale stood!"

Thompson, Counsel for the Defendants. "If the challenge be not good, there must be a defect in it either in point of law, or in point of fact. I pray that the Crown may either demur or traverse."—*Jeffreys.* "This discourse is only for discourse sake. I pray the jury may be sworn." —*Lord Chief Justice Saunders.* "Ay, ay, swear the jury." The defendants were, of course, all found guilty, and as there were among them the most eminent of Jeffreys's old City friends, he exerted himself to the utmost not only in gaining a conviction, but in aggravating the sentence.[1]

But this was only a case of misdemeanor, in which he could ask for nothing beyond fine and imprisonment. He was soon to be engaged in prosecutions for high treason against the noblest of the land, in which his savage taste for blood might be gratified. The Rye-house plot broke out, for which there was some foundation, and after the conviction of those who had planned it, Lord Russell was brought to trial at the Old Bailey, on the ground that he had consented to it.

Jeffreys, in the late state trials, had gradually been encroaching on the Attorney and Solicitor General, Sir

[1] 9 St. Tr. 187.

Robert Sawyer and Sir Heneage Finch, and in Lord Russell's case, to which the government attached such infinite importance, he almost entirely superseded them. To account for this unexampled zeal, we must remember that the office of Chief Justice of the King's Bench was still vacant, Saunders having died a few months before, and Lord Keeper North having strongly opposed the appointment of Jeffreys as his successor.

Lord Russell had certainly been present at a meeting of the conspirators, when there was a consultation about seizing the King's guards; but he insisted that he came in accidentally, that he had taken no part in the conversation, and that he was not acquainted with their plans. The aspirant Chief Justice saw clearly where was the pinch of the case, and the Attorney General, who was examining Colonel Rumsey, being contented with asking —" Was the prisoner at the bar present at the debate?" and receiving the answer "Yes," Jeffreys started up, took the witness into his own hands, and calling upon him to draw the inference which was for the jury, pinned the basket by this leading and highly irregular question— "Did you find him averse to it or agreeing to it?" Having got the echoing answer which he suggested— "*agreeing to it*"—he looked round with exultation, and said—" If my Lord Russell now pleases to ask any questions, he may!"

Jeffreys addressed the jury in reply after the Solicitor General had finished, and much outdid him in pressing the case against the prisoner, while he disclaimed with horror the endeavor to take away the life of the innocent.[1] He thus concluded: "You have a Prince, and a merciful one, too. Consider the life of your Prince, the life of his posterity, the consequences that would have attended if this villainy had taken effect. What would have become of your lives and religion? What would have become of that religion we have been so fond of preserving? Gentlemen, I must put these things home upon your consciences. I know you will remember the horrid murder of the most pious Prince, the Martyr, King Charles I. Let not the greatness of any man corrupt you,

---

[1] " Jefferies would show his zeal and speak after him, but it was not an insolent declaration, such as all were his were, full of fury and indecent invectives."—*Burnet*, ii. 216.

but discharge your consciences both to God and the King, and to your posterity."[1]

Jeffreys had all the glory of the verdict of *Guilty*, and as the Lord Chief Justice Pemberton had rather flinched during this trial, and the Attorney and Solicitor General were thought men who would cry CRAVEN, and as the next case was not less important and still more ticklish, all objections to the proposed elevation of the favorite vanished, and he became Chief Justice of England, as the only man fit to condemn Algernon Sydney.[2]

CHAPTER C.

CONTINUATION OF THE LIFE OF LORD CHANCELLOR JEFFREYS TILL HE RECEIVED THE GREAT SEAL.

THE new Chief Justice was sworn in on the 29th of September, 1683, and took his seat in the Court of King's Bench on the first day of the following Michaelmas term.[3]

Sydney's case was immediately brought on before him in this Court, the indictment being removed by *certiorari* from the Old Bailey, that it might be under his peculiar

---

[1] 9 St. Tr. 654.

[2] Evelyn, Oct. 4, 1683. Sir Geo. Jefferies was advanced, reputed to be most ignorant but most daring." This is the very day on which the diarist saw "The Duchess of Portsmouth in her dressing-room within her bed-chamber in her morning loose garment, her maids combing her newly out of bed, his Majesty and the gallants standing about her."

Till the exploit of Lord Russell's conviction the objections to Jeffrey's appointment as Chief Justice were so strong that even Charles II. himself would not consent to it. Extract of letter from Lord Sunderland to Lord Rochester, dated Newmarket, March 10th, 1683:—" Upon the news of my Lord Chief Justice being ill, I spoke to the King of Jeffries, but I found him very much unresolved and full of objections against him, as that all the Judges would be unsatisfied if he were so advanced, and that he had not law enough."

[3] We learn from Burnet the impression made by this appointment on the public mind, "All people were apprehensive of very black designs, when they saw Jefferies made Lord Chief Justice, who was scandalously vicious and was drunk every day; besides a drunkenness of fury in his temper that looked like enthusiasm. He did not consider the decencies of his post; nor did he so much as affect to seem impartial as became a Judge; but ran out upon all occasions into declamations that did not become the bar much less the bench."—*Own Times*, ii. 231.

care. The prisoner wishing to plead some collateral matter, was told by the Chief Justice that, if overruled, sentence of death would immediately be passed upon him. Though there can be no doubt of the illegality of the conviction, the charge against Jeffreys is unfounded, that he admitted the MS. treatise on Government to be read without any evidence of its having been written by the prisoner, beyond " similitude of hands." Two witnesses, who were acquainted with his handwriting from having seen him indorse bills of exchange, swore that they believed it to be his handwriting, and they were corroborated by a third, who, with his privity, had paid notes purporting to be indorsed by him, without any complaint ever being made. But the undeniable and ineffaceable atrocity of the case was the Lord Chief Justice's doctrine, that "*scribere est agere*," and that therefore this MS. containing some abstract speculations on different forms of government, written many years before, never shown to any human being, and containing nothing beyond the constitutional principles of Locke and Paley, was tantamount to the evidence of a witness to prove an overt act of high treason. "If you believe that this was Colonel Sydney's book, writ by him, no man can doubt that it is a sufficient evidence that he is guilty of compassing and imagining the death of the King. It fixes the whole power in the parliament and the people. The King, it says, is responsible to them; the King is but their trustee. Gentlemen, I must tell you I think I ought more than ordinarily to press this upon you, because I know the misfortune of the late unhappy rebellion, and the bringing of the late blessed King to the scaffold, was first begun with such kind of principles. They cried he had betrayed the trust that was delegated to him by the people, so that the case rests not upon two but upon greater evidence than twenty-two witnesses, if you believe this book was writ by him."

The Chief Justice having had the satisfaction of pronouncing with his own lips the sentence upon Sydney, of death and mutilation, instead of leaving the task as usual to the senior puisne judge,—a scene followed which is familiar to every one.—*Sydney.* "Then, O God! O God! I beseech thee to sanctify these sufferings unto me, and impute not my blood to the country; let no inquisition be made for it,—but if any,—and the shedding of blood that is innocent must be revenged,—let the weight of it fall only upon those that maliciously persecute me for righteousness' sake."—*Lord C. J. Jeffreys.* "I pray God work in you a temper fit to go unto the other world, for I see you are not fit for this."—*Sydney.* "My Lord, feel my pulse [holding out his hand], and see if I am disordered. I bless God I never was in better temper than I now am."—By order of the Chief Justice, the lieutenant of the Tower immediately removed the prisoner.

A very few days after, and while this illustrious patriot was still lying under sentence of death,[1] the Lord Chief Justice Jeffreys, and Mr. Justice Withins, who sat as his brother Judge on the trial, went to a gay City wedding, where the Lord Mayor and other grandees were present. Evelyn, who was of the party, tells us that the Chief and the puisne both "danced with the bride, and were exceeding merry." He adds, "These great men spent the rest of the afternoon until eleven at night in drinking healths, taking tobacco, and talking much beneath the gravity of Judges who had but a day or two before condemned Mr. Algernon Sydney."[2]

The next exhibition in the Court of King's Bench which particularly pleased Jeffreys and horrified the public, was the condemnation of Sir Thomas Armstrong. It will be recollected that this gentleman was outlawed while beyond the seas, and being sent from Holland within the year, sought, according to his clear right in law, to reverse the outlawry.[3] I have had occasion to reprobate the conduct of Lord Keeper North in refusing him his writ of error, and suffering his execution; but Jeffreys may be considered the executioner. When brought up to the King's Bench bar, Armstrong was attended by his daughter, a most beautiful and interesting young woman, who, when the Chief Justice had illegally overruled the plea, and pronounced judgment of death under the outlawry, exclaimed, "My Lord, I hope you will not murder my father."—*Chief Justice Jeffreys.* "Who is this woman? Marshal, take her into custody.

---

[1] 5th Dec.
[2] Mem. 530.
[3] Stat. 6 Ed. 6 enacted that if any outlaw yielded himself to the Chief Justice, &c., within a year, he should be discharged of the outlawry, and entitled to a jury.

Why, how now? Because your relative is attainted for high treason, must you take upon you to tax the courts of justice for murder when we grant execution according to law? Take her away."—*Daughter.* "God Almighty's judgments light upon you."—*Chief Justice Jeffreys.* "God Almighty's judgments will light upon those that are guilty of high treason."—*Daughter.* "Amen. I pray God."—*Chief Justice Jeffreys.* "So say I. I thank God I am clamor proof." [The daughter is committed to prison, and carried off in custody.]—*Sir Thomas Armstrong.* "I ought to have the benefit of the law, and I demand no more."—*Chief Justice Jeffreys.* "That you shall have, by the grace of God. See that execution be done on Friday next, according to law. You shall have the full benefit of the law!!!" Armstrong was hanged, emboweled, beheaded, and quartered accordingly.

When Jeffreys came to the King at Windsor, soon after this trial, "the King took a ring of good value from his finger and gave it to him for these services. The ring upon that was called his *blood stone*."[1] In the reign of William and Mary, Armstrong's attainder was reversed. Jeffreys was then out of reach of process, but for the share which Sir Robert Sawyer had in it as Attorney General, he was expelled the House of Commons.[2]

Jeffreys had now the satisfaction of causing an information to be filed against Sir William Williams for having, as Speaker of the House of Commons, under the orders of the House, directed the printing of "Dangerfield's Narrative,"—the vengeful tyrant thus dealing a blow at once to an old enemy, who had reprimanded him on his knees, and to the privileges of the House, equally the object of his detestation. He was in hopes of deciding the case himself, but he left it as a legacy to his successor, Chief Justice Herbert, who, under his auspices, at once overruled the plea, and fined the defendant £10,000.[3]

Not only was Jeffreys a Privy Councillor, but he had become a member of the Cabinet, where, from his supe-

[1] Burn. Own Times, i. 580. "The King accompanied the gift with a piece of advice somewhat extraordinary from a King to a Judge: "*My Lord, as it is a hot summer, and you are going the circuit, I desire you will not drink too much.*'"
[2] 10 St. Tr. 105. See a beautiful reference to this case by Lord Erskine, in defending Hardy.—24 St. Tr. 944.
[3] 13 St. Tr. 1436. 2 Shower, 471. Lord Campbell's Speeches, 284.

rior boldness and energy, as well as his more agreeable manners, he had gained a complete victory over Lord Keeper North, whom he denounced as a "Trimmer,"—and the Great Seal seemed almost within his grasp.¹ To secure it, he still strove to do everything he could devise to please the Court, as if hitherto nothing base had been done by him.² When, to his great joy, final judgment was entered up against the City of London on the *quo warranto*, he undertook to get all the considerable towns in England to surrender their charters on the threat of similar proceedings; and with this view, in the autumn of 1684, he made "a campaign in the North," which was almost as fatal to corporations as that "in the West," the following year, proved to the lives of men. To show to the public the special credit he enjoyed at Court, the London Gazette, just before he set out, in reference to the gift bestowed upon him for the judgment against Sir Thomas Armstrong, announced "that his Majesty, as a mark of his royal favor, had taken a ring from his own finger and placed it on that of Lord Chief Justice Jeffreys." In consequence, although when on the circuit he forgot the caution against hard drinking, with which the gift had been accompanied, he carried everything before him,—" charters fell like the walls of Jericho,"³ and he returned laden with his hyperborean spoils.

I have already related the clutch at the Great Seal which he then made, and his temporary disappointment.⁴ He was contented to "bide his time." There were only two other occasions when he had it in his power to pervert the law, for the purpose of pleasing the Court, during the present reign. The first was on the trial of Hampden, the grandson of the great Hampden, for a trifling misdemeanor. Although this young gentleman was only heir apparent to a moderate estate, and not in possession of any property, he was sentenced to pay a fine of £40,000, —Jeffreys saying that the clause in MAGNA CHARTA, "Liber homo non amercietur pro magno delicto nisi salvo contenemento suo," does not apply to fines imposed by the King's Judges.⁵—The other was the inquisition in the

---

¹ For the disputes between them, see ante, p. 285.
² ———— "In omnia præceps,
   Nil actum credens, dum quid superesset agendum,
   Instat atrox."
³ Wool. 103, 104.   ⁴ Ante, p. 285.   ⁵ 9 St. Tr, 1125

action of *scan. mag.* brought by the Duke of York against Titus Oates, in which the jury, under his direction, awarded £100,000 damages.[1]

Ever since the disfranchisement of the City of London, the Ex-Recorder had ruled it with a rod of iron. He set up a nominal Lord Mayor and nominal Aldermen; but, as they were entirely dependent upon him, he treated them with continual insolence.[2]

On the sudden death of Charles II., Jeffreys no doubt thought the period was arrived when he must be rewarded for the peculiar zeal with which he had abandoned himself to the service of the successor; but he was at first disappointed, and he still had to "wade through slaughter" to the seat he so much coveted.

Not dismayed, he resolved to act on two principles: 1st, If possible, to outdo himself in pleasing his master, whose arbitrary and cruel disposition became more apparent from the hour that he mounted the throne. 2ndly, To leave no effort untried to discredit, disgrace, disgust, and break the heart of the man who stood between him and his object.

Being confirmed in the office of Chief Justice of the King's Bench, he began with the trial for perjury of Titus Oates,—whose veracity he had often maintained, but with whom he had a personal quarrel, and whom he now held up to reprobation,—depriving him of all chance of acquittal. The defendant was found guilty on two indictments, and the verdict on both was probably correct; but what is to be said for the sentence?—"To pay on each indictment a fine of 1,000 marks; to be stripped of all his canonical habits; to be imprisoned for life; to stand in the pillory on the following Monday, with a paper over his head, declaring his crime; next day to stand in the

[1] 10 St. Tr. 125. It is curious to observe that, in this case, after judgment by default, the inquisition being before the Court of King's Bench *in banco*, the Sheriffs of Middlesex attending in person, sat covered before the Judges, and the counsel began their speeches, "May it please your Lordships, you Mr. Sheriffs, and gentlemen of the Jury."

[2] Sir John Reresby, giving an account of his dining with Sir James Smith, the Lord Mayor, says: "This gentleman complained to me that he enjoyed no more than bare title of Lord Mayor, the Lord Chief Justice Jeffries usurping the power; that the city had no sort of intercourse with the King but by the intervention of that Lord, and that himself and the aldermen were looked upon by the Court as no better than his tools; that upon all occasions his Lordship was so forgetful of the high dignity of the City, as to use him and his brethren with contempt."—*Reresb. Mem.* 207.

pillory at the Royal Exchange, with the same inscription; on the Wednesday to be whipped from Aldgate to Newgate; on the Friday to be whipped from Newgate to Tyburn; upon the 24th of April in every year, during life, to stand in the pillory at Tyburn, opposite the gallows; on the 9th of August in every year to stand in the pillory opposite Westminster Hall Gate; on the 10th of August in every year to stand in the pillory at Charing Cross; and the like on the following day at Temple Bar; and the like on the 2nd of September, every year, at the Royal Exchange;"—the Court expressing deep regret that they could not do more, as they would "not have been unwilling to have given judgment of death upon him."¹

Next came the trial of Richard Baxter, the pious and learned Presbyterian divine, who had actually said, and adhered to the saying, "Nolo episcopari," and who was now prosecuted for a libel, because in a book on church government he had reflected on the Church of Rome in words which might possibly be applied to the Bishops of the Church of England. No such reference was intended by him; and he was known not only to be of exemplary private character, but to be warmly attached to monarchy, and always inclined to moderate measures in the differences between the established church and those of his own persuasion.² Yet, when he pleaded *not guilty*, and prayed on account of ill health, that his trial might be postponed, Jeffreys exclaimed, "Not a minute more to save his life. We have had to do with other sort of persons, but now we have a Saint to deal with; and I know how to deal with Saints as well as Sinners. Yonder stands Oates in the pillory, [Oates was at that moment suffering part of his sentence in Palace Yard, outside the great gate of Westminster Hall,] and he says he suffers for the truth; and so says Baxter; but if Baxter did but stand on the outside of the pillory with him, I would say *two of the greatest rogues and rascals in the kingdom stood there together.*" Having silenced the defendant's counsel by almost incredible rudeness, the defendant himself wished to speak, when the Chief Justice burst out, "Richard, Richard, thou art an old fellow and an old knave; thou hast written books enough to load a cart; every one is as

¹ 10 St. Tr. 1315. ² Fox's Hist. James, ii. 96.

full of sedition, I might say treason, as an egg is full of meat; hadst thou been whipt out of thy writing trade forty years ago, it had been happy. Thou pretendest to be a preacher of the gospel of peace, and thou hast one foot in the grave; it is time for thee to begin to think what account thou intendest to give; but leave thee to thyself, and I see thou wilt go on as thou hast begun; but, by the grace of God, I'll look after thee. Gentlemen of the jury, he is now modest enough; but time was when no man was so ready at *Bind your Kings in chains, and your nobles in fetters of iron,* crying, *To your tents, O Israel!* Gentlemen, for God's sake do not let us be gulled twice in an age." The defendant was, of course, found guilty, and thought himself lucky to escape with a fine of £500, and giving security for his good behavior for seven years.[1]

The Lord Chief Justice, for his own demerits, and to thrust a thorn into the side of Lord Keeper Guilford, was now raised to the peerage by the title of "Baron Jeffreys of Wem,"—the preamble of his patent narrating his former promotions—averring that they were the reward of virtue,—and after the statement of his being appointed to preside in the Court of King's Bench, adding, "ubi etiamnum justitiam et tutelam subditis nostris ad normam legis intrepide et fideliter administrans: quarum ejus virtutum intuitu eum inter pares hujus regni cooptandum esse censuimus," &c.

He took his seat in the House of Lords on the first day of the meeting of James's only parliament, along with nineteen others either raised in the peerage or newly created since the dissolution of the Oxford parliament,—the junior being John, Lord Churchill, afterwards Duke of Marlborough. The Journals show that Lord Jeffreys was very regular in his attendance during the session, and as the House sat daily and still met at the same early hour as the Courts of law, he must generally have left the business of the King's Bench to be transacted by the other Judges. He was now occupied day and night with plans for pushing the already disgraced Lord Keeper from the woolsack.

I have already, in the Life of Lord Guilford, related how these plans were conducted in the Cabinet, in the

[1] 11 St. Tr. 495. 3 Mod. Rep. 68.

royal circle at Whitehall, and in the House of Lords—particularly the savage treatment which the "staggering statesman" received on the reversal of his decree in *Howard* v. *Duke of Norfolk*, after which he never held up his head more.[1] The probability is, that although he clung to office so pusillanimously in the midst of all sorts of slights and indignities, he would now have been forcibly ejected if his death had not appeared to be near at hand, and if there had not been a demand for the services of "Judge Jeffreys" in a scene very different from the drowsy tranquillity of the Court of Chancery.

By the month of July Monmouth's rebellion had been put down, and he himself had been executed upon his parliamentary attainder without the trouble of a trial; but all the jails in the West of England were crowded with his adherents, and, instead of Colonel Kirke doing military execution on more of them than had already suffered from his "Lambs," it was resolved that they should all perish by the flaming sword of justice—which, on such an occasion, there was only one man fit to wield.

No assizes had been held this summer on the Western circuit; but for all the counties upon it a special Commission to try criminals was now appointed—at the head of which Lord Chief Justice Jeffreys was put—and by a second Commission, he, singly, was invested with the authority of Commander-in-Chief over all his Majesty's forces within the same limits.[2]

On entering Hampshire he was met by a brigade of soldiers, by whom he was guarded to Winchester. During the rest of his progress he never moved without a military escort—he daily gave the word—orders for going the rounds, and for the general disposal of the troops, were dictated by him—sentinels mounting guard at his

---

[1] Ante, p. 290 *et seq.* From the slight passed upon the Lord Guilford at the opening of the session, and the elevation of Jeffreys to the peerage, a speedy transfer of the Great Seal seems to have been generally anticipated. Evelyn, in his Memoirs, under May 22, 1685, after giving an account of the meeting of parliament, thus proceeds: "There was no speech made by the Lord Keeper after his Majesty as usual. It was whispered he would not be long in that situation, and many believe the bold Chief Justice Jefferies, who was made Baron of Wem, in Shropshire, and who went through stitch in that tribunal, stands fair for that office. I gave him joy the morning before of his new honor, he having been always very civil to me."

[2] There is preserved in the War Office an order dated 24th August, 1685, for furnishing horse and foot at his request.

lodgings, and the officers on duty sending him their reports.

I desire at once to save my readers from the apprehension that I am about to shock their humane feelings by a detailed statement of the atrocities of this bloody campaign in the West, the character of which is familiar to every Englishman. But, as a specimen of it, I must present a short account of the treatment experienced by Lady Lisle, with whose murder it commenced.

She was the widow of Major Lisle, who had sat in judgment on Charles I., had been a Lord Commissioner of the Great Seal under Cromwell, and, flying on the Restoration, had been assassinated at Lausanne.[1] She remained in England, and was remarkable for her loyalty as well as piety. Jeffrey's malignant spite against her is wholly inexplicable; for he had never had any personal quarrel with her, she did not stand in the way of his promotion, and the circumstance of her being the widow of a regicide, can not account for his vindictiveness. Perhaps without any personal dislike to the individual, he merely wished to strike terror into the West by his first operation.

The charge against her, which was laid capitally, was that after the battle of Sedgemoor she had harbored in her house one Hickes, who had been in arms with the Duke of Monmouth—*she knowing of his treason*.[2] In truth she had received him into her house—thinking merely that he was persecuted as a nonconformist minister, and the moment she knew whence he came, she (conveying to him a hint that he should escape) sent her servant to a justice of peace to give information concerning him. There was the greatest difficulty even to show that Hickes had been in the rebellion, and the Judge was worked up to a pitch of fury by being obliged himself to cross-examine a Presbyterian witness, who had showed a leaning against the prosecution. But the principal traitor had not been convicted, and there was not a particle of evidence to show the *scienter*—*i. e.* that the supposed accomplice, at the time of the harboring, was acquainted

---

[1] Ante, vol. iii., p. 360 *et seq.*
[2] Another person of the name of Nelthorp was mentioned in the indictment; but with respect to him there was not the shadow of a case made in evidence.—11 St. Tr. 297.

with the treason. Not allowed the benefit of counsel, she herself, prompted by natural good sense, took the legal objection that the principal traitor ought first to have been convicted, " because, peradventure, he might afterwards be acquitted as innocent after she had been condemned for harboring him;" and she urged with great force to the jury, " that at the time of the alleged offense, she had been entirely ignorant of any suspicion of Hickes having participated in the rebellion ; that she had strongly disapproved of it, and that she had sent her only son into the field to fight under the royal banner to suppress it."

It is said by almost all the contemporary authorities, that thrice did the jury refuse to find a verdict of *guilty*, and thrice did Lord Chief Justice Jeffreys send them back to reconsider their verdict.[1] In the account of the proceeding in the STATE TRIALS, which has the appearance of having been taken in short-hand, and of being authentic, the repeated sending back of the Jury is not mentioned; but enough appears to stamp eternal infamy on Jeffreys, if there were nothing more extant against him. After a most furious summing up, " the Jury withdrew, and staying out awhile, the Lord Jeffreys expressed a great deal of impatience, and said he wondered that in so plain a case they would go from the bar, and would have sent for them, with an intimation that, if they did not come quickly, he would adjourn, and let them lie by it all night; but, after about half an hour's stay, the jury returned, and the foreman addressed himself to the Court thus: ' My Lord, we have one thing to beg of your Lordship some directions in before we can give our verdict; we have some doubt whether there be sufficient evidence that she knew Hickes to have been in the army.' —*L. C. J.* ' There is as full proof as as proof can be ; but you are judges of the proof; for my part, I thought there was no difficulty in it.'—*Foreman.* ' My Lord, we are in some doubt of it.'—*L. C. J.* ' I can not help your doubts; was there not proved a discourse of the battle and the army at supper time?'—*Foreman.* ' But, my Lord, we are not satisfied that she had notice that Hickes was in the army.'—*L. C. J.* ' I can not tell what would satisfy you. Did she not inquire of Dunne whether Hickes had

---

[1] See Coke's Detection, ii. 1719. Kennet, iii. 433. Rapin, v. 750. Oldmixon, i. 706. Echard. 1068. Ralph, i. 839.

been in the army? and when he told her he did not know, she did not say she would refuse him if he had been there, but ordered him to come by night, by which it is evident she suspected it. . . . But if there were no such proof, the circumstances and management of the thing is as full a proof as can be. I wonder what it is you doubt of.' —*Lady Lisle.* 'My Lord, I hope——' —*L. C. J.* 'You must not speak now.'— The Jury laid their heads together near a quarter of an hour, and then pronounced a verdict of *Guilty.*—*L. C. J.* 'Gentlemen I did not think I should have had any occasion to speak after your verdict; but finding some hesitancy and doubt among you, I can not but say I wonder it should come about; for I think, in my conscience, the evidence was as full and plain as could be, and if I had been among you, and she had been my own mother, I should have found her guilty.'"

He passed sentence upon her with great *sang froid*, and I really believe, would have done the same had she been the mother who bore him,—" That you be conveyed from hence to the place from whence you came, and from thence you are to be drawn on a hurdle to the place of execution, where your body is to be burnt alive till you be dead. And the Lord have mercy on your soul."

The King refused the most earnest applications to save her life, saying that he had promised Lord Chief Justice Jeffreys not to pardon her: but, by a mild exercise of the prerogative, he changed the punishment of burning into that of beheading,—which she actually underwent. After the Revolution, her attainder was reversed by act of parliament, on the ground that "the verdict was injuriously extorted by the menaces and violence, and other illegal practices of George, Lord Jeffreys, Baron of Wem, then Lord Chief Justice of the Kings' Bench."[1]

From Winchester the "Lord General Judge" proceeded to Salisbury, where he was obliged to content himself with whippings and imprisonments for indiscreet words, the Wiltshire men not having actually joined in the insurrection. But when he got into Dorsetshire, the county in which Monmouth had landed, and where many had joined his standard, he was fatigued, if not satiated, with shedding blood. Great alarm was excited, and not with-

[1] 11 St. Tr. 381. Stat. 1 W. & M.

out reason, by his being seen to laugh in church, both during the prayers and sermon, which preceded the commencement of business in the Hall,—his smile being construed into a sign that he was about "to breathe death like a destroying angel, and to sanguine his very ermine in blood."[1] His charge to the Grand Jury threw the whole county into a state of consternation: for he said he was determined to exercise the utmost rigor of the law, not only against principal traitors, but all aiders and abettors, who, by any expression, had encouraged the rebellion, or had favored the escape of any engaged in it, however nearly related to them,—unless it were the harboring of a husband by a wife, which the wisdom of our ancestors permitted, because she had sworn to obey him.

Bills of indictment for high treason were found by the hundred, often without evidence, the Grand Jury being afraid that, if they were at all scrupulous, they themselves might be brought in "aiders and abettors." It happened, curiously enough, that as he was about to arraign the prisoners, he received news, by express, that the Lord Keeper Guilford had breathed his last at Wroxton, in Oxfordshire. He had little doubt that he should himself be the successor, and very soon after, by a messenger from Windsor, he received assurances to that effect, with orders "to finish the King's business in the West." Although he had no ground for serious misgivings, he could not but feel a little uneasy at the thought of the intrigues which in his absence might spring up against him in a corrupt Court, and he was impatient to take possession of his new dignity. But what a prospect before him, if all the prisoners against whom there might be indictments, here and at other places, should plead "not guilty," and *seriatim* take their trials! He resorted to an expedient worthy of his genius by openly proclaiming, in terms of vague promise but certain denunciation, that "if any of those indicted would relent from their conspiracies, and plead *guilty*, they should find him to be a merciful Judge; but that those who put themselves upon their trials (which the law mercifully gave them all, in strictness, a right to do), if found guilty, would have very little time to live; and, therefore, that such as were conscious they had no

[1] Wool. 200.

defense, had better spare him the trouble of trying them."[1]

He was at first disappointed. The prisoners knew the sternness of the Judge, and had some hope from the mercy of their countrymen on the Jury. The result of this boldness is soon told. He began on a Saturday morning, with a batch of thirty. Of these only one was acquitted for want of evidence, and the same evening he signed a warrant to hang thirteen of those convicted on Monday morning, and the rest the following day. An impressive defense was made by the constable of Chard-stock, charged with supplying the Duke of Monmouth's soldiers with money,—whereas they had actually robbed him of a considerable sum, which he had in his hands for the use of the militia. The prisoner having objected to the competency of a witness called against him, "Villain! Rebel!" exclaimed the Judge, "methinks I see thee already with a halter about thy neck." And he was specially ordered to be hanged the first,—my Lord jeeringly declaring, "that if any with a knowledge of the law came in his way, he should take care to *prefer them!*"

On the Monday morning, the court sitting rather late on account of the executions, the Judge, on taking his place, found many applications to withdraw the plea of *Not Guilty*, and the prisoners pleaded *Guilty* in great numbers; but his ire was kindled, and he would not even affect any semblance of mercy. Two hundred and ninety-two more received judgment to die, and of these seventy-four actually suffered,—some being sent to be executed in every town, and almost in every village, for many miles round. While the whole county was covered with the

[1] " He did 'um to confess, if e'er they hope
To be reprieved from the fatal rope :
This seem'd a favor, but he'd none forgive;
The favor was a day or two to live,—
Which those had not that troubled him with tryal,
His business blood, and would have no denyal.
Two hundred he could sentence in an hour," &c.
Jeffery's Elegy.

" The prisoners to plead to his Lordship did cry.
But still he made answer and thus did reply :
'We'll hang you up first, and then after we'll try.'
Sing hev, brave Chancellor ! O, fine Chancellor !
Delicate Chancellor, O !"
Song on Chancellor Jeffreys, to the tune of " Hey, brave Popery."
See 11 St. Tr. 302. Wool. 203.

gibbeted quarters of human beings, the towns resounded with the cries of men, and even of women and children, who were cruelly whipped for sedition, on the ground that by words or looks they had favored the insurrection. The case of John Tutchin, afterwards the noted political writer satirized by Pope, may be taken as a specimen of these minor cruelties. He was tried at Dorchester, on the charge of having said "Hampshire is up in arms for the Duke of Monmouth," and on his conviction was sentenced to be whipped through every market town in the county for seven years. One of the officers of the court called forth the resentment of the Judge, by venturing to observe, that "the culprit was very young, and that the sentence would reach to once a fortnight for seven years," and the unhappy youth himself in vain petitioned for the more lenient punishment of the gallows. Luckily for him he was seized with the small-pox in prison and discharged,— to prevent the spreading of the contagion,—so that he was not "flagrant from the scourge" till the succeeding reign.

Jeffreys next proceeded to Exeter, where one John Foweracres, the first prisoner arranged, had the temerity to plead *Not guilty*, and being speedily convicted, was sent to instant execution. This had the desired effect; for all the others confessed, and his Lordship was saved the trouble of trying them. Only thirty-seven suffered capitally in the county of Devon, the rest of the two hundred and forty-three against whom indictments were found being transported, whipped, or imprisoned.

Somersetshire afforded a much finer field for indulging the propensities of the Chief Justice, as in this county there had not only been a considerable rising of armed men for Monmouth, but processions,—in which women and children had joined, carrying ribbons, boughs, and garlands to his honor. There were five hundred prisoners for trial at Taunton alone. Jeffreys said, in his charge to the Grand Jury, "it would not be his fault if he did not purify the place." The first person tried before him here was Simon Hamling, a dissenter of a class to whom the Judge bore a particular enmity. In reality, the accused had only come to Taunton, during the rebellion, to warn his son, who resided there, to remain neuter. Conscious of his innocence, he insisted on pleading *Not guilty;* he called witnesses, and made a resolute defense,—which was considered great presumption. The committing magistrate, who was sitting on the bench, at last interposed, and said, "There must certainly be some mistake about the individual."—*Jeffreys.* "You have brought him here, and, if he be innocent, his blood be upon your head." The prisoner was found guilty, and ordered for execution next morning. Few afterwards gave his Lordship the trouble of trying them, and one hundred and forty-three are said here to have been ordered for execution, and two hundred and eighty-four to have been sentenced to transportation for life. He particularly piqued himself upon his *bon mot* in passing sentence on one Hucher, who pleaded, in mitigation, that, though he had joined the Duke of Monmouth, he had sent important information to the King's general, the Earl of Feversham. "You deserve a double death," said the impartial Judge;—"one for rebelling against your Sovereign, and the other for betraying your friends."[1]

He showed great ingenuity in revenging himself upon such as betrayed any disapprobation of his severities. Among these was Lord Stawell, who was so much shocked with what he had heard of the Chief Justice, that he refused to see him. Immediately after, there came forth an order that Colonel Bovet, of Taunton, a friend to whom this Cavalier nobleman had been much attached, should be executed at Cothelstone, close by the house where he and Lady Stawell and his children then resided.

A considerable harvest here arose from compositions levied upon the friends of twenty-six young virgins, who presented the invader with colors, which they had embroidered with their own hands. The fund was ostensibly for the benefit of "the Queen's maids of honor," but a strong suspicion arose that the Chief Justice participated in bribes for these as well as other pardons. He thought that his *peculium* was encroached upon by a letter from Lord Sunderland, informing him of "the King's pleasure to bestow one thousand convicts on several courtiers, and one hundred on a favorite of the Queen,—security being given that the prisoners should be enslaved for ten years in some West India Island." In his remonstrance he said that "these convicts would be worth

[1] Toulmin's History of Taunton, 162, 529.

ten or fifteen pounds a-piece," and with a view to his own claim, returned thanks for his Majesty's gracious acceptance of his services. However, he was obliged to submit to the royal distribution of the spoil.[1]

Where the King did not personally interfere, Jeffreys was generally inexorable if he did not himself receive the bribe for a pardon. Kiffin, a nonconformist merchant, had agreed to give £3,000 to a courtier for the pardon of two youths, his grandsons, who had been in Monmouth's army; but the Chief Justice would listen to no circumstances of mitigation, as another was to pocket the price of mercy.[2] Yet, to a buffoon who attended him on the circuit and made sport by his mimicry,—in an hour of revelry at Taunton, he tossed the pardon of a rich culprit, expressing a hope "that it might turn to good account."

The jails at Taunton being incapable of containing all the prisoners, it was necessary to adjourn the Commission to Wells, where the same horrible scenes were again acted, notwithstanding the humane exertions of that most honorable man, Bishop Ken, who afterwards, having been one of the seven Bishops prosecuted by King James, resigned his see at the Revolution, rather than sign the new tests.

The Cornishmen had all remained loyal, and the city of Bristol only remained to be visted by the Commission. There were not many cases of treason here, but Jeffreys had a particular spite against the Corporation magistrates, because they were supposed to favor dissenters, and he had them very much in his power by a discovery he made, that they had been in the habit of having in turn assigned to them prisoners charged with felony, whom they sold, for their own benefit, to be transported to Barbadoes. In addressing the Grand Jury, (while he complained of a fit of the stone, and was seemingly under the excitement of liquor), he said:

"I find a special Commission is an unusual thing here, and relishes very ill; nay, the very women storm at it, for fear we should take the upper hand of them, too; for by-the-by, Gentlemen, I hear it is much in fashion in this city for the women to govern and bear sway." Having

[1] Letters in State Paper Office, 14, 15, 19, 22 Sept. 1685.
[2] Kiffin's Memoirs, p. 54.

praised the mild and paternal rule of King James, he thus proceeded: "On the other hand, up starts a puppet Prince who seduces the mobile into rebellion, into which they are easily bewitched; for I say, rebellion is like the sin of witchcraft. This man, who had as little title to the Crown as the least of you (for I hope you are all legitimate), being overtaken by justice, and by the goodness of his Prince brought to the scaffold, he has the confidence (good God, that men should be so impudent!) to say that God Almighty did not know with what joyfulness he did die (a traitor!). Great God of heaven and earth! what reason have men to rebel? But, as I told you rebellion is like the sin of witchcraft: *Fear God and honor the King* is rejected for no other reason, as I can find, but that it is written in St. Peter. Gentlemen, I must tell you, I am afraid that this city hath too many of these people in it, and it is your duty to find them out. Gentlemen, I shall not stand complimenting with you: I shall talk with some of you before you and I part, I tell you: I tell you I have brought a besom, and I will sweep every man's door, whether great or small. Certainly here are a great many of those men whom they call Trimmers: a Whig is but a mere fool to those; for a whig is some sort of a subject in comparison of these; for a Trimmer is but a cowardly and base-spirited Whig; for the Whig is but the journeyman prentice that is hired and set over the rebellion, whilst the Trimmer is afraid to appear in the cause." He then opens his charge against the Aldermen for the sale of convicts, and thus continues: "Good God! where am I?—in Bristol? This city it seems claims the privilege of hanging and drawing among themselves. I find you have more need of a special commission once a month at least. The very magistrates that should be the ministers of justice, fall out with one another to that degree they will scarcely dine together; yet I find they can agree for their interest; if there be but a *kid* in the case; for I hear the trade of *kidnapping* is much in request in this city. You can discharge a felon or a traitor, provided they will go to Mr. Alderman's plantation in the West Indies. Come, come, I find you stink for want of rubbing. It seems the dissenters and fanatics fare well amongst you, by reason of the favor of the magistrates; for example, if a dissenter, who is a notorious and obstinate offender comes before them, one alderman or another stands up and says, *He is a good man* (though three parts a rebel). Well then, for the sake of Mr. Alderman, he shall be fined but five shillings. Then comes another, and up stands another goodman Alderman, and says, *I know him to be an honest man* (though rather worse than the former). Well, for Mr. Alderman's sake, he shall be fined but half-a-crown; so *manus manum fricat;* you play the knave for me now, and I will play the knave for you by-and-by. I am ashamed of these things, but, by God's grace, I will mend them: for, as I have told you, I have brought a brush in my pocket, and I shall be sure to rub the dirt wherever it is, or on whomsoever it sticks." "Thereupon," says Roger North, "he turns to the Mayor, accoutered with his scarlet and furs, and gave him all the ill names that scolding eloquence could supply; and so, with rating and staring as his way was, never left till he made him quit the bench and go down to the criminal's post at the bar; and there he pleaded for himself as a common rogue or thief must have done; and when the Mayor hesitated a little, or slackened his pace, he bawled at him, and stamping, called for his guards, for he was still general by commission. Thus the citizens saw their scarlet chief magistrate at the bar to their infinite terror and amazement."[1]

Only three were executed for treason at Bristol, but Jeffreys looking at the end of his campaign to the returns of the enemy *killed*, had the satisfaction to find that they amounted to 330,—besides 800 *prisoners* ordered to be transported.[2]

He now hastened homewards to pounce upon the Great Seal. In his way through Somersetshire, with a regiment of dragoons as his life-guards, the Major took the liberty to say that there were two *Spokes* who had been convicted, and that one of these left for execution was not the one intended to suffer, the other having contrived to make his escape, and that favor might perhaps still be

---

[1] Life of Guilford, ii. 113. Wool. 225.
[2] In a letter from Bristol dated 22nd Sept. 1685, he boasts of his victory over that most factious city, where he had committed the mayor and an alderman for selling to the plantations men whom they had unjustly convicted with a view to such a sale, and pledges himself that Bristol and the county of Somerset should know their duty both to God and their King before he leaves them.

shown to him whom it was intended to pardon. "No!" said the General-Judge; "his family owe a life—he shall die for his namesake!" To render such narratives credible, we must recollect that his mind was often greatly disturbed by fits of the stone, and still more by intemperance. Burnet speaking of his behavior, at this time, says, "He was perpetually either drunk or in a rage, liker a fury than the zeal of a judge."[1]

I shall conclude my sketch of Jeffreys as a Criminal Judge with his treatment of a prisoner whom he was eager to hang, but who escaped with life. This was Prideaux, a gentleman of fortune in the West of England, who had been apprehended on the landing of Monmouth, for no other reason than that his father had been Attorney General under Cromwell. A reward of £500, with a free pardon, was offered to any witnesses who would give evidence against him; but none could be found, and he was discharged. Afterwards two convicts were prevailed upon to say that they had seen him take part in the insurrection, and he was again cast into prison. His friends, alarmed for his safety, though convinced of his innocence, tried to procure a pardon for him, when they were told "that nothing could be done for him, as the King had *given him to the* Chief Justice" (the familiar phrase for the grant of an estate about to be forfeited). A negotiation was then opened with Jennings, the avowed agent of Jeffreys for the sale of pardons—and the sum of £15,000 was actually paid to him by a banker for the deliverance of a man whose destruction could not be effected by any perversion of the formalities of law.[2]

There is to be found only one defender of these atrocities. "I have, indeed, sometimes thought," says the author of A CAVEAT AGAINST THE WHIGS, "that in Jeffrey's Western circuit, justice went too far before mercy was remembered, though there was not above a fourth part executed of what were convicted. But when I consider in what manner several of those lives then spared were afterwards spent, I can not but think a little more *hemp* might have been usefully employed upon that occasion."

A great controversy has arisen—"Who is chiefly to be blamed, Jeffreys or James?" Sheffield, Duke of Bucking-

---

[1] Burnet, ii. 334.   [2] Common's Journals, May 1, 1689.

ham, declares that "the King never forgave the cruelty of the Judge in executing such multitudes in the West against his express orders." Père d'Orléans says, "Le Roi fut trop tard averti de ce désordre, mais on ne l'en eut pas plustot informé qu'il en témoigna de l'indignation; et si des services importans, qu'il avoit reçu de ceux qui en étoient accusez, l'obligea de les épargner, il repara autant qu'il put leur injustice, par le pardon general qu'il accorda à ceux des revoltez qui etoient encore en etat d'eprouver les effets de sa clemence." And reliance is placed by Hume[1] on the assertion of Roger North, that his brother, the Lord Keeper, going to the King, and moving him "to put a stop to the fury, which was in no respect for his service, and would be counted a carnage, not law or justice,—orders went to mitigate the proceeding."

I have already demonstrated that this last assertion is a mere invention[2]—and though it is easy to fix deep guilt on the Judge, it is impossible to exculpate the Monarch. Burnet says that James "had a particular account of his proceedings writ to him every day, and he took pleasure to relate them in the drawing-room, to foreign ministers, and at his table, calling it *Jeffreys' campaign*—speaking of all he had done in a style that neither became the majesty nor the mercifulness of a great Prince." Jeffreys himself (certainly a very suspicious witness), when in the Tower, declared to Tutchin, that "his instructions were much more severe than the execution of them; and that at his return he was snubbed at Court for being too merciful." And to Dr. Scott, the divine who attended him on his death-bed, he said, "Whatever I did then, I did by express orders; and I have this further to say for myself, that I was not half bloody enough for him who sent me thither." We certainly know from a letter written to him by the Earl of Sunderland, at Dorchester, that "the King approved entirely of all his proceedings." And though we can not believe that he stopped short of any severity which he thought would be of service to himself, there seems no reason to doubt (if that be any palliation) that throughout the whole of these proceedings his object was to please his master, whose disposition was now most vindictive, and who thought that, by such terrible

[1] Vol. viii. 236   [2] Ante, p. 293.

examples, he should secure to himself a long and quiet reign.[1]

The two were equally criminal,[2] and both had their reward. But in the first instance, and till the consequences of such wickedness and folly began to appear, they met each other with mutual joy and congratulations. Jeffreys returning from the West, by royal command stopped at Windsor Castle. He arrived there on the 28th of September; and after a most gracious reception, the Great Seal was immediately delivered to him with the title of Lord Chancellor.

We learn from Evelyn that it had been three weeks in the King's personal custody. "About six o'clock came Sir Dudley North, and his brother, Roger North, and brought the Great Seal from my Lord Keeper, who died the day before. The King went immediately to Council—everybody guessing who was most likely to succeed this great officer. Most believed it would be no other than Lord Chief Justice Jeffreys, who had so rigorously prosecuted the late rebels, and was now gone the Western

---

[1] One of the strongest testimonies against James is his own letter to the Prince of Orange, dated Sept. 24, 1685, in which, after giving him a long account of his fox-hunting, he says, "As for news, there is little stirring, but that the Lord Chief Justice has almost done his campaign. He has already condemned several hundreds, some of which are already executed, some are to be, and the others sent to the plantations."—*Dalrymple's App.* part ii. 165.—The only public man who showed any bowels of compassion amidst these horrors was Lord Sunderland, who entreated repeatedly with Jeffreys, but in vain, for a youth named William Jenkins. His father, an eminent Nonconformist clergyman, having died in Newgate in consequence of a long and unjust imprisonment, he distributed mourning rings with the inscription, "William Jenkins murdered in Newgate." He was in consequence confined in Ilchester jail till released by Monmouth's army, which he followed.—*Letter from Sunderland to Jeffreys,* Sept. 12, 1685. *State Paper Office.*—Whig party writers are at great pains to exculpate Polexfen, the great Whig lawyer, who conducted all these prosecutions as counsel for the Crown; but I think he comes in for no small share of the infamy then incurred, and he must be considered as principal *aide de camp* to Jeffreys in the *Western campaign.* He ought to have told the jury that there was no case against the Lady Lisle, and when a few examples had been made he ought to have stopped the prosecutions, or have thrown up his briefs. See Life of James II. vol. ii. p. 44. Mackintosh's Works, vol. ii. p. 34.

[2] I hope I have not been prejudiced in my estimate of James's character by the consideration that when acting as Regent in Scotland he issued an order (afterwards recalled) for the utter suppression of the name of CAMPBELL, "which," says Mackintosh, "would have amounted to a proscription of several noblemen, a considerable body of gentry, and the most numerous and powerful tribe in the kingdom."—*Works,* ii. 109.

circuit to punish the rest that were secured in the several counties. and was now near upon his return." [1]

The London Gazette of October 1, 1685, contains the following notice:—

"Windsor, Sept. 28.

" His Majesty taking into his royal consideration the many eminent and faithful services which the Right Honorable George, Lord Jeffreys, of Wem, Lord Chief Justice of England, has rendered the Crown, as well in the reign of the late King, of ever blessed memory, as since his Majesty's accession to the throne, was pleased this day to commit to him the custody of the Great Seal of England, with the title of Lord Chancellor." [2]

CHAPTER CI.

CONTINUATION OF THE LIFE OF LORD CHANCELLOR JEFFREYS TILL THE GREAT SEAL WAS TAKEN FROM HIM BY JAMES II. AND THROWN INTO THE RIVER THAMES.

THE new Lord Chancellor, having brought the Great Seal with him from Windsor to London, had near a month to prepare for the business of the term.

He took a large house in Duke Street, Westminster; and there fitted up a Court, which was afterwards consecrated as a place of public worship, and is now called " Duke Street Chapel." [3]

[1] Mem. i. 569.
[2] The Crown Office Minute Book, not imitating the amusing circumstantiality of the old entries on the Close Roll, after stating the death of the late Lord Keeper on the 5th of September, the delivery of the Seal next day to the King, "who keep it in his own custody till the return of the Lord Jeffreys from the Western circuit,"—merely states, that, " on the 28th of the same September, his Majesty was pleased to deliver the Seal to him with the title of Lord Chancellor."—p. 121. Burnet relates, that as a further reward he was created a Peer (ii. 335); and Hume and most subsequent historians repeat the statement, although it is quite certain that he had been created a Peer before the meeting of the parliament, months before, and had taken an active part in the House of Lords before Monmouth's rebellion broke out. As such mistakes are little noticed, I am encouraged to hope that those I may fall into may be overlooked or forgiven.
[3] Pennant, in his " London," speaking of Jeffreys's house, says, " It is

He had only a very slender acquaintance with Chancery proceedings, and he was by no means thoroughly grounded in common-law learning; but he now fell to the study of equity pleading and practice, and though exceedingly inferior to his two immediate predecessors in legal acquirements, his natural shrewdness was such, that, when entirely sober, he contrived to gloss over his ignorance of technicalities, and to arrive at a right decision. He was seldom led into temptation by the occurrence of cases in which the interests of political parties, or religious sects, were concerned; and, as an Equity Judge, the multitude rather regarded him with favor.

He took his place in the Court of Chancery on the 23rd of October, the first day of Michaelmas term. I find no account of his procession from Duke Street to Westminster Hall; and I rather suspect that, on account of the offense he had given to so many persons by his brutal manners and his general unpopularity, it was not well attended. When he took the oaths in the Court of Chancery, there were present "the Earl of Rochester, Lord Treasurer, the Earl of Clarendon, Lord Privy Seal, the Duke of Beaufort, the Earl of Derby, the Earl of Sunderland, the Earl of Craven, the Earl of Burlington, Lord Fauconbridge, and several other persons of honor, who only stayed while he heard one motion, and then departed, leaving him sitting."[1]

The public and the profession were much shocked to see such a man at the head of the law; but as soon as he was installed in his office, there were plenty ready enough to gather round him, and, suppressing their real feelings, to load him with flattery and to solicit him for favors.

Evelyn, who, upon his appointment as Chief Justice, describes him as "most ignorant, but most daring," now assiduously cultivated his notice; and, having succeeded in getting an invitation to dine with him, thus speaks of him:

easily known by a large flight of stone steps, which his royal master permitted to made into the park adjacent, for the accommodation of his Lordship. These steps terminate above in a small court, on three sides of which stands the house. The cause room was afterwards converted into a place of worship called Duke Street Chapel, and is on the left. When Jeffreys found it inconvenient to sit at Westminster or Lincoln's Inn, he made use of this court." [1] Cr. Off. Min. B. fol. 122.

"31st Oct., 1685.
"I dined at our great Lord Chancellor Jeffreys', who used me with much respect. This was the late Chief Justice, who had newly been the Western Circuit to try the Monmouth conspirators, and had formerly done such severe justice amongst the obnoxious in Westminster Hall, for which his Majesty dignified him by creating him first a Baron, and now Lord Chancellor; is of an assured and undaunted spirit, and has served the Court interest on all hardiest occasions; is of nature civil, and a slave of the Court."[1]

A slave of the Court he still continued, till the wicked and insane measures which he unscrupulously supported proved the ruin of himself and his master. He who originated and commanded these measures incurred much less moral blame, as he was a sincere believer in the religion he wished to establish in the country; and it may be forgiven to a King to desire to extend his prerogative. Had he been resisted by a firm and virtuous minister, he might have continued to reign prosperously, and have transmitted his Crown to his posterity;—

> "How oft the sight of means to do ill deeds,
> Makes deeds ill done! Hadst not thou been by,
> A fellow by the hand of nature mark'd,
> Quoted and sign'd to do a deed of shame,
> This murder had not come into my mind."

The very first measure which James proposed to his new Chancellor was, literally, the hanging of an alderman. He was still afraid of the mutinous spirit of the City, which, without some fresh terrors, might again break out, although the charters were destroyed; and no sufficient atonement had yet been made for the hostility constantly manifested by the metropolis to the policy of his family for half a century. His Majesty proposed that Alderman Clayton, a very troublesome agitator, should be selected as the victim. The Chancellor agreed that "it was very fit an example should be made, as his Majesty had graciously proposed; but if it were the same thing to his Majesty, he would venture to suggest a different choice. Alderman Clayton was a bad subject, but Alderman Cornish was still more troublesome, and more dangerous." The King readily acquiesced, and Alderman Cornish was im-

[1] Mem. i. 617.

mediately brought to trial before a packed jury, and executed on a gibbet erected in Cheapside, on pretense that some years before he had been concerned in the Ryehouse plot.¹ The apologists of Jeffreys say (and as it is the only alleged instance of his gratitude I have met with, I have great pleasure in recording it) that he was induced to save Sir Robert Clayton from recollecting that this alderman had been his pot companion, and had greatly assisted him in obtaining the office of Common Sergeant.²

Monmouth's rebellion in England, and Argyle's in Scotland, being put down, and the City of London reduced to subjection, James expressed an opinion, in which the Chancellor concurred, that there was no longer any occasion to disguise the plan of governing by military force, and of violating at pleasure the solemn acts of the legislature. Parliament reassembled on the 9th of November, when Jeffreys took his seat on the Woolsack. The King alone (as had been concerted) addressed the two Houses, and plainly told them that he could rely upon "nothing but a good force of well disciplined troops in constant pay," and that he was determined to employ "officers in the army, not qualified by the late tests, for their employments."³

When the King had withdrawn, Lord Halifax rose, and said, sarcastically, "They had now more reason than ever to give thanks to his Majesty, since he had dealt so plainly with them, and discovered what he would be at."

This the Chancellor thought fit to take as a serious motion, and immediately put the question as proposed by a noble Lord, "that an humble address be presented to his Majesty to thank him for his gracious speech from the throne." No one ventured to offer any remark, and it was immediately carried, *nemine dissentiente*. The King returned a grave answer to the address, "That he was much satisfied to find their Lordships were so well pleased with what he said, and that he would never offer

---

¹ 11 St. Tr. 381-465. This iniquitous attainder was reversed by act of parliament, 1 W. & M.
² Steward's Anecdotes: "Jeffries." However, the prosecution of Cornish excited such general horror, that even Sir John Trevor, the Master of the Rolls, vainly remonstrated against it, and told Jeffries that "if he pursued that unfortunate man to execution, it would be no better than murder."— Yorke's *Tribes of Wales*, 110. ³ 4 Parl. Hist. 1369.

anything to their House that he should not be convinced was for the true interest of the kingdom."[1]

But the Lords very soon discovered the false position in which they had placed themselves, and the Bishops were particularly scandalized at the thought that they were supposed to have thanked the King for announcing a principle upon which Papists and Dissenters might be introduced into every civil office, and even into ecclesiastical benefices.

Accordingly, Compton, Bishop of London, moved "that a day might be appointed for taking his Majesty's speech into consideration," stating, "that he spoke the united sentiments of the Episcopal bench when he pronounced the Test Act the chief security of the Established Church." This raised a very long and most animated debate, at which King James, to his great mortification, was present. Sunderland, and the popishly inclined ministers, objected to the regularity of the proceeding, urging that, having given thanks for the speech, they must be taken to have already considered it, and precluded themselves from finding fault with any part of it. The Lords Halifax, Nottingham, and Mordaunt, on the other side, treated with scorn the notion that the constitution was to be sacrificed to a point of form, and entering into the merits of the question, showed that if the power which the Sovereign now, for the first time, had openly claimed were conceded to him, the rights, privileges, and property of the nation lay at his mercy.

At last the Lord Chancellor left the woolsack, and not only bitterly attacked the regularity of the motion after an unanimous vote of thanks to the King for his speech, but gallantly insisted on the legality and expediency of the power of the Sovereign to dispense with laws for the safety and benefit of the state. No Lord Chancellor ever made such an unfortunate exhibition. He assumed the same arrogant and overbearing tone with which he had been accustomed from the bench to browbeat juries, counsel, witnesses, and prisoners, and he launched out into the most indecent personalities against his opponents. He was soon taught to know his place, and that frowns, noise, and menaces would not pass for arguments there.

[1] 4 Parl. Hist. 1367.

While he spoke he was heard with marked disgust by all parts of the House; when he sat down, being required to retract his words by those whom he had assailed, and finding all the sympathies of the house against him, he made to each of them an abject apology, "and he proved by his behavior that insolence, when checked, naturally sinks into meanness and cowardice."[1]

The Ministerialists being afraid to divide the House,—Monday following, the 23rd of November, was fixed for taking the King's speech into consideration.

But a similar disposition having been shown by the other House,—before that day parliament was prorogued, and no other national council met till the Convention Parliament after the landing of King William.[2]

James, far from abandoning his plans, was more resolute to carry them into effect. The Earl of Rochester, his own brother-in-law, and others who had hitherto stood by him, having in vain remonstrated against his madness, resigned their offices; but Jeffreys still recklessly pushed him forward in his headlong career. In open violation of the Test Act, four Catholic Lords were introduced into the Cabinet, and one of them, Lord Bellasis, was placed at the head of the Treasury in the room of the Protestant Earl of Rochester. Among such colleagues the Lord Chancellor was contented to sit in Council, and the wonder is, that he did not follow the example of Sunderland and other renegades, who, at this time, to please the King, professed to change their religion, and were reconciled to the Church of Rome. Perhaps, with his peculiar sagacity, Jeffreys thought it would be a greater sacrifice in the King's eyes to appear to be daily wounding his conscience by submitting to measures which he must be supposed inwardly to condemn.

As a grand *coup d'état*, he undertook to obtain a solemn decision of the Judges in favor of the dispensing power, and for this purpose a fictitious action was brought against Sir Edward Hales, the Lieutenant of the Tower, an avowed Roman Catholic, in the name of his coachman, for holding an office in the army without having taken the oath of supremacy, or received the sacrament according to the rites of the Church of England, or signed the declaration against transubstantiation. Jeffreys had put

[1] Hume, viii. 241.   [2] 4 Parl. Hist. 1367—1387.

the Great Seal to letters patent, authorizing him to hold the office without these tests, "*non obstante*" the act of parliament. This dispensation was pleaded in bar of the action, and upon a demurrer to the plea, after a sham argument by counsel, all the Judges except one (Baron Street) held the plea to be sufficient, and pronounced judgment for the defendant.[1] It was now proclaimed at Court that the law was not any longer an obstacle to any scheme that might be thought advisable.

The Earl of Castlemaine was sent to Rome, regularly commissioned as ambassador to his Holiness the Pope, a Papal nuncio being reciprocally received at St. James's. But assuming that religion was not embraced in the negotiations between the two courts, however impolitic the proceeding might be, I do not think that the King and the Chancellor are liable to be blamed, as they have been, by recent historians, for having in this instance violated acts of parliament. If all those are examined which had passed from the commencement of the Reformation down to the "Bill of Rights," it will probably be found that none of them can be applied to a mere diplomatic intercourse with the Pope, however stringent their provisions may be against receiving bulls or doing anything in derogation of the King's supremacy.[2]

There can be no doubt of the illegality of the next measure of the King and the Chancellor. The Court of

[1] 11 St. Tr. 1165.
[2] The statutes 5 Eliz. c. 1, and 13 Eliz. c. 5, are chiefly relied upon, but I think they were passed *alio intuitu*. Neither in the Declaration of Rights nor Bill of Rights is the embassy to Rome enumerated among the infractions of law by which James had tried to subvert the liberties and religion of the country. Lord Castlemaine was prosecuted by the Convention Parliament—but it was on a charge of going on a mission "to reconcile the realm of England to the Roman see." And if he could have made out his defense that he only carried a letter of compliment from James II. to the Pope as a temporal prince, he would have been immediately discharged. 12 St. Tr. 618.

Whether diplomatic intercourse with the Pope is now forbidden, depends upon the construction to be put upon words, " shall hold *communion* with the see or church of Rome " in the Bill of Rights. This seems to refer to *spiritual* communion only, or the Queen would hold communion with the successor of Mahomet by appointing an ambassador to the Sublime Porte. *

* This question has been since settled by stat. 11 & 12 Vic., c. 108, which expressly legalized diplomatic intercourse with the Pope, but unfortunately contained a prohibition against receiving any person as minister from him who is in holy orders,—which Pio Nono himself assured me has rendered it of no avail.—Aug. 1856.

High Commission was revived with some slight modification, although it had been abolished in the reign of Charles I. by an act of parliament, which forbade the erection of any similar Court,—and Jeffreys, having deliberately put the Great Seal to the patent creating this new arbitrary tribunal,[1] undertook to preside in it. The Commissioners were vested with unlimited jurisdiction over the Church of England, and were empowered, even in cases of suspicion, to proceed inquisitorially like the abolished Court, "*notwithstanding any law or statute to the contrary.*" The object was to have all ecclesiastics under complete control, lest any of them should oppose the intended innovations in religion.[2]

Jeffreys selected as his first victims, Sharp, Rector of St. Giles's, called "the railing parson," who had made himself very obnoxious to the government by inveighing against the errors of Popery,—and Compton, Bishop of London, his diocesan, who had raised the storm against the dispensing power in the House of Lords. A mandate was issued to the Bishop to suspend the Rector, and this being declined on the ground that no man can be lawfully condemned till he has been heard in his defense, both were summoned before the High Commission.

The Bishop appearing and being asked by the Chancellor why he had not obeyed the King's orders by suspending Dr. Sharp, prayed time to prepare his defense, as his counsel were on the circuit, and he begged to have a copy of the commission. A week's time was given; but as to the commission, he was told "all the coffee-houses had it for a penny." On the eighth day the business was resumed; but the Bishop still said he was unprepared, having great difficulty to procure a copy of the commission; when the Chancellor made him a bantering apology. "My Lord, in telling you our commission was to be seen in every coffee-house, I did not speak with any design to reflect on your Lordship, as if you were a haunter of coffee-houses. I abhor the thoughts of it!" A further indulgence of a fortnight was granted.

---

[1] The erection of this Court is the third grievance enumerated by the Bill of Rights, 1 W. & M. sess. 2, c. 2.

[2] Burnet says that Jeffreys had been declining at Court, and that, jealous of the rising favor of Herbert, the Chief Justice, he, to please the King, suggested the bold measure of reviving the Court of High Commission.—ii. 370.

At the day appointed, the Bishop again appeared with four Doctors of the civil law,—who were so frightened, that they hardly dared to say a word for him ; but he himself firmly though mildly argued, "that he had acted *jurisperitorum consilio*, and could not have had any bad motive ; that he should not have been justified in obeying an illegal order; that he had privately recommended to Dr. Sharp not to preach ; that this advice had been followed, so that the King's wish was complied with and that if he had committed any fault, he ought to be tried for it before his Archbishop and brother Bishops."

Several of the Commissioners were inclined to let him off with an an admonition ; but Jeffreys obtained and pronounced sentence of *Suspension during the King's pleasure*, both on the Bishop and the Rector.[1]

There was another political trial where justice was done to the accused, although Jeffreys presided at it. A charge was brought against Lord Delamere, the head of an ancient family in Cheshire, that he had tried to excite an insurrection in that county in aid of Monmouth's rebellion. An indictment for high treason being found against him, he was brought to trial upon it, before Jeffreys as Lord High Steward and thirty Peers-triers. The King was present, and was very desirous of a conviction, as Lord Delamere, when a member of the House of Commons, had taken an active part in supporting the Exclusion Bill

Jeffreys did his best to gratify this wish. According to the habit he had lately acquired in the West, he at first tried to induce the noble prisoner to confess,—in the hope of pardon "from the King's known clemency." "My Lord," said he, "if you are conscious to yourself that you are guilty of this heinous crime, give glory to God, make amends to his vicegerent the King, by a plain and full discovery of your guilt, and do not, by any obstinate persisting in the denial of it, provoke the just indignation of your Prince, who has made it appear to the world that his inclinations are rather to show mercy than inflict punishment."

Lord Delamere, to ease his mind from the anxiety to know whether the man who so spoke was to pronounce upon his guilt or innocence, said, " I beg your Grace would please to satisfy me whether your Grace be one of my

[1] 11 St. Tr. 1123—1166.

judges in concurrence with the rest of the Lords?"—*L. H. Steward.* "No, my Lord, I am Judge of the Court, but I am none of your triers."[1]

A plea to the jurisdiction being put in, Lord Delamere requested his Grace to advise with the other Peers upon it, as it was a matter of privilege.—*L. H. Steward.* "Good my Lord, I hope you that are a prisoner at the bar are not to give me direction who I should advise with, or how I should demean myself here."

This plea was properly overruled, and *Not guilty* pleaded,—when his grace, to prejudice the Peers-triers against the noble prisoner as a notorious exclusionist, delivered an inflammatory address to them before any evidence was given,—thus beginning: "My Lords, I know you can not but well remember what unjust and insolent attempts were made upon the rightful and unalterable succession to the imperial crown of these realms, under the pretense of that which has been so often found to be the occasion of rebellion, I mean the specious pretense of religion, by the fierce, froward, and fanatical zeal of some members of the House of Commons in the last parliaments under the late King Charles II., of ever blessed memory; which by the wonderful providence of Almighty God not prevailing, the chief contrivers of that horrid villainy consulted together how to gain that advantage upon the monarchy by open force which they could not obtain by a pretended course of law."

To create a farther prejudice, poor Lord Howard was called to repeat once more his oft-told tale of the Rye-house plot, with which it was not pretended that the prisoner had any connection. The charge in the indictment was only supported by one witness, who himself had been in the rebellion, and who swore that Lord Delamere, at a time and place which he specified, had sent a message by him to Monmouth, asking a supply of money to maintain 10,000 men to be levied in Cheshire against King James. An *alibi* was clearly proved. Yet his Grace summed up for a conviction, and took pains "for the sake

---

[1] When a Peer is tried in parliament before the House of Lords, the Lord High Steward votes like the rest of the Peers, who have all a right to be present; but if the trial be out of parliament, the Lord High Steward is only the Judge to give direction in point of law, and the verdict is by the Lords-triers specially summoned.

of the numerous and great auditory, that a mistake in point of law might not go unrectified, which seemed to be urged with some earnestness by the noble Lord at the bar, *that there is a necessity there should be two positive witnesses to convict a man of treason."*

To the honor of the Peerage of England, there was an unanimous verdict of acquittal.[1] James himself even allowed this to be right, wreaking all his vengeance on the witness for not having given better evidence, and swearing that he would have him first convicted of perjury, and then hanged for treason. Jeffreys seems to have struggled hard to behave with moderation on this trial; but his habitual arrogance from time to time broke out, and must have created a disgust among the Peers-triers very favorable to the prisoner. "My lords," said he, "I would always be very tender of the privilege of the Peers; but truly I apprehend according to the best of my understanding, that this Court is held before me: it is my warrant that convenes the prisoner to the bar: it is my summons that brings the Peers together to try him; and so I take myself to be the Judge of the Court."[2]

Jeffreys, still pretending to be a strong Protestant, eagerly assisted the King in his mad attempt to open the Church and the universities to the intrusion of the Catholics. The Fellows of Magdalen College, Oxford, having disobeyed the royal mandate to elect, as head of their College, Anthony Farmer, who was not qualified by the statutes, and was a man of infamous character,—and having chosen the pious and learned Hough,—were summoned before the Court of Ecclesiastical Commission. Jeffreys observed that Dr. Fairfax, one of their number, had not signed the answer of the College to the charge of disregarding the King's recommendation. Fairfax asking leave to explain his reasons for declining to sign the answer, Jeffreys thought that he was willing to conform, and exclaimed, " Ay, this looks like a man of sense, and a good subject. Let's hear what he will say."—*Fairfax.* " I don't object to the answer, because it is the vindication of my College; I go further: and as, according to the rules of the Ecclesiastical Courts, a libel is given to the party that he may know the grounds of his accusation, I demand that libel; for I do not know otherwise wherefore

[1] 11 St. Tr. 593.   [2] Ibid. 592.

I am called here, and besides this affair should be discussed in Westminster Hall."—*Jeffreys*. "You are a Doctor of *Divinity*, not of *Law*."—*Fairfax*. "By what authority do you sit here?"—*Jeffreys*. "Pray, what commission have you to be so impudent in Court? This man ought to be kept in a dark room. Why do you suffer him without a guardian? Why did you not bring him to me? Pray let my officers seize him."[1]

Three members of the Ecclesiastical Commission were sent to Oxford to represent that formidable body, and they annulled the election of Hough, expelled the refractory Fellows, and made Magdalen College, for a time, a Popish establishment—the Court in London, under the presidency of Jeffreys, confirming all their proceedings.

The Lord Chancellor next involved the King in the prosecution of the Seven Bishops, which, more than any other act of misrule during his reign, led to his downfall.[2] On the 25th of April, 1688, a new "Declaration of Indulgence" came out under the Great Seal; and, that it might be the more generally known and obeyed, an order was sent from the Council to all Bishops in England, enjoining that it should be read by the clergy in all churches and chapels within their dioceses during divine service. A petition signed by Sancroft, the Archbishop, and six other prelates, was laid before the King, praying in respectful language that the clergy might be excused from reading the Declaration; not because they were wanting in duty to the Sovereign, or in tenderness to the dissenters, but because it was founded upon the dispensing power, which had often been declared illegal in parliament, and on that account they could not, in prudence, honor, or conscience, be such parties to it as the reading of it in the church would imply.

Even the Earl of Sunderland and Father Peter represented to the King the danger of arraying the whole Church of England against the authority of the Crown, and advised him that the Bishops should merely be admonished to be more compliant. But with the concur-

[1] 11 St. Tr. 1143—1148. 12 St. Tr. l. 26 n.
[2] In James's Memoirs, all the blame of this prosecution is thrown upon Jeffreys; but it is more probable that he only recklessly supported his master.

rence of Jeffreys he resolved to visit them with condign punishment, and they were ordered to appear before the Council, with a view to obtain evidence against them, as the petition had been privately presented to the King. When they entered the Council Chamber, Jeffreys said to them, "Do you own the Petition?" After some hesitation, the Archbishop confessed that he wrote it, and the Bishops that they signed it.—*Jeffreys*. "Did you publish it?" They, thinking he referred to the *printing* of it, of which the King had loudly complained, denied this very resolutely,—but they admitted that they had delivered it to the King at Whitehall palace, in the county of Middlesex.[1] This was considered enough to fix them with a publication, in point of law, of the supposed libel; and Jeffreys, after lecturing them on their disloyalty, required them to enter in a recognizance to appear before the Court of King's Bench, and answer the high misdemeanor of which they were guilty. They insisted, that, according to the Privileges of the House of Peers, of which they were members, they could not lawfully be committed, and were not bound to enter into the required recognizance. Jeffreys threatened to commit them to the Tower as public delinquents.—*Archbishop*. "We are ready to go whithersoever his Majesty may be pleased to send us. We hope the King of Kings will be our protector and our judge. We fear nought from man; and having acted according to law and our consciences, no punishment shall ever be able to shake our resolutions."

If this struggle could have been foreseen, even Jeffreys would have shrunk from the monstrous impolicy of sending these holy men to jail, on what would be considered the charge of temperately exercising a constitutional right in defense of the Protestant faith, so dear to the great bulk of the nation;—but he thought it was too late to resile. He, therefore, with his own hand, drew a warrant for their commitment, which he signed, and handed round the Board. It was signed by all the Councillors present, except Father Peter, whose signature the King excused—

---

[1] On their trial they were, after all, about to be acquitted for want of evidence, when Lord Sunderland was sent for, and proved a statement which had been made to him that they were going into the King's closet to present the Petition.

to avoid the awkward appearance of Protestant Bishops being sent to jail by a Jesuit.

It is not for me to relate the progress of these pious confessors to the Tower of London, or the interesting vicissitudes of their trial;[1] but there are some circumstances connected with their acquittal in which Jeffreys personally appears.

Seeing how he had acquired such immense favor, there were other lawyers who tried to undermine him by his own arts. One of the most formidable of these was Sir John Trevor, Master of the Rolls, who, some authors say, certainly would have got the Great Seal had James remained longer on the throne, but whom Jeffreys had hitherto kept down by reversing his decrees. The Chancellor's alarm was now excited by a report that Sir William Williams (who, from being Speaker of the last Westminster parliament, and fined £10,000 on the prosecution of the Duke of York, was become the caressed Solicitor-General to James II.) had a positive promise of the Great Seal if he could obtain a conviction of the Seven Bishops.[2] His brutal conduct to them during the whole trial, which was no doubt reported to Jeffreys, would confirm the rumor and increase his apprehensions. The jury having sat up all night in the Court of King's Bench without food, fire, or candle, to consider of their verdict, the Lord Chancellor, while they were still inclosed, had come down to Westminster Hall next morning, and taken his seat in his own Court. When he heard the immense shout arise which soon made the King tremble on Hounslow Heath, he smiled and hid his face in his nosegay—"as much," observes the relator of the anecdote, "as to say, *Mr. Solicitor, I keep my Seal.*"[3]

However, the part he had taken in sending the Bishops to the Tower, had caused such scandal, that the University of Oxford would not have him for their Chancellor, although in the prospect of a vacancy he had received

---

[1] 12 St. Tr. 183–433.

[2] The arrangement of counsel in this celebrated case was very whimsical. The Bishops were defended by Pemberton, the Ex-Chief Justice, who had presided at several of the late state trials, by Levinz, Sawyer, and Finch, who had conducted them very oppressively for the Crown, and by Polexfen, Treby, and Somers, considered steady Whigs.

[3] On the authority of Lord Hardwicke. See Yorke's *Tribes of Wales*, 110 n. 12 St. Tr. 183.

many promises of support. The moment the news arrived of the death of the old Duke of Ormond, his grandson was elected to succeed him: and next day a mandate coming from Court to elect Lord Jeffreys, an answer was returned, that an election had already taken place which could not be revoked.

Suspecting that things were now taking an unfavorable turn, he began privately to censure the measures of the Court, and to insinuate that the King had acted against his advice, saying, " It will be found that I have done the part of an honest man; but as for the Judges, they are most of them rogues."

About this time he was present at an event which was considered more than a counterpoise to recent discomfitures, but which greatly precipitated the crisis by taking away the hope of relief by the rightful succession of a Protestant heir.—Being suddenly summoned to Whitehall, he immediately repaired thither, and found that the Queen had been taken in labor. Other Councillors and many ladies of quality soon arrived, and they were all admitted into her bed-chamber. Her Majesty seems to have been much annoyed by the presence of the Lord Chancellor. The King calling for him, he came forward, and stood on the step of the bed to show that he was there. She then begged her consort to cover her face with his head and periwig; for she declared " she could not be brought to bed, and have so many men look on her." However, the fright may have shortened her sufferings; for James III., or " the Old Pretender," very speedily made his appearance, and the midwife having made the concerted signal that the child was of the wished-for sex, the company retreated.[1]

Considering the surmises which had been propagated ever since the Queen's pregnancy was announced, that it was feigned, and that a supposititious child was to be palmed upon the world, Jeffreys was lamentably deficient in duty to the King in not having recommended steps to convince the public from the beginning, beyond all possibility of controversey, of the genuineness of the birth.

[1] The attendance of Jeffreys at Whitehall on this occasion was celebrated in doggerel verse:—
" Then comes great George, of England Chancellor,
   Who was with expedition call'd to th' labor."

When the story of the "warming pan" had taken hold of the public mind, many witnesses were examined before the Privy Council to disprove it;[1] but it continued an article of faith with thorough Anti-jacobites during the two succeeding reigns.

The birth of a son, which the King had so ardently longed for, led to his speedy overthrow. Instead of the intrigues between the discontented at home and the Prince and Princess of Orange, hitherto regarded as his successors, being put an end to, they immediately assumed a far more formidable aspect. William, who had hoped in the course of a few years to wield the energies of Britain against the dangerous ambition of Louis XIV., saw that if he remained quiet he should with difficulty even retain the circumscribed power of Stadtholder of the United Provinces. He therefore gladly listened to the representations of those who had fled to Holland to escape from the tyranny exercised in their native country, or who sent secret emissaries to implore his aid; and he boldly resolved to come to England—not as a military conqueror, but for their deliverance, and to obtain the Crown with the assent of the nation. That he and his adherents might be protected against any sudden effort to crush them, a formidable fleet was equipped in the Dutch ports, and a considerable army, which had been assembled professedly for a different purpose, was ready on a short notice to be embarked in it.

James, who had been amusing himself by making the Pope godfather to his son, and had listened with absolute incredulity to the rumors of the coming invasion, suddenly became sensible of his danger, and, to avert it, was willing to make any sacrifice to please his people. The slender merit of the tardy, forced, and ineffectual concessions which were offered is claimed respectively by the apologists of the King, of Jeffreys, and of the Earl of Sunderland, but seems due to the last of the three. James's infatuation was transcendant,—he was so struck with judicial blindness,—being doomed to destruction, he was so demented, that, if let alone, he probably would have trusted with confidence to his divine right and the protection of the Virgin, even when William had landed at Torbay. As far as I can discover—from the time when

[1] 12 St. Tr. 123.

Jeffreys received the Great Seal, he never originated any measure, wise or wicked, and, without remonstrance, he heartily co-operated in all those suggested by the King, however illegal or mischievous they might be. I do not find the slightest foundation for the assertion that, with all his faults, he had a regard for the Protestant religion, which made him stand up in its defense. The "Declaration of Indulgence," to which he put the Great Seal, might be imputed to a love of toleration (to which he was a stranger), but what can be said of the active part he took in the High Commission Court, and in introducing Roman Catholics into the Universities and in the Church? The Earl of Sunderland, though utterly unprincipled, was a man of great discernment and courage: he could speak boldly to the King; and he had joined in objecting to the precipitate measures for giving ascendency to his new religion, which had produced this crisis. His seemingly forced removal from office he himself probably suggested, along with the other steps now taken to appease the people.

Whoever might first propose the altered policy, Jeffreys was the instrument for carrying it into effect, and thereby it lost all its grace and virtue. He took off the suspension of the Bishop of London, and, by a *supersedeas* under the Great Seal, abolished the High Commission Court. He annulled all the proceedings respecting Magdalen College, and issued the necessary proceedings for reinstating Dr. Hough and the Protestant Fellows. He put the Great Seal to a general pardon.

But the reaction was hoped for, above all, from the restoration of the City charters.[1] On the 2nd of October the Chancellor sent a flattering message to the Mayor and Aldermen to come to Whitehall in the evening, that they might be presented at Court by "their old Recorder." Here the King told them that he was mightily concerned for the welfare of their body, and that at a time when invasion threatened the kingdom, he was determined to show them his confidence in their loyalty, by restoring the rights of the City to the state in which they were before the unfortunate *quo warranto* proceedings had been instituted in the late reign. Accordingly, on the following day, a meeting of the Common Council was

[1] See Diary of second Lord Clarendon, 3rd Oct. 1688.

called at Guildhall, and the Lord Chancellor proceeded thither in his state carriage, attended by his purse-bearer, mace-bearer, and other officers, and, after a florid speech, delivered them letters patent under the Great Seal, which waived all forfeitures, revived all charters, and confirmed all liberties the City had ever enjoyed under the King or any of his ancestors. Great joy was manifested ; but the citizens could not refrain from showing their abhorrence of the man who brought these glad tidings—and on his return they hissed him, and hooted him, and gave him a foretaste of the violence he was soon to experience from an English mob.

It is said that, upon a rumor that the Prince of Orange had suffered some disaster, the King repented of these concessions, and ordered them to be recalled ; but, in truth, the assent of the Crown was expressed by the Chancellor to the restoration of Treby to the office of Recorder, and to the election of Sir John Shorter, a churchman, as Mayor, in the room of Eyles, an anabaptist, who had been appointed by the Crown, that he might be succeeded by a Roman Catholic. The forfeited and surrendered charters were likewise restored to the other corporations in England. These popular acts, however, were generally ascribed to fear, and the coalition of all parties, including the preachers of passive obedience, to obtain a permanent redress of grievances by force, continued resolute and unshaken.

When William landed, the frightful severities of Jeffreys in the West had the effect of preventing the populace from flocking to his standard, but he met with no opposition, and soon persons of great consideration and influence sent in their adhesion to him.

When we read in history of civil commotions and foreign invasions, we are apt to suppose that all the ordinary business of life was suspended. But on inquiry, we find that it went on pretty much as usual, unless where interrupted by actual violence. While the Prince of Orange was advancing to the capital, and James was marching out to give him battle—if his army would have stood true—the Court of Chancery sat regularly to hear "exceptions" and "motions for time to plead ;" and on the very day on which the Princess Anne fled to Nottingham, and her unhappy father exclaimed, in the extremity of his agony, "God help me! my own children have forsaken me," the Lord Chancellor decided, that "if an administrator pays a debt due by bond before a debt due by a decree in Equity, he is still liable to pay the debt due by the decree."[1]

Change of dynasty was not yet talked of, and the cry was for "a free parliament." To meet this, the King resolved to call one in his own name; and the last use which Jeffreys made of the Great Seal was by sealing writs for the election of members of the House of Commons, who were ordered to meet on the 15th of January following.[2]

This movement only infused fresh vigor into the Prince of Orange, who now resolved to bring matters to a crisis; and James finding himself almost universally deserted—as the most effectual way, in his judgment, of annoying his enemies—very conveniently for them, determined to leave the kingdom. Preparatory to this he had a parting interview with Jeffreys, to whom he did not confide his secret, but he obtained from him all the parliamentary writs which had not been issued to the sheriffs, amounting to a considerable number, and these, with his own hand, he threw into the fire—so that a lawful parliament might not be assembled when he was gone. To increase the confusion, he required Jeffreys to surrender the Great Seal to him—having laid the plan of destroying it, in the belief that without it the government could not be conducted.

All things being prepared, and Father Peter and the Earl of Melfort having been informed of his intentions, which he still concealed from Jeffreys,—on the night of the 10th of December, James, disguised, left Whitehall, accompanied by Sir Edward Hales, whom he afterwards created Earl of Tenterden. London Bridge (which they durst not cross) being the only one then over the Thames, they

---

[1] 24th Nov. 1688. 2 Vernon, 88, Searle v. Lane. By a reference to the minute-books in the Registrar's Office, it appears that Jeffreys sat again on Monday, Nov. 26th, when he decided Duval v. Edwards, a case on exceptions, nine in number, giving a separate judgment on each. He did not sit on the 27th, but he did on the 28th, which was the last day of Term. So late as the 8th of December he sat and heard several petitions. In the evening of this day the Great Seal was taken from him. The Court of Chancery was held by the Master of the Rolls and certain Masters up to Christmas.

[2] See diary of second Earl of Clarendon, Nov. 28, 29, 1688.

drove in a hackney-coach to the Horse Ferry, Westminster, and as they crossed the river with a pair of oars, the King threw the Great Seal into the water, and thought he had sunk with it for ever the fortunes of the Prince of Orange. At Vauxhall they found horses in readiness for them, and they rode swiftly to Feversham, where they embarked for France.

CHAPTER CII.

CONCLUSION OF THE LIFE OF LORD CHANCELLOR JEFFREYS.

INSTEAD of narrating the adventures of the monarch, when he was intercepted at Feversham, we must confine ourselves to what befell the unhappy Ex-Chancellor. He heard early next morning of the royal flight, and was thrown into a state of the greatest consternation. He was afraid of punishment from the new government which was now to be established, and being asked by a courtier if he had heard "what the *heads* of the Prince's declaration were?" he answered, "I am sure that my *head* is one, whatever the rest may be." He dreaded still more the fury of the mob, of which the most alarming accounts were soon brought him. In the existing state of anarchy, almost the whole population of the metropolis crowded into the streets in quest of intelligence;[1] the excitement was unexampled; there was an eager desire to prevent the King's evil counselors from escaping along with him; and many bad characters, under a pretense of a regard for the Protestant religion, took the opportunity to gratify their love of violence and plunder.

The first object of vengeance was Father Peter; but it was found that in consequence of the information of the King's intentions conveyed to him and the Earl of Melfort, they had secretly withdrawn the day before, and

[1] See Hubert's description to King John of the smith swallowing the tailor's news,—
"With his sheers and measure in his hand,
Standing on slippers, which his nimble haste
Had falsely thrust upon contrary feet."

were now in safety. The Pope's Nuncio was rescued from imminent peril by the interposition of the Lords of the Council, who had met, and exercising temporarily the powers of government, were striving to preserve the public tranquillity.

The next victim demanded was Jeffreys, who (no one knowing that the Great Seal had been taken from him) still went by the name of "the Chancellor," and who, of all professing Protestants, was most obnoxious to the multitude. He retired early in the day from his house in Duke-street to the obscure dwelling of a dependent in Westminster, near the river side,—and here, lying concealed, he caused preparations to be made for his escape from the kingdom. It was arranged that a coal-ship, which had delivered her cargo, should clear out from the Custom House as for her return to Newcastle, and should land him at Hamburg.

To avoid, as he thought, all chance of being recognized by those who had seen him in ermine or gold-embroidered robes, with a long white band under the chin, his collar of SS round his neck, and on his head a full-bottom wig, which had lately become the attribute of judicial dignity, instead of the old-fashioned coif, or black-velvet cap,—he cut off his bushy eyebrows, wont to inspire such terror,—he put on the worn-out dress of a common sailor, —and he covered his head with an old tarred hat that seemed to have weathered many a blast.[1]

Thus disguised, as soon as it was dusk he got into a boat; and the state of the tide enabling him to shoot London Bridge without danger, he safely reached the coal-ship, lying off Wapping. Here he was introduced to the captain and the mate, on whose secrecy he was told he might rely; but, as they could not sail till next day,— when he had examined his berth, he went on board another vessel that lay at a little distance, there to pass the night. If he had not taken this precaution, he would

---

[1] Other accounts, varying a little from this, were given of his disguise, as we learn from contemporary ballads:—

"He took a *collier's* coat to sea to go—
Was ever Chancellour arrayed so?"

"Jeffreys was prepared for sailing
In his *long tarpaulin gown;*
Where is now his furious railing,
And his blood-congealing frown?"

have been almost immediately in the power of his enemies. The mate, without waiting to see what became of him hurried on shore, and treacherously gave information to some person who had been in pursuit of him, that he was concealed in the Newcastle collier. They applied to Justices of the peace in the neighborhood for a warrant to arrest him,—which was refused, on the ground that no specific charge was sworn against him. They then went to the Lords of the Council, whom they found sitting, and who actually gave them a warrant to apprehend him for high treason,—under the belief that the safety of the state required his detention. Armed with this, they returned to the coal-ship in which he had taken his passage, but he was not there, and the captain, a man of honor, baffled all their inquiries.

He slept securely in the vessel in which he had sought refuge; and had it not been for the most extraordinary imprudence, leading to the belief that he was fated speedily to expiate his crimes, he might have effected his escape. Probably, with a view of indulging more freely his habit of intemperance, he next morning came ashore, and made his appearance at a little ale-house bearing the sign of "The Red Cow," in *Anchor and Hope Alley, near King Edward's Stairs, Wapping*,—and called for a pot of ale. When he had nearly finished it,—still wearing his sailor's attire, with his hat on his head, he was so rashly confident as to put his head out from an open window to look at the passengers in the street.[1]

I must prepare my readers for the scene which follows, by relating, in the words of Roger North, an anecdote of the behavior of Jeffreys to a suitor in the heyday of his power and arrogance. "There was a scrivener of Wapping brought to hearing for relief against a *bummery bond*.[2] The contingency of losing all being showed, the bill was going to be dismissed;[3] but one of the plaintiff's counsel said that the scrivener was a strange fellow, and sometimes went to church, sometimes to conventicles, and none

---

[1] To heighten the effect, some relate that the captain of the collier was in the mean time waiting for him, and that he lost the tide and his life by his love of drinking.

[2] "Bottomry bond." This contraction shows the etymology of an elegant English word from "bottom," which Dr. Johnson chooses to derive from the Dutch word "bomme."

[3] *i. e.* The principal being put in hazard, the interest was not usurious.

could tell what to make of him; and *it was thought he was a trimmer*. At that the Chancellor fired; and '*A trimmer!*' said he; '*I have heard much of that monster, but never saw one. Come forth, Mr. Trimmer—turn you round, and let us see your shape*,' and at that rate talked so long that the poor fellow was ready to drop under him; but at last the bill was dismissed with costs, and he went his way. In the hall one of his friends asked him how he came off? '*Came off*,' said he: 'I am escaped from the terrors of that man's face, which I would scarce undergo again to save my life, and I shall certainly have the frightful impression of it as long as I live.'"[1]

It happened, by a most extraordinary coincidence, that this very scrivener was then walking through *Anchor and Hope Alley* on the opposite side of the way, and immediately looking towards "The Red Cow," thought he recollected the features of the sailor who was gazing across towards him. The conviction then flashed upon his mind that this could be no other than the Lord Chancellor who had so frightened him out of his wits before pronouncing a decree in his favor about the "*bummery bond*." But hardly believing his own senses, he entered the tap-room of the ale house to examine the countenance more deliberately. Upon his entrance, Jeffreys must have recognized "the Trimmer;" for he coughed, turned to the wall, and put the quart-pot before his face. An immense multitude of persons were in a few minutes, collected round the door by the proclamation of the scrivener, that the pretended sailor was indeed the wicked Lord Chancellor Jeffreys. He was now in the greatest jeopardy, for unlike the usual character of the English mob, who are by no means given to cruelty, the persons here assembled were disposed at first to tear him limb from limb, and he was only saved by the interposition of some of the more considerate, who suggested that the proper course would be take him before the Lord Mayor.

The cry was raised, "To the Lord Mayor!" but before he could be secured in a carriage to be conveyed thither, they assaulted and pelted him;[2] and might have proceeded to greater extremities, if a party of the train-

---

[1] Life of Guilford, ii. 118.
[2] Some accounts say that he died of the wounds he now received, but I do not think that any serious injury was inflicted upon him.

bands had not rescued him from their fury. They still pursued him all the way with whips, and halters, and cries of "Vengeance! Justice! Justice!"[1] Although he lay back in the coach, he could still be discovered in his blue jacket, and with his sailor's hat flapped down upon his face.[2] The Lord Mayor, Sir John Chapman, a nervous, timid man, who had stood in tremendous awe of the Lord Chancellor, could not now see him, disguised as a sailor, without trepidation,—and instead of ordering him to stand at the bar of his justice-room,—with much bowing and scraping, and many apologies for the liberty he was using, requested that his Lordship would do him the honor to dine with him, as, it being now past twelve o'clock, he and the Lady Mayoress were about to sit down to dinner. Jeffreys, though probably with little appetite, was going to accept the invitation,—when a gentleman in the room exclaimed, " The Lord Chancellor is the Lord Mayor's prisoner, not his guest; and now to harbor him is treason, for which anyone, however high, may have to answer with his own blood." The Lord Mayor swooned away, and died (it is said of apoplexy) soon after.

The numbers and violence of the mob had greatly increased from the delay in examining the culprit, and they

[1] The feelings of the mob are thus described in some doggerel verses, which I copy for the epigrammic point at the end:—

"Limb him they would, as boys at Shrovetide do:
Some cried I am for a wing, an arm; for what are you?
I am for his head, says one; for his brains, says t'other;
And I am for his nose; his ears, another.
Oh, cries a third, I am for his buttocks brave;
Nine pounds of steaks from them I mean to have.
I know the rogue is fleshy, says a fourth,
His heart to me will be of greatest worth.
Yes, quoth another, but not good to eat,—
A heart of steel will ne'er prove tender meat."

A better specimen of the street ballads on this occasion contains the following lines:—

" Now you may hear the people as they scoure
Along, not fear to damn the Chancellore,
Then women, too, and all the tender crew
That used to pity, all now laugh at you."

[2] Burnet says, "*After many hours tossing him about*, he was carried to the Lord Mayor." But this seems to be a great exaggeration, for they must have arrived at the Lord Mayor's about mid-day; and, considering the season of the year, the discovery at Wapping could not have been much before nine in morning.—*O. T.* ii. 542.

loudly threatened to take the law into their own hand.¹
Some were for examining him before an Alderman, and
leading him out by a back way for that purpose; but he
himself showed most prudence by advising that, without
any previous examination, he should be committed to
the Tower for safe custody, and that two other regiments
of the train-bands should be ordered up to conduct him
thither. In the confusion, he offered to draw the warrant
for his own commitment. This course was followed, but
was by no means free from danger, the mob defying the
matchlocks and pikes of the soldiers, and pressing round
the coach in which the noble prisoner was carried, still
flourishing the whips and halters, and expressing their
determined resolution to execute summary justice upon
him for the many murders he had committed. Seeing the
imminent danger to which he was exposed, and possibly
conscience-struck when he thought he was so near his
end, he lost all sense of dignity, and all presence of mind.
He held up his imploring hands, sometimes on one side
of the coach, and sometimes on the other, exclaiming,
" For the Lord's sake, keep them off! For the Lord's
sake, keep them off!" Oldmixon, who was an eyewitness
of this procession, and makes loud professions of compassion for malefactors, declares that he saw these agon-
izing alarms without pity.²

The difficulty was greatest in passing the open space on
Tower Hill. But at length the carriage passed the draw-
bridge, and the portcullis descended. Within all was
still. Jeffreys was courteously received by Lord Lucas,
recently appointed Lieutenant, and in a gloomy apartment which he never more left, he reflected in solitude on

<blockquote>
" At fessi tandem cives, infanda furentem
Armati circumsistunt ipsumque domumque,
Atque ad supplicium præsenti morte reposcunt."
</blockquote>

² " I saw him and heard him, and, I truly say, without pity; though I
never saw any malefactor in this distress without compassion or concern."—
i. 762. I am afraid that Oldmixon would not have scrupled on this occasion
to act the part of Judge LYNCH.
" So dreadfully did his own insolence and barbarity recoil upon his own
head ; and so much was he to suffer as a criminal, who, as a Judge, had
brought such sufferings on others. Every face that he saw was the face of a
jury ; every grasp that he felt he had reason to think was that of the demon
that waited for him ; every voice that he could distinguish in so wild an up-
roar overwhelmed him with reproaches ; and his conscience echoed within
him that he deserved them all."—*Ralph*, i. 1063.

the procession which had just terminated,—so different from those to which he had been accustomed for some years on the first day of each returning Term, when, attended by the Judges and all the grandees of the law, he had moved in state to Westminster Hall, the envy and admiration of all beholders.

A regular warrant for his commitment was the same night made out by the Lords of the Council,[1] and the next day a deputation from their body, consisting of Lords North, Grey, Chandos, and Ossulston, attended to examine him at the Tower. Four questions were asked him. 1. "What he had done with the Great Seal of England?" He answered "that he had delivered it to the King on the Saturday before, at Mr. Cheffnel's, no person being present, and that he had not seen it since." He was next asked, 2. "Whether he had sealed all the writs for the parliament, and what he had done with them?" "To the best of his remembrance," he said, "the writs were all sealed and delivered to the King" (suppressing that he had seen the King throw a great many of them in the fire). 3. "Had he sealed the several patents for the then ensuing year?" He declared "that he had sealed several patents for the new Sheriffs, but that he could not charge his memory with the particulars." Lastly, he was asked "whether he had a license to go out of the kingdom." And to this he replied, "that he had several licenses to go beyond sea, which were all delivered to Sir John Friend." He subscribed these answers with an affirmation, that "they were true upon his honor,"—and the Lords withdrew.

But no sympathy did he meet with from any quarter, and he was now reproachfully spoken of even by the King, to please whom, he had "his eternal jewel given to the common enemy of man."[2] The news of the outbreak against him coming speedily to Feversham, the fugitive monarch, who then meditated an attempt to remount his throne, thought that his Chancellor might possibly be accepted by the nation as a scapegoat, and laid upon him

[1] This recited that he had been removed to the Tower at his own desire, to secure him from the violence of the people.

[2] What visions he had in the Tower we are not exactly told; but his career does strongly remind us of the stories of men selling themselves to the Devil for a term of prosperous fortune, and then being claimed according to the bond they had signed.

all the sins of his reign. It happened, strangely enough, that the Inn to which James had been carried when captured off Sheerness, was kept by a man on whom Jeffreys, for some supposed contempt of Court, had imposed a very heavy fine, which had not yet been levied. Complaining of this arbitrary act to his royal guest,—who had admitted him to his presence, and had asked him, in royal fashion, "his name, his age, and his history,"—James desired him to draw a discharge as ample as he chose,—and, establishing a precedent, which has been often followed since, for writing in a seemingly private and confidential document what is intended afterwards to be communicated to the public, he subjoined to his signature these remarkable words, which were immediately proclaimed in Feversham and transmitted to London, "I am sensible that my Lord Chancellor hath been a very ill man, and hath done very ill things."

Jeffreys was assailed by the press in a manner which showed how his cruelties had brutalized the public mind. A poetical letter, addressed to him, advising him to cut his own throat, thus concluded:—"I am your Lordship's OBEDIENT SERVANT in anything of this nature. From the little house over against Tyburn, where the people are almost dead with expectation of you."

This was followed by "A Letter from Hell from Lord Ch——r Jeffreys to L—— C—— B—— W——d." His "Confession," hawked about the streets, contained an exaggerated statement of all the bad measures of the latter part of the preceding, and of the present reign. Then came his "Last Will and Testament," commencing, "In the name of AMBITION, the only god of our setting and worshipping, together with CRUELTY, PERJURY, PRIDE, INSOLENCE, &c., I, George Jeffreys, being in sound and perfect memory, of high commissions, *quo warrantos*, dispensations, pillorizations, floggations, gibbetations, barbarity, butchery, &c., do make my last will," &c. Here is the concluding legacy:—"Item, I order an ell and a half of fine cambric to be cut into handkerchiefs for drying up all the wet eyes at my funeral; together with a half a pint of burnt claret for all the mourners in the kingdom."

When he had been some weeks in confinement, he received a small barrel, marked "Colchester Oysters," of which, ever since his arrival in London when a boy, he had been been particularly fond. Seeing it he exclaimed, " Well, I have some friends left still ;" but on opening it, the gift was—a halter !

An actual serious petition was received by the Lords of the Council of England, from "the widows and fatherless children in the West," beginning, " We, to the number of a thousand and more widows and fatherless children of the counties of Dorset, Somerset, and Devon; our dear husbands and tender fathers having been so tyrannously butchered and some transported; our estates sold from us, and our inheritance cut off, by the severe and brutish sentence of George, Lord Jeffreys, now we understand in the Tower of London a prisoner," &c. After enumerating some of his atrocities, and particularly dwelling upon his indecent speech (which I may not copy) to a young lady who asked the life of her lover convicted before him, the petitioners thus concluded :—" These, with many hundred more tyrannical acts, are ready to be made appear in the said counties by honest and credible persons, and therefore your petitioners desire that the said George Jeffreys, late Lord Chancellor, the vilest of men, may be brought down to the counties aforesaid, where we, the good women of the West, shall be glad to see him, and give him another manner of welcome than he had there three years since."

Meanwhile, the Great Seal, the *Clavis Regni*, the emblem of sovereign sway, which had been thrown into the Thames that it might never reach the Prince of Orange, was found in the net of a fisherman near Lambeth, and was delivered by him to the Lords of the Council, who were resolved to place it in the hands of the founder of the new dynasty ;[1] and James, after revisiting the capital,

---

[1] This fishing up of the Great Seal calls forth from Sir John Dalrymple the observation, " that Heaven seemed by this accident to declare that the laws, the constitution, and the sovereignty of Great Britain were not to depend on the frailty of man.

" Dum domus Æneæ Capitoli immobile saxum
  Accolet, imperiumque pater Romanus habebit."

Bishop Burnet represents that the Great Seal was not fished up till the following summer, his narrative displaying his usual inaccuracy and credulity. " A fisherman, between Lambeth and Vauxhall, was drawing a net pretty close to the channel : *and a great weight, not without some difficulty drawn to the shore*, which, when taken up, was found to be the Great Seal of England." One would suppose from this that " the Seal " was as large and heavy as a millstone, or at least as the fish whose name it bears,—whereas the fisherman

and enjoying a fleeting moment of popularity, had finally bid adieu to England, and was enjoying the munificent hospitality of Louis, at St. Germaine's.

The provisional government, in deference to the public voice, issued an order for the more rigorous confinement of the Ex-Chancellor, in the Tower, and intimated a resolution that he should speedily be brought to trial for his misdeeds; but amidst the stirring events which rapidly followed, he was allowed quietly to languish out the remainder of his miserable existence. While the elections were proceeding for the Convention Parliament—while the two Houses were struggling respecting the "abdication" or "desertion" of the throne—while men were occupied with discussing the "Declaration of Rights"—while preparations were making for the coronation of the new Sovereigns—while curiosity was keenly alive in watching their demeanor—and while alarms were spread by the adherence of Ireland to the exiled King—the national indignation, which at first burst forth so violently against the crimes of Jeffreys, almost entirely subsided, and little desire was evinced to see him punished as he deserved.

However, considerable sensation was excited by the news that he was no more. He breathed his last, in the Tower of London, on the 19th of April, 1689, at thirty-five minutes past four in the morning. Those who take a vague impression of events without attention to dates, may suppose, from the crowded vicissitudes of his career, that he must have passed his grand climacteric; but he was still only in the forty-first year of his age. Next day, many handbills, some in prose and some in verse, were hawked through the streets of London, pretending to give an account of his death, and of his character.[1]

could have experienced no difficulty in pulling home his net containing it, and could not have supposed that he had caught more than a good-sized trout.

[1] From the kindness of my friend, Mr. J. Payne Collier, the originals of two of these now lie before me, and I copy them for the amusement of the reader:—

"A FULL AND TRUE ACCOUNT OF THE DEATH OF
GEORGE, LORD JEFFRIES,
LATE LORD CHANCELLOR OF ENGLAND,
WHO DIED IN THE TOWER OF LONDON, APRIL 18th, 1689.
Licensed, April 18*th*.—JAMES FRASER.

We have no accounts that can be implicitly relied upon, either of the manner in which he passed his time during his imprisonment, or of the immediate cause of his death.

"Many and great have been the expectations of the people about the event of the commitment of the late Lord Chancellor to the Tower; and their wishes have been as various as they have been affected to him. Many (who had entertained a just indignation against him for his late ill conduct of affairs) longed for his being brought to his trial, that he might receive that justice that his irregularities that he was committed for were thought to have deserved. But divine Providence has disappointed them herein by calling him to a higher bar, where he must give a just account of all his actions, and receive the just reward that is due to him for the same unless he has prevented it by his repentance and God's infinite mercy.

"As to the manner of his death it was as followeth: He has been very much tormented with his old distemper, the stone and rheumatism, almost ever since he has been in the Tower, and there has not been any help wanting that skill or art could invent for the continuation of his life; but it has been all as ineffectual and vain as the supplications of the distressed were sometimes to him in the time of his power. For about this month last past he has been in a very languishing condition, still wasting away more and more, in which time he has hardly been in a capacity to take any thing to sustain nature, unless a little sack to revive it when it has been almost spent. About three weeks since he had a mind to a bit of salmon, which he had, but could not digest it, nor scarce any thing else unless a poached egg. So he continued decaying till the 18th of this instant, April, 1689, when, about half an hour after three in the morning, he died, in the forty-first year of his age; after having lived to see many ambitious designs disappointed, and their most gracious Majesties King William and Queen Mary seated on the throne: WHOM GOD LONG PRESERVE!"

"AN ELEGY
ON
SIR GEORGE JEFFREYS,
WHO DIED PRISONER IN THE TOWER OF LONDON, APRIL 18th, 1689.

"Poor widows' tears and begging orphans' cries
Sound forth his life, and sing his obsequies;
Then neither praise nor stigmatize his name,
His life 's indented on the wings of fame;
That fame which will his cruel deeds recall,
And make them fresh to generations all.

"But since Death's issues do belong to God,
Who makes such Judges oft a nation's rod,
Judge not his soul, for God (and only he)
In Christ can set the greatest sinners free."

EPITAPH.

"Here England's great Lord Chancellor is laid,
Who King and Kingdom, Church and State betray'd;
But may his crimes and bloodshed silent lie,
And ne'er against the English nation cry.

"At the request of the Widows of the West, whose husbands were hanged without trial by this Lord Chancellor."

Some say that he died of a broken heart; others, of repeated attacks of the stone, a disease under which he had long suffered ; others, that he killed himself by brandy;[1] and others, that he was visited by madness, and died like a furious wild beast. The last may be rejected as a fable, invented to please the lovers of the marvelous; and we may safely believe that he sunk under the combined effects of bodily pain, mental anguish, and habitual intemperance. It is said that he profited by the spiritual ministrations of Dr. John Scott, a pious divine, but that he never could be induced to express any contrition for his cruelties in the West,—laboring, in his dying hours, under the delusion that he was excused in the sight of God and man by the consideration, " that all the blood he had shed fell short of the King's demand."[2]

His body was buried privately in the Tower, where it remained quietly for some years. A warrant was afterwards signed by Queen Mary, while William was on the Continent, directed to the Governor of the Tower, "for his delivering the body of George, late Lord Jeffreys, to his friends and relations, to bury him as they think fit." On the 2nd of November, 1693, the body was disinterred, and buried a second time in a vault under the communion-table of St. Mary, Aldermanbury. In the year 1810, when the church was repaired, the coffin was inspected by the curious, and was found still fresh with the name of " Lord Chancellor Jeffreys " inscribed upon it.

Little remains to be said of him as a statesman or as a Criminal Judge. His acts, which I have detailed, show him in both capacities to deserve reprobation such as no language could adequately express. He can not, like his

[1] Oldmixon is the most positive as to this, representing the termination to his career as a Roman death. "He chose to save himself from a public death by large draughts of brandy, which soon dispatched him."—Oldm. *Hist.* i.

[2] For the last part of Jeffreys's career, see Memoirs of James, Echard, Rapin, Buckingham, Ralph, Oldmixon, Ellis's Corresp., North's Life of Guilford, Burnet, Dalrymple, M'Pherson. Throughout the whole of this memoir I have derived great assistance from the Life of Judge Jeffreys, by Humphry W. Woolwrich. "The Merciful Assize, or a Panegyric on the late Lord Jeffreys," though clever, is so much in the taste of satire, or rather lampoon, that I have placed no reliance upon it.

predecessors, Lord Clarendon and Lord Nottingham, be accused of bigotry, for all religious creeds as well as all political opinions seem to have been really indifferent to him, and in his choice of those which he professed he was guided only by his "desire to climb." Even the strong hatred against Dissenters which he affected when he had changed sides, he could (as in Rosewell's case), to please the government, entirely lay aside or suspend. From his daring and resolute character, he probably felt a genuine contempt for "a Trimmer," and having no personal antipathy to an opponent who boldly went into extremes like himself, his bile was excited by watching a struggle between conscience and convenience. The revival of the Court of High Commission is the only great unconstitutional measure which he has the credit of having originated; but there were no measures, however illegal or pernicious, proposed by Charles or James, to the execution of which he did not devotedly and recklessly abandon himself. England, happy in the integrity and mildness of her Judges in the 18th century, and in our own times,—during the Stuart reigns was cursed by a succession of ruffians in ermine, who, for the sake of Court favor, violated the principles of law, the precepts of religion, and the dictates of humanity;—but they were all greatly outstripped by Jeffreys, and though the infamous Scroggs, with whom his name is generally coupled, was next to him, there was a long interval between them.[1]

As a Civil Judge he was by no means without high qualifications, and in the absence of any motive to do wrong, he was willing to do right. He had a very quick perception, a vigorous and logical understanding, and an impressive eloquence. He must, at the bar, have severely felt his imperfect legal education, and his want of experience in civil cases.[2] He was quite young enough, when appointed Chief Justice, by industry to have, in a

[1] The following is his character, by Sir John M'Pherson, which, in quaint and affected terms, expresses much truth:—"A man of outrageous abilities and violent principles; bold and intrepid from a fixed disregard of the world; profligate from a contempt of virtue; fair only to those whom he feared; a tyrant to the unfortunate, and a fawning slave to the great."—*M'Pherson,* i. 402.

[2] We may judge of his reputation as a lawyer by Maynard's reply to him, when he had with his usual brutality, told the Sergeant opposed to him in a cause, that from his great age he had forgotten his law. "Yes, Sir George, I have forgotten more than you ever learned."

measure, supplied these defects; but, instead of sitting down to pore over the MS. treatises on Equity practice then in circulation, he spent his afternoons and evenings in intriguing against the Lord Keeper, or in carousing with his boon companions. When he had to decide questions respecting fines and recoveries, executory devises and contingent remainders, he could not resort, as on trials for treason, to the "fashionable doctrine of supporting the King's prerogative in its full extent, and without restriction or limitation,—which rendered, to such as espoused it, all that branch of the law called constitutional, extremely easy and simple."[1] Though not learned in his profession, what was wanting in knowledge he made up by positiveness, and he was very imperious with his colleagues as well as with the bar.

We find a number of his common-law judgments in Shower, Skinner, and 3 Modern; but law reporters give an inadequate notion of the demeanor of a Chief Justice, as they do not tell us what was furnished to him by others, and they generally suppress what falls from him that is inconsiderate. One of the best specimens of Jeffreys's judicial powers is his argument in the case of the East India Company against Sandys,[2] in which the question arose as to the validity of the charter giving to the plaintiffs the exclusive right of trading to all countries to the east of the Cape of Good Hope. Contrary to our notions on the subject, he insisted very elaborately and ingeniously that such a charter might be granted by the Crown, so as to create a monopoly, without any confirmation by parliament, and that the defendant by trading within the prescribed limits was liable to the action. Thus he concluded:—"The King by his charter makes the plaintiffs as it were his ambassadors to concert peace with the Indians, and Mr. Sandys has complained that he is not one of them. Because the King may pardon every offender, but will not pardon any highwayman now in Newgate, must these jail-birds therefore think themselves injured in their liberty and property? The Company have been at the trouble of discovering places, of erecting forts, of keeping forces, of settling factories, and of making leagues and treaties; and it would be against natural equity to wrest the benefits from them which they

[1] Fox's History of James II. c. 2.   10 St. Tr. 519.

have thus earned. Let there be judgments for the plaintiffs."[1]

When quite sober, he was particularly good as a Nisi Prius Judge. His summing up, in what is called "The Lady Ivy's case,"[2] an ejectment between her and the Dean and Chapter of St. Paul's, to recover a large estate at Shadwell, is most masterly. The evidence was exceedingly complicated, and he gives a beautiful sketch of the whole, both documentary and parol; and, without taking the case from the Jury, he makes some admirable observations on certain deeds produced by the Lady Ivy, which led to the conclusion that they were forged, and to a verdict for the Dean and Chapter.[3]

Considering the systematic form which Equity jurisprudence had assumed under his two immediate predecessors, Jeffreys must have been been very poorly furnished for presiding in Chancery. He had practiced little before these Judges, and none of their decisions were yet in print; so that if he had been so inclined, he had not the opportunity to make himself familiar with the established practice and doctrines of the Court. Roger North says, "he came to the Seal without any concern at the weight of the duty incumbent upon him; for at the first, being merry over a bottle with some of his old friends, one of them told him, that he would find the business heavy. '*No*,' said he, '*I'll make it light.*' "[4]

Although he must often have betrayed his ignorance, yet with his characteristic boldness and energy he contrived to get through the business without any signal disgrace, and among all the invectives, satires, and lampoons by which his memory is blackened, I find little said against his decrees. He did not promulgate any body of new orders according to recent custom; but, while he held the Great Seal, he issued separate orders from time to time, some of which were very useful. He first put an end to a very oppressive practice, by which a plaintiff, having filed a frivolous and vexatious bill, might dismiss it on paying merely 20s. costs, and he directed that the defend-

---

[1] It is curious to think that this is the company which has become the sovereign of one hundred millions of subjects. [2] 10 St. Tr. 555.
[3] Down to this time trials at Nisi Prius had not assumed their present shape. The issue being read to the Jury, the evidence was given, and with hardly any speeches from counsel, all seems to have been left to the Judge.
[4] Life of Guilford, ii. 120.

ant should be allowed all the costs he had incurred, to be properly ascertained by an officer of the Court.¹ He then checked the abuse of staying actions at law for the examination of witnesses abroad, by requiring, before a commission to examine them issued, an affidavit specifying the names of the witnesses, and the facts they were expected to prove.² By subsequent orders which he framed, vexatious applications for rehearings were guarded against, and an attempt was made to get rid of what has ever been the opprobrium of the Court,—controversies about settling the minutes of a decree after it has been pronounced.³

Vernon, the Chancery Reporter, has selected and dressed up a considerable number of his decisions, so as to make them appear respectable, and to be occasionally cited as authority at this day.⁴ As might be expected, Lord Chancellor Jeffreys was little inclined to defer to fixed rules which stood in his way, saying that "he had as good a right to make precedents to succeeding times as those who had gone before him had made precedents for him;⁵ and he showed a disposition to return to the old notion of the Chancellor's equitable jurisdiction by his observation, that "he was to make decrees according to his conscience, and every case was to stand upon its own bottom."⁶

I will give one or two short specimens of his style as an Equity Judge. In Hobley v. Weedon, a bill was filed against the devisee of an heir of the obligor, who had died after a verdict against him on the bond, but before final judgment. *Lord Chancellor.* "Dismiss the bill. There is no color of equity in the case, unless you will have it that the defendant died maliciously, before the day in bank, on purpose to defeat the plaintiff of his death."⁷

¹ 1 Vernon, 334. This matter is now regulated by 4 Anne, c. 15, s. 23. In the late case of Mendizabel v. Merchado, the Vice-Chancellor cited and acted upon this order. 2 S. & S. 484.
² Beames's Orders in Chancery, 265–288. ³ Ibid.
⁴ From p. 334 of vol. i. to the end, and from the beginning to p. 90 of vol. ii. in Hardwicke's "Tribes of Wales" (110 n.) we are told that he was considered the author of Vernon's Reports; which could not well be, as they come down to the year 1718, when he had been thirty years in his grave.
⁵ Burnet, ii. 236.
⁶ Earl of Rivers v. Earl of Derby, 2 Vern. 74.
⁷ 1 Vern. 400.

In Gale *v.* Lindo, A., on a treaty of marriage of his sister with B., let her have a sum of money, that her fortune might appear equal to what B. demanded, and took a bond from her to repay him; the executor of A. put the bond in suit against the executor of the sister, who survived her husband, and there being no defense at law, the bill was filed for relief. *Lord Chancellor.* "You admit the husband might have been relieved on a bill brought by him and his wife; that which was once a fraud will be always so; and the accident of the woman's surviving the husband will not better the case. Decree the bond to be delivered up, and a perpetual injunction against it."[1]

In the case of Sir Basil Firebras *v.* Brett, in which he granted an injunction against an action to recover money lost at play, he delivered an edifying discourse against gaming; for, notwithstanding his own practices, he was always most furious in denouncing the vices of others.[2]

In cases of great magnitude, he had the good sense to call in the assistance of the common-law Judges, and by the advice of Lord Chief Justice Beddingfield, and Lord Chief Baron Atkyns, he decreed that he had jurisdiction to enforce a trust of lands in Ireland, the trustees residing in England;[3] and by the advice of Lord Chief Justice Jones, and Lord Chief Baron Montague, that a grant of lands by the Crown might be set aside in equity on the ground of fraud.[4]

The oft-repeated compliment to bad Chancellors, "none of his decrees were reversed," is bestowed upon Jeffreys. I find only one appeal brought against a decree of his, and this, notwithstanding suspicion and prejudice, terminated to his honor. When his son was about to be married to the heiress of the late Earl of Pembroke, a suit was instituted to determine whether a large sum of money belonged to her or to her father's creditors. The Chancellor decided in her favor, and the marriage was celebrated. Loud and deep reflections were made upon the Judge's honesty, and a ballad came out with these lines—

"Old Tyburn must groan,
For Jeffreys is known
To have perjur'd his conscience to marry his son."

---

[1] 1 Vern. 475. See Kemp *v.* Coleman. Salk, 156.   [2] 1 Vern. 489.
[3] The Earl of Kildare *v.* Eustace, Ibid. 419.
[4] Attorney General *v.* Vernon, Ibid. 369.

But he had used the precaution to call in the assistance of the Master of the Rolls, Mr. Justice Lutwich, and Mr. Justice Powell, and though the appeal was heard after the Revolution, the decree was first affirmed by the Lords Commissioners of the Great Seal, and then by the House of Lords.[1]

The most weighty testimony in his favor is the Speaker, Onslow, who, from the tradition of Sir Joseph Jekyll, said, "he had great parts, and made a great Chancellor in the business of that Court. In mere private matters he was thought an able and upright Judge." But this can not outweigh the contemporary testimony against him—particularly that of an eye-witness, who, after candidly saying, "When he was in temper, and matters indifferent came before him, he became his seat of justice better than any other I ever saw in his place," adds, "he seemed to lay none of his business to heart, nor care what he did or left undone; and spent in the Chancery Court what time he thought fit to spare. Many times, on days of causes at his house, the company have waited five hours in a morning, and after eleven he hath come out inflamed and staring as one distracted."[2]

He was excusably annoyed by the custom, which seems then to have prevailed, of having on the same side a great host of counsel, who necessarily repeated each other. "It was troublesome," he said,—"it was impertinent,—he could not bear it." His occasional rudeness to counsel appears incredible. Mr. Wallop, a gentleman of eminence at the bar, who defended the famous Richard Baxter, arguing against the opinion expressed by the Court upon the construction of a writing, Jeffreys said, "Mr. Wallop, I observe you are in all these dirty causes; and were it not for you gentlemen of the long robe, who should have more wit and honesty than to support and hold up these factious knaves by the chin, we should not be at the pass we are at." *Mr. Wallop:* "My Lord, I humbly conceive that——" *Jeffreys:* "You humbly conceive! and I humbly conceive! Swear him! swear him!" Mr. Bradbury, a junior counsel, having ventured to make an observation, which was received with courtesy, as it agreed with my Lord's view of the case, was by this encouraged to follow his leader in supporting a new ob-

---
[1] 2 Vern. 51, 213.   [2] Life of Lord Guilford, ii. 118.   11 St. Tr. 499.

jection thought by his Lordship not to be tenable. *Jeffreys:* "Lord, Sir! you must be cackling, too. We told you your objection was very ingenious; that must not make you troublesome; you can not lay an egg but you must be cackling over it."[1]

Attorneys fared much worse. When they did anything to displease him, he gave them what he called "a lick with the rough side of his tongue;" and he "terrified them with his face and voice, as if the thunder of the day of judgment broke over their heads." He had to decide upon a Petition against a great City attorney with whom he used to get drunk, and who had given him a great many briefs at Guildhall when still obscure; and one of the affidavits swore, that when the attorney was threatened with being brought before my Lord Chancellor, he exclaimed, "My Lord Chancellor! I *made* him!" —meaning that he had laid the foundation of his fortune by bringing him early into City business. *Jeffreys:* "Well! then will I lay my MAKER by the heels." He thereupon instantly ordered a commitment to be made out, and sent off his old friend to the Fleet.[2]

But "he would drink and be merry, kiss and slaver with these boon companions over night, and the next day fall upon them ranting and scolding with insufferable virulence."[3] I rather find an inclination to praise him as a civil lawyer, which I can only explain from the desire to assume an air of impartiality, and to make a contrast between his actual bad qualities and the good ones invented for him; but I believe, take him for all in all, that in civil cases, as well as in criminal, he was, in the words of Mr. Justice Foster, "the very worst Judge that ever disgraced Westminster Hall."

The manner in which Jeffreys, while Chancellor, attacked the independence of the Judges, was most out-

[1] 10 St. Tr. 626.
[2] Life of Guilford, ii. 118. "I was under the painful necessity of relating this anecdote in my argument in Stockdale *v.* Hansard to show that Judges might abuse their privileges as well as the House of Commons."—*Lord Campbell's Speeches*, 128.
[3] Very different from Lord Mansfield's vengeance on Dr. Brocklesby, the famous physician, who, having met him in society overnight, and being examined before him in Court next morning, chose to be offensively familiar. *Lord Mansfield, summing up to the Jury*—"Gentlemen, the next witness is one Rocklesby or Brocklesby, Brocklesby or Rocklesby, and, first, he swears that he is a physician."

rageous. The trial of the Seven Bishops coming on, he removed from the office of Chief Justice of the King's Bench, Sir Edward Herbert, who might have been expected to be tolerably subservient, to make room for his creature, Sir Robert Wright, so notoriously incompetent from ignorance, stupidity, and immorality, that the courtly Lord Keeper Guilford had long withstood the wish of Charles II. to make him a puisne Baron of the Exchequer.

When the question of the dispensing power arose upon issuing the last Declaration of Indulgence, Jeffreys showed a fixed purpose to obtain a unanimous opinion of the Judges in favor of it. He first summoned the reluctant ones to Chiffinch's lodgings at Whitehall, to talk over the subject with himself and the King, assisted by Sunderland, Rochester, and Godolphin. Baron Nevil tried to escape by saying that he would consider of it, but to a peremptory question declared against the prerogative. Jeffreys, by sending for him to his own house in Duke Street, still tried to bend him—and finding him inflexible, forwarded to him his quietus. Sir Thomas Street, a Judge of the Common Pleas, and that most able and upright man, Sir John Powell, a Judge of the King's Bench, being labored in the same manner to as little purpose, shared the same fate—Powell, on account of his high character, having a respite till the end of the term, from Jeffreys, who went so far as to say "he was sorry so good a Judge should be turned out for so trifling a cause."[1] He was quite indifferent as to the qualifications of their successors if they were obedient to his will, and it became necessary for William to make a sweeping change on the Bench as one of the first acts of the new reign.[2]

I have discovered one benevolent opinion of this cruel Chancellor, and, strange to say, it is at variance with that of the humane magistrates who have adorned Westminster Hall in the nineteenth century. "The Prisoners' Counsel Bill" was condemned and opposed by almost all

---

[1] These facts came out from an examination of the Judges before a committee of the House of Commons after the Revolution.

[2] It was then that Holt was made Chief Justice of the King's Bench, and Atkyns, Dolben, Gregory, and John Powell, who had been removed during the two preceding reigns for their honesty, being restored to the Bench, the Courts were presided over by the best set of Judges that Westminster Hall has ever seen.

the Judges in the reign of William IV., yet even Jeffreys was struck with the injustice and inequality of the law, which, allowing the accused to defend himself by counsel "for a two-penny trespass," refuses that aid "where life, estate, honor, and all are concerned," and lamented its existence while he declared himself bound to adhere to it.[1] The venerable sages who apprehended such multiplied evils from altering the practice must have been greatly relieved by finding that their objections have proved as unfounded as those which were urged against the abolition of "*peine forte et dure;*" and the alarming innovation, so long resisted, of allowing witnesses for the prisoner to be examined under the sanction of an oath.

Jeffreys only sat in parliament for a few weeks, and all we know of his performances there is that he bullied his predecessor, Lord Keeper Guilford, and that he himself broke down when, by his indiscriminating arrogance, he had set all the Peers of England against him. He was nearly the only Chancellor of the seventeenth century who was not an author; but we can not trace to him the publication even of a speech, a pamphlet, or a law tract.

We have no very distinct account of him in domestic life. Having lost his first wife, whom he had espoused so generously, within three months from her death he again entered the married state. The object of his choice was the widow of a Montgomeryshire gentleman, and daughter of Sir Thomas Bludworth, who had been Lord Mayor of London, and for many years one of the City representatives. I am sorry to say there was much scandal about the second Lady Jeffreys, and she presented him prematurely with a full-grown child. It is related that he was once disagreeably reminded of this mistake: when cross-examining a flippant female, he said to her, "Madam, you are very quick in your answers." "Quick as I am, Sir George," cried she, "I was not so quick as your lady."[2] Even after the marriage she is still said to

[1] 10 St. Tr. 267.
[2] The following is an extract from a long poem published on the occasion, in February, 167, :—

    "When old St. George did dragon slay,
    He sav'd a maid from cruel fray;
    But this Sir George, whom knaves do brag on,
    Mist of the maid, and caught the dragon.
    Marriage and hanging both do go

have encouraged Sir John Trevor, M.R., and other lovers, while her husband was indulging in his cups.

"He had a set of banterers for the most part near him, as in old times great men kept fools to make them merry. And these fellows, abusing one another and their betters, were a regale to him."[1] But there can be no doubt that he circulated in good society. He was not only much at Court, but he exchanged visits with the nobility and persons of distinction in different walks of life. In the social circle, being entirely free from hypocrisy and affectation,—from haughtiness and ill-nature,—laughing at principle,—courting a reputation for profligacy,—talking with the utmost freedom of all parties and all men,—he disarmed the censure of the world,—and, by the fascination of his manners, while he was present, he threw an oblivion over his vices and his crimes.

The second Earl of Clarendon, shortly before the landing of the Prince of Orange, having visited him at Bulstrode, his country seat, on some business, which could not be entered upon by the default of absentees, gives us in his diary the following account of the manner in which the Chancellor amused him till the hour for the banquet. "I went in his calash with him. He talked very freely to me of all affairs; called the Judges a thousand fools and knaves; that Chief Justice Wright was a beast.[2] He said the King and Queen were to dine with him on Thursday next; that he had still great hopes the King would be moderate when parliament met.[3] When we came to Dr. Hickman's my Lord was inclined to be merry; saying he had papists and spies among his own servants, and therefore must be cautious at home."

From Sir John Reresby we learn how very pleasant (if not quite decorous) must have been his parties in Duke Street. "I dined with the Lord Chancellor, where the Lord Mayor of London was a guest, and some other

> By destiny. Sir George, if so,
> You stand as fairly both to have
> As ever yet did fool or knave.
> What then, you fool? Some wives miscarry
> And reckon June for January."

[1] Life of Guilford, ii. 117.

[2] This is the man he had just made Chief Justice of the King's Bench to try the Seven Bishops.

[3] The parliament about to be called when the Prince of Orange was approaching.

gentlemen. His Lordship having, according to custom, drank deep at dinner, called for one Mountford, a gentleman of his, who had been a comedian, an excellent mimic; and to divert the company, as he was pleased to term it, he made him plead before him in a feigned cause, during which he aped the Judges and all the great lawyers of the age in their tone of voice, and in their action and gestures of body, to the very great ridicule, not only of the lawyers, but of the law itself, which to me did not seem altogether so prudent in a man in his lofty station in the law: diverting it certainly was, but prudent in the Lord Chancellor I shall never think it."[1]

On one occasion, dining in the City with Alderman Duncomb, the Lord Treasurer and other great Courtiers being of the party, they worked themselves up to such a pitch of loyalty by bumpers to "Confusion to the Whigs," that they all stripped to their shirts, and were about to get upon a sign-post to drink the King's health, when they were accidentally diverted from their purpose, —and the Lord Chancellor escaped the fate which befell Sir Charles Sedley, of being indicted for indecently exposing his person in the public streets. But this frolic brought upon him a violent fit of the stone, which nearly cost him his life.[2]

I should have expected that, boldly descending to the level of his company and conscious of great mental power, he would have despised flattery; but it is said that none could be too fulsome for him, and this statement is corroborated by some Dedications to him still extant. The pious author of the "History of Oracles and the Cheats of the Pagan Priests,"[3] after lauding his great virtues and actions, thus proceeds:—" Nor can the unthinking and most malicious of your enemies reproach your Lordship with self-interest in any of your services, since all the world knows that when they were thought criminal, nay, even punishable,—you had nothing left you but HONOR, JUSTICE, and INNOCENCE."

He was not only famous, like the Baron of Bradwardine,

[1] Sir John Reresby, 229.
[2] Ibid. 231. The warmest defense I find of his sobriety is by Bevil Higgins, in his Review of Burnet's History, who says, " If my Lord Jeffries exceeded the bounds of temperance now and then in an evening, it does not follow that he was drunk on the Bench and in council."—Vol. ii. 263.
[3] Published in 1668.

for his *chansons à boire*, but he had a scientific skill in music, of which we have proof at this day. There being a great controversy which of the two rival organ-builders, Smith or Harris, should be the artist to supply a new organ to the Temple Church, it was agreed that each should send one on trial, and that the Lord Chancellor should decide between them. He decreed for Smith,—the deep and rich tones of whose organ still charm us. Harris's went to Wolverhampton, and is said to be of hardly inferior merit.[1]

There is an anecdote related of him respecting his interference in a contested election, which, however extraordinary, is rather characteristic in some of its circumstances, and I am not at liberty to reject it. The scene is laid at Arundel, where, upon a vacancy in the representation, there was a keen struggle, to which the government attached great importance,—and Jeffreys, who had recently got the Great Seal, was asked to go down to countenance the Tory candidate. He not only did so, but entered the Town Hall while the poll was going forward, and the Mayor, who was the returning officer, having rejected a Tory voter, he rose in a great passion, and contending imperiously that the vote was clearly good, insisted upon it being admitted. The Mayor tried to silence him.—*Jeffreys*. "I am the Lord Chancellor of this realm."—*Mayor*. "Impossible! were you the Lord Chancellor, you know that you have nothing to do here where I alone preside. Officers, turn that fellow out of Court." Jeffreys, for once abashed, withdrew to his inn, and wishing to hush the matter up, in the evening asked the Mayor to sup with him. The virtuous magistrate declining this suspicious honor, the Chancellor boldly went to his house, and introducing himself, said, "Sir, notwithstanding we are in different interests, I can not help revering one who so well knows and dares so nobly execute the law; and though I myself was somewhat degraded thereby, you did but your duty. You, as I have learned, are independent, but you may have some relation who is not so well provided for; if you have, let me enjoy the pleasure of presenting him with a considerable place in my gift now vacant." This was irresistible; his worship said he had a nephew to whom the place, which his Lord-

---

[1] Granger's Biog. Hist. by Noble, ii. 363.

ship so generously offered, would be very suitable, and the appointment was immediately made out and signed.[1]

He had never forgiven his father for so obstinately wishing to make him a tradesman, and uttering such sinister prophecies as to the termination of his career, and he had not visited or corresponded with him since the riotous assault upon Acton when he was Chief Justice of Chester.[2] Become a Peer and Lord High Chancellor, he intimated, in the long vacation of 1686, an intention of coming to ask his father's blessing; but the venerable Squire, hurt by past neglect, shocked by the stories of his son which reached his ears, and thinking that George was now actuated merely by a desire to show his greatness in his native place, harshly refused to receive him, and sent him a blessing, with a prayer for his reformation.

It is said that, shortly before the coming of the Prince of Orange, the Chancellor was in such high favor that he was about to be raised to an Earldom. Some assert that the patent was prepared and was ready to pass the Great Seal; and there certainly was extant, in the middle of the last century, a book entitled " Dissertatio Lithologica, auctore Joanne Grœnevelt, Transisalano, Daventriensi M. D. E. Col. Med. Lond.," dedicated " Honoratissimo Domino, D. Georgio Comiti Flintensi, Vicecomiti de Wickham, Baroni de Wem, supremo Angliæ Cancellario, et serenissimo Jacobo Secundo, Regi Angliæ a secretioribus Consiliis." If the Dutch fleet had met with a storm, he might have lived and died Earl of Flint, and then who can tell whether he would not have appeared in different colors to posterity?

He had children by both his wives; but of these only one son grew up to manhood, and survived him. This was John, the second Lord Jeffreys, who has acquired celebrity only by having rivaled his father in the power of drinking, and for having, when in a state of intoxication, interrupted the funeral of Dryden, the poet. He was married, as we have seen, to the daughter of the Earl of Pembroke, but dying in 1703, without male issue, the title of Jeffreys happily become extinct. He soon dissipated large estates, which his father, by such unjustifiable

---

[1] Wool. 310. [2] Ante, p. 325.

means, had acquired in Shropshire, Buckinghamshire, and Leicestershire.[1]

On the meeting of the Convention Parliament attempts were made to attaint the late Chancellor Jeffreys,—to prevent his heirs from sitting in parliament,—and to charge his estates with compensation to those whom he had injured;—but they all failed, and no mark of public censure was set upon his memory beyond excepting him, with some other Judges, from the act of indemnity passed at the commencement of the new reign.

In his person he was rather above the middle stature, his complexion (before it was bloated by intemperance) inclining to fair, and he was of a comely appearance. There was great animation in his eye, with a twinkle which might breed a suspicion of insincerity and lurking malice. His brow was commanding, and he managed it with wonderful effect, whether he wished to terrify or to conciliate. There are many portraits of him, all, from his marked features, bearing a great resemblance to each other, and, it may be presumed, to the original. The best was by Sir Godfrey Kneller, painted in 1687, and hung up in the Inner Temple Hall. Although that society had been eager to show their respect for him when he was made Chancellor, and voted £50 for a full length of him in his robes, that during dinner the students might be stimulated to imitate his conduct in the hope of reaching his elevation,—when misfortune overtook him, the Benchers, expecting a visit from King William and Queen Mary, ordered it to be taken down and hid in a garret. There it remained till the year 1695, when, at "a parliament," the following resolution was passed:—"That Mr. Treasurer do declare to the Lord Jeffreys that, at his Lordship's desire, the House do make a present to his Lordship of his father's picture, now in Mr. Holloway's

---

[1] Nichols's Leicestershire, i. 114. In Yorke's "Life and Character of the late Lord Chancellor Jeffreys," he observes:—"He left only one son, and with him ended the name, the honor, and the estate, and this in so short a time, that some of those very servants who had lived with the Chancellor when he was hardly worth a shilling, and lived to see him acquire an estate of twelve thousand a year, continued still in the family, till the whole was spent and squandered."

———"Qui nimios obtabat honores,
Et nimias poscebat opes, numerosa parabat
Excelsæ turris tabulata, unde altior esset
Casus, et impulsæ præceps immane ruinæ."

chambers, who is desired to deliver the same to his Lordship or his order." The son accepted the ungracious present, and sent it to Acton; but it was swept away with other family portraits, to pay his debts.

An engraving of the father was published soon after his capture at Wapping, which had a prodigious sale, as it represented "the Lord Chancellor taken in disguise and surrounded by the mob." [1]

A very few sentences will be sufficient to notice the changes in the law, and the manner in which it was administered, in the reign of James II. His single parliament sat only for a few weeks, and the only legislative improvement upon our jurisprudence attempted was the enactment, that in case of a son dying intestate and without children, after the death of his father, the personal property, instead of all going to the mother, shall be divided in equal portions between her and the brothers and sisters of the intestate.[2] Of judge-made law (which always bears a large proportion to parliamentary[3]) there was great abundance, but it was of the worst quality, and happily, a great part of it was speedily overturned. Jeffreys presiding in the Court of Chancery, and Wright in the King's Bench, their brethren were of the same stamp,—men of learning and independence being chased from the Bench ; and not only was the King's power to dispense with laws carried to an extent which, if acquiesced in, would have established a pure despotism, but private rights and private property were becoming insecure, and all those objects were endangered for the preservation of which civil government is established. However, James would subvert the religion as well as the liberties of his subjects, and he was hurled from the throne.

It is consoling to me to think that, after the irksome

[1] I have in my possession a copy of a similar print that was published in Holland, where the fate of Jeffreys seems to have excited almost as much interest as in his own country. It is entitled " DE LORD CANTZELIER WERD GEDEGUISKERT, in Wapping gevangen." Jeffreys is dressed like a Dutch sailor with several pairs of breeches on, surrounded and hustled by officers of justice and the populace. Out of their mouths severally are coming the following words :—" Wel broer Peters wat segje nu ;" " By Jaen neen fult hangen ;" " Denkt opt Westen ;" " Heugdu d'Heer Cornish ;" " Denkt opt de Bischoppe ;" " Slaahem de kop in ;" " Denktan St. Magdalena Coll." Being thus reproached with his misdeeds, the words come from his own mouth, " Scheurd my aar stukken."   [2] 1 Jac. 2, c. 17, s. 7.

[3] Pemberton, C. J., used to boast that, "in making law, he had outdone King, Lords, and Commons."

task of relating the actions of so many men devoid of political principle, and ready to suggest or support any measures, however arbitrary or mischievous, for the purpose of procuring their own advancement,—a brighter prospect now opens, and I see rising before me, Chancellors distinguished for their virtues as well as for their talents. To preserve the essential distinctions between right and wrong, to consult the best interests of mankind, I am obliged to expose to reprobation such characters as Shaftesbury, Guilford, and Jeffreys; but it will be far more congenial to my feelings to present for applause and imitation a Somers, a Cowper, a King, and a Hardwicke.

CHAPTER CIII.

LORDS COMMISSIONERS OF THE GREAT SEAL ON THE ACCESSION OF WILLIAM AND MARY; AND LIFE OF LORD COMMISSIONER MAYNARD, FROM HIS BIRTH TILL THE REVOLUTION OF 1688.

THE interregnum, which began on the 10th of December, 1688, when James II. fled from London, after throwing the Great Seal into the Thames, ceased on the 13th of February, 1689, when the Prince and Princess of Orange, accepting the tender of the crown from the Lords and Commons, under the conditions specified in the " Declaration of Rights," were proclaimed King and Queen. Most of the high offices of state were immediately filled up; and nearly all the common-law Judges being very properly removed on account of their corruption and insufficiency, the Bench was replenished with a most excellent new set,—Holt being at their head, as Chief Justice of England. So far no difficulty was experienced in determining and executing what was fit to be done in Westminster Hall. But much doubt and hesitation arose respecting the disposition of the Great Seal.

A rumor was propagated, which I think rests on no sufficient grounds, that it was seriously offered—with the title of Lord Chancellor—first to Lord Nottingham, and then to Lord Halifax; and that they both declined it.¹ The perversion of law, through the instrumentality of corrupt courts, having mainly brought about the Revolution, William and his ministers were anxious above all things to obtain credit for a satisfactory administration of justice, and it would require strong evidence to convince us that they proposed appointments to which the public could hardly have submitted under the exiled sovereign. Equity had now assumed a systematic form; the decisions of the Chancellor were reported and cited as authority, like those of the common-law Judges; Guilford and Jeffreys, however venal where the Crown was concerned, were regularly trained lawyers, and they were capable of deciding satisfactorily between subject and subject. It is impossible, therefore, that, to please Tories or Whigs, there could have been any real intention of placing as Supreme Judge in the Court of Chancery any nobleman, however respectable, who had, from the day of his leaving the University, devoted the whole of his time to fashionable amusement or political intrigue. I believe, upon the accession of William, it was resolved as a permanent arrangement, instead of a single Judge presiding in the Chancery, to resort to the plan adopted during the Commonwealth, of having several Judges sitting there co-ordinately,—after the model of the common-law Courts.²

Recollecting the fantastical as well as arbitrary acts of which late Chancellors had occasionally been guilty, "single-seated justice"³ was then in great disrepute; and very fallacious hopes were entertained that the long-standing evils of the Court of Chancery might be cured by severing it from all connection with politics, and appointing to the bench there several deep lawyers who should have nothing to distract them from their judicial duties.⁴

¹ See 3 Kennet, 550. 3 Burnet, O. T. 4.
² On examining the Books of the Privy Council, I find the following order, made so early as 18th February, 1688-89:—
"Present,
"The King's Most Excellent Majesty, &c.
"It is this day ordered by his Majesty in Council, that Mr. Aaron Pingrey, one of the Clerks of the Petty Bag in Chancery, do cause copies forthwith to be made of all commissions that were granted by Oliver, the Protector, for custody of the Great Seal, and send them to Sir Robert Atkyns for his perusal."
³ The Benthamite term for a tribunal with a single judge.
⁴ It has been said that the reason for putting the Great Seal into commis-

Accordingly on the 4th of March, Sir JOHN MAYNARD, *Anthony Keck, Esq.*, and *Mr. Sergeant Rawlinson*, were named Lords Commissioners of the Great Seal. On the following day they were sworn in before the King in Council at Whitehall, and the two last received the honor of knighthood.¹

Keck and Rawlinson are wholly uninteresting characters, and there could be no amusement or instruction in recording the dates of their birth, of their going to the university, of their being called to the bar, and of their death—which would comprehend the whole of their known history, beyond their accidental appointment to their present office.² But the career of the first Lord Commissioner is very curious, were it for nothing else than that it lasted much longer than that of any other English lawyer or statesman, as he had been called to the bar and sat in the House of Commons in the year 1625, in the very beginning of the reign of Charles I., and he held a high office in the law, and was a member of the House of Commons, in the year 1690, in the second year of the reign of William and Mary. Having been engaged in the most important state trials during that period—having been a representative of the people in every intermediate parliament, whether held by Kings or Protectors—having assisted in passing the "Bill of Rights," as well as the "Petition of Right."—having seen the government carried on by prerogative for many years without popular assemblies,—the constitution first reformed and then subverted by the Long Parliament—the vicissitudes of the civil war—the trial and execution of the King—the establishment of mili-

sion was to multiply offices; but Keck and Rawlinson were men without political claims or influence.

¹ "At the Court at Whitehall, the 5th of March, 1688-89.
"Present,
"The King's Most Excellent Majesty.
"The Right Honorable Sir John Maynard, Knight, having taken the oaths enjoined to be taken by the late act of parliament, instead of the oaths of allegiance and supremacy, was this day, by His Majesty's command, sworn one of the Lords Commissioners for the custody of the Great Seal of England." A similar entry follows with respect to each of the other two, with the addition of the words, "and at the same time received the honor of knighthood from his Majesty."—*Books of Privy Council.* See also Crown Off. Min. Book, fol. 131. 2 Vernon's Rep. 95.

² "Their name, their years, spelt by the unlettered muse,
The place of fame and elegy supply."

tary despotism—the recall of the ancient dynasty—two turbulent reigns, in which the voice of the law and the lessons of experience were despised—he lived to see the Stuarts forever banished from their native country, and the foundation laid of a constitutional monarchy, which still flourishes, and has conferred upon Britons a greater degree of civil and religious freedom, and of public prosperity than ever fell to the lot of any other nation.

This remarkable man—reminding us of the patriarchal race, who could plant an acorn, and recline under the spreading boughs of the unwedgeable and gnarled oak which sprang from it—was the eldest son of Alexander Maynard, Esq., a gentleman of good family, in the county of Devon.[1] He was born at Tavistock, in the year 1602. At the age of 16 he was entered of Exeter College, Oxford, where he took the degree of A.B. We have no account of his academical habits, but his eager and dogged love of application was innate, and must have early marked him for eminence. Being destined to the legal profession, he was removed to the Middle Temple, where luckily he found a set of hard reading men, including Noy, Selden, and Rolle. Now he acquired that taste for black-letter law which stuck by him through life, and made him prefer the "YEAR BOOKS" to *Shakespeare* or *Ben Jonson*, insomuch that when he grew rich and kept his coach, he never took an airing in it without having a volume of these Reports as a companion, and he solaced his old age by publishing an edition of them.[2] At the same time he was a diligent attender at "moots," and labored to acquire the faculty of prompt speaking, according to his noted saying, which he was fond of repeating to his dying day, that "the Law is ARS BABLATIVA."[3]

On account of his extraordinary proficiency, he was called to the bar before the usual curriculum of study at his inn of court had expired; and his countrymen in the West being proud of him, and pushing him on, he got into practice much more rapidly than he otherwise would

---

[1] I do not find any relationship stated between the Devonshire Maynards and the Essex family of the same name, ennobled by Charles I., and represented by the present Viscount Maynard.

[2] Roger North thus describes Maynard's well known passion for the Year Books. "He had such a relish of the old Year Books, that he carried one in his coach to divert his time in travel, and said he chose it before any comedy. Life of Guilford, i. 28.   [3] Ibid. ii. 27.

have done, notwithstanding all his merits.[1] He likewise derived great advantage from the patronage of Noy, to whom he was recommended by his industry and acuteness, and he had the reputation of being the chief favorite of the future inventor of ship money. However, he was not by any means injured by "prepropera praxis." Every case intrusted to him he studied profoundly, and whatever leisure he enjoyed from the business of his clients, he devoted to his law books, that he might keep up and extend his stock of legal lore. Ever familiar with the ancient history as well as with the newest fashions of the law, he could, from his retentive memory, his copious common-place book, and his daily experience, readily tell all the decided cases on any question which might arise, from the reign of Edward I. till the day on which his opinion was asked, or on which he had to argue in Court. He naturally took to the Western Circuit, and, from inclination or economy, he several times traveled it all the way round on foot.[2] He soon got employment upon it, and was the decided leader of it above half a century.

In the first parliament of Charles I. he was returned to the House of Commons, and he made his maiden speech in opposing the supply which was demanded under the pretense of a Spanish war, said to be impending. When he had inveighed against the extravagance of the Court, he declared at the same time that "he was for carrying on an open maritime war with Spain, whereby the nation might acquire riches and glory."[3]

He spoke for the "Petition of Right," but it would not appear that he ever had much success as a debater in parliament, and his efforts there were afterwards chiefly confined to giving an opinion upon questions of law, or of constitutional learning, which incidentally arose. His grand object continued to be to support his ascendency at the bar, whatever faction or whatever form of government might prevail. He voted steadily with the country party in the early parliaments of this reign, without making himself prominent like Coke, Hollis, or Eliot,—or sharing

[1] This laudable spirit to support "a worthy of Devon," has constantly subsisted down to recent times;—two instances of which I may mention, Sir Vicary Gibbs and Lord Gifford. Maynard's name first appears in the Reports as counsel in Cro. Car. 3 Charles I. A.D. 1628; but the law reporters of those days often report cases without mentioning the names of counsel.

[2] Roger North's Study of the Law, p. 34.   [3] 2 Parl. Hist. 32.

the glory with them of being sent to the Tower, or being prosecuted in the Star Chamber.

During the long intermission of parliaments he comforted himself for the suppression of popular rights by counting his gains at the end of every term and circuit, and finding, on comparison, that there was no falling off from the corresponding portion of the preceding year.

He was a member of the "Short Parliament," abruptly dissolved in the beginning of 1640, and voted for the inquiry into grievances before granting a supply. At the meeting of the "Long Parliament," he was returned for Totness, and still took the liberal side, but with moderation. Lord Clarendon gives the following candid testimony to his merits, and those of another holder of the Great Seal, with both of them he then co-operated, but to both of whom he was afterwards violently opposed:—
"John Maynard and Bulstrode Whitelock were men of eminent parts and great learning out of their professions, and in their professions of signal reputation; and though they did afterwards bow their knees to Baal, and so swerved from their allegiance, it was with less rancor and malice than other men: they never led, but followed, and were rather carried away with the torrent than swam with the stream, and failed through these infirmities, which less than a general defection, and a prosperous rebellion, could not have discovered."[1] Maynard without, like Hyde, renouncing his profession, and without materially sacrificing his practice for his parliamentary duties, as many lawyers then did—contrived to have much influence with the country party, and considerable weight in the House of Commons. He was a member of the committee to inquire into ship-money, and other abuses, from which the principal measures against the Court originated. He acted as one of the managers of the House of Commons on the impeachment of Lord Strafford, and of Archbishop Laud, but he grudged the time which these "unpaying occupations" consumed, and he did not gain much distinction from them. Although he was abundantly zealous, he was wanting in general political information, as well as in courtesy to the accused.[2]

[1] Life of Clarendon, i. 59.
[2] 3 St. Tr. 1456. Evelyn, in his graphic account of Lord Stafford's trial, enumerates among the managers, "Sergeant Maynard, the great lawyer, the

Before the civil war broke out, I find only one speech of his given at any length; but on this he seems to have bestowed prodigious pains, and he must himself have reported and published it.[1] It was made in the Committee of the House of Commons which sat at Guildhall, under the protection of the city train-bands, after Charles's mad attempt to arrest the five members in St. Stephen's Chapel,—and it thus begins:—" Mr. Chairman, the intermission of parliaments so long together hath been the only cause, I confidently believe, of all those evils and troubles that have happened upon this and the other his Majesty's kingdoms. The perverse nature of man is so froward and crooked, that it is always inclined and bent to do nothing but that which is evil: without restriction either by the powerful preaching of the word of God, wholesome and pious discipline in the exercise of religion, and good laws made for the strict observance and performance of the same, under the pain of severe punishment for not obeying thereof: I say, without restraint by such means, the corrupt nature of the flesh is not to be curbed; but will go on to the committing of all manner of wickedness, both against God, his king and country: and, sir, the only means to preserve and enjoy the sincere and pure teaching of God's word, and pious discipline, by wholesome laws enacted and made for that purpose, is by a parliament, by that great and wise council, expert in all the sciences of good government, either of a church or commonwealth. A parliament, sir, is the clearest looking-glass for a state perfectly to see itself in that ever was made; there is no disease, infirmity, or misery that it groans under the burden of, but in this glass it may be perspicuously perceived, and the original and prime causes that have produced the same; this glass is not only clear and bright to look in, but it is medicinal, and of that sovereign power and efficacy, that it can cure and remedy all the grievances of the spectators therein, of what personage, degree, or dignity soever they be, of whatever condition or quality soever the disease be, they are infected withal; of what profession or function soever,

same who prosecuted the Earle of Strafford forty years before, being now neere eighty yeares of age." Diary, 30th Nov. 1680, vol. i. 328.

[1] It came out in a pamphlet along with the speeches on the same occasion of Mr. Grimson and Mr. Glyn. "Printed by Francis Constable, 1642." 2 Parl. Hist. 1020.

whether spiritual or temporal, they are of, if they do but look herein." He then goes on at infinite length, with unbounded tediousness, and much mixture of metaphor, to prove how "this glass is a cure for pride, haughtiness of heart, and tyranny over the King's good people, and above all for the diseases of the clergy, viz. ease, idleness, plenty, covetousness, luxury, wantonness, and all manner of lasciviousness."[1] But this specimen is enough to show that our orator was now thoroughly imbued with puritanical notions, and dealt largely in puritanical cant.

He zealously attached himself to the Presbyterian sect; he subscribed the "Solemn League and Covenant," and he sat as a lay member of the famous Assembly of Divines at Westminster, which prepared the catechism and chief standards of doctrine still adhered to by the Presbyterian Church of Scotland. He was likewise about the same time appointed a Commissioner along with Bulstrode Whitelock to meet the Lord Chancellor of Scotland and other Commissioners of that kingdom, to treat of the best mode of establishing Presbyterianism over the whole island of Great Britain. Whitelock, in his "Memorials," gives us a very amusing specimen of those consultations: "One evening very late Maynard and I were sent for by the Lord General [Essex] to Essex House, and there was no excuse to be admitted, nor did we know beforehand the occasion of our being sent for: when we came to Essex House we were brought to the Lord General, and with him were the Scots Commissioners, Mr. Hollis, Sir Philip Stapleton, Sir John Meyrick, and divers others of his special friends. After compliments, and that all were set down in council, the Lord General spake to us to this effect :—' Mr. Maynard and Mr. Whitelock, I sent for you upon a special occasion to have your advice and counsel, and that in a matter of very great importance concerning both kingdoms, in which my Lords the Commissioners of Scotland are concerned for their state, and we for ours ; and they as well as we knowing your abilities and integrity are very desirous of your counsel in this great business.'—*Maynard.* 'We are come to obey your Excellency's commands, and we shall be ready to give our faithful advice

[1] 2 Parl. Hist. 1026.

in what shall be required of us.'—*L. Gen.* 'My Lord Chancellor of Scotland, and the rest of the Commissioners of that kingdom, desired that you two by name might be consulted with upon this occasion, and I shall desire my Lord Chancellor, who is a much better orator than I am, to acquaint you what the business is.'—*L. Chancellor.* 'Master Maynard and Master Whitelock, ye ken vary weele that Lieutenant General Cromwell is no freend of oors, and since the advance of our army into England he hath used all underhand and cunning means to take off from our honor and merit of this kingdom; an evil requital of all our hazards and services, but so it is, and we are nevertheless fully satisfied of the affection and gratitude of the gude people of this nation in general.' [After dilating at some length on Cromwell's enmity to Scotland and the Presbyterian church, on the suspicion that he was no well-wisher to his Excellency, and on the necessity, for the benefit of the *twa* kingdoms, that some course should be taken for prevention of impending mischief, his Lordship proceeds] 'Ye ken vary weele the accord twixt the twa kingdoms, and the union by the Solemn League and Covenant, and if any be *an incendiary between the twa nations*, how he is to be proceeded against: now the matter is wherein we desire your opinions, what you tak the meaning of this word *incendiary* to be, and whether Lieutenant General Cromwell be not sike an *incendiary* as is meant thereby, and whilke way wud be best to tak to proceed against him if he be proved to be sike an *incendiary*, and that will clepe his wings from soaring to the prejudice of our cause. Now you may ken that by our law in Scotland we clepe an *incendiary* whay kindleth coals of contention, and raiseth differences in the state to the public damage, and he is *tanquam publicus hostis patriæ;* whether your law be the same or not, you ken best who are mickle learned therein, and therefore with the faveure of his Excellency, we desire your judgments in these points.'—*L. Gen.* 'My Lord Chancellor hath opened the business fully to you, and we all desire your opinions therein.'—*Maynard.* 'Your Excellency and my Lord Chancellor are pleased to require our advice in this great business, and we shall deal clearly and freely with your Lordships, which I think will be most acceptable to you, and will in conclusion be best for your service.

The word *incendiary* is not much conversant in our law, nor often met with in our books, but more a term of the civil law or of state, and so to be considered in this case, and to be taken according to the expression wherein it is used in the ACCORD of the two kingdoms, and in the sense of the parliaments of both nations. That sense of it which my Lord Chancellor hath been pleased to mention, it doth bear *ex vi termini;* and surely he that kindles the coals of contention between our brethren of Scotland and us, is an *incendiary*, and to be punished as it is agreed on by both kingdoms. But, my Lord, there must be proof made of such particulars of words or actions upon which there may be sufficient ground for a parliament to declare their judgment that he who used such words or actions endeavored thereby to raise differences, and to kindle the fire of contention among us, and so that he is an *incendiary*. Lieutenant General Cromwell is a person of great favor and interest with the House of Commons and with some of the House of Peers likewise, and therefore there must be proofs, and the more clear and evident against him to prevail with the parliament to adjudge him to be an *incendiary*. I confess, my Lords, I do not in my private knowledge assure myself of any such particulars, nor have we heard of any here; and I believe it will be more difficult than perhaps some of us may imagine to fasten this upon him. And if it be difficult and doubtful, it is not fit for such persons as my Lord General and the Commissioners of the kingdom of Scotland as yet to appear in it, but rather first to see what proofs may be had of particular passages which will amount to a clear proof, upon which judgment may be grounded that he is an *incendiary*. And when such proofs shall be ready to be produced, we may again wait upon your Excellency, and the business will then be the more ripe for your Lordships' resolution; in the mean time, my humble opinion is that it may be deferred.'"[1] Hollis and some hot Presbyterians present were for instantly denouncing Cromwell as an *incendiary*,—a step which might have changed the history of the country, but Whitelock having joined in the wary advice of his brother barrister, he thus concludes his narrative: " The Scots Commissioners were not so forward to adventure upon it

[1] Whit. Mem. 116.

for the reasons given by Mr. Maynard and me until a further inquiry were made of particulars for proof to make him an *incendiary*, the which at length was generally consented to, and about two o'clock in the morning, with thanks and compliments, Mr. Maynard and I were dismissed; and he had some cause to believe that at this debate some who were present were false brethren, and informed Cromwell of all that passed among us; and after that, Cromwell, though he took no notice of any particular passages at that time, yet he seemed more kind to me and Mr. Maynard than he had been formerly, and carried on his design more actively of making way for his own advancement."

Maynard, notwithstanding his Presbyterianism, was cautious enough to avoid quarreling outright with the Independents, and he never was expelled the House of Commons.

Always true to his party, with a considerable regard for his personal safety,—on one occasion he displayed spirit,—knowing that the Independents would not then proceed to extremities against him. Being a friend to monarchy, while he wished greatly to curtail the prerogatives of the Crown, he opposed the resolution brought forward when the King was a prisoner in the Isle of Wight, against holding any further communication with him,—the tendency of which was the establishment of a republic. He urged "that by this resolution of making no more addresses to the King, they did, as far as in them lay, dissolve the parliament; and that from the time of that determination, he knew not with what security, in point of law, they could meet together, or any join with them in their counsels; that it was of the essence of parliament that they should upon all occasions repair to the King, and that his Majesty's refusal at any time to receive their petitions, or to admit their addresses, had been always held the highest breach of their privilege, because it tended to their dissolution without dissolving them; and therefore if they should now, on their parts, determine that they would receive no more messages from him, nor make any more address to him, they did upon the matter declare that they were no longer a parliament; and then how could the people look upon them as such?"[2] The resolu-

---

[1] Whit. Mem. 117.   [2] Clarendon iii. 142.   3 Parl. Hist. 831.

tion, however, was carried by a large majority, the influence of the Presbyterians in the House having very much declined.

To intimidate Maynard from repeating any such effort, articles of impeachment were soon after framed against him, accusing him of high treason, and were sent up to the Lords. The pretext for this prosecution was a tumult which had taken place in the month of July preceding, when a band of apprentices had marched from the City of London to Westminster, with a view to induce parliament to revoke certain ordinances respecting the City militia, which had been passed at the instance of Cromwell and the army. It was alleged that the defendant had incited and encouraged this insurrection, and that it amounted to high treason as a "levying of war against the parliament."[1] Maynard being brought to the bar of the House of Lords in custody of the lieutenant of the Tower, to plead to these articles, he positively refused to do so, saying with unanswerable reason, "that he, being a commoner of England, and a free-born subject, ought to be tried as a commoner by bill or indictment in the inferior courts of justice."[2] He likewise refused to kneel when required so to do, observing sarcastically that "he did admire the justice of the *Council Table* (against which they had made such complaints), in regard of the arbitrary proceedings against him in what was called a *Parliament*."

The Lords imposed a fine of £500 upon him for his contumacy, and committed him to prison during pleasure. However, upon a secret understanding that he was to be quiet for the future, the impeachment was dropped, and he was soon after restored to liberty.

He remained very quiet for several years, keeping aloof from politics,[3] till the Protectorate being established, he thought, like Hale, Rolle, and other great lawyers, that

[1] 3 Parl. History, 839. [2] Ibid. 845.
[3] It has been recently said that Maynard strongly opposed the Ordinance for the trial of Charles I., and that he entered a protest against that proceeding; but there is no contemporary evidence of his having taken any part in the discussion. It is exceedingly improbable that he should have done an act for which he never could have been forgiven, as it was the policy of his life "so to live with his enemies that he might be reconciled to them as friends," and he was accused of pleading "as if he had taken fees on both sides; one while magnifying the gallant deeds of the army, then *firking* them for their remonstrance." See *Chalmer's Biography:* "Maynard."

it was the part of a good citizen to submit to the existing government, however much he might condemn the hypocrisy and ambition of the man who was at the head of it. He accordingly consented to take the degree of the coif under a writ in the name of OLIVER, and he actually became a "Protector's Sergeant," whereby he was placed at the head of the bar.[1]

When the Crown was offered to Oliver, Maynard, as a lover of monarchy, joined Whitelock, Glyn, and St. John in strongly advising him to accept it, urging "that no new government could be settled legally but by a king; till then, all they did was like building upon sand, and every man that had been concerned in the war and in the blood that was shed—above all, the King's—was still obnoxious to punishment, and no warrants could be pleaded but what were founded on, or approved of by, a law passed by King, Lords, and Commons; and as no man's person was safe till that was done, so they said all the grants and sales that had been made were null and void, all men that had gathered or disposed of the public money were forever accountable. So, on public grounds, monarchy was the form of government suitable to all our institutions, and to the genius of the people, and the title of King, with defined prerogatives, was more favorable to liberty than that of Protector, who was often driven to do arbitrary acts from the novelty of his dominion."[2] But he was answered by the fanatics, who said "this was a mistrusting of God and a trusting to the arm of flesh: they had gone out in the simplicity of their hearts to fight the Lord's battles, to whom they had made the appeal; he had heard them, and appeared for them, and now they could trust him no longer; they had pulled down monarchy with the monarch, and would they now build that up which they had destroyed? they had solemnly vowed to be true to the Commonwealth without a king or kingship, and under that vow, as under a banner, they had fought and conquered; would

---

[1] In 1653, Oliver, Protector, Maynard was, by writ dated February 1, called to the degree of Sergeant-at-law, having before taken the engagement; and, on May 1st, was made the Protector's Sergeant, and pleaded in his and in the then Commonwealth's behalf against several Royalists that were tried in the pretended high court of parliament, whereon several generous cavaliers and noble hearts received the dismal sentence of death."—*Anthony Wood*.

[2] "Res dura et regni novitas me talia cogunt."

they go back to Egypt? if kings were invaders of
God's right, and usurpers upon men's liberties, why must
they have recourse to such a wicked engine?"[1] These
arguments, fortified by private threats of assassination,
prevailed, and the name of OLIVER I. is not inscribed in
the list of English sovereigns, although his statute is very
properly to appear in the new Palace at Westminster,
among our distinguished generals and statesmen.

Maynard continued to practice at the bar with his usual
assiduity. Notwithstanding his dignity of "Protector's
Sergeant," he did not long conduct the government prosecutions, and he sometimes was counsel for those who
were illegally proceeded against by his Highness's Attorney
General. He gave a written opinion in favor of Lilburne,
which the defendant read to the jury, and which greatly
contributed to his acquittal.[2] Afterwards, when Cony
had been imprisoned for refusing to pay a tax imposed
without authority of parliament, Sergeant Maynard
moved the Court of Upper Bench for a *habeas corpus* in
his favor, and "demanded his liberty with great confidence, both upon the illegality of the commitment, and
the illegality of the imposition, as being laid without any
lawful authority." The Judges, not being able to maintain or defend either, pretty plainly declared what their
sentence would be, and thereupon the Protector's Attorney
required a further day to answer what had been urged.
Before that day Maynard was committed to the Tower,
for presuming to question or make doubt of his Highness's
authority.[3] But I am sorry to say that Maynard again

[1] Burnet 94. It is curious to consider what would have been the effect if
he had accepted the offer, and after being proclaimed King he had lived long
enough to assemble a parliament which had passed an act ratifying all
that had been theretofore done, and pardoning all past offenses. His Majesty,
King Oliver, would probably have soon been assassinated or dethroned ; but
there is great difficulty in seeing how those who sentenced Charles I. to death
could have afterwards been brought to trial.

[2] 5 St. Tr. 348, 443. The defendant had earnestly prayed for further time
" in regard the counsel assigned him refused to appear for him, *only Sergeant
Maynard who was sick.*" This sickness was suspected to have been brought
on by a dread of the Tower.

[3] 5 St. Tr. 935. 3 Clarendon, Hist. Reb. 985. The noble historian adds:
"The Judges were sent for and severely reprehended for suffering that
license. When they with all humility mentioned the law and MAGNA
CHARTA, Cromwell told them with terms of contempt and derision, ' Their
MAGNA F—— should not control his actions, which he knew were for the
safety of the Commonwealth.' He asked them, 'who made them Judges?
whether they had any authority to sit there but what he gave them?' and if

showed that he had no taste for being a martyr. When he and Sergeant Twisden and Mr. Wadham Wyndham, who had been imprisoned along with him for the same cause, had lain three or four days in custody, "they unworthily petitioned to be set at liberty, acknowledging their fault, and promising to do so no more, choosing rather to sacrifice the cause of their client, whereon that of their country was eminently concerned, than to endure a little restraint with the loss of a few fees." [1]

Maynard was soon again on good terms with the Protector, and might have been one of his Peers, but he wisely would not accept any promotion which would take him from the practice of his profession; and while parliaments sat under Oliver, he continued a member of the House of Commons as representative for Newton, and afterwards for Bearlstone. He is recorded as having entered a solemn protest against two evils which have continued to visit subsequent parliaments—"excessive legislation, and long speeches." "A parliament," said he, "hath passed more laws in one month, than the best student in England can read in a year, and well if he can understand them then. We had a speech to-day (Sir Arthur Haslerig's) which lasted from nine to twelve: if you go on at this rate to have one speech a day, the Dutch will give you £2,000 a day to do so." [2]

On Oliver's demise, Maynard immediately swore allegiance to his successor, and had his patent renewed, as "Protector's Prime Sergeant." But in consequence of the proved incapacity of Richard, and the confusion which followed, the Presbyterians resolved to recall Charles II., trusting to the comprehension promised them privately by Hyde, and by the King's public declaration from Breda,—and Maynard, as one of their leaders, took an active part in the measures devised for supporting Monk's movement to crush the Commonwealth. He was a member of the Council of State, in whom the executive government

his authority were at an end, they knew well enough what would become of themselves;' and dismissed them with a caution that they should not suffer the lawyers to prate what it would not become them to hear." Notwithstanding this coarse and violent ebullition, it should be recollected that "in all matters which did not concern the life of his jurisdiction he seemed to have great concern for the law," and that, pressing the Judges to act under him, he said "he would rather rule by *red gowns* than by *red coats*." [1] 5 St. Tr. 936.

[2] *Burton's Diary.* Our only consolation is to read of an American legislator being "five days in possession of the floor."

ernment was for some time vested,¹ and he took his seat once more as representative for Totness on the restoration of the Rump. Being returned for Beralstone to the "Convention Parliament," he was very useful in repressing the republican spirit, which still showed itself in considerable strength.²

Charles, on his arrival at Whitehall, very cordially received the Sergeant, now well stricken in years, and little expecting to live to sit in another "Convention Parliament," or to see the expulsion of the dynasty now so enthusiastically supported. He submitted to the ceremony of again taking the coif under a royal writ, which treated his former sergeantcy as a nullity;—and, to reward his loyalty, he was made a King's Sergeant, and received the honor of knighthood.³ Sir John was likewise offered the situation of a puisne judge, but he preferred his lucrative practice at the bar.

Now comes the most discreditable part of his career. Along with Sergeant Glyn, who had acted as the Protector's Chief Justice, he appeared at Westminster among the Crown lawyers to sustain the prosecution of Sir Harry Vane for high treason,—the only overt act being that he (like the two sergeants) had acted under the authority of the Commonwealth:—an instance of tergiversation which even shocked the warmest royalists, and which is thus held up to scorn by Butler :—

"Did not the learned Glyn and Maynard,
To make good subjects traitors strain hard?"³

Maynard, however, strenuously resisted the measures introduced by Clarendon, by which faith was broken with the Presbyterians.

Though baffled in the unequal contest, he showed great moderation on the fall of their capital enemy, by contending that none of the offenses charged against him

---

¹ Martyn's Life of Shaftesbury, i. 231.   ² 4 Parl. Hist. i. 164.
³ Dugd. Or. Jur. 115.
⁴ Pepys's Diary likewise shows the public scandal excited by the two republican Sergeants become royalists. He thus concludes his account of the coronation: "Thus did the day end with joy everywhere, and, blessed be God, I have not heard of any mischance to anybody through it all, but only to Sergeant Glynne, whose horse fell upon him yesterday, and is like to kill him, which people do please themselves to see how just God is to punish the rogue at such a time as this, being now one of the King's Sergeants, and rode in the cavalcade with MAYNARD, *to whom people wish the same fortune.*"

amounted to high treason. "No man," said he, "can do what is just, but he must have what is true before him; where life is concerned, you ought to have a moral certainty of the thing, and every one be able to say, *upon this proof, in my conscience, this man is guilty.* Common fame is no ground to accuse a man where matter of fact is not clear. To say an evil is done, therefore this man hath done it, is strange in morality, more strange in logic."[1]

He was now counsel for the Crown in all government prosecutions:[2] but though he had precedence of the Attorney and Solicitor General, he did not take a prominent part in any case which occurred, till Lord Shaftesbury was brought up before the Court of King's Bench on a *habeas corpus*, having been committed to the Tower by the House of Lords for contending that the parliament was dissolved.[3] The question now arose for the first time, "whether a warrant of commitment by either House of Parliament must be framed with the same strictness as a warrant of commitment by an inferior tribunal," the warrant merely ordering the defendent to be "imprisoned during pleasure, for high contempts committed against this House." Objection was taken "that the cause of commitment was not sufficient, for the general allegation of high contempts is too uncertain, as the Court can not judge of the contempt if it doth not appear in what act it consists." But Maynard argued that the House of Lords was a branch of the legislature and the Supreme Court of the realm, and that its resolutions on its own privileges could not be adjudicated upon by inferior tribunals, whose judgments it was entitled to review. He admitted, that "if the commitment had been by a magistrate, or by the Common Pleas, or Exchequer, it could not have been supported; but it was by a Court not under the control of the Court desired to quash it, and whether the contempts should be specified, was a matter within the deliberation of that Court, not of this; that when a question of privilege incidentally arises in a common-law action, it may be determined by the com-

[1] 4 Parl. Hist. 572, 577.
[2] See Rex v. Tonge and others for high treason, 6 St. Tr. 252. Lord Morley's Trial, ib. 776. Lord Mordaunt's Trial, ib. 796.
[3] Ante, Chap. LXXXVIII.

mon-law judges; but here the question was, whether the Lords had capacity to determine their own privileges, and whether this Court can reverse their decision, and discharge a Peer whom they have committed for contempt. The Judges had often demanded of the Lords how the law is, and how a statute should be expounded; and, *à fortiori*, this Court ought to demand their opinions when a doubt ariseth on an order made by the House of Lords, respecting their own privilege and one of their own members, instead of adjudicating this order to be erroneous."

Luckily for parliamentary privilege, the government wished to detain Shaftesbury in custody, or this unanswerable reasoning might not have prevailed; but the Judges unanimously adopted it, the prisoner was remanded to the Tower, and the precedent has hitherto been universally followed, where the question of the validity of the commitment by either House of Parliament has arisen on a *habeas corpus*, although an attempt has been made to throw a doubt upon the principle where the question arises in an action.[1]

During the reign of Charles II. Maynard went on steadily devoting himself to his profession, and eschewing politics as much as he decently could, consistently with preserving his reputation as a leader of the Presbyterians; but he occasionally came forward in the House of Commons on great constitutional questions. His arguments in the dispute with the House of Lords respecting the jurisdiction of that House to hear appeals from Courts of Equity, although they proved nugatory, were so pleasing to the Commons that they were ordered *in perpetuam rei memoriam* to be entered in the Journals. In the discussions on the "Declaration of Indulgence," in 1673, he boldly denied the dispensing power.[2] Likewise, when the bill was proposed, two years after, for Purity of Election, he strongly supported it, saying, "This bribing men by drink is a lay simony. *Electiones fiant liberè.* What do men give hogs drink for? To be

---

[1] 6 St. Tr. 1269. S. C. 1 Freeman, 153. 1 Mod. 144. 3 Keble, 792. And see Murray's Case, 1 Wils. 299. Brass Crosby's Case, 19 St. Tr. 1137. Oliver's Case, 2 Sir. W. Bl. 758. Flower's Case, 8 T. R. 314. Sir John Hobhouse's Case, 3 Barn. and Ald. 420. Case of Sheriffs of Middlesex, 11 Ad. and Ell. 275. Lord Campbell's Speeches, 240–251.

[2] 4 Parl. Hist. 377. Ib. 783.

carried on the shoulders of drunken fellows." He was, nevertheless, for a high property qualification in the representatives. The franchise of the electors hardly seems to have been generally considered in England from the reign of Henry VI., when it was confined in counties to freeholders of 40 shillings, till the reign of George III., when the discussions originated which terminated in the "Reform Bill."

Maynard took an active part in the prosecutions which arose out of the Popish plot, conducting some before a jury as counsel for the Crown, and others before the Lords as a manager for the House of Commons. He was particularly conspicuous on the trials of Coleman and of Lord Stafford, repeating on both occasions his favorite quotation: "Multi ob stultitiam non putabant, multi ob ignorantiam non videbant multi ob pravitatem non credebant, et non credendo conjurationem adjuvabant."

In these cases he might be carried away by popular enthusiasm, but I must strongly reprobate a cold-blooded attempt he made (from no motive that I can discover, except the professional passion for getting the verdict) to convict of murder the minor peer, Lord Cornwallis, who had, by mere mischance, killed another schoolboy. Although no evidence was given for the accused, no case being made out against him—after the Solicitor General had replied for the Crown, the old Sergeant delivered a furious address to the Lord High Steward and the Peers-triers, calling on them to convict, and concluding with these words: "Thus stands the case before your Grace and my Lords; it is a case of blood, and it cries loud." But, to the honor of the Peerage, the poor boy was acquitted, one or two Lords finding it manslaughter, and all the rest saying generally, *Not Guilty*.[1]

I must likewise hold up to indignation the attempt which he made in Lord Danby's case to pervert the famous Statute of Treasons, 25 Edward III., by laying down that "it was only binding on the inferior Courts, while in a proceeding by way of parliamentary impeachment, anything may be declared treason;" for he must have been well aware that the power to declare new treasons was to be exercised only by prospective legislation,

[1] 7 St. Tr. 144-158.

and that an impeachment for treason, as well as an indictment, could only properly be for an offense declared to be treason before it was committed. Swift, with his usual keenness, remarks on the Sergeant's casuistry in this case respecting the power of parliament to declare new treasons—"Yes, by a new act, but not by a retrospective one: Maynard was a knave and a fool, with all his law."[1]

When the "Exclusion Bill" was brought forward, he supported it on the ground that the hopes of a Popish successor encouraged the Popish plot. "Shall we be led," he exclaimed, "like an ox to the slaughter, or a fool to the stocks, and not apprehend our danger?" While the measure was pending, he slipped away to the circuit without leave of absence. This being discovered, his son was instructed to inform him that "if he did not return forthwith, he should be sent for in custody, he being treated thus tenderly in respect of his having been long the Father of the House."[2]

In the critical parliament at Oxford which followed, he was so far carried away by faction as to forget what he had said when he was himself imprisoned for high treason, and to abet Shaftesbury in the unconstitutional attempt to try Fitzharris, a commoner, on a similar impeachment for high treason, at the bar of the House of Peers ; but no better reasoning could be adduced by him than the following :—" This damnable Popish plot is still on foot in England, and I am sure in Ireland too ; and what arts and crafts have been used to hide this plot ! It began with the murder of a magistrate ; then with perjury and false subornation, and this of Fitzharris is a second part of that. We sent up an impeachment to the Lords against Fitzharris, and told the Lords that in due time he would bring up articles against him, and the Lords refuse to try him. In effect they make us no parliament. If we are the prosecutors, and they will not hear our accusation, their own lives as well as ours are concerned. This is a strange way of proceeding; the same day we impeach Fitzharris, they vote we shall not prosecute him: now, when all is at stake, we must not prosecute. If this be so, Holland must submit, and let the French run over all. This is a strange breach

[1] 2 Burn. O. T. 58.   11 St. Tr. 599.   [2] Com. Journ. vol. viii.

of privilege of parliament, and tends to the danger of the King's person, and the destruction of the Protestant religion; and I hope you will vote it so."[1] It was so voted; but the public condemned the attempt to deprive an Englishman of his birth-right, the benefit of a trial by his own peers, and the King dissolved the parliament with the general applause of the nation.[2]

Now came out the Earl of Roscommon's "Ghost of the Old House of Commons to the New One, appointed to meet at Oxford," in which the old Sergeant is handled very roughly by the nephew and godson of Strafford.[3]

> "The robe was summon'd, Maynard in the head,
> In legal murder none so deeply read;
> I brought him to the bar where once he stood
> Stain'd with the (yet unexpiated) blood
> Of the brave Strafford, when three kingdoms rung
> With his accumulative hackney tongue;
> Prisoners and witnesses were standing by,
> These had been taught to swear, and those to die,
> And to expect the arbitrary fates,
> Some for ill faces, some for good estates.
> To fright the people and alarm the town,
> Bedloe and Oates employ'd the reverend gown;
> But while the triple mitre bore the blame,
> The King's three crowns were their rebellious aim."

Maynard was immediately after subjected to a great mortification, in being required, as King's Ancient Sergeant, to prosecute before a jury the very Fitzharris who the Commons had voted could not, without a gross breach of their privileges, be proceeded against according to the course of the common law; the impeachment in the name of the Commons of England being to be considered as depending notwithstanding a dissolution. After due deliberation, the old lawyer preferred the performance of

---

[1] 4 Parl. Hist. 1335.
[2] Ante, Chap. XCIII. This subject is very ably treated in the Edinburgh Review, No. clxviii. p. 329. The learned and ingenious writer, taking the opposite side,—in answer to precedents, authorities, and general arguments, relies almost exclusively on the *dictum* of Selden,—which would have been entitled to much respect but for the reasoning by which it was supported. If, indeed, the Commons upon an impeachment were, as Selden supposes, "instead of a jury," a commoner might be tried before them for his life, but they are simply "accusers" as much as the Attorney General, and the Lords exclusively decide both upon the law and facts of the case. The Lords do *try* the delinquent, as well as pass *judgment* upon him.—There is not a single instance in our records of a commoner being capitally convicted by the Lords, and surely the weight of authority is greatly against such a proceeding.
[3] See Johnson's Life of Roscommon.

his professional dignity; and Fitzharris having pleaded the pendency of the impeachment in abatement of the indictment, Sergeant Maynard contended with Sergeant Jeffreys, his brother counsel, that the plea was so vicious, that it ought to be quashed without the Attorney General being even called upon to demur to it. The plea was quashed accordingly, and the prisoner was convicted and executed.[1]

It was said of Maynard that, "as a lawyer, all parties were willing to employ him, and he was equally willing to be employed by all." Accordingly, after the victory gained by the Court in the City of London, he was counsel for Papillon in the famous action brought against him as Sheriff by the late Lord Mayor for a false arrest, on the ground that Papillon and Dubois had not been duly elected Sheriffs, and that all acts done by them in executing process were unlawful. This I think is the Sergeant's most eloquent forensic effort; but it had no effect upon a packed jury, who found a verdict for the plaintiff with £10,000 damages, and merited this compliment from Chief Justice Jeffreys: "Gentlemen, you seem to be persons that have sense about you, and consideration for the government. You have given a good verdict, and are greatly to be commended for it."[2]

Nevertheless, Maynard was always very courteous and respectful to the Judges, even amidst their worst atrocities, and he had been so careful not to give any mortal offense to the government, that on the demise of the crown he was reappointed "Ancient Sergeant" by James II., and he was employed in this capacity to assist in the investigation respecting the birth of the Prince.[3]

During this reign he was placed in a very awkward situation, being subpœnaed as a witness by Titus Oates, when that miscreant was indicted for perjury. The Sergeant, who had so often supported his veracity, was examined to his character and required to state on oath some particulars that had occurred on the trial of Lord Stafford.—*Serg. Maynard.* "I know nothing truly, nor can I remember anything of it now."—*C. J. Jeffreys.* "He says he remembers nothing."—*Serg. Maynard.* "If Mr. Oates had told me before-hand, when he subpœnaed me, what time and what particular things he would have

[1] 8 St. Tr. 243-309. [2] 10 St. Tr. 372. [3] 12 St. Tr. 125

examined me to. probably, if I was there, I have notes that I then took; but I can never swear to my memory for any cause so long ago."—*Oates.* "My Lord, I am very sorry Mr. Sergeant Maynard's age should so impair his memory."—*C. J. Jeffreys.* "I dare say you are not more sorry for his age than he is."[1] We cannot help suspecting that this supposed lapse of memory from senility was affected, as five years later the same individual took an important part in the settlement of the kingdom, on the landing of the Prince of Orange, and was actually intrusted with the custody of the Great Seal.

In the only parliament of James II., Maynard still represented Beralstone, and he now displayed more than his usual boldness. A bill was brought in to make words disparaging the King's person or government high treason, which it was supposed would have embraced any thing spoken against the King's religion. "This was chiefly opposed by Sergeant Maynard, who in a very grave speech laid open the inconvenience of making words treason; 'they were often ill heard, and ill understood, and were apt to be misrecited by a very small variation; men in a passion, or in drink, might say things they never intended; therefore, he hoped they would keep to the law of Edward III., by which an overt act was made the necessary proof of all intentions.' When others insisted that 'out of the abundance of the heart the mouth speaketh,' he brought the instance of our Saviour's words, 'Destroy this Temple,' &c., and showed how near *the* Temple was to *this* Temple, *pronouncing it in Syriac,* so that the difference was almost imperceptible. 'There was nothing more innocent than these words as our Saviour meant and spoke them, but nothing more criminal than the setting on a multitude to destroy the Temple.' This made some impression at that time; but if the Duke of Monmouth's landing had not brought the session to an early conclusion, that, and everything else, which the officious courtiers were projecting, would have certainly passed."[2]

After the suppression of Monmouth's rebellion, a supply was proposed to keep up a standing army, which was to be commanded by Roman Catholic officers. The Sergeant joined in stoutly opposing this plan of military

---

[1] 10 St. Tr. 1162.   [2] Burn. O. T. 323.

government. After showing that, by the existing law, and the powers vested in Sheriffs and Lord Lieutenants, the internal tranquillity of the country was sufficiently provided for, and that we were at peace with all foreign nations, he observed, "If you give this supply, it is for an army; and then, may not this army be made of those that will not take the test? which act was not designed a punishment for the Papists, but a protection for ourselves."[1]

A vote for a supply was carried by a ministerial majority; but such a storm was excited, that the King immediately dissolved the parliament, and ruled thereafter without the pretense even of being restrained by law, till his combined violence and folly precipitated him from the throne.

CHAPTER CIV.

CONCLUSION OF THE LIFE OF LORD COMMISSIONER MAYNARD.

AT the meeting of the Convention Parliament, Maynard was returned by Plympton, as well as by Beralstone, and chose to serve for the former borough. From his great age and experience, he was looked up to as an oracle of constitutional law in the discussions which arose respecting the vacancy of the throne. The House, according to his advice, having gone into a Grand Committee "on the state of the nation," he strongly supported the resolution that "King James II., having endeavored to subvert the constitution of the kindom by breaking the original contract between King and people, and by the advice of Jesuits and other wicked persons, having violated the fundamental laws, and having withdrawn himself out of this kingdom, has abdicated the government, and that the throne is thereby vacant." In answer to the objection that they were deposing the King, and making the monarchy elective, he said, "The question is not whether we can depose the King, but

[1] 4 Parl. Hist. 1375. 5 Parl. Hist. 26.

whether the King has not deposed himself. It is no new project; our government is mixed—not monarchical and tyrannous, but has had its beginning from the people. There may be such a transgression in the Prince, that the people will be no more governed by him." He admitted that the King being a Papist did not thereby make himself incapable of the Crown, there being hitherto no law to that effect; but he insisted that by James's multiplied violations of the constitution, he had broken the contract between the Crown and the people, and that he was to be considered as *civiliter mortuus*, with this unexampled accompaniment, that being *naturally alive* his heir was not designated; and it devolved upon the two Houses of Parliament to restore the equilibrium of the constitution by appointing to the throne,—which they would best do by offering it to Protestants descended from the royal family, who might most worthily fill it for the public good.[1]

This resolution passed by a vast majority in the Commons, but was far from being agreeable to the Upper House, where a vote for a Regent was very nearly carried. The Lords insisted that the word "deserted" should be substituted for "abdicated," and that the clause respecting the "vacancy of the throne" should be entirely omitted.

This dispute between the two Houses leading to a "Free Conference" in the Painted Chamber, Maynard was appointed one of the managers to conduct it on the part of the Commons, and he boldly combated the high Tory doctrines of the Earl of Nottingham, and the managers for the Lords.

"When there is," said he, "a present defect of one to exercise the administration of the government, I conceive the declaring a vacancy, and provision for a supply for it, can never make the Crown elective. The Commons apprehend that there is such a defect now; and, by consequence, a present necessity for the supply of the government. My Lords, the constitution, notwithstanding the vacancy, is the same; but if there be an irreparable breach of the constitution, that is an abdication, and an abdication infers a vacancy. It is not that the Commons do say the Crown of England is always and perpetually elective; but it is necessary there be a supply where there

[1] 5 Parl. Hist. 36, 40, 45.

is a defect, and the doing of that will be no alteration of the monarchy from hereditary to elective. As to the pretended Prince of Wales succeeding rightfully as heir, I say no man can now be called heir of James II. We have a maxim in law as certain as any other, *Nemo est hæres viventis.* His heir is now *in nubibus.* What shall we do till he is dead? The Crown can not descend till then."

The Earl of Pembroke tried to answer this technical reasoning by saying, "I can not directly name him that hath the immediate right; but it is enough to prevent a vacancy that there is, and must be, an heir or successor, let he be who he will."—*Maynard.* "But your Lordship will neither agree that it is vacant, nor tell us how it is full. Is James King? Then obey him. But you allow that he is not to be obeyed. Then he is not King. Tell us, then, who is King, if King James be not. But if there be now no King, the throne is vacant."—*Pembroke.* "Sure, Mr. Sergeant, you agree, that notwithstanding Charles II. was abroad at his father's death, and did not actually exercise the government, yet in law he was not the less heir for that; nor was the throne vacant."—*Maynard.* "That is not like this case, because there the descent was legally immediate; but there can be no hereditary descent during King James's life. Therefore, unless we declare and fill up the vacancy, there must be an everlasting war entailed upon us; his title continuing, and we opposing his return to the exercise of his prerogatives. Pray, my Lords, consider the condition of the nation till there be a government; no law can be executed, no debts can be compelled to be paid, no offenses can be punished, no one can tell what to do to obtain his right or defend himself from wrong. You still say the throne is not void, and yet you will not tell us who fills it. If once you will agree that the throne is vacant, it will then come orderly in debate how it should, according to our law, be filled. If our law is silent, then we must look to the law of nature (above all human laws), and provide for the public weal in such an exigency as this."

The two parties separated, probably without any change of private opinion among them; but the Lords, frightened by the horrors of anarchy which Maynard had painted, next day resiled, and sent a message that they agreed to the resolution of the Commons without any amendment.

"The Declaration of Rights" soon followed, and William and Mary were upon the throne.[1]

Maynard strongly supported the first measure of the new reign, which was by resolution to prevent the dissolution of the "Convention," although it had been called—not by royal writs—but by letters from the Prince of Orange. He was conscious that the high Churchmen and the Tories had already forgot their recent dangers and deliverance, and, if a new parliament had been summoned, would generally have voted for adherents of the abdicated sovereign. He said, therefore, "On the consequence of this debate will be the safety of the nation, and of the Protestant religion. I think we are a parliament. What is a parliament but King, Lords, and Commons? The convention in which I sat, 12 Charles II., resolved, that without a writ from the King we were a parliament. We acted on the greatest law in the world, which is recorded in the Twelve Tables, *Salus populi suprema lex esto*. We sat here before the King was declared, and much more may we now. There is a great danger in sending out writs at this time, if you consider what a ferment the nation is in; and I think the clergy are out of their wits; and I believe if the clergy had their wills, few of us would be here again. You will not declare yourselves no parliament, unless *you* are out of your wits. As for the clergy, I have much honor for high and low of them; but I must say they are in a ferment; there are pluralists among them, and when they should preach the gospel, they preach against the parliament and the law of England."[2] His advice was followed, and there was no dissolution till the following year, when men's minds were more tranquilized, and William's success in Scotland had weakened the doctrine of divine right, although even then a majority of Tories was returned.

The resolution being taken to separate the judicial from the political duties hitherto intrusted to the one individual who held the Great Seal, and to have several Judges sitting together to dispatch the business in the Court of Chancery, the offer was made to the veteran Maynard to place him at the head of them. Although he was now in his 88th year, his mental faculties remained

[1] 5 Parl. Hist. 72, 89, 90, 103.   [2] Ibid. 124, 128, 131.

quite unimpaired. Such activity and spirits did he likewise possess, that, in spite of several generations of younger leaders who had successively sprung up to compete with him, his practice at the bar remained with him undiminished. Forgetting how short a period he could by the course of nature now enjoy it, he felt a severe pang when required to sacrifice his fees for an office which he dreaded might be very precarious. However, after some hesitation he accepted it, intending, perhaps, after various examples of that age, if he should lose it, again to practice as an advocate, and to argue that all such of his judicial decisions as, when cited against him, should appear to impugn the positions he had to sustain for his new clients, were erroneous. His brother Commissioners, Keck and Rawlinson, though considered sound lawyers, were unknown to the public; and he had nearly as much *éclat* as if he had been appointed Lord Chancellor.

They received the Great Seal in Hilary vacation,[1] and on the first day of Easter Term they were duly inaugurated in Westminster Hall. "Before they entered upon any business, they took the oaths usually administered to the Lord Chancellor or Lord Keeper (*mutatis mutandis*), the book being held to them by the Master of the Rolls,[2] and the oaths read to them by the Clerk of the Crown."

King James's Great Seal, fished up from the river Thames, was for some time used, but on the 23rd of May an order was made by the King in Council for a new Great Seal, representing William and his spouse sitting together lovingly on the throne; and this being soon engraved, was used till Mary's death.

Serious difficulties, however, arose respecting the jurisdiction and precedence of the Lords Commissioners; for, except during the Commonwealth, such an arrangement

[1] On account of the interregnum, Hilary Term had not been kept, and the administration of justice had been completely suspended. In consequence an act was passed (1 W. & M. c. 4) "for renewing actions and process lately depending in the Courts at Westminster, and discontinued by the not holding of Hilary Term, and for supplying other defects relating to proceedings at law," whereby it was enacted, among other things, that all offenses committed during the interregnum, which was reckoned from the 11th December, 1688, to the 12th March, 1689, should be laid in indictments, to be instead of " contra pacem *Regis*," " contra pacem *Regni*."
[2] Cro. Office Min. fol. 133

for the transaction of Chancery business had never been attempted, and no weight was given to Cromwellian precedents. To obviate these difficulties, an Act was passed " for enabling Lords Commissioners of the Great Seal to execute the office of Lord Chancellor or Lord Keeper," which enacted that they should have the same power as as the Lord Chancellor or Lord Keeper, two being required to put the Great Seal to any instrument, and one being authorized to hear interlocutory motions—all having precedence next after Peers, and the Speaker of the House of Commons.[1]

Maynard continued to hold his office along with Keck and Rawlinson till the end of Easter Term, in the following year. They were allowed to be diligent, patient, and upright, but their dispatch of business did not give so much satisfaction as was expected. People began to suspect that Equity suits, differing so much from actions at law, were better adapted to the cognizance of a single judge; the Lords Commissioners sometimes differed in a manner not edifying: Maynard without official political functions, still continuing a member of the House of Commons, used to attend there when his presence was needed in the Court of Chancery; and being deprived of the exercise which he had taken for above sixty years by walking up and down Westminster Hall, and making speeches at the bar, his health suffered, and his infirmities multiplied upon him.

The printed Reports of Chancery during his year of office give us a very imperfect notion of his judicial powers, as they almost all begin the judgment with the words " *Per curiam*," without distinguishing what was said by the several Commissioners.

Once I find what I consider doubtful doctrine laid

---

[1] 1 W. & M. c. 21. There are some curious entries in the journals respecting the progress of this bill through the Two Houses. A clause was introduced in the Lords to forbid the sale of the office of Master in Chancery, which "Lord Maynard" contrived to get thrown out. This might have induced Swift to write in the margin of his copy of Burnet, where an anecdote is related to Maynard's honor, " He was an old rogue for all that." See last edition of O. T. iii. 341. The bill was brought in and read a first time the 18th of March. The clause about selling masterships was added in committee on the 25th of March; but, after a conference between the Two Houses on the 20th of June, was rejected, and clauses forbidding the sale of the office of *Custos Rotulorum* were substituted for it —*Lords' Journ.* 1688-89.

down "*Per Lord Maynard*,"[1] that unless a submission to arbitration contains the words "*ita quod* an award be made *de et super præmissis*, &c.," an award on a part is binding, although it leaves the residue of the controversy unsettled;[2] but in the only other case in which his separate opinion was given respecting the right of the half blood to have administration, and an equal share of personal property with the whole blood—the decree which he recommended, being appealed from, after civilians and common lawyers had been heard on both sides, it was affirmed by the House of Lords.[3]

There being then no statute to vacate seats in the House of Commons on accepting an office of profit under the Crown, or to disqualify any commoner for sitting in that assembly, Maynard not only continued to represent Plympton during the remainder of the Convention Parliament, but he was re-elected for the same place in the Parliament called in the spring of the following year, and he took rather a prominent part in the debates till he finally retired from public life. In the spirit of the Whigs of that day, he strongly supported the Bill for disarming Roman Catholics, saying, "We are so mealy-mouthed and soft-handed to the Papists that it occasions their insolence. I think it is fitting that all Papists should resort to their own dwellings, and not depart without licenses from the next justices; and another thing, that all those of that religion bring all their fire-arms in, unless for the necessary defense of their houses, to officers appointed. I would not imitate their cruelty. I would let them have their religion in their private houses—but no harboring of Priests or Jesuits. And if any Papist have a hand in firing houses, he should be compelled to help to rebuild them."[4] The Lord Commissioner was carried away so far by religious zeal that he not only spoke in favor of reversing the cruel sentence upon Titus Oates, but actually stood up for the veracity of that impostor, and seemed still alarmed by the perils of the Popish plot.[5]

---

[1] He was always so designated while Commissioner of the Great Seal, the title of "Lord" added to the Christian name being given to the Chief Justices, as "Lord Hale," "Lord Holt;" while in Scotland the custom was and is for a Judge to be called Lord with his family name, or the name of his estate, at his election, as "Lord Jeffrey," "Lord Corehouse."

[2] Hide *v*. Cooth, 2 Vernon, 10).   [3] Crooke *v*. Watt, 2 Ibid. 124.
[4] 5 Parl. Hist. 182, 183.   [5] Ibid. 293, 294.

His next appearance is more creditable to him. Sir Adam Blair and other commoners had been detected in distributing a declaration of King James, from Ireland, where he was then established, denouncing the Prince of Orange as an usurper of the English throne; and it was proposed that the House of Commons should impeach them before the Lords for high treason. Maynard, taking a juster view of this subject than in the Parliament at Oxford, said, "I am against impeachment of these persons, that they may be punished. Prosecute them by way of indictment, and then you may punish them severely and legally. One man condemned and punished at common law will work more upon the people than ten impeachments."[1] This opinion was overruled, but the impeachment proved abortive.[2]

Holding an office at the pleasure of the Crown, but not being a member of the cabinet, the old patriot showed his independence by occasionally censuring the conduct of the government. He was particularly severe against the administration of the navy. "I hear," said he, "there are young men put to command ships that never were at sea before, because they are well affected to the present settlement. The question used to be, '*Is he a godly man?*' and he was employed. I asked them '*Can a godly man, because he is godly, make a watch or a pair of boots?*'"[3]

On the question of privilege, which arose on the arrest of the young Earl of Danby, then a member of the House of Commons, for sailing in his pleasure yacht, Maynard violently took part against the Earl of Nottingham, who had issued the warrant, saying, "At this rate we may all be imprisoned and whipped to our lives' end."[4]

Having sat in parliament with the great-great-grand-

[1] 5 Parl. Hist. 306. [2] 12 St. Tr. 1207-1234. [3] 5 Parl. Hist. 332.
[4] Ibid. 365. This reminds me of a speech I heard the first circuit I went—from Mr. Justice Heath who was then as old as Maynard, and might almost have remembered him. A man charged with felonious violence to a female appearing to be innocent, by reason of the consent of the prosecutrix, the Judge said, "Gentlemen of the jury, acquit the prisoner. If such a scandalous prosecution were to succeed, *which of us is safe?*"—At the same assizes, a man convicted of murdering his wife, being asked what he had to say why sentence of death should not be passed upon him, gave a very moving account of his wife's misconduct, and the provocation he had received from her. *Heath, J.* "Prisoner, you were wrong *in point of law*. You must therefore be taken from hence to the place from whence you came, and from thence to the place of execution, and there you must be hanged by the neck till you are dead; and may the Lord have mercy on your soul!"

fathers of some of the present members, he seems to have been permitted considerable license in debate. A young gentleman who opposed the bill for restoring corporations, drew down upon himself this reprimand.—*Sergeant Maynard.* "I have heard that to-day which makes my ears to tingle. There is a bill brought in to restore corporations. It has been committed, and ordered to be engrossed, and a gentleman starts up and prays that it may be thrown out; certainly he is but a young parliament-man. If those surrenders of charters stand, they may make what parliament they will at court; and, formerly, he that should have named such a thing should not have come to the bar, but gone to the Tower."[1]

But, not afraid of unpopularity, Maynard boldly counteracted the attempt of the Tories to cripple the new government by withholding the necessary supplies. Said he, "The King must not be left necessitous, or the people will suffer. The revenue of the crown-land is gone; it is aliened from him; he can have nothing but from parliament. Consider *quantum, quomodo, et quamdiu,* and bear in mind that the grant is for the necessary preservation of your liberties."[2]

Maynard's last speech in parliament was on the Regency Bill,—for vesting in the Queen the powers of government in England while the King should be absent in Ireland. With many professions of respect for Mary, he condemned this arrangement,—rather on narrow and technical grounds,—saying,

"If the Bill pass as it is, all the justices of the peace in England are gone. All the regal power is at present acted in the name of the King and Queen; how are they now to be distinguished in the whole regal government? In the King's absence do you take all power from the King, that he can do nothing but by commission from the Queen? This noble lady, the Queen, has so demeaned herself, that all would readily trust her personally, but no wise man will trust where he can not remedy. If this new commission be granted by authority, does not the former authority determine? Being derivative from it, the King has it no more; it is wholly in the Queen. All that we have done for our religion and properties, on a sudden to

[1] 5 Parl. Hist. 511.   [2] Ibid, 552.

be put on a moot point like this! We are fallen into a wilderness entangled by our enemies; God send us well out of it! No man can wish better to the commonwealth than I do; if that stand, I care not what becomes of me. The King to have power in Ireland, and none here! The thing is so great, that I am upon my knees lest we should be swallowed up by enemies, or betrayed by our friends."[1]

The act nevertheless passed,[2] and none of the evils which haunted the imagination of the Lord Commissioner arose out of it. William continuing a confiding husband, and Mary a most submissive wife,—on his return after the battle of the Boyne, the frame of government, as settled by the Bill of Rights, was in all respects restored.

Whether Lord Commissioner Maynard's last speech gave offense to the Court, or was suppose to smell of apoplexy, and therefore he was displaced against his will,—or whether he spontaneously wished to retire, from the consciousness of increasing infirmities, from the apprehension of the growing complaints of the suitors in Chancery, or from a Christian wish to have a little space for contemplation before the great change which he was certain could not be far distant,—in a few days after the Regency Bill received the royal assent, another commission passed for executing the office of Chancellor, the new Commissioners being Sir JOHN TREVOR, Sir William Rawlinson, and Sir George Hutchins. I have in vain tried to trace the true cause of Maynard's removal or voluntary resignation; and I will not substitute plausible conjecture for authenticated fact. He appeared in his place in the Court of Chancery, for the last time, on the 14th of May, 1690, when he gave judgment in the important case of *Levet* v. *Needham*, on the construction of a will.[3] Next day the new Lords Commissioners were sworn in, and he—destined never more to revisit Westminster Hall or St. Stephen's Chapel—retired to his country-house at Gunnersbury, near Ealing, afterwards famous as the residence of the Princess Amelia, daughter of George II. Here he enjoyed but short repose from the labors of his profession and the anxieties of politics A complication of diseases soon assailed him, which, per-

---
[1] 5 Parl. Hist., 617, 623.   [2] Wm. & Mary, c. vi.   [3] 2 Vern. 137.

haps, he was the less able to combat from having no mental occupation, and being deprived of the pleasure of casting up his fee-book or calculating when another gale of salary would become due. He expired on the 9th day of October, 1690, in the eighty-ninth year of his age. He is said, with his last breath, to have "railed at the Papists."

He had amassed an immense fortune from his professional gains. On one Western circuit, in the year 1647, he received in fees £700, the largest sum theretofore made on one circuit by any barrister;[1] but in the prosperous times which followed, his profits must have been still more considerable. At his death his possessions were equally divided between his two granddaughters and co-heiresses, Lady Hobart, wife of Sir John Hobart, Bart., and Mary, Countess of Stamford.[2]

For the mere pleasure of what he considered a clever legal trick [or *trickum in lege*], he is said to have rendered nugatory the settlement made on his marriage with his third wife. But he was so much hated and envied by thorough-going churchmen, who piously believed that all Presbyterians should be burnt for the good of their souls, that, although he was by no means a man of high moral qualities, the grosser stories to his disadvantage should be received with some distrust.

According to Roger North, who was intimately acquainted with him, and had a great spite against him, he once brought a very foolish action of slander against a man who had told an anecdote concerning his cheating a client on the circuit. Having, by virtue of his privilege as a Sergeant, sued in the Court of Common Pleas, and laid the venue in Middlesex, the trial came on, at Nisi Prius, before Lord Chief Justice North, who was determined to make game of the old republican.[3] "The witness, telling the story as he swore the defendant told it, said that a client came to the Sergeant and gave him a basket of pippins, and every pippin had a piece of gold in

---

[1] Whitelock, leader of the Oxford circuit, records the fact in a tone of wondering envy. "I attended the house, and Maynard and I talking of our circuit gains, he told me that he got on the last circuit £700, which I believe was more than any one of our profession got before." Mem. 273, Oct. 1649.

[2] The line of his descendants is recited in a private act, which received the royal assent 6th August, 1844.

[3] He used to be called reproachfully "one of the tribe of forty-one." Life of Jeffreys, 73.

it. *Those were golden pippins*, quoth the Judge. The Sergeant began to puff, not bearing the jest: so the witness went on. And then, said he, the other side came and gave him a roasting pig (as it is called in the West), and in the belly of that there were fifty broad pieces. *That's good sauce to a pig*, quoth the Judge again. This put the Sergeant out of all patience, and speaking to those about him, *This*, said he, *is on purpose to make me ridiculous.*" The Sergeant ultimately failed in his action, for the story "used to be told of Noy, and all the cock lawyers of the West, and had been repeated by the defendant of Maynard, the reigning cock, as mere merriment, over ale, without intent to slander." [1]

Roger, whose soul must have migrated into Jemmy Boswell, gives us the following anecdote of Maynard, in which he himself makes rather a contemptible figure. " One afternoon at the *nisi prius* Court of the Common Pleas in Westminster Hall, before the Judge sat, a poor, half-starved old woman, who sold sweetmeats to schoolboys and footmen at the end of the bar, desired the Sergeant to pay her two shillings for keeping his hat two terms. She spoke two or three times, and he took no notice of her; and then I told the Sergeant *the poor woman wanted her money*, and *I thought he would do well to pay her*. The Sergeant fumbled a little, and then said to me, *Lend me a shilling. Ay, with all my heart*, quoth I, *to pay the poor woman.* He took it, and gave it to her; but she asked for another. I said, *I would lend him that also to pay the woman. No, don't, boy*, said he, *for I never intend to pay you this.* And he was as good as his word, for however he came off with that woman, having been, as they say, a wonderful charitable man, I am sure he died in my debt. But in this manner (as I guess he intended) I stood corrected for meddling." [2]

"A great man," however, Roger pronounces him to

---

[1] Life of Guilford, i. 235.
[2] Ibid. 236. The following passage respecting Samuel Johnson must be by the narrator of the above anecdote of Sergeant Maynard. " One day, I owned to him that I was occasionally troubled with a fit of *narrowness*. 'Why, Sir,' said he, 'so am I. *But I do not tell it*.' He has now and then BORROWED A SHILLING of me; and when I asked him for it again he seemed rather out of humor. A droll little circumstance once occured ; as if he meant to reprimand my minute exactness as a creditor, he thus addressed me :—' Boswell, *lend* me sixpence—NOT TO BE REPAID.' "—*Boswell's Life of Johnson*, iv. 203.

have been, "since his natural and acquired abilities, *and the immense gains he had by his practice,* justly entitle his name to that epithet;" adding this character of him— "to give him his due, he was, to his last breath, at the bottom true as steel to the principles of the late times when he first entered upon the stage of business. Being an artful as well as learned lawyer, he would lay notable snares; but when discovered, never persisted, but sat down, and for the decorum of bar practice of the law, was an excellent pattern."[1]

Sometimes he was suspected of inventing law authorities to mislead the Judges. Chief Justice Pemberton having ruled a point according to a case which the Sergeant cited from memory and which never could be found, afterwards complained of having been bamboozled by him, saying, "My brother Maynard might as well have tossed his cap into the air, or have laughed in my face." Yet such was his reputation for law, that even Judge Jeffreys was sometimes afraid to overrule him. This ermined ruffian having, on one occasion, almost annihilated Mr. Ward, a junior barrister, who argued a point before him, and severely rebuked him, saying, "Do not make such discourses *ad captandum populum* with your flourishes; I will none of your enamel, nor your garniture,"—the Sergeant, who was his leader, having got a hearing, quietly stated how the law really stood, and so clearly demonstrated his position to the satisfaction of all the bar and all the bystanders, that the Chief Justice was for once shamed out of his insolence, and acquiesced.

Beyond the precincts of the law Maynard's vision was very contracted. Along with wiser men who lived in the sixteenth and seventeenth centuries, he had a great dread of the increasing size of the metropolis. He was alarmed by the town being extended so far to the west as St. Giles's; and he warmly supported a bill, which was rejected, "to prevent further building in London or the neighborhood." "This building," he said pathetically, "is the ruin of the gentry and ruin of religion, leaving so many good people without churches to go to. This enlarging of London makes it filled with lackeys and pages. In St. Giles's parish, scarce the fifth part can come to church, and we shall have no religion at last."

[1] Life of Guilford, i. 238.

The most elaborate character of Maynard is by Bishop Warburton, in a parallel between him and his contemporary, Whitelock. "They were both lawyers of family, and in the Long Parliament; both of the Presbyterian faction; both learned and eminent in their profession; moderate, sage, and steady. So far they agreed. In this they differed: Maynard had strong parts, with a serious modesty; Whitelock was weak and vain, and, by these defects only, more self-interested. A sense of honor made Maynard stick to the Presbyterian faction, and to fall *with* them; but, as he had much phlegm and caution, not, like Hollis and Stapleton, to fall *for* them. So that he was never marked out by the Independents for their first sacrifices. On the contrary, Whitelock forsook his party in distress; but, as he had the other's moderation, it was by slow and gentle degrees; and so as it happened, decently. Maynard, by adhering steadily, but not violently, to the party he set out with, was reverenced by all; and, had he not been more intent on the affairs of his profession than on public business, might have become considerable by station. He went through the whole reigns of Charles and James II. with the same steady pace, and the same adherence to his party; but, by his party, I rather mean presbytery for the sake of civil liberty, than to civil liberty for the sake of presbytery."[1]

I ought to make special mention of Maynard's "Edition of the Year Books," a work to which he devoted himself as eagerly and delightedly as ever refined critic did to an edition of Homer or Shakespeare.[2]

[1] Warburton's Letters to Hurd, p. 211.
[2] I subjoin the title-page of the first volume, the gipsy jargon of which may amuse the reader:—

"LES
REPORTS
DES
CASES
argue & adjudge in le Temps del'
Roy Edward le Second,
Et auxy Memoranda del' Exchequer en Temps le
Roy Edward le Primer.
Selonq; les ancient manuscripts ore remanent les maines de Sir Jehan
Maynard
Chevaler Serjeant de la ley al sa Tres Excellent Majesty
Le Roy Charles le Second.
ovesq; un perfect Table les Matters en les dits Cases de Temps de l'Roy
Edward le Second colligee per le mesme Serjeant.
1678."

Yet, from the mouth of this same dull black-letter lawyer came two of the most felicitous sayings in the English language—to be envied by Congreve or Sheridan. Jeffreys having once rudely taunted him with having grown so old as to forget his law: "True, Sir George," replied he, "I have forgotten more law than you ever learned."

When the Prince of Orange first took up his quarters at Whitehall, on James's flight, different public bodies presented addresses to him, and Maynard came at the head of the men of the gown. The Prince took notice of his great age, and observed that he must have outlived all the lawyers of his time, "If your Highness," answered he, "had not come over to our aid, I should have outlived the law itself."[1]

We ought to value still more highly his encomium on the great palladium of our freedom: "Trial by Jury," said he, "is the subject's birthright and inheritance, as his lands are; and without which he is not sure to keep them or anything else. This way of trial is his fence and protection against all frauds and surprises, and against all storms of power."[2]

CHAPTER CV.

LIFE OF LORD COMMISSIONER TREVOR.

NOTWITHSTANDING the complaints raised against the Court of Chancery under Lord Commissioner Maynard, the King and his Ministers thought that the experiment of having several co-ordinate Judges jointly to do the business there had not yet been fairly tried, and a new commission (as we have seen) was issued, with Sir JOHN TREVOR at the head of

---

[1] 2 Burn. O. T. 550. The exact contemporary of Maynard, to whom he was introduced by William, was the Duke of Schomberg, killed a few months after at the battle of the Boyne, in his eighty-third year,—who, a short time before he set off for Ireland, being asked whether he did not mean to give himself the repose to which his years entitled him, replied, "a good general makes his retreat as late as he can." By his subsequent conduct, as well as courage, he added greatly to the glory of the octogenarians.

[2] Grey's Debates, i. 447.

it.[1] Rawlinson, one of the former commissioners, was continued, and Sir George Hutchins, another new one, was introduced, but, though a sensible man and a sound lawyer, he likewise was too obscure and uninteresting to deserve further notice.

If I were to select for commemoration those only who displayed amiable and praiseworthy qualities, I fear that Sir John Trevor ought equally to be consigned to oblivion; but it is my duty to trace his career, for, though devoid of principle, he was gifted with singular energy and versatility, and he acted a conspicuous part in the most interesting period of our history.

He was descended from Edward ap David, an illustrious Welshman, who, no doubt carrying up his own pedigree to Noah, was the common ancestor of several noble and distinguished families taking the surname of Trevor.[2] Our John was the second son of John Trevor, of Brynkinalt, in the county of Denbigh, Esq., by an aunt of Lord Chancellor Jeffreys. He was born during the civil war in the reign of Charles I. Notwithstanding the high "Welsh *plood* in his *pody*, which all the water in Wye could not wash out," his family was at this time in reduced circumstances, and, being a younger brother, great difficulty was found in procuring him education, and giving him a start in life. It is certain that he never was at the university, and it is supposed that he never was at any higher seminary than a village school. He likewise had the misfortune to have a cast in his eye, which alarmed all who saw him. Arthur Trevor, a cousin, who was an eminent barrister, hearing how sadly the Brynkinalt folks were at a loss to dispose of "squinting Jack," took compassion upon them, and sent for the lad to London. On his arrival, he displayed very lively parts, although his manners were rather uncouth, and he could not speak a sentence of correct English. He was now put to copy papers and go messages. Roger North gives us an amusing description of this part of his career. "He was bred a sort of clerk in old Arthur Trevor's chamber, an eminent and worthy professor of the law in the Inner Temple. A gentleman that visited Mr. Arthur Trevor, at his going out observed

---

[1] Books of Privy Council, June 3, 1690. Cr. Off. Min. fol. 137.
[2] Among others, that of Theodore Trevor, Earl of Hereford. Yorke's Royal Tribes of Wales. Collins's Peerage.

a strange looking boy in his clerk's seat (for no person ever had a worse sort of squint than he had), and asked who that youth was? '*A kinsman of mine,*' said Arthur Trevor, '*that I have allowed to sit here to learn the knavish part of the law.*' This John Trevor grew up, and took in with the gamesters, among whom he was a great proficient: and being well grounded in the law, proved a critic in resolving gaming cases and doubts, and had the authority of a judge among them; and his sentence for the most part carried the cause."[1]

But, in truth, though he occasionally kept loose company, it was with a view to his own advancement, and his office of " Lord Chancellor of the Jockey Club," he only considered as a stepping stone to the woolsack. From his arrival in London, he cogitated night and day how he was to become rich and great, and he made his love of pleasure always subservient to his avarice and ambition. Being entered a student of the Inner Temple, he studied law with much assiduity, and rendered himself well versed in all branches of his profession. Ever looking to the main chance, he had formed an extensive connection among attorneys and their clerks while in the office of his cousin Arthur; and when he was called to the bar, being particularly skilled in " the knavish part of the law," he soon got into extensive practice, although not of the most reputable description.

His countryman and cousin, Jeffreys, was rising into high repute, and showed his kindness. Through the interest of Sir George, who had now renounced Shaftesbury and the Whigs, he was made a King's counsel, introduced at Court, returned a member to the House of Commons, and put in the way to the highest preferments. I am sorry, from the constant allusions to the topic in contemporary writings, to be obliged to mention that he was likewise supposed to owe his advancement to another member of the same family. He had been a lover of the gay widow of a Montgomeryshire squire,—daughter of Sir Thomas Bludworth, Lord Mayor of London,—and this *liaison* was still supposed to continue, after she became Lady Jeffreys, and he had been advanced to high stations, in which gravity of character and purity of morals

---

[1] Life of Guilford, ii. 27, 28.

ought especially to be preserved.[1] It was said that Sir George was not unaware of his own disgrace, and a story went, that Scroggs and he once having quarreled in their cups, the former taunted him with it, but that they were very soon good friends again, and jointly pursued their infamous designs against law, justice and humanity."[2]

Trevor never seems to have made any figure in the House of Commons as an orator, but he was busy and bustling, and by activity and intrigue acquired considerable influence among the members. He occasionally spoke, and he made up for his want of eloquence by the slavish doctrines which he inculcated. The exercise of

[1] These publications are generally too gross for the present day; but to show the manners of the age, I will venture on one more modest specimen from a Ballad published on Jeffreys soon after his second marriage—(which the ladies may skip).

"But to allay the secret so hot,
George from the Court has knighthood got,
Bestowed upon him for his bauling,
A royal mark for catterwauling.
There's something more that George has got
(For Trevor left him who knows what)
A teeming lady-wife, &c."

[2] This story is referred to in the following doggerel:—

"But one thing more must not be past
When George with Clodpate* feasted last
(I must say Clodpate was a sinner,
To jeer his brother so at dinner).
He by his almanack did discover
His wife scarce thirty weeks went over,
Ere she, poor thing in pieces fell,
Which made Mouth† stare and bawl like hell.
What then, you fool! some wives miscarry,
And reckon June for January.
This Clodpate did assert as true,
Which he by old experience knew;
But all his canting would not do,
George put him to't upon denial,
Which set him hard as Wakeman's trial.‡
They rail'd and bawl'd, and kept a pother,
And like two curs did bite each other,
Which brought some sport but no repentance;
So off they went to Harris's§ sentence,
Which soon they pass'd against all laws
To glut their rage with popish cause,
For which injustice, knaves! we hope
You'll end together in the rope."‖

* Scroggs. † Jeffreys. ‡ For the Popish Plot.
§ See Harris's trial for a libel, 7 St. Tr. 928. ‖ Life of Jeffreys, 39

the royal prerogative he maintained was by no means to be inquired into by parliament. " 'Tis the King's prerogative," said he, " to make peace or war; 'tis he that makes it, and he that breaks it. The disciples came to our Saviour in the ship, and said, ' Lord, save us or we perish;' and we say no more to the King." When the Popish plot broke out, falsely thinking to please Charles II., who, in this instance, displayed more generosity than he had credit for, he said, " I would satisfy the loyal subjects of England, and pass a vote in plain English to make an address to the King that the Queen and her family, together with all reputed or suspected papists may be removed from Whitehall." The vote was carried by acclamation, but was censured by his majesty.

Trevor took an active part in the infamous prosecution of Lord Stafford, saying, " Upon the evidence, I am satisfied clearly that this Lord Stafford is guilty, and so I would make no manner of bones to demand judgment. I would have no more delay, but go up and demand judgment." What was more to his credit, he boldly, though ineffectually, attempted to defend Jeffreys when attacked in the House of Commons for obstructing the right of petitioning in the great controversy between the " Petitioners " and the " Abhorrers." " This gentleman," said he, " has been Recorder of London many years, and it is a place of great authority ; and it is his happiness that there is no evidence against him that he ever packed a jury, or has gone about to clear the guilty. He has been counsel for the King when persons were indicted for the horrid plot, and labored himself worthily; and, if I may say so, he was too forward in prosecuting : if so, that may make some atonement for his forwardness in other matters. I hope in some measure you will take pity of him." Jeffreys was deprived of his recordership, but soon rallied from the blow, and revenged himself upon his enemies.[1]

Such was Trevor's reputation as a high prerogative lawyer, that at the meeting of James II.'s only parliament, in May, 1685, he was proposed by the government as Speaker, and of course, was elected.[2] He succeeded in getting one supply bill passed. Presenting it according to the custom which then prevailed, that the King pending the session might pass it in person, he said :—

[1] See 4 Parl. Hist. 543, 990, Grey's Debates.   [2] Ibid. 1349.

"We bring not with it any bill for the preservation or security of our religion, which is dearer to us than our lives: in that we acquiesce, entirely rely, and rest wholly satisfied in your Majesty's gracious and sacred word, repeated declarations and assurance to support and defend the religion of the Church of England as it is now by law established. We present this revenue to your Majesty without the addition of any conditional appropriating or tacking clauses, and we humbly beseech your Majesty to accept of it, and along with it our hearty prayers, that God Almighty would bless you with a long life and happy reign to enjoy it."

Everything went smoothly during the first short session, till it was interrupted by Monmouth's rebellion; but when parliament again met in the end of the year, notwithstanding all the Speaker's efforts to repress free discussion, such symptoms appeared in the House of Commons of resistance to tyranny, that a speedy dissolution took place, with a resolve to rule thereafter by prerogative alone. In the meanwhile, Trevor was rewarded with the office of Master of the Rolls,[1] Jeffreys having received the Great Seal, as Chancellor, about a month before.[2] From this time their friendship was at an end, and they became rivals and enemies.[3]

Trevor's ambition was only inflamed by past success; and with little disguise he now aimed at the Great Seal. For this purpose he began to disparage Jeffreys as a lawyer; but Jeffreys, being Chancellor, was revenged of him by reversing his decrees and discharging his most common orders.[4] "Nay, more, it is said that the Chancellor set up officers of his own appointment to affront the Master of the Rolls by questioning his authority, and insulting him publicly on his seat, although they had not learning or credit to support their objections."[5] However, Trevor,

---

[1] Rot. Pat. 1 Jac. 2, m. 32.   [2] Cr. Off. Min. fol. 121.
[3] The scandalous Chronicle asserted that his Honor now likewise broke with Lady Jeffreys, and was superseded in her affections by one Mountfort, a comedian taken into the service of the Chancellor, to make him laugh by mimicking the Judges—as a substitute for the ancient fool—an officer who does not seem to have been professedly kept by King or Chancellor after the Restoration. A libel on Jeffreys said,
"He now wears horns that are by M——t made,
T——r engaging in a different trade."
[4] Life of Guilford, ii. 28. Yorke's Royal Tribes, 109, 110.
[5] Life of Jeffreys, 326.

far from succumbing with the abject submission which was expected, was bold enough to turn again when trampled upon; and, resolutely standing his own ground, watched for an opportunity when Jeffreys might commit some serious mistake, or from some unlucky combination of circumstances might get into disgrace. Roger North says, that Trevor at this time, "like a true gamester, fell to the good work of supplanting his patron and friend, and had certainly done it if King James's affairs had stood right up much longer; for he was advanced so far with him as to vilify and scold with him publicly at Whitehall."[1]

Trevor tried to excite an outcry in respect of the prosecution of Alderman Cornish, whom Jeffreys had pointed out as a victim, and declared "that if he pursued that unfortunate man unto execution, it would be no better than murder."[2] He had the address still to keep his footing at Court; and, if Jeffreys on any occasion hesitated for a moment in complying with James's illegal and mad schemes, denounced him, in the royal circle, as disloyal, and, as soon as Jeffreys complied, contrived to have him denounced to the public as the author of a pernicious and unconstitutional measure.

Trevor had a formidable competitor in Williams, the Solicitor General, who conducted the prosecution against the Seven Bishops, and to whom the Great Seal was promised if he could obtain a conviction. By unbounded subserviency, Jeffreys did contrive to keep his office till after the landing of the Prince of Orange; but Trevor was gaining upon him, and, in July, managed to get himself sworn of the Privy Council, which was not then, as it often now is, a mere empty honor, but entitled the person on whom it was conferred to take a part in the measures of government. The entry in the Diary of Henry, Earl of Clarendon, recording the batch of Privy Councillors now made, is rather amusing: "July 6, 1688. Sir John Trevor, Master of the Rolls; Caloner Tytus and Mr. Vane, Sir Henry Vane's son, were sworn of the Privy Council. Good God bless us! What will the world come to?"

When acting with the advice of such counselors, James discovered that his nephew, the Prince of Orange, having landed in England, was a candidate for the throne.

---

[1] Life of Jeffreys, 326. [2] Ante, p. 357.

Trevor for a while stood aloof to see which would be victorious. On the return of the deluded monarch from Rochester,—misled by the transient symptoms of a reaction in his favor, Trevor declared for him, attended his levee at Whitehall, and assisted with Hamilton, Berkeley, Craven, Preston, and Godolphin, the only other counselors who remained faithful, in preparing a proclamation for suppressing tumultuary outrages—which was published in the London Gazette, and was the last act of sovereignty ever performed by a legitimist monarch in England. On James's final flight, Trevor joined the high Tories, who were desirous first of appointing William as Regent, and, when they were beaten, of doing everything to embarrass his government,—having devised a plan with a double aspect,—whereby the King should either be compelled to go back to Holland, or to choose the Tory leaders for his ministers.

As soon as William and Mary were proclaimed King and Queen, and William entered on the administration of the government, Trevor was removed from his office of Master of the Rolls, and Henry Powle, a good Whig, was appointed in his place.[1] Though returned to the Convention Parliament, he had taken no open part in the discussions respecting the settlement of the throne, from the hope that he might give no offense, and, as he was allowed to be a good Equity Judge, his political misdeeds might be overlooked; but as soon as he was removed, he entered into furious opposition, and did everything in his power to thwart the measures of the government. Still, he was no orator, and although he occasionally made short speeches, he was chiefly prominent in guiding the measures of his party.[2] The only occasion when he took a leading part in the Convention Parliament was in opposing a Bill to disfranchise the borough of Stockbridge for bribery and corruption. He then delivered the earliest speech I find on record against parliamentary reform: "I never heard of boroughs dissolved before. I am afraid if this question pass, you, Mr. Speaker, and I, shall sit no more in that chair. I have the honor to serve for a borough in Devonshire (Beralstone), for which I am

---

[1] He sat for Beralstone; Sergeant Maynard, who was first returned for that borough, having elected to serve for Plympton, for which likewise he was returned.   [2] See 5 Parl. Hist. 298, 410, 422, 432, 491, 520, 533.

obliged to a member of the House (Lord Commissioner Maynard) and to the gentlemen of that country. If you break the ancient constitution of elections, I know not the consequences." He then goes on to show that it was only on the petition of boroughs themselves that they had ever been exempted from sending representatives to parliament, and that the franchise once granted ought always to be preserved—thus concluding: "The security of the nation was ever thought in the mixture of this House. What shall then become of merchants to inform you of trade? The House stands upon ancient constitutions, and I hope you will not remove old landmarks." The Bill was dropped—contrary to the interest of the Jacobites; for I am afraid it must be confessed that it was in the small corrupt boroughs that the strength of the liberal party chiefly lay,—the county constituencies continuing long in favor of the exiled family.

The Convention Parliament having been dissolved, and a new one being called, there was a violent struggle at the elections between the contending factions, but the returns showed a decided majority in favor of the Tories. Of these a considerable number were zealous friends to King James, and would eagerly have recalled him at all hazards; but many, from a dread of Popery, were willing for the present to support the new *régime*, in the hope that something might hereafter occur to re-establish hereditary right; and a still greater number were only impatient to wrest power and place from the Whigs, and and were ready, on their own terms, loyally to serve King William. At the head of this last section appeared the ex-Master of the Rolls. Being disappointed in his wish to represent his native county, he had been returned for a rotten borough,—and shortly before the commencement of the session, after meeting with his friends who were assembling in London, he made an overture to the Court, that, if restored to the chair of the House of Commons, which he had filled under James II., he not only would himself support King William, but that he would exert all the interest he possessed among the Tory party to bring over adherents. His proposal was agreed to,—and, to strengthen his arguments in favor of "Revolution principles," he was furnished with large sums of money to be distributed by him among the members of the new

House of Commons who were thought formidable and venal.

Accordingly, on the first day of the session, the Commons being desired to choose a Speaker, Sir John Lowther, Vice-Chamberlain to the King, rose and said, "that he conceived Sir John Trevor, both for his great experience in parliamentary affairs and knowledge in the laws, was every way qualified for that employment." The Tories were delighted with their apparent triumph, and the Whigs of course acquiesced in the nomination of the government. Trevor, who had been dismissed from his office exactly a twelvemonth before, as an adherent of "Popery and arbitrary power," was unanimously elected Speaker of William's first regular parliament. Being conducted to the chair by his mover and seconder, he acknowledged the great honor the House had conferred upon him, withal saying, "that he feared they had done themselves a great prejudice in making choice of him, and therefore he desired leave to disable himself before the royal throne, that they might thereby have an opportunity of making a better choice."[1] This farce of "disabling" was acted at the bar of the House of Lords, but Lord Chief Baron Atkyns, by the King's command, declared, "that the Commons could not by possibility have made a better choice than the ex-Master of the Rolls."

Trevor honorably performed his part of the contract, and not only himself did what he could in the chair for the government, but with the assistance of the money supplied to him, made many converts from the doctrine of "divine indefeasible right," and was in such favor with William that, at the end of a few weeks, still continuing Speaker, on the removal of Maynard, he was created First Lord Commissioner of the Great Seal. He afterwards obtained this compliment from Burnet :—

"The Speaker of the House of Commons, Sir John Trevor, was a bold and dexterous man, and knew the most effectual ways of recommending himself to every government: he had been in great favor in King James's time, and was made Master of the Rolls by him, and if Lord Jeffreys had stuck at anything, he was looked on as the man likeliest to have had the Great Seal: he now got himself to be chosen Speaker, and was made First Com-

[1] 5 Parl. Hist. 547.

missioner of the Great Seal: being a Tory in principle, he undertook to manage that party, provided he was furnished with such sums of money as might purchase some votes; and by him began the practice of buying off men, in which hitherto the King had kept to stricter rules. I took the liberty," adds the Bishop, "once to complain to the King of this method; he said he hated it as much as any man could do, but he saw it was not possible, considering the corruption of the age, to avoid it, unless he would endanger the whole."[1]

Such satisfaction did Sir John Trevor continue to give, as Speaker, in removing the scruples of refractory members when they came privately to consult him in his chamber on points of order, and in smoothing the progress of the measures of Government through the House, that on the sudden death of Powle, his Whiggish substitute, he was appointed to succeed him;[2] so that he was, at the same time Master of the Rolls, First Lord Commissioner of the Great Seal, and Speaker of the House of Commons.

The Great Seal continued in the hands of the three Lords Commissioners, Trevor, Rawlinson, and Hutchins, till the beginning of the following month of May, but complaints had been multiplying against the administration of justice in the Court of Chancery, and these became so loud that they could no longer be neglected. Trevor was frequently absent on account of his political avocations; the other two were sometimes divided: when agreeing, their opinion did not carry much weight, and now that one of the three was Master of the Rolls, there was no satisfactory mode of reviewing the decisions of that Judge. Besides, the experiment having been tried above three years, the profession and the public came to the conviction, which I believe has been since generally entertained, that from the nature of Equity suits they are best disposed of by a single judge, he having the power, when legal questions arise, of referring them to a court of common law, or calling in common-law judges to assist him.[3]

[1] O. T. iii. 57.
[2] He was sworn before the Lords Commissioners Rawlinson and Hutchins, himself still First Commissioner. Cr. Off. Min. fol. 140.
[3] "All people were now grown weary of the Great Seal being in Commission; it made the proceedings in Chancery to be both more dilatory and more ex-

Considerable difficulty had likewise been felt respecting the Speakership of the House of Lords, where, according to immemorial usage, a Lord Chancellor or Lord Keeper ought to have presided. At a meeting of the Convention Parliament, the Lords chose the Marquis of Halifax their Speaker, and, in the exercise of the power belonging to them to chose one of themselves Speaker in the absence of the Lord Chancellor or any Speaker named by the Crown, they continued day by day to re-elect the Marquis of Halifax, till the 19th day of October, 1689.[1] On that day Sir Robert Atkyns, Chief Baron of the Exechequer and Knight of the Bath, produced in the House letters patent, addressed to him, authorizing him "to do and execute all such things as the Lord Chancellor or Lord Keeper of the Great Seal should or might in that behalf do if he were personally present in the Upper House of Parliament." By virtue of this commission, he constantly acted as Speaker till the 14th of March, 1693, when he prorogued parliament in the name of their Majesties;[2] but serious inconvenience was experienced from the occupier of the woolsack, not only not being a member of the House, but not being a member of the Government, and knowing nothing of the measures to be brought forward and carried. According to the then existing system, there neither was, nor was there any chance of there

pensive; and there were such exceptions made to the decrees of the Commissioners, that appeals were brought against most of them, and frequently they were reversed." 3 Burn. O. T. 148.

The Great Seal has never since been in commission, unless during a temporary embarrassment about the appointment of a Lord Keeper or Lord Chancellor; but the offices of Lord High Treasurer and Lord High Admiral have been in commission almost ever since the reign of Queen Anne.

[1] Till then the Journal each day begins with an entry in this form: "Marquis of Halifax chosen Speaker;" and thus concludes: Marquis Halifax, Orator Procerum pro tempore, declaravit præsen. convent continuand. esse usque in diem Veneris videlicet 25um diem instantis Januarii 168$\frac{8}{9}$, hora decima auror. Dominis sic decernentibus."—*Lords' Journal*.

[2] On these occasions "he went to the usual place by the state."

On the 21st of January, 1691, "the Speaker was ordered for the future, when he shall speak to any lord, or other person, to speak sitting with his hat on." On the 15th of January, 1693, an order was made which it would be highly for the advantage of the House if the Lord Chancellor would now enforce. "The Speaker is ordered to stop proceedings in case Lords are at the fire, sitting on the woolsacks, &c., requiring them *by name* to go to their places."—*Lords' Journals*. Anciently the Lords always sat on their appropriated benches according to their degrees and seniority—but the right reverend Prelates alone now regard this usage. If *precedence* is waived, *order* ought still to be preserved.

afterwards being, a law lord in the House ; which, not only in deciding appeals and writs of error, but in passing bills connected with jurisprudence and in discussing great constitutional questions, was thus likely to remain lamentably *inops concilii.*

Great weight was, no doubt, likewise given to the consideration that there was now a most distinguished individual to whom, singly, all the duties of the highest office in the law might be intrusted with the applause of the nation. The Great Seal was therefore taken from the Commissioners, and intrusted to Sir JOHN SOMERS, as Lord Keeper.[1]

Rawlinson and Hutchinson immediately sank back into the insignificance from which they had been accidently raised ; but Trevor, still Speaker and Master of the Rolls —with singular activity of mind and talent for intrigue— continued to play an important part before the public, and, if it had not been for his extreme indiscretion when he became the *bribed* instead of the *briber*, he probably would have reached the grand object of his ambition since, as before, the Revolution—which was to become Lord Chancellor, and to be created a peer.

So "dexterous" was he, that he not only continued in favor with William, but, with a view to the next reign, he contrived to insinuate himself into the confidence of the Princess of Denmark, and her maid or mistress, so that he was privately consulted by them in all that regarded the succession. While some discussion was going on in parliament respecting the designation of those on whom the Crown was limited, a meeting of the Princess and her friends was held, of which the following minute was made by Sir John Trevor :—[2]

"Tuesday evening, 22nd Jan., 1694, at Berkley House, Present, E. of Marlborough.

"*Princess,*—That she understood Debate in the House about the words ' Heirs and Succo^m' in the Style of Acts of Parliament. That she did desire that this matter should not interrupt their Consultations, or obstruct the King's business for the support of the Gover^t. That she had considered this matter, and was confident of the King's kindness and justice, and therefore did desire me

[1] Cr. Off. Min. fol. 140.
[2] The original, in his handwriting, now lies before me.

that I would acquaint the House that she was willing and desirous that the words 'Heirs and Succors' might still continue in the style.

"I replyed that this was a matter of a high nature for me to deale in. That I was willing to serve her R. H. in anything that might consist wth my Duty and Service to ye King and the House. But for my owne Justification, and least I might mistake in the matter of this importance, I did desire her Commands in writing, under her hand; else I most humbly begged her excuse. To which she agreed."

Accordingly, in an envelope bearing the indorsement in Sir John Trevor's hand, "The Princess's Letter to me —Heirs and Succ^rs," and in a more modern hand, "From Queen Anne," there is the following letter, "For the Right Honble Sir John Trevor, Speaker of the House of Comons," in the handwriting of the Princess herself:

"I have heard there was some question in the House concerning the words '*Heirs and Successors;*' as to the concern I may have in it, I am very far from desiring any alteration of the style, and wish only that it may bee determined in such a way as may bring the least obstruction or delay to the King's affairs in Parliament."[1]

Trevor might have acquired a complete ascendency over Anne, and have become her Lord Chancellor and chief adviser, but a blow was now impending over him which forever marred his fortunes.

In the beginning of 1695, the cry against bribery was violent, and the belief gained ground that the Court, the camp, the city, nay, parliament itself, was tainted, and that universal corruption prevailed. A motion was made in the House of Commons which must have caused general alarm, but which no one had courage to oppose—for the appointment of a committee "to inquire into the charges which were made against members,—with power to send for persons, papers, and records." On the 7th of March, the Committee reported "that there having been in the preceding session a bill pending in the House of Commons, promoted by the City of London, called

[1] I am indebted for these valuable relics, now first submitted to the public, to the kindness of Sir John Trevor's representative, the present Lord Dungannon, who has himself written a very interesting account of those times. See Trevor's Life of William III.

'the Orphans Bill,' whereby a power was to be given to lay assessments on the public for the benefit of the Corporation, an entry had been found in the books of the Common Council, '. That Mr. Chamberlain do pay to the hon. Sir John Trevor, knight, Speaker of the House of Commons, the sum of 1,000 guineas, so soon as the said bill be passed into an act of parliament,'—that a hint had been given to the Common Council, that unless this sum were paid, the bill would not pass—that Mr. Speaker knew of the order being made while the bill was pending —that when the bill passed, two Aldermen and the Chamberlain waited on Mr. Speaker, with a compliment of thanks in the name of the City, for his kindness in furthering the bill, and an order for the said guineas, which Mr. Speaker accepted—that two or three days after, Mr. Speaker sent a messenger into the City with the said order, and received the said guineas,—and that the said order was forthcoming with this indorsement thereon: 'The within mentioned 1,000 guineas were delivered and paid unto the hon. Sir John Trevor, this 22nd June, 1694, in the presence of Sir Robt Clayton and Sir Jas. Houblon, which at 22s. exchange, comes to £1,100.'"

Corruption being thus traced to the Chair, with a reasonable suspicion that it had communicated the taint to many members by the way, it was impossible for the House to retain any degree of credit with the people unless they declared their abhorrence of the guilt they had discovered, however much they might regret the exposure or pity the victim. Accordingly a resolution was moved, and seems to have passed without much discussion, "That Sir John Trevor, Speaker of this House, receiving a gratuity of 1,000 guineas from the City of London after the passing of the Orphans Bill, is guilty of a high crime and misdemeanor." The Speaker was subjected to the unparalleled humiliation of putting the resolution from the Chair, of declaring that the "ayes" had it,—and of adding that it was carried *nemine dissentiente*.[1]

[1] Trevor's Life of William III. ii. 250; Com. Jour. 1694–95; 5 Parl. Hist. 906. "On receiving and debating this report, therefore, the Speaker himself, in virtue of his office, was exposed to all the shame and confusion of face which a man could bear and live, in putting the following questions, viz., &c. And so much grace did he discover upon the occasion, that he chose to abdicate rather than be deposed."—*Ralph*, ii. 547. "He was forced or yielded to put the question upon himself, 'As many as are of opinion that Sir

The House immediately adjourned, and the last act which Trevor did as Speaker was to sign the "Votes" containing this resolution, which appeared in print next day. That he might escape the additional disgrace of putting the motion for his own expulsion, he forthwith sent a letter to the Clerk, which was delivered to him at the table, in these words: "Mr. Jodrell; I desire you to present the inclosed to the House and in that you will oblige, Sir, your servant, J. TREVOR, Speaker. March 13, 1694." The Clerk then read the inclosure to the House: "Gentlemen; I did intend to have waited upon you this morning; but, after I was up, I was taken suddenly ill with a violent colick; I hope to be in condition of attending you to-morrow morning: in the mean time I desire you will be pleased to excuse my attendance. I am with all duty, Gentlemen, your most obedient humble servant, J. TREVOR, Speaker. March 13, 1694."[1]

After the reading of these letters a scene of much confusion arose. Some proposed that they should forthwith proceed to the choice of a new Speaker, but an objection was taken, that this could not be done without the authority of the Crown, and that Sir John Trevor still detaining the mace, no motion could be made, and no debate could proceed, till it was brought and laid under the table. Precedents were looked for; but none in point could be found. This irregular conversation having gone on for about two hours, the House adjourned till the following morning at ten o'clock.

All the members in London having then assembled, the Sergeant brought the mace, and laid it under the table, and delivered to the Clerk the following letter from Sir John Trevor, which was immediately read to the House: "Mr. Jodrell; My illness still continues, which makes me unable to come abroad; wherewith I desire you to acquaint the House, and that I humbly pray they will please to excuse me for not attending them. I am, your

John Trevor is guilty, &c.;' and in declaring the sense of the House declared himself guilty. The House rose, and he went his way and came there no more."—*North's Life of Guilford*, ii. 28, 29. A curious difficulty might have arisen, if continuing Speaker, a motion had been made for his expulsion; for the instant the motion was carried, he ceased to be Speaker or a member, although perhaps the resolution would not have had full operation till announced from the Chair. Then he must have been turned out of the House, or taken into custody as "*a stranger.*" [1] This is old style.

friend and servant, J. TREVOR, Speaker. March 14, 1694[5]."

But he had intimated to the King his wish to resign the Chair, and Mr. Wharton, the comptroller of the household, now said, " he was commanded by his Majesty to inform the House that the late Speaker, Sir John Trevor, from indisposition, could not further attend the service of the House ; and that his Majesty gave leave to the House to proceed to the choice of a new Speaker." He accordingly proposed Sir Thomas Littleton, but the House, by a majority of 179 to 146, elected Mr. Foley, who had been chairman of the committee of inquiry.[1]

As soon as the new Speaker was allowed by the Crown, and business could recommence, a motion was made, " that Sir John Trevor, late Speaker of this House, being guilty of a high crime and misdemeanor, by receiving a gratuity of 1,000 guineas from the City of London after passing the Orphans Bill, be expelled the House,"—which was carried without opposition, and a new writ was issued for the election of a burgess for the borough he had represented.

Strange to say, not only no further proceedings were taken against him to punish him for the bribery of which he had been guilty, or to make him refund the bribe, but he was permitted to retain his high judicial office of Master of the Rolls—taking precedence of the Lord Chief Justice of the Common Pleas and the Lord Chief Baron of the Exchequer—and to administer justice in the Court of Chancery, after his expulsion from the House of Commons—for the long period of two-and-twenty years,—under Lord Chancellor Somers, Lord Keeper Wright, Lord Chancellor Cowper, Lord Chancellor Harcourt, and Lord Chancellor Cowper again.[2]

His offense could not have been regarded by his contemporaries by any means in the same serious light in which we should regard it. Even in the resolution of the

---

[1] 3 Burnet, O. T. 199.
[2] " Whether the members thought that the being so basted in the Chair was punishment enough, or for his taking such gross correction so patiently and so conformably, or else, a matter once out of the way was thought of no more, it is certain that he never was molested further about that matter, but continued in his post of Master of the Rolls, equitable Judge of the subjects' interests and estates, to the great encouragement of prudent bribery for ever after."— *North's Life of Guilford,* ii. 29.

House of Commons, the *bribe* is tenderly designated "a gratuity;" and, in those times, although judicial corruption would have been strongly reprobated, yet to give or to receive money for voting in parliament was only called "the way of the world." The sin was reckoned to be in the discovery,—not in the act.[1]

Trevor never was accused or suspected of taking bribes from the suitors in his Court, and he was not only an upright, but an enlightened Judge.[2] Being now free from political distraction, he devoted himself to the business of his Court, and, having much more experience than any of the holders of the Great Seal who were placed over him, he pronounced many decrees which to this day are considered of high authority. He first laid down the doctrine that marriage and the birth of a child shall revoke a will, —or, rather, that a will of an unmarried person is made subject to the implied condition, that under such a new state of circumstances it shall not stand good.

The following anecdote shows the weight of his authority in the Court of Chancery, Lord Harcourt having expressed an opinion, that certain process issued against a wife during her husband's absence abroad was irregular, but being met by an observation from counsel which staggered him, said "he would ask the Master of the Rolls and be guided by his opinion." Trevor, coming into Court, declared the process to be regular, and so it was ruled to be.—Lord Harcourt did not venture to reverse any of Trevor's decrees, and on one occasion set an example which might be usefully followed by "affirming Chancellors;"—coming back to Court from attending a

---

[1] "Corrumpere et corrumpi seculum vocatur." Roger North thus slurs over a bribe taken by Sir Edward Turner, another Speaker in the reign of Charles II.: "This gentleman had served long as Speaker of the parliament, and had been useful to the Crown and also to himself. But on the discovery of *a small present* made to him by the East India Company, he was blown in the House of Commons. The anti-Court party took all advantages against the Court, and made a mountain of this mouse: for it was but a trifle. However, it cost him much of his credit and authority in the Chair which he used to have; and he thought fit to give way, and not to sit there longer to be exposed to the affronts which would continually be thrown at him." However, he was made Solicitor General, and afterwards Lord Chief Baron of the Exchequer.—*Life of Guilford*, i. 97.

[2] He has been absurdly blamed for hearing cases at his private house,—a practice which all Equity Judges must occasionally follow. He had a villa at Knightsbridge, then considered almost a day's journey from London, now forming a division of Belgravia.

Council, and finding the Master of the Rolls, who had been sitting for him, in the act of giving a judgment, he said, "I am of the same opinion—to prevent a rehearing before myself."[1]

On the dissolution of the parliament, after his expulsion, he had the hardihood to propose to be again returned as a representative of the people; but, says Somers, writing to Shrewsbury, "The King said he had in a manner commanded the Master of the Rolls not to come into the House of Commons, on purpose to prevent the inconvenience the reviving that matter would occasion."[2]

He lived ever afterwards very privately, and found his chief delight in accumulating money. He became so great an economist, that he even grudged a glass of wine to a poor relation. It is recorded of him, that he had dined by himself one day at the Rolls, and was drinking his wine quietly, when his cousin, Roderic Lloyd, was unexpectedly introduced to him from a side door: "You rascal," said his Honor to the servant, "and you have brought my cousin, Roderic Lloyd, Esquire, Prothonotary of North Wales, Marshal to Baron Price, &c., &c., &c., up my *back stairs*. Take my cousin, Roderic Lloyd, Esquire, Prothonotary of North Wales, Marshal to Baron Price, &c., &c., &c., take him instantly back down my *back stairs*, and bring him up my *front stairs*." Roderic in vain remonstrated, and, while he was conveyed down the back stairs and up the front stairs, the bottle and glasses were removed by his Honor,—some law books and papers taking their place.[3]

On another occasion he behaved kindly to this same cousin, having an opportunity of doing so without incurring any expense. "Roderic was returning rather elevated from his club one night, and ran against the pump in Chancery Lane. Conceiving somebody had struck him, he drew, and made a lunge at the pump. The sword

---

[1] See Vernon, vol. ii.; Peere Williams, vol. i.; Mod. vols. vi. vii. xi. He made an order for regulating the Six Clerks' Office, which curiously illustrates the manners of the times: "That noe under-clerke in the said office shall from henceforth duering the time of his clerkeshipp presume to weare any sword either in or out of the said office within the cities of London or Westminster or the libertyes thereof, or to be covered or weare his hatt in the said office in the presence of any one of the sworne clerkes." 9 Dec. 1693., Sand. i. 398.

[2] Shrewsbury Correspondence, 1695.

[3] Yorke's Royal Tribes, 108, 109.

entered the spout, and the pump, being crazy, fell down. Roderic concluded he had killed his man ; left his sword in the pump, and retreated to his old friend's house at the Rolls. There he was concealed by the servants for the night. In the morning his Honor, having heard the story, came himself to deliver him from his consternation and confinement in the coal-hole."[1]

I find only one political anecdote of him after his retirement. He was so incensed by the promotion to the primacy of Tillotson, whom he considered a low churchman, that, passing him one day near the House of Lords, he could not refrain from muttering, loud enough to be heard by the object of his spleen, " I hate a fanatic in lawn sleeves." "And I," retorted the Primate, "hate a knave in any sleeves."[2]

Sir John Trevor being near eighty years of age, at last died, on the 20th of May, 1717, at his house in Chancery Lane, and was buried in the Rolls Chapel.[3]

The unfortunate obliquity of his vision is perceptible in the portraits and prints we have of him, and made the wags assert that "Justice was blind, but at the Rolls Equity was now seen to squint." While in the chair, as Speaker, two members in different parts of the House were often equally confident of having "*caught his eye.*"

He is said to have been rough to the bar, and to have caused great consternation in those on whom he frowned, the effect of his squinting being aggravated by a dark truculent visage, and a tremendous pair of bushy eyebrows. His enemies even alleged that he uttered something so harsh to a very promising nephew of his own, practicing before him, as to cause the young man's death from vexation. But recollecting the factious times in which he lived, and the triumph which his enemies gained over him, we should receive with suspicion every statement to his disadvantage which is not supported by positive proof. With all his faults, we must admire the energy, enterprise, and perseverance which, under so many disadvantages, raised him from being a barrister's

---

[1] Yorke's Royal Tribes, 109; Noble's Granger, i. 172.
[2] Life of Jeffreys, 329, n.
[3] He was succeeded by Sir Joseph Jekyll,
——" that good old Whig,
Who never changed his principles or wig."

clerk to the highest offices of the state, and which, with a little more luck, might have given him a respectable name in English history. I have pleasure in recording of him, that he discovered the merit of Atterbury, and appointed him Preacher at the Rolls.[1]

By the death of his elder brother, he succeeded to the paternal estates at Brynkinalt, which, with large possessions of his own acquisition, have descended, through a female, to the present Viscount Dungannon, the very honorable representative of his family.[2]

CHAPTER CVI.

LIFE OF LORD SOMERS,[3] FROM HIS BIRTH TILL THE REVOLUTION.

IT is most consolatory to me at last to reach a Chancellor eminent as a lawyer, a statesman, and a man of letters—the whole of whose public career and character I can conscientiously praise—and whose private life embellished by many virtues, could not have been liable to any grave imputation, since it has received the unqualified approbation of Addison.[4] But my pleasure is chastised by considering the difficulty of the task on which I enter. While we so often see men eager for notoriety and present applause, Lord Somers acted on the maxim which he took for his motto,—" PRODESSE QUAM CONSPICI." He has left us no memoir of himself, and he was so careless about his speeches and his writings, that there are hardly the means of fairly appreciating him as an orator, or as an author. He has had a

---

[1] The Jacobite divine naturally had a high opinion of his patron, who treated him with great familiarity. Writing to Bishop Trelawny, in 1704, he says: "The Master of the Rolls drank the healths of your Lordship and of the whole family quite through to me on Sunday."—*Atterbury Correspondence by Nicholls.*

[2] See Collins's *Peerage*—" Trevor," " Dungannon," " Hampden."

[3] In all the entries respecting Lord Somers in the books of the Middle Temple till he was called to the Bench in 1689, his name is spelt Somer, and then Somers.—He himself afterwards sometimes wrote his name SOMMERS, and generally SOMERS, with a circumflex; but I adhere to that which must now be considered the historical orthography, SOMERS.

[4] Freeholder, No. XXXIX., Friday, May 4, 1716.

great share of general reputation as a consummate Judge, and as the chief founder of the constitutional monarchy under which the country has flourished above a century and a half: but no biographer has yet appeared who can be said to have done him justice.[1] From long neglect several important parts of his career must for ever remain obscure; few personal anecdotes of him are preserved; and materials for his Life must be sought in College Registers, County Chronicles, Peerages, Parliamentary Debates, State Trials, Equity Reports, Party pamphlets, doggerel verses, such scandalous publications at home as Mrs. Manley's "New Atalantis," and such scarce foreign books as Bonaventuri's "Life of Vincenzio Filicaja." Let me then bespeak the indulgence of the reader for an attempt which I deeply feel must be unworthy of its object.[2]

Lord Somers, although the architect of his own fortune, was by no means "sprung from the dregs of the people," as it suited his vituperators to represent.[3] His family had long been owners of a small estate in the parish of Severn-Stoke, in the county of Gloucester.[4]

[1] The author of "The Life of Lord Somers,"—published in 1716, soon after his death, and the foundation of the subsequent Lives of him,—was so grossly ignorant and incurious as to avow that he could not tell at which university his hero had studied: and the "Essay on the Life and Character of Lord Somers," by Cooksey, his kinsman, supposed to contain the most authentic account of his early career, states that he was entered a student of the Middle Temple, in 1676, which was the year he was called to the bar, after having been entered there above seven years. There is much valuable information to be found in a Life of Lord Somers by a most learned and honorable man, the late HENRY MADDOCK, Esq., the first part of which was published in 4to. in the year 1812, and the Second Part of which I have been permitted to peruse in MS.; but the personal narrative is overlaid by general disquisitions on politics and law. The very erudite author would have had much more success if he had borne in mind the caution to biographers by Cornelius Nepos in the commencement of the "Life of Pelopidas;" "Vereor, ne, si res explicare incipiam, non vitam, ejus enarrare, sed historiam videar scribere."

[2] Says Lord Brougham in his interesting "Sketches,"—"Of Lord Somers, indeed, we can scarcely be said to know anything at all. It is now unfortunately too late to fill up the outline which the meagre records of his time have left us."—Vol. i. p. 17.

[3] EXAMINER, No. 26, by Swift; New Atalantis, iv. 62.

[4] Of this family was the famous Admiral Sir George Somer, one of the discoverers of the *Bermudas,* or "*Somer* Islands," celebrated by Waller for their beauty when explored, though long shunned for their supposed dangers and enchantments.

"Heaven sure has kept that charming spot uncurst,
To show how well things were created first."

The old mariner's answer to King James, when persecuted for refusing to yield to the wishes of the Court, seems to show that the feeling of indepen-

They had likewise another possession, the site of a dissolved nunnery, called "The White-ladies," a short distance beyond the walls of the city of Worcester. After the expulsion of the nuns, the dormitory remained entire, and the old hall and refectory had been fitted up into a modern mansion. This property had been granted to the Somers's at the Reformation, and here they received Queen Elizabeth, in her progress through Worcestershire, in the year 1585; the bed in which she slept, and the cup from which she drank, being preserved by them as precious relics, even when they took to the republican side.

The Chancellor's father, John Somers, to increase his patrimonial fortune, was bred to the law, and was established in practice as the most eminent attorney in the county of Worcester when the civil war broke out. Although the city and the chief part of the county of Worcester supported the royal cause, he sided with the parliament, raised a troop of horse, and served under Cromwell. He was for some time quartered at Upton, near his estate, and, while he lay there, used to frequent the parish church of Severn-Stoke. The clergyman, an intrepid supporter of divine right and passive obedience, though often warned against "politics in the pulpit," could not forbear from introducing in his sermons violent invectives against the opposite party. To cure him effectually of this propensity, Captain Somers, in the transport of one of these furious harangues, fired a pistol over his head, and lodged a ball in the sounding-board, the mark of which is shown, and the history of it related, by the clerk of the parish, to this very day.[1]

The battle of Worcester, Cromwell's "crowning mercy," having crushed the royal cause, and established tranquillity in the country, the captain changed his service, and, supported by JOHN DOE and RICHARD ROE, prepared for warfare at Westminster. He resumed his profession, and, from his great skill in it, had *cavaliers* as well as *roundheads* for his clients. A sort of sanctity had

dence was very strong in the blood of Somers: "I wish that as I am the first, so I may be the last, of sacrifices in your times. When from private appetite it is resolved that a creature shall be sacrificed, it is easy to pick up sticks enough from any thicket whither it hath strayed to make a fire to offer it with."—*Life of Bacon,* prefixed to folio edition of his Works," p. 22.

[1] Cooksey, p. 7.

been attached by both sides to the White-ladies, so that it was left uninjured when all the rest of the suburb to which it belonged, including St. Oswald's Hospital, had been demolished during the sieges which the city had stood.[1] In this mansion, thus venerated and considered neutral ground, King Charles II. took up his abode prior to the fatal fight; and having shifted himself here after his defeat, while a council of war was held at Burbourne Bridge, he went off in disguise through the fields adjoining the house, to Estwood, and thence to Boscobel, leaving behind him his garters, two pairs of fine fringed gloves, a waistcoat, and a pair of trunk hose,—which were afterwards added by the family to the memorials of Queen Elizabeth.

John Somers, the father, had been married in the year 1649, to Catherine Ceavern, of a respectable family in Shropshire, and she had brought him a daughter, Elizabeth, afterwards Lady Jekyll. She was now again pregnant, and he placed her for safety in the sanctuary at White-ladies, not many days after Charles had left it. Here, in the spring of the following year, she gave birth to John, the future Chancellor. From the disturbed state of the country no register is to be discovered of the baptism of these two children, and the exact day of the birth of either of them has not been ascertained.[2]

I find no further notice of the boy till a prodigy announced his future greatness. He was much under the care of an aunt married to a noted Presbyterian of the name of Blurton, and " the good lady walking with him in her hand amongst her poultry, a beautiful roost-cock flew upon his curly head, and while perched there, crowed three times very loudly."[3]

[1] In a MS. of Mr. Townshend, of Elmley House, who was in the city during the first siege, and kept a regular diary, under the date of 26th March, 1646, there is this entry: " The citizens and soldiers in the town destroyed St. Oswald's Hospital, but spared Mr. Somers's house at the White Ladies, which was a strong stone building, capable of holding 500 men with safety."
—*Nash, Hist. Worcestershire*, ii. 97.

[2] Some accounts state the 4th of March as the Chancellor's birthday, but without any authority cited. Mary and Catherine, the two younger daughters, are regularly registered in St. Michael's parish, in the city of Worcester.

[3] Cooksey, a relation of the family says, " This tradition comes well attested to me from the Rev. Mr. Pixall, who derived it from his grandmother, who lived at the time in intimacy with the family, and had no doubt of the fact.'
—p. 10.

However, for a long time there seemed to be little prospect of his ever rising higher than being, like his father, an eminent country solicitor. He was put to the College School at Worcester, the master of which then was Dr. Bright, a distinguished classical scholar and a very skillful teacher. Such a practical love of communicating knowledge had this meritorious man, that after he was a prebendary of the Cathedral, and proprietor of a considerable landed estate, he continued with unwearied assiduity and patience to ply his pedagogical labors. From him young Somers imbibed that taste for elegant literature which adhered to him through life. At this seminary we know that he was thoroughly grounded in Greek and Latin, but how long he continued there is uncertain, and there is great difficulty in tracing him during his early youth. He appears to have been put for a short time to a private academy at Walsall, in Staffordshire, and to another at Sheriff-Hales, in Shropshire.[1] He was always remarkably studious and contemplative. "Though the brightest boy in the College School, instead of joining his young companions in their boyish amusements, he was seen walking and musing alone, not so much as looking on while they were at play."[2]

His biographers represent that as soon as his school education was finished, he was placed in his father's office to learn the business of an attorney, and they defer his first entrance at the University till the year 1675, when he was in the twenty-fifth year of his age; but although he certainly did reside at Oxford at the time they suppose, I have ascertained that, in the year 1667, when he was only sixteen years old, he was matriculated and admitted of Trinity College.[3]

The records of the University have been searched in vain to discover any other notice respecting him. I am inclined to believe that his residence at Oxford at this

---

[1] Buck's MSS. Brit. Mus. No. 4223.   [2] Seward's Anecdotes, ii. 114.
[3] Copy of Matriculation:—"Mar. 23, 1667, Johannes Somers an n. 16, fil. Joh. Somers de Worcester Genri."
Copy of admission in his own handwriting:—"Ego Johannes Somers, Filius Johannis Somers generosi in civitate, Vigorniæ natus, admissus sum commensalis 3 mensæ in Col. Trin: Oxon: sub tutamine M^{gi} Campion, 1667." Then follow these words in another hand: "Termino Paschalis. Tandem Summus Angliæ Cancellarius." His biographers have been misled by the entry of another John Somers, in 1674, who is described " of the city of Exeter."

period of his life was extremely short, and that while still very young he did become an apprentice in the manner supposed, with the view of being his father's partner and successor. A few years afterwards we find him occupying a desk in the office at White-ladies. The drudgery to which he was there expected to submit did not by any means suit his taste, and he soon made it apparent that he could not succeed in this department of the profession. However, idleness could never be imputed to him; nor did he now cross his father's soul by penning a stanza when he should engross, for it was not till some years after that he first displayed his poetical vein, when initiated into fashionable society by the young Earl of Shrewsbury he drank champagne with the wits. At this period he devoted himself to severe study, insomuch that, "by the exactness of his knowledge and behavior, he discouraged his father and all the young men that knew him; they were afraid to be in his company."

He was sometimes allowed to retire to the family house in the parish of Severn-Stoke, and the room which he occupied, and in which he read night and day, used afterwards, when he became a great man, to be pointed out as "Somers's study." But he chiefly resided at White-ladies, the society of which he was not sorry to exchange for his books. A scheme of life prevailed there of a very extraordinary description. Somers, the father, having at the Restoration obtained a pardon under the Great Seal (which is still preserved in the family), and continuing to flourish in his profession, had his office established in the old Nunnery.[2] The mansion was inhabited by several other families connected by blood or marriage, and they consorted in a style of which it is now difficult to give or to form an idea.

"Their mornings were employed by each in their respective occupations—the culture of a large farm—the clothing trade, then in a flourishing state—the producing and manufacturing teasels, woad, madder, and all dyeing materials—the making of bricks and tiles in immense

---

[1] Seward's Anecdotes, vol. ii. 114; Buck's MSS. Brit. Mus. No. 4223.

[2] He is not supposed to have committed any offense requiring a special pardon beyond firing over the head of the parson at Severn-Stoke while in the pulpit; but, being a lawyer, he perhaps remembered the observation of Sir Edward Coke, "That good men will never refuse God and the King's pardon, because every man doth often offend both of them." 3 Inst. C. 105.

quantities, to supply the demand occasioned by rebuilding the ruined city and suburbs.[1] The labors of the day over, they repaired for refreshment to one common table in the great hall of the old Nunnery, where seldom fewer than twenty or thirty relations and friends of the families assembled daily, and spent their evenings in the utmost cheerfulness and conviviality. The products of the farm, the supplies of fish and game, and viands of every kind, received constantly from their country connections, furnished their table with abundant plenty, and entitled such contributors to a place at it without ceremony or reserve. The annual slaughter of two brawns marked the festivity of Christmas."[2]

Old Somers managed the parliamentary elections for the County, for the City, and for the boroughs of Evesham, Droitwich, and Bewdley. To White-ladies came the candidates and representatives to consult him and plan their electioneering operations, and to White-ladies were summoned the leading electors to receive a good dinner and promises of preferment.

The most distinguished individual in the group for some years was the great lawyer, Sir Francis Winnington, afterwards Solicitor General, who was now rising rapidly at the bar, and represented the city of Worcester in parliament.[3] He saw the merit of young Somers, and recommended that he should study for the bar, pointing out how Littleton and other Worcestershire men had risen to be Judges. The wary attorney was very averse to such a hazardous experiment, particularly as he had no younger son to inherit the fine business which he had established; but at last he yielded, and on the 24th of May, 1669, the future Chancellor was carried to London, and entered a student of the Middle Temple.[4] This ceremony being

---

[1] From which, Lord Somers was afterwards, in abusive ballads, called the *Brickmaker's Son*.   [2] Cooksey, 14.

[3]   " But how at church and bar all gape and stretch,
        If Winnington but plead, or South or Only preach !"
                                                    Dispensary, canto v.

But by all prose accounts, although Sir Francis was a deep jurisconsult, he was a very indifferent orator. In 1674, he was made Solicitor General. Orig. Jur. 119.

[4] By the kindness of the benchers and the sub-treasurer of the Middle Temple, I have been able to ascertain this date ; and I subjoin a copy of his admission from the books of the Society:—

gone through, he immediately returned into the country, and read law privately in his father's house under the direction of Winnington, till the spring of the following year. A small set of chambers was then bought for him in Elm Court, in the Temple, and he began to keep his terms.[1] He had now "the run of his friend's chambers," and he was there so constantly to see and to assist in the business which was going forward, that some said "he began the law by being the clerk of Sir Francis Winnington;"[2] but, in truth, he was only his pupil. The "Readings" and "Moots" by which the study of the law had been carried on since the establishment of the Inns of Court were falling into desuetude, the "Exercises" by which proficiency was tested were now becoming empty forms, such as we find them, and the system of pupilage was beginning. This has since very imperfectly supplied the place of the training for the profession in England which prevails elsewhere under regular professors appointed to teach the law of nations, the civil law, the different branches of the municipal law, and medical jurisprudence,—with examinations and theses, to show that the aspirant is fit to be trusted with the duties of an advocate, and is qualified to fill the offices to which, as an advocate, he may be appointed.[3]

Maij 24to 1669°.

Somer J. adh.   Mr. Johes Somer filius et heres apparens Johis Somer de pochia Scti Michis in Bedwerdine in Com. Worcestr'. gen. Admissus est in Societatem Medij Templi spealiter. Et obligatur una cum. Et dat ℔ fine. 03.10.00

Februarij 26to 1669°.

Somer, J. ad. Ca.   Ex Assignacone et sursum reddicone Executor: ultime voluntat et Testamenti Thome Connesby gen. nup. Defunct. M^r. Johes Somer Admissus est in totam illam Cameram cum prtimentij et Scituat ex Australi parte de le Elm Co^{er} quarti gradus Habend. totatam. illam Cameram prdict cum prtinentij et prdict m^{ro} Somer pr termino vite ipsus Johis. Et dat ℔ fine. .   02.00.00

[2] Life of Somers, 8vo. 1716, p. 10.
[3] The bencher who, according to the present system, "publishes a bar-

As yet young Somers, while in London, associated only with lawyers, his chief companion being Jekyll, afterwards his brother-in-law—the "good old Whig," Sir Joseph, celebrated by Pope. His vacations he spent at White-ladies, where the society was very little relished by him—till the year 1672, when it was enlivened by a gay and gallant young courtier, who was not only an accomplished scholar, but was familiarly acquainted with the leaders on both sides in politics, and with the intrigues of fashionable life. Somers, the attorney, along with the estates of other great families, had managed those of the Earls of Shrewsbury. The head of this illustrious house had been killed some years before in a duel with the Duke of Buckingham,—his countess, as it was said, disguised as a page, holding the Duke's horse, and rewarding his prowess by sleeping with him in the shirt stained with her husband's blood.[1] The young Earl, after being much courted by Charles II., had met with some disgust from the monarch or his ministers, and, still in early youth, resolved to retire into the country. Grafton, then the chief residence of the family, being found much out of repair, he accepted an invitation from his steward to White-ladies. It was vacation-time, and young John, the student of the Middle Temple, was an inmate. At once a friendship was contracted between them which lasted through life, unabated even by some deviation of the Earl, when become Duke of Shrewsbury, from the political principles which they long held in common. They now engaged in the same studies and amusements, and for months were inseparable. Somers from this time visibly changed his manners, and acquired that "exquisite taste of politeness" for which, as well as "the greatest strength of good sense," he was afterwards celebrated.[2] There is, however, a suspicion

rister" in the hall, in token of his proficiency, may appropriately address him in the words of Horace:

"Lusisti satis, *edisti satis* atque bibisti,
Tempus abire tibi est."

However, I am happy to say that there are now in the Inns of Court symptoms of improvement.

[1] ——"How chang'd from him
That life of humor and that soul of whim,
Gallant and gay in Cliefden's proud alcove,
The bower of wanton Shrewsbury and love.

[2] Freeholder, No. 39. Ralph, ii. 785. He seems to have accomplished the union which Pliny thought so difficult and important. Severitatem istam

that his morals underwent a change, not so favorable, about the same time, and (with what foundation I do not certainly know, perhaps only from political spite) libertinism was afterwards imputed to him.

Upon their return to London they still lived much together, and Shrewsbury introduced his friend as well to Dryden and other distinguished men of letters as to the nobility residing in Queen Street, in Lincoln's Inn Fields, and in Aldersgate Street. Somers now felt the disadvantages of a defective education, which must have arisen either from a very short stay at the University, or from idleness while resident there. Suspending professional pursuits, and sacrificing professional gains, he nobly resolved yet to go through a regular course of academical discipline. He was confirmed in this purpose by the advice of Dr. William Hopkins, a very learned man, Prebendary of the Cathedral, and Master of St. Oswald's Hospital at Worcester. Accordingly, in the year 1674, when he was in his twenty-fourth year, he returned to his College and established himself there, but still contriving to keep his terms at the Middle Temple, and spending his vacations at White-ladies. "As a member of Trinity College," says Cooksey, "he lived as other students lived; his exercises of which I have seen some, are no wise remarkable; and I find there nothing recorded of him, or worthy to be recorded, except an entry in Bursar's book of the year 1675, the year after he entered, of his giving them five pounds towards the repair of the chapel, which I should not mention but as a proof of the liberality with which his father supported him there, few students being in those times enabled to spare a donation, small as this may seem, out of the usual allowance to young men of his rank."[1]

But though he does not appear, either at school or the University, to have composed anything which might have prognosticated his future eminence, his character, even at this early age, was such as to inspire no common respect. His father, we are told, used to visit London during the terms, the system of agency between country

---

pari jucunditate condire, summæque gravitati tantum comitatis adjungere, non minùs difficile quàm magnum est." Plin. Ep. Lib. iv. Ep. 3.

[1] Cooksey, 24. In 1682 he contributed a further donation of £100 for the same purpose.

and London attorneys not then being established, and on his way, he usually left his horse at the George Inn at Acton, where he often mentioned " his hopeful son at the Temple." The landlord one day, in reply to these panegyrics, said, "Why don't you let us see him, sir?" Mr. Somers, in consequence, requested his son to accompany him as far as Acton, on his return home; but on his arrival at the George, taking the landlord aside, said, " I have brought him, Cobbett, but you must not talk to him as you do to me; he will not suffer such fellows as you in his company."[1]

On the 5th of May, 1676, when he was of seven years' standing as a student of law, the period then regularly required, he was called to the bar,[2] and in the following year he was admitted to a larger set of chambers in Pump Court,[3] but he did not begin to lay himself out for practice for five years after; still making Oxford his principal place of abode during all this time, though he occasionally visited London and Worcester. He thus became a ripe and good scholar as well as lawyer, and, regard being had to his acquaintance with modern languages and literature, perhaps the most accomplished man that ever rose to high eminence as a professional jurist in England. Having mastered the common law under Winnington, he now devoted himself to the civil law, and acquired a knowledge of it which is very unusual among English barristers, and which he found to be of the most essential service to him in his subsequent career. The French writers had come into great vogue soon after the Restoration, and,

[1] Life of Lord Somers, 1716, p. 11.
[2] Ad Parliament. tent. 5° die Maij. 1676°.
Barristers called. Mr Somer J. Hetherington H. Leach J. Freke J. Barton C and Broughton P., are called to the degree of the utter barr. Mr. Davys M. Plouden F. and Dobbins R. are likewise of grace and favour called to the same degree.

[3] Julij. 10mo.

Somer J. ad Ca.	Mr. Johes Somer de le utter barr admissus est in totam illam Cameram cum ptinentijs M^{rl} Samuelis Kecke de le Utter barr Scituat in passagio inter le Pumpe Co^{rt}. et Wine Co^{rt}. prim gradus. Ac in loco et vice dci M^{rl} Kecke J. qui eandem ea intencone sursum reddidit et dat ℔ fine.	02.00.00

being familiar with them, he was on a footing with those whom he met in good society; Italian was now much less known in England than it had been in the reign of Elizabeth: nevertheless, to gain distinction, or rather to gratify his own fine taste, he acquired a critical knowledge of that noble dialect, and he perused and reperused all the great poets, as well as prose writers, who composed in it from Petrarca to his own contemporary Filicaja, whom he justly considered the greatest genius Italy had produced since the author of GERUSALEMME LIBERATA.[1]

He began now likewise to take a very active part in politics. He had been introduced in London to Shaftesbury, Lord Russell, Sydney, Sir William Jones, and all the eminent Whigs, and—contrary to his interest,—upon conviction, he eagerly joined them. He ever remained true to his principles, and, from his enlightened views, his great talents, and his unsullied integrity, he is to be considered the greatest ornament of the Whig party. But let those who embrace the notion very common in England, that a gentleman, having merely gone through the ordinary routine of education at school and college, and having afterwards spent his life in rural amusements, in reading the newspapers, and occasionally attending parliament, is qualified at any time to fill a high office under the crown, and to act as a consummate statesman, remember that this was not the way in which Somers learned how to rescue a nation from tyranny, to bring about a revolution without bloodshed, and nicely to balance the antagonist forces of a constitutional monarchy. He studied politics as a science. Making himself master of the history and antiquities of his own country, and collecting and reading all that had been published on both sides during the memorable struggle between the King and the Parliament, which terminated before his birth, but of which he had heard so much from his father; he applied himself diligently to the civil history of other countries, ancient and modern; and he attentively pondered all that had been written on constitutions and the art of government, from Aristotle to Hobbes. Knowing that without the habit of composition little eminence can

[1] We shall see hereafter that this admiration was reciprocal, and that Somers was celebrated by Filicaja (among other things) for being able to speak seven languages without having ever been out of England.

be acquired in speaking or in thinking, he from time to time wrote essays and treatises, several of which he gave to the world,—not out of vanity, but to enlighten the public mind. He is said first to have appeared in print as reporter of " The memorable case of Denzil Onslow, Esq., tried at the assizes in Surrey, touching his election at Haslemere, wherein is much good matter touching the due ordering of elections for Parliament."[1]

The next work in which Somers engaged was of far more importance, and gave him full opportunity to display his constitutional learning and his logical method of reasoning. It arose out of the famous " Exclusion Bill," and was undertaken at the request of Lord Shaftesbury. The lovers of absolute prerogative and the adherents of the Church of Rome, eager that James should succeed on a demise of the crown, denied the power of parliament to change the succession, which they contended was regulated entirely by the law of God. The object of the Whigs was to establish the authority of parliament to limit, restrain, or qualify the right to the succession—which no temperate inquirer into our constitutional history could venture to deny, and which has not only been repeatedly acted upon, but is also expressly recognized and confirmed by statute.[2] The tract came out opportunely while the Bill to set aside the Duke of York was pending. The title of it was "A History of the Succession, collected out of the Records and the most authentic Historians."[3] It was well received, and made many converts, as it presented a clear exposition of the principles by which the succession to the crown had been governed from the earliest times—with striking historical illustrations to enforce the doctrine which was inculcated. However, the unconstitutional expedient dexterously proposed of suspending or abridging the prerogatives of a Popish successor, was generally preferred to the entire exclusion of the right heir, and the nation became alarmed and disgusted by Shaftesbury's mad scheme of setting up the legitimacy of the Duke of Monmouth.

[1] Somers's Tracts, vol. i. 374. Lord Glenbervie's Election Cases, vol. i. 341. This report was quoted and much relied upon in a recent case in the Common Pleas, in which the Court held that it is legal to purchase a small freehold for the express purpose of acquiring a vote in a county, and that no valid objection can be made to a vote so acquired.
[2] 13 Eliz. c. 1, and Anne, c. 7.   [3] Somers's Tracts, vol. xvi. 167.

After the breaking of the Oxford Parliament, which gave such a complete triumph to the Court, there was issued a royal "Declaration," framed by Lord Chief Justice North, in explanation of the causes which had led to the two last dissolutions,—inveighing in bitter terms against those who had opposed the government, and had advocated the Exclusion Bill.[1]

This was answered by a tract entitled "A just and modest Vindication of the two last Parliaments," which was at first ascribed to Sir William Jones. Burnet says that Sydney contributed to it; but there is now no doubt that it was chiefly composed by Somers.[2] It is a very masterly vindication of the rights of Parliament, and of the policy of the liberal party under Shaftesbury in their attempt to alter the succession for the safety of the people and the preservation of the monarchy. The author certainly goes too far in denying the power of the Crown to dissolve parliament at pleasure, although he is fully justified in animadverting on the manner in which this power had been recently exercised.[3] An unfounded charge was brought against the publication, that it advocated democracy. Somers was through life a sincere and zealous friend to limited monarchy. On this very occasion he says, "The preservation of every government depends upon an exact adherence unto its principles, and the essential principle of the English monarchy being that well proportioned distribution of powers whereby the law doth at once provide for the greatness of the King and the safety of the people, the government can subsist no longer than whilst the monarch, enjoying the

---

[1] Life of Guilford, ante, p. 262.

[2] Lord Hardwicke mentions that a copy of it in the handwriting of Lord Somers was amongst the MSS. which were destroyed in the fire at the chambers of the Honorable C. Yorke. State Papers, vol. ii. p. 399; and the internal evidence of the authorship is equally strong. The first edition was published 8th April, 1681.

[3] Sydney had contended that after the statutes requiring parliaments to be called at least once a year, and oftener if necessary, the Crown was bound to call parliaments annually, and could not evade the law by a dissolution. In a treatise entitled the "Antiquities of the Parliament of England," ascribed to Mr. Justice Dodderidge, it is laid down, that "Parliament ought not to be dissolved until every petition is answered, and that the King is guilty of perjury if he acts differently." But the "most critical and delicate trust," of dissolving as well as calling parliaments is undoubtedly vested in the Crown, and is indispensably necessary for the preservation of the monarchical branch of the constitution. See Burke's Works, vol. ii. 634. 4to. ed.

power which the law gives him, is enabled to perform the part which it allows him, and the people are duly protected in their rights and liberties." In reply to the taunt that his party were "lovers of commonwealth principles," he says, "If they mean by those *lovers of commonwealth principles* men passionately devoted to the public good, and to the common service of their country,—who believe that kings were instituted for the good of the people, and the government ordained for the sake of those that are to be governed, and therefore complain or grieve when it is used to contrary ends, every humane and honest man will be proud to be ranked in that number. To be fond of such principles becomes every Englishman." These are the principles on which, seven years later, the Revolution was conducted, and this is almost the language of the Prince of Orange and the leaders of the Convention Parliament. According to Burnet, the pamphlet, though very able, "had no great effect, the spirit of the party being spent;" but it increased the reputation of Somers as a constitutional lawyer, and it must have had a salutary influence by explaining the just object of political institutions, and defining the boundaries between the duty of obedience and the right of resistance.

A few months after, Somers published another tract, which was very popular on its first appearance, and may now be perused with satisfaction. The attempt to prosecute Lord Shaftesbury for high treason in the City of London having been defeated by the famous "IGNORAMUS," various pamphlets issued from the press, under the patronage of the government, to abuse the grand jury who had returned this verdict. By way of answer there came out a tract entitled, "The Security of Englishmen's Lives: or the Trust, Power, and Duty of Grand Juries of England." This likewise was ascribed to Jones and other Whig leaders. Burnet represents that it passed as written by Lord Essex, though, says he, "I understood afterwards it was written by Somers, who was much esteemed, and often visited by Lord Essex, and writ the best papers that came out in that time,"[1] It contains an able exposition of the advantages of the institution of Grand Juries, condemns the doctrine that they are bound to find a true bill upon any evidence which may be laid before them,

[1] See North's Examen. p. 508.

and forcibly points out the misconduct of the judges, who, by an examination of witnesses in open court, and by a perversion of the law and facts of the case, had recently striven to have a bill found against an innocent nobleman, on which he would immediately have been capitally convicted before a partial Lord Steward and a packed selection of peers. The author still avowed his attachment to the monarchy, saying:—

"The greatness and honor of a prince consist in the virtue, multitude, wealth, and prowess of his people, and his greatest glory is to encourage virtue and piety by the excellence of his government. The King's interest is more concerned in the protection of the innocent than in the punishment of the guilty. The law has not been less careful for the reputation of the subjects of England than for their lives and estates, and this seems to be one reason why, in criminal cases, a man shall not be brought to an open, legal trial by a petit jury, till the grand jury have first found the bill. If, for fear of being unworthily reproached as *ignoramus jurymen, obstinate fellows, that obstruct justice and disserve the King*, the grand jury shall suffer the judges or the King's counsel to prevail with them to indorse *Billa vera*, when their consciences are not satisfied in the truth of the accusation, they act directly against their oaths,—oppress the innocent, whom they ought to protect,—as far as in them lies, subject their country, themselves, and posterity, to arbitrary powers, pervert the administration of justice, and overthrow the government which is instituted for the obtaining of it and subsists by it. Every design of changing the constitution ought to be most warily observed and timely opposed: nor is it only the interest of the people that such fundamentals should be duly guarded, for whose benefit they are at first so carefully laid, and whom the judges are sworn to serve; but of the King too, for whose sake those pretend to act who would subvert them."

Thus early did Somers deserve to be described as—

'Form'd 'twixt the people and the Crown to stand,
And hold the scales of right with even hand."

In the midst of these laborious compositions he sedulously kept up his classical reading. To improve his prose style he was in the habit of diligently translating from the Greek, and he now contributed " the Life of Alcibidas ' to a new translation of PLUTARCH. He likewise occasionally amused himself with rhyming. After the instance of Cicero we can not say decidedly that he might not have considered himself a great poet, but the probability is that he only sought by his metrical experiments to improve his taste and to unbend his mind. He must have supposed, however, that he had reached some skill in versification, as he now published translations from Ovid, of the Epistles of "Dido to Æneas," and "Ariadne to Theseus." He is certainly very inferior to Dryden, his contemporary; and, now that every shop-boy and milliner's apprentice can write smooth lines of ten syllables, we are astonished to find some of his couplets so uncouth as well as prosaic; but, closely following his original, he occasionally renders the sense with some felicity. Thus he makes the deserted Tyrian queen reproach in English her ungrateful fugitive:

> "With cruel haste to distant lands you fly;
> You know not whose they are, or where they lie.
> On Carthage and its rising walls you frown,
> And shun a scepter which is now your own.
> But tho' all this succeeded to your mind,
> So true a wife no search could ever find.
> All day Æneas walks before my sight,
> In all my dreams I see him every night;
> But see him still ungrateful as before,
> And such as, if I could, I should abhor.
> But the strong flame burns on against my will,
> I call him false, but love the traitor still."

And thus he represents the deserted Ariadne reproaching the deceitful Theseus:

> "Ah! see this wounded breast worn out with sighs,
> And these faint arms stretched to the seas and skies!
> See these few hairs yet spared by grief and rage,
> Some pity let these flowing tears engage!
> Turn back, and if I'm dead when you return,
> Yet lay my ashes in the peaceful urn."

He was praised by political partisans out of hatred to Dryden, who had recently lashed Shaftesbury and the Whigs so successfully in "Absalom and Achitophel," and the "Medal;"—but had Somers only been a versifier, his name never would have reached us, and his "immortal strains" must soon have perished. We now examine them because we can not free ourselves from a little curiosity to know how the great lawyer and statesman succeeded in the poetic vein.

Shortly after, a deep sensation was excited by an anonymous poem, entitled "Dryden's Satire to his Muse," which, if not recommended by flights of fancy and mellifluous numbers, was highly seasoned with ribaldry and scandal. It was universally believed to be Somers's, but he denied it. There is no positive evidence to prove that it was his; and Pope, who ought to have been well acquainted with the literary history of the age immediately preceding his own, said that it was untruly ascribed to him.[1] The disavowal of such a production does not amount to much; and a comparison of some parts of it with the acknowledged publications of Somers in prose and verse, affords strong evidence in support of his putative authorship. Horace Walpole objects that "the gross ribaldry of it can not be supposed to have flowed from so humane and polished a nature as Lord Somers;"[2] but we can not well judge of the license which the times might allow to an anonymous political satirist. "The poem," says Johnson, "whosesoever it was, has much virulence and some sprightliness. The writer tells all the ill that he can collect of Dryden and his friends." The personal attack on Dryden, the most pungent part of this satire, is too coarse to be transcribed, and the reader must be contented with an eulogistic character of the Duke of Ormond, who is strongly contrasted with the Tory leaders:

> "Barzillai's praise I could rehearse again,
> And make the labor of my second pen;
> Wise, valiant, loyal, rich, of high descent,
> Born t' all that fortune for her darlings meant.
> Who nobly scorned a private happiness,
> When he beheld the sovereign in distress:
> To arms he flew, but, with bold Cato's fate,
> Espoused the cause that fortune seemed to hate.
> Striving to save the head that wore the crown,
> He pulled the mighty ruin on his own."

Somers likewise practiced Latin composition, and, some may think, with more felicity. The following epitaph on his unmarried sister, who died young, may be admired both for the rhythm and the sentiment:—

[1] In the "Life of Dryden," Johnson having said that "both his person and his party were exposed in their turns to the shafts of satire which, though neither so well pointed nor perhaps so well aimed, undoubtedly drew blood," adds, "one of these poems is called 'Dryden's Satire on his Muse;' ascribed *though as Pope says falsely*, to Somers, who was afterwards Chancellor."
[2] Works, vol. i. 432.

> "Moribus illa vultuque modesto
> Omnes callebat artes
> Quæ virginem decebant:
> Quid plura? Hic unà jacent
> Parentum deliciæ, et decus, et dolor!"

He still kept up his intimacy with the Earl of Shrewsbury, and they seemed inseparable, whether in the Metropolis, at Oxford, or at White-ladies. Cooksey positively asserts that " here, and at this period of their lives, Mr. Somers and his gay young friend amused themselves with sketching, from the life, the characters of PETER, JACK, and MARTIN, and their ludicrous disputes about the fashion of their coats,"—adding, circumstantially, that " Somers's uncle, Blurton, furnished the portraiture of the Church of England man; his grandfather, Somers, a rigid Calvinist, was Jack; and that Peter had his lineaments from Father Peter and the Jesuits, with whom the young Earl was constantly beleaguered." This biographer represents that the two real authors of the " Tale of a Tub" trusted their MS. to Shaftesbury—who showed it to Sir William Temple—from whom it was obtained by Swift, who kept it by him till 1703, and then published it.[1] I make no doubt that Cooksey is sincere, but, though a relation, he can make no stronger case than " the private tradition of the family," together with certain supposed " internal evidence:" and, although there is no direct proof upon the subject, I think the probabilities are infinitely stronger in favor of the common belief, that the " Tale of a Tub" was Swift's own composition. Johnson sometimes *doubted*, and sometimes entertained a strong belief in the negative. " That Swift was its author," he writes, "though it be universally believed, was never owned by himself; but no claimant can be produced, and he did not deny it when Archbishop Sharpe and the Duchess of Somerset, by showing it to the Queen, debarred him from a bishopric." Again,—" his *Tale of a Tub* has little resemblance to his other pieces. It exhibits a vehemence and rapidity of mind, a copiousness of images, and vivacity of diction, such as he afterwards never possessed or never exerted."[2] And in conversation, the great critic observed to Boswell, " I doubt if the *Tale of a Tub* was his; it has so much more thinking, more knowledge, more power, more color than any of the works which are

---

[1] Cooksey, p. 18 *et sep*. [2] Life of Swift. Tour to Hebrides.

indisputably his : if it was his, I shall only say he was *impar sibi*." But Swift's dedication of the piece to Lord Somers when they were on good terms, and their subsequent quarrel without any complaint or reproach of literary theft on either side, seem entirely at variance with Cooksey's story. Sheridan, in his Life of Swift, says that soon after the publication of the work, a Mr. Waryng, a chamber-fellow of Swift's, declared he had read the first sketch of it in Swift's handwriting.[1] Dr. Hawksworth observes, that the Dean corrected an edition of the Tale of a Tub, a short time before his understanding was impaired;[2] and Blackmore, imputing the work to Swift, denounces him as " an insolent derider of the worship of his country," while in his ESSAY OF WIT, in praising what he considers excellent, he says—

"'Twill SOMERS' scales and Talbot's test abide,
And with their mark please all the world beside."

The argument from superiority to acknowledged compositions weighs much more strongly against Somers and the Earl of Shrewsbury than against Swift,—and Peter, Martin, and Jack do not exhibit the peculiarities of individuals seen at White-ladies, but the characteristics of the three great divisions of Christians. The statement in the " Apology for a Tale of a Tub," that " the greatest part of this work was written many years since, when the author was young, his invention at the height, and his reading fresh in his head," supposing it to be serious, would apply to Swift himself as well as to Somers.[3] But we are quite certain that the whole work could not have been composed in the lifetime of Lord Shaftesbury ; for the incident of " Jack getting on a great horse and eating custard " undoubtedly alludes to Sir Humphry Edwin, Lord Mayor of London, going in state to a Presbyterian meeting-house in the reign of Queen Anne. Dryden is very severely handled in it ; but Swift started as a Whig. Upon the whole, I think we may safely conclude that Somers, notwithstanding the broad assertion of his kinsman, can neither have credit for the wit, nor be made responsible for the coarseness, of this extraordinary performance. The author, whoever he was, is not fairly chargeable with irreligion ; and if he had been made a

[1] Sheridan's Life of Swift, p. 6. [2] Nicoll's edition of Swift, i. p. 5.
[3] The first edition was published in 1704.

bishop, I doubt not he would ever after have proved an exemplary father of the church.[1]

Other anonymous pieces Somers did write about this time. One of these, a popular poetical effusion, an impudent pretender had the effrontery to claim as his own. This person being introduced to Lord Somers, when Chancellor, and asked by him if he knew who wrote it, "Yes, my Lord," he replied, "'tis a trifle: I did it off hand." At this his Lordship laughed heartily, and the pretended poet withdrew in confusion.[2]

It seemed as if Somers had entirely renounced the law, and meant to devote himself to literature and politics. He was thirty years of age, and, although he had been called to the bar five years, he had not yet put on his gown. If such were his views, he now suddenly changed them on the death of his father[3]—when he resolved steadily to follow his profession, and thereby to advance himself to wealth and station.[4]

[1] See Porson's Tracts by Kidd, p. 316. [2] Life, 1716, p. 124. [3] Ibid. p. 15.
[4] His father died in 1681. His mother survived many years, and enjoyed his greatness and his fame. Both parents being buried at Severn-Stoke, Lord Somers erected in the church there a monument to their memory, with the following elegant inscription which he himself composed:—

M. S.
JOHANNIS et CATHARINÆ SOMERS
AMORE OLIM ET FIDE CONJUGALI,
DUM UNA VIXERE,
JAM ET TUMULO CONJUNCTORUM,
QUI
NON FICTA IN DEUM PIETATE,
IN UNIVERSOS CHARITATE,
COMITATE, SIUMUL ET PRUDENTIA,
VITAM SIBI IPSIS JUCUNDAM
ALIIS UTILEM GRATAMQUE
EGERE.
ADEOQUE HINC IPSORUM DISCESSUS
AETATE LICET PROVECTIORE,
ALTERIUS SC. SEXAGESIMO ÆTATIS ANNO
ALTERIUS OCTOGESIMO SEXTO,
SUIS IMO CUNCTIS
ACERBUS PLANE VISUS EST ATQUE
IMMATURIS
VIRI MORTEM LONGUM VIDUA DEFLEVIT.
PRISTINO DEHINC IN IPSUM AMORE
AD CARISSIMA PIGNORA, COMMUNES LIBEROS
CONVERSO ;
SIC OPTIME DEFUNCTI MEMORIAM COLENS,
SIC VERE SUUM MONSTRANS AFFECTUM ;
TRIUSQUE AUTEM OBITUM,
BONI DIUTISSIME DEFLEBUNT.

Whether he was influenced by finding, from the ample provision made for his sisters, the inheritance to which he succeeded much smaller than he expected,—or that after the ascendency which the Court had gained, and which all his writings could not shake, it was no longer safe to play the patriot,—or that, from the indifferent reception of his poetry among impartial judges, he despaired of gaining celebrity by the Muses, we shall never know. But certain it is, that now he bade a final adieu to Oxford:[1] he was admitted to chambers in Pump Court,[2] —he regularly attended the Courts at Westminster—and he rode the Oxford Circuit, on which he expected that his paternal connection would be useful in bringing him business. Probably no man ever commenced practice as an advocate in England with such high and varied qualifications. He was consummately skilled as a lawyer,— from the practice of commencing an action, which he had learned when a lad in his father's office, to the most abstruse doctrines of real property, which he had imbibed from Winnington, and the most enlarged views of general jurisprudence, with which he had become familiar from his civil law studies at Oxford. He was moreover deeply

[1] I believe that he never took any degree, although I have not been able clearly to ascertain the fact. There are entries of "John Somers" having taken the degree of B.A. 17th October, 1678, and of M.A. 14th June, 1681; but these seem to relate to a John Somers who matriculated 20th March, 1674-5, described as being "the son of John Somers, of Exeter, plebian, and in the 15th year of his age,"—Lord Somers being the son of an attorney at Worcester— always describing his father as "generosus," and being then in his 23rd or 24th year.

[2]
"Somer J. ad Ca. {
"Julij 9ⁿᵒ 1681°.
Die et anno pʳ dict.
Virtute actus Parliamenti medij Templi ibᵐ fact 4° die ffebruarij 1678° Mʳ Johes Somer de le Utter barr admissus est in totam illam Cameram scituat in novis Edificijs nup erect sup Australem partem cujusdam loci vocat le Pump Coʳᵗ primi gradus in parte Edificion—pʳ dict. ppime adjacent le Middle Temple Lane et ex orientali parte graduum pʳ dict., et in octavum partem Cellarij sub Edificijs pʳ dict. Habend totam illam Cameram pʳ dict. cum ptinentijs pʳ dco Mʳ Somer J. Executoribz Admstratoribus et Assignalis suis pro termino vite ipius Johis et pʳ duabus Assignaconibus post mortem ejus et dat pʳ fine virtute Actus parliamenti pʳ dict." } nil.

versed in all constitutional learning, and, besides being a fine classical scholar, he was familiarly acquainted with the languages and the literature of all the polished nations on the continent of Europe. Above all, he had steady habits of application, and he could not only make the necessary active exertion, but undergo the necessary drudgery, and submit to the necessary sacrifices, to insure success at the English bar.

Accordingly his progress was rapid and brilliant. By his learned arguments and his modest demeanor, he was very favorably noticed by Lord Chancellor Nottingham,[1] and in a few years his professional profits amounted to £700 a year, a very large sum for those times.[2]

The first considerable case in which he was counsel was the trial before Lord C. J. Saunders, at Guildhall, of Pilkington and Shute, the late Sheriffs, Alderman Cornish, Lord Grey de Werke, and others, for a riot on Midsummer-day, 1681, when the great struggle took place for enslaving the City of London, and the poll for the election of Sheriffs had been continued after the Lord Mayor, who had been gained over by the Court, had illegally attempted to adjourn it. Somers was retained as Junior, on the recommendation of his old master, Sir Francis Winnington, of Holt, and of the other distinguished Whig lawyers who were to lead for the several defendants.

It was well known that a packed jury had been summoned, and, on consultation, it was resolved " to challenge the array." Somers, as Junior, drew and signed the " *Challenge*," which duly stated the grounds on which the objection rested.

At the commencement of the trial, when the Jury appeared, Mr. Somers said, " My Lord I challenge the array ; " and he put in the " *Challenge.*" When it had been read by the Clerk with the signature at the end of it, Jeffreys, then a King's Sergeant and conducting the prosecution, exclaimed, " Here's a TALE OF A TUB indeed ! "

---

[1] Ante, Chap. XCIII.

[2] Life, 1716, p. 15. "That unwearied diligence which followed him through all the stages of his life gave him such a thorough insight into the laws of the land that he passed for one of the greate**st** masters of his profession at his first appearance in it. Though he made a regular progress through the several honors of the long robe, he was always looked upon as one who desired a superior station to that he was possessed of, till he arrived at the highest dignity to which those studies could advance him."—ADDISON, *Freeholder*, No. xxxix.

—*Lord C. J. Saunders.* "Ay, it is nothing else;"¹ and the challenge was immediately overruled. Somers does not appear to have again addressed the Court. The defendants were of course all found guilty and severely punished.²

But the greatest distinction which Somers acquired at the bar, previous to the Revolution, was on the trial of the Seven Bishops. The proposal that he should be one of their counsel rather shocked some of the Right Reverend defendants, who at last, driven to question the prerogative of the Crown when directed against the exclusive immunities of the Church, had often preached the doctrine of passive obedience, and had heard this rising young lawyer denounced as "nothing better than a Whig;" but "old Pollexfen insisted upon him, and would not be himself retained without him, representing him as the man who would take most pains, and go deepest into all that depended on precedents and records."³

Perhaps it was from the industry and zest with which Somers prepared for this trial that Addison, in reference to him, afterwards said, "I have heard one of the greatest geniuses this age has produced, who has been trained up in all the polite studies of antiquity, assure me, upon his being obliged to search into several rolls and records, that, notwithstanding such an employment was at first very dry and irksome to him, he at last took an incredible pleasure in it, and preferred it even to the reading of Virgil or Cicero."⁴

The result of his researches he fully and freely communicated to Pollexfen and his other seniors, his object being to procure the acquittal of his clients, not to gain *éclat* for himself—"*prodesse non conspici.*"

At the trial he powerfully argued in support of the technical objection, that, as the Attorney General could not at first show that the petition of the Bishops had been presented to the King at Whitehall, there was no

---

¹ Had the "Tale of a Tub" been then published, this dialogue would have been cited as strong authority to prove that it was generally imputed to Somers; but the first edition did not come out till 20 years later,—Swift was still a boy of 16, and although, according Cooksey's theory, the piece had then been written by Somers and the Earl of Shrewsbury, it was communicated to no one except Lord Shaftesbury and Sir William Temple, till Swift purloined it.

² 9 St. Tr. 187.   ³ 3 Ken. Hist. 513, n.   ⁴ Spectator, No. 447.

evidence of a publication of the supposed libel in Middlesex, the county in which the venue was laid. He insisted that "if the criminal act is not proved to have been committed in the county in which it is alleged to have been committed, the party accused is innocent, and ought to be absolved; for, though he may have committed another offense elsewhere, he has not committed the offense with which he was charged."

Against the opinion of that upright Judge, Mr. Justice Powell, the trial was allowed to proceed, and, while the lawyers were squabbling, Lord Sunderland, the Lord President of the Council, was sent for, and proved the publication in Middlesex.

Upon the merits, involving the great question of the "dispensing power," all the defendants' counsel were heard, and Somers, though coming last (like Erskine in *Rex* v. *Baillie*[1]) made by far the most impressive speech. He cited, with much effect, the great case of *Thomas* v. *Sorrel*, in the Exchequer-chamber, upon the validity of a dispensation of the statute of Edward VI. touching the selling of wine.[2] Here the Judges laid it down as a settled position, that there never can be an abrogation, or a suspension (which is a temporary abrogation), of an act of parliament but by the legislative power. He thus concluded:—

"My Lord, by the law of all civilized nations, if the Prince does require something to be done which the person who is to do it considers unlawful, it is his duty *rescribere Principi*. This is all that was done here, and in the most humble manner that could be thought of. Your Lordships will please to observe how careful the defendants were that they might not any way justly offend the King; they did not voluntarily interpose, as they might have done, by giving their advice as peers; they never stirred till a command which they deemed unlawful was laid upon themselves. When they made their Petition, they only went so far as to ask that they might not be compelled to read the Declaration—without even praying that it might be revoked. My Lord, as to all the matters of fact alleged in the Petition,—that they are perfectly true we have shown by the Journals of both Houses. In every instance which the petitioners men-

[1] 21 St. Tr. 31.   [2] Vaughan, 330.

tion, this power of dispensation was considered in Parliament, and, on debate, declared to be contrary to law. They could have no design to diminish the prerogative, because the King hath no such prerogative. Seditious, my Lord, the Petition could not be, nor could it possibly stir up sedition in the minds of the people, because it was presented to the King in private and alone. False it could not be, for the matter of it must be seen to be strictly true. There could be nothing of malice, for the occasion, instead of being sought, was forced upon them. A libel it could not be, for the intent of the defendants was innocent, and they kept strictly within the bounds set by the law, which gives the subject leave to apply to his Prince by petition when he is aggrieved."[1]

The acquittal which followed was mainly ascribed to this speech of Somers, the effect of which upon the jury was greatly heightened by the modesty and grace with which it was delivered. He now and ever merited the praise that "his pleading at the bar was masculine and persuasive—free from everything trivial or affected."

The Revolution immediately followed.

CHAPTER CVII.

CONTINUATION OF THE LIFE OF LORD SOMERS TILL HE RECEIVES THE GREAT SEAL.

FROM the unostentatious character of Lord Somers, there is much difficulty in ascertaining the exact share which he had in originating the bold scheme to expel from the throne, for misrule, him who was the right heir of William the Conqueror and of the Saxon Kings; but there can be no doubt that the Whig leaders, who were now driven to resort to the sacred right of resistance, and who thought there was a sufficient chance of rescuing the nation from tyranny to justify the attempt, in conducting the enterprise were mainly guided by his advice. From this time he was "the life, the soul, the spirit of his party."[2] Tindal says that "he was admitted into the most secret councils of the Prince of Orange, and

[1] 12 St. Tr. 396. [2] Letter of Lord Sunderland to King Willliam.

was one of those who concocted the measure of bringing him over."[1]

On the very day of the acquittal of the Bishops, and probably by the hand of their junior counsel, was drawn the " Association,"—a paper enumerating the various acts of James's tyrannical government, and inviting William to rescue the nation from Popery and arbitrary power. Somers did not put his own name to it, but, along with the Earl of Devonshire, the Earl of Danby, Lord Lumley, the Bishop of London, Admiral Russell, and other men in high station, it was signed by his bosom friend the Earl of Shrewsbury, with whom he had always continued to live in the closest intimacy. This nobleman soon after secretly left England, and joined the Prince of Orange at the Hague, bringing with him a supply of £40,000, a considerable part of which he was said to have borrowed from Father Peter, and other Catholics,—" holding it no sin to impoverish and spoil the enemy."[2]

The Prince's " Declaration," which came out soon after, and in which he announced his design to proceed to England " to have a free and lawful parliament assembled for the preservation of the Protestant religion, and for securing to the whole nation the free enjoyment of their laws and liberties ;"—if not framed by Somers, certainly had his previous approbation.

When William had landed in England, Somers still avoided making himself conspicuous, but he attended all the meetings of the Whig leaders, prompted their measures, and, on the flight of James, he concurred in the advice that a Convention should be assembled—to guard against the notion of a change of dynasty by conquest, and to lay the foundations of a free monarchy on the constitutional basis of the national will. He had declined the overtures made to him to be returned to the House of Commons in the two last parliaments held in the reign of Charles II., and in the parliament summoned by James II.; but he was now prevailed upon openly to adventure on the stormy sea of public life. In his thirty-seventh year he was elected to the Convention Parliament as representative for his native city of Worcester.

From the first meeting of the two Houses a difference of sentiment appeared between them. The Commons

[1] Continuation of Rapin, vol. ii. 770.   [2] Ibid.

were almost unanimously for dethroning James, and disregarding the claims of his son; while a majority of the Lords, with a strong feeling in favor of the divine right of kings, were desirous of some expedient whereby immediate danger to religion and liberty might be warded off without violating the order of succession to the crown.

Somers from the first led the deliberations of the Lower House. In a maiden speech he laid down the true principles of limited monarchy; he showed that James had forfeited his right to allegiance, and he pointed out a parallel case which had occurred in the history of Sweden, when King Sigismund, having attempted to subvert the laws and religion of his native country, and having fled to a foreign state, was set aside, and Charles VIII. was set upon the throne. He concluded by moving a committee of the whole House "on the state of the nation."¹ The debate terminated in the memorable Resolution which he drew—not in the language which he himself would have selected, but in such as might be suited to the opinions and prejudices of others: "That King James II., having endeavored to subvert the constitution of the kingdom by breaking the original contract between King and People, and by the advice of Jesuits and other wicked persons having violated the fundamental laws, and having withdrawn himself out of this kingdom, has abdicated the government, and that the throne is thereby become vacant."²

The following day Somers gained a signal triumph in the agreement of the House of Commons, by acclamation, to the principle on which the "Exclusion Bill" had been framed, and their vote, without a dissentient voice, "that it hath been found by experience inconsistent with the safety and welfare of this Protestant kingdom that it should be governed by a Popish Prince."³ There is evidently a broad distinction between the Crown and any subordinate political office; nor can it be considered at all inconsistent with the doctrine of toleration to require for the public security that the Chief Magistrate shall be

---

¹ 5 Parl. His. 42.   ² Ibid. 50.
³ Somers's Tract on the Exclusion Bill, entitled "A History of the Succession, &c.," was republished soon after William landed, and had a considerable effect upon the public mind.

of the religion of the majority of the nation, leaving him of course full liberty of conscience, and of worship in a private station. In Saxony and other states a different rule has been observed, and some confidence might be placed in a well-defined prerogative, and in the forbearance of modern times · but there is an evident advantage in the Sovereign being of the national religion :—which may fairly be secured by the penalty of loss of power for dissent. This restraint of course never can be complained of by the present royal family of England, as it was the condition on which they accepted the throne; and if it be unjust, we should transfer our allegiance to the Duke of Modena, who is sprung from Charles I., and is the lineal heir of the monarchy.

The two resolutions being sent up to the Lords for their concurrence, the latter was carried unanimously; but the former, guarded and qualified as it was, raised among their Lordships great alarm and opposition. In order to save a nominal allegiance to the late King, it was first proposed that there should be a *Regency*—" with the administration of regal power under his name, as the best and safest way to preserve the Protestant religion and the laws of this kingdom." This was supported by all sections of the Tories—as well by those who really meant to exclude James from the enjoyment of power, such as the Earl of Nottingham, its great promoter, as by those who, like the Earl of Clarendon, were anxious for his return upon terms of security for their religion and liberty. The motion was negatived only by a majority of two,—the numbers being 51 to 49. Next came a close division of 55 to 46 on the abstract resolution, "that there is an original contract between King and people," which perhaps was necessary by way of negativing the doctrine of the divine origin of kingship—opposed to any human legislation in regulating the descent of the crown. But in coming to the "*abdication,*" and the "*vacancy of the throne,*" the tide turned, and by a majority of 55 to 41, it was resolved to substitute the word "*deserted*" for "*abdicated,*" and entirely to omit the clause declaring "the throne to be vacant;" Lord Danby and his friends considering the young Prince as spurious, and wishing that the Princess of Orange should be declared successor by hereditary right.[1]

[1] The credit pretended to be given to the story of "the warming-pan" is

The amendments were reported to the Commons—with the request of a Conference. This was carried on by written reasons, and at the end of it the Commons determined, by 282 to 151, to adhere to the words of their resolution.

Then followed the celebrated " Free Conference " between the two Houses, which was conducted by *vivâ voce* debate. Somers was one of the managers for the Commons, and the cause of " abdication and the vacancy of the throne " rested chiefly on his shoulders. It must be confessed that the speeches on this occasion are by no means what might have been expected from enlightened statesmen settling the constitution of a great nation, and rather remind us of the quibbling argumentations of pleaders in a court of law on a special demurrer to a declaration or plea for want of form. Somers defends the word " abdicate " by quotations from Grotius, Calvin's Lexicon Juridicum, Bressonius de Verborum Significatione, Budæus, Pralejus, and Spicilegius; and then he falls foul of the word " desert," which, from its etymology and its use, he contends is wholly inapplicable to a permanent renunciation, and means only a voluntary relinquishment —with the power of resumption.[1] " The vacancy of the throne," he chiefly defends from the record in 1 Hen. IV. where it is said that upon the deposition of Richard II. " *Sedes regalis fuit vacua, et confestim, ut constabat ex præmissis, regnum Angliæ vacare,* then Henry riseth up out of his place as Duke of Lancaster, and claims the Crown *dictum regnum Angliæ sicut præmittitur vacans una cum corona vendicat.*"[2] Yet it is to Mr. Somers's reasons, such

the great blot on the Revolution, and is discreditable to all parties; but it was most eagerly caught at by the Tories, that they might reconcile their transference of allegiance to their doctrine of indefeasible right. There are very few persons now alive who could so satisfactorily be shown to be sprung from their lawful parents as the infant Prince, by evidence then before the world, was demonstrated to be the son of James II. and Mary of Modena, his queen.

[1] Burton, in his work on " Melancholy," first published in 1621, uses the word 'abdicated " in the same sense as Mr. Somers. So Molinæus, in his " Treatise on Fiefs," says—"Sequitur quod non potest alienari, *abdicari*, nec præscribi."

[2] 5 Parl. Hist. 68. " The dispute about the words 'abdicate' or 'desert,'" says Bolingbroke, " might have been expected in some assembly of pedants, where young students exercised themselves in disputation, but not in such an august assembly of the Lords and Commons in solemn conference upon the most important occasion."

as they are, that Nottingham and the other managers for the Lords chiefly apply themselves in supporting their word "desert," and insisting that, by the constitution of England, the throne never can by possibility be in contemplation of law one moment vacant. Amidst these technicalities, the real struggle was, whether there should be a change of dynasty, or the experiment should be made of Protestant Regents governing in the name of Popish Sovereigns. Somers and the Whigs were not only afraid of the public confusion which might follow from such an anomalous administration of the government, but were strongly convinced that there could be no permanent reformation of abuses till, by a break in the succession, the doctrine of "divine right" should be necessarily renounced and discountenanced by the family on the throne.

The conference closed without any convert being made; but, the Commons remaining firm, and William threatening to return to Holland, the Lords, by a majority of sixty-two to forty-seven, resolved not to insist on their amendments to the original vote; and they precipitately followed this up by a resolution "that the Prince and Princess of Orange shall be declared King and Queen of England, and the dominions thereunto belonging."[1] The object now probably was to avoid any recognition of the Whig notion of a contract between the governors and the governed. "But the Commons, with a noble patriotism, delayed to concur in this hasty settlement of the Crown, till they should have completed the declaration of those fundamental rights and liberties for the sake of which alone they had gone forward with this great revolution."[2] A committee had been appointed, of which Somers was the leading member, "to bring in general heads of such things as were absolutely necessary to be considered for the better securing our religion, law, and liberties." The Committee made their Report the day after the last vote of the Lords; and though it is little noticed by historians who have looked only to the "Declaration of Rights," and the "Bill of Rights," which sprang from it, it is a most interesting document, and re-

[1] 5 Parl. Hist. 93; Lords' Jour. Feb. 6. The Scottish parliament proceeded in a more manly manner, by a direct vote that James had *forefaulted* the crown. [2] Hall. Const. Hist. iii. 134.

flects immortal honor on the name of Somers. The careful reader will perceive that he here suggests some few grievances and remedies which were omitted by the two Houses in their ensuing vindication of public liberty; but the discrimination, the moderation, and the firmness displayed by him and his party at this crisis are above all praise, and contrast most favorably with the blind enthusiasm of the French National Assembly a century later, and with the spoliation and violence which have generally marked revolutionary movements. The maxim of the Whig patriots was to change only what was necessary to be changed for the good government of the country. They therefore departed as little as possible from the hereditary succession to the throne, and they only strengthened and secured our ancient constitution and laws. Hence the settlement was lasting, and we pray that IT MAY BE PERPETUAL!

The Report was divided into twenty-eight heads, partly pointing out infringements of existing rights, and partly new safeguards for public freedom:—" 1. The pretended power of dispensing or suspending of laws, or the execution of laws, by regal prerogative, without consent of Parliament, is illegal.[1] 2. The commission for erecting the late Court of Commissioners for ecclesiastical causes, and all other Commissioners and Courts of the like nature, are illegal. 3. Levying money for, or to the use of, the Crown by pretense of prerogative, without grant of Parliament, for longer time or in any other manner than the same shall be so granted, is illegal.[1] 4. It is the right of the subject to petition the King, and all commitments and prosecutions for such petitioning are illegal.[1] 5. The Acts concerning the militia are grievous to the subject. 6. The raising or keeping a standing army within this kingdom in time of peace, unless it be with the consent of Parliament, is illegal.[1] It is necessary for the public safety that the subjects (which are Protestants) should provide and keep arms for their common defense, and that the arms which have been seized and taken from them be restored.[1] 8. The right and freedom of electing members of the House of Commons,[1] and the rights and privileges of Parliament and members, as well in the intervals of Parliament as during their sitting, to be preserved.

[1] Adopted in the Bill of Rights.

9. That Parliament ought to sit frequently, and that their frequent sitting be secured.¹ 10. No interrupting of any session of Parliament till the affairs which are necessary to be dispatched at that time are determined. 11. That the too long continuance of the same Parliament be prevented. 12. No pardon to be pleadable to an impeachment of Parliament.² 13. Cities, universities, towns, corporate boroughs, and plantations, to be secured against *quo warrantos* and surrenders, and restored to their ancient rights. 14. None of the royal family to marry a Papist.³ 15. Every King and Queen of this realm, at the time of their entering into the exercise of their royal authority, to take an oath for maintaining the Protestant religion, and the laws and liberties of the nation, and that the coronation oath be revived.⁴ 16. Effectual provision to be made for the liberty of Protestants in the exercise of their religion, and for uniting all Protestants in the matter of public worship, as far as may be. 17. Constructions upon the statutes of treason, and trials, and proceedings, and writs of error, in cases of treason, to be regulated.⁵ 18. Judges' commissions to be made *Quamdiu se bene gesserint*, and their salaries to be ascertained and established, to be paid out of the public revenue only, and not to be removed nor suspended from the execution of their office but by due course of law. 19. The requiring excessive bail of persons committed in criminal cases, and imposing excessive fines and illegal punishments, to be prevented.⁶ 20. Abuses in appointing sheriffs, and in the execution of their office, to be reformed. 21. Jurors to be duly impanneled and returned, and corrupt and false verdicts prevented.⁶ 22. Informations in the Court of King's Bench to be taken away. 23. The Chancery and other courts of justice, and the fees of office, to be regulated. 24. That the buying and selling of offices may be effectually provided against. 25. That upon return of habeas corpuses and mandamuses the subject may have liberty to traverse such return. 26. That all grants of fines and forfeitures are illegal and void; and that all such persons as procure them be liable to punishment." ⁶

¹ Triennial Act, 6 W. & M. c. 10. ² 12 & 13 W. 3, c. 2.
³ 13 W. 3, c. 2. ⁴ 1 W. & M. st. 2; 12 & 13 W. 3, c. 2.
⁵ Stat. 7 W. 3, c. 3, respecting trials for treason.
⁶ "Declaration of Rights" and "Bill of Rights."

The last two heads of grievance are against the collection of Hearth-money,[1] and the abuses of the Excise.

The "Declaration of Rights," prepared by another committee under the management of Somers, was wisely confined to the declaratory part of the Report, and being agreed to by the Lords, was made the basis on which the Crown was tendered to, and was accepted by, William and Mary. Most of the other articles in the Report were embraced in the Act of Settlement and other constitutional statues which followed, but the obligation to serve in the militia[2] continued as a necessary evil; and it has always been thought that it would be dangerous to limit the prerogative of the crown to prorogue or dissolve Parliament at pleasure,[3] the constant necessity for votes of supply abundantly securing the summoning and the sitting of legislative assemblies. The law respecting *Quo Warrantos* and Informations in the King's Bench, though not substantially altered, has been regulated in practice so as to avoid all oppression or abuse. Somers's views were disappointed only with respect to the Church.[4] Preserving all respect for the property and the rights of the clergy, he evidently contemplated a larger measure of religious freedom than he was able to accomplish, or than was enjoyed in England till very recent times; and, wishing to repair the bad faith of Lord Clarendon at the Restoration, he was in hopes that the establishment might be made more comprehensive.[5] It may further be observed that the "Declaration of Rights" and the "Bill of Rights" supplied a deficiency in the "Report" by embracing the recent illegal prosecutions in violation of Parliamentary privilege, and in requiring security for the liberty of the press.

We can not sufficiently admire the skill with which Somers encountered the difficulties opposed to him. Notwithstanding the strong prejudices of the Tory party, comprehending a large proportion of the wealth and rank of the country, he contrived, with a few exceptions, to have the constitution placed on what he considered its true basis. There was a small republican party still subsisting; but he by no means belonged to it, for he thought that under a limited monarchy, enlightened pub-

---

[1] Abrogated by 1 W. & M. c. 10.
[2] Art. 5.   [3] Arts. 9 and 10.   [4] Arts. 13, 22.   [5] Art. 16.

lic opinion had the greatest influence, and general prosperity was best secured.[1]

When the ministry was formed after the proclamation of William and Mary as King and Queen, the merits of Somers were by no means overlooked. The leaders who had been guided by his advice were desirous still to avail themselves of his services, and through the Earl of Shrewsbury he had been made personally known to William, who, from their first interview, placed more confidence in him than in any English politician. We are surprised therefore to find him only in the subordinate office of Solicitor General. But he would not renounce politics by becoming a common-law judge; the aristocratic Whigs have ever been slow to associate with themselves in high office any one who can not boast of distinguished birth;[2] he would not leave the bar for the precarious appointment of Lord Commissioner of the Great Seal; and, agreeing to become a law-officer of the Crown, he confessed that Sir George Treby, who was to be his colleague, and who was greatly his senior, could not be asked to serve under him.—At the same time he submitted to be knighted.[3]

But, though never eager to put himself forward, he had much more weight in the House of Commons than the Attorney General, and, while he was desirous of affording all fair assistance to the Government, he never forgot the principles of civil and religious liberty which he had before professed. His first official speech was in support of the "Bill for declaring the Convention a Parliament," contrary to the opinion of those who questioned its legality because it was not summoned by Royal writ. "He

---

[1] With the exception of Parliamentary Reform, which was then little thought of, although a more equal representation of the people will be found referred to in some of the pamphlets of that day, there is hardly any constitutional improvement which may not be traced to the recommendation of the patriots of 1689.

[2] The most striking instance of this is the exclusion of Edmund Burke from the Cabinet on the formation of the Rockingham administration, after he had led the opposition for years in the House of Commons. The exclusion of Sheridan from the Cabinet in 1806 would be still more extraordinary, if it were not accounted for by the unfortunate habits he had then contracted.

[3] He was immediately made a Bencher of the Middle Temple.

"Ad Parliamentu tentu 10mo die Maij 1689°.
"M^r. John Somers being made ye Kings Solicitor Generall is called to the bench."

About the same time he was elected Recorder of the city of Gloucester.

said, 'If this were not a legal parliament, they who had taken the oaths which it prescribed were guilty of high treason; the laws repealed by it were still in force; all concerned in levying, collecting, or paying taxes under its statutes, were highly criminal, and the whole nation must presently return to King James.' This he spoke with much zeal, and such an ascendent of authority, that none was prepared to answer it; so the bill passed without any more opposition. This was a great service done in a very critical time, and contributed not a little to raise Somers's character."[1]

He carried through the Toleration Act,[2] which, if its conditions had been strictly enforced, would have been found a most scanty measure of religious liberty.[3] He found that the scheme of comprehension which he had contemplated for England was impracticable. But he had the satisfaction of successfully advising the King to agree to the establishment in Scotland of the Presbyterian religion,—devotedly cherished by the vast majority of the inhabitants of that kingdom,—whereby the most discontented, turbulent, and miserable nation in Europe soon became loyal, peaceable, and prosperous.

The next important question agitated was whether the revenue granted during the life of King James had expired? The courtiers, to please William, contended that this revenue was vested in their present Majesties during the natural life of the abdicated monarch; but Somers, "*qui potius patriæ opes augeri quam regis maluit*," argued, that, "looking to the preamble of the act granting the revenue which specifies the purpose of the grant when it was limited to the *King's life*, it must be intended *for his reign*; abdication works a demise of the crown; after which the natural life of him who had reigned can not be recognized." He therefore suggested a more rational and constitutional course, and the House of Commons being of opinion that the revenue had expired, an act passed "granting a present aid to their Majesties."[4]

---

[1] Burnet, iii. 57.　　　　　　[2] 1 W. & M. st. 1, c. 18.
[3] Its benefits were confined to Dissenters, who professed a belief in almost all the doctrines of the Church of England; but it was very liberally in'erpreted, and, by and by, the most crying grievances of the Dissenters were practically remedied by the annual Indemnity Act.
[4] 1 W. & M. c. 8. The statute provided that all Acts passed should have reference to the 13th of February as the first day of the Session,—being the

He then assisted in the grand reform of appropriating the revenue to the public service—making the King a proper allowance for his personal and household expenses —which was one of the most important results of the Revolution, a sovereign having previously plunged the nation into foreign war, that he might obtain money to lavish upon his mistresses. Somers never used overbearing language in parliament, and on this occasion he modestly concluded his speech with the words, "Settle it as you please."[1]

When the terms of the coronation oath came to be discussed, he supported an amendment, the adoption of which would have saved much unnecessary pain to royal consciences, and would have deprived bigotry of an unfair weapon. Instead of the words, "Will you, to the utmost of your power, maintain the true profession of the Gospel and the Protestant reformed religion *established by law?*" Mr. Hampden moved to insert the words, "the true profession of the Gospel and the Protestant reformed religion *as it may be established according to the laws for the time being.*" Somers contended that the words to be added were an improvement, as obviating all doubt respecting the power of the legislature. He met the argument "that they were going about to alter the government of the Church," by urging that though the constitution be as good as possible for the present time, none can be good at all times. "Therefore," said he, "I am for the word *may*, and that will be a remedy at all times." But the amendment was negatived by a majority of 188 to 149,[2] and the foundation was laid for the argument that the coronation oath is binding on the sovereign in his legislative capacity, and is violated by giving the royal assent to such laws as "The Catholic Relief Bill," or "The Bill for repealing the Test Act," or "The Bill for granting an additional Endowment to Maynooth,"—an argument which has great weight with many well-meaning persons although it was scouted even by Lord Kenyon in his correspondence with George III.

Somers was defeated in another attempt, for which he has been a good deal censured, although I think unjustly.

---

day when the King and Queen agreed to take the government.—See Grey's Debates, p. 93. [1] 5 Parl. Hist. 144.
[2] Ibid. 204. Stat. 1 W. & M. c. 6; 12 & 13 W. 3, c. 2.

Into the "Bill for restoring Corporations," he introduced a clause which excluded, for the space of seven years, from municipal offices of trust "all who had acted or were concerned in surrendering charters." This was, no doubt, intended to maintain the superiority of the Whigs; but the profligate activity and cowardly submissiveness of the opposite party, by which all free municipal institutions had been swept away in the late reign, seemed to deserve this censure; and the measure could by no means be put on a level with the Corporation Act of Charles II., which created perpetual disabilities. "As the Dissenters, unquestioned friends of the Revolution, had been universally excluded by that statute, and the Tories had lately been strong enough to prevent their readmission, it was not unfair to provide some security against men who, in spite of their oaths of allegiance, were not likely thoroughly to have abjured their former principles."[1] Notwithstanding the strenuous support of the Solicitor General, the clause was lost, so that those who had come into corporations by very ill means, retained their power, and, as appeared at the next general election, the Revolution party was alarmingly weakened.[2]

In looking through and considering Somers's speeches in the House of Commons, I find one instance, and one only, in which he maintains what I consider unconstitutional and dangerous doctrine. To the "Bill for regulating Trials for High Treason," passed by the Commons, the Lords had added a proviso, which was objected to on the ground that it would interfere with the supposed right of the Commons to proceed by impeachment for other treasons than those specified in 25th Edward III., and which by that statute are reserved for the judgment of parliament by the words "in doubtful treasons the judges shall tarry and not proceed till the parliament have declared the same." I have expressed a strong opinion that these words only reserve the power of parliament legislatively and prospectively to declare new treasons; and certainly there would be no safety for mankind, if, upon a parliamentary impeachment, a man may be punished as a traitor for any act which the Commons charge, and the Lords find, to be treason, although never before

---

[1] Hall Const. Hist. iii. 155.
[2] See Com. Jour. ii. 10, Jan. 1690. 5 Parl. Hist. 508.

considered to have this character. Mr. Solicitor, however, makes a speech against the amendment not very courteous to the Upper House. "The more dark," says he, "the Lords' amendments are, the more they are to be suspected. The House of Commons go from their dignity and lessen themselves by listening to such amendments. The power of impeachment ought to be like Goliah's sword, kept in the Temple, and not used but on great occasions. The security of your constitution is lost when you lose this power. The statute of 25th Edward III. did foresee that men would be above the law, and I believe did not take away those that were treasons at common law. *Seductio Regis* can be punished no otherwise than in parliament. Let us adhere to our Bill as we passed it."[1] In consequence of this unwise controversy stirred up between the two Houses, the passing of a most useful law, allowing to the accused, in prosecution for treason, a copy of the indictment, a list of the jury and of the witnesses, and a full defense by counsel, was postponed for some years.[2] But the doctrine of the power of parliament, judicially and retrospectively to declare new treasons, upon which such outrages were perpetrated in the time of Charles I., both by the court and the popular party, has been heard of no more.

Somers, in conducting prosecutions officially before courts of justice, was most mild, candid, and merciful. The first state trial in the reign of William and Mary was that of Lord Preston; and it is a true refreshment to peruse the report of it, as it is in every respect a striking contrast to all that had preceded it. Mr. Macaulay justly observes, that "The earlier volumes of the STATE TRIALS are the most frightful record of baseness and depravity in the world. Our hatred is altogether turned away from the crimes and the criminals, and directed against the law and its ministers. We see villainies as black as ever

---

[1] 5 Parl. Hist. 677-680, 712. This being the last occasion of my mentioning Somers as a Member of the House of Commons, I must express my deep sorrow for the inadequacy of our means of judging of his oratory from the very imperfect reports we have of his speeches there. He did that justice to others which he himself has not experienced. During the first session of the Convention Parliament he took notes of the Debates, which are still preserved, and which, being full, clear, and spirited, give us a very lively notion of the eloquence of the leaders on both sides.—See Hardwicke State Papers, vol. ii 401, &c. [2] See 7 W. 3, c. 3. 7 Anne, c. 21.

were imputed to any prisoner at any bar, daily committed on the bench and in the jury box."[1] It is difficult to believe, that little more than three years had elapsed between the prosecution of the Seven Bishops and the prosecution of Lord Preston, as we seem suddenly transferred to another age, or to a distant country, where the principles of justice are held sacred instead of being violated and despised. The Judges were Holt, Pollexfen, and Atkyns, the three chiefs of the common-law courts, who had been selected for their learning, talents, and integrity. A decent excuse was found for the absence of the King's Sergeant and the Attorney General;—and, to consult the credit of the Government, the case for the Crown was conducted by Mr. Solicitor Somers.

After some preliminary objections had been answered and overruled in a tone of kindness, he opened the case to the jury with beautiful simplicity and moderation,—laying down the law of treason with perfect correctness as well as precision, never overstating the facts which were afterwards to be proved, and abstaining from all observations which could tend to raise a prejudice against the accused. He thus concluded: "Gentlemen, we shall now proceed to the evidence, first calling the living witnesses, and then reading the papers which will be proved to be in the handwriting of the prisoner, or to have been found in his possession; and when you have heard what the witnesses say, and what the papers contain, we must leave it to your consideration, and submit all to the direction of the Court."

The evidence was then adduced, every iota of it being such as would be received by those upright Judges, Lord Chief Justice Denman and Lord Chief Justice Tindal, and it clearly established the charge that Lord Preston had engaged in a Jacobite plot to dethrone King William and Queen Mary by means of the invasion of a French army. While Lord C. J. Holt was summing up, the prisoner frequently interrupted him,—and a specimen of the dialogue between them may be instructive. The Judge commenting upon a paper which purported to be "Heads for a declaration by the King of France on his landing, that he did not come to make an entire conquest," Lord Preston interposes: "My Lord, with sub-

[1] Macaulay's Essays, vol. ii. p. 270.

mission to your Lordship, I hope you will please to remember and observe to the Jury that paper was not found about me." *Lord C. J. Holt.*—" No, my Lord, it was not; but, good my Lord, give me your favor, I will certainly observe everything that is fitting, but I can not speak all my words at once. Gentlemen, my Lord Preston insists upon it that this paper was not found about him. It is true, but you have three witnesses—Mr. Townshend, Mr. Bland, and Mr. Warr were produced— to prove the paper to be in my Lord's hand; Mr. Townshend tells you he was acquainted pretty well with my Lord's hand; he was one of his clerks in the office of the wardrobe; he says he has seen my Lord write several times, and does believe the writing to be his hand, and to the same purpose says Bland, and Warr, who has seen him write, swears that he believes it to be his hand." *Lord Preston.*—" I hope your your Lordship will please to observe to the Jury that this is only a proof by similitude of hands." *Lord C. J. Holt.*—" They only say they believe it to be your hand. Nobody says they saw you write it." *Lord Preston.*—" I give your Lordship thanks for observing that the paper was not proved to have been taken upon me; but I beg pardon for interrupting of your Lordship." *Lord C. J. Holt.*—" Interrupt me as much as you please, if I do not observe right; I will assure you I will do you no wrong willingly." The summing up being concluded Lord Preston begged permission again to address the Jury before they went out. *Lord C. J. Holt.*—" Your Lordship should have said what you had to say before, it is contrary to the course of all proceedings in such cases to have anything said to the Jury after the Court has summed up the evidence. But we will dispense with the rule. What has your Lordship to say?" *Lord Preston.*— " My Lord, I humbly thank your Lordship; I am not acquainted with such proceedings." *Lord C. J. Holt.*— " You know I permitted your Lordship to interrupt me as much as you would, which was never done before in any such case." He was then patiently heard, and he chiefly complained that, after the Revolution, when he had been deprived of the places which he held under King James, and wished to live a retired life, he had been twice imprisoned in the Tower, which filled him with a desire to leave the country. Holt mildly answered,

"Suppose your Lordship did think yourself hardly used, yet your Lordship must remember it was in a time of danger that your Lordship was taken up, and you had showed your dissatisfaction with the present government, and therefore they were not to be blamed if they secured themselves against you."[1]

The Jury, who had been most impartially selected, after retiring for half an hour, brought in a verdict of *guilty*—upon which Lord C. J. Pollexfen calmly remarked, "I think truly, gentlemen, you have done according to your evidence; and though it be a hard case upon particular men who have brought themselves into these inconveniences, yet it is necessary that justice should have its due course, or else there is no safety for any society or government."

The merit of the conduct of this prosecution can not be fully appreciated without recollecting that the case was intensely political; that if the prisoner's party had prevailed, the Judges and the counsel would have exchanged places with him; and that, to all former precedents, he ought to have been convicted without being heard, or to have been attainted by act of parliament, and immediately led out to execution. But the majesty of the law being vindicated,—on the recommendation of Somers, Lord Preston received a free pardon.[2]

While still Solicitor General, Somers was consulted confidentially by the Government on all public measures, and to him was assigned the task of drawing the declaration of war against France. This is a very able state paper,—although, the denial of the new Sovereign's right to the crown not being referred to, the list of grievances does not appear very formidable; and, to tickle the national vanity, it was considered necessary to complain that Louis had not recognized our sovereignty of the narrow seas,—which had been virtually renounced by Charles II in his last treaty with the Dutch: "The right of flag inherent in the crown of England," William is made to say, "has been disputed by orders of the French King, in violation of our sovereignty of the narrow seas, which in all ages has been asserted by our predecessors, and we

[1] "Res dura, et regni novitas, me taila cogunt
  Moliri, et late fines custode tueri."
[2] 12 St. Tr. 646—822.

are resolved to maintain for the honor of our crown and of the English nation." After denouncing the ill treatment which English subjects had experienced in France, it magnanimously concludes with an assurance " that all Frenchmen in the British dominions behaving themselves peaceably shall be safe in their persons and estates, and free from molestation and trouble of any kind."

On the 2nd of May, 1692, Somers was promoted to be Attorney General in consequence of the appointment of Sir George Treby to succeed Pollexfen as Lord Chief Justice of the Court of Common Pleas. He had previously been the first man in point of practice at the bar, being retained in all private causes of any importance, as well as conducting the prosecutions of the Government. He was counsel for the plaintiff in the great case of the *Duke of Norfolk* v. *Germaine*, the first instance on record of an action peculiar to England, and not very creditable to our jurisprudence—to recover a pecuniary compensation for criminal conversation with the plaintiff's wife. It was now established, contrary to the opinion of the early English reformers, and contrary to the practice of all other Protestant countries, that marriage could not be dissolved, even for adultery, by the ordinary tribunals: but in the case of Lord de Roos the legislature had granted relief to the injured husband by a special act of parliament. On the authority of this precedent the Duke presented a divorce bill in the House of Lords, on the ground of adultery between the Duchess and Sir John Germaine, as he had obtained a sentence of separation *à mensâ et thoro;* but, as the evidence was doubtful, the bill was negatived. He was then advised to have the fact proved in a court of law, and he brought the present action, laying the damages at £100,000. The trial came on before Lord Chief Justice Holt; and the new Attorney General appeared for the plaintiff. Instead of a lengthy and exaggerated statement of the wrongs of the injured husband, such as would now be expected, he stated the nature of the case in a few plain sentences, saying, "Our proofs are such as I am ashamed to repeat them." There being a plea of the Statute of Limitations, the difficulty was to give the requisite evidence within six years before the commencement of the action. The jury found a verdict for the plaintiff, with 100 marks damages. " Upon which they had a severe reprimand from the Court for giving so small and scandalous a fine,"—but without sufficient cause, as there was great reason to suspect that the Duke had connived at his own dishonor. He was not able to carry his divorce bill till Somers was Chancellor.[1]

The only other case of much importance in which this distinguished Attorney General is recorded to have appeared as counsel at the bar, was that of Lord Mohun, indicted for the murder of William Mountford. The trial took place before the House of Peers, the Marquis of Carmarthen acting as Lord High Steward. Mr. Attorney General Somers conducted the prosecution, and again furnished a most valuable illustration of the duties of an officer of the Crown upon such an occasion. After a few observations on the law of the case, he said, "My Lords, it is my part to give an account of the nature of the evidence, to the end that your Lordships may more easily go along with the witnesses as they are examined, and more readily make your observations on what they say. This I shall do as shortly and exactly as I can, without pretending to aggravate anything, which I could never think did become any one in my station, and I am sure would be to very little purpose upon such a judicature as this; for, after all, your Lordships will found your judgments upon the fact, not as it is represented by us, but as it appears upon the oaths of the witnesses."

The deceased, a favorite comic actor, had been a lover of the celebrated Mrs. Bracegirdle, and had been killed in an affray which arose out of an attempt forcibly to carry her off from Drury Lane. After many abstract questions put to the Judges respecting the crime of murder, the noble prisoner was acquitted by a majority of 69 to 14; but, as we shall see, he was again tried for a similar murder, and he was at length killed in a duel.[2]

Before Somers left the bar, he on one occasion got into a very disagreeable embarrassment from his conflicting duties as member of the House of Commons, and assessor to the House of Lords. While sitting in St. Stephen's Chapel as Chairman of a Committe of the whole House, the Lords sent for him to advise them in the case of Lord

---

[1] See 12 St. Tr. 833–950; Macqueen's Practice of House of Lords, 562.
[2] 12 St. Tr. 950; 1 Salk. 104; Skyn. 683; Swift's Journal to Stella, 15th Nov. 1712.

Banbury, who, being charged with murder, had pleaded his peerage. He immediately left the Chair and broke up the Committee, which gave some disgust to the Commons; and the Lords, because they had waited some time for him, instituted an inquiry whether the Attorney General is not obliged by his post to attend their House, and presented an address to the Crown, praying that he might be directed to do so.[1]

Somers remained Attorney General rather less than one year. In the new parliament which met in the spring of 1693, he was again returned as representative for the city of Worcester, and in sixteen days after the the commencement of the Session he was Lord Keeper of the Great Seal. The complaints of the administration of justice in the Court of Chancery had become so loud that they could be neglected no longer, and all eyes were turned to the man who, practicing with unrivaled brilliancy, had shown, as an advocate, moderation, candor, and good temper, which were sure to qualify him to preside as a Judge.

The Tory section in the Government, while they could not deny his merit, being afraid of his influence, urged various pretenses for delaying his promotion; while the Whigs were eager to see him the ostensible head, as he had long been the most efficient leader, of their party. Rumors were spread of a speedy transfer of the Great Seal to abler hands. "Haud semper errat fama; aliquando et elegit." On the 23rd of March it was officially announced that "the Great Seal, having been surrendered by the Lords Commissioners, Trevor, Rawlinson, and Hutchins, had been delivered to Sir John Somers, their Majesties' Attorney General, as Lord Keeper, who was

---

[1] See Lords' and Com. Jour. 1693. The Attorney General is summoned to the House of Lords by a writ in all respects the same as that of a peer, omitting the words "ad consentiendum." On the trial of a peer he sits without the bar, if he be a member of the House of Commons, and within the bar if he is not. If he returns his writ, he may sit on the woolsacks; but then he is precluded from pleading in any private cause at the bar. From 1620 to 1670 no Attorney General continued a member of the House of Commons after his appointment. Since then he has always been a member, unless casually, since the Reform Bill, from the difficulty of finding a seat. Previously a seat was found for him by the Treasury, at the fixed price of £500.—His proper official place in the King's Bench is under the Judges, on the left hand of the Master of the Crown Office.—Ralph ascribes the proceedings taken on this occasion against Somers to the spite of the Jacobites.

at the same time sworn of their Majesties' Most Honorable Privy Council."[1]

[1] London Gazette, March 23, 1693. "His Majesty was this day graciously pleased to commit the custody of the Great Seal to the Right Honorable Sir John Somers, their Majesties' Attorney General, who was accordingly sworn Lord Keeper of the Great Seal of England, and one of their Majesties' Most Honourable Privy Council, and then took his place at the Board." The biographers of Somers have generally stated that he was appointed Lord Keeper on the day of his installation, 3rd May. Evelyn brings it forward a few days, writing of what had been determined upon, although not formally completed. " 19th March. The Attorney General Somers made Lord Keeper, —a young lawyer of extraordinary merit."—*Diary*.

www.ingramcontent.com/pod-product-compliance
Lightning Source LLC
Chambersburg PA
CBHW032027150426
43194CB00006B/185